TAGHeuer

WHAT ARE YOU MADE OF ?

CONTENTS

AUTOCOURSE 2004–2005

is published by:
Hazleton Publishing Ltd,
5th Floor, Mermaid House,
2 Puddle Dock, London,
EC4V 3DS.

Colour reproduction by
Radstock Repro,
Midsomer Norton, Somerset

Printed in England by
Butler and Tanner Ltd,
Frome, Somerset

Hazleton Publishing Ltd is a member
of Profile Media Group Plc.

ISBN: 1 903135 35 4

DISTRIBUTORS

UNITED KINGDOM
Vine House
Waldenbury
Chailey
East Sussex
BN8 4DR

Tel: 01825 723398
email: sales@vinehouseuk.co.uk

REST OF THE WORLD
Menoshire Ltd
Unit 13
21 Wadsworth Road
Perivale
Middlesex UB6 7LQ
Telephone: 020 8566 7344
Fax: 020 8991 2439

**Dust-jacket: Michael Schumacher
(main picture); celebrates after
winning the Spanish Grand Prix.**

**Title page: BAR mechanics await
the arrival of one of their men for a
refuelling stop.**
All photographs: Darren Heath

FOREWORD by Michael Schumacher	5
EDITOR'S INTRODUCTION	6
THE TOP TEN DRIVERS OF 2004 Ranked by the Editor	13
MAKING GOOD Tony Dodgins examines the career of Jenson Button	24
WHERE NEXT? Eric Silbermann charts the evolution of F1	28
PLAYING SECOND FIDDLE? Nigel Roebuck assesses the ideal qualities of the number-two driver	32
GLOBAL REACH Adam Cooper on F1's new venues	36
FORMULA 1 REVIEW by Bob Constanduros, Maurice Hamilton and Alan Henry	41
2004 GRANDS PRIX by Alan Henry and Adam Cooper	73
2004 FORMULA 1 STATISTICS compiled by David Hayhoe and Emma Henry	220
FORMULA 3000 REVIEW by Simon Arron	222
FORMULA 3 REVIEW by Andrew van de Burgt	226
SPORTS & GT REVIEW by Gary Watkins	228
TOURING CARS REVIEW by Charles Bradley	232
US RACING REVIEW by Gordon Kirby	234
MAJOR WORLDWIDE RESULTS compiled by David Hayhoe	242

Acknowledgements

The Editor of AUTOCOURSE wishes to thank the following for their assistance while compiling the 2004–2005 edition. **Eire:** Jordan Grand Prix (Eddie Jordan, Ian Phillips, Charlotte Anderson and Helen Temple). **France:** ACO, Fédération Française du Sport Automobile, FIA (Max Mosley, Bernie Ecclestone, Alan Donnelly, Richard Woods, Agnes Kaiser, Anouk , Charlie Whiting, Herbie Blash and Pat Behar), Michelin (Pierre Dupasquier and Severine Ray), Renault F1 (Flavio Briatore, Pat Symonds, Patrizia Spinelli and Bradley Lord). **Germany:** Formula 3 Vereinigung, BMW Motorsport (Mario Theissen and Jorg Kottmeier), Mercedes-Benz (Norbert Haug, Wolfgang Schattling, Frank Reichert and Tanya Severin), Sabine Kehm. **Great Britain:** Autocar, British American Racing (David Richards, Geoff Willis, Hugh Chambers, Nick Fry, Alastair Watkins, Tracy Novak, Emma Bearpark and Jane Chapman), Martin Brundle, Bob Constanduros, Paul Edwards, Laura Fell, Peter Foubister, Maurice Hamilton, Emma Henry, Nick Henry, Ian Hutchinson, Cosworth Engineering (Bernard Ferguson), Ford (Jost Capito,), Jaguar Racing (Tony Purnell, David Pitchforth, Mark Gillan, Stuart Dyble, Nav Sidhu, Jane Stewart and Carrie Bond), McLaren International (Ron Dennis, Martin Whitmarsh, Adrian Newey, Justine Blake, Beverley Keynes, Ellen Kolby, Clare Robertson, Claire Bateman, Lyndy Redding, Simon Points, Neil Oatley, Steve Hallam and Peter Stayner), Stan Piecha, Nigel Roebuck, Eric Silbermann, Sir Jackie Stewart, Jules Kulpinski, Professor Sid Watkins, WilliamsF1 (Sir Frank Williams, Patrick Head, Dickie Stanford, Sam Michael, Frank Dernie, Jonathan Williams, Claire Williams, Jim Wright, Silvia Hoffer Frangipane and Liam Clogger). **Italy:** Commisione Sportiva Automobilistica Italiana, Scuderia Ferrari (Jean Todt, Ross Brawn, Antonio Ghini, Luca Colajanni, Stefania Bocci, Jane Parisi and Regine Rettner), Minardi F1 team (Paul Stoddart, Graham Jones and Fabiana Valenti), 'George' Piola. **Japan:** Bridgestone (Hirode Hamashima, Hisao Suganuma, Adrian Atkinson and Rachel Ingham), Honda Racing (Robert Watherston and Charlie Reid), Toyota (Tsutomu Tomita, John Howett, Mike Gascoyne, Andrea Ficarelli, Chris Hughes and Silke Albus). **Switzerland:** Sauber (Peter Sauber, Hans-Peter Brack and Ilka Wendlandt). **USA:** CART, Daytona International Speedway, Indianapolis Motor Speedway, NASCAR, Roger Penske, SportsCar.

Photographs published in AUTOCOURSE 2004–2005 have been contributed by:

Chief Photographer: Darren Heath; Chief Contributing Photographers: Bryn Williams/crash.net; Peter Nygaard/GP Photo; LAT Photographic; (Phil Abbott, Lorenzo Bellanca, Jeff Bloxham, Glenn Dunbar, Malcolm Griffiths, Leland Hill, Andre Irlmeier, Michael Kim, Walt Kuhn, Mike Levitt, Lesley-Ann Miller, Robert Le Sieur, Bill Stafford, Dan Streck, Denis Tanney, F. Pierce-Williams

editor
ALAN HENRY

publisher
EDDIE TAYLOR

text editor
IAN PENBERTHY

art editor
STEVE SMALL

sales promotion
LAURA FELL

results and statistics
DAVID HAYHOE
EMMA HENRY

f1 illustrations
ADRIAN DEAN

chief photographer
DARREN HEATH

chief contributing photographers
BRYN WILLIAMS/crash.net
PETER NYGAARD/GP PHOTO
LAT PHOTOGRAPHIC

AUTOCOURSE
www.autocourse.co.uk

FOREWORD
by MICHAEL SCHUMACHER

I urgently have to stop thinking I am living a dream. A dream that unites me and Ferrari, and that seems to be unstoppable at the moment, but then, to be honest, I like this idea.

No, seriously, I can only repeat that I find all that happens to us incredible. What we achieved again in this season is just the icing on the cake made from the performances of the past years. When I joined Ferrari, we never imagined that all our hard work could pay out like this. And, you know – this is the good part of it – we really worked for our success, in long exhausting hours and with a lot of depressing moments that we managed to overcome. That's why now we can really be proud about that.

When we won the constructors' title in Budapest, we all flew back and celebrated the success in Maranello at Ferrari's headquarters with all the people who work at the Gestione Sportiva. I found that more than appropriate. It is easy to forget the extreme importance of the work of all the people back in the factory if you just look at all the glitz and media hype at the racing track. But it is these people who gave us a car that did not suffer a technical failure for around 50 races. We can trust them, they are the soul of the racing team of which I am just one part. The victories and titles are for all of us.

At Ferrari, we are very much aware that sooner or later other times will come. Our current successes will give us the strength for those harder times. But be sure about one thing – we will try to ensure that those harder times happen later rather than sooner!

SAME AGAIN?

Overwhelmingly, the 2004 FIA Formula 1 World Championship delivered more of the same. After an ominous wobble in late-season form very nearly dropped Michael Schumacher's sixth title into the eagerly awaiting clutches of McLaren's Kimi Räikkönen, Ferrari and Bridgestone bounced back impressively to ensure that his campaign for his seventh crown was probably the most dominant of all.

Main photograph: The unmistakable profile of seven-time champion who continues to dominate his chosen sport in unprecedented fashion.

Above: Will life ever be different? Michael and Ferrari clinched their fifth successive title in 2004.
Photographs: Darren Heath

The Ferrari F2004 came out of the starting traps in storming style to post a 1-2 finish in the Australian Grand Prix at Melbourne, and after that the Prancing Horse just kept on winning. Michael eventually posted an all-time record 13 race victories in the 18-race season – the longest in F1 history – while team-mate Rubens Barrichello bagged another two. That left only three golden moments for the opposition to pick up. And all were brilliant. Jarno Trulli's victory at Monaco in the Renault R24, Kimi Räikkönen's triumph at Spa with the McLaren MP4/19B and Juan Pablo Montoya's close win over Räikkönen in the season finale at Interlagos were truly top-flight performances by the drivers and teams concerned.

Ironically, the team that made the strongest impression on the year was the BAR Honda squad, which took a superb second place to Ferrari in the constructors' championship and carried Jenson Button to third place in the drivers' points table. Button and BAR really were a revelation. The team's emergence as a consistently competitive contender said much for Honda's renewed zeal on the engine development front as well as David Richards's management qualities.

As for Button, he drove superbly race after race, highlighting his season with brilliant second-place finishes to Schumacher in the San Marino and German Grands Prix. Yet all was not as it seemed. Just as one began to be tempted to draw a comparison with the way in which Nigel Mansell had grown to stardom with Williams in the 1980s, the seemingly sunny relationship between Button and BAR was darkened by unexpected storm clouds.

In the middle of the season, Button announced that he would be off to Williams in 2005, his management team citing irregularities over the way in which BAR had exercised its option for the following year. What was not explained was why Button was looking to escape; whatever the reason, it transpired that he had been badly advised.

In similar cases in the past, a lot of noise has been made by the teams involved, followed by a period of calm during which some discreet financial arrangements have been made to ensure the transfer of the driver to the team of his choice. That's what most F1 insiders believed would happen on this occasion. After all, they concluded, nobody would force a driver to stay with a team he wanted to leave.

That theory, however, reckoned without the tenacity of BAR's team principal, David Richards. From the outset, he was implacable in his determination that his team's contract with Button would prevail. He referred the matter to the FIA Contracts Review Board, who agreed that Button's BAR contract took priority over the agreement with Williams. Sheepishly, Button confirmed that he would be staying with BAR after all. Williams, not amused by all the costs involved in reaching an unsuccessful conclusion to the issue, was left casting around for another driver to pair with Mark Webber in 2005.

Meanwhile, other issues were impinging on the health of the F1 business, particularly those of costs and who, in the long-term, will control the commercial-rights income, variously estimated at between $450 and $800 million annually. Bernie Ecclestone's grip on that income suddenly appeared under greater threat than ever before when the three creditor banks that control 75 per cent of the business, through their stake in Ecclestone's SLEC company, dramatically intensified their efforts to challenge his omnipotence.

Ecclestone remained stoic and unimpressed by this bid to undermine his control of the business. Yet what had become very clear by the end of 2004 was the harsh reality that either costs needed to be brought quickly under control or the share of the commercial-rights income accruing to the teams radically increased. The vulnerability of F1 as a business model was also thrown into sharp focus when Ford announced that it was putting the Jaguar F1 team up for sale at the end of the year, apparently because it was unable to make a compelling business case for remaining in the grand prix game.

Suddenly a chill wind rippled through the paddock. The knock-on effect of selling or closing Jaguar could have dire implications. Engine specialist Cosworth was also up for sale, threatening the already struggling Jordan and Minardi teams with another body blow. Yet Ford's decision on Jaguar seemed strangely perverse given that the company was a founder member of the GPWC power base, which collectively had professed huge confidence in

Far left: Let the domination begin. Michael Schumacher in his Ferrari surrounded by all the paraphenalia of the F1 business on the starting grid at Melbourne.

Below: Fighting his corner. Bernie Ecclestone found himself under presure from all sides but remained as cool and controlled as ever.
Photographs: Darren Heath

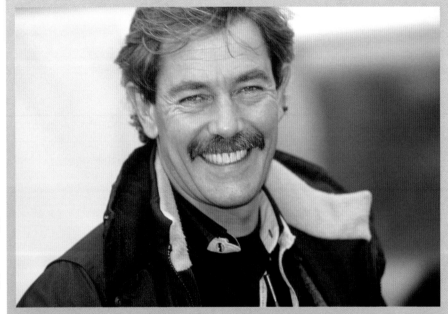

Near right: Olivier Panis called time on his F1 career at the end of 2004. The popular and amiable Frenchman will continue to be invovd with Toyota in a testing role.

Top right: Jarno Trulli took a memorable victory at Monaco for Renault It was one of only three Grands Prix not won by Ferrari.

Bottom right: It was the end of the road for Jaguar, but the team was rescued and will appear in Red Bull colours in 2005
All photographs: Darren Heath

the future potential of the F1 business.

GPWC itself finally tired of trying to cut a long-term deal with Ecclestone over the division of income within F1. Having agreed a Memorandum of Understanding with SLEC in December 2003, GPWC withdrew from it in April 2004 after concluding that Ecclestone had been dragging his feet to an unacceptable degree. By the end of the year, GPWC was busy formulating its own administrative structure to run F1 after the expiry of the current Concorde Agreement at the end of 2007. It remains to be seen how far this dispute will run before a compromise solution is seriously inked.

As far as the F1 calendar was concerned, the world's appetite for grand prix racing appears insatiable. The calendar expanded to 18 races, accommodating the spectacular new government backed fixtures in Bahrain and Shanghai, based on multi-million-dollar, Hermann Tilke designed tracks; the signs are that there will be more to come, with Turkey joining the F1 club in 2005, while both Mexico and South Africa are waiting in line for a possible chance the following year.

The advent of these new races and the forthcoming ban on tobacco sponsorship in F1 have conspired to place many traditional

European venues under huge pressure. Ecclestone's continued ambivalence toward the British Racing Drivers' Club, owner of Silverstone, almost inevitably placed the future of the British Grand Prix on the line as protracted negotiations ground on for much of the year to secure the event's future. Thankfully the matter was resolved in early December when the BRDC signed a five-year deal with Ecclestone which guarantees the race until 2009.

Wherever future F1 races may be held in the UK – be it Silverstone or even on the streets of London, an Olympian dream riding on the back of a brilliantly successful F1 demonstration in the West End during the summer – they will almost certainly be with significantly slower cars than we saw in 2004. With 2.4-litre V8 engines and a standard control tyre – probably from a single supplier – due to be initiated in 2006, the 4s or so trimmed from lap times during 2004 could be reversed. FIA President Max Mosley is particularly keen on such safety driven moves, even though many of the teams question the efficacy of the steps the FIA has supported to reach this conclusion.

In the USA, while NASCAR continues to thrive, the open-wheel racing situation seems as much in a state of flux as ever. Chevrolet, which has been badging Cosworth engines in the IRL, is dumping its programme. What that means for the future is unclear. Honda is dominating the IRL, and there are signs that Toyota may quit the series in the foreseeable future, and almost certainly compete in the NASCAR Nextel Cup, maybe as soon as 2006.

Meanwhile, Champ Car leading light Kevin Kalkhoven seems to have secured continuity of engine supply for his series, buying into the Cosworth US operation based in Torrance, California. The two series seem set to continue charting uneasy parallel courses almost ten years after the famous split that rent asunder the American front-line single-seater racing categories. There is still no real sign of the long awaited and much needed reconciliation.

As far as the European second-division categories are concerned, Vitantonio Liuzzi dominated the International F3000 series, and Britain's Jamie Green notched up an impressive success in the F3 Euroseries, a category that has already produced such promising F1 newcomers as Timo Glock, Christian Klien and Ryan Briscoe.

Yet F1 continues to suck such vast resources from the global motorsporting infrastructure that most other European based categories look threadbare by comparison. One major evolving exception to that rule may be the FIA GT Series, which looks set for healthy expansion over the coming years with the promise of Aston Martin, Maserati, Ferrari, Lamborghini and Chevrolet all doing battle in what they hope will develop into a fully fledged World Sports Car Championship.

Time was when sports car racing was motorsport's international 'big deal' and F1 was a nickel-and-dime affair by comparison in financial terms. Then along came Bernie Ecclestone, and the global motorsport eco-system changed irrevocably. In 2004, he continued to hold sway over the F1 business, but there were definite cracks appearing in the columns that support his commercial edifice. Where we go from here is real crystal-ball stuff, but like everything in this complex and colourful sport, it promises to be an exciting ride.

Alan Henry,
Tillingham,
Essex
December 2004

JOHN WALTON • An Appreciation

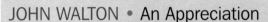

Photograph: LAT Photographic

JOHN Walton's funeral in Oxford on 19 July, 2004, said everything about the huge regard for one of the most popular men in the paddock. St Aloysius Roman Catholic Church was overflowing with a wide cross-section of motor sport people. The majority were mechanics representing the teams 'John Boy' had worked with since arriving in England from his native Dublin in the 1970s. The presence of individuals from such organisations as Ferrari, however, indicated the genuine affection and respect in which he had been held among the sometimes selfish and hard-nosed F1 community.

It could hardly have been otherwise for someone who was tough, but fair, and backed up his tireless work ethic with a rich sense of fun and wry humour. Walton had developed that during his early days as Eddie Jordan's mechanic, and needed it latterly when working as team manager for Minardi.

In between, 'John Boy' had gathered useful knowledge at Toleman, where he was mechanic to Ayrton Senna during the Brazilian's formative F1 year in 1984, and where he later became chief mechanic. Joining Jordan Grand Prix when Eddie Jordan formed his F1 team in 1990 had been a natural move, and he assumed the role of team manager before moving on to Prost and then Arrows.

The last two had been hamstrung by financial difficulties, but at least that gave Walton valuable experience that he put to good use when he joined Minardi in 2001, practically managing the team on a day-by-day basis. Walton took care of the Italian side of the operation, and was the man at the pit wall to whom everyone would turn at times of uncertainty and crisis during a race weekend. He knew the rulebook backwards and was quick to make the most of any changes in procedure that might favour his impoverished team.

Throughout, Walton retained a sharp sense of reality. His down-to-earth summary of whatever was going on was laced with a cutting wit, and delivered in a devastating Dublin brogue and with an inevitable twinkle in the eye.

Walton was a great friend and ally to young drivers, race crews and journalists alike: a reliable and diplomatic source of information with a healthy take on the latest gossip. Nothing was ever too much trouble. It was while preparing for an F1 demonstration in London – the last thing anyone needed with just a week between the French and British Grands Prix – that he suffered a severe heart attack without warning. Louise Goodman, his partner, was by his side and stayed there with his family until he passed away four days later. The F1 community and motor sport in general shared the profound loss of a really good man. John Walton was 47.

Maurice Hamilton

[ultimate performance]

[innovation and performance]

With expertise spanning more than four decades, Cosworth Racing is a world leader in the design, development and manufacture of ultra-high performance engines for all applications. Cosworth provides powerplant technology and design solutions for teams in Formula One, the World Rally Championship, Champ Cars and GP motorcycle racing.

Cosworth Racing also offers its knowledge and experience to provide complete technological solutions to a variety of commercial clients across a multitude of disciplines. From consultancy to clean sheet engine design, for high performance road, race or rally applications, Cosworth Racing has the solution.

Cosworth Racing, Commercial Dept
The Octagon, St James Mill Road
Northampton NN5 5RA, United Kingdom
Tel: +44 [0]1604 598169 E: mresl@cosworth-racing.com

Cosworth Racing Inc, Commercial Dept
3031 Fujita Street
Torrance, CA 90505, USA
Tel: +1 310 534 1390 E: cosinc@cosworth-racing.com

POWER BY COSWORTH

www.cosworth.com

[reliability • performance • innovation • excellence]

FIA FORMULA 1
WORLD CHAMPIONSHIP 2004

TOP TEN DRIVERS

Chosen by the Editor,
taking into account their
racing performances
and the equipment at
their disposal

Photography by
Darren Heath

1	Date of birth: *3 January 1969*
	Team: *Scuderia Ferrari Marlboro*
	Grand Prix starts in 2004: *18*
	World Championship placing: *1st*
	Wins: *13*
	Poles: *8*
	Points: *148*

MICHAEL
SCHUMACHER

MICHAEL Schumacher's competitive durability remains the most remarkable quality that underpins the near-serene character of the seven times world champion. In 2004, he bagged another 13 grand prix victories, yet there is no sign that his appetite for success is in any way losing its edge. The stresses and strains of relentless and consistent performance at the highest level imaginable seem to take nothing out of him. Every race win is greeted with the spontaneous delight one associates with the psyche of a first-time winner.

Out of the cockpit, Michael is as immaculate as the style he deploys behind the wheel. When he strolled into the paddock at Melbourne's Albert Park at the start of the dominant 2004 campaign, it was as if one had rewound a videotape recorded during any one of the past half-dozen years. It says much for the 35-year-old's mental resilience and sheer durability that one has to study the detailing of the sponsorship patches on his overalls to pinpoint precisely the year in question.

In a sense, that's the whole key to Schumacher. Twelve years at the very pinnacle of F1 achievement have yielded virtually no physical wear and tear. Just like the lack of mechanical wear and tear on his Ferrari helped steer him inexorably towards his seventh world championship in 2004.

Nominating the best performances from his 2004 canvas remains a difficult task. Possibly the most marginal of all was in Malaysia, where the punishing temperatures were expected to offer a decisive performance advantage to the Michelin opposition. It didn't quite work out that way, but Michael still had to extend himself to keep Juan Pablo Montoya's Williams-BMW under control. At Magny-Cours, he had to pull out all the stops after Maranello's pit-wall tactician, Luca Baldisserri, worked out that switching to a four-stop strategy was the best route to clinching victory over Fernando Alonso's Renault, but unquestionably his best drive was that explosive recovery from a first-lap spin at Monza to finish second, hard on the heels of Rubens Barrichello.

Alongside that, his slips at Shanghai and Interlagos were merely inconsequential footnotes that served to heighten the magnitude of his achievements as a whole. Some day, somebody will topple Schumacher. But who? And when? Don't start holding your breath yet.

2 JENSON BUTTON

Date of birth: **19 January 1980**

Team: *Lucky Strike BAR Honda*

Grand Prix starts in 2004: **18**

World Championship placing: **3rd**

Wins: **0**

Poles: **1**

Points: **85**

IT was disappointing that Jenson Button's season was punctuated by the ructions that stemmed from his desire mid-year to leave the BAR Honda team in favour of a switch to Williams in 2005. It was also a measure of the maturity displayed by both Button and the BAR crew that they managed to conduct themselves with such professionalism while moving through the eye of that particular storm, such that their on-track form was hardly ruffled by the tensions of the dispute.

In the end, Button reconciled himself to remaining with BAR in 2005 after the FIA's Contracts Recognition Board decreed that the team's deal with the 24-year-old took precedence over the contract he had signed with Williams. Button took it on the chin and knuckled down to the job. And what a job he did.

Ironically, by the start of the 2004 season, it appeared as though Button had developed an extremely close working relationship with BAR team principal David Richards. They seemed very close and displayed the congenial informality that is usually only the preserve of genuinely good friends. Understandably, that relationship was dented by the dispute over the contract, an issue that was not handled at all well by Button's management.

That said, none of the contractual strife could alter the reality that Button became a world-class F1 driver in 2004.

He took his first podium with a strong third place in the Malaysian Grand Prix. By the end of the season, there would be nine more top-three finishes, including a superb second from pole at Imola and an amazing second from 13th on the grid at Hockenheim. That last race forced all the critics who had pigeon-holed Button as a quick driver who couldn't overtake to eat their words. Yet the first victory proved frustratingly elusive, although there was a point at Monza where it looked as though he was bang on course to win the Italian Grand Prix. Then, however, both the Ferrari drivers began demonstrating what the F2004s could really do – and Button had to settle for third.

Date of birth: *17 October 1979*	
Team: *West McLaren Mercedes*	
Grand Prix starts in 2004: *18*	
World Championship placing: *7th*	
Wins: *1*	
Poles: *1*	
Points: *45*	

McLaren Chairman Ron Dennis believes that there is something in the Finnish temperament that contributes to Kimi Räikkönen's mental equilibrium. 'Part of the ingredient for success in Formula 1 is to have the best available drivers, and while it is almost coincidental that Kimi followed on from Mika [Häkkinen], it is not entirely so,' he postulated. 'There's a core determination that is often found in Finns. Perhaps it's the extreme nature of the climate which affects their mind-set. There's an icy determination in Finnish people which I've experienced when working with them. They [also] have the highest percentage of rally drivers and lots of talent in skiing and ski jumping.'

Frank Williams, whose enthusiasm and respect for F1 drivers as a genre has not been dimmed after more than 30 years in the business, is another huge fan of Räikkönen. 'Kimi is the genuine act, the real deal,' he said. 'You look at drivers and some have something special…and some don't. When you look at Kimi, you know he's one of the ones who've got it, just like Juan Pablo Montoya.'

The irony behind those remarks is that Montoya is on course to succeed David Coulthard as Räikkönen's team-mate in 2005, if not before. McLaren will then have a super team to compare with the dynamic pairing of Ayrton Senna and Alain Prost in 1988–89. Räikkönen remains sanguine about the prospect.

The 2004 season certainly tested Räikkönen's resolve. He was understandably frustrated by the poor form displayed by the original McLaren MP4/19 during the first part of the season, a brutal disappointment after coming so close to the title crown after Ferrari wobbled ominously in 2003. Yet when the new MP4/19B arrived mid-season, the Finn rose to the occasion superbly and was right on the pace at Silverstone, Hockenheim (where a rear wing failure pitched him into an accident) and Spa, where he emerged victorious ahead of not one, but both of the Ferraris.

'I have my place in the team,' said Räikkönen quietly. 'I don't care who my team-mate is because I concentrate on my own thing.'

It is that tightly focused attitude that wins world championships. Not 2005 perhaps, but certainly very soon.

KIMI RÄIKKÖNEN

FERNANDO Alonso gave the impression of having peaked ever so slightly during the first half of 2004, yet that perception stemmed mainly from the stupendous form displayed by his team-mate, Jarno Trulli, during the early races of the year, notably his dominant win at Monte Carlo. However, it is all too easy to forget that Alonso was easily best of the rest at the opening race of the year in Melbourne, running a lonely schedule in third place, not quick enough to keep up with the dominant Ferraris, but quite capable of out-distancing the rest of the pack.

While Trulli was winning at Monaco, Alonso was having a fraught afternoon, ending up with his Renault R24 clattering along the guard rail at the exit of the tunnel after an incident he felt Ralf Schumacher had triggered through a lack of attention. This was followed by a disappointing North American tour, which saw him suffer driveshaft failure accelerating away from the start in Montreal, and a puncture and ensuing shunt while chasing the Ferraris for all he was worth at

Indianapolis. Then came Magny-Cours, however, and a superb pole position for the French Grand Prix, followed by a run in the race that was so promising that Michael Schumacher's Ferrari was switched from a three- to four-stop refuelling strategy to ensure that he got the upper hand over the Spaniard.

The rest of the season was one of consistently solid achievement. Third places in both the German and Hungarian races, plus a fourth in China, reaffirmed Alonso's steady progress to maturity. He rounded off the season by leading the Brazilian Grand Prix at Interlagos, a performance that, if sustained to the finish, would have closed the gap to BAR Honda in the constructors' championship table, although not by sufficient to wrest second place from that rival.

Alonso drove well in 2004, but the quality of Ferrari's opposition was a major factor standing between him and more race victories. For 2005, he will need a slightly better car. And slightly more consistency to go with his unquestioned speed.

Date of birth: *29 July 1981*

Team: *Renault*

Grand Prix starts in 2004: *18*

World Championship placing: *4th*

Wins: *0*

Poles: *1*

Points: *59*

FERNANDO ALONSO

RUBENS BARRICHELLO

5

Date of birth: *23 May 1972*

Team: *Scuderia Ferrari Marlboro*

Grand Prix starts in 2004: *18*

World Championship placing: *2nd*

Wins: *2*

Poles: *4*

Points: *114*

JUDGING Rubens Barrichello is perhaps the most exacting task in this volume. He's quick, he's consistent, he wins grands prix, and in any other set of circumstances he would be capable of challenging for the championship. Yet he is Michael Schumacher's team-mate, a role that is at one and the same time stimulating and frustrating. Stimulating because he is always being compared with the greatest of the age in the same car. Frustrating for the same reason. No matter how well prepared Barrichello may be at the start of a season, Schumacher will be better prepared. No matter how pumped up, Michael will be more so.

Yet there have been occasions when Barrichello has given the maestro a genuine race, most notably in the US and Canadian Grands Prix, when it looked as though the rub of the green was going in the Brazilian's direction. On both occasions, Schumacher dug deeper, and fortune went his way, while Barrichello was second. Yet he opted for what proved to be the winning strategy at Monza, heading the world champion across the line, and he picked up the Ferrari baton with aplomb to win the inaugural Chinese Grand Prix on a day when everything went wrong for his team-mate.

Barrichello is popular within the Ferrari squad. The obvious pleasure Schumacher gains when Rubens squeezes in a win is too spontaneous to be the contrived amusement of one who regards his team-mate as a makeweight. Schumacher has genuine respect and regard for the colleague whom he regards as a friend.

There were other fine days too. The inspired overtaking move Barrichello pulled on Jarno Trulli's Renault on the last lap at Magny-Cours. The front-row start at Silverstone, pole at Indianapolis, Monza, Shanghai and Interlagos. The dogged run to third at Spa after almost losing a lap on the leader after his Ferrari's rear wing needed changing. The first podium in a decade of trying in front of his home crowd at São Paolo, although sadly not the win that would symbolically have cemented his position alongside Emerson Fittipaldi, Nelson Piquet and his great hero, Ayrton Senna, in the panoply of Brazilian racing greats.

JUAN PABLO MONTOYA

JUAN Pablo Montoya's hair-trigger response to a group of irreverent hecklers that caused him to storm out of a sponsor's press conference in the run-up to the Australian Grand Prix placed further question marks over the Colombian driver's temperament as he prepared for the 2004 season.

Yet the Colombian's convincing victory in the Brazilian Grand Prix at Interlagos, 18 races later, not only wrapped up his four-year association with the BMW Williams squad on a convincing note, it also sent a message to Kimi Räikkönen – beaten into second place in Brazil – that the 2005 season, when they are partnered together at McLaren, will be an extremely close-fought affair with no quarter given or asked.

Prior to Interlagos, Montoya had been on the podium just once in 2004, a third-place finish behind Michael Schumacher and Jenson Button in the San Marino Grand Prix at Imola. In general, his year was scrappy. Montoya had expected much more from his final season with Sir Frank's team. The belief was that the team could build on its record of four wins in 2003 and launch a bid to

challenge at the front of the grid. But the new FW26 was far from perfect.

Montoya showed flashes of his innate driving genius, but not often, as the machinery didn't always allow that talent to shine through. He outqualified Ralf Schumacher 7–2 through the first nine races of the season until the US Grand Prix, when the younger Schumacher suffered the crash that sidelined him for much of the season. Considering 2004 in its entirety, the two Williams drivers were seldom on form together, and if Montoya hadn't managed to round off the year with that fine win in Brazil, his team-mate's strong run to second place behind brother Michael's Ferrari at Suzuka would have gone down as the best Williams performance of the year.

In so many ways, Montoya is a contradiction: supremely talented, yet irritatingly wilful; gregarious and very fast, yet moody and inconsistent. He likes his pals, his family and his burgers. Whether he can shift up a gear to handle Räikkönen in equal cars during 2005 remains one of the most tantalising of F1 imponderables.

Date of birth: *20 September 1975*

Team: *BMW WilliamsF1 Team*

Grand Prix starts in 2004: *18*

World Championship placing: *5th*

Wins: *1*

Poles: *0*

Points: *58*

JARNO Trulli's victory in the Monaco Grand Prix was one of the very best driving performances of the 2004 F1 world championship season. His pole winning lap was sublime, and the way in which he fended off Jenson Button's robust challenge in the closing stages of the chase marked him out as a man who'd finally unlocked the door to sustained success. Yet somehow his initial promise seemed to become psychologically unravelled. In many ways, the turning point was the French Grand Prix at Magny-Cours. He looked on course to complete a Renault 2-3 behind Schumacher's Ferrari and his own team-mate, Fernando Alonso, when he made a slight slip toward the end of the final lap; Barrichello got a run at him and squeezed through almost within sight of the chequered flag.

Understandably, the Renault team was disappointed, but implied criticism of Trulli's lapse seemed to be out of all proportion to the offence, bearing in mind that he had often shaded the ostensibly more talented Alonso during the first part of the championship campaign. Then, during the British Grand Prix at Silverstone, he suffered a big accident due to a mechanical problem, slamming into the barrier on the exit of Bridge corner. Thankfully, he walked away without a scratch, but the shunt certainly shook him up.

Thereafter, his performances tailed off and he complained that his R24 never felt quite right, although there was no serious suggestion that this lack of confidence was an after-effect of the accident. His relationship with Flavio Briatore's management company was also coming to an end, and his impending departure from the Renault squad was announced a few days before it was confirmed that Giancarlo Fisichella would replace him for 2005.

Well before the end of the year, Trulli signed a contract to drive for Toyota alongside Ralf Schumacher in 2005, a challenging opportunity that once more would see the popular Italian paired with a very quick team-mate. In many ways, 2005 could be the defining year for Trulli, who is still trying to muster a really consistent streak as he faces his ninth season in the F1 business.

JARNO TRULLI

Date of birth: *13 July 1974*

Teams: *Renault, Panasonic Toyota Racing*

Grand Prix starts in 2004: *17*

World Championship placing: *6th*

Wins: *1*

Poles: *1*

Points: *46*

GIANCARLO FISICHELLA

8

VERY much perceived as a close contemporary of his compatriot, Jarno Trulli, Giancarlo Fisichella has enjoyed a racing career that has paralleled that of his slightly younger rival, but neither has quite made the consistent performance breakthrough they had hoped for. Both have a single grand prix win to their credit, but while Trulli's victory was a high-profile success in the most famous race on the calendar, Fisichella's came in confused circumstances driving a Jordan-Ford Cosworth at Interlagos in 2003.

It would be a brave man who could make the definitive call as to whom is better. In this annual assessment, Trulli just gets the nod on the strength of that dynamic success through the streets of Monte Carlo. Yet Fisichella helped raise the profile and competitive pitch of the Sauber Petronas squad, often running with a heavier fuel load with the intention of making a two-stop strategy work to his advantage compared to the three-stoppers employed by many of his rivals.

Fisichella's arrival at Sauber was a key moment in his career. Although he'd won for Jordan in Brazil during 2003, lack of cash meant that the Silverstone based team had struggled against the odds, and Fisichella needed to turn back up the ladder of opportunity in a bid to sustain his career momentum. At Imola, he started 19th and finished ninth; at Silverstone, he was 20th on the grid and hauled through to sixth at the chequered flag. He was a regular points scorer and quickly proved himself to be a popular asset in Peter Sauber's equally popular team. Above all, Fisichella is a fighter, an experienced driver who races hard.

Flavio Briatore, who recruited him to replace Trulli at Renault for 2005, also believes he is a finisher, a driver who delivers a consistent performance from the first lap to the last. He takes every opportunity that comes his way, and he knows the team well, doesn't have a big ego and isn't interested in internal politics. The Renault boss is convinced that the combination of Fisichella and Alonso will be spectacular in 2005. Who would bet against him giving Alonso more trouble than he may be expecting?

Date of birth: 14 January 1973

Team: Sauber Petronas

Grand Prix starts in 2004: 18

World Championship placing: 11th

Wins: 0

Poles: 0

Points: 22

MARK WEBBER

9

IN the capricious F1 business, the sheer quality of a driver is often measured by less obvious yardsticks than simply his performance on the circuit. Mark Webber has a self-effacing quality about him, conceding that ultimately his credentials are built on the foundations of a fifth-place finish for Minardi in the 2002 Australian Grand Prix. In truth, either that's an excessively modest assessment, or the ripple effect of that achievement was good enough for Frank Williams to opt for his services in 2005. Either way, Webber consolidated his reputation in 2004 as one of F1's most promising contenders, although a measly seven world championship points reflected neither the true capability of the mild mannered Australian nor the strength in depth of the underfunded Jaguar team.

Webber started the season on a strong note, qualifying sixth in Australia and second in Malaysia, but neither race yielded a finish. Sixth place from 11th on the grid at Hockenheim was particularly satisfying, but otherwise his frugal tally of points was accumulated in dribs and drabs. Yet Webber's greatest strength was his genuine confidence in the Jaguar Racing workforce at a time when it was under increasing threat from Ford's economic bottom line. In retrospect, it seems clear that Webber had concluded quite early in the season that Ford was not going to deliver the necessary resources to enable Jaguar to compete at the highest level. In fact, the reality would be a lot worse, as now we all know.

Webber's even temperament and consistent approach undoubtedly gave strength to the Jaguar workforce, helping it stay motivated and focused with remarkable self-discipline right to the very last race. This straightforward and practical character clearly struck a chord with Frank Williams and Patrick Head, who together identified in Webber the qualities that they have admired in the past. Webber has now served his F1 apprenticeship and looks set to flourish at the centre of one of the most exacting team environments in the business.

Date of birth: 27 August 1976

Team: Jaguar Racing

Grand Prix starts in 2004: 18

World Championship placing: 13th

Wins: 0

Poles: 0

Points: 7

TAKUMA SATO

10

Date of birth: *28 January 1977*

Team: *Lucky Strike BAR Honda*

Grand Prix starts in 2004: *18*

World Championship placing: *8th*

Wins: *0*

Poles: *0*

Points: *34*

IN many ways, the genial Takuma Sato was one of the revelations of the 2004 world championship season. After an erratic start, the Japanese driver progressively honed and moderated his driving style without losing any of his raw speed. 'Taku' started the year with a good fifth place in Bahrain followed by another fifth from third on the grid at Barcelona, then an electrifying start at Monaco, which saw him clip Michael Schumacher's Ferrari as he rocketed off the line toward Ste Devote.

His early Monaco sprint proved all too brief, as his Honda V10 unstitched itself spectacularly after a couple of laps, laying an impenetrable wall of smoke in which Giancarlo Fisichella was unable to prevent his Sauber from vaulting over the back of David Coulthard's McLaren, eliminating them both from the contest.

In the European Grand Prix at the Nürburgring, Sato collided with Barrichello's Ferrari in the course of an over-optimistic passing manoeuvre, then spun in front of both Italian cars at Montreal, just as they were about to lap him. By this stage in the season, there were murmurs to the effect that the team management was getting a little bored with Sato's inconsistency – there were even suggestions that the team's third driver, Anthony Davidson, might replace him – but Sato rescued his reputation with a flawless run to third in the US Grand Prix behind Schumacher and Barrichello.

Yet still he made slight errors. A superb third place on the grid at the Hungaroring evaporated into a disappointing sixth in the race after his brimming enthusiasm caused him to run wide at the first corner. But then he finished the year with a reassuringly consistent run: fourth at Monza and in Japan, sixth in China and Brazil. It goes without saying that Sato was cheered to the echo each time he accelerated out on to the circuit at Suzuka, and he has been largely responsible for the huge resurgence of interest in F1 in Japan, which is now approaching the levels we saw in Ayrton Senna's heyday more than a decade ago.

Jenson Button
MAKING GOOD

By TONY DODGINS

JENSON Button truly emerged in 2004. His talent had been obvious from the outset at Williams in 2000, but at Benetton in 2001/2, it had all started to go wrong. The 2001 Benetton-Renault had been a dog and, in Giancarlo Fisichella, Jenson had found himself up against one of F1's underrated talents. He had finished the year 17th in the championship with only two points to his name.

The Benetton years did Jenson no favours and his image suffered. The problem, if such a word is apposite, was disastrous underperformance from Benetton coinciding with a 21-year-old Button having a 22-metre Princess yacht in pride of place in the Monte Carlo harbour when the F1 circus rolled into town.

The Ferrari was in the garage, there was the pad in Weybridge's exclusive St George's Hill and now the boat. And what had he achieved? There hadn't even been a podium, and now not the slightest sniff of one. Jealousy is an ugly trait, but omnipresent. Jenson had the playboy lifestyle, the pretty girl-friend, all the trappings, but apparently no substance.

A year earlier, he could do no wrong. He had been Britain's new hope, the boy wonder; now he was attracting a different kind of ink. It was an early lesson in media fickleness.

Button could have done with a sense of perspective. His Princess 22 was worth around £1 million, but his salary was estimated at anything up to five times that, thanks to the astute husbandry of David Robertson, who had managed his career since shelling out for Jenson's title winning British Formula Ford season. Button was earning from both Williams and Benetton, and the boat, pro rata, was to his pocket about as significant as a secondhand Ford Mondeo to a man earning the average British wage.

Unfairly, Button found himself having to re-establish his reputation, and in BAR Honda and Jacques Villeneuve, he found the perfect vehicle.

Villeneuve was diametrically opposite to Fisichella. If the Italian had been the under-appreciated talent who never had a car worthy of him, Villeneuve was the former champion who arrived in F1 with the right name and a vastly superior car. Reputation in excess of substance. Villeneuve knew Jenson would be trouble. Button, now with three years' experience, fancied it, and was right to. There were some early mind games to negotiate, which he did without problem. Once Button's natural speed proved superior, the psychology was irrelevant, and Villeneuve's days and dollars were numbered. Jenson was quick, personable and marketable; all in the garden seemed rosy. All the more so when the 006, the first BAR directly influenced by technical director Geoff Willis, flew in pre-season testing.

The doubters weren't convinced. There were accusations of showboating and sponsor wooing. But Melbourne confirmed the pace to be genuine. Jenson qualified on the second row, half a second behind the Ferraris, and only a fuel-rig problem prevented him from finishing fourth.

Next time out, at Sepang, he scored that elusive first podium, finishing third behind Schumacher and Montoya. Button and his loyal father, John, fell into each other's arms. He followed up with another in Bahrain, then took pole and finished second at Imola.

This was seriously impressive. Suddenly, BAR's aims of being best of the rest behind Ferrari looked anything but fanciful. Six months on and Jenson was all on his own behind the Maranello drivers in the final championship classification, with 85 points, four second places and ten podiums. And his team had achieved its ambition to be championship runner-up.

So how on earth did Jenson find himself at the centre of a tug-of-love in front of F1's Contracts Recognition Board? Never forget that F1 is business. Yes, there had been a load of blather about the 'new' Jenson, the marvellous new communications channelling that had sparked such progress at

Facing page: Jenson Button, happy with his performances in 2004.

Left: David Richards, who battled successfully to keep his prize asset for the 2005 season.

Above: The combination of Button and BAR proved to be the most consistent challenger to Ferrari, even though a victory was elusive.
Photographs: Darren Heath

Clockwise, from above: In the big league. Jenson is congratulated by Michael Schumacher on his superb drive in San Marino; despite the tension, Button and BAR maintained a professional working reationship; John Byfield, one of Button's management team who sought to move their man to Williams; Button emerged as one of the sport's top stars in 2004; Jenson in action at the Canadian Grand Prix in Montreal.

Facing page: An eye on the title – Button's long-term goal.

Photographs: Darren Heath

BAR, and so on and so forth. Doubtless, David Richards's management capabilities are first rate – his record in business reflects that – but let's not over-complicate things. Geoff Willis had designed a fast racing car, Honda had screwed together a quick engine, and Button was the same talented driver he had always been, with added experience and confidence.

It should have been no surprise that his management was talking to Williams. They are paid to maximise his opportunities. Forget about loyalty and all that hokum. Richards hired Button because he is a quick driver; Button joined BAR at a time when he had few options. If a team like Williams wanted Jenson back, obviously he'd listen.

A few short months earlier, the decision would have been a no-brainer. But by the time 'Buttongate' erupted, most inconveniently as F1 went on its summer holidays, the logic was not so clear cut. BAR was having a memorable season, while BMW Williams was struggling with its FW26 and, rumour had it, there were a few rumblings of discontent among a backroom staff noted for its stability. Patrick Head had just taken a step back to allow Australian Sam Michael to emerge at the forefront of the technical team, and Mark Webber, a fellow Aussie, was a shoe-in for one Williams seat.

Button's attempted defection, when it came, was handled appallingly. You can understand that, perhaps, it was necessary for BAR and David Richards to be kept in the dark for as long as possible to minimise their chances of closing contractual loopholes that Jenson's legal team would try to exploit.

It would have been nice and honourable for Jenson to have gone to Richards, shaken his hand and said, 'Look, David, I'm awfully sorry, but this is what is about to kick off.' And doubtless highly impractical, too. But when the muck hit the fan, leading to Jenson and his dad being sat solus, on different tables, at the BAR motorhome in Hungary, like a couple of lepers at a tea party, Button did seem highly perplexed at the intensity of the backlash. He looked like a rabbit on the M25 in rush hour.

Perhaps, at that point, he should have taken control, accepted responsibility for his actions, properly explained the issues to the press and why it had had to happen like it did. And perhaps he should have phoned Richards the moment it all began, so that at least when DR had been confronted by national media inquiries, he hadn't been left clutching a fistful of straws.

Williams had moved to re-sign Button because it had been told that the conditions allowing BAR to take up its 2005 option had not been met, centring on the certainty of Honda works engine supply, a condition of the option. The Japanese manufacturer had stated publicly that its contract contained a get-out clause if it was unhappy with potential F1 rule changes.

There were suggestions that, technically, the absence of such certainty had been legitimately argued in front of the CRB, but that the matter had been overridden by one of Button's representatives accepting verbally, in front of witnesses, that all the criteria allowing BAR Honda to exercise its 2005 option had been satisfied. Before acting, Williams allegedly asked Button's management whether this affirmation had been made, and was told that it had not.

The whole matter was regrettable. Jenson's state of mind was nicely illustrated by a TV interview. 'It's not that I wanted to leave,' he said, 'just that I wanted to go somewhere else.' We knew what he meant. The only reason he had considered moving teams was because he had thought his BAR contract was not valid for 2005, and it turned out that he had been wrongly advised.

Can BAR and Jenson go on as if nothing has happened? Time will tell. But by the end of the season, they had already done it for three months without any fall-off in performance.

'We've got to convince Jenson, quite clearly,' said Richards in Brazil at the final race, as the pair went through the motions of a kiss-and-make-up for the benefit of the media hordes.

'Jenson, why did you think the future would have been brighter at Williams? Do you have doubts about the technical side at BAR,' came the question.

'I think I've already said enough in the press about that,' was Jenson's lame response.

'Let me just interrupt there on Jenson's part,' offered the erudite Richards. 'Clearly, we're a young team. It's quite clear that the records of others are far more established. It's a fact I can't get away from, so it's not unreasonable for a young driver to wonder if BAR is going to be able to deliver in the long term. I say that we can, but there must be question marks, quite clearly. But now we are committed to working together to make sure it happens next year.'

Let's hope that they can. Jenson the driver is fully mature; Jenson the politician is still learning.

WHERE NEXT?

By ERIC SILBERMANN

Above: Michael Schumacher and Ferrari out in front – no matter which way the rules are framed.

Right: Max Mosley, imposing engine capacity reductions for 2006.

Top right: Big players such Luca di Montezemolo (left) and Norbert Haug (right) represent the manufacturers' interests.

Far right: Still calling the shots, Bernie Ecclestone.

Photographs: Darren Heath

FORMULA 1 is to undergo a radical shake-up of its technical and sporting regulations over the next two years, but at the time of writing – a week after the 2004 season finale – it is not yet clear exactly what those changes will be, and that's typical of the malaise affecting the sport. Given that only 19 weeks separate the final race of 2004 from the 2005 curtain raiser, that the future of three teams is uncertain, and that the F1 boffins usually like doodling a new car on their 'Etch A Sketch' pads six months ahead of a new season, it is not unreasonable to talk of a crisis.

All the F1 movers and shakers are in agreement that change is needed to achieve the three objectives of reducing speeds, cutting costs and improving the show. However, when it comes to the means of implementing these admirable principles, the team owners cannot agree among themselves, let alone with the governing body, the FIA.

Now read that sentence again and apply it to any other sport. Can you imagine football managers rewriting the offside rule, or tennis players rejigging the scoring system? Of course not, as it smacks of self-interest. A football manager with a short, long-armed goalkeeper would be lobbying for a very wide goal with a low crossbar, and a tennis player with an excellent return of serve would request points scored against service to count double.

On 6 July 2004, scepticism notwithstanding, the FIA asked the teams to put forward a new set of rules. Inevitably, the 6 September deadline passed without any agreement having

been reached, so the FIA came up with three sets of proposals for the teams to chose from. Guess what? Still no agreement. Then, in Brazil, in the tone of a headmaster ticking off his pupils for not submitting their course work on time, the FIA issued a final set of rules that, in the absence of anything constructive from the teams, would be applied for 2005.

'The TWG [Technical Working Group] met most recently on October 15, 2004, but still failed to vote 8 to 2 in favour of any one of the three packages within the 45 days specified by Article 7.5,' intoned the FIA missive. 'The World Motor Sport Council was therefore free to impose its own measures from October 21, 2004, to come into force no sooner than three months from publication. On October 21, 2004, the WMSC decided to impose Package 2 and that those parts of it which apply to 2005 would come into force on March 1, 2005 and the remainder on January 1, 2006.'

Without going into detail, the main changes specify less downforce, engines that last for two entire grand prix weekends, rather than one, and only one set of tyres per driver for qualifying and the race. For 2006, a new 2.4-litre V8 engine formula comes into being, much to the displeasure of many of the big car companies that currently dominate the sport.

Apparently sent by second-class post, as it landed in the Brazil media centre a couple of days later, came another FIA release, this time outlining the new qualifying format. The governing body would have us believe that all its decisions are the result of long deliberation and much contemplative

beard stroking, but the new timetable was evidently a knee-jerk reaction to the Suzuka 'cram-it-all-into-one day' formula, dictated by the threat of a typhoon.

Having final qualifying on race morning is a great idea, giving the Sunday spectators something to watch now that the warm-up session is no more. The Saturday session will no longer serve simply to decide the running order for qualifying proper. Instead, the times from both sessions will be aggregated, and the first session will be run in reverse finishing order of the previous grand prix, thus favouring the winner, rather than penalising him with running first, as was the case in 2004.

At this point, the Interlagos paddock echoed to the sound of hooves clippety-clopping down the pit lane as team owners tried to shut the stable door, apparently unaware that the F1 horse had already bolted. They convened no fewer than three meetings in Brazil to try to draw up their own set of rules. Also in attendance was one Bernard Charles Ecclestone. I know some of the team bosses are well into their second half-century, but did they really believe 'The Bolt' was still running the Brabham team? Maybe Bernie just fancied reprising his greatest role, when he starred in the FISA-FOCA wars back in the '80s.

I'm not sure how the old magician did it, but Bernie encouraged them to draw up a plan centred on a two-day grand prix weekend, with testing during the actual season reduced to just ten days, and four hours of free testing on the Friday of the grand prix weekend. These were the very proposals he had been banging on about for years, as inevitably it would lead to far more money generating races on the calendar and, of course, Mr E doesn't earn a bean from testing.

Combining all the skills of a modern-day Machiavelli with those of a vaudeville hypnotist, Ecclestone then produced his master-stroke: he persuaded the team bosses to link these proposals to the fate of the French and British Grands Prix. Get these rules approved and the teams could split all the revenue from the two events. It was only at this final meeting

that the team bosses realised that one horse, the Prancing Horse, was still chewing at its hay net and refusing to budge from the stable.

It was crystal clear to everyone that Ferrari would refuse to sign up to a testing ban. While other team owners have used their capital to build palatial factories that might eventually serve as mausoleums for their F1 aspirations, or simply trousered their sponsorship money to spend on yachts and private jets, Ferrari has invested heavily in two test tracks. Cynics might add that, having watched the dismal performance of the F2004/Bridgestone tyre combo in the damp conditions at Interlagos, Ferrari really needs to do as much testing as possible!

Et voila! Having tried unsuccessfully to blame the Silverstone crisis on the BRDC, then on the British teams for refusing his financial package, Ecclestone could now point the finger at the Evil Empire that is Ferrari. As for Mosley, he congratulated his charges on their diligence, but pointed out that unless Ferrari signed, he could only score them nine out of ten for their efforts, and that without unanimity, sadly, he could not accept their proposals.

So where does that leave F1 in 2005? The new weekend format should provide a better show for the paying public, and the new technical rules (whatever is eventually decided) might improve the racing and produce more overtaking. On the down side, making an engine last for two weekends seems a ridiculous move for the blue-riband category of motor racing, when eight-year-old kids who go karting don't face such restrictions. As a driver, going to a grand prix knowing that you have already lost ten places on the grid because your motor went pop a fortnight ago will be hard to swallow, and for the fans, hard to follow.

Any major rule changes, however, always favour the best teams, who have the resources and brain power to find ways around them. The only conclusion, therefore, is that we should prepare ourselves for yet another season of Ferrari domination.

Facing page: Under threat. Kimi Räikkönen and his McLaren-Mercedes racing at Silverstone in the British Grand Prix. At one point it looked as though this venue might be a thing of the past.

Below: Ferrari, the most powerful force in Formula 1.
Photographs: Darren Heath

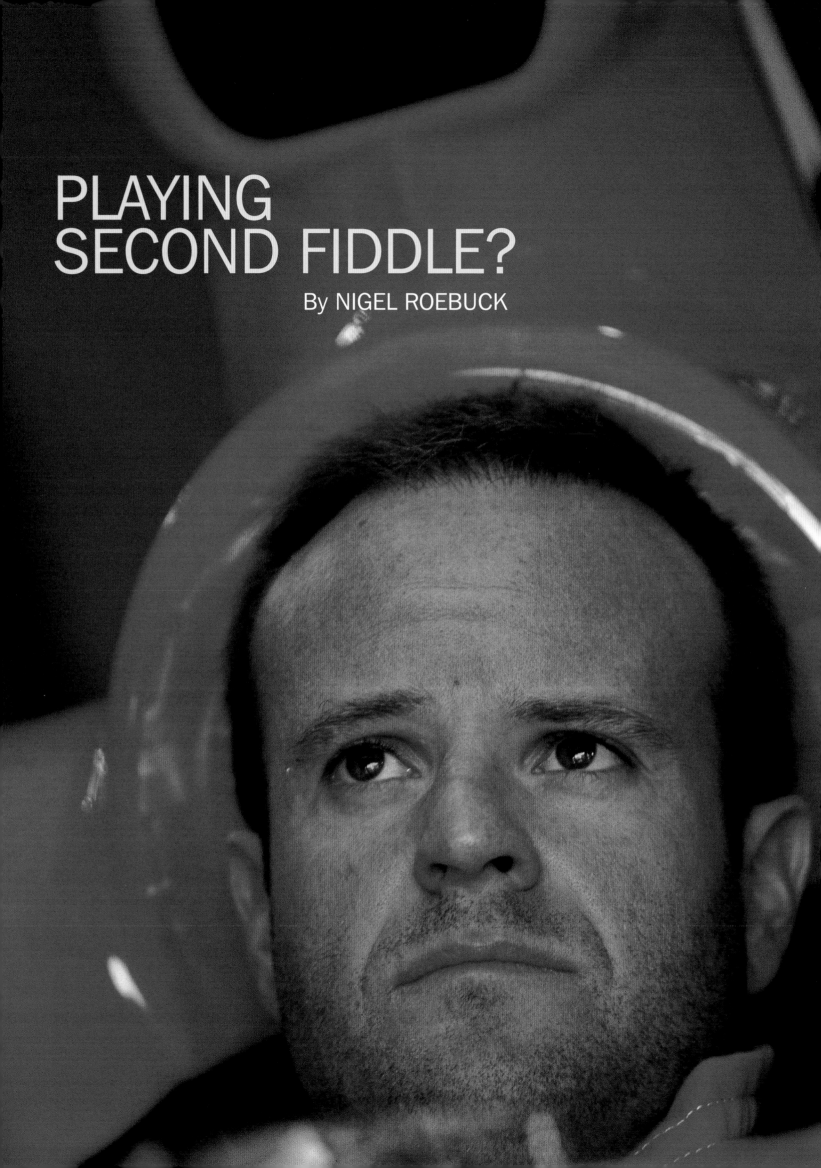

PLAYING
SECOND FIDDLE?

By NIGEL ROEBUCK

Facing page: The second-best seat in the house? A pensive Rubens Barrichello.

Right: Jarno Trulli took a dominant win at Monaco, but his status at Renault was such that he soon became dispensable.

Below: Test driver Ricardo Zonta grabbed the opportunity of replacing Toyota's under-achieving number-two driver Cristiano da Matta.

Photographs: Darren Heath

Above: Felipe Massa battled hard with Giancarlo Fisichella.

Above centre: The inexperienced Christian Klien was rarely able to match his team leader, Mark Webber.

Photographs: Darren Heath

What are the qualities that define the ideal number-two F1 driver? They depend to a great extent on where you're standing.

'When I was a driver,' said Gerhard Berger, 'for me, it was simple: the ideal team-mate was a guy three seconds slower! When I was working for BMW, with Williams, I wanted two drivers who were both super-quick, to push each other…' And two drivers, of course, capable of winning grands prix, which Berger had with Juan Pablo Montoya and Ralf Schumacher.

The role of the 'number two', though, is not clearly defined, in that it does not amount to the same thing in every team. During the 2004 season, it was obvious that Takuma Sato was number two to Jenson Button at BAR, and the same was true of Felipe Massa at Sauber, Cristiano da Matta at Toyota, Christian Klien at Jaguar and Giorgio Pantano at Jordan.

Elsewhere, the situation was, by shades, somewhat different. At McLaren, David Coulthard was obviously the *de facto* number two to Kimi Räikkönen, but Ron Dennis never publicly described him as such. And it was much the same at Renault, where Fernando Alonso was the 'golden boy' – but Monaco winner Jarno Trulli outpaced him for much of the season.

In other ways, too, the situation varies from team to team. Most, for example, allow their drivers to race with each other, figuring that this is healthy for both, and asking them only not to take out each other along the way.

This was not the situation at Ferrari, however, where Rubens Barrichello continued to partner Michael Schumacher. 'I don't think there's any doubt,' said the team's technical director, Ross Brawn, 'that Rubens has the toughest job in Formula 1, in that he's got the same equipment as the strongest driver there's been for a very long time. When you're up against someone like Michael, it's so easy to overstretch yourself and go down the other side of the slope.

'In so many ways, though, Rubens is the ideal team-mate for Michael. He's never been malicious toward him – all right, in Austria a couple of years ago, he got upset, but he didn't say, "You're all a bunch of bastards." He just said, "I don't agree with what's going on; it's not fair," and that was the end of it. You know where you are with Rubens: he's a great team member and a *very* talented driver. But, of course, he's in the shadow of Michael, and it tends to reflect on him somewhat.'

Eddie Irvine, Barrichello's predecessor at Ferrari, approached the job in a very different way, publicly acknowledging from the start that Schumacher was on another plane, and thereby creating the impression that finishing second to him was almost like winning. In time, this prompted Irvine fatuously – and surely facetiously – to suggest that, while Schumacher was clearly the best on earth, he was the second best.

Not once, though, did Irvine win a race against Schumacher; not once did he beat him for sheer pace. Barrichello, however, has done that on a number of occasions – not always, but usually toward the end of a season, when yet another of Schumacher's championships had been put to bed. Could this be because Michael had backed off a touch – or because Rubens, finally, had found himself on a level playing field?

The fact is that Barrichello was not truly a number-two driver at all. When Williams was casting about for a team leader

Above: Thumbs-up from Barrichello on the grid at Indianapolis, while Jean Todt (left) appears in relaxed mood.

Photograph: Darren Heath

for 2005, the offer was made to Rubens, but he turned it down, preferring to commit himself to another couple of years' apparent slavery with Ferrari.

At the time, many were critical, in effect suggesting that he was afraid to go out into the big, wide world, to accept the responsibilities of team leadership, and so on. Barrichello shrugged at that, pointing out that he was in F1 for success, and that, even with all the strictures implicit in being Schumacher's team-mate, his chances of achieving it were greater at Ferrari than anywhere else.

There was no defying his logic. Since Barrichello had joined the team, at the beginning of the 2000 season, Ferrari had won more than two-thirds of the races, and although, at the time of writing, 'only' nine of the victories had come his way, how many races might he have won with another team?

That's the strictly hard-headed approach, though. The daily frustration of Barrichello's professional life in 2004 was

that he, far more than any other F1 driver, was very obviously considered 'secondary' to his team-mate. Had he been partnered with Montoya at Williams or Räikkönen at McLaren, he could at least have gone into every race with the thought that if he could win it, he could win it…

Rubens becomes defensive when this is suggested: 'Before I joined the team, I said to Jean Todt, "Look, I'm very happy to come to Ferrari – it's the chance of my life – but if you tell me that it will be in my contract that I have to let Michael by, I'll go somewhere else." And it's never written like that. I bet you that all 20 of the drivers have a clause in their contract, saying that if the team makes a decision, they should respect it. It's as simple as that.'

Perhaps so, but the devil, as ever, is in the detail, in the *application*. Unless a situation arises when the world championship is reaching a crucial point, and only one of their drivers has a serious shot at the title, there are no

Twice – in 2001 and 2002 – Rubens was ordered to yield to Michael on the very run up to the line, and on the second occasion it was for the win.

'I want to have the freedom to win if I'm there because I deserve it,' Barrichello said, when he signed for Ferrari. 'And I hope, in those circumstances, that the team will be happy for me to win. But, until I start driving alongside Michael, we probably won't find out…'

In Austria, he found out. 'When I was at Stewart, I had a special relationship with Jackie, and I have something like that with Todt – but it's only a small percentage of what Michael has with him, and it's not going to change.'

Barrichello, loyal and faithful to his team, and also more than capable of outpacing Schumacher on occasion, of winning races on merit, was undoubtedly as ideal a number two to Michael as Ferrari could ever find. Why? Because he wasn't really a number two at all.

'Michael does not like to be beaten, that's for sure,' Rubens smiled, perhaps a touch ruefully. 'I have a good relationship with him, and I don't want to say too much, because it could be quite political. But it's a fact he doesn't like to be beaten. I very much feel that God gave me this chance of driving for Ferrari. It's just that I have a small stone in my shoe which is called Michael…'

Below: Barrichello took two end-of-year victories in Italy and China.

Bottom: 'Stone in the Schu.'
Photographs: Darren Heath

team orders at such teams as Williams, McLaren and Renault. But unless Schumacher has had a qualifying problem and is back on the grid – or, perhaps, has already sewn up the latest of his umpteen championships – Barrichello goes into every race knowing that, at some point, Todt may be on the blower to him: 'In the best interests of the team…' Which is to say, Michael.

Time was when the only team orders at Ferrari were that, in the event of the cars running first and second, they should cross the line in the order in which they assumed those positions. More recently, in the multiple-stop 'refuelling era' – in the course of which, a 1-2 for Ferrari has become the monotonous norm – the crucial moment has been the final stops: whoever is ahead afterwards shall win the race. Unless, of course, it is Barrichello and Schumacher's latest title has yet to be clinched…

The A1-Ring became a place of notoriety for that reason.

GLOBAL REACH
F1'S WIDENING HORIZONS

By ADAM COOPER

ONE of the big stories of the 2004 season was the addition of Bahrain and China to the world championship schedule. To put that double whammy into perspective, in the previous 30 years only four completely new venues had been added to the calendar, namely Japan (1976), Australia (1985), Hungary (1986) and Malaysia (1999).

There have been other occasions when the circus has returned to a country that had held a race in the past, but two visits in one year to hitherto uncharted territories is without recent precedent. In July 2005, the sport is due to visit yet another new location in Turkey, on the border between Europe and Asia. And still they're queuing up to play host to F1. In October 2004, Bernie Ecclestone revealed plans for a race in Cancun in Mexico as early as 2006, while he has also endorsed efforts to hold a race in Cape Town. Many other projects are in the pipeline.

All this activity suggests that the sport is in a healthy state, but Ecclestone has given himself a problem. How does he fit in all the races? The answer, at least in the short term, is by making the calendar busier.

As long ago as 1977, the annual schedule expanded to 17 grands prix, although the total subsequently stabilised at 16. The higher figure was not reached again until 1997, remaining sacrosanct until 2004, when it was finally breached. Eight of the record 18 events took place outside Europe.

The teams had always resisted enlargement of the schedule, but the Concorde Agreement ensured that they were suitably compensated for the addition of an 18th race. After some brinkmanship from Ecclestone, the 'extra' event turned out not to be China, Bahrain or even a return to Belgium, but Canada. Go figure.

At the time of writing, the definitive 2005 calendar had yet to be published, but the original version released by the FIA World Motor Sport Council in October listed 19 events, all the existing races being joined by Turkey. Almost half, however, had some form of provisional label attached to them, or did not yet have a definite date. It was farcical, and further proof that even Ecclestone was struggling to fit in everything and please everybody. At the heart of discussions was the ongoing debate about the British and French Grands Prix, both of which faced uncertain futures.

The human cost of expansion seems to count for little. The 2004 schedule was tough for all concerned, and the tired faces at São Paulo Airport on Monday 25 October were not just the result of the previous night's end-of-season partying.

'Some of our guys are already saying, "Where does this leave us?"' said Adrian Newey. 'People have got wives and children. If you look at the calendar, it's more than just the extra races. Quite a few of them are back to back, and for the mechanics that means weeks away from home.'

It may or may not have been a coincidence that the Silverstone saga came to a head at the same time as the Cancun and Cape Town projects were announced. Whatever the case, it's hard not to see a correlation between the expansion overseas and a reduction in the number of European races. It's a trend that worries a lot of people in the sport, including FIA President Max Mosley.

'I'm all for globalisation, but not at the expense of our traditional events,' said Mosley. 'We've got to be very careful about destroying the roots of F1. I think it's a little bit worrying that we've got question marks over both the British and French

GPs. One view is that it's market forces. Another view is what creates the market? If you don't have the traditional events, then maybe the product becomes different and the market changes. I think it needs to be looked at very carefully.'

Nevertheless, Mosley acknowledges that there will be more new races: 'There are lots of different possibilities. Really that's Bernie's department. Bernie's job is to make F1 work commercially, and also to look after the shareholders in his company. My job is to look at the wider interests of motor sport. My job and Bernie's are not always the same, therefore there are different interests. We nearly always manage to find a good compromise.'

'I'm very happy, as long as we don't forget Europe,' agreed Flavio Briatore. 'The grand prix in France is very important, the grand prix in England is very important. But I don't care if the race is in London city or Silverstone. This is not my problem. Bernie's done an incredible job. When we arrive there, everything's done, but the negotiations and convincing people to spend this kind of money is not really simple.'

It's thought that the lowest annual fee paid to Formula One Management by a European promoter is around $13.5 million, and the price paid by government funded 'flyaways' is certainly a lot more than that. On top of that fee, circuits also have to update their facilities each year to the standards required by the FIA and FOM, and provide all the necessary personnel and equipment to run a grand prix meeting. Their sole income comes from gate receipts.

It became public knowledge in 2004 that a typical Bernie deal also involves a ten-per-cent compound increase over each year of a five-year contract, a highly unusual arrangement. But most seem happy to agree to it, making life extremely difficult for the likes of Silverstone and Magny-Cours.

The other impetus for going beyond Europe is the desperate effort to extend the life of tobacco sponsorship. In that sense, most of the major teams have a vested interest in expansion to new venues.

'Bernie is trying to protect tobacco and have different races that guarantee us tobacco,' confirmed Briatore. 'Tobacco is big, big income, not only for Renault, but for everyone in F1, and we don't want to lose it.'

Cynics might assume that Ecclestone simply goes where the money is and does the deals that suit him. Whatever one thinks of the commercial arrangements, however, there are few complaints about the venues he has added to the schedule. Herrmann Tilke continues to receive rave reviews both for his actual circuit designs and the facilities that he builds alongside them.

More importantly, the new events fill huge voids in the sport's global reach. The benefits to major international players like Toyota and Bridgestone are obvious, and every F1 marketing man and sponsor agent now has extra ammunition with which to tempt sponsors. Potentially, there are also funds to be sourced locally. China, in particular, could be a rich source of revenue, although it may take time.

'I think F1 has to understand patience,' said Ron Dennis. 'But it's inevitable that there will be relationships between racing teams and Chinese companies. I think China sees the world as its market, and the world sees China vice versa.'

'It's very exciting, but we need to educate them a little bit,' agreed Jordan's Ian Phillips. 'There's no racing culture there, but what is great is that the signs are that they're going to em-

Main photograph: **Red ship of the desert.
Michael Schumacher in Bahrain.**

Inset: **Flyaway package. Formula 1's
equipment crated up in Brazil.**
Photographs: Darren Heath

brace it. They won't be giving it away without good reason, that's for sure. It reminds me of Japan in the eighties.'

At the end of the day, F1 is built around the TV audience, and it could be argued that it matters little to the casual viewer where a race is held. However, there is an important side issue. The bulk of Ecclestone's TV income comes from the major European broadcasters, who are increasingly concerned about losing their traditional Sunday-afternoon slots. Asian events kick off early in the morning, when live audiences are small; American races hit early-evening prime time, but create havoc by disrupting regular schedules.

'You head west, and it helps your audience,' said ITV's Martin Brundle. 'You head east, and it hurts your audience.' The counter argument, of course, is that other parts of the world can see more races at a convenient time.

It remains to be seen how Ecclestone will squeeze all the

events he wants into the schedule – his support of efforts to cut testing in 2005 was part of a campaign to free up time for races. Some observers question how he can continue to justify having two races apiece in Italy and Germany, even if the current popularity of the Ferrari/Schumacher combination guarantees interest. However, times change. Three years ago, dreary Barcelona appeared to be surplus to requirements, but the emergence of Fernando Alonso has made the Spanish Grand Prix a colourful, emotionally charged weekend.

Despite his antagonism toward Silverstone, Ecclestone has demonstrated an appreciation of traditional names in the past. Over the years, he's taken us back to revamped versions of Spa, Interlagos, Nürburgring, Kyalami, Mexico City, Buenos Aires and the Österreichring, although the last four eventually disappeared for a second time. It's no coincidence that, after endless discussions with would-be promoters, he selected

Indianapolis as the venue for the United States Grand Prix.

'We'll have to see,' said Ecclestone. 'Maybe we'll lose some races outside Europe and replace them. China was super, and I was delighted with it. We were trying for ten years to do something there. It's very important. All the teams were thinking I was totally mad thinking of going to China, and now obviously they've seen it. Bahrain services that part of the world. I've always wanted South Africa; it's on the same time zone as Europe, so it's good for TV. We're a world championship. When we started in Europe, some of these countries weren't even invented. I don't want to lose Silverstone, contrary to popular belief. We just need to upgrade it a bit.'

Inevitably, Tilke's government funded projects have raised the bar to an impossible level for any venue that has to operate on a commercial basis, or even with modest support from local authorities.

'Bernie is a very intelligent man,' said Jackie Stewart as he surveyed the paddock in Shanghai. 'He knows that this could not have been achieved by private enterprise. And it could not have been achieved in an Italy, a France, a Germany, in almost any other country. The countries that have spent large sums, like Malaysia and Bahrain, have done it through the monarchy or a government that has decided to make a major statement. I applaud them for that, but what you can't have is a basis where private enterprise is not permitted to continue.'

'Others may not be able to match it,' said Mosley of China. 'But it's quite realistic to set it as the target, because in the end, that will become the world level. One of the reasons they got the Olympic Games is that they can do what's necessary. The UK is trying to do what's necessary in 2012. If they can compete with China for the Olympic Games, why not for the Grand Prix? It's not our problem where the money comes from.'

Insets, clockwise from top left: Souvenir stalls outside the Indianapolis Speedway.
Photograph: Darren Heath

Bungalows inside the Shanghai circuit.
Photograph: Bryn Williams/crash.net

Exuberant fans in Australia contrast with the polite and restrained crowd at Suzuka.
Photographs: Darren Heath

Formula 1 review

Contributors
BOB CONSTANDUROS
MAURICE HAMILTON
ALAN HENRY

F1 illustrations
ADRIAN DEAN

SCUDERIA FERRARI MARLBORO

1

MICHAEL SCHUMACHER

Photograph: Darren Heath

2

RUBENS BARRICHELLO

Photograph: Darren Heath

© ADRIAN DEAN

FERRARI F2004

SPONSORS	Philip Morris, Vodafone, Fiat, Shell, Bridgestone, AMD, Olympus
ENGINE	**Type:** Ferrari 053 **No. of cylinders (vee angle):** V10 (90°) **Sparking plugs:** NGK **Electronics:** Magneti Marelli **Fuel:** Shell **Oil:** Shell
TRANSMISSION	**Gearbox:** Ferrari seven-speed longitudinal automatic
CHASSIS	**Front suspension:** double wishbones, pushrod-activated torsion bars **Rear suspension:** double wishbones, pushrod-activated torsion bars **Dampers:** Sachs
	Wheel diameter: front: 13 in rear: 13 in **Tyres:** Bridgestone **Brake pads:** Brembo **Brake discs:** Brembo **Brake calipers:** Brembo
	Steering: Ferrari power-assisted **Battery:** Magneti Marelli
DIMENSIONS	**Wheelbase:** 3050 mm **Track:** front: 1470 mm rear: 1405 mm **Formula weight:** 600 kg including driver

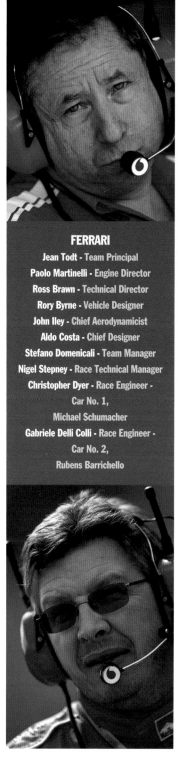

FERRARI

Jean Todt - Team Principal

Paolo Martinelli - Engine Director

Ross Brawn - Technical Director

Rory Byrne - Vehicle Designer

John Iley - Chief Aerodynamicist

Aldo Costa - Chief Designer

Stefano Domenicali - Team Manager

Nigel Stepney - Race Technical Manager

Christopher Dyer - Race Engineer - Car No. 1,

Michael Schumacher

Gabriele Delli Colli - Race Engineer - Car No. 2,

Rubens Barrichello

Above left: Michael Schumacher, superb as always.

Above: Ross Brawn and the Maranello technical team surpassed themselves again in 2004.

Top: Jean Todt kept his usual steady hand on the management tiller.
Photographs: Darren Heath

YET another remarkable season for Ferrari saw more mind boggling statistics cascading into the F1 record books. The Scuderia completed more laps (2,196) and therefore more kilometres (10,745) than any other team during the 2004 season, the longest in the history of Formula 1. These facts, along with an extraordinary set of results – 15 wins, 12 pole positions, 14 fastest race laps, eight 1-2 finishes and 262 points scored out of a total of 324 – underpinned another remarkable year of achievement in a dominant era that looks in no danger of coming to a close.

'The 2003 season was a close call for us, and a wake-up call in that sense,' said technical director Ross Brawn. 'We had a fantastic season in 2002, and perhaps that both invigorated our opposition and maybe we were a little conservative in a lot of areas. In that sort of position, you are always a little bit cautious about pushing things too hard because you are seeking to consolidate your position.

'So we got into 2003 and saw that perhaps we'd not progressed as much as we should have done, on the cars, on the tyres, on the engine. And it takes a while to react to these things. So in 2003, we did sort ourselves out, and I think 2004 reflects that, and we're trying to avoid the mistakes that maybe we made in 2002.'

So how does the well-honed Ferrari infrastructure avoid becoming lulled into a warm sense of complacency? What pro-active steps can the management take to head off such problems?

'I think we all know that can happen, but sometimes I think you need the prod of losing a race to rejuvenate the situation,' said Brawn. 'When you consider in F1 that [there are] different chassis, different engines, different tyres, different drivers, different designers, you appreciate just how competitive this business is when they end up within a few tenths of each other. If you've got an advantage, you seek to emphasise that in terms of reliability and make sure your car finishes [races], and you emphasise that side of it. When you are behind in terms of performance, then the balance is different. So we're just making a judgement all the time as to where we should be putting our efforts and where our priorities should be.

'We have also done some reorganisation internally. Rory [Byrne] has done a fantastic job at Ferrari and will continue to do a

fantastic job at Ferrari, but he's identified that in the next few years, he wants to perhaps reduce his role at Ferrari. So we're developing people internally to take up the mantle, and that's given some interesting fresh impetus to the organisation, given some people some new responsibilities, but all under Rory's watchful eye. That's what we call dynamic stability. We want to keep it moving – continuity without it going stale.'

The Ferrari F2004 exploded out of the box in Melbourne and delivered such a dominant 1-2 result that the opposition was wrong-footed from the very start of the season. Brawn confirmed that the car was pretty much as good as it looked, with no hidden shortcomings or potential areas of technical concern to ruffle the serene progress of the Maranello campaign.

'To be honest, it's been a very good car,' he said. 'It's had its reliability niggles, but nothing major, just the little bits that go wrong. I think there have been one or two close calls, occasions when we've got back to the factory and found a crack in a piston, perhaps. Then there was the issue of the exhaust failure in Spain.'

Brawn admitted that the exhaust problem had been a nerve-racking issue that could have gone either way. 'That was a close one,' he said. 'I went and had a [close] look at the car during a pit stop, and radioed Michael and told him, "Carry on, but I don't think we're going to finish this one." But in fact, the pit stop was the worst scenario for the problem, as the exhaust gas was getting on to some bodywork and the whole thing flared up.

'So literally as he went to pull away and he got on to the throttle, the whole thing went up in flames, but I could see that it had blown itself out by the time he'd got down the pit lane.'

Brawn acknowledged that his thoughts had turned to the Monaco Grand Prix of several years before, when Schumacher had lost the race because an overheating exhaust had damaged a rear suspension member. 'Since then, what we did was fit sensors on the suspension, so we were able to look at the data to see if the suspension was in fact getting hot,' he continued, 'but it wasn't, and so we were comfortable to let the car run.

'In fact, the exhaust was blowing on the bodywork, which was not critical, so the pit stop had been the worst case because for the few seconds after the refuelling had finished, Michael had his

Above: Barrichello in Hungary, where he finished a strong second to his team-mate.

Right: Test driver Luca Badoer was not needed on race days, but was an integral part of the team.

Below: The Ferrari pit crew – vigilant, unflappable, relentlessly efficient.

Photographs: Darren Heath

Facing page: Barrichello rose to the occasion to win the Italian and Chinese GPs with flawless precision.

Photograph: Darren Heath

foot on the throttle, so there was no air going through there and massive exhaust build-up. So in fact, for the next stop, we told Michael not to go on the throttle and pull out of the pits as quietly as he could. Which worked fine for us.'

Brawn was reluctant to nominate a best race for Ferrari in 2004, but allowed that the team's overall progress had been aided by Bridgestone's development pace. 'We've certainly had an advantage in racing conditions with the tyres,' he said. 'The tyres have been great in the races, even though they've perhaps not had the one-lap performance on occasion which Michelin have enjoyed, so

sometimes we've been stuck in potentially strong situations, but not been able to use the performance of the car.

'So sometimes we had to take strategic decisions which put the driver on to a bit of track where there was nobody around. So the switch to the four-stop strategy at Magny-Cours was only about getting the jump on Alonso and then being able to use the car. If you did the calculations, the four-stop wasn't faster, but if you're being held up in traffic a second a lap, you're just stuck there hoping you're going to get the jump in the pit stop, which is not so predictable.

'So a lot of the season has been around accepting the fact that we may not always be on pole, but we would always have a very competitive car during the race, using the strategy to play to our strengths and compensate for any weaknesses.'

Michael Schumacher, of course, delivered another virtually flawless season's performance, winning 13 of the 18 races on his way to his seventh world championship crown. Brawn, like all his team colleagues, was unstinting in his admiration for the German driver, who continued to be the key motivating element within the extraordinary winning machine that is Ferrari. His respect for Rubens Barrichello, the winner of two races and runner-up in the title chase, is correspondingly well-honed.

'I think Rubens has one of the toughest jobs in Formula 1,' said Brawn. 'It's difficult in that Michael has been the reference point for the past decade. He's relentless and hardly ever has a bad day, so you can't rely on that if you're trying to beat him. You've got to have an exceptional day to beat Michael most of the time.

'Of course, each year Rubens spends his winter psyching himself up, getting fit and determined to beat Michael, and he comes back to find that Michael has done the same job, or even more. Rubens does a great job, a fantastic job. But he just has this guy with the same equipment alongside him who is the reference point.

'We had a little bit of a quiet time at the start of the season, when Rubens realised that Michael had raised his game again. But all credit to Rubens, he's come back, found some extra performance from somewhere. He made a brave choice at Monza, going on the wet-weather tyres, and made it work for him.'

Monza also saw Schumacher close in dramatically on Barrichello before holding station over the last few laps. 'We try to look after the machinery,' said Brawn. 'Michael's finishing record is not an accident because he looks after the equipment so well. He never over-stretches an advantage. In these days of one-race engines, you have to manage the engine throughout the weekend, so if you get the opportunity to turn the revs down and consolidate the situation, you try and take it.

'The drivers have freedom until they get to the last pit stops. If you haven't got past by the last pit stop, you're into risking a fairly hairy overtaking manoeuvre. So we do ask the drivers to be sensible in the last stint. But that means for a fair chunk of the race, they're going hard: in Canada and the USA, for example, where they really had a good pop at each other!'

Alan Henry

The Ferrari team celebrates winnning the
constructors' championship after the race
in Budapest.
Photograph: Darren Heath

3

JUAN PABLO MONTOYA

MARC GENÉ

4

RALF SCHUMACHER

ANTONIO PIZZONIA

Photographs: Bryn Williams/crash.net

© ADRIAN DEAN

WILLIAMS FW26-BMW

SPONSORS	Hewlett Packard, Castrol, Petrobras, Accenture, Allianz, Budweiser, FedEx, Hamleys, NiquitinCQ, Reuters, Michelin, Boysen, MAN, Oris, Oz Racing, MMO2, Puma, PPG Industries, Wurth, Gore
ENGINE	Type: BMW P84 No. of cylinders (vee angle): V10 (90°) Sparking plugs: Champion Electronics: BMW Fuel: Petrobras Oil: Castrol
TRANSMISSION	Gearbox: WilliamsF1 seven-speed longitudinal semi-automatic Driveshafts: Pankl Clutch: AP Racing hand-operated
CHASSIS	Front suspension: torsion bars Rear suspension: torsion bars Dampers: WilliamsF1 Wheel diameter: front: 13 in rear: 13 in
	Wheels: OZ Racing Tyres: Michelin Brake discs: Carbone Industrie Brake pads: Carbone Industrie Calipers: AP Racing Steering: power-assisted
	Radiators: Marston Fuel tank: ATL Capacity: 135 litres Instruments: WilliamsF1
DIMENSIONS	Formula weight: 600 kg including driver

'THE target is to do something that we haven't achieved for the last five years, and that's to come out at the beginning of the following season with a car that can run at the front right from the very first race. That's the challenge.'

That was Williams's then technical director, Patrick Head, quoted in AUTOCOURSE 2003–2004. Sad to say, the target was not met in 2004 either, and Head blamed himself to such an extent that he handed over the technical director's responsibility to Sam Michael at mid-season. The latter explained, 'We took some wrong directions on three or four different fronts over the winter – mechanical and aerodynamic, which is basically the whole car. We also made some mistakes with the gearbox design, which has cost us points in three or four grands prix. So basically we didn't do a good enough job, and in some ways not only did we not do a good enough job performance-wise, but we made bad decisions which compromised this year.'

Head took up the story: 'One of the technical director's responsibilities is to guide the continuous detailed technical decisions and approve the continuous detailed technical decisions that form the make-up of the specification of the car. I was obviously pretty disappointed that I didn't pick up and avoid the errors that occurred over the winter. One of the reasons for that was because of the fact that I was probably present at the factory for 50 hours a week, living in London, having a young family at a later age.

'I was present for 50 hours a week, and to guide and make all those decisions, I think you need to be present for more than that. If you go back ten or 20 years or whatever, I was present in the factory for maybe 80, 90, 100 hours, seven days a week. I'm not doing that now, and I'm not prepared to do that now.

'I'd already made the decision [to stand down], and Frank was well aware of it, that there was going to be a change at the end of 2004, but the results of our winter work were so disappointing that I considered that it was appropriate to make the change earlier, and that that should be an important part of getting back to a competitive position, both through 2004 and for 2005.

'Also, Sam lives a lot closer to the factory and he is very, very committed. He's at the right age and the right time. He's got enough experience to be in that critical position.'

So, just before the North American double-header, Sam Michael became BMW WilliamsF1's technical director. 'Half of my role has changed and half of it's the same,' he said. 'It's obviously changed operationally at the track, because now I have a serious race engineer, Bob Gearing, who works for me and does a lot of the work that I used to do at the track, but at the same time, half of my job as technical director I was already doing anyway with Patrick.

'Really, right from the start, when I came to Williams, half of my role was fulfilling a TD's role anyway, but that's obviously expanded quite a bit since then.'

When Sam Michael took over after seven races, Juan Pablo Montoya had been on the front row once and on the podium twice. Team-mate Ralf Schumacher had achieved neither. Both drivers knew their future didn't lie with the team. This reality, and the lack of competitive machinery, probably affected their motivation, according to Head.

'I think drivers have a habit of winding themselves up over the winter and putting up very high expectations, and then if it's not achieved, they can go through a big dip,' explained Head. 'Their response to things not being particularly good was affected by the fact that they knew that their long-term futures weren't going to be with the team.

'In our aerodynamics department, there was a view that the car was going to be very good, and it took them some time to realise that it wasn't as good as they thought it was. It wasn't a question of a lack of hard work, but of course, the moment you start thinking you're doing well is the moment you start going backwards.'

However, that all looked as though it would change in Montreal. Ralf Schumacher claimed the team's first pole position of the year, Montoya was fourth. Ralf led the early stages, but Ferrari brought Michael Schumacher up to win from sixth on the grid. Ralf was second and Montoya fifth, the team's best finishing position so far, until both cars were disqualified for illegal brake ducts, which would scarcely have altered the cars' performance.

Above: Juan Pablo Montoya headed the Williams team's fitful challenge to be the best of the rest behind Ferrari.

Below: Patrick Head stood back from the front line mid-season, handing Sam Michael the reins as technical director.
Photograph: Darren Heath

Right: Ralf Schumacher's final season with Williams was disrupted by injury, but he bounced back to take second in Japan.

Below, top to bottom: Sir Frank Williams, still the most passionate F1 enthusiast in the paddock; Sam Michael, who took over as technical director in mid-season; chief designer Gavin Fisher.
Photographs: Darren Heath

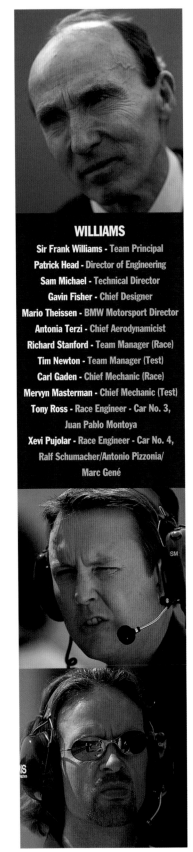

WILLIAMS

Sir Frank Williams - Team Principal

Patrick Head - Director of Engineering

Sam Michael - Technical Director

Gavin Fisher - Chief Designer

Mario Theissen - BMW Motorsport Director

Antonia Terzi - Chief Aerodynamicist

Richard Stanford - Team Manager (Race)

Tim Newton - Team Manager (Test)

Carl Gaden - Chief Mechanic (Race)

Mervyn Masterman - Chief Mechanic (Test)

Tony Ross - Race Engineer - Car No. 3,
Juan Pablo Montoya

Xevi Pujolar - Race Engineer - Car No. 4,
Ralf Schumacher/Antonio Pizzonia/
Marc Gené

'When we were leaving Montreal, we thought, "Well, it can't get much worse than this,"' said Sam Michael. 'Then it did.'

Montoya and Schumacher qualified fifth and sixth for the following weekend's US Grand Prix at Indianapolis. When the external starter failed to engage on his car on the grid, Montoya switched to the spare, but too late within the regulations; he was eventually disqualified when holding fifth. Ralf Schumacher was sixth when he crashed heavily due to a puncture. Later, he was diagnosed as suffering from hairline fractures of the 11th and 12th vertebrae.

The team was surrounded by controversy. Why had Ralf crashed? Why had he been left in the car for two laps before medical assistance had arrived? Why had it taken the FIA so long to disqualify his team-mate? Eventually, the FIA explained that the last two points had been within their guidelines, while it was thought that debris on the track had caused a number of punctures.

Montoya continued to carry the Williams flag, assisted by test drivers Marc Gené for the next two races, and Antonio Pizzonia for another four. The Spaniard's finishing positions were in double figures, and despite doing a reasonable job, he was replaced by the Brazilian, who scored three seventh places, with a best grid spot of sixth in Hungary, where he outqualified Montoya.

The Colombian, meanwhile, had twice put the car on the front row and had scored a succession of fifth places. Ralf Schumacher returned for the final three races of the year, when both drivers shifted up a gear to finish the season. Montoya scored another fifth and a seventh, then brilliantly won the Brazilian Grand Prix; Schumacher came back with fifth on the grid in China, only to retire controversially after a collision with David Coulthard. Subsequently, the German scored second place from second on the grid in Japan, and took a late fifth in Brazil.

By this stage, Williams's engineers had done all they could to make the car competitive. It had started out quite differently mechanically and aerodynamically to the previous car, particularly with its distinctive 'walrus' nose.

'We ran the car at the start of January, which was obviously an early launch because we had had reliability problems the year before,' explained Michael. 'It improved the general reliability by running early, but we couldn't get on top of the problems that we had with the gearbox early enough. There are a lot of things that are fundamental which are difficult to change during the course of the year. The problem with gearboxes is that they can be inconsistent, so you can think you've solved a problem, but you really need a lot of statistical data to really prove that you have.

'Aerodynamically, we had quite an aggressive development programme, and the car, as it was at the end of the season, was definitely not too bad and would have been a reasonable starting point at the start of year. But the way Formula 1 is, you've got your development, and if you add that on to not a very good baseline, it's not enough to catch up during the course of the year. We knew, throughout February and March that it wasn't good enough. I think you do know that early.'

The team did 14,705 km of pre-season testing. 'Probably 50 per cent of our mileage and budgets goes on tyre testing,' said Michael. A development programme meant that there were three or four changes, mechanically and aerodynamically, at every race.

'We couldn't attack the fundamental problems until later on in the year,' he added. 'Aero-wise, it's quite easy to see the major steps we made on the car in terms of engine cover and side-pod package at Magny-Cours. We changed the front wing and nose at Hungary, and then we changed the bodywork at Spa with different flip-ups and things. We changed one thing on the front suspension and two things on the rear suspension for Silverstone.'

BMW became more involved with various aspects of the car (including the transmission) during the year, but Head explained, 'The biggest thing the major manufacturer can do for a Formula 1 team is to give them a massive power advantage. BMW did than in 2001/2002 and maybe 2003, but by their own statement, they haven't in 2004, but they will attend to that.'

BMW's P83 was a development of the previous P82 due to the fact that the regulations required it to be used for 800 km. 'We tackled the target of double mileage in three steps,' said BMW's Mario Theissen. 'The first step was to have a reliable 800-km engine for the first race, without losing too much power and without gaining too much weight. That was achieved. We had close to 900 bhp, a bit less at the first race, and the weight increase was below five per cent.

'We thought for these regulations it would be more important to keep top power and top engine speed for the race distance, rather than improve peak power for qualifying and then step back, so the second target was to go up to 19,000 rpm, even for the race, even in top gear, which means, for instance, you keep 19,000 rpm for about ten seconds at Indianapolis. And the third step was power development throughout the season, as in years before.'

BMW doubled the mileage with testing on the dyno as well as on the track to cope with the increased endurance demands on the engine: 'On the other hand, we built less engines than during the years before – it's still more than 200 – so in total, there has been a cost saving. Fifty per cent of an engine manufacturer's budget is parts costs. If you reduce the number of engines built, it has a significant effect on overall cost.'

BMW had just one engine failure in a race with Ralf Schumacher in Malaysia. 'Apart from that, I am very satisfied with the reliability which was achieved,' said Theissen. 'I expected more engine failures generally during the first half of the season. I think our engineers did a very good job.'

Having completed a second, full-size wind-tunnel prior to the end of the season, and with restructuring throughout the company and a win in the last race of the season, Williams was ready to start 2005 on a different footing, perhaps finally fulfilling Patrick Head's expectations.

Bob Constanduros

BMW.WilliamsF1 Team
Technical Sponsor

First flight over the Atlantic.

First car over the sound barrier.

First team over 19,000 rpm.

Three firsts that have pushed motor engineering further and faster than ever before. We're proud to have played our part in all of them. Through our partnership with the BMW WilliamsF1 Team, we're always searching for the next breakthrough. So motoring keeps progressing from the skies to the deserts. From the racetrack to the road.

A Successful Formula

Photograph: Darren Heath

DAVID COULTHARD

Photograph: Darren Heath

KIMI RÄIKKÖNEN

INITIALLY, it was a bruising year for McLaren Mercedes, although by the end of the season a sequence of consistently competitive race performances from Kimi Räikkönen, most notably an impressive and decisive victory in the Belgian Grand Prix at Spa-Francorchamps, helped assuage lingering memories of the team's painful progress through the first few races of the season.

Prior to the Australian Grand Prix, McLaren had been cautiously upbeat about prospects for the new MP4/19. The machine had been undergoing testing since well before Christmas, the benefit of refining the abortive MP4/18 concept, which never raced in 2003. The MP4/19 featured tightly packaged bodywork, particularly around the rear end, and another new Mercedes V10, which, it was hoped, would contribute to a car that was capable of going head to head with the best.

The chassis profile was the same as the MP4/18, but the internal architecture of the monocoque had been completely changed. As a result, the MP4/19 chassis was stiffer and stronger with no weight penalty, and it had a lower centre of gravity, which helped stability under acceleration and braking. The cockpit was very compact, which made for a tight fit for the drivers, particularly tester Alex Wurz, who needed the fire extinguisher repositioning before he could get comfy.

The new car featured a quick-change engine facility, which had been pioneered on the MP4/18. This had been prompted by the new rules that require engines to last a full race weekend; in the event of a practice accident, it may be necessary to switch a V10 into a new chassis at short notice to avoid incurring a penalty.

Initial testing of the MP4/19 had been promising, but then the clouds rolled in big time in Melbourne, where Räikkönen spun off with an engine failure caused by loss of coolant from a broken radiator. His team-mate, David Coulthard, fared dismally, ending up a lapped eighth, The team and its drivers concluded that it could be mid-way through the European season before modifications could be made to allow the new McLaren to unlock its much heralded pre-season promise.

'We were not where we wanted to be with the car in Melbourne,' said Coulthard. 'Having said that, looking back on 2003, Ferrari's gap in qualifying [in Australia] was significantly more than in 2004, so if that trend follows, we will be much closer generally.

'Melbourne was not a big surprise to us, more a surprise to other people because I think we [the team] knew what to expect. Before we even reached the first race, the McLaren MP4/19B was already in the pipeline. Changes were already in process.

'Those changes that can be accelerated will be. I don't have

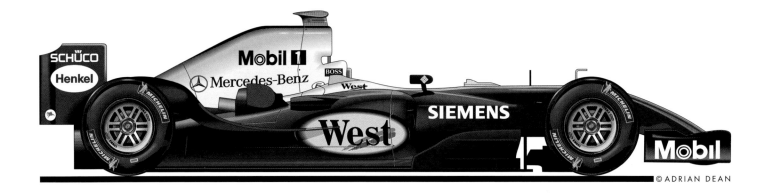

© ADRIAN DEAN

McLAREN MP4/19B-MERCEDES-BENZ

SPONSORS	West, EXXONMobil, Siemens, Michelin, BAE Systems, Computer Associates, Sun Microsystems, SAP, Warsteiner, Hugo Boss, Schueco, TAG Heuer, T-Mobile
ENGINE	**Type:** Mercedes-Benz FO110Q **No. of cylinders (vee angle):** V10 **Electronics:** McLaren **Fuel:** Mobil **Oil:** Mobil 1
TRANSMISSION	**Gearbox:** seven-speed longitudinal semi-automatic **Driveshafts:** McLaren **Clutch:** hand-operated
CHASSIS	**Front suspension:** double wishbones, pushrod/bell-crank-activated torsion bars and dampers **Rear suspension:** double wishbones, pushrod/bell-crank-activated torsion bars and dampers **Dampers:** Multimatic/McLaren **Wheels:** Enkei **Tyres:** Michelin **Brake pads:** Carbone Industrie **Brake discs:** Carbone Industrie
	Brake calipers: AP Racing **Steering:** McLaren power-assisted **Fuel tank:** ATL **Battery:** GS **Instruments:** McLaren
DIMENSIONS	**Formula weight:** 600 kg including driver

a date, but I think we can expect significant changes to the car half-way through the European season.'

Frankly, McLaren's management was slightly confused over the performance shortfall of the new car. This was compounded immediately after the Australian race when the team's test driver, Pedro de la Rosa, set very competitive times while testing at Spain's Valencia circuit, emphasising the complex interaction between aerodynamics, suspension characteristics, engine and tyre performance that governs the performance of a contemporary F1 car.

'Pedro had a really good test in Spain,' said Ron Dennis, McLaren's chairman. 'To be honest, our lack of pace at Melbourne was slightly baffling. At every test during the off-season, the new car ran over a second quicker than last year's chassis each time it appeared. It may be that we just fell out of the ideal tyre operating window in Australia. But we're confident that things will improve.'

Martin Whitmarsh, McLaren Racing's managing director, agreed that everybody in the team had been seriously disappointed with the MP4/19's performance in Melbourne. 'We had some good tests at Jerez and Valencia during the winter,' he said, 'but that was followed by a poor test at Barcelona and, in retrospect, perhaps we did not read the signals with the correct degree of amplification.

'That doesn't alter the fact that no part of our technical package was as good as it should have been in order to go out and win races or challenge for championships. But our challenge is now to be a bit stronger in Malaysia and a bit stronger again in Bahrain. We just have to get on with it and graft away.'

There was also initial concern over the Mercedes V10 engine's shortage of power. It was rumoured that the unit in the MP4/19 was at least 50 bhp down on the rival BMW engine used by Williams. Mercedes wouldn't comment on the matter, saying that it was a team issue and not for debate in public.

The affair was complicated further by the fact that Mercedes owns 40 per cent of the McLaren shares (it is tipped to buy out the balance over the next couple of years). This meant that all the team's senior personnel had to choose their words carefully on the subject. 'If I say the engine is a concern to me, it doesn't put a positive spin on our relationship with Mercedes,' said

Dennis. 'If I say no, it would be an indication that this wasn't an area where we need improvement.

'The right answer is that the performance of a grand prix car is controlled by a number of parameters, and every one of those parameters needs to be strong. You can't carry an aerodynamic problem, you can't carry an inferior driver, you can't carry being with the wrong tyre company, you can't carry not having the best engine. It's as simple as that.'

For Räikkönen, the early part of the season was utterly disastrous with mechanical failures in the first three races; the Finn managed to score just a single championship point in the first seven races on the schedule. But McLaren and Mercedes Ilmor were working incredibly hard behind the scenes, and immediately after the European Grand Prix at the Nürburgring, the wraps came off the new MP4/19B, and the team set out on the long road back to competitiveness.

Räikkönen's initial assessment that the revised car was very promising, voiced after the preliminary test at Silverstone, was tempered by memories of him saying much the same about the disastrous, never-to-be-raced MP4/18 in 2003. At its second major test at Jerez, Kimi was joined by David Coulthard, and test drivers Alex Wurz and Pedro de la Rosa. Between them, they completed well over 600 laps in blistering conditions with encouraging mechanical reliability.

The MP4/19B had been built around a new monocoque, had a rear aerodynamic treatment that was similar to the Renault R24 and was equipped with a modified Mercedes V10 engine with an uprated lubrication system. The main problem with the original MP4/19, namely a variable handling imbalance caused by inconsistencies between the front and rear tyre temperatures, seemed to have been licked.

By this stage in the year, Mercedes Ilmor had become the responsibility of McLaren Mercedes CEO Martin Whitmarsh. 'It is an interesting and exciting challenge,' he said, 'and perhaps even more demanding than I anticipated.' For the rest of the year, there was a steady and heartening improvement in engine performance to match the much better chassis.

The MP4/19B made its race debut in the French Grand Prix, where Räikkönen and Coulthard finished fifth and sixth, the car's much improved front-to-rear handling balance being

Above: **Kimi Räikkönen suffered a succession of mechanical failures during 2004, but highlighted his season with a fine win in Belgium.**
Photograph: Darren Heath

53

McLAREN

Ron Dennis - Team Principal

Martin Whitmarsh - CEO Formula One

Norbert Haug - Vice-President
(Mercedes-Benz Motorsport)

Jonathan Neale - Managing Director

Adrian Newey - Technical Director

Mario Illien - Technical Director
(Mercedes-Ilmor)

Neil Oatley - Executive Director
of Engineering

Mike Coughlan - Chief Designer

Dave Ryan - Team Manager

Stephen Giles - Chief Mechanic

Phil Prew - Race Engineer - Car No. 5,
David Coulthard

Mark Slade - Race Engineer - Car No. 6,
Kimi Räikkönen

Top: Ron Dennis continued to preside over the team for his 23rd year as team principal.
Photograph: Bryn Williams/crash.net

Above: Martin Whitmarsh saw his responsibilities expand within the McLaren Mercedes empire in 2004.

Above right: David Coulthard had a mixed ninth, and final, season with the team.
Photographs: Darren Heath

complemented by a welcome improvement in reliability levels. At Silverstone, the Finn qualified on pole and gave Michael Schumacher's Ferrari a great run for its money, the McLaren finishing second; at Hockenheim, Räikkönen hounded the German ace in the early stages until a rear wing failure spun him into the first-corner tyre barrier at considerable speed, but thankfully without injury.

Then came Räikkönen's superb win at Spa, which really put a spring back into the McLaren team's collective step. 'It wasn't just a race win for Kimi and the team,' said team principal Ron Dennis, 'it was where it was done. It was how it was done. He didn't win from the front. He didn't win because of some freak qualifying situation, or some freak weather conditions. There was no element of the success which was in any way gifted to Kimi or the team. It was a clear-cut victory.

'For an hour or so after the race, the feeling was great. But I felt on reflection that we could have won more races this season. At Hockenheim, we were strong, and also pretty competitive in Brazil. Of course, one is better than none, but three is better than one. Both our next year's drivers were dominant in Brazil, of course.'

Dennis had been referring to the close victory over Räikkönen by Juan Pablo Montoya in his last race for the rival BMW Williams squad. The Colombian had been signed to McLaren for 2005 as successor to the outgoing David Coulthard and partner to Räikkönen. McLaren had come through the eye of the storm and was confident that it would get the best from its dynamic new super-team pairing. It certainly promises to be well worth watching.

Alan Henry

Designed for life

TURNING COMMUNICATION AROUND

www.siemens.com/sk65
or call us on 08457 400 700

THE NEW SIEMENS SK65 WITH CONVENIENT MESSAGING.

Now using BlackBerry e-mail push technology is even easier. Send e-mails,
receive e-mails and have your calendar automatically updated, with the perfect
keyboard for perfect mobile messaging. The future of communication is here.

SIEMENS

Photograph: Bryn Williams/crash.net

JARNO TRULLI

JACQUES VILLENEUVE

7

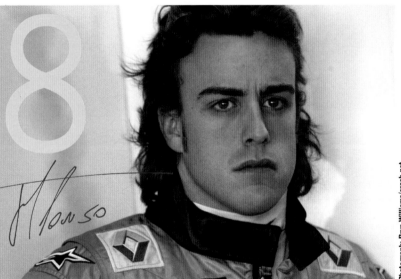

Photograph: Bryn Williams/crash.net

Photograph: Darren Heath

FERNANDO ALONSO

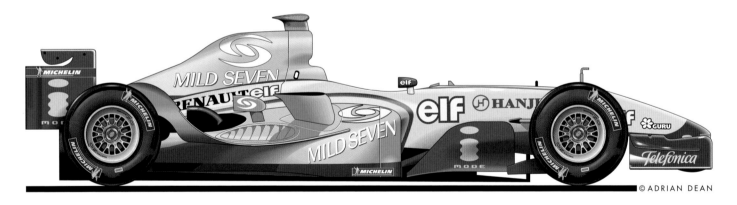

© ADRIAN DEAN

RENAULT R24

SPONSORS	Mild Seven, Elf, Michelin, Hanjin, i-mode, Telefonica, Guru, 3D Systems, Magneti Marelli, Charmilles, Novell
ENGINE	**Type:** Renault F1 R24 **No. of cylinders:** V10 **Sparking plugs:** Champion **Electronics:** Magneti Marelli **Fuel:** Elf **Oil:** Elf
TRANSMISSION	**Gearbox:** Renault F1 six-speed longitudinal electro-hydraulic **Driveshafts:** Renault F1 integrated tri-lobe **Clutch:** hand-operated
CHASSIS	**Front suspension:** double wishbones, pushrod-activated torsion bars **Rear suspension:** double wishbones, pushrod-activated torsion bars
	Dampers: Penske **Wheel diameter:** front: 13 in rear: 13 in **Wheels:** OZ **Tyres:** Michelin **Brake pads:** Hitco **Brake discs:** Hitco
	Brake calipers: AP Racing **Steering:** Renault F1 power-assisted **Radiators:** Marston **Fuel tank:** ATL **Instruments:** Renault F1
DIMENSIONS	**Track:** front: 1450 mm rear: 1420 mm **Gearbox weight:** 40 kg **Chassis weight (tub):** 60 kg **Formula weight:** 600 kg including driver

I T was almost as if the gods of the 2004 season were having a laugh at Renault's expense. Having finished fourth at the end of 2003, the Anglo-French team started out with the realistic intention of moving up a place 12 months later. It did exactly that, but it wasn't happy. For much of the year, Renault had held second place. It had been there on merit, the best of the rest, which, when you consider Ferrari's all-round brilliance, was as good as anyone not wearing a red shirt could have hoped for. Then, with three races to go, second place slipped away as BAR Honda continued to make a strong showing while Renault faltered slightly.

That's all it took, although, as ever, a championship is not won or lost in the final furlong. In this case, it was the sum of 18 races, and Renault will forever look back to the middle of June when a disastrous race in Canada did most of the damage at a critical point. What happened that day in Montreal – and, to a lesser extent, two months later with an oil seal problem – was not indicative of Renault's season as a whole. It was a combination of those annoying little things that make up the fabric of motor racing, with its incredible highs and in-your-face lows.

Although BAR Honda took the second spot, Renault was by no means disgraced. It had seen off McLaren Mercedes and BMW Williams. And no one, certainly not Renault's seasoned technical chiefs Bob Bell and Pat Symonds, took that as a given when the Renault R24 was unveiled in Palermo on 29 January.

With the benefit of hindsight, there was a certain omen attached to the timing of that launch. Britain had ground to its usual pathetic standstill following an inch of snow that had fallen the previous night, and the majority of the British media could not make the trip. There was disappointment all round. Any social event involving Flavio Briatore is worth the trouble. But there was more than that.

Renault was continuing the upward trend that had begun with the absorption of Benetton in 2000, followed by the restructuring of the team and the estimable engine division in Viry Châtillon. There had been a return to a narrow-angle V10 in addition to the streamlining of the technical department and race team in Oxfordshire, and, of course, one of the potentially strongest partnerships in Jarno Trulli and Fernando Alonso, two quick drivers who enjoyed each other's company and worked well together.

Renault made a strong start to the season, both drivers scoring points in the first five races. Then it got even better. In what may be remembered as the weekend of his life, Trulli took pole at Monaco with the sort of performance that indicated, for once, that he would soak up whatever pressure came his way. The Italian led from start to finish, scoring his first win. Alonso, who had been shaded by Trulli for much of the season thus far, was shoved into the barrier while lapping Ralf Schumacher, which added to his mounting frustration.

Nonetheless, Renault was a comfortable second in the table, with Trulli leading Alonso by ten points. Significantly, Jenson Button was ahead of them both. He had been doing the lion's share of point scoring for BAR; there was no doubt that BAR could be a force if, like Renault, both drivers consistently collected points. Put another way, there could be trouble if Renault faltered. That moment came three weeks later in Montreal.

Despite losing track time with electrical problems on Friday, Trulli produced a typically strong qualifying lap, good enough for third on the grid. Alonso would have been higher than fifth but for a mistake. But the Ferraris – and, more to the point, Bridgestone – were in trouble with one-lap qualifying. With Button on the front row, alongside pole man Ralf Schumacher, there was all to play for. In theory, Renault could have had both drivers on the podium.

A keen sense of anticipation was delivered a blow within ten seconds of the start as Trulli coasted to a halt with a broken driveshaft. After a strong 45 laps, Alonso lost fourth place with a similar problem. What made these retirements even more difficult to swallow was that everyone, with the exception of Ferrari, had a bad day. Renault could have stolen a significant psychological advantage as the season reached the half-way point.

'It was most odd,' said engineering director Pat Symonds. 'The failures occurred at different stages of the race. The component design had been around for a while; it wasn't anything new. We were putting more load through the driveshafts this year because we had more torque and a lot more grip. Canada does put specific additional stresses through the driveshafts, particularly when coming off a kerb with a wheel spinning freely, then hitting the ground, gripping and putting that shock load in. Unfortunately, we

Above: **Fernando Alonso at speed.**
Photograph: Darren Heath

Below: **Test driver Franck Montagny must have been bitterly disappointed to have been passed over in favour of Villeneuve after Trulli's abrupt departure.**
Photograph: Bryn Williams/crash.net

Right: Jarno Trulli often outpaced Fernando Alonso, and he won in Monaco, but a dip in results thereafter saw him dropped from the team.

Below: Flavio Briatore.

Photographs: Darren Heath

RENAULT

Patrick Faure - Team President

Flavio Briatore - Managing Director

Bernard Dudot - Deputy Managing Director (France)

Bob Bell - Technical Director

Rob White - Engine Technical Director

Pat Symonds - Executive Director of Engineering

Denis Chevrier - Head of Race Engineering (Engine)

Tim Densham - Chief Designer

Mark Smith - Chief Designer (2004)

Dino Toso - Head of Aerodynamics

Steve Nielsen - Sporting Manager

Jonathan Wheatley - Chief Mechanic

Alan Permane/Nicholas Chester/Fabrice Lom -

Race Engineers - Car No. 7,

Jarno Trulli/Jacques Villeneuve

Paul Monaghan/Rod Nelson/Rémi Taffin -

Race Engineers - Car No. 8,

Fernando Alonso

Above: Pat Symonds.

Photograph: Bryn Williams/crash.net

Right: Jacques Villeneuve failed to bring the team precious points, and it lost out to BAR in the race for second place in the constructors' championship.

Photograph: Darren Heath

found the limit of it in a race rather than a test because of the nature of the circuit.'

It was around this point that a subtle change crept in. Trulli appeared to lose momentum, a strong drive from the back of the grid at Indianapolis being spoiled by the loss of third place to, of all people, Takuma Sato. It was even worse two weeks later in France, where Trulli threw away a place on the podium for Renault's home race when he let Rubens Barrichello snatch third at the last corner. Not even Alonso's second place would console an incandescent Briatore. Trulli's season with Renault more or less ended right there, and he went through the motions before parting company with three races to go. It was definitely a year of two halves for the Italian.

'I think you can say the same happened, but in the opposite way, in 2003,' said Symonds. 'When Fernando won in Hungary that year, I think Jarno had an inward look at himself and he reacted extremely well in the latter part of the year. The fantastic thing is he brought the whole mental attitude through to 2004.

'He was very, very strong through the first half of the season. Then he had a few disappointments, some tough luck and things like that. And it appeared to have affected him; it's very difficult to say why. I know he has the equipment to do the job, and the results were not what he is capable of. I know that he can do better.

'Fernando had to work a bit harder than he'd expected. It was a lovely, well-balanced team, pushing each other in very a nice way in the first part of the season. That seemed to disappear a little bit, and it probably wasn't helped by all the talk about Jarno's future. When you get into the psychology of the thing, it is difficult to understand. Different people react in different ways to disappointment; bad news challenges. I think it is probably not coincidence that his run of bad luck seemed to coincide with indications that he hadn't got a guaranteed place with Renault for 2005.

'As for Fernando, if there is an area for improvement, then it probably is during qualifying. He has not taken to the single-lap qualifying quite as well as some. In Malaysia, he spun off, and Barcelona was disappointing. But his spin in Bahrain was definitely a brake problem. Apart from that, Fernando's races were very good. He gave it everything, as usual.'

Both drivers were helped by Renault continuing to have the edge at the start, the blue and yellow cars rocketing off the line and gaining a couple of valuable places. Apart from that, though, they were not easy to drive.

'The R24 has not been as good as we would have hoped,' said Bob Bell. 'But the engine has come on superbly during the year and vindicated the decision to switch from the wide-angle V10. The problem with the R24 is that it hasn't been as easy a car to drive as its predecessor was. It's quick over one lap, but more difficult for the drivers to extract time from consistently during a race. We've worked hard over the year to get to the bottom of those technical problems which were inherent in its fundamental design, but not at the expense of the normal development process of putting performance enhancing bits on the car.'

You could argue that replacing Trulli with Jacques Villeneuve for the last three races was hardly performance enhancing just as the team needed to counter BAR Honda's continuing surge. The former champion never looked like scoring points in China and Japan, by which time Renault's second place was more or less a memory.

'There were times when we stretched the lead [in second place] and thought that we were looking good,' said Bell. 'But then we suffered misfortunes on the track and it closed back up again. Nonetheless, our objective was to finish third, and I take enormous pride in what the team has achieved during what has been a difficult year.'

Maurice Hamilton

9

JENSON BUTTON

Photographs: Darren Heath

10

TAKUMA SATO

OF all the pretenders to Ferrari's throne, no team deserved to win a grand prix more than BAR, yet it was denied that reward. After five mainly fruitless seasons, the writing had been on the wall at the end of 2003 – the 2004 season would see the team finally come good – and BAR and Honda duly delivered.

The team claimed only its third ever podium in the second race of the season, then scooped another 11. BAR Honda established itself in fourth place in the constructors' series at the start of the season, then brilliantly moved ahead of Williams with Jenson Button's pole position and second place at the San Marino Grand Prix. When Button and team-mate Takuma Sato finished third and fourth at Monza, BAR overtook Renault to claim a solid second in the championship at year's end.

Button scored four second places and six thirds on his way to a well-deserved third in the championship, while his less experienced team-mate started the European Grand Prix from the front row of the grid, a first for Japan, and two races later stood on the rostrum for the first time at Indianapolis.

There were few blips along the way, although Button was largely condemned when he stated that he was turning his back on the team that had given him such success to rejoin Williams, a decision ultimately overthrown by the Contracts Recognition Board. It was to his credit and that of the team that any bad feeling was overcome. Takuma Sato's five engine failures were also unfortunate, as was Button's third retirement of the year in the final race of the season in Brazil for the same reason.

As far as team principal David Richards and technical director Geoff Willis were concerned, the success was all down to planning. 'I read that you can't talk about three-year plans or management plans in Formula 1,' said Willis. 'Well, I've probably learned to disagree with that. I've learned that good business practice, good sensible robust management is what you need to make a complex business like Formula 1 work.'

Richards continued on that theme: 'It hasn't suddenly become successful this year. We've worked to get it there for the last three years. We put the plans in place right from the outset to achieve what we have today. The first year was about reorganisation, the second was about consolidation and getting ourselves working as a cohesive unit, the third year was always going to be a year when we started to show the full performance potential on the track.'

In this case, the three-year plan worked. 'The infrastructure was put in place at the factory,' Richards continued. 'Nick Fry has put in an awful lot of processes in the organisation, Geoff has worked very diligently in getting all the technical side structured properly, the team at the track under Ron Meadows [team manager], Alastair Gibson [chief mechanic] and Craig Wilson [chief race engineer] is really coming together, so it has really been a case of all the individual ingredients just quietly being put in place.'

A great part of that cohesive unit was Honda. 'The relation-

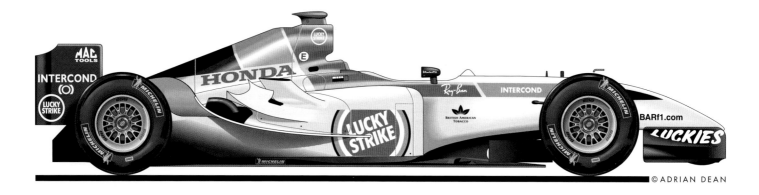

© ADRIAN DEAN

BRITISH AMERICAN RACING BAR 006-HONDA

SPONSORS	**Lucky Strike, Honda, Michelin, Intercond, Brunotti, Ray-Ban, Alpinestars**
ENGINE	**Type:** Honda RA004E **No. of cylinders (vee angle):** V10 (90°) **Sparking plugs:** NGK **Electronics:** Honda Athena **Fuel:** Elf **Oil:** Nisseki
TRANSMISSION	**Gearbox:** seven-speed longitudinal semi-automatic **Driveshafts:** Pankl **Clutch:** Sachs carbon plate, hand-operated
CHASSIS	**Front suspension:** double wishbones, pushrod-activated torsion bars **Rear suspension:** double wishbones, pushrod-activated torsion bars **Suspension dampers:** Koni
	Wheel diameter: front: 330 mm **rear:** 330 mm **Wheels:** BBS **Tyres:** Michelin **Brake pads:** Brembo **Brake discs:** Brembo **Brake calipers:** Alcon
	Steering: power-assisted rack-and-pinion **Radiators:** IMI Marston/Showa **Fuel tank:** ATL **Fuel capacity:** 140 litres **Battery:** Yuasa **Instruments:** BAR
DIMENSIONS	**Wheelbase:** 3131 mm **Track: front:** 1453 mm **rear:** 1414 mm **Formula weight:** 600 kg including driver

ship with Honda has changed fundamentally,' Richards explained. 'Two years ago, it was very much Honda the engine supplier and BAR the chassis, and there wasn't a very close collaboration. The following year, Honda started working on chassis development programmes in parallel to our own, and although they did some very good work in that area, it wasn't a very efficient way of working.

'Now we work as a cohesive team, with Honda engineers totally integrated into Geoff's technical team, 28 engineers working in individual departments. Not only that, but they access facilities back in Japan, so it really is tapping into the enormous resource and potential that Honda have in Japan.'

Honda Racing Development had also reorganised, as its vice-president, Otmar Szafnauer, explained: 'It wasn't so much different people coming in and out, but just the way they approached the problem of making the best engine in F1. I think that's helped significantly. I think we're unique in the way we go about designing and building our engines. It's in the way we're organised.'

The latest engine was brand new at the start of the year. 'The block, everything was brand new, mainly because our focus was threefold,' said Szafnauer. 'Firstly, reliability, because we had to consider the engine having to last all weekend, and we didn't want penalties. Then we realised that we had to reduce weight significantly, and the last thing is ingrained in Honda engineers – power. You never have to tell them we need power. It happens by default.

'We needed reliability all year long, but we decided that on the weight and power front, instead of taking many steps as we like to do, we would take more significant and fewer ones. The first significant step in power was at Imola [resulting in Button's first pole and second place]. The first weight reduction, which was up high, came at Monaco.

'The next increase in power came at Canada with another up-high reduction in weight. We had another power increase and weight reduction for Monza, and the last one was the Suzuka Special, which was again an increase in power and reduction in weight, actually introduced a race early in China. By that time, we believed that we'd got the most power and one of the lightest engines on the grid.'

Szafnauer reckoned HRD still produced nearly 200 engines, but that the one engine/one race format had probably saved it between 18 and 36 engines. Of course, it no longer built parts for short-life engines, so there had been a saving – but not much.

Honda's effort was matched by BAR's. 'The 2003 car was really built on the background of much more solid and reliable engineering,' explained Willis, 'but we still had reliability issues. But a lot of them were really what you might call operational issues. We hadn't quite mastered the knack of supplying all the parts, checking them all, not having little drop-offs.

'But that gave us confidence to really work much harder and set ourselves much higher targets with the 2004 car. This was quite a big step for us. We took a lot of weight out of the car, worked in certain very specific aerodynamic areas and introduced some bolder steps.

'We also introduced our concept car at the end of November 2003, in which we started track testing the 2004 engine and gearbox, hydraulic assembly, the whole back end of the car. That considerably extended the amount of our testing – probably twice as much as the previous year – and gave us a very very reliable car.'

Slightly complicating the situation was the potential, but still unconfirmed, move from Bridgestone to Michelin at the end of the 2003 season. Willis – described as a committed Michelin man – surreptitiously had to steer his designers toward the French tyres. Once the move had been made, revised rear suspension was needed to cope with the different balance between the sidewall and tread stiffness of the Michelins.

A slight mid-season slump in race pace was caused by a lack of communication between the team and its new tyre supplier – even though it considered itself Michelin's number-one test team. 'I think we were caught out a little bit on tyre usage, and there were some issues where I think Michelin assumed we'd know more about the tyres than we did,' said Willis.

Helping to ascertain tyre wear on Fridays was Anthony Davidson, who drove the third car to great effect, frequently trading fastest times with Michael Schumacher, although admittedly using a few more revs than the regular drivers.

The team was also quite innovative in that it introduced what Willis described as a 'loophole' rear wing with vanes, which was banned before it could be raced at Sepang. In addition, BAR debuted a front torque transfer device at Hockenheim, which was intended to improve the car's stability under braking. This was disputed by the FIA, but reintroduced at Monza. Other innovations included an award winning, new carbon-composite gearbox casing and what Willis called 'some quite clever uprights'.

There were aerodynamic updates at Imola, and more bits at Barcelona, Montreal and Indianapolis, while a change at Silverstone didn't work as expected. There was a final update at Shanghai.

Certainly the drivers had great confidence in the car, something that Willis ensured with the design of the safety-critical parts. The ever improving Sato even had to be restrained from over-driving, building his confidence and relieving self-imposed pressure.

The sting in the year's tail came when Prodrive's contract to run the team was terminated with two years still to run, and Honda took a 45-per-cent stake in the team.

Bob Constanduros

GIANCARLO FISICHELLA

FELIPE MASSA

SAUBER PETRONAS

11

12

Photographs: Bryn Williams/crash.net

FOR a few races mid-season, it seemed that Sauber had made that miraculous jump back up to fifth place in the championship, as the team led McLaren. It was no surprise, however, that the men from Woking took back what, for them, was a lowly fifth, but Sauber can be proud that, as top privateer, it beat the factory teams from Jaguar and Toyota, as well as the other two privateers, on its way to equalling 2003's sixth place.

The big event for the Hinwil team in 2004 was the opening of its full-scale, $50-million wind-tunnel, and although Sauber's engineers weren't multi-shifting or using the facility 24 hours a day, it began to produce benefits from Imola onward, with a constant stream of wings, turning vanes and engine covers, all of which seemed to improve performance. That, coupled with the latest Ferrari engine and some excellent tactics – usually focusing on a pit stop less than many rivals – resulted in a constant string of minor points scoring placings, often ahead of more prestigious teams.

The one thing that does change quite often at Sauber is its driver line-up. So gone were the Mönchen-Gladbach pair of Heinz-Harald Frentzen (to enforced retirement) and Nick Heidfeld (to Jordan); in came Giancarlo Fisichella (from Jordan) and the returning Felipe Massa, who had spent a year at finishing school in Maranello as test driver.

Of the major staff, only Rémy de Cortanze had left, his job as chief engineer at the race track having been taken by the indefatigable Jacky Eckelaert. The team remained at around 300 people with its usual excellent atmosphere, nurtured by Josef Leberer and Beat Zehnder, free from politics and aggravation. This makes Sauber a popular location for many staff, although the travelling, as in any team, takes its toll.

Sauber's faithful sponsors stayed on board in 2004, so the budget was the same as in 2003, although the reduction in the value of the US dollar hit the team. It was one reason why Sauber didn't have a third driver, the only team that was allowed to have one, but didn't. 'The third driver would have been quite useful for tyre evaluation and long runs,' explained technical director Willy Rampf. 'But if we had to pay for everything for a third driver, then we would rather invest the money in the aerodynamic department. It was economics.' Several more data engineers would have been necessary, said the team, for minimum advantage.

The two main influences on the C23 were the new regulations requiring a single engine per weekend, and a low engine cover developed at the end of 2003. 'This year's concept was quite different,' explained Rampf. 'We changed the package quite a lot, and also had to adapt the car because we used the Ferrari engine and the gearbox as well, which is a quite different installation.'

So why use the Ferrari gearbox when the team had successfully produced its own for many years? 'Ferrari had a very short gearbox, and we wanted to have the same package of engine and gearbox,' said Rampf. 'The reasons were firstly cost, and secondly we learned a lot by using this gearbox because it's short and compact. Furthermore, to reduce the overall risk of the one-engine-per-weekend regulation, we took over the engine and gearbox as a complete package.' Cost came into it too, as Sauber were intending to produce a titanium box for 2005.

With the shorter Ferrari gearbox, it was no surprise that the car dis-

© ADRIAN DEAN

SAUBER C23-PETRONAS

SPONSORS	Petronas, Credit Suisse, Red Bull, Adelholzener Alpenquellen, Adnovum Informatik, AMD, AS Lifts, Balzers, Bridgestone, Brütsch/Rüegger, Catia/Enovia Solutions, Cisco Systems, DaimlerChrysler, Dalco, Druckerei Flawil, Egro, Elektro Frauchiger, Emil Frey, Ericsson, Fluent Deutschland, Gamatech Bottarlini, Italdesign/Giugiaro, Jacques Germanier, Kaeser Kompressoren, Klauke, Lista, Magneti Marelli, Microsoft, Mobile Telesystems, MSC, MTS, Ozalid, Paninfo, Philips, Pilatus, Plenexis
ENGINE	Type: Petronas 04A No. of cylinders: V10 Sparking plugs: NGK Electronics: Magneti Marelli Fuel: Primax Oil: Syntium
TRANSMISSION	Gearbox: Ferrari seven-speed longitudinal Clutch: AP hand-operated
CHASSIS	Front suspension: Sachs double wishbones, pushrod-activated inboard spring/damper units Rear suspension: Sachs double wishbones, pushrod-activated inboard spring/damper units Wheel diameter: front: 13 in rear: 13 in Wheels: OZ Tyres: Bridgestone Brake pads: Brembo Brake discs: Brembo Brake calipers: Brembo Steering: power-assisted Radiators: Calsonic
DIMENSIONS	Wheelbase: 3100 mm Track: front: 1400 mm rear: 1390 mm Formula weight: 600 kg including driver

played similarities to the Ferrari F2004, but the team refuted utterly any suggestion that Maranello engineers had worked in the new wind-tunnel: 'Apart from the opening party, no one from Ferrari was ever in our wind-tunnel.'

The team was unable to afford more than one more person on the wind-tunnel staff. 'We have single shifts,' said Rampf, 'but we get up to 12 hours if we have to catch up, longer shifts up to 18 hours, but more is not possible. We just don't have the people. The wind-tunnel is still a prototype, it still needs more maintenance at the beginning, but this is normal.'

The flow of developments from this relatively limited team was impressive. After a fairly slow and uncharacteristic start, power steering was the first new feature, being introduced in Bahrain. There was a new rear wing at Imola, plus some minor changes. More came in Barcelona, particularly to the turning vanes.

Monaco is always a special race, due to higher downforce requirements, but Sauber had its new V-type water radiators, a new rear wing and a roll-hoop wing. At the Nürburgring, there was a new engine-cover wing, while there was a new front wing assembly and different rear suspension to accommodate increased brake demands in Canada. This caused Massa's big accident, however, so there were more changes a week later at Indianapolis, where new wishbones were used.

At Magny-Cours, the team ran a new front wing, while the changes for Silverstone were the greatest all season and included a new engine cover. Fisichella claimed that he had never made such a big step forward in one race in all the years he had been in F1. He was consistently 0.3s faster.

At Hockenheim, Sauber introduced yet another engine-cover wing, while there were revised rear wings and modifications to the front wing at Budapest. For the medium-downforce Belgian Grand Prix, the team reverted to an earlier specification, while Monza, requiring a low-downforce set-up, meant more new front wings and

rear configuration, plus an older-spec engine cover. In Shanghai, there were new turning vanes.

Although Sauber started out with the same engine spec as Ferrari, there was only one step forward at Magny-Cours. This included a small drop in weight and a noticeable increase in power. However, the team seemed to suffer more engine glitches than Ferrari. Fisichella retired with an engine problem at the Nürburgring, while engine troubles forced Massa to retire from the first race of the year.

When Sauber did take a hit on an engine change – and Fisichella started on the back row three times – the team revealed its relatively cautious strategy, although this would often be rewarded with points.

'Our tendency is that we use harder tyres than Ferrari, but we also have different strategies,' admitted Rampf. 'We had a few races where we were quite competitive with longer stints and one stop less.' The British Grand Prix was a classic example: Fisichella started 20th and finished sixth. Such tactics are decided by Rampf with the engineers, but it is Zehnder who decides strategy from the pit wall.

Generally speaking, 2004 was a good season for Sauber. Massa had improved a lot since his first season and was telling the engineers what he wanted, rather than simply listening and learning. 'He still has one or two, perhaps three or four, moments,' said a team member.

Fisichella was hugely popular, but very quiet, 'a Roman gentleman,' said one team member. 'He's a really fine person, a fantastic driver, particularly at race speed. He's very good at qualifying, but even better in the race. You hardly see him, but at the end, he's there, fourth or sixth. It's so sad that he's leaving.'

Bob Constanduros

SAUBER

Peter Sauber - Team Principal

Willy Rampf - Technical Director

Osamu Goto - Head of Powertrain

Seamus Mullarkey - Senior Aerodynamicist

Beat Zehnder - Team Manager

Urs Kuratle - Chief Mechanic

Giampaolo Dall'Ara - Race Engineer - Car No. 11, Giancarlo Fisichella

Mike Krack - Race Engineer - Car No. 12, Felipe Massa

Top: Giancarlo Fisichella had a promising year with the Swiss team.

Above centre: Peter Sauber kept smiling through good times and bad times.

Above: Willy Rampf had a steady hand on the technical fortunes of the team.

Left: Felipe Massa at Monaco.

MARK WEBBER

CHRISTIAN KLIEN

JAGUAR RACING

A MEDIA briefing nine days into 2004 summed up Jaguar Racing and the season ahead. Held in the factory at Milton Keynes, the informal gathering pulled no punches. David Pitchforth, the managing director, went straight to the heart of the matter when he waved his hand around the workshop and pointed to the Jaguar R5. 'No poshness,' he said. 'Nothing palatial here. Everything has gone into that car.'

It may have been a wry reference to the grandeur of the McLaren Technology Centre, due to be opened by royalty a few months later, but it said everything about a team that was fighting for survival, not just within F1, but in the minds of board members at the Ford Motor Company in Detroit. Money would continue to be tight, but, according to CEO Tony Purnell, neither the build nor the running of the car would be compromised. 'There has been no resource lacking to make a really good car,' he said. 'Our target is to convert qualifying into race performance. We want to be higher up the running order in the races. We know it won't be easy, but that's the aim.'

Did Jaguar achieve its goal? Yes and no. The car ran reliably, but it was never fast. That is fast enough to keep the attention of the Ford Motor Company. By the end of the season, the parent company had put Jaguar Racing up for sale. It was a kick in the teeth for a compact, efficient team that had done all it could with the limited resources available.

Ford's narrow-minded approach had not been matched by Jaguar's technical group. With the revised regulations calling for engines to last for the entire weekend, reliability was a major factor that had to be addressed by Cosworth Racing and Dr Mark Gillan, the head of vehicle performance.

'Right from the outset, we set ourselves a specific test matrix of items we wanted to cover from chassis and aero, all the way through the various systems in the car,' said Gillan. 'We specified 650 km as a distance that would be acceptable on a race weekend. To make sure we always hit that target from the engine side, we would run up to 800 km during testing and sign off various increments in performance based on an 800-km race weekend, but working to 650 km. That worked very successfully.'

In one sense, the statistics demonstrate that success, with very few technical DNFs. In another, however, the actual results suggest a disappointing overall performance. Mark Webber collected points just four times, a sixth place at Hockenheim being his best. That result was matched by Christian Klien in Belgium, the Austrian's only points finish.

The R5 may have been running after 190 miles of flat-out racing, but the results were about as good as they were ever going to be. The irony was that moments of great potential – a brilliant second on the grid for Webber in Malaysia; running eighth at Monaco – were scuppered by the few problems to come the team's way. In

© ADRIAN DEAN

JAGUAR R5-COSWORTH

SPONSORS	HSBC, Lear, Castrol, AT&T, Becks, UGS PLM, Dupont, Hangar-7
ENGINE	**Type:** Cosworth CR6 **No. of cylinders (vee angle):** V10 (90°) **Sparking plugs:** Champion **Electronics:** Pi VCS system **Fuel:** Castrol **Oil:** Castrol
TRANSMISSION	**Gearbox:** Jaguar seven-speed longitudinal semi-automatic **Clutch:** AP Racing hand-operated
CHASSIS	**Front suspension:** double wishbones, pushrod-activated torsion bars **Rear suspension:** double wishbones, pushrod-activated coil springs **Dampers:** Koni
	Wheel diameter: front: 13 in rear: 13 in **Wheels:** OZ **Tyres:** Michelin **Brake pads:** Carbone Industrie or Brembo
	Brake discs: Carbone Industrie or Brembo **Brake calipers:** AP Racing
DIMENSIONS	**Formula weight:** 600 kg including driver

JAGUAR

Tony Purnell - Team Principal
David Pitchforth - Managing Director
Mark Gillan - Director of Vehicle Performance
David Stubbs - Team Manager
Pete Harrison - Race Engineer - Car No. 14, Mark Webber
Stefano Sordo - Race Engineer - Car No. 15, Christian Klien
Ron Hartvelt - Race Engineer - Spare car, Björn Wirdheim

many respects, that performance in Sepang, coming two weeks after qualifying sixth in Melbourne, would be one of the few highlights of the season.

'Last year, we had a good qualifying car and it suffered more in the race,' said Gillan. 'This year, we paid a lot of attention to upping the race performance, but not detracting from qualifying. We spent the race weekends concentrating on race performance, knowing that the reliability is there and hopefully trying to extract the most from the car.

'We took an informed approach strategy-wise to make sure we were set optimal for the race, which means you might not look as good in qualifying. That said, in Malaysia, the car was extremely quick. Some circuits suit some cars more than others. In 2003, for instance, in Brazil we were very quick irrespective of fuel.

'The marked difference between this and previous seasons is how good the other teams have been. BAR did a really, really good job. I think we did a good job and brought the fight to Toyota, and had a go at them for most of the season. The reliability is much better, although the hydraulics and gearbox have probably been the weakest areas. On the control side, our start performance at the beginning of the season wasn't that great and let us down, particularly in Malaysia. On the aero and power-train side, we moved along quite nicely, although there was still room for improvement. There always is!'

Jaguar also made significant progress on the tyre front (Gillan: 'Michelin have been absolutely super in terms of their help.'), the team working on tyre maintenance and management through the race weekend. In the past, the green cars had been among the worst of the Michelin runners in terms of graining and blistering, but for 2004, the Jaguars were no longer the heaviest users of rubber.

The tyres were put to a stringent test, particularly by Webber, who pushed the R5 to the absolute limit. His qualifying lap on the testing Suzuka circuit was a prime example of the quality that had helped make him an attractive proposition for Williams for 2005. Apart from a dog of a day at Spa, where he threw away the opportunity presented by an excellent seventh on the grid by hitting Rubens Barrichello at the first corner and then colliding with Takuma Sato, Webber was the model of consistency and effort.

Christian Klien had a tough baptism. Given that he had been viewed with suspicion by the media from the outset, because of the fat Red Bull cheque poking out of his back pocket, Klien did a sensible job as he climbed the massively steep learning curve. It was not until Spa at the end of August that his possible potential began to emerge. But that was more or less the sum of his year, a performance that left many wondering just how much progress Justin Wilson might have made had he been given a full season.

In the end, the supreme effort by the loyal members of the team counted for little, as Ford put the company in the 'For Sale' column. There had been a warning of sorts at that informal gathering in January. Richard Parry-Jones had noted that the general escalation of costs in F1 could not be sustained, Ford's chief technical officer hinting that F1 would not be an attractive investment for prospective sponsors.

It summed up Ford's confused logic as the motor giant went into the fray at half-cock, relying too much on outside support and whingeing pathetically when it didn't materialise. In the four turbulent years since Ford had bought the team outright from Stewart Grand Prix – the company in which it had already invested handsomely – Jaguar had finished third twice. Now it fell to Dietrich Materschitz's Red Bull company to purchase the team, lock, stock and barrel, in November 2004 in a bid to carry on the fight.

Maurice Hamilton

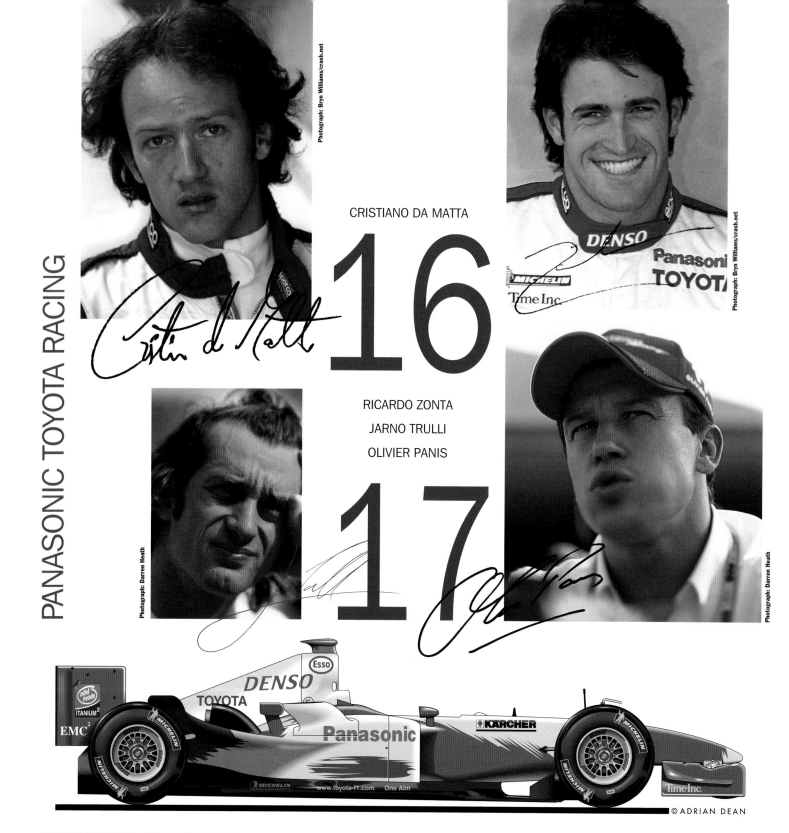

PANASONIC TOYOTA RACING

CRISTIANO DA MATTA

16

RICARDO ZONTA

JARNO TRULLI

OLIVIER PANIS

17

Photograph: Bryn Williams/crash.net

Photograph: Bryn Williams/crash.net

Photograph: Darren Heath

Photograph: Darren Heath

© ADRIAN DEAN

TOYOTA TF104/TF104B

SPONSORS	**Panasonic, Avex, Denso, Ebbon Dacs, ESPN Star Sports, Intel, Kärcher, KDDI, Time Inc,**
ENGINE	**Type:** Toyota RVX-04 **No. of cylinders (vee angle):** V10 (90°) **Sparking plugs:** Denso **Electronics:** Magneti Marelli **Fuel:** Esso **Oil:** Esso
TRANSMISSION	**Gearbox:** Toyota seven-speed longitudinal semi-automatic
CHASSIS	**Front suspension:** pushrod-activated torsion bars **Rear suspension:** pushrod-activated torsion bars **Dampers:** Toyota/Sachs
	Wheel diameter: front: 13 in rear: 13 in. **Wheels:** BBS **Tyres:** Michelin **Brake pads:** Brembo **Brake discs:** Brembo **Brake calipers:** Brembo
	Steering: Toyota power-assisted **Battery:** Panasonic
DIMENSIONS	**Wheelbase:** 3090 mm **Track:** front: 1425 mm rear: 1411 mm **Formula weight:** 600 kg including driver

Toyota unveiled its new TF104 challenger at the start of the season with some satisfaction, because the new RVX-04 V10 engine had sustained 2003's 900 bhp output, despite having to double its performance requirement from 400 km.

The new Toyota chassis had also evolved from the 2003 car, having been designed by Gustav Brunner and his team before the arrival of former Renault tech chief Mike Gascoyne, who had taken over as chassis technical director for the Japanese squad.

'The TF103 and TF104 may appear visually similar, but we have looked at every single part of the car, studied it, redesigned it and improved it,' said Brunner. 'There is no carry-over from last year's car, but we have worked on every single part to make it lighter, stiffer, more reliable and with better overall performance.'

Changes to the technical rules had affected the engine department much more than the chassis department, according to Toyota's executive vice-president, Toshiro Kurusu. 'Nevertheless, we have had to produce a bigger engine cover, larger rear end plates and use only two elements in the rear wing rather than three,' he said. 'However, I do not believe that these changes to the chassis design will greatly affect the overall performance of the car.'

Gascoyne arrived from Renault at the start of December 2003 and was shrewd enough not to intervene in any aspect of the TF104 at that point, as it was virtually complete. Even so, he quickly concluded that there was still a long way to go before the team would be fully competitive.

'Coming from Renault, when I first saw the car, it was fairly clear that there was still a way to go,' he explained. 'To be honest, the mechanical package was not too far away, but it was obvious to me that the most potential for improvement was going to come from aerodynamic improvements. But for the moment, the immediate priority was simply to get the car on its wheels, test it and work on its reliability.'

With Olivier Panis and Cristiano da Matta on the driving strength, supplemented by test drivers Ricardo Zonta and Ryan Briscoe, Toyota clearly was not taking too many gambles. Initially, results were modest. The team didn't score its first helping of championship points until round six at Monaco, where da Matta finished sixth, Panis eighth.

By that stage of the season, the TF104 had been subjected to its first significant revamp. 'We repackaged the car in time for Imola,' said Gascoyne, 'generally lowering it and introducing some aerodynamic improvements.' But it wasn't until Hockenheim in July that the TF104B arrived on the scene, based around a stiffer, lower and 9-kg lighter monocoque. It had a totally new aero package, including front wing and end plates. At the rear, there were new exhaust exit chimneys, a tighter waisting of the bodywork ahead of the rear wheels, and new winglets on the edges of the bodywork.

However, the TF104B's maiden race proved to be a big disappointment. Da Matta qualified disappointingly in 15th place, then spun off with a punctured tyre, while Panis stalled at the start and joined in late from the pit lane. 'There's nothing wrong with the car, not a single problem,' said Gascoyne at Hockenheim. 'I've always said that if you do the wind-tunnel testing properly and make it work to the right level of accuracy, then what you have in the tunnel is what you have at the track, as has been the case with this car.'

A few days later, Toyota rocked the F1 world with the news that da Matta would be stood down from the team for the final six races of the season, to be replaced by test driver Zonta.

Officially, da Matta was sidelined because of his disappointing form in the previous three races, but the matter-of-fact manner in which team principal Tsutomu Tomita commented on Olivier Panis's continued inclusion in the squad hardly amounted to a ringing endorsement of the Frenchman either.

'We believe it is fair to offer Ricardo the chance to show his potential in full race conditions, before we enter into the final step of our driver evaluation for the 2005 season,' said Tomita. 'We decided to retain Olivier Panis as a race driver for the rest of this season, based on the fact that he is the driver who has secured the team's best race result of the year so far [fifth at Indianapolis] and has collected the higher number of championship points [five].'

Ryan Briscoe would take over as the team's third driver for the Friday free practice sessions and general testing duties.

Gascoyne considered the TF104B to represent reasonable progress, but soon afterwards the team began working flat out to develop the 2005 car. 'That quickly became the main priority,' he explained, 'and I am confident that was the right way to go.'

Engine reliability was generally pretty good, although Zonta's retirement from a strong fourth place at Spa-Francorchamps with a rare failure was a big disappointment. 'We usually had no problems with engine mileage and didn't have to adopt a policy of restricted running to conserve the machinery,' said Gascoyne.

Toyota's new technical chief certainly didn't attach any real blame to the drivers for the team's performance during the year. 'They didn't have a car quick enough to get the results,' he said. 'They put in several strong drives, but we switched da Matta because we wanted to assess whether Ricardo could perform competitively in the race and qualifying situations.'

In the summer, there was a major reshuffle in the squad, team manager Ange Pasquali and senior engineer Norbert Kreyer leaving. This was followed by the signing of first Ralf Schumacher and then Jarno Trulli for the 2005 season.

Gascoyne continued, 'I have a lot of time for both our new drivers. Ralf is very quick and reacts positively to having the right team-mate. Trulli is a nice guy and also very quick, his only weak area perhaps being his consistency. Both like to tackle their racing in the right frame of mind, and we are confident we can give them the right environment in which they can produce their best in the future.'

Alan Henry

Top left: **Technical director and chassis guru Mike Gasgoyne.**
Photograph: Darren Heath

Top right: **Test driver Ryan Briscoe.**
Photograph: Bryn Williams/crash.net

Above: **Olivier Panis took honourable retirement at year's end.**

Left: **Cristiano da Matta was released in mid-season.**
Photographs: Darren Heath

TOYOTA

Tsutomu Tomita - Team Chairman
John Howett - Team President
Toshiro Kurusu - Executive Vice-President
Luca Marmorini - Technical Director (Engine)
Mike Gascoyne - Technical Director (Chassis)
Keizo Takahashi - Director Techical
Co-ordination
Gustav Brunner - Chief Designer
Richard Cregan - Team Manager
Gerard Le Coq - Chief Mechanic
Dieter Gass - Chief Race Engineer
Humphrey Corbett/Remi Decorzent -
Race Engineers - Car No. 17,
Olivier Panis/Ricardo Zonta
Humphrey Corbett/Ossi Oikarinen -
Race Engineers - Car No. 16,
Cristiano da Matta/Ricardo Zonta/Jarno Trulli

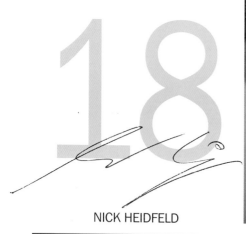

18

NICK HEIDFELD

19

TIMO GLOCK

GIORGIO PANTANO

JORDAN FORD

UNTIL the beginning of 2004, Jordan's most recent difficulties had been of an ethereal nature – at least in the mind of the team's owner. For the eternally optimistic Eddie Jordan, there would always be tomorrow; things would be different then. True enough, Jordan Grand Prix had actually won a race at the beginning of 2003. At the end of the season, however, the team had been next to last in the championship.

There could be no getting away from that fact in 2004 when you walked through the paddock. There was the yellow ensemble, parked alongside Minardi at the fag end of the F1 social order. It was a massive drop in every sense for the team that had been third in line just a few years before.

If 2003 had been difficult, the following 12 months would merely confirm the extent of the problem. As Jordan's 14th season drew to a close, it seemed that it might be the team's last. That's how serious things had become as the spending gap between the 'haves' and the 'have-nots' grew even wider. In fact, for much of the time, Jordan had very little at all.

The biggest blow over the winter had been the final departure of Gary Anderson, the technical chief whose hands-on ability had pulled the team through many a crisis. With no funds to employ a replacement, Jordan relied heavily on technicians and engineers who, while extremely competent in their own areas, lacked the experience to take control of the overall scheme. John McQuilliam, a talented and loyal servant, continued as chief designer in close association with colleagues whose total number would not have filled a single department at McLaren or Ferrari.

Because of the lack of money, the fundamental design parameter was to keep the 2004 car simple. The green light was not given for the EJ-14 until November, an impossibly late start that saw the team arrive in Melbourne with barely a handful of laps beneath the car's wheels. Or its tyres, to be precise. Bridgestone, in the interim, had been racing ahead with development, but Jordan had little knowledge of it.

'The new car ran at Silverstone, and that was about it,' said Ian Phillips, Jordan's director of business affairs. 'There were the usual new-car problems, which meant we went to Australia with barely a dozen flying laps under its belt. The tyre development had moved on massively during the winter, but we hadn't really participated in any serious testing; we had run the old car, but really it was a case of renting drivers out to generate some money.

'When we got to Melbourne, we found that some of the tyres we

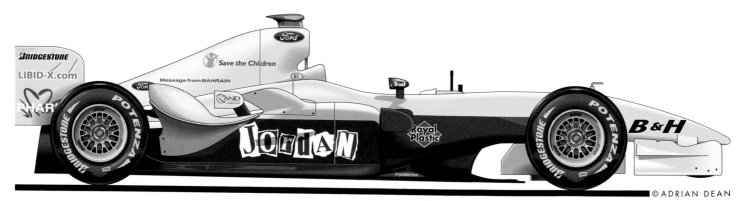

© ADRIAN DEAN

JORDAN EJ-14-COSWORTH

SPONSORS	Ford Cosworth, Bridgestone, Benson & Hedges/Sobranie, Re/MAX, Kingdom of Bahrain, Deutsche Post Speed Academy,
	Libid-X, Trust, B&Q China, Beijing Chateau, Citibank China
ENGINE	Type: Ford Cosworth RS2 No. of cylinders (vee angle): V10 (90°) Sparking plugs: Champion Electronics: Pi Fuel: Elf Oil: Elf
TRANSMISSION	Gearbox: Jordan seven-speed longitudinal electro-hydraulic sequential Driveshafts: Pankl Clutch: Jordan/AP triple-plate
CHASSIS	Front suspension: double wishbones, pushrod-activated torsion bars and dampers Rear suspension: double wishbones, pushrod-activated torsion bars and dampers
	Dampers: Jordan Penske Wheels: BBS Tyres: Bridgestone Fuel tank: ATL
DIMENSIONS	Track: front: 1400 mm rear: 1418 mm Formula weight: 600 kg including driver

had tested were not available to us anyway, because Bridgestone had not settled on the specification for their new tyre until quite late and they took a long time to produce. So, for the first two races, we were floundering around: there wasn't enough grip and the drivers weren't familiar with the car.'

Jordan had settled on Nick Heidfeld. He was not paid, but neither did the German bring any money. Instead, he contributed the experience and speed developed over 66 grands prix, and he proved a useful asset as the team tried to find its feet. Despite such a shaky start, the initial signs were very encouraging.

'We knew,' said Phillips, 'that the Bridgestones were not particularly good as one-lap qualifying tyres, but they were fantastic as a race tyre. Our lap times in the races were fairly competitive. We thought we would be in reasonably good shape once we returned to Europe, and got to understand the car and the tyres.'

The engine powering the Jordan was architecturally the same as the V10 designed and built by Cosworth for Jaguar, but there the similarity ended.

'We were running it in a specification demanded by Cosworth to make sure it didn't blow up!' said Phillips. 'At a conservative estimate, we were probably 70 bhp down on Jaguar. And it got worse toward the end of the season, when Cosworth were up for sale and needed to show they produced a reliable engine. It was all a bit of a farce.'

By the time Jordan reached the final three races, the state of the engine was almost irrelevant. The team was marking time, much as it had done ever since the mid-season realisation that the hoped-for improvement was not going to happen.

'By the time we got to North America, everyone else had major upgrades of cars and engines, and we hadn't.' said Phillips. 'We actually had a B-spec car [lightweight chassis and new aero package] designed, but we couldn't afford to build it.

'By Hockenheim, it was more delay, more delay. Previously, we were looking to mix it with Toyota, the second Jaguar and occasionally have a go at Massa, but we could not afford to make the changes simply because we had to stay in business. It was a decision we did not want to take, but we had no option. The points simply were not there to be had, although when they presented themselves in Canada, we were in a position to grab such a rare opportunity.'

The Jordans were classified seventh and eighth in Montreal, Heidfeld being led home by Timo Glock. It was an auspicious debut for the young Austrian, who was standing in for Giorgio Pantano following a hiccup in the Italian's payments because of a row between his family and his manager.

'Giorgio had impeccable credentials,' said Phillips. 'He had

speed, but he was very wild. He was starting to settle down, and then this dispute arose which had nothing to do with the team, but we had to suspend him for one race. He was beginning to get to grips with F1, even though, by his own admission, it caught him by surprise just how much he needed to learn.

'As the season went on, he started getting desperate, completely over-driving the car and making ridiculous mistakes. Monza was the final straw. We thought it was best for everyone's sake to draw a line under it right then, and Glock moved up from being the Friday driver.'

Glock had been tested during the winter, and it was immediately apparent that his clear and concise interpretation of what the car was doing made him a decent prospect for the team's third driver.

'Because we did very little testing, the presence of an intelligent third driver on Fridays helped us a lot, particularly with tyres,' said Phillips. 'Timo fulfilled the role really well, right up to his first race in Canada. He over-drove totally in qualifying, but had a bloody good race and was luckily rewarded with some points, which was great. Certainly, we had no qualms about using him again as a race driver once Giorgio had left.'

Jordan survived 2004, being prudent enough to avoid making any of its 200 staff redundant. There was intense speculation over the team's future, much as there had been before. The difference this time was that Eddie Jordan's bullish optimism was less evident than usual. That was a bad sign. The sincere hope in the paddock was that this colourful and immensely popular team would be around in 2005.

Maurice Hamilton

Above: Giorgio Pantano ran short of funds and was replaced by test driver Timo Glock (top right).

Above left: Nick Heidfeld squeezed the maximum from the Jordan-Cosworth package for little reward.
Photographs: Darren Heath

Top centre: Dutchman Robert Doornbos, an F3000 front-runner, took on testing duties for the last three races.

Left: The ever-optimistic Eddie Jordan.

JORDAN

Eddie Jordan - Team Principal
Richard O'Driscoll - Chief Operating Officer
Ian Phillips - Director of Business Affairs
James Robinson - Head of Race and Test Engineering
John McQuilliam - Chief Designer
Nicolo Petrucci - Head of Aerodynamics
Mike Wroe - Head of Electronics
David Williams - Head of Production
Tim Edwards - Team Manager
Gerrard O'Reilly - Assistant Team Manager
Andy Stevenson - Chief Mechanic
Gerry Hughes - Race Engineer - Car No. 18, Nick Heidfeld
Dominic Harlow - Race Engineer - Car No. 19, Giorgio Pantano/Timo Glock

Photograph: Darren Heath

20

GIANMARIA BRUNI

Photograph: Bryn Williams/crash.net

21

ZSOLT BAUMGARTNER

WHEN you're bumping along on the bottom of Formula 1, every little success helps. So the fact that Minardi made a small profit in 2004 and scored a point marked two such successes. That, at the end of the year, the team didn't know where its next engine was coming from, nor what regulations it would be running to were the minus points.

As usual, it was all change at the beginning of the year, at least as far as drivers were concerned. Gone were the experienced Jos Verstappen, Justin Wilson (who had moved on to Jaguar) and Wilson's replacement, Nicholas Kiesa; in came Zsolt Baumgartner and Gianmaria Bruni.

'Financially, it was better for us, but I think the biggest advantage was that we had a clearer and earlier decision on our drivers, and therefore we knew where we were going,' said team principal Paul Stoddart.

Baumgartner had driven a couple of races for Jordan in 2003, as replacement for Ralph Firman. 'Zsolt, in particular, has just got better and better,' Stoddart said of the likeable Hungarian. 'I think he's earned a lot of respect around here. A lot of people thought he was simply a pay driver and nothing but that, but he's actually improved. He's very, very reliable. He'll bring the car home for you, and when you're Minardi, you need that. You need to be there for that odd occasion like Indianapolis this year, where you can score the point by being reliable and being there at the end of the race.'

Bruni came to Minardi with perhaps better credentials. 'Gimmi had a blinding start,' continued Stoddart, 'but then had a bit of a mid-season struggle. He had some unlucky races, but toward the end of the season, he was totally motivated again and he was delivering some good performances.'

The pair were joined by Belgian F3000 driver Bas Leinders, who did most of Minardi's test and development on the Fridays of grand prix weekends. Otherwise, the team only did a day's testing at Imola before the start of the season, a day at Mugello, another at Misano and the pre-Italian Grand Prix test at Monza.

Gabriele Tredozzi's stable, 17-strong technical team once again modified the design that was based on the chassis first built in 2002. For once, it was working with the same Cosworth CR3 engine and gearbox from the previous year, which allowed it to concentrate elsewhere.

At one time, following the purchase of the last Arrows, it was thought that some of its features would be incorporated in the latest Minardi, but this wasn't the case. 'We pushed to improve everywhere we could to the maximum,' explained Tredozzi. 'We improved the stiffness in the suspension, the engine mounting, and we worked the maximum we could from the aero point of view, but we didn't spend huge time in the wind tunnel.' In fact,

© ADRIAN DEAN

EUROPEAN MINARDI PS04B-COSWORTH

SPONSORS	Superfund, Cosworth Racing, Bridgestone, Magneti Marelli, Brevi, Puma, 3D Systems, Cimatron, Aurora Engineering, Fedem, Beta, CD adapco Group,
	IT Unlimited, Nescalibur, Feedback, Tosinvest, CIB Lizing, Uniqa, Standox, Santogal, Fondmetal, Golden Palace, Allegrini, OzJet
ENGINE	**Type:** Cosworth CR3 **No. of cylinders (vee angle):** V10 (72°) **Sparking plugs:** Champion **Electronics:** Magneti Marelli **Fuel:** Elf **Oil:** Elf
TRANSMISSION	**Gearbox:** Minardi six-speed longitudinal semi-automatic sequential **Driveshafts:** Minardi **Clutch:** AP Racing triple-plate carbon
CHASSIS	**Front suspension:** double wishbones, pushrod-activated torsion bars **Rear suspension:** double wishbones, pushrod-activated torsion bars **Dampers:** Sachs
	Wheel diameter: front: 13 in rear: 13 in **Wheels:** OZ Racing **Tyres:** Bridgestone **Brake pads:** Hitco Brembo **Brake discs:** Hitco Brembo **Brake calipers:** Brembo
	Steering: Minardi power-assisted rack-and-pinion **Radiators:** Minardi/Secan **Fuel tank:** ATL **Battery:** Fiamm **Instruments:** Magneti Marelli
DIMENSIONS	**Wheelbase:** 3097 mm **Track:** front: 1400 mm rear: 1410 mm **Formula weight:** 600 kg including driver

Above: Oh Lucky Man. Zsolt Baumgartner grabbed the team's only point in a season of toil for the perennial backmarkers.

Below left: Gianmaria Bruni had an up-and-down year.

Below: Paul Stoddart continued to tilt at windmills as his Minardi team survived aganst the odds.
Photographs: Darren Heath

Below left: Dream On. Test driver Bas Leinders plugged away in the hope of a full-time ride in Formula 1.
Photograph: Bryn Williams/crash.net

there was no aero time at all between January 2003 and February 2004. 'This was because of resources,' explained Tredozzi. 'After that, a few sessions and we gained something.' Indeed, there were modifications to the body and the diffuser.

Development continued throughout the season. 'There were lots of little things,' said Tredozzi. 'We wanted to package everything as well as possible, but also change the weight distribution, keep the centre of gravity lower, and improve the aerodynamics and decrease the weight. 'There was a big package in the middle of the season, with a different floor and side-pod inlets, bargeboards and front wing end plates. It was a good package, although it wasn't easy to find a balance. It isn't when you introduce it at a race weekend.

'But the performance was a huge improvement in comparison to the previous year. Admittedly, some of that also came from the tyres. Maybe the gap to the big teams remained the same, but the big teams have pushed very hard, like never before.'

Cosworth's CR3 engine had to last a weekend, and generally speaking did so. 'We had some engine changes, but not a lot,' admitted Tredozzi. It was never a great penalty to do so.

Only once did the engine let go in a race, and interestingly, it achieved a remarkable top speed at Monza, where Leinders, running with very little downforce, was timed at 224 mph on the pit straight. Even Tredozzi was surprised: 'Maybe he had a bit of a tow; it was more than our target.'

In most cases, it was Bridgestone who suggested which tyres the team should use due to its lack of testing. Minardi did request a change of rear construction during the year, which the tyre company supplied.

Unlike in 2003, the Minardi was fairly reliable. Driver error accounted for 50 per cent of the retirements, while there was a gearbox issue early in the season that was resolved. Baumgartner suffered an early ECU failure.

For Tredozzi, the best race was Spa, where both cars were consistent and closer than ever to fellow independent Jordan, even though neither car actually finished due to accidents. 'I like to remember Indianapolis too, because we scored a point,' he said.

Off the track, the team contracted to 90 people, 'because we didn't do an awful lot of development, because we didn't know what we were developing to', but the budget was slightly better. That said, costs were higher.

The team's greatest tragedy, however, was the loss of popular sporting director John Walton, who died after a severe heart attack in July. 'It was the most tragic event, not only of the year, but of my involvement in F1,' said Stoddart. 'He was a total leader of the guys, and there's not a week goes by when we don't miss him.'

As F1's fourth-oldest team ended its 20th season, Stoddart reflected on how the sport's politics continued to blight his outfit: 'I'm worse off because of the politics this year, because there's absolutely no stability. I opened this year hoping for a new Concorde Agreement. We had an MOU signed between Bernie and the manufacturers – that disappeared. We had promises that we were going to see a new commercial agreement – that hasn't happened. We had the commercially affordable engines – that didn't happen, and now we don't know whether we even have an engine for next year, or whether we are going to have to do it ourselves.'

Life, then, continues to be tough for the minnows in Formula 1, but they continue to survive and perhaps to act as an inspiration for those considering entering the sport. There must be occasions, though, when Paul Stoddart wishes that the business was less frustrating.

Bob Constanduros

MINARDI

Paul Stoddart - Team Principal

Gian Carlo Minardi - Director
(young driver development)

Gabriele Tredozi - Technical Director

Andy Tilley - Senior Engineer

Andrea Rochetto - Senior Aerodynamicist

John Walton - Sporting Director (deceased)

Massimo Rivola - Team Manager

Paulo Piancastelli - Chief Mechanic

Ricardo Adami - Race Engineer -
Car No. 20, Gianmaria Bruni

Laurent Mekies - Race Engineer -
Car No. 21, Zsolt Baumgartner

GRANDS PRIX 2004

BY ALAN HENRY & ADAM COOPER

AUSTRALIAN GP	74
MALAYSIAN GP	84
BAHRAIN GP	92
SAN MARINO GP	100
SPANISH GP	108
MONACO GP	116
EUROPEAN GP	124
CANADIAN GP	132
UNITED STATES GP	140
FRENCH GP	148
BRITISH GP	156
GERMAN GP	164
HUNGARIAN GP	172
BELGIAN GP	180
ITALIAN GP	188
CHINESE GP	196
JAPANESE GP	204
BRAZILIAN GP	212

Ferrari and Michael Schumacher's ruthless
domination of the 2004 season began in
Melbourne.
Photograph: Darren Heath

MELBOURNE
AUSTRALIANGP

FIA F1 WORLD CHAMPIONSHIP • ROUND 1

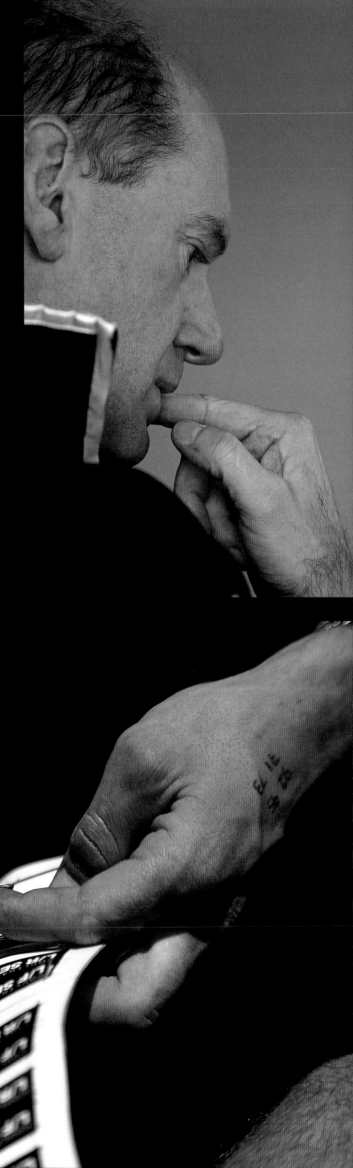

RULE CHANGES FOR 2004

On 15 October, 2003, the FIA announced a number of changes to the Sporting Regulations for the 2004 F1 season.
• Friday morning's private test session and the first qualifying session were abandoned. Instead, the opening day's track action would comprise two one-hour practice sessions, in which all teams, bar the top four from the 2003 championship, would be allowed to run a third car (see below).
• As in 2003, Saturday's schedule would feature two 45-minute practice sessions, which would be followed by a new two-part qualifying session, effectively 2003's Friday and Saturday sessions back to back, with only a two-minute break in between (see below).

Race Weekend Schedule
Friday
11.00–12.00 Free practice
14.00–15.00 Free practice
During both sessions, all teams, other than those who finished in the top four positions of the previous year's World Championship for Constructors, would be permitted to run a third car provided any driver of it was not one of the team's nominated drivers for the event in question, held a Super Licence and had not driven in more than six world championship events during the two previous world championships.

   If one of the team's nominated drivers was deemed unable to drive at some stage after initial scrutineering, and the stewards agreed to a change of driver, the driver of a third car could take part in the remainder of the event. Under such circumstances, a driver who started the event as a 'third' driver would have to continue with the same engine for the remainder of the event.

   The third car could be run in a different livery, unless it was used as the team's spare car during the remainder of the event.

Saturday
10.00–10.45 Free practice
11.15–12.00 Free practice
14.00 Qualifying begins
The qualifying session would be held in two parts, separated by two minutes. During the first part, each driver would carry out a single timed lap, starting in the order they had finished in the previous race. At the first race of the year, the order of the last event of the previous year's world championship would be used (in both cases, any new drivers would be arranged in numerical order). Any car stopping in the first part would not be allowed to take part in the second; if the car was brought back to the pits before the end of the session, it had to remain in parc fermé until the end of the session. Refuelling rigs would be allowed in the first part subject to everyone wearing suitable clothing and photographers being restricted as for a race. The running order for the second part would be determined by reversing the order of the times achieved in the first part. Cars would run with race fuel and race settings, as in 2003. In both sessions, cars would be released as the previous one crossed the line to start its flying lap; in both sessions, the sixth, 11th and 16th cars in sequence would be released two minutes after the previous car finished its flying lap.

Sunday
14.00 Race (or at other times according to the relevant schedule).

Tyre use and allocation
• The number of dry-weather tyres available to each driver during the event would remain the same at 20 front and 20 rear. Each driver would be allocated three sets of dry-weather tyres for use on Friday, which could not be used at any other time during the event. No tyres from the remaining seven sets could be used on Friday. The choice of dry-weather tyre for qualifying and the race had to be made by 9.00 am on Saturday (either specification of tyre could be used for the free practice sessions on Saturday). However, if both Friday sessions were declared wet, the choice could be postponed until 1.00 pm on Saturday.
• The number of wet-weather tyres available to each driver during the event would remain the same at 14 front and 14 rear. Extreme-weather tyres would continue to be permitted, but could only be used when authorised.

Parc fermé procedures
These would remain the same as in 2003, but the practice of using fuel circulation for engine cooling would be prohibited.

Number of drivers per car
Each team would be allowed to employ four drivers during each season, excluding any third driver running in the Friday sessions.

Pit-lane speed limit
The speed limit for qualifying and the race would be raised to 100 km/h for most events, although a lower limit would be considered at tracks with particularly narrow pit lanes.

MELBOURNE QUALIFYING

PAINFUL SHOWING FOR MP4/19

Instead of celebrating the debut of a highly competitive car, McLaren's chairman, Ron Dennis, found himself convening an urgent technical post-mortem on the team's disastrous failure in the Australian Grand Prix, where the all-new MP4/19 challenger had been totally outclassed by its key rivals.

The first of the new 2004 cars to appear in testing (in November 2003), the McLaren had a terrible season opener, which raised questions about the organisation of the design teams, both at McLaren's factory in Woking and at the headquarters of its engine partner, Mercedes Ilmor, at Brixworth, near Northampton.

After Kimi Räikkönen's early retirement with engine failure and David Coulthard's uncompetitive drive to eighth place, it was clear that urgent work was required to improve the car's handling balance and extract more power from its Mercedes V10 engine.

It was a serious problem for the British team, coming so soon after the failure of its MP4/18, which had been tested exhaustively in 2003, but never raced following a spate of technical failures and two serious crashes.

'It was certainly a race which reflects a significant differential between one tyre manufacturer and another, and as the majority of the quick cars are on Michelin, you've got a lot of them struggling for grip,' said Dennis. 'The ambient temperature dropped so low that we suffered probably more than most, as our own performance wasn't up to where we thought it should be. I am absolutely sure that we have the resource and expertise to resolve the issues. How fast, we will have to wait and see.'

He added, 'We do know where the weaknesses are. The performance of all the Michelin runners will be better in Malaysia. But Ferrari are in a league of their own at the moment, and it will be difficult for any other team to match that performance. Alonso's performance was particularly impressive in the circumstances, but our own efforts...we know where we are going and what we need to do.

'The engine is certainly one area of the package we need to improve. Obviously, an engine failure is not great, but it would be completely unfair to attribute all the performance to any one component.'

Coulthard was also asked why he thought the MP4/19 was so slow despite four months of testing. 'That's a very good question,' he replied. 'Despite all the initial hype from all the winter tests, when we've been running on track with others, we've always been around the midgrid. We need to improve. We can't hide from it. We need to work hard and make improvements.

'It's like all these things, if you knew exactly what the one problem was, then you would be working flat out on that, but I think generally we're not making the most of the tyres on one lap, the car is difficult to position, and our race pace isn't good enough. So you could say every area, whether that be finding horsepower, downforce or mechanical grip.'

Above left: McLaren technical director Adrian Newey certainly seemed to have quite an engineering conundrum on his hands at the first race, given the disappointing form of the new MP4/19.

Left: Stickers for the all-important art of tyre management in 2004.

Right: Jean Todt's inscrutable visage belied the satisfaction he derived from another crushing Maranello 1-2.

Photographs: Darren Heath

Schumacher's qualifying pace in the new Ferrari was astounding, so it came as no surprise that he started from pole. In 2003, there had been a premium on going for banzai lap times in the Friday session because earning a slot to run late on Saturday, when the times were reversed, meant that you would be out on the circuit when it was at its rubbered-in best, offering maximum grip. Under the controversial new format, with the sessions separated not by 24 hours, but by two minutes, this was not an issue. By the time the first car ran in the second session, more than enough rubber had been laid down to provide all the grip anybody could require.

'It's rubbish,' said Flavio Briatore of the new format. 'It's too long for TV and makes no sense. It needs to be changed. It's stupid for us, stupid for the spectators.' Bernie Ecclestone, correctly judging when F1 was on to a loser, concluded the same, calling on the FIA and the teams to get together and change it as quickly as possible.

Michael Schumacher managed a 1m 24.408s best, just squeezing out Barrichello by 0.074s. It was certainly a testimony to Bridgestone's development work during the off-season, The team had a new, wider front tyre at its disposal, and the way the new Ferrari F2004 changed direction through the fast swerves was simply dazzling.

Juan Pablo Montoya's Williams FW26 emerged best of the rest with third-fastest time on 1m 24.998s, although this was only after several off-track excursions during practice. Nevertheless, he admitted that the car felt much better than it had in the Friday sessions.

'Yesterday, we struggled a bit with tyres, and it took us a while to get the set-up working properly,' he admitted. 'I was amazed by the time I set in the first qualifying, but then I tried too hard in the second session, made a mistake in the third sector and lost my advantage.'

Team-mate Ralf Schumacher could only manage a 1m 25.925s, putting him eighth on the grid, which suggested he was carrying rather more fuel than Montoya. In reality, he didn't push hard enough through the first few corners, then made a slight mistake toward the end of his lap, costing him a crucial few seconds.

Impressively, Jenson Button matched Montoya's time to claim fourth place on the grid, confounding the team's critics, who had suggested his off-season testing form had been flattered by running the new BAR 006 under the weight limit to produce competitive times. Now it was clear that Button was genuinely competitive and, come the race, his performance would be thrown into even clearer relief when he ran an opening stint just as long as his key rivals.

For Renault, there was a measure of disappointment, Fernando Alonso (1m 25.699s) and Jarno Trulli (1m 26.290s) lining up fifth and ninth, separated by Mark Webber's Jaguar R5 (1m 25.805s), Takuma Sato's BAR-Honda (1m 25.851s) and Ralf Schumacher's Williams. The Renault guys had opted for a soft race compound, which would pay dividends on race day when the weather turned out to be unseasonably cool, ensuring they had grip to spare.

McLaren's Kimi Räikkönen could only manage a tenth-fastest 1m 26.297s in the twitchy and nervous MP4/19, but at least that was the best part of a second quicker than Coulthard, who again came unstuck in his attempts to get to grip with the pressures of one-lap qualifying. Coming out of the final corner to complete his run, he went wide and bounced over the grass for a long while, but kept his foot in it and survived with only superficial damage to the car.

Splitting the McLarens was Felipe Massa in the best-placed Sauber C23 on 1m 27.065s, while in the Toyota garage there was a general air of gloom, as Cristiano da Matta (1m 27.823s) could not better 13th-fastest time, and an electrical glitch prevented team-mate Olivier Panis from making his run. Consequently, he had to start at the back of the grid, a fate he shared with Jaguar's Christian Klien, who had suffered a hydraulic malfunction, and Minardi's Gianmaria Bruni.

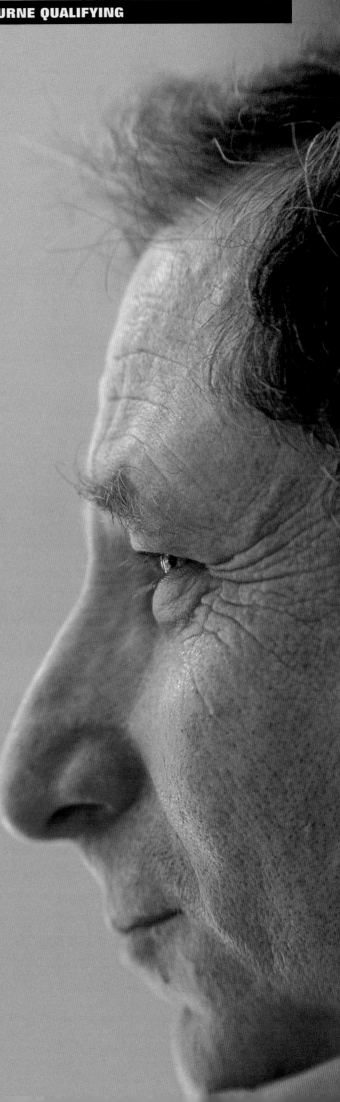

RUNNERS AND RIDERS FOR 2004

SCUDERIA FERRARI MARLBORO

Michael Schumacher and Rubens Barrichello defending Maranello's pre-eminence with an outwardly conservative, evolutionary version of 2003's car. The key difference is that for the past two seasons, Ferrari has run an updated car in the first few races. The new F2004, powered by the latest type 053 version of Ferrari's V10 engine, is easily capable of running 800 km under new regulations. Engine wizard Paolo Martinelli says cylinder heads have been reinforced, but with no extra weight penalty.

Photographs: Darren Heath

BMW WILLIAMSF1 TEAM

A radically new FW26 for Juan Pablo Montoya and Ralf Schumacher features aerodynamic package working in conjunction with twin-keel front suspension pick-up points (above), a first for Williams and a modification that benefits the entire airflow over and under the car. Short-wheelbase configuration is the same as 2003's FW25, which played well to the requirements of one-lap qualifying. Fuel-tank capacity is slightly smaller than its predecessor, which had one of the smallest cells anyway.

WEST MCLAREN MERCEDES

The new MP4/19 features extremely tightly packaged bodywork, particularly around the rear end, and another new Mercedes V10 engine. The chassis profile is unchanged from the shelved MP4/18, but the internal architecture of the monocoque is completely different. The chassis is stiffer and stronger as a result with no weight penalty. The car has a lower centre of gravity to enhance stability under acceleration and braking.

MILD SEVEN RENAULT F1 TEAM

The R24 is the first of the Renault F1 generation to break cover since Mike Gascoyne moved to Toyota as technical director. Development now headed by former McLaren engineer Bob Bell. In order to tightly package the rear end of the R24, the wide-angle ,106-degree V10 has been ditched in favour of a more upright, 72-degree unit, which has its antecedence in the engines that powered Damon Hill and Jacques Villeneuve to their championships in 1996 and 1997.

LUCKY STRIKE BAR HONDA

The BAR 006 is an evolutionary version of 2003's promising 005, seeking finally to bury the team's reputation for financial profligacy and pathetic results. Technical director Geoff Willis admits he was somewhat more ambitious in his design approach to the car, and Honda is confident that the lighter, lower RA004E V10 will get the job done. The new chassis is stiffer and has a lower centre of gravity. It also features a smaller fuel capacity to reflect the revised qualifying rules and raised pit-lane speeds. A new carbon-fibre gearbox is fitted, which, together with a narrow, lightweight gear set, affords a very substantial weight reduction at the rear of the car.

SAUBER PETRONAS

The C23 is the most controversial car of the year, touted as a Ferrari F2003 copy by its rivals, an allegation roundly denied by both Maranello and the Swiss team. Twin-keel, lower front suspension pick-up points, very much a recent Sauber speciality, abandoned on this car in favour of a single-keel arrangement. All-new driver line-up of Giancarlo Fisichella and returnee Felipe Massa, back in the fold after a season test driving for Ferrari.

JAGUAR RACING

With a relatively modest $120 million available for its entire programme, including the Cosworth CR6 engine, Jaguar understandably pursued a cautious evolutionary route with its R5 for Mark Webber and new boy Christian Klien (above). The R5's nose section is mounted lower than on the R4, and the wind-tunnel numbers confirmed that it is more efficient than its predecessor. Single-keel, lower front suspension pick-up points are retained. The latest 90-degree Cosworth CR6 V10 should be slightly lighter than last year's engine and slightly less powerful in 800-km form.

JORDAN FORD

Another all-new driver line-up with Nick Heidfeld and late recruit Giorgio Pantano (above) handling the all-new EJ-14, which has benefited from what the team claims was a highly productive, winter aerodynamic development programme. Fitted with the latest 90-degree Cosworth V10 engine, giving Jordan theoretical parity on power with the rival Jaguar squad.

PANASONIC TOYOTA RACING

Japan's top car company seriously ramping up its efforts with the all-new TF104 as it prepares for its third racing season in F1. The TF104 monocoque is very different from 2003, being higher at the front and therefore requiring a revised seating position for drivers Olivier Panis and Cristiano da Matta. Toyota's latest RVX-04 engine is the same length and has the same crankshaft axis as its predecessor, but the centre of mass is lower than 2003's V10. It features an all-new, lighter, stiffer titanium-cased gearbox.

EUROPEAN MINARDI COSWORTH

New boys Zsolt Baumgartner and Gianmaria Bruni signed to drive the new Minardi PS04B after a few months spent assessing the old Arrows A23s, which the team had purchased at auction the previous summer. After conducting back-to-back tests with the Arrows, Minardi concluded that little could be learned from this bought-in technology and pressed ahead with their own Cosworth-engined car.

THERE was always the private hope, nurtured deep within the F1 collective psyche, that Maranello might stumble slightly. That the mental effort of winning that sixth world championship in 2003 could conceivably have gone some way toward drying up Michael Schumacher's seemingly bottomless pit of personal motivation. Or even that Michelin, having appeared to push Bridgestone on to its back foot the previous summer, would have raised its game so dramatically that somehow it would catapult Renault, BMW Williams and McLaren-Mercedes into a head-to-head confrontation with the Prancing Horse.

Instead, the fans were treated to a double dose of *deja-vu* in the first race of the 2004 season. And when the celebration was over, the empty champagne bottles discarded, Michael Schumacher changed out of his trademark red jumper, donned a black helmet and black visor, and sneaked anonymously out of Melbourne's Albert Park circuit on a borrowed motorcycle to join his family at their nearby luxury hotel.

If they had not eased their pace in the closing stages of the race, Michael and team-mate Rubens Barrichello might well have lapped Juan Pablo Montoya's Williams-BMW FW26 before the end of the 58-lap race; the Colombian finished over a minute behind the scarlet Ferrari F2004s in fifth place. They did briefly lap Jenson Button's sixth-place BAR-Honda, but the British driver was able to get back on the tail of the winning lap as Michael and Rubens slowed toward the finish.

After all the pre-season hype and frenzied anticipation, any hopes that Williams and McLaren would finally take the fight to Ferrari seemed to lie in tatters as Schumacher and Barrichello cruised imperiously to another 1-2 success.

Although their performance edge had been given a spectacular boost by the unseasonably cool conditions, which played to the

strength of their Bridgestone tyres, by Sunday evening, paddock insiders were speculating whether the legendary Italian team might even win all the events in what promised to be a gruelling 18-race season.

F1 doesn't usually work like that, of course. Yet from the moment the two Ferrari F2004s sailed effortlessly away from the front row of the grid at the Albert Park circuit, you could have been forgiven for concluding that Schumacher's seventh world championship title was little more than a formality.

Barrichello took a long look down the inside as the pack scrambled into the first turn, but his sense of prudence and self-discipline served to remind him that this was not the time or place for any extrovert heroics. He moved dutifully back into line behind Michael, just as the fans' attention was grabbed by the fast starting Fernando Alonso, who jinked his Renault R24 to the left as he accelerated away from the pack, briefly took to the grass and surged through to fourth place, wheel-to-wheel with Montoya's Williams as they raced for the first turn.

Alonso was on the grippy racing line and knew that the Williams driver might be in trouble if he attempted to eyeball it out all the way into the braking area. Alonso went deep, but Juan Pablo went deeper. It wasn't the best strategy. On the dusty side of the circuit, he ploughed straight off on to the grass, allowing Alonso to duck around behind him into third place.

'I didn't get off the line too well, but I was coming back along-side Alonso like a rocket when both my front wheels locked going into the first corner, which was a little strange, as I had the brake bias adjusted right back to the rear,' said Montoya. 'I lost four places, which was a little frustrating.'

Alonso saw it from a slightly different perspective. 'I made a great start, even though Montoya forced me on to the grass,' he

claimed. 'After he outbraked himself at the first corner, I found myself third, and from then on had a pretty easy race.

'After that, I was too slow to fight with the Ferraris, and I was a little bit quicker than Jenson and the [two] Williams. I was in the middle of nowhere and didn't have any big problems.'

Farther back, Jarno Trulli felt his Renault being hit quite hard from behind. Takuma Sato's BAR 006 had nudged the Italian's car under braking for the first corner and damaged the R24's dif-fuser, as well as slightly damaging his own nose section. It left an exasperated Trulli struggling for grip for the rest of the afternoon.

By the end of the opening lap, Michael Schumacher was a full second ahead of Barrichello. By lap four, he was 1.8s in front of the Brazilian and 4s ahead of Alonso's Renault, which in turn was easing away from Jenson Button's BAR. Trulli was next up and doing his best to hang on ahead of the recovering Montoya, the Williams driver having energetically barged aside team-mate Ralf Schumacher.

Barrichello kept his team leader under strong pressure from the start, only to slow slightly after overheating his brakes in the chase. 'It was a tough one because at the beginning, for the first half of the race before Rubens had some problems, he was push-ing very, very hard, and it was a really close fight,' admitted Michael Schumacher.

'I couldn't allow any mistakes and it was very exciting, I have to say. But the car is going well, we've seen this all weekend long, and the great thing from my personal point of view is that I've come home with two more points than I scored last year after the first three races. So that's a good start of the season for me.'

On lap 11, Barrichello, Alonso and Button all made their first refuelling stops after short opening stints. Farther back, the McLaren MP4/19s had been mired in the mid-field ruck. Both

Kimi Räikkönen and David Coulthard had qualified poorly, even allowing for the fact that they were relying on two-stop strategies to boost their race prospects.

Räikkönen had dropped behind Coulthard after a poor start and soon realised that his engine was losing power. Battling with Felipe Massa's Sauber for 11th place, he spun off at turn three on lap ten after the rear wheels locked. Later, it was established that a radiator core had failed, causing the water pressure to drop and the engine to seize.

Schumacher's Ferrari came in for its first stop (9.4s) on lap 12, resuming in the lead, while Mark Webber's Jaguar R5 briefly showed in third place before coming in for a 10.2s refuelling stop on lap 13. With 14 laps completed and the race settling down again, Schumacher and Alonso were separated by 7.4s in first and third places respectively.

Alonso made his second stop on lap 24, by which time Schumacher was easing away from Barrichello, the Brazilian being troubled by a soft brake pedal after those earlier exertions.

'I kept pressing and trying to pass him [Schumacher] up to the point of the second refuelling stop,' said Barrichello, who came in on lap 29, again one lap before his team leader. 'But after the stop, the brakes did not seem to have cooled very much and I had a very long pedal. Combined with the extra fuel load, I was worried that I might crash if I pushed too hard, so from then on I backed off.'

Meanwhile, there had been disappointment in the Jaguar camp. After his first refuelling stop, Webber had rejoined in a strong eighth place, close behind Montoya's Williams. It looked as though he was on course for a championship point in front of his home crowd, but it wasn't to be. He lost sixth gear on lap 27, and seventh gear shortly afterwards, leaving him no alternative but to pull in and retire.

'The balance of the car was good, and to have lost those gears was very frustrating, since we have not had this problem before through 6,000 kilometres of testing,' he shrugged. 'Roll on Malaysia!'

The victorious Ferraris duly made their third scheduled refuelling stops on lap 44 (Barrichello) and 45 (Schumacher) before easing their pace and running out the remaining race distance in their customary commanding formation. They crossed the finishing line 13.605s apart, with Alonso another 21.06s back in an excellent third place.

The Williams drivers were slightly disappointed by the performance of their FW26s, even allowing for the fact that the cool conditions had reduced the grip from their Michelin tyres. Ralf Schumacher finished fourth, 8.1s ahead of team-mate Montoya, but it was certainly an uninspiring debut for the new twin-keel Williams.

On the plus side, the BMW P84 engines ran faultlessly all weekend on the Albert Park track, which is the third most gru-

DIARY

November 2003

Christian Klien given Jaguar F1 test after Jacques Villeneuve indicates he has 'no interest' in paying for a drive – with Jaguar or anybody else.

McLaren confirms that Juan Pablo Montoya has signed a contract to drive for them in 2005.

The BAR Honda team confirms a switch from Bridgestone to Michelin tyres for 2004.

December 2003

The new McLaren-Mercedes MP4/19 makes its testing debut at Barcelona, driven by David Coulthard.

The future of the French GP in 2004 remains uncertain, as there is still $10 million owed to Bernie Ecclestone's F1 Management company in respect of fees due from the 2003 race. However, a new contract covering the years 2005–09 is finalised.

GPWC agrees a 'Memorandum of Understanding' with Bernie Ecclestone, the F1 teams and the bankers holding the shares of the now-bankrupt Kirch media group, which the car manufacturers hope will produce a more equitable division of the sport's commercial-rights income in future.

Ralf Schumacher confirms that negotiations with Frank Williams for an extension of his contract into 2005 have stalled.

January 2004

New Williams-BMW FW26 makes its testing debut at Barcelona.

Christian Klien confirmed as Mark Webber's team-mate at Jaguar Racing.

Bahrain GP organisers confirm that their new circuit will be ready in time for the third round of the world championship on 4 April.

Louis Stanley, one-time managing director of the BRM F1 team, dies at the age of 92.

February 2004

Jos Verstappen and Eddie Jordan fail to agree on terms for the Dutch driver to join the Silverstone based team. Italy's Giorgio Pantano gets the drive instead.

Former Renault test driver Allan McNish joins Audi sports car team.

elling from the point of view of full-throttle running (63 per cent of the lap) and the need for hard engine braking.

'The worrying thing,' said Ralf Schumacher, 'is that at this race we were missing a second a lap compared with Ferrari, which I certainly didn't expect, and is mainly down to the design of their car as well as some tyre graining for us. The whole package needs to improve slightly, and this is going to take maybe a couple of races, but I am confident we can make it.'

Behind Montoya, Jenson Button and the new BAR-Honda 006 punched well above their weight to finish sixth, the car showing commendable speed on its race debut, although the team was slightly disappointed after qualifying fourth.

'My start wasn't particularly great,' said Button, 'and it was very slippery out there, but I managed to hold on for fourth for some time. Ralf was able to get past me in the pit stop when we had a delay with the refuelling nozzle.

'Then Montoya got past me out on the circuit. I think we need a little more in the way of race pace, but it's certainly a solid start to the season. We had good reliability, but then so did everybody else.'

Trulli finished seventh after a difficult drive in his Renault, ahead of a philosophical David Coulthard, who was a lapped eighth in the new McLaren. He was followed by Takuma Sato, who changed his nose section – following contact with Trulli in the first-corner scramble – at his second refuelling stop.

Yet it was as well to tiptoe past the McLaren garage at the end of the afternoon. To Coulthard, it wasn't a total surprise. 'I did the [last] Imola test, so to an extent I think I've always felt I'm the prophet of doom,' he admitted. 'People get so excited about a single quick lap time during a test, saying, "Oh, we're quick," and I have to say, "Hold on a minute, it's not about one lap in testing, it's about averaging out all those tests." I saw Ferrari's pace in the 15th lap in a test at Imola, and they were a second quicker than anybody.'

For the Toyota team, the TF104 produced nowhere near enough downforce, leaving drivers Cristiano da Matta and Olivier Panis struggling two laps down at the chequered flag. Paddock gossip suggested that they'd been so concerned about the pre-season form of their new car that they had tested it secretly back to back with the 2003 season's machine. The old car had been reportedly quicker.

The shattered Toyota mechanics were consoled by their newly recruited technical director, Mike Gascoyne. 'Think what a mess Renault was in two years ago, and look at them now,' he remarked. 'We can do the same and we will.'

Gascoyne, of course, had been the man who'd steered Renault to its current state of re-emergence. Now he seemed to be targeting the world champions. A tall order, and a long journey? Perhaps, but Gascoyne had never been short on confidence. Just like Ferrari, in fact.

MELBOURNE – ALBERT PARK

LAUDA 160/258 (5)
70/113 (3)
175/282 (6)
MARINA
CLARK 60/97 (2)
WAITE 130/209 (5)
HILL 180/290 (6)
mph/km/h (gear)
WHITFORD 130/209 (5)
180/290 (6)
SENNA 45/72 (2)
ASCARI 70/113 (3)
50/81 (2)
BRABHAM
FANGIO 180/290 (6)
JONES CHICANE
185/298 (6)
PROST 80/129 (4)
STEWART 130/209 (4)

CIRCUIT LENGTH: 3.295 miles/5.303 km

FIA F1 WORLD CHAMPIONSHIP • ROUND 1

FOSTER'S
AUSTRALIAN GRAND PRIX

MELBOURNE 5–7 MARCH 2004

Photograph: Darren Heath

RACE DISTANCE: 58 laps, 191.117 miles/307.574 km   RACE WEATHER: Bright and warm (track 22°C, air 18°C)

Pos.	Driver	Nat.	No.	Entrant	Car/Engine	Tyres	Laps	Time/Retirement	Speed (mph/km/h)	Gap to leader	Fastest race lap	
1	Michael Schumacher	D	1	Scuderia Ferrari Marlboro	Ferrari F2004-052 V10	B	58	1h 24m 15.757s	136.086/219.010		1m 24.125s	29
2	Rubens Barrichello	BR	2	Scuderia Ferrari Marlboro	Ferrari F2004-052 V10	B	58	1h 24m 29.362s	135.722/218.423	+13.605s	1m 24.179s	8
3	Fernando Alonso	E	8	Mild Seven Renault F1 Team	Renault R24-RS4 V10	M	58	1h 24m 50.430s	135.160/217.519	+34.673s	1m 25.088s	10
4	Ralf Schumacher	D	4	BMW WilliamsF1 Team	Williams FW26-BMW P84 V10	M	58	1h 25m 16.180s	134.479/216.424	+60.423s	1m 25.824s	11
5	Juan Pablo Montoya	COL	3	BMW WilliamsF1 Team	Williams FW26-BMW P84 V10	M	58	1h 25m 24.293s	134.266/216.081	+68.536s	1m 25.286s	42
6	Jenson Button	GB	9	Lucky Strike BAR Honda	BAR 006-Honda RA004E V10	M	58	1h 25m 26.355s	134.212/215.994	+70.598s	1m 25.982s	24
7	Jarno Trulli	I	7	Mild Seven Renault F1 Team	Renault R24-RS4 V10	M	57			+1 lap	1m 26.275s	9
8	David Coulthard	GB	5	West McLaren Mercedes	McLaren MP4/19-Mercedes F0110P V10	M	57			+1 lap	1m 26.328s	13
9	Takuma Sato	J	10	Lucky Strike BAR Honda	BAR 006-Honda RA004E V10	M	57			+1 lap	1m 26.077s	43
10	Giancarlo Fisichella	I	11	Sauber Petronas	Sauber C23-Petronas 04 V10	B	57			+1 lap	1m 26.282s	39
11	Christian Klien	A	15	Jaguar Racing	Jaguar R5-Cosworth CR6 V10	M	56			+2 laps	1m 27.840s	6
12	Cristiano da Matta	BR	16	Panasonic Toyota Racing	Toyota TF104-RVX04 V10	M	56			+2 laps	1m 27.820s	41
13	Olivier Panis	F	17	Panasonic Toyota Racing	Toyota TF104-RVX04 V10	M	56			+2 laps	1m 27.807s	35
14	Giorgio Pantano	I	19	Jordan Ford	Jordan EJ-14-Cosworth RS V10	B	55			+3 laps	1m 28.523s	15
	Felipe Massa	BR	12	Sauber Petronas	Sauber C23-Petronas 04 V10	B	44	Engine			1m 26.846s	11
	Nick Heidfeld	D	18	Jordan Ford	Jordan EJ-14-Cosworth RS V10	B	43	Collision in pits			1m 27.503s	27
	Gianmaria Bruni	I	20	European Minardi Cosworth	Minardi PS04B-Cosworth CR3 V10	B	43			+15 laps	1m 30.161	10
	Mark Webber	AUS	14	Jaguar Racing	Jaguar R5-Cosworth CR6 V10	M	29	Gearbox			1m 25.952s	15
	Zsolt Baumgartner	H	21	European Minardi Cosworth	Minardi PS04B-Cosworth CR3 V10	B	13	Engine			1m 30.621s	8
	Kimi Räikkönen	FIN	6	West McLaren Mercedes	McLaren MP4/19-Mercedes F0110P V10	M	9	Engine			1m 27.936s	7

Fastest lap: Michael Schumacher, on lap 29, 1m 24.125s, 141.009 mph/226.933 km/h (record).

Previous lap record: Kimi Räikkönen (McLaren MP4/17D-Mercedes F0110M V10), 1m 27.724s, 135.224 mph/217.623 km/h (2003).

19th: CHRISTIAN KLIEN Jaguar-Cosworth

17th: ZSOLT BAUMGARTNER Minardi-Cosworth

15th: NICK HEIDFELD Jordan-Cosworth

13th: CRISTIANO da MATTA Toyota

11th: FELIPE MASSA Sauber-Petronas

20th: GIANMARIA BRUNI Minardi-Cosworth

18th: OLIVIER PANIS Toyota

16th: GIORGIO PANTANO Jordan-Cosworth

14th: GIANCARLO FISICHELLA Sauber-Petronas

12th: DAVID COULTHARD McLaren-Mercedes

Grid order	1	2	3	4	5	6	7	8	9	10	11	12	13	14	15	16	17	18	19	20	21	22	23	24	25	26	27	28	29	30	31	32	33	34	35	36	37	38	39	40	41	42	43	44
1 M. SCHUMACHER	1	1	1	1	1	1	1	1	1	1	1	1	1	1	1	1	1	1	1	1	1	1	1	1	1	1	1	1	1	1	1	1	1	1	1	1	1	1	1	1	1	1	1	1
2 BARRICHELLO	2	2	2	2	2	2	2	2	2	2	2	2	2	2	2	2	2	2	2	2	2	2	2	2	2	2	2	2	2	2	2	2	2	2	2	2	2	2	2	2	2	2	2	2
3 MONTOYA	8	8	8	8	8	8	8	8	8	8	7	14	8	8	8	8	8	8	8	8	8	8	8	8	8	9	8	8	8	8	8	8	8	8	8	8	8	8	8	8	8	8	8	8
9 BUTTON	9	9	9	9	9	9	9	9	9	9	4	8	5	9	9	9	9	9	9	9	9	9	9	9	8	4	4	4	4	4	4	4	4	4	4	4	4	4	4	4	4	4	4	4
8 ALONSO	7	7	7	7	7	7	7	7	7	8	5	9	4	4	4	4	4	4	4	4	4	4	4	4	7	7	9	9	9	9	9	9	9	9	9	3	3	3	3	3	3	3	3	3
14 WEBBER	4	3	3	3	3	3	3	3	3	4	14		4	4	7	7	7	7	7	7	7	7	7	3	14		3	3	3	3	3	3	3	3	3	9	9	9	9	9	9	9	9	9
10 SATO	3	4	4	4	4	4	4	4	4	14	9	7	12	3	3	3	3	3	3	3	3	3	3	7	9	3	7	7	7	7	7	7	7	7	7	7	7	7	7	7		7	7	7
4 R. SCHUMACHER	14	14	14	14	14	14	14	14	14	10	10		9	7	14	14	14	14	14	14	14	14	14	14	3	5	5	5	5	5	5	5	5	5	5	5	5	5	5	5	5	5	5	5
7 TRULLI	10	10	10	10	10	10	10	10	10	5	5	12	3	5	5	5	5	5	5	5	5	5	5	5	5	14	14	12	12	12	12	12	12	10	10	10	10	10	10	10	10	10	10	10
6 RÄIKKÖNEN	5	5	5	5	5	5	5	5	5	12	12		3	14	15	15	10	10	10	10	10	10	10	10	12	12	14	10	10	10	10	10	12	12	12	12	12	12	12	12	12	12	12	12
12 MASSA	6	6	6	6	6	6	6	6	6	3	3	10	18	10	10	12	12	12	12	12	12	12	12	12	10	10	10	15	15	15	15	15	15	11	11	11	11	11	11	11	11	11	11	11
5 COULTHARD	12	12	12	12	12	12	12	12	12	16	16	18	15	12	19	18	18	16	16	16	16	16	11	11	11	11	11	11	11	11	11	11	18	18	18	18	18	15	15	15	15	16	16	16
16 DA MATTA	16	16	16	16	16	16	16	16	16	18	18	19	19	16	18	16	16	11	11	11	11	11	15	15	15	15	16	16	16	16	16	15	15	15	15	15	15	16	16	16	16			
11 FISICHELLA	11	18	18	18	18	18	18	18	18	19	19	11	11	18	16	11	11	15	15	15	15	15	16	16	16	16	16	16	16	16	16	16	16	16	16	15	15	15	15	16				
18 HEIDFELD	18	11	11	11	11	11	11	15	15	20	20	9	16	17	16	16	16	16	16	16	16	16	19	19	19	19	19	19	19	19	19	19	19	19	19	19	19	19	19	19	19	19	17	17
19 PANTANO	19	20	20	20	15	15	21	20	20	19	17	12	11	11	19	19	19	19	19	19	19	19	17	17	17	17	17	17	17	17	17	17	17	17	17	17	17	17	17	17	17	17	18	
21 BAUMGARTNER	20	19	19	15	20	20	20	19	19	11	11	11	17	21	17	17	17	17	17	17	17	17	20	20	20	20	20	20	20	20	20	20	20	20	20	20	20	20	20	20	20	20		
17 PANIS	15	15	15	19	19	19	19	17	17	21	20	20	20	20	20	20	20	20	20	20	20	20	20																					
15 KLIEN	17	17	17	17	17	17	17	21	21	11	21	21																																
20 BRUNI	21	21	21	21	21	21	21	11	11																																			

Pit stop
One lap behind leader

82

QUALIFYING

Sunny and hot (track 38°C, air 24°C)

Pos.	Driver	Lap time	Sector 1	Sector 2	Sector 3
1	Michael Schumacher	1m 24.408s	28.168s	22.519s	33.721s
2	Rubens Barrichello	1m 24.482s	28.234s	22.694s	33.554s
3	Juan Pablo Montoya	1m 24.998s	28.169s	22.703s	34.126s
4	Jenson Button	1m 24.998s	28.454s	22.796s	34.748s
5	Fernando Alonso	1m 25.699s	28.504s	22.938s	34.257s
6	Mark Webber	1m 25.805s	28.675s	22.860s	34.270s
7	Takuma Sato	1m 25.851s	28.675s	22.959s	34.217s
8	Ralf Schumacher	1m 25.925s	28.891s	22.813s	34.221s
9	Jarno Trulli	1m 26.290s	28.582s	23.222s	34.486s
10	Kimi Räikkönen	1m 26.297s	28.662s	23.055s	34.580s
11	Felipe Massa	1m 27.065s	29.169s	23.237s	34.659s
12	David Coulthard	1m 27.294s	28.844s	23.144s	35.306s
13	Cristiano da Matta	1m 27.823s	29.431s	23.419s	34.973s
14	Giancarlo Fisichella	1m 27.845s	29.729s	23.917s	35.199s
15	Nick Heidfeld	1m 28.178s	29.298s	23.574s	35.306s
16	Giorgio Pantano	1m 30.140s	30.062s	23.926s	35.152s
17	Zsolt Baumgartner	1m 30.681s	30.291s	24.049s	36.341s
18	Olivier Panis	No time	–	–	–
19	Christian Klien	No time	37.155s	23.961s	–
20	Gianmaria Bruni	No time	–	–	–

PRACTICE 1 (FRIDAY)

Dry, slight cloud (track 27°C, air 21°C)

Pos.	Driver	Laps	Time
1	Michael Schumacher	4	1m 25.127s
2	Rubens Barrichello	9	1m 25.361s
3	Jarno Trulli	10	1m 27.025s
4	David Coulthard	5	1m 27.264s
5	Fernando Alonso	14	1m 27.359s
6	Juan Pablo Montoya	12	1m 27.462s
7	Ralf Schumacher	11	1m 27.675s
8	Jenson Button	7	1m 27.867s
9	Anthony Davidson	25	1m 27.921s
10	Mark Webber	6	1m 28.089s
11	Ricardo Zonta	17	1m 28.118s
12	Kimi Räikkönen	5	1m 28.233s
13	Takuma Sato	6	1m 28.874s
14	Cristiano da Matta	11	1m 27.955s
15	Giancarlo Fisichella	6	1m 29.120s
16	Olivier Panis	12	1m 29.169s
17	Nick Heidfeld	11	1m 29.826
18	Björn Wirdheim	24	1m 30.033s
19	Christian Klien	7	1m 30.046s
20	Giorgio Pantano	18	1m 30.100s
21	Timo Glock	12	1m 30.618s
22	Zsolt Baumgartner	14	1m 32.886s
23	Gianmaria Bruni	8	1m 33.236s
24	Felipe Massa	1	No time

PRACTICE 2 (FRIDAY)

Dry and sunny (track 39°C, air 22°C)

Pos.	Driver	Laps	Time
1	Michael Schumacher	15	1m 24.718s
2	Rubens Barrichello	22	1m 24.826s
3	Jarno Trulli	23	1m 25.757s
4	Jenson Button	15	1m 25.786s
5	Fernando Alonso	22	1m 25.853s
6	Ralf Schumacher	26	1m 25.882s
7	Juan Pablo Montoya	19	1m 26.206s
8	David Coulthard	17	1m 26.215s
9	Mark Webber	17	1m 26.312s
10	Kimi Räikkönen	18	1m 26.579s
11	Giancarlo Fisichella	27	1m 26.601s
12	Takuma Sato	15	1m 26.967s
13	Felipe Massa	26	1m 26.969s
14	Ricardo Zonta	25	1m 27.165s
15	Anthony Davidson	11	1m 27.516s
16	Cristiano da Matta	11	1m 27.710s
17	Christian Klien	20	1m 27.724s
18	Olivier Panis	16	1m 27.807s
19	Nick Heidfeld	15	1m 27.826s
20	Björn Wirdheim	30	1m 28.781s
21	Gianmaria Bruni	18	1m 28.991s
22	Zsolt Baumgartner	9	1m 29.708s
23	Giorgio Pantano	18	1m 30.061s
24	Timo Glock	4	1m 30.291s

PRACTICE 3 (SATURDAY)

Sunny and warm (track 36°C, air 19°C)

Pos.	Driver	Laps	Time
1	Michael Schumacher	13	1m 25.786s
2	Rubens Barrichello	8	1m 26.159s
3	Juan Pablo Montoya	13	1m 26.195s
4	Ralf Schumacher	11	1m 26.390s
5	David Coulthard	5	1m 26.428s
6	Fernando Alonso	7	1m 26.610s
7	Kimi Räikkönen	6	1m 26.725s
8	Mark Webber	5	1m 26.804s
9	Jarno Trulli	14	1m 26.817s
10	Jenson Button	11	1m 26.995s
11	Oliver Panis	16	1m 27.107s
12	Cristiano da Matta	14	1m 27.717s
13	Giancarlo Fisichella	9	1m 27.744s
14	Felipe Massa	15	1m 28.341s
15	Takuma Sato	12	1m 28.438s
16	Christian Klien	7	1m 28.572s
17	Giorgio Pantano	13	1m 30.057s
18	Nick Heidfeld	13	1m 30.233s
19	Gianmaria Bruni	12	1m 31.310s
20	Zsolt Baumgartner	14	1m 32.295s

PRACTICE 4 (SATURDAY)

Sunny and hot (track 37°C, air 23°C)

Pos.	Driver	Laps	Time
1	Michael Schumacher	13	1m 25.093s
2	Juan Pablo Montoya	9	1m 25.255s
3	Ralf Schumacher	9	1m 25.628s
4	Rubens Barrichello	12	1m 25.649s
5	Fernando Alonso	11	1m 25.908s
6	Olivier Panis	14	1m 25.916s
7	Jarno Trulli	9	1m 25.927s
8	Mark Webber	11	1m 26.066s
9	Kimi Räikkönen	8	1m 26.127s
10	David Coulthard	11	1m 26.133s
11	Jenson Button	14	1m 26.403s
12	Cristiano da Matta	17	1m 26.597s
13	Christian Klien	14	1m 27.088s
14	Felipe Massa	13	1m 27.172s
15	Giancarlo Fisichella	12	1m 27.195s
16	Takuma Sato	9	1m 27.592s
17	Nick Heidfeld	14	1m 27.755s
18	Giorgio Pantano	12	1m 28.825s
19	Gianmaria Bruni	16	1m 30.496s
20	Zsolt Baumgartner	13	1m 31.763s

CHASSIS LOG BOOK

	Driver	Chassis
1	Michael Schumacher	F2004/234
2	Rubens Barrichello	F2004/236
	Spare	F2004/235
3	Juan Pablo Montoya	FW26/05
4	Ralf Schumacher	FW26/03
	Spare	FW26/02
5	David Coulthard	MP4/19-03
6	Kimi Räikkönen	MP4/19-04
	Spare	MP4/19-01
7	Jarno Trulli	R24/03
8	Fernando Alonso	R24/02
	Spare	R24/01
9	Jenson Button	006/01
10	Takuma Sato	006/02
	Anthony Davidson	006/03
	Spare	006/03
11	Giancarlo Fisichella	C23/02
12	Felipe Massa	C23/03
	Spare	C23/01
14	Mark Webber	R5/03
15	Christian Klien	R5/01
	Björn Wirdheim	R5/02
	Spare	R5/02
16	Cristiano da Matta	TF104/02
17	Olivier Panis	TF104/03
	Ricardo Zonta	TF104/04
	Spare	TF104/04
18	Nick Heidfeld	EJ-14/03
19	Giorgio Pantano	EJ-14/02
	Timo Glock	EJ-14/01
	Spare	EJ-14/01
20	Gianmaria Bruni	PS04B/02
21	Zsolt Baumgartner	PS04B/01
	Spare	PS04B/04

Photograph: Darren Heath

9th: JARNO TRULLI Renault

7th: TAKUMA SATO BAR-Honda

5th: FERNANDO ALONSO Renault

3rd: MONTOYA Williams-BMW

Pole: MICHAEL SCHUMACHER Ferrari

10th: RÄIKKÖNEN McLaren-Mercedes

8th: RALF SCHUMACHER Williams-BMW

6th: MARK WEBBER Jaguar-Cosworth

4th: JENSON BUTTON BAR-Honda

2nd: RUBENS BARRICHELLO Ferrari

46	47	48	49	50	51	52	53	54	55	56	57	58	
1	1	1	1	1	1	1	1	1	1	1	1	1	1
2	2	2	2	2	2	2	2	2	2	2	2	2	2
8	8	8	8	8	8	8	8	8	8	8	8	8	3
4	4	4	4	4	4	4	4	4	4	4	4	4	4
3	3	3	3	3	3	3	3	3	3	3	3	3	5
9	9	9	9	9	9	9	9	9	9	9	9	9	6
7	7	7	7	7	7	7	7	7	7	7	7	7	7
5	5	5	5	5	5	5	5	5	5	5	5		8
10	10	10	10	10	10	10	10	10	10	10	10	10	
11	11	11	11	11	11	11	11	11	11	11	11	11	
15	15	15	15	15	15	15	15	15	15	15	15	15	
16	16	16	16	16	16	16	16	16	16	16	16		
19	19	19	19	19	19	17	17	17	17	17	17		
17	17	17	17	17	19	19	19	19	19	19			

FOR THE RECORD

First grand prix start

Gianmaria Bruni

Christian Klien

Giorgio Pantano

4,000 laps led

Michael Schumacher

POINTS: CONSTRUCTORS

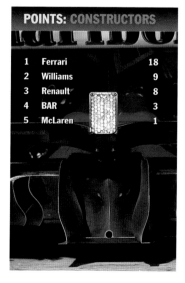

1	Ferrari	18
2	Williams	9
3	Renault	8
4	BAR	3
5	McLaren	1

POINTS: DRIVERS

1	Michael Schumacher	10
2	Rubens Barrichello	8
3	Fernando Alonso	6
4	Ralf Schumacher	5
5	Juan Pablo Montoya	4
6	Jenson Button	3
7	Jarno Trulli	2
8	David Coulthard	1

Photographs: Darren Heath

The Ferraris of Michael Schumacher and Rubens Barrichello lead Juan Pablo Montoya's Williams FW26 through the first long right-hander at Sepang. By the end of lap two, Barrichello had made a slight slip on a damp track surface and dropped to fourth, but Schumacher fended off Montoya all the way to the finish.
Photograph: Darren Heath

FIA F1 WORLD CHAMPIONSHIP • ROUND 2

MALAYSIANGP
SEPANG

Right: **Bubbling tyre tread compounds, cooking in the stifling Malaysian heat.**
Photograph: Darren Heath

Bottom: **Kimi Räikkönen boosted McLaren with fastest time on Friday, but his hopes of repeating his 2003 victory were dashed by another retirement.**
Photograph: Bryn Williams/crash.net

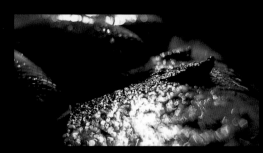

SEPANG QUALIFYING

The capricious and unpredictable nature of the F1 business was highlighted in Friday free practice when Kimi Räikkönen's hitherto troubled McLaren MP4/19 set fastest time, raising speculation that the Mercedes-engined machine would display better overall form in the torrid conditions at Sepang.

Yet Friday free practice sessions have always been notoriously unreliable barometers of F1 form, as drivers are always experimenting with different tyre compounds and varying fuel loads. Räikkönen, who had won in Sepang 12 months before, was being scrupulously cautious about his prospects, even though the MP4/19 sported a new front wing that had been tested with encouraging results by Pedro de la Rosa at Valencia during the break between the first two races.

'It was a productive practice session and, of course, it's pleasing to be fastest,' he said. 'The car feels good and is handling well, but it's definitely too early to say how much we have improved since Melbourne, but I'm looking forward to the rest of the weekend.'

He was right to be cautious, although when the 2003 winner dropped to fifth in the final grid order, it didn't look too bad, except that his 1m 34.164s best was more than a second away from Michael Schumacher's pole winning Ferrari F2004.

Schumacher did the job superbly when the track temperature was hovering around the 51°C mark, edging Mark Webber's superb Jaguar R5 by 0.7s. 'It was a mind blowing lap, I have to say,' recalled Schumacher with obvious satisfaction. 'Just everything was perfect and spot on. We worked very well with the car. We were looking in difficulty yesterday, but we managed to work the car very well and put it back on the road. I hope the numbers are true, but I am slightly concerned and we will have to work out what today's overall showing means for the race tomorrow.'

With Barrichello opting for the slightly harder Bridgestone choice and winding up on the inside of row two on 1m 33.756s, Webber capitalised on the new Jaguar's potential to line up second on 1m 33.715s.

'The team have done a really good job, and this is making it easier for me to get the most from the R5,' he said. 'Versus where we were last year with the R4, there is really no comparison. It is a great deal better.'

In the BMW Williams garage, there was guarded optimism. The FW26s had been strong and consistent during long runs in practice, but Juan Pablo Montoya made a slight error on his qualifying run, which probably cost him a place on the front row of the grid. As it was, he ended up fourth on 1m 34.054s, team-mate Ralf Schumacher languishing back in seventh on 1m 34.235s. 'We should have run the cars lighter in the first session,' said Williams chief operations engineer Sam Michael. 'That would have allowed us to run the second session in slightly cooler conditions later in the afternoon.'

Splitting the two Williams-BMWs were Räikkönen and Jenson Button, who managed a 1m 34.221s for sixth fastest in the BAR-Honda 006. 'I'm a bit disappointed with sixth, to be honest,' shrugged Jenson. 'I had two really good first sectors, particularly the high-speed part, but then I lost quite a bit of time in the final sector because I had too much oversteer, and two tenths on my best time this morning.'

Nevertheless, this was significantly better than Takuma Sato, who wound up 18th and last after spinning into a gravel trap, adding to his woes after knocking off his car's nose section in Friday free practice. Behind him were Giorgio Pantano, who had to switch to the spare Jordan EJ-14 due to an engine problem and went to the back of the grid as a result, plus 2003's pole winner, Fernando Alonso, who spun off on his qualifying run.

'I made a mistake under braking for turn 14, lost the back end and the car spun,' explained Fernando. 'Of course, it's disappointing, particularly for the team who have worked hard this weekend. But I'm still confident. We know the car is quick, and even starting last I think we can fight for points.'

Jarno Trulli, meanwhile, qualified his Renault R24 eighth on 1m 34.413s, just ahead of David Coulthard's McLaren (1m 34.602s) and the two Sauber C23s of Felipe Massa (1m 35.039s) and Giancarlo Fisichella (1m 35.061s). The Swiss machines were the next two Bridgestone runners on the grid after the Ferraris, and both drivers complained of poor high-speed stability on their qualifying runs.

The Toyota TF104s of Cristiano da Matta (1m 34.917s) and Olivier Panis (1m 35.617s) wound up tenth and 14th, split by the Saubers and Christian Klien's Jaguar (1m 35.158s), while Nick Heidfeld's Jordan and the two Minardis completed the list of those who recorded a valid qualifying time, ahead of the luckless trio at the back who didn't.

THIS was the day the Michelin brigade should have carried the fight to Michael Schumacher's Bridgestone-shod Ferrari. Yet only two weeks after outclassing the field to win the opening race of the year in unseasonably cool conditions at Melbourne, the world champion again proved too good for the opposition in the sweltering heat at Kualar Lumpur's splendid Sepang circuit. It was Schumacher's 72nd grand prix victory, and although he had been under some pressure from Juan Pablo Montoya's Williams-BMW FW26, which eventually finished second, the hard facts were that Sir Frank's blue-riband team had so far failed to meet its pre-season objective, namely to mount a genuine wheel-to-wheel challenge against its legendary Italian rival.

Of course, the absence of sweltering track temperatures in Australia was certainly a factor that had played to the strengths of Ferrari's Bridgestone rubber. Malaysia would be different, said the pundits. But it wasn't.

After qualifying on pole position in conditions that saw the track temperature soar to 57°C, Schumacher capitalised on the slightly cooler conditions that prevailed on race day and pulled away strongly from the start. He had gambled on the use of the softer of the two Bridgestone tyre compounds, which gave him added grip from the outset.

It was a finely balanced choice. He qualified running a lightish fuel load, which meant that he made his first stop early, on lap nine of the 56-lap race. He successfully ran the gauntlet of a brief shower during the opening stages, then settled down to domi-

nate the proceedings in the marginally less punishing 42°C track conditions.

With Mark Webber's Jaguar R5 having qualified second to join Schumacher on the front row of the grid, it seemed just possible that the Australian might inject something of a wild card into the proceedings, at least for the first few laps of the race. But when the final starting light went out, Webber got badly bogged down due to a glitch in the Cosworth V10's anti-stall software and was passed on all sides as Schumacher neatly accelerated his Ferrari toward the first corner.

Michael led by 2.0s at the end of the opening lap, and successfully brushed aside the consequences of a fleeting light rain shower that dampened part of the circuit for the first few miles of the contest. Initially, Barrichello held second, but ran wide second time around and dropped to fourth behind Juan Pablo Montoya's Williams FW26 and Kimi Räikkönen's McLaren MP4/19, which earlier had spun on the formation lap in the damp. Jarno Trulli was fifth on the opening lap, but Jenson Button winged past him at the end of lap two, the British driver having bumped the Italian as they all scrambled around Webber in the traffic jam at the start.

Meanwhile, the Jaguar team leader was trying to claw his way back into contention. He moved up to eighth on lap three, but then was savaged from behind by Ralf Schumacher's Williams, an incident that sent the green machine into the pit lane for attention at the end of lap five. It was the start of a downward spiral for Web-

ber, which eventually would see him spin off after 23 laps.

'I had a bad start with the car and things didn't get much better after that,' he shrugged. 'After overtaking Ralf Schumacher, he twice hit me from behind, and my right rear tyre picked up a puncture and the car may have suffered some damage too.

'I then had to limp to the pits to be refuelled and have the tyres changed. A drive-through penalty added to my troubles, and after then going off line several times to let other people past, I spun under braking. A very difficult end for us, which should not have been the case.'

In the meantime, Michael Schumacher was piling on the pressure. On lap six, he turned a time of 1m 34.819s, which stood as the race's fastest until lap 28, when Montoya bettered it by 0.596s. The Ferrari number one ducked in for his first refuelling stop three laps later. That left Montoya leading by 6.2s from the hard charging Button, but when they both pitted at the end of lap 12, Michael regained a 6.4s lead over the Colombian, with Räikkönen third, then Trulli and Button nose-to-tail for the next couple of places, and a rather frustrated Barrichello sixth, making the best he could of the harder-compound Bridgestone tyres he'd elected to use.

So could Montoya close the gap? At one point, it certainly looked like a finely balanced equation between the two leading runners. By lap 13, Schumacher was 6.4s ahead, but within another five laps, this was down to 3.3s, after which there was a 7s gap back to Räikkönen, the Finn having his work cut out beating

Above: It's not Bahrain yet Rubens!

Top: Final preparations for Jaguar on the grid. Mark Webber's brilliant effort in earning a place on the front row came to nought in the race.
Photographs: Darren Heath

Left: Two years after his Renault had been pushed down to fourth by Michael Schumacher's recovering Ferrari on the last lap of the Malaysian GP, Jenson Button scored the first podium finish of his F1 career with third in the BAR-Honda 006. It would be the first of many.
Photograph: Darren Heath

BAR DELIGHT AT BUTTON PODIUM

The most emotional moment of the Malaysian GP weekend came about ten minutes after Jenson Button emerged from the post-race media conference. As he jogged through the paddock toward the BAR Honda team garage, he came face to face with his father, John, and the two men hurled themselves into each other's arms.

John Button had nurtured Jenson's early career as a pre-teenage kart racer, not just footing the bills, but often preparing his machinery as well. Since his boy's graduation into F1 in 2000, Button senior had been a regular member of the grand prix scene, but always standing quietly in the background and never seeking to lay claim to any of his son's reflected glory.

'He did it all himself, he deserves it,' said John Button with a modest grin as Jenson was engulfed by the rest of the BAR squad, jostling, cheering and reaching out to touch the man who'd given them a taste of the respectability and credibility they had been craving since their debut in 1999.

For Button, that podium finish had been a long time coming. Two years earlier, he had been on course for third place at Sepang when his Renault suffered suspension problems in the closing stages and Michael Schumacher's Ferrari, climbing back through the field after an early collision, had swept ahead of him on the final lap.

It was also a hugely satisfying result for David Richards, the BAR team principal, who was brought in by shareholders BAT to turn around the team's fortunes after founder Craig Pollock had failed to achieve any serious success.

'Jenson and the team have worked very hard for this result,' said Richards, 'and to get his first podium finish in a straight fight with the best in Formula 1 is real proof of how far we have come.'

off a challenge from Trulli. Button was next ahead of Barrichello, then came Coulthard in the McLaren with Alonso right on his tail.

Alonso had started at the back of the grid after his slip during qualifying, but was up to tenth by the end of the opening lap. The Renault team decided to change the Spaniard's fuel strategy in a bid to vault him ahead of Coulthard, but going into lap 24 – when he was scheduled to make his second stop – he got past the Scot going around the outside of the first turn.

Thus, the Renault led the McLaren in at the end of the lap, but with Coulthard's stop taking just 7.9s and Alonso stationary for 11.2s as his car was fuelled for a non-stop run to the finish, Coulthard got back out ahead of him.

On lap 26, Schumacher and Montoya made their second refuelling stops, allowing Barrichello through into the lead, but he completed the following lap just 2.6s ahead of the world champion and relinquished the lead when he made his own second stop at the end of lap 28. Now only 6.6s separated the Ferrari and the Williams at the head of the field, with Button third from Räikkönen, Barrichello, Trulli, Coulthard, Takuma Sato in the other BAR-Honda 006 and Alonso.

So could Montoya chase down Schumacher? For a few tantalising laps, it certainly looked possible. By lap 31, the Colombian was 5.1s adrift. He had trimmed that to 4.4s by lap 34, then to 3.7s by lap 37. But then the world champion responded, opening his advantage to 4.3s on lap 38.

On lap 39, Montoya came in for a 7.9s third refuelling stop. Schumacher came next time around for a 7.6s top-up, just as Räikkönen's McLaren rolled to a halt out on the circuit, trailing an ominous cloud of smoke from an apparent driveshaft failure. The Finn stalked away from his steaming machine, pushing aside a marshal who stepped out to guide him behind the barrier. You could understand his frustration over his second retirement in as many races.

At this point, Michael Schumacher put the hammer down and finished the job. He went into his final lap 10s ahead of the Williams, but coming out of the final corner to take the chequered flag and wave to his pit crew, he eased off, allowing Montoya to close to within 5s. Yet most observers believed that the German driver's unflustered and composed style throughout the race concealed the fact that he'd refrained from asserting his true potential advantage.

Montoya felt that Barrichello, running third at the time, had held him up slightly on lap 40 while Schumacher had ducked in for that final stop. The Ferrari driver denied this vehemently, claiming that Juan Pablo had been nowhere near close enough to be thinking of overtaking.

Even so, Montoya finished the day in an upbeat mood. 'I think it

went pretty well,' he said. 'In the first few laps, I got in front of Rubens. He made a mistake. Then I was trying to catch Michael toward the end of the race. The car got better, the tyres were just getting better and better.

'It was a shame that I came out of the last stop behind Rubens. I went to pass him straight away, but he blocked me. In a non-Ferrari, it's better to back off than try to…you know. It's better to go home with eight points than be out of the race.'

For his part, Michael Schumacher acknowledged that he'd been kept on his toes by Montoya.

'In the moment where we needed to be quick, we were just quick enough, at the beginning of the stint and at the end of the stint,' he said. 'But the beginning of the race was very tough, as it was so unpredictable, where the water was, and how much there was. Being the first car having no reference didn't really help, so I had to be cautious and, at the same time, be careful of Juan and not give him an opportunity.'

Meanwhile, Jenson Button, had captured the imagination of the 90,000-strong crowd by storming home to finish third in his BAR-Honda 006, claiming the first podium finish of his career in the process. He had qualified sixth and had been in the thick of the action from the very start of the chase, getting up to fifth by the end of the second lap after coming into contact with Jarno Trulli's Renault R24. Thereafter, he never put a wheel wrong in a performance that underlined that both he and the team have significantly raised their game to become potential challengers for world championship points in every race.

Button was also kept on his toes by instructions from the pit to activate the pump that circulated lubricant from the secondary oil tank after some worrying signs from the telemetry, concerns that were heightened when Takuma Sato's Honda V10 expired spectacularly in the closing stages. But all went well he duly delivered the result he had been promising for so long.

'It was amazing.' said Button. 'The team has worked so hard, obviously not the pinnacle of what we want, but a step in the right direction. I'm ecstatic.'

He added, 'Melbourne was our first race on Michelins, and we gained a lot of information to help me how to use them. Initially, here we had too much understeer, but I didn't want to go into the race with an oversteery car. But we sorted that out, which was good.

'At the start, as we passed Mark Webber, I bumped wheels with Jarno [Trulli], which I worried might have damaged the car, but it was all fine. We've worked so hard and it's been a struggle to get on the podium for the first time. It's a fantastic feeling.'

Mechanical reliability was good across the field. The small group of retirements included Ralf Schumacher's Williams FW26 (a BMW engine failure), the hapless Kimi Räikkönen's McLaren-Merc and Sato's BAR.

For his part, Barrichello was a little disappointed with his eventual fourth place. 'I pushed hard all race long, doing as much as I could,' he said. 'I made a different tyre choice, which did not pay off. On top of that, in the opening laps when it rained, my tyres quickly lost temperature and that's why I lost a few places. Unfortunately, the two seconds that kept me away from Button in the fight for the podium were lost when I was overtaking Baumgartner [in the Minardi]. In any case, I'm satisfied with the car, which confirmed its potential.'

Behind Coulthard and Alonso, Felipe Massa claimed the final point of the day with eighth place in his Sauber C23. 'I had a bit of a clutch problem from the start of the race, which made all my pit stops a bit nerve-racking,' he explained. He also had a close moment when he straight-lined one of the grassy run-off areas and was narrowly missed by Schumacher. Team-mate Giancarlo Fisichella's engine stalled during both his second and third refuelling stops, which contributed to his distant 11th behind Cristiano da Matta's Toyota TF104 and Christian Klien's Jaguar R5.

A frustrated Olivier Panis struggled home 12th after being nudged into an early spin, which was followed by an unscheduled pit stop due to a radio glitch and a subsequent drive-through penalty for speeding in the pit lane. 'A real pity,' he shrugged, 'because the car felt good and was handling well.'

With two races down, 16 to go, Ferrari was leading two-nil. 'Ah yes, but wait until Bahrain,' said the insiders. 'It will all be different there.' They didn't explain why. Probably because they couldn't.

DIARY

Marc Gené demonstrates a Williams-BMW FW25 at Bahrain during the official inauguration of the Sakhir circuit, prompting claims from rivals that the British team has gained an unfair advantage in preparing for the new track.

Former Jaguar F1 driver Justin Wilson signs to drive for Conquest Racing Champ Car team.

IRL champion Scott Dixon agrees an F1 test programme with Williams.

Bobby Rahal's team abandons Champ Car in favour of the rival IRL series.

Rally ace Colin McRae tests a Prodrive Ferrari 550 Maranello in preparation for his Le Mans debut in June.

Above far left: Ralf Schumacher got up to fourth at Sepang before his Williams-BMW checked out with engine failure.

Above left: David Coulthard finished sixth for McLaren Mercedes, a disappointing 53.09s behind the winning Ferrari.

Left: On the mark. Michael Schumacher pits to perfection.

Below: Juan Pablo Montoya chased hard, but second place was the best he could do in the Michelin-shod Williams FW26
Photographs: Darren Heath

PETRONAS MALAYSIAN GRAND PRIX

SEPANG 19–21 MARCH 2004

SEPANG

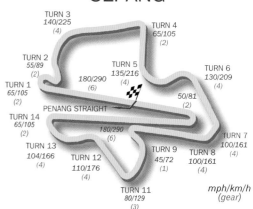

TURN 3 140/225 (4)
TURN 4 65/105 (2)
TURN 2 55/89 (2)
TURN 5 135/216 (4)
180/290 (6)
TURN 6 130/209 (4)
TURN 1 65/105 (2)
PENANG STRAIGHT
50/81 (2)
TURN 14 65/105 (2)
180/290 (6)
TURN 7 100/161 (4)
TURN 13 104/166 (4)
TURN 12 110/176 (4)
TURN 9 45/72 (1)
TURN 8 100/161 (4)
TURN 11 80/129 (3)
mph/km/h (gear)

CIRCUIT LENGTH: 3.444 miles/5.543 km

RACE DISTANCE: 56 laps, 192.878 miles/310.408 km **RACE WEATHER:** Hot and overcast (track 42°C, air 33°C)

Pos.	Driver	Nat.	No.	Entrant	Car/Engine	Tyres	Laps	Time/Retirement	Speed (mph/km/h)	Gap to leader	Fastest race lap	
1	Michael Schumacher	D	1	Scuderia Ferrari Marlboro	Ferrari F2004-052 V10	B	56	1h 31m 07.490s	126.998/ 204.384		1m 34.819s	6
2	Juan Pablo Montoya	COL	3	BMW WilliamsF1 Team	Williams FW26-BMW P84 V10	M	56	1h 31m 12.512s	126.881/ 204.196	+5.022s	1m 34.223s	28
3	Jenson Button	GB	9	Lucky Strike BAR Honda	BAR 006-Honda RA004E V10	M	56	1h 31m 19.058s	126.730/ 203.952s	+11.568s	1m 34.967s	28
4	Rubens Barrichello	BR	2	Scuderia Ferrari Marlboro	Ferrari F2004-052 V10	B	56	1h 31m 21.106s	126.682/ 203.876	+13.616s	1m 35.350s	7
5	Jarno Trulli	I	7	Mild Seven Renault F1 Team	Renault R24-RS4 V10	M	56	1h 31m 44.850s	126.124/ 202.977	+37.360s	1m 35.039s	12
6	David Coulthard	GB	5	West McLaren Mercedes	McLaren MP4/19-Mercedes F0110P V10	M	56	1h 32m 00.588s	125.776/ 202.418	+53.098s	1m 35.852s	26
7	Fernando Alonso	E	8	Mild Seven Renault F1 Team	Renault R24-RS4 V10	M	56	1h 32m 15.367s	125.440 /201.877	+67.877s	1m 35.888s	7
8	Felipe Massa	BR	12	Sauber Petronas	Sauber C23-Petronas 04 V10	B	55			+1 lap	1m 36.570s	7
9	Cristiano da Matta	BR	16	Panasonic Toyota Racing	Toyota TF104-RVX04 V10	M	55			+1 lap	1m 36.544s	22
10	Christian Klien	A	15	Jaguar Racing	Jaguar R5-Cosworth CR6 V10	M	55			+1 lap	1m 37.031s	12
11	Giancarlo Fisichella	I	11	Sauber Petronas	Sauber C23-Petronas 04 V10	B	55			+1 lap	1m 36.675s	54
12	Olivier Panis	F	17	Panasonic Toyota Racing	Toyota TF104-RVX04 V10	M	55			+1 lap	1m 35.951s	23
13	Giorgio Pantano	I	19	Jordan Ford	Jordan EJ-14-Cosworth RS V10	B	54			+2 laps	1m 39.527s	41
14	Gianmaria Bruni	I	20	European Minardi Cosworth	Minardi PS04B-Cosworth CR3 V10	B	53			+3 laps	1m 39.911s	11
15	Takuma Sato	J	10	Lucky Strike BAR Honda	BAR 006-Honda RA004E V10	M	52			DNF	1m 35.679s	13
16	Zsolt Baumgartner	H	21	European Minardi Cosworth	Minardi PS04B-Cosworth CR3 V10	B	52			+4 laps	1m 40.123s	12
	Kimi Räikkönen	FIN	6	West McLaren Mercedes	McLaren MP4/19-Mercedes F0110P V10	M	40	Transmisson			1m 35.156s	12
	Nick Heidfeld	D	18	Jordan Ford	Jordan EJ-14-Cosworth RS V10	B	34	Gearshift			1m 37.433s	15
	Ralf Schumacher	D	4	BMW WilliamsF1 Team	Williams FW26-BMW P84 V10	M	27	Engine			1m 35.607s	10
	Mark Webber	AUS	14	Jaguar Racing	Jaguar R5-Cosworth CR6 V10	M	23	Spun off			1m 36.922s	9

Fastest lap: Juan Pablo Montoya, on lap 28, 1m 34.223s, 131.595 mph/211.782 km/h (record).

Previous lap record: Michael Schumacher (Ferrari F2002-051 V10), 1m 36.412s, 128.607 mph/206.974 km/h (2003).

19th: GIORGIO PANTANO Jordan-Cosworth
Demoted after switching to spare car

17th: ZSOLT BAUMGARTNER Minardi-Cosworth

15th: NICK HEIDFELD Jordan-Cosworth

13th: CHRISTIAN KLIEN Jaguar-Cosworth

11th: FELIPE MASSA Sauber-Petronas

20th: FERNANDO ALONSO Renault

18th: TAKUMA SATO BAR-Honda

16th: GIANMARIA BRUNI Minardi-Cosworth

14th: OLIVIER PANIS Toyota

12th: GIANCARLO FISICHELLA Sauber-Petronas

Grid order	1	2	3	4	5	6	7	8	9	10	11	12	13	14	15	16	17	18	19	20	21	22	23	24	25	26	27	28	29	30	31	32	33	34	35	36	37	38	39	40	41	42	43
1 M. SCHUMACHER	1	1	1	1	1	1	1	1	1	3	3	3	1	1	1	1	1	1	1	1	1	1	1	1	1	1	2	1	1	1	1	1	1	1	1	1	1	1	1	1	1	1	1
14 WEBBER	2	3	3	3	3	3	3	3	9	9	9	3	3	3	3	3	3	3	3	3	3	3	3	1	2	3	3	3	3	3	3	3	3	3	3	3	9	2	2	2			
2 BARRICHELLO	3	6	6	6	6	6	6	6	6	1	1	6	6	6	6	6	6	6	6	6	6	6	9	9	3	9	9	9	9	9	9	9	9	9	9	9	6	3	3	3			
3 MONTOYA	6	2	2	2	2	2	2	2	4	6	7	7	7	7	7	7	9	9	9	9	9	6	2	4	9	6	6	6	6	6	6	6	6	6	6	2	9	9	9			
6 RÄIKKÖNEN	7	9	9	9	9	9	9	9	7	6	2	2	2	2	2	2	7	2	2	2	2	4	9	2	2	2	2	2	2	2	2	2	2	2	3	7	7	7					
9 BUTTON	9	7	7	7	7	7	7	7	4	7	2	2	2	2	2	2	2	2	2	2	5	8	4	6	6	7	7	7	7	7	7	7	7	7	5	7	7	7					
4 R. SCHUMACHER	5	5	5	5	5	5	5	5	1	2	10	10	5	5	5	5	5	8	8	8	5	7	7	7	5	5	5	5	5	5	5	5	5	8	8	8							
7 TRULLI	4	4	14	8	8	8	8	8	5	18	18	5	5	10	8	8	8	8	4	4	4	5	10	10	10	10	10	10	10	10	8	8	8	8	10	10	10						
5 COULTHARD	14	14	8	14	4	4	4	4	8	17	10	8	8	4	4	4	4	4	7	7	7	12	10	10	8	8	8	8	8	8	10	10	10	10	12	12	12						
16 DA MATTA	8	8	4	12	18	18	18	18	18	5	8	4	12	12	12	12	12	12	12	10	8	12	12	12	12	12	12	17	17	17													
12 MASSA	10	12	12	12	18	18	18	18	5	8	4	12	10	10	10	10	10	10	10	11	12	17	17	17	17	17	17	11	11	11													
11 FISICHELLA	12	18	18	18	16	16	16	16	16	17	12	15	15	15	15	11	11	11	11	12	17	16	16	16	16	16	16	16	15	15													
15 KLIEN	18	16	16	16	15	15	15	17	8	12	15	14	14	14	11	11	15	15	15	15	15	15	15	15	15	16	16	16	16	11	11												
17 PANIS	16	15	15	15	11	11	11	17	12	15	11	17	17	17	17	17	17	17	17	19	19	19	19	19	19	15	19	19	19														
18 HEIDFELD	15	10	10	11	17	17	11	11	16	16	16	16	18	18	18	18	18	19	19	19	19	19	19	20	20	20																	
20 BRUNI	11	17	17	20	20	20	10	10	11	11	16	18	18	18	18	18	18	18	18	18	18	18	20	20	21	21	21																
21 BAUMGARTNER	20	20	11	20	10	20	20	20	20	20	20	20	20	14	19	19	19	21	21	21	21	21	21	21																			
19 PANTANO	17	21	20	10	21	21	21	21	19	19	20	20	20	20	20	20	21	20	20	21	21	21	20	20																			
8 ALONSO	21	11	21	21	19	19	19	19	20	21	21	21	14	14	14	14	14	20	21	20	21	21																					
10 SATO	19	19	19	19	14	14	14	14	14	14	14	14	14	21	21	21	21	21	21	21	21																						

QUALIFYING

Sunny and very hot (track 57°C, air 38°C)

Pos.	Driver	Lap time	Sector 1	Sector 2	Sector 3
1	Michael Schumacher	1m 33.074s	24.064s	30.607s	38.403s
2	Mark Webber	1m 33.715s	24.393s	30.850s	38.472s
3	Rubens Barrichello	1m 33.756s	24.217s	30.881s	38.658s
4	Juan Pablo Montoya	1m 34.054s	24.333s	31.224s	38.497s
5	Kimi Räikkönen	1m 34.164s	24.409s	31.355s	38.400s
6	Jenson Button	1m 34.221s	24.443s	31.068s	38.710s
7	Ralf Schumacher	1m 34.235s	24.240s	31.306s	38.689s
8	Jarno Trulli	1m 34.413s	24.528s	31.263s	38.622s
9	David Coulthard	1m 34.602s	24.438s	31.417s	38.747s
10	Cristiano da Matta	1m 34.917s	24.626s	31.416s	38.875s
11	Felipe Massa	1m 35.039s	24.432s	31.555s	39.052s
12	Giancarlo Fisichella	1m 35.061s	24.473s	31.470s	39.118s
13	Christian Klien	1m 35.158s	24.698s	31.556s	38.904s
14	Olivier Panis	1m 35.617s	24.654s	31.942s	39.021s
15	Nick Heidfeld	1m 36.569s	24.854s	31.963s	39.752s
16	Gianmaria Bruni	1m 38.577s	25.045s	32.862s	40.670s
17	Zsolt Baumgartner	1m 39.272s	25.320s	33.002s	40.950s
18	Giorgio Pantano	1m 39.902s	25.556s	32.988s	41.358s
19	Fernando Alonso	No time	24.247s	31.014s	43.851s
20	Takuma Sato	No time	24.504s	31.283s	43.480s

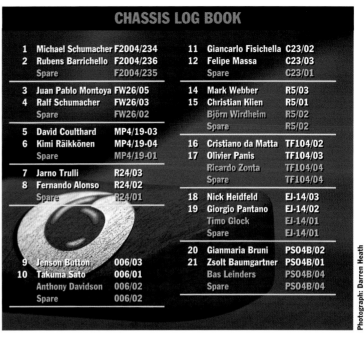

1	Michael Schumacher	F2004/234
2	Rubens Barrichello	F2004/236
	Spare	F2004/235
3	Juan Pablo Montoya	FW26/05
4	Ralf Schumacher	FW26/03
	Spare	FW26/02
5	David Coulthard	MP4/19-03
6	Kimi Räikkönen	MP4/19-04
	Spare	MP4/19-01
7	Jarno Trulli	R24/03
8	Fernando Alonso	R24/02
	Spare	R24/01
9	Jenson Button	006/03
10	Takuma Sato	006/01
	Anthony Davidson	006/02
	Spare	006/02
11	Giancarlo Fisichella	C23/02
12	Felipe Massa	C23/03
	Spare	C23/01
14	Mark Webber	R5/03
15	Christian Klien	R5/01
	Björn Wirdheim	R5/05
	Spare	R5/02
16	Cristiano da Matta	TF104/02
17	Olivier Panis	TF104/03
	Ricardo Zonta	TF104/04
	Spare	TF104/04
18	Nick Heidfeld	EJ-14/03
19	Giorgio Pantano	EJ-14/02
	Timo Glock	EJ-14/01
	Spare	EJ-14/01
20	Gianmaria Bruni	PS04B/02
21	Zsolt Baumgartner	PS04B/01
	Bas Leinders	PS04B/04
	Spare	PS04B/04

Photograph: Darren Heath

PRACTICE 1 (FRIDAY)

Sunny and very hot (track 50°C, air 35°C)

Pos.	Driver	Laps	Time
1	Michael Schumacher	11	1m 34.437s
2	Rubens Barrichello	8	1m 35.380s
3	Anthony Davidson	21	1m 35.970s
4	Ricardo Zonta	21	1m 36.147s
5	Ralf Schumacher	11	1m 36.229s
6	Kimi Räikkönen	5	1m 36.314s
7	Mark Webber	6	1m 36.478s
8	Juan Pablo Montoya	9	1m 36.606s
9	Jenson Button	5	1m 37.018s
10	Fernando Alonso	13	1m 37.119s
11	David Coulthard	4	1m 37.438s
12	Olivier Panis	12	1m 37.590s
13	Jarno Trulli	10	1m 37.816s
14	Giancarlo Fisichella	5	1m 37.995s
15	Takuma Sato	6	1m 38.023s
16	Björn Wirdheim	18	1m 38.086s
17	Christian Klien	11	1m 38.554s
18	Cristiano da Matta	11	1m 38.734s
19	Timo Glock	18	1m 38.788s
20	Nick Heidfeld	8	1m 38.831s
21	Giorgio Pantano	14	1m 39.860s
22	Gianmaria Bruni	6	1m 41.149s
23	Zsolt Baumgartner	14	1m 42.556s
24	Felipe Massa	5	1m 42.718s
25	Bas Leinders	15	1m 43.424s

PRACTICE 2 (FRIDAY)

Sunny and very hot (track 55°C, air 38°C)

Pos.	Driver	Laps	Time
1	Kimi Räikkönen	17	1m 34.395s
2	Ralf Schumacher	24	1m 34.693s
3	Mark Webber	20	1m 35.054s
4	Michael Schumacher	22	1m 35.094s
5	Juan Pablo Montoya	23	1m 35.100s
6	Jarno Trulli	20	1m 35.115s
7	Felipe Massa	21	1m 35.288s
8	Fernando Alonso	20	1m 35.300s
9	David Coulthard	13	1m 35.301s
10	Rubens Barrichello	19	1m 35.373s
11	Jenson Button	19	1m 35.407s
12	Olivier Panis	19	1m 35.524s
13	Ricardo Zonta	27	1m 35.850s
14	Christian Klien	19	1m 35.996s
15	Takuma Sato	6	1m 36.292s
16	Giancarlo Fisichella	28	1m 36.353s
17	Anthony Davidson	5	1m 36.708s
18	Björn Wirdheim	21	1m 36.883s
19	Cristiano da Matta	7	1m 36.907s
20	Nick Heidfeld	19	1m 37.725s
21	Gianmaria Bruni	19	1m 37.818s
22	Zsolt Baumgartner	10	1m 38.588s
23	Timo Glock	27	1m 38.796s
24	Giorgio Pantano	16	1m 39.324s
25	Bas Leinders	23	1m 41.485s

PRACTICE 3 (SATURDAY)

Sunny and very hot (track 51°C, air 36°C)

Pos.	Driver	Laps	Time
1	Michael Schumacher	7	1m 33.391s
2	Fernando Alonso	12	1m 34.175s
3	Ralf Schumacher	8	1m 34.239s
4	Rubens Barrichello	9	1m 34.362s
5	David Coulthard	9	1m 34.415s
6	Jarno Trulli	14	1m 34.482s
7	Juan Pablo Montoya	12	1m 34.547s
8	Mark Webber	5	1m 34.770s
9	Jenson Button	11	1m 34.839s
10	Giancarlo Fisichella	9	1m 35.516s
11	Cristiano da Matta	4	1m 35.678s
12	Takuma Sato	16	1m 35.697s
13	Olivier Panis	10	1m 35.697s
14	Felipe Massa	10	1m 35.813s
15	Christian Klien	8	1m 36.106s
16	Nick Heidfeld	9	1m 37.194s
17	Giorgio Pantano	11	1m 38.302s
18	Zsolt Baumgarnter	13	1m 39.013s
19	Gianmaria Bruni	11	1m 39.209s
20	Kimi Räikkönen	4	No time

PRACTICE 4 (SATURDAY)

Sunny and very hot (track 51°C, air 37°C)

Pos.	Driver	Laps	Time
1	Michael Schumacher	11	1m 33.526s
2	Juan Pablo Montoya	8	1m 33.563s
3	Ralf Schumacher	8	1m 33.973s
4	Jarno Trulli	12	1m 34.041s
5	Rubens Barrichello	9	1m 34.061s
6	Jenson Button	13	1m 34.128s
7	Kimi Räikkönen	10	1m 34.163s
8	David Coulthard	10	1m 34.181s
9	Fernando Alonso	10	1m 34.194s
10	Mark Webber	12	1m 34.381s
11	Olivier Panis	16	1m 34.929s
12	Felipe Massa	5	1m 34.943s
13	Christian Klien	16	1m 34.953s
14	Giancarlo Fisichella	10	1m 35.036s
15	Takuma Sato	13	1m 35.144s
16	Cristiano da Matta	15	1m 35.441s
17	Nick Heidfeld	11	1m 36.607s
18	Giorgio Pantano	12	1m 38.059s
19	Gianmaria Bruni	13	1m 38.554s
20	Zsolt Baumgartner	13	1m 39.893s

9th: DAVID COULTHARD McLaren-Mercedes   7th: RALF SCHUMACHER Williams-BMW   5th: KIMI RÄIKKÖNEN McLaren-Mercedes   3rd: RUBENS BARRICHELLO Ferrari   Pole: MICHAEL SCHUMACHER Ferrari

10th: CRISTIANO DA MATTA Toyota   8th: JARNO TRULLI Renault   6th: JENSON BUTTON BAR-Honda   4th: JUAN PABLO MONTOYA Williams-BMW   2nd: MARK WEBBER Jaguar-Cosworth

44	45	46	47	48	49	50	51	52	53	54	55	56	
1	1	1	1	1	1	1	1	1	1	1	1	1	1
3	3	3	3	3	3	3	3	3	3	3	3	3	2
2	9	9	9	9	9	9	9	9	9	9	9	9	3
9	2	2	2	2	2	2	2	2	2	2	2	2	4
7	7	7	7	7	7	7	7	7	7	7	7	7	5
5	5	5	5	5	5	5	5	5	5	5	5	5	6
8	8	8	8	8	8	8	8	8	8	8	8	8	7
10	10	10	10	10	10	10	10	10	12	12	12		8
12	12	12	12	12	12	12	12	12	16	16	16		
17	16	16	16	16	16	16	16	16	15	15	15		
16	17	17	17	15	15	15	15	15	11	11	11		
15	15	15	17	17	17	17	17	17	17	17	17		
11	11	11	11	11	11	11	11	17	19	19			
19	19	19	19	19	19	19	19	19	20				
20	20	20	20	20	20	20	20	20					
21	21	21	21	21	21	21	21	21					

Pit stop

One lap behind leader

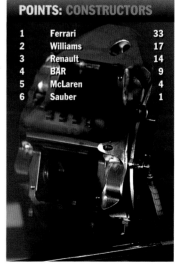

POINTS: DRIVERS

1	Michael Schumacher	20
2	Rubens Barrichello	13
3	Juan Pablo Montoya	12
4	Jenson Button	9
5	Fernando Alonso	8
6	Jarno Trulli	6
7	Ralf Schumacher	5
8	David Coulthard	4
9	Felipe Massa	2

FOR THE RECORD

50 grand prix points

Jenson Button

POINTS: CONSTRUCTORS

1	Ferrari	33
2	Williams	17
3	Renault	14
4	BAR	9
5	McLaren	4
6	Sauber	1

Photographs: Darren Heath

Main photograph: New circuit, fresh challenge, same winner. Michael Schumacher dominated the first race to be held at the spectacular Sakhir circuit.

Left: Three wins out of three races was clearly setting a trend.
Photographs: Darren Heath

FIA F1 WORLD CHAMPIONSHIP • ROUND 3

BAHRAINGP
SAKHIR

BRINGING BAHRAIN INTO THE F1 FOLD

The first impression of the Sakhir circuit borders on the surreal. Its grandstands and control tower loom into view like an ocean liner emerging from the mist as one travels through the arid desert about 30 km south of Manama, the gulf kingdom's capital city.

Although it was a brand-new circuit, the teams had begun preparing for the race well before the season began. Pat Symonds, Renault's executive director of engineering, explained that preparation for the Bahrain track started as soon as the first accurate circuit map had been published, from which the trajectory of the car along the racing line could be described mathematically in three dimensions.

'Once the circuit configuration has been finalised, detailed maps are issued by the FIA, and work can begin,' he said. 'The boundaries of the tarmac are digitised and fed into the first stage of the simulation program to determine the ideal racing line. This is what a skilled driver does intuitively.

'Once the racing line has been established, a car model with an "average" set-up is introduced. From this, a variety of wing settings and gear ratios can be evaluated to get the basis of the set-up calculated.'

Nobody doubted that the Bahrain authorities had done a brilliant job in building the circuit in just over 18 months, and the unfavourable comparisons with those older established European races, many of which do not benefit from unlimited government funding, is understandable in today's highly political F1 environment.

Bernie Ecclestone commented, 'My message to some of the European circuits is, "Watch your backs."

'This is a Formula One World Championship. Nobody wants to abandon the European races. What we want them to do – and particularly Silverstone – is what I've been asking them to do for the last five years, is to raise their standards. They will never raise it to the sorts of levels achieved here in Bahrain, but they can raise it.'

The Sakhir track was the product of Hermann Tilke's Aachen based company, which previously had produced the Sepang circuit in Kuala Lumpur. The company had been working on the Bahrain and Shanghai projects simultaneously, which added to the pressure.

In Bahrain, the challenge was very unusual. More than 60,000 tonnes of Welsh granite were imported to build the circuit, which was constructed on the site of a former camel farm and oasis at Sakhir. In the process, several thousand palm trees were planted, reportedly at a cost of around £1,500 each.

SAKHIR QUALIFYING

Ferrari was on top of its game from the outset at Sakhir, but even so it looked as though one of the Williams-BMW FW26s might squeeze its way on to the front row. As it turned out, however, both Juan Pablo Montoya and Ralf Schumacher made slight errors that consigned them to the second row.

'It's a shame,' said Montoya after posting a third-fastest 1m 30.581s, 'because I was having a very good lap and I was really quick in the first and second sectors. I lost all my advantage and even more in the third sector, in the last corner actually, where I was trying to find a bit more speed. [But] I'm not sure I could have set the pole without that problem at the last corner, because Michael was really quick.'

That was a masterly understatement from the Colombian. Michael Schumacher was full on for pole position, turning a decisive 1m 30.139s even though he deemed the lap far from perfect. 'I was right on the limit and sometimes over it,' he said. 'I think that this is because the track is technically demanding and difficult, but of course we're not supposed to be here for an easy life.'

The qualifying format had been modified for this race, the two runs on Saturday being split into separate sessions, the first formally dubbed 'pre-qualifying'. BAR Honda team boss David Richards slammed this tinkering as 'about as much use as rearranging the deck-chairs on the Titanic.'

He added, 'Moving the whole schedule forward an hour isn't going to do much. What the hell is there to say about it? The whole thing is irrelevant. The thing we have got to do is collectively sit down, all the signatories of the Concorde Agreement, and let Bernie Ecclestone offer up one, maybe two proposals which he thinks will get the TV coverage right. Under those circumstances, he will have our mandate for sure.'

Barrichello joined Schumacher on the front row with a lap of 1m 30.530s, which he felt was reasonable considering that he had not been too happy with his brakes and had driven a conservative lap as a result. Meanwhile, Ralf Schumacher completed the leading quartet with 1m 30.633s, reporting that his car felt very good and predicting that it would be capable of a strong showing come the race.

Despite more oversteer than he judged ideal, Takuma Sato (1m 30.827s) did a great job in the BAR-Honda 005, bagging fifth ahead of team-mate Jenson Button (1m 30.856s). Button was rather baffled by a deterioration in grip during his qualifying run and admitted to being quite disappointed.

Renault's Jarno Trulli did well to line up seventh on 1m 30.971s, but Fernando Alonso grappled with a locking brake, which caused him to miss the apex of the first corner on his qualifying run and later to run wide in Turn 14. The best he could salvage was a 1m 34.130s, which consigned him to a 16th-place start.

Olivier Panis (1m 31.686s) and Cristiano da Matta (1m 31.717s) continued the two-by-two parade for Toyota in eighth and ninth places, while David Coulthard's McLaren MP4/19 (1m 31.719s) and Giancarlo Fisichella's Sauber C23 (1m 31.731s) were next up.

'Our difficult weekend continues, as we have just not been able to get the package working to our advantage,' said Coulthard crisply. 'The car feels okay through corners 11 and 12, but apart from that it's really difficult to find the speed.'

After an engine change on Friday, Kimi Räikkönen would have dropped ten places from his qualifying time, so the team decided to change tactics and not make the timed run, allowing the Finn to start at the back with a good fuel load and new tyres. 'Hopefully, this strategy will pay off,' he said rather forlornly.

A couple of uncharacteristic driving errors prevented Mark Webber from unlocking what he regarded as the Jaguar R5's full potential, and he lined up 14th on 1m 32.625s, 0.3s and two places behind Christian Klien. 'The grip levels reduced slightly in my second session [qualifying] and I made a couple of minor mistakes in sector one, and obviously this was frustrating for me,' said Webber.

Klien added, 'My lap was not perfect this afternoon and so I am not best pleased with my final qualifying position. If you go off-line, the track is really dirty, and this could make overtaking slightly more challenging.'

Behind Webber's Jaguar was Giorgio Pantano's Jordan (1m 34.105s). Alonso and Gianmaria Bruni in the Minardi (1m 34.584s) completed the list of drivers who'd set benchmark times. Starting at the back after taking penalties were Nick Heidfeld (Jordan), Räikkönen and Zsolt Baumgartner (Minardi).

Top: Rubens Barrichello again gave his all, and again had to settle for second behind the master.

Photograph: Bryn Williams/crash.net

Above: The control tower and hospitality suites at Sakhir raised F1 standards yet another notch.

Photograph: Darren Heath

JENSON Button stormed to the second successive podium finish of his career at the Bahrain Grand Prix, driving another flawless race in his BAR-Honda 005 while traditional key rivals, BMW Williams and McLaren Mercedes, collapsed yet again in the face of another Maranello grand slam, delivered with surgical precision by Michael Schumacher and the Ferrari team.

For Schumacher, this was business as usual, the world champion producing another dominant performance to win his 73rd career victory from pole position. A fortnight earlier, Juan Pablo Montoya's Williams had given him a good run for his money in Malaysia, but now Ferrari resumed the form we'd seen in the season opener in Melbourne, with Rubens Barrichello dutifully following Schumacher home for another 1-2 success.

As Button joined the two Ferrari drivers on the rostrum, where they shared a heady non-alcoholic mix of rosewater and pomegranate juice rather than the usual champagne, in deference to Arab protocol, the Englishman could reflect on the fact that he was third in the world championship. Moreover, he could be confident that there was more to come from both himself and his team as he surveyed the remaining 15 races of the season.

'This is only our third race with Michelin tyres, and working out how they work is not as easy as it seems,' said Button. 'We're gaining experience, and hopefully by the next race we can make another step forward.'

Williams started race day with quiet confidence, Montoya and Ralf Schumacher having qualified their FW26s third and fourth in blistering track conditions on Saturday. Yet Sunday was very different. The first rain experienced in Bahrain for two months fell during the morning, and a gusting wind made the low flypass by an Airbus A340 airliner – owned by Gulf Air, the race's sponsors – even more spectacular than it might otherwise have been.

More significantly, the track temperature plunged to 31°C at the start – ideal for Ferrari's soft-compound Bridgestone tyres. Although Schumacher locked a front wheel as he braked hard for the first corner, the Williams-BMWs were tumbled from the very start, and when the two Ferraris slammed across the timing line 1.5s apart at the end of the opening lap, it was all over bar the shouting.

'I had hoped that some short-term rain might help just because my brakes were a little bit too cold,' said Barrichello, 'and I needed to warm them up, but at the same time I needed to save fuel a little bit on the out lap.

'I almost had to avoid Michael at the first corner, and then he was very, very fast for the next couple of corners. So he got a gap and it was difficult to follow, but I was within two- or three-tenths.'

Montoya led the pursuit from the BAR-Honda of Takuma Sato, Ralf Schumacher's Williams-BMW, Jarno Trulli's Renault and Button's BAR-Honda in the opening stages. Fernando Alonso, attempting to make up ground from his 16th-place starting spot, knocked the nose off his Renault R24 on the opening lap and had to pit for a replacement.

Second time around, Michael Schumacher opened his lead to 2.7s, while farther down the pack Christian Klien was racing wheel to wheel with Kimi Räikkönen's McLaren-Mercedes MP4/19, the young Jaguar driver clearly not having got the message that it's impossible to overtake in F1!

By lap five, the world champion was 4.4s ahead, with Montoya still third, while Sato had his BAR's mirrors full of Ralf Schumacher's Williams. On lap seven, this close contest became a little too close as the Williams driver edged ahead on the outside of his Japanese rival, then simply turned across him as if he were suddenly going to de-materialise. Ralf spun off and then limped back to the pits for a precautionary check while Sato continued in fifth.

'The tangle with Ralf Schumacher was disappointing because we should have got through Turn Two side by side,' said Sato, 'but he just closed the door and turned in on me.' Ralf saw it from a subtly different perspective, commenting, 'The collision with Sato was an unfortunate race incident from my point of view. However, he was a bit optimistic in thinking [he could] get back the position he had simply just lost.'

On lap eight, Räikkönen's brief race came to an end as his McLaren's Mercedes engine failed dramatically in a huge spurt of smoke and flame, the disconsolate Finn pulling off out on the circuit after another exasperating disappointment. He'd started from the back of the grid after an engine failure prior to qualifying, so this race performance really was the final straw.

On lap nine, Michael Schumacher made his first refuelling stop (7.2s), which briefly allowed Barrichello into the lead, but Rubens stopped next time around, being followed into the pit lane by Montoya and Trulli. This allowed Sato into the lead for a short period on lap 11 until he too pitted for fuel and tyres at the completion of the lap.

Then Jenson Button slipped ahead before making a 12.0s stop

DIARY

Honda celebrates the inaugural Bahrain GP by announcing that its F1 website will be available in Arabic.

The Duke of York and Spain's King Juan Carlos are among the dignitaries attending the race at Sakhir.

Ralf Schumacher formally announces that he is not poised to quit Williams to join Toyota in 2005.

Jenson Button (above) confirms that it is '100-per-cent certain' that he will be driving for BAR Honda in 2005.

Below: Fernando Alonso raced to sixth from 16th, after being squeezed out at the start by one of the Jaguars and having had to stop for a replacement nose. 'I did the maximum possible today,' claimed the Spaniard after the race.
Photograph: Darren Heath

at the end of lap 12, during which his pit crew made a front wing adjustment, as he had been experiencing quite severe understeer. The race now settled down, with the two Ferraris separated by 11.7s at the head of the pack, and Montoya third from Trulli, Sato and Button.

On lap 17, Sato ran wide over a kerb, slightly damaging the nose section of his BAR-Honda, which forced him to make an unscheduled 11.0s stop for a replacement at the end of lap 18. That dropped him back to 14th, but the plucky Japanese driver just put his head down and started to cut his way back through the pack, undaunted by his disappointment.

Michael Schumacher had extended his advantage over Barrichello to 14.7s by the end of lap 23; he made a second refuelling stop (8.1s) at the end of lap 24. Barrichello stayed out in the lead until lap 27 before making his second stop (7.5s), and the chase settled down once again, with Montoya ahead of Trulli, the dynamic Button, David Coulthard in the McLaren MP4/19 and the irrepressible Sato. It didn't take long for Sato to deal with Coulthard, the BAR slipping ahead of the McLaren on lap 33.

Meanwhile, Button was running strongly in fifth, closing on Trulli, and it was clear that the Renault driver's fourth place might be vulnerable as they went into the third round of refuelling stops. Trulli made an 8.3s stop on lap 38, but Button stayed out for another two laps and just squeezed out ahead of the Italian.

'Our guys in the pit stops normally do fantastic jobs at our team,' Jenson enthused after the race, 'and this was no exception. We do a lot of practice, as every team does, but they are simply very good, and I think our strategy really paid off this weekend.'

Thereafter, Button concentrated on hunting down Montoya's third-place Williams. The Colombian's car developed a gearbox problem with about ten laps to go, so he was a sitting duck, and Button stormed through into third place with eight laps remaining.

'It was a great first race here and a brilliant result for the team,' said Button. 'I didn't get a very good start and I was stuck behind Ralf in Turn One, so I dropped back to eighth initially, which left me with plenty of work to do.'

As Montoya fell away to finish a dejected 13th, Ralf Schumacher recovered to seventh place, which at least brought with it the meagre consolation of two championship points for the blue-riband British team. 'It is clear that we are not quick enough to match Ferrari at the moment, but today we were the quickest on Michelin tyres, which is very important for us,' said Montoya. 'But I still had a good pace and would have come third if I hadn't had that gearbox problem. We were beaten fair and square by Michael and Rubens.'

Trulli wound up reasonably satisfied in fourth, reporting that his Renault R24 had been fine through the first two stints of the race, but then unaccountably had lost grip after his third refuelling stop. Sato took a worthy fifth, while Alonso recovered well to gain sixth, the best he felt he could have done under the circumstances.

'Quite honestly, I was very surprised by how some cars were being driven today,' said Fernando. 'A Jaguar nearly put me in the wall, and then some other drivers were a little too difficult to overtake. I started this race half a minute behind everybody else after my first stop and just pushed all the way.'

Behind Ralf Schumacher's Williams, Mark Webber's Jaguar R5 was the first of the lapped runners in eighth place ahead of the Toyota TF104s of Olivier Panis and Cristiano da Matta.

'It was really good to get our first point of the season here,' said Webber. 'I started well and was up to tenth position on my first lap, which to be honest is where I should have qualified. During my first pit stop, we made a slight flap change, but it was perhaps too much and I had a minor off on Turn 13. It made no real difference in the end, but I was lucky to catch it.'

For McLaren, the Bahrain GP was one of the team's worst showings in living memory. Coulthard was battling for sixth when loss of pneumatic pressure to the Mercedes engine's valve gear sidelined him eight laps from the chequered flag. In the aftermath of the race, the team seemed utterly shell shocked with embarrassment that things could have gone so badly, particularly since the hapless Räikkönen – widely tipped as a championship contender – had failed to finish in any of the season's first three races.

At least McLaren and Williams received some words of comfort from former World Champion Niki Lauda, who had won the third of his titles in a McLaren 20 years before. 'Both Williams and McLaren will analyse what went wrong and work hard to improve,' he said. 'There is no doubt that they will be back, but if Ferrari keeps winning like this, it will be too late for the championship.

'Williams fights with its drivers and, while the McLaren drivers seem to have harmony with each other, their car doesn't work.'

Lauda's capacity for hitting the nail on the head, regardless of whose fingers become bruised in the process, was right on target as usual.

Main photograph: Sandblasted. The rear wing of the McLaren shows the wear and tear of racing action.
Photograph: Darren Heath

Far left: Takuma Sato finished fifth in his BAR-Honda after a collision with Ralf Schumacher and a nose damaging off-track moment.

Left: Gearbox problems caused Juan Pablo Montoya's retirement in the closing stages at Sakhir.

Below left: Jarno Trulli's Renault R24 split the BARs with a fourth-place finish.
Photographs: Darren Heath

GULF AIR
BAHRAIN GRAND PRIX

Photograph: Darren Heath

BAHRAIN 2–4 APRIL 2004

BAHRAIN INTERNATIONAL CIRCUIT

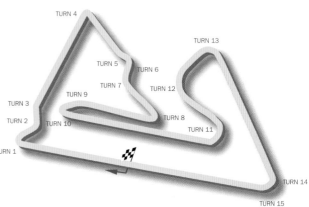

TURN 4
TURN 5
TURN 6
TURN 7
TURN 9
TURN 12
TURN 13
TURN 3
TURN 8
TURN 2
TURN 10
TURN 11
TURN 1
TURN 14
TURN 15

CIRCUIT LENGTH: 3.366 miles/5.417 km

RACE DISTANCE: 57 laps, 191.707 miles/308.523 km RACE WEATHER: Light rain, cloudy (track 31–33°C, air 30°C)

Pos.	Driver	Nat.	No.	Entrant	Car/Engine	Tyres	Laps	Time/Retirement	Speed (mph/km/h)	Gap to leader	Fastest race lap	
1	Michael Schumacher	D	1	Scuderia Ferrari Marlboro	Ferrari F2004-052 V10	B	57	1h 28m 34.875s	129.851/208.976		1m 30.252s	7
2	Rubens Barrichello	BR	2	Scuderia Ferrari Marlboro	Ferrari F2004-052 V10	B	57	1h 28m 36.242s	129.818/208.922	+1.367s	1m 30.876s	29
3	Jenson Button	GB	9	Lucky Strike BAR Honda	BAR 006-Honda RA004E V10	M	57	1h 29m 01.562s	129.202/207.932	+26.687s	1m 30.960s	24
4	Jarno Trulli	I	7	Mild Seven Renault F1 Team	Renault R24-RS4 V10	M	57	1h 29m 07.089s	129.069/207.717	+32.214s	1m 31.421s	24
5	Takuma Sato	J	10	Lucky Strike BAR Honda	BAR 006-Honda RA004E V10	M	57	1h 29m 27.335s	128.582/206.933	+52.460s	1m 31.101s	55
6	Fernando Alonso	E	8	Mild Seven Renault F1 Team	Renault R24-RS4 V10	M	57	1h 29m 28.031s	128.565/206.906	+53.156s	1m 30.654s	39
7	Ralf Schumacher	D	4	BMW WilliamsF1 Team	Williams FW26-BMW P84 V10	M	57	1h 29m 33.030s	128.446/206.714	+58.155s	1m 30.781s	56
8	Mark Webber	AUS	14	Jaguar Racing	Jaguar R5-Cosworth CR6 V10	M	56			+1 lap	1m 32.277s	19
9	Olivier Panis	F	17	Panasonic Toyota Racing	Toyota TF104-RVX04 V10	M	56			+1 lap	1m 32.401s	22
10	Cristiano da Matta	BR	16	Panasonic Toyota Racing	Toyota TF104-RVX04 V10	M	56			+1 lap	1m 32.319s	23
11	Giancarlo Fisichella	I	11	Sauber Petronas	Sauber C23-Petronas 04 V10	B	56			+1 lap	1m 32.329s	40
12	Felipe Massa	BR	12	Sauber Petronas	Sauber C23-Petronas 04 V10	B	56			+1 lap	1m 32.690s	44
13	Juan Pablo Montoya	COL	3	BMW WilliamsF1 Team	Williams FW26-BMW P84 V10	M	56			+1 lap	1m 30.977s	28
14	Christian Klien	A	15	Jaguar Racing	Jaguar R5-Cosworth CR6 V10	M	56			+1 lap	1m 32.533s	38
15	Nick Heidfeld	D	18	Jordan Ford	Jordan EJ-14-Cosworth RS V10	B	56			+1 lap	1m 33.284s	56
16	Giorgio Pantano	I	19	Jordan Ford	Jordan EJ-14-Cosworth RS V10	B	55			+2 laps	1m 34.032s	9
17	Gianmaria Bruni	I	20	European Minardi Cosworth	Minardi PS04B-Cosworth CR3 V10	B	52			+5 laps	1m 35.130s	40
	David Coulthard	GB	5	West McLaren Mercedes	McLaren MP4/19-Mercedes F0110P V10	M	50	Engine			1m 31.861s	19
	Zsolt Baumgartner	H	21	European Minardi Cosworth	Minardi PS04B-Cosworth CR3 V10	B	44	Engine			1m 34.555s	24
	Kimi Räikkönen	FIN	6	West McLaren Mercedes	McLaren MP4/19-Mercedes F0110P V10	M	7	Pneumatics			1m 33.527s	7

All results and data © FOM 2004

Fastest lap: Michael Schumacher, on lap 7, 1m 30.252s, 134.262 mph/216.074 km/h (record for new track).

19th: KIMI RÄIKKÖNEN McLaren-Mercedes
Demoted after engine change

17th: GIANMARIA BRUNI Minardi-Cosworth

15th: GIORGIO PANTANO Jordan-Cosworth

13th: FELIPE MASSA Sauber-Petronas

11th: GIANCARLO FISICHELLA Sauber-Petronas

20th: ZSOLT BAUMGARTNER Minardi-Cosworth
Demoted after engine change

18th: NICK HEIDFELD Jordan-Cosworth
Demoted after engine change

16th: FERNANDO ALONSO Renault

14th: MARK WEBBER Jaguar-Cosworth

12th: CHRISTIAN KLIEN Jaguar-Cosworth

Grid order	1	2	3	4	5	6	7	8	9	10	11	12	13	14	15	16	17	18	19	20	21	22	23	24	25	26	27	28	29	30	31	32	33	34	35	36	37	38	39	40	41	42	43	44
1 M. SCHUMACHER	1	1	1	1	1	1	1	1	1	2	9	1	1	1	1	1	1	1	1	1	1	1	1	1	2	2	2	1	1	1	1	1	1	1	1	1	1	1	1	1	2	2	1	
2 BARRICHELLO	2	2	2	2	2	2	2	2	2	3	1	9	2	2	2	2	2	2	2	2	2	2	2	3	3	1	2	2	2	2	2	2	2	2	2	2	2	2	2	1	1	2		
3 MONTOYA	3	3	3	3	3	3	3	3	3	10	10	2	3	3	3	3	3	3	3	3	3	3	3	1	1	3	3	3	3	3	3	3	3	3	3	3	3	9	3	3	3	3		
4 R. SCHUMACHER	10	10	10	10	10	10	7	7	7	7	2	3	7	7	7	7	7	7	7	7	7	7	9	9	7	7	7	7	7	7	7	7	7	7	9	9	3	9	9	9	9			
10 SATO	4	4	4	4	4	4	10	10	10	9	3	7	10	10	10	10	9	9	9	9	9	9	7	7	9	9	9	9	9	9	9	9	9	9	7	7	7	7	7	7				
9 BUTTON	7	7	7	7	7	7	9	9	1	18	18	9	9	9	9	10	10	5	5	11	11	11	5	5	5	5	5	10	10	10	10	5	8	8	4	4	4	4						
7 TRULLI	9	9	9	9	9	14	14	11	11	7	10	18	5	5	5	5	14	14	14	14	14	8	10	10	10	10	5	5	5	5	5	10	10	4	10	10	10							
17 PANIS	17	17	17	17	17	14	5	5	14	15	19	5	5	14	14	14	11	11	11	11	11	4	5	14	14	14	8	8	8	8	8	14	10	10	8	8	8							
16 DA MATTA	5	14	14	14	14	5	11	11	5	18	5	14	11	11	11	11	17	16	16	8	8	5	10	10	8	8	8	14	14	14	14	4	5	5	5	5	5							
5 COULTHARD	14	5	5	5	5	11	12	12	15	19	14	11	11	17	17	17	8	4	4	12	12	14	17	17	17	17	17	17	17	17	4	10	11	11	11	11	14							
11 FISICHELLA	11	11	11	11	17	6	15	12	17	11	17	17	16	16	16	16	16	8	8	4	4	4	4	4	17	16	12	12	12	14	14	17												
15 KLIEN	12	16	16	16	16	16	15	18	5	17	16	15	15	12	12	8	4	12	12	16	16	16	11	11	16	16	16	16	11	14	14	14	12	17	16									
12 MASSA	16	12	12	12	12	12	16	19	9	14	16	16	15	15	12	8	4	10	17	17	17	16	11	11	11	11	11	11	11	12	12	11	16	16	16	16	12							
14 WEBBER	6	6	6	6	6	6	18	21	17	16	12	12	8	8	4	4	10	10	17	16	16	4	12	12	12	12	12	12	12	12	12	16	16	16	16	12	16							
19 PANTANO	15	15	15	15	15	19	17	21	12	15	8	4	15	15	15	19	19	19	19	19	19	18	18	18	18	18	15	15	15	15	15	15	15	15	15	15	15							
8 ALONSO	18	18	18	18	18	18	21	16	16	8	8	4	19	19	19	18	18	18	18	15	15	19	19	19	19	19	19	19	19	19	19	19	19	18	18	18								
20 BRUNI	19	19	19	19	19	4	8	8	4	4	19	19	18	18	18	15	15	15	15	18	18	15	15	15	15	15	18	18	18	18	18	18	18	19	19	19								
18 HEIDFELD	21	21	21	21	21	21	4	4	21	21	21	21	21	21	21	21	21	21	21	21	21	21	21	21	21	21	21	21	21	21	21	21	21	21	21	21								
6 RÄIKKÖNEN	8	8	8	8	8	8	20	20	20	20	20	20	20	20	20	20	20	20	20	20	20	20	20	20	20	20	20	20	20	20	20	20	20	20	20	20								
21 BAUMGARTNER	20	20	20	20	20	20	20																																					

TIME SHEETS

QUALIFYING

Sunny and very hot (track 47–51°C, air 31–32°C)

Pos.	Driver	Lap time	Sector 1	Sector 2	Sector 3
1	Michael Schumacher	1m 30.139s	29.505s	38.715s	21.919s
2	Rubens Barrichello	1m 30.530s	29.533s	38.731s	22.266s
3	Juan Pablo Montoya	1m 30.581s	29.387s	38.686s	22.508s
4	Ralf Schumacher	1m 30.633s	29.387s	39.058s	22.188s
5	Takuma Sato	1m 30.827s	29.734s	38.676s	22.417s
6	Jenson Button	1m 30.856s	29.626s	38.907s	22.323s
7	Jarno Trulli	1m 30.971s	29.460s	39.054s	22.457s
8	Olivier Panis	1m 31.686s	29.823s	39.543s	22.320s
9	Cristiano da Matta	1m 31.717s	29.743s	39.445s	22.529s
10	David Coulthard	1m 31.719s	29.988s	39.159s	22.572s
11	Giancarlo Fisichella	1m 31.731s	29.809s	39.348s	22.574s
12	Christian Klien	1m 32.332s	30.157s	39.457s	22.178s
13	Felipe Massa	1m 32.536s	30.577s	39.301s	22.658s
14	Mark Webber	1m 32.625s	30.814s	39.353s	22.458s
15	Nick Heidfeld	1m 33.506s	30.436s	40.043s	23.027s
16	Giorgio Pantano	1m 34.105s	30.802s	40.318s	22.985s
17	Fernando Alonso	1m 34.130s	30.427s	39.046s	23.923s
18	Gianmaria Bruni	1m 34.584s	30.414s	40.844s	23.326s
19	Zsolt Baumgartner	1m 35.787s	30.713s	41.420s	23.654s
20	Kimi Räikkönen	No time	–	–	–

CHASSIS LOG BOOK

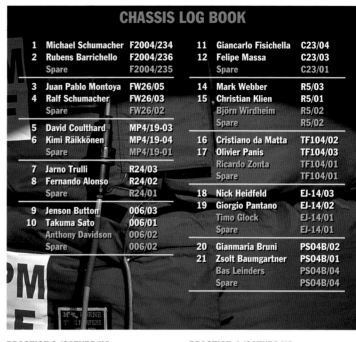

1	Michael Schumacher	F2004/234		11	Giancarlo Fisichella	C23/04
2	Rubens Barrichello	F2004/236		12	Felipe Massa	C23/03
	Spare	F2004/235			Spare	C23/01
3	Juan Pablo Montoya	FW26/05		14	Mark Webber	R5/03
4	Ralf Schumacher	FW26/03		15	Christian Klien	R5/01
	Spare	FW26/02			Björn Wirdheim	R5/02
					Spare	R5/02
5	David Coulthard	MP4/19-03		16	Cristiano da Matta	TF104/02
6	Kimi Räikkönen	MP4/19-04		17	Olivier Panis	TF104/03
	Spare	MP4/19-01			Ricardo Zonta	TF104/01
					Spare	TF104/01
7	Jarno Trulli	R24/03		18	Nick Heidfeld	EJ-14/03
8	Fernando Alonso	R24/02		19	Giorgio Pantano	EJ-14/02
	Spare	R24/01			Timo Glock	EJ-14/01
					Spare	EJ-14/01
9	Jenson Button	006/03				
10	Takuma Sato	006/01		20	Gianmaria Bruni	PS04B/02
	Anthony Davidson	006/02		21	Zsolt Baumgartner	PS04B/01
	Spare	006/02			Bas Leinders	PS04B/04
					Spare	PS04B/04

PRACTICE 1 (FRIDAY)

Sunny, very hot (track 42–47°C, air 32–33°C)

Pos.	Driver	Laps	Time
1	Michael Schumacher	13	1m 32.158s
2	Rubens Barrichello	13	1m 32.651s
3	Anthony Davidson	19	1m 32.958s
4	Juan Pablo Montoya	14	1m 33.027s
5	Jenson Button	13	1m 33.898s
6	David Coulthard	10	1m 34.023s
7	Ricardo Zonta	21	1m 34.289s
8	Felipe Massa	12	1m 34.488s
9	Kimi Räikkönen	10	1m 34.603s
10	Takuma Sato	12	1m 34.610s
11	Ralf Schumacher	13	1m 34.619s
12	Jarno Trulli	6	1m 34.796s
13	Fernando Alonso	11	1m 34.810s
14	Nick Heidfeld	11	1m 34.872s
15	Giorgio Pantano	17	1m 34.967s
16	Giancarlo Fisichella	8	1m 35.388s
17	Timo Glock	16	1m 35.760s
18	Mark Webber	11	1m 35.905s
19	Olivier Panis	14	1m 35.981s
20	Cristiano da Matta	16	1m 36.359s
21	Christian Klien	12	1m 36.645s
22	Zsolt Baumgartner	12	1m 37.049s
23	Gianmaria Bruni	12	1m 37.347s
24	Björn Wirdheim	12	1m 37.443s
25	Bas Leinders	18	1m 37.792s

PRACTICE 2 (FRIDAY)

Sunny, very hot (track 50–51°C, air 32–34°C)

Pos.	Driver	Laps	Time
1	Rubens Barrichello	19	1m 31.450s
2	Juan Pablo Montoya	21	1m 31.451s
3	Anthony Davidson	29	1m 31.488s
4	Michael Schumacher	22	1m 31.732s
5	Christian Klien	20	1m 31.789s
6	Ralf Schumacher	25	1m 31.842s
7	Jenson Button	22	1m 31.879s
8	Mark Webber	24	1m 32.041s
9	Fernando Alonso	23	1m 32.234s
10	Ricardo Zonta	27	1m 32.335s
11	David Coulthard	17	1m 32.495s
12	Takuma Sato	16	1m 32.680s
13	Giorgio Pantano	18	1m 32.708s
14	Cristiano da Matta	21	1m 32.761s
15	Felipe Massa	23	1m 33.031s
16	Olivier Panis	18	1m 33.049s
17	Giancarlo Fisichella	23	1m 33.061s
18	Jarno Trulli	12	1m 33.437s
19	Timo Glock	27	1m 33.695s
20	Zsolt Baumgartner	14	1m 34.054s
21	Björn Wirdheim	25	1m 34.317s
22	Gianmaria Bruni	16	1m 34.791s
23	Bas Leinders	25	1m 36.248s
24	Nick Heidfeld	5	1m 40.573s
25	Kimi Räikkönen	1	No time

PRACTICE 3 (SATURDAY)

Sunny, very hot (track 49°C, air 32°C)

Pos.	Driver	Laps	Time
1	Jenson Button	11	1m 30.062s
2	Juan Pablo Montoya	9	1m 30.121s
3	Michael Schumacher	10	1m 30.545s
4	Rubens Barrichello	10	1m 30.616s
5	Ralf Schumacher	13	1m 30.651s
6	Kimi Räikkönen	14	1m 31.003s
7	Takuma Sato	10	1m 31.090s
8	David Coulthard	9	1m 31.341s
9	Fernando Alonso	9	1m 31.485s
10	Jarno Trulli	17	1m 31.644s
11	Christian Klien	4	1m 31.692s
12	Olivier Panis	16	1m 31.962s
13	Cristiano da Matta	10	1m 32.183s
14	Giancarlo Fisichella	10	1m 32.210s
15	Mark Webber	9	1m 32.276s
16	Nick Heidfeld	12	1m 33.404s
17	Giorgio Pantano	11	1m 33.474s
18	Gianmaria Bruni	11	1m 33.863s
19	Zsolt Baumgartner	9	1m 35.696s
20	Felipe Massa	1	No time

PRACTICE 4 (SATURDAY)

Sunny, very hot (track 50°C, air 33°C)

Pos.	Driver	Laps	Time
1	Jenson Button	14	1m 29.552s
2	Ralf Schumacher	9	1m 29.690s
3	Juan Pablo Montoya	13	1m 29.696s
4	Takuma Sato	19	1m 30.239s
5	Michael Schumacher	11	1m 30.407s
6	Jarno Trulli	10	1m 30.472s
7	Cristiano da Matta	12	1m 30.499s
8	Rubens Barrichello	11	1m 30.513s
9	Fernando Alonso	12	1m 30.774s
10	Olivier Panis	13	1m 30.934s
11	Kimi Räikkönen	9	1m 31.320s
12	Christian Klien	12	1m 31.331s
13	Mark Webber	12	1m 31.384s
14	Giancarlo Fisichella	11	1m 32.433s
15	Felipe Massa	12	1m 32.557s
16	Nick Heidfeld	12	1m 32.816s
17	Giorgio Pantano	7	1m 33.342s
18	Gianmaria Bruni	11	1m 34.590s
19	Zsolt Baumgartner	7	1m 35.901s
20	David Coulthard	4	No time

9th: CRISTIANO DA MATTA Toyota

7th: JARNO TRULLI Renault

5th: TAKUMA SATO BAR-Honda

3rd: JUAN PABLO MONTOYA Williams-BMW

Pole: MICHAEL SCHUMACHER Ferrari

10th: DAVID COULTHARD McLaren-Mercedes

8th: OLIVIER PANIS Toyota

6th: JENSON BUTTON BAR-Honda

4th: RALF SCHUMACHER Williams-BMW

2nd: RUBENS BARRICHELLO Ferrari

45	46	47	48	49	50	51	52	53	54	55	56	57	
1	1	1	1	1	1	1	1	1	1	1	1	1	1
2	2	2	2	2	2	2	2	2	2	2	2	2	2
3	3	3	3	9	9	9	9	9	9	9	9	9	3
9	9	9	9	3	7	7	7	7	7	7	7	7	4
7	7	7	7	3	3	3	10	10	10	10	10		5
4	10	10	10	10	10	10	8	8	8	8	8	8	6
10	8	8	8	8	8	8	4	4	4	4	4	7	7
8	5	5	5	4	4	4	4	3	3	14			8
5	4	4	4	5	14	14	14	14	14	17			
14	14	14	14	14	14	17	17	17	17	17	16		
17	17	17	17	17	16	16	16	16	16	11			
16	16	16	16	16	11	11	11	11	11	12			
11	11	11	11	11	12	12	12	12	12	3			
12	12	12	12	12	15	15	15	15	15	15			
15	15	15	15	15	18	18	18	18	18	18			
18	18	18	18	18	19	19	19	19	19				
19	19	19	19	19	20	20							
20	20	20	20	20	20								

Pit stop

One lap behind leader

POINTS: DRIVERS

1	Michael Schumacher	30
2	Rubens Barrichello	21
3	Jenson Button	15
4	Juan Pablo Montoya	12
5 =	Fernando Alonso	11
5 =	Jarno Trulli	11
7	Ralf Schumacher	7
8 =	Takuma Sato	4
8 =	David Coulthard	4
10 =	Felipe Massa	1
10 =	Mark Webber	1

FOR THE RECORD

600 laps led

Rubens Barrichello

POINTS: CONSTRUCTORS

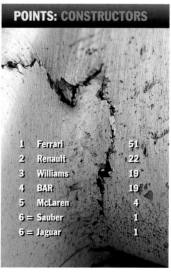

1	Ferrari	51
2	Renault	22
3	Williams	19
4	BAR	19
5	McLaren	4
6 =	Sauber	1
6 =	Jaguar	1

'Forza Michael!' Schumacher hugs the pit wall after taking his fourth straight win of the year, acknowledging the plaudits of the Maranello pit crew.
Photograph: Darren Heath

FIA F1 WORLD CHAMPIONSHIP • ROUND 4

SAN MARINOGP
IMOLA

IMOLA QUALIFYING

Facing page: Jenson Button started his BAR-Honda 006 from pole position and opened a huge lead over Michael Schumacher's Ferrari at the end of the opening lap, an achievement that really held the world champion's attention.
Photograph: Darren Heath

Above: Gianmaria Bruni working the Minardi through one of the Imola chicanes. He retired with a brake problem.
Photograph: Bryn Williams/crash.net

Below: Taking notes. Patrick Head keeps track of changes during practice.
Photograph: Darren Heath

The 2004 San Marino Grand Prix was the first time since Ayrton Senna's McLaren had qualified fastest at the 1992 Canadian Grand Prix that Honda power had propelled an F1 pole winner. With a lap of seamless efficiency and matchless precision, Jenson Button continued his ascendancy in Saturday qualifying by prising top spot on the starting grid from Michael Schumacher's expectant grasp.

Yet it was not just the 900+ bhp generated by the latest Honda RA004E V10 that powered F1's top Brit to the front of the grid. His BAR 006 also displayed tremendous handling poise, riding the high kerbs at the evocatively titled Autodromo Dino e Enzo Ferrari with an unflustered composure that rivalled Maranello's superb F2004.

It was the stuff of dreams. During testing, Button had quickly latched on to the potential of the new BAR and had been sandbagging ever so slightly to attract the minimum of attention. Now came the pay-off, and with Schumacher losing control of his Ferrari at the Variante Alta at the top of the hill before Rivazza, a slip that cost him about 0.3s, Button was effectively unchallenged as he raced to the first pole of his F1 career.

'It was a great lap,' grinned Button with understandable satisfaction, 'and I enjoyed it very much. In pre-qualifying, I was a little wide, because I had very low grip, but in proper qualifying it seemed to be all there. So I was very happy and I don't think there were any mistakes.'

Takuma Sato, meanwhile, had been less successful, reporting that his car had displayed a general lack of grip that caused him to ride the kerbs a little too much. He wound up seventh on 1m 20.913s.

Barrichello similarly failed to get as close to Schumacher as he would

have liked. Initially, he'd been unhappy with the set-up of his F2004, but made some changes for qualifying, only to lose crucial fractions in the final sector of the lap. That placed him fourth on 1m 20.451s, a fraction off Juan Pablo Montoya's best in the Williams-BMW FW26.

'I think it went really well,' said the Colombian in upbeat mood. 'As you can see, we took little fuel in the first qualifying because we wanted to run last [in the second], and as you see, the track got better and it worked quite well for us. I think we've got a very good race car. I was actually lacking in pace on new tyres, and with the work we did it seemed to come to me a little bit. It's the first time I've outqualified Ralf here, so it's good.'

Ralf Schumacher had to be content with fifth fastest on 1m 20.538s after grappling with minor handling problems, while the Renault R24s were sixth and ninth in the hands of Fernando Alonso and Jarno Trulli, separated by Sato's BAR and Mark Webber's Jaguar R5.

'Sixth is a good position for us, as I think the car is quick in race conditions,' said Alonso, 'and that we can be very consistent on the long runs.' Trulli added, 'It was a pretty good qualifying session for me. I made some little mistakes in the first and third sectors, but that only cost me maybe a couple of tenths. I think we are capable of scoring good points.'

Toyota's Cristiano da Matta (1m 12.087s) and Olivier Panis (1m 21.558s) wound up tenth and 13th, the Brazilian judging that he'd pushed a little too hard, while Olivier admitted that he had been a touch unsettled by an electrical glitch on his out-lap, which almost brought his car to a standstill.

The prospects for both Sauber and McLaren were blighted by the need for Giancarlo Fisichella and Kimi Räikkönen respectively to start at the back of the grid. The former had dropped out of qualifying due to a gearbox problem, while Räikkönen's disadvantage had resulted from an engine change. That left Coulthard and Massa, the best placed McLaren and Sauber runners, in 11th and 12th on the grid.

Behind Panis came Christian Klien's Jaguar (1m 21.949s), the two Jordans of Giorgio Pantano (1m 23.352s) and Nick Heidfeld (1m 23.488s), plus the two Minardis. Zsolt Baumgartner had flown off the road at the Variante Alta during his qualifying run, but had sustained rather more damage than Michael Schumacher.

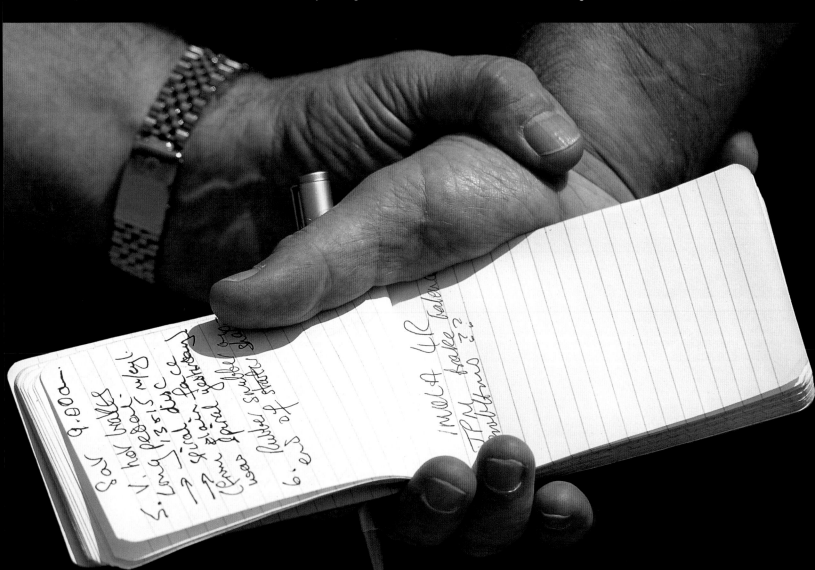

AS Jenson Button was feted after his brilliant run to second place in the San Marino Grand Prix, winner Michael Schumacher was accused of being 'either blind or stupid' by Juan Pablo Montoya. The two men had been involved in a lurid skirmish while battling for second place on the opening lap of what could conceivably have been the last grand prix at Imola's Autodromo Enzo e Dino Ferrari.

As the two rivals battled hard, Button made good his escape to lead the first eight laps in glorious style. Sure enough, he was jumped by the world champion during the first round of refuelling stops, but by then he had such a commanding cushion that he was easily able to stay ahead of third-placed Montoya to the chequered flag.

Fourth and fifth spots fell to the Renault R24s of Fernando Alonso and Jarno Trulli, a disappointed Rubens Barrichello bringing the other Ferrari F2004 home sixth. The remaining points scorers were Ralf Schumacher in the Williams-BMW FW26 and Kimi Räikkönen in the McLaren-Mercedes MP4/19.

The Ferrari fans were understandably confident that Michael Schumacher would deliver another home victory. Button, however, having bagged the first pole position of his career, had other ideas and was determined to make Maranello's finest work harder for his living than perhaps had been the case so far in 2004.

Thus, Jenson made a perfect start from the front, while Montoya accelerated his Williams-BMW up from fourth place to within inches of the world champion's Ferrari as they jinked and weaved their way through the sequence of ess-bends on the outward leg of the circuit. The Colombian was absolutely hell-bent on pressing home his attack in the brief window of opportunity theoretically available while Schumacher's Bridgestone tyres took their customary lap or so to reach optimum working temperature.

On the first straight, Schumacher weaved across in front of Montoya to prevent him from making an overtaking bid, and then pushed him off the road as he attempted to go around the outside of the Ferrari on the tricky uphill, left-hand Tosa hairpin.

'Well, you know Michael had a poor start,' said Montoya. 'He was slow out of the first chicane, you know, the first Turns Two and Three. I went to pass, he closed the door on me and I had to back off. Then he did the same out of the next corner and closed the door.

'So I went for the inside and I'm coming beside him, and the next thing I see he's just coming straight at me, hit me and put me up the grass. It's very disappointing to see racing like that, but I'll

be surprised if he gets away with it, but it's up to the FIA.'

He added, 'I actually got in front while we were braking, and he says, oh, he didn't see me there. No chance. You've got to be either blind or stupid not to see me. But you know, it is racing.'

Asked if he thought it was a bit too optimistic to try the outside line at Tosa, Montoya replied, 'I've done it before and it has quite a lot of grip. I understand he has got to defend his position, but how far do you go to defend your position? That's the question. Or how far are you allowed to go?'

Schumacher refused to be drawn on the matter, declining to comment, but looking extremely sheepish and embarrassed as he sat in the post-race media conference listening to Montoya criticise his driving techniques with a relaxed insouciance. In the event, the world champion had the last laugh, as the FIA stewards judged it to be an incident that merited no sanction.

Schumacher escaping without a penalty seemed supremely ironic to the Williams driver, given that he had been penalised in 2003's US Grand Prix for pulling a similar move on Rubens Barrichello's Ferrari early in the race.

Not that Montoya's Williams-BMW was in the same class as Schumacher's Ferrari, of course. Once he caught his stride, the world champion dropped the rest of the field at around a second a lap as he went on the offensive, relentlessly hunting down Button, who had capitalised on the chaos behind him to open a 2.7s lead over the Italian car by the end of the opening lap. By lap four, however, Schumacher had trimmed the Englishman's advantage to 0.9s, but Button refused to be ruffled by the pressure. Schumacher admitted he was impressed.

'It was mind blowing what Jenson put up in front,' he said. 'I just thought that it was raining in front of me and it was dry for him. He was just disappearing into the distance, and I was really wondering.

'It took quite a few laps until everything got going and we were able to chase. His first stint. Well, I saw the lap times in the low 1m 21s, and he was still pulling away, so I thought that this was going to be a very busy and tough afternoon. Luckily, whatever happened, we sort of kept our pace and they [BAR] dropped off a little bit from their initial pace.'

Button ducked in to make his first refuelling stop in 9.7s at the end of lap nine, after which Schumacher really piled on the pressure before making his first stop at the end of lap 11. Two staggeringly quick laps transformed, indeed reversed, the race order, emphasising quite dramatically just how deeply Michael could dig

BRAWN PRAISES BUTTON'S PROWESS

Ross Brawn, Ferrari's technical director, praised Jenson Button's performance at Imola and hinted that the British driver may come to be considered as a potential successor to Michael Schumacher at Maranello when the multiple world champion hangs up his helmet.

'It was an exciting start to the race because we didn't know quite how much fuel Jenson had on board,' he said. 'He stopped after nine laps, which meant he had 6 kg less than Michael, and that was crucial. Michael blitzed his way around the extra two laps he was able to remain out before refuelling. That is why he got ahead and was able to control the pace. But it was, nevertheless, a very impressive performance by Jenson.'

He continued, 'BAR are serious contenders and they did a great job. Jenson had a good race. I am very impressed with him. The signs were there when he was at Williams, and his present form just goes to show that when a driver gets the right engineers, the right environment and the team believe in him, then he raises his game. For him to have taken pole ahead of Schumacher was fantastic, and he is learning to work with the team. He is going to become very hot property over the next couple of years.'

Then Brawn added the most telling comment of all: 'One day, Michael is going to stop, and then we will have to look around for a replacement and see who is the best at that stage. Jenson will be on that list.'

ttled
. Schu-

was really
ap on the first
pace in the first
ter we refuelled, I
hael.'

dded, 'In the race, it's
ed more windy today and
e had expected. It was a lit-
hose problems, the pace was

ng stops, Montoya led the pursuit
fourth ahead of Ralf Schumacher,
stage, Michael Schumacher was lap-
an Button and had stretched his advan-
of lap 15, and 9.9s next time around. By lap
7s in front, and with 23 laps completed, But-
d.

his second stop (7.5s) at the end of lap 27, a lap
nd resumed 18.3s ahead. Jenson stopped again in
, but Schumacher kept the Ferrari out until lap 46, re-
n a 26.5s edge over the gallant BAR driver. Thereafter,
cher held his lead without challenge to beat Button by just
ne seconds after easing back on the final lap.
Montoya wound up a distant third, frustrated by the fact that the
ew Williams-BMW was clearly unable to challenge the Ferrari
F2004 in a straight fight.

'Jenson had an incredibly fast pace. Therefore, third was the
best I could do today, since our car was just not quick enough,' explained Montoya. 'We need to improve our complete package to be
competitive in order to catch up with the leaders.'

Alonso and Jarno Trulli drove energetically to bring their Renaults home fourth and fifth ahead of Rubens Barrichello's Ferrari,
the Spanish driver surviving a brush with Ralf Schumacher under
braking for the uphill Tosa hairpin while battling for what looked
like an ultimate third place.

Alonso had driven superbly, staying out until lap 48 before making his third and final refuelling stop, which vaulted him into fifth
ahead of Trulli and Barrichello. On lap 50, Ralf had tried to squeeze
Alonso as he attempted to outbrake the Williams, but the German
driver was pitched into a spin, dropping to an eventual seventh.

Alonso agreed that it had been a tough contest. 'It was a very
good result after a tough race for me,' he said. 'I made a bad start,
the car just lacked traction, and then Coulthard almost took me out
at the first corner. Some parts [of his car] actually hit my helmet.

'By then, though, I had lost too much time to be able to fight
with the leaders, so I followed the cars in front and made the most
of my opportunities around the [refuelling] stops to pass them. The
car was a little bit nervous, but I still managed to push. As for the

incident with Ralf, from where I was [sitting], he just closed the door on me, but fortunately it didn't damage the car.'

Barrichello had strained every sinew in a bid to grasp fourth place from Trulli as they came plunging down into Rivazza on the final lap. The Brazilian was clearly extremely disappointed. 'My race was spoilt by traffic,' he shrugged. 'I always found myself with a slower car ahead of me and so I was never able to push my car as hard as it would go. Ralf Schumacher especially blocked me several times, at the start for example, when he made a move that saw me go off the track. It's a shame, as I knew I had a great car and was convinced I could have a good race.'

Kimi Räikkönen's McLaren came home eighth on a two-stop strategy that carried him through from his starting place at the back of the grid. 'I'm pleased at least to have finished my first race of the year,' he said grimly, 'but obviously we want to be fighting for the lead, not for eighth place. The track is very narrow, so it's quite difficult to overtake, and when you are so far back you inevitably get stuck.'

Coulthard struggled back to 12th place after being switched to a three-stop strategy following his return to the pits at the end of the opening lap to have a replacement nose section fitted.

Splitting the two McLarens were the Sauber C23s of Giancarlo Fisichella and Felipe Massa, the Italian just losing out to Räikkönen in the battle for the final championship point of the afternoon. 'I got held up by one of the Minardis in the final corner,' shrugged Fisichella, 'at a point when Kimi had fresher tyres, and, with the better traction out of the corner, he got a run at me and overtook me on the straight.'

Behind Massa, Olivier Panis brought the sole surviving Toyota TF104 home 11th after team-mate Cristiano da Matta had slid off the track in the wake of a bizarre sequence of events. The recipient of a drive-through penalty, he had followed his normal procedure as he came into the pit lane. 'This involves pressing two buttons, one for the pit-lane speed limiter and one for the launch control,' he explained. 'But the launch control button also disables the traction control and, of course, this time I was not actually stopping. I got to the first chicane, where I was caught out by not having any traction control and went off the circuit. It is a mistake, but very frustrating…'

Nobody ever said F1 was easy.

Main photograph: Can't get enough of it. Michael Schumacher accepts the adulation of the passionately loyal tifosi.
Photograph: Darren Heath

Inset, below left: Jarno Trulli continued to display impressive form with the Renault at Imola, fighting off Rubens Barrichello in the closing stages in a battle for fifth.
Photograph: Bryn Williams/crash.net

Inset, bottom left: Pit stop for Giancarlo Fisichella's Sauber C23. After ducking out of qualifying due to a gearbox problem, he started last and finished ninth, hard on the heels of Kimi Räikkönen's McLaren.
Photograph: Darren Heath

DIARY

Gerhard Berger demonstrates the ex-Ayrton Senna JPS Lotus-Renault 98T (below) at Imola on the tenth anniversary of the death of his friend and former team-mate.

Photograph: Darren Heath

FIA President Max Mosley unveils a dramatic range of changes to the F1 regulations that will come into force from the start of 2008. They include 2.4-litre V8 engines plus manual gearboxes and clutches.

Motorcycle ace Valentino Rossi samples an F1 Ferrari at Fiorano.

Williams admits that it might give Jacques Villeneuve a test drive sometime during the season.

Vitantonio Liuzzi wins the opening round of the F3000 championship on the eve of the San Marino Grand Prix.

IMOLA – AUTODROMO DINO E ENZO FERRARI

PIRATELLA
105/169
(4)

TOSA
55/89
(2)

ACQUE
MINERALI
70/113
(3)

VARIANTE ALTA
75/121
(3)

VILLENEUVE
85/137
(3)

mph/km/h
(gear)

175/281
(6)

TRAGUARDO
55/89
(2)

RIVAZZA
65/105
(2)

TAMBURELLO
100/161
(3)

VARIANTE BASSA
180/290
(6)

GRAN PREMIO FOSTER'S DI
SAN MARINO
IMOLA 23–25 APRIL 2004

CIRCUIT LENGTH: 3.065 miles/4.933 km

Photograph: Darren Heath

RACE DISTANCE: 62 laps, 189.896 miles/305.609 km   RACE WEATHER: Warm and sunny (track 38–41°C, air 26–29°C)

Pos.	Driver	Nat.	No.	Entrant	Car/Engine	Tyres	Laps	Time/Retirement	Speed (mph/km/h)	Gap to leader	Fastest race lap	
1	Michael Schumacher	D	1	Scuderia Ferrari Marlboro	Ferrari F2004-052 V10	B	62	1h 26m 19.670s	131.982/212.405		1m 20.411s	10
2	Jenson Button	GB	9	Lucky Strike BAR Honda	BAR 006-Honda RA004E V10	M	62	1h 26m 29.372s	131.735/212.008	+9.702s	1m 21.201s	28
3	Juan Pablo Montoya	COL	3	BMW WilliamsF1 Team	Williams FW26-BMW P84 V10	M	62	1h 26m 41.287s	131.434/211.523	+21.617s	1m 21.870s	27
4	Fernando Alonso	E	8	Mild Seven Renault F1 Team	Renault R24-RS4 V10	M	62	1h 26m 43.324s	131.382/211.440	+23.654s	1m 21.650s	59
5	Jarno Trulli	I	7	Mild Seven Renault F1 Team	Renault R24-RS4 V10	M	62	1h 26m 55.886s	131.066/210.931	+36.216s	1m 21.666s	11
6	Rubens Barrichello	BR	2	Scuderia Ferrari Marlboro	Ferrari F2004-052 V10	B	62	1h 26m 56.353s	131.054/210.912	+36.683s	1m 21.873s	31
7	Ralf Schumacher	D	4	BMW WilliamsF1 Team	Williams FW26-BMW P84 V10	M	62	1h 27m 15.400s	130.577/210.144	+55.730s	1m 21.689s	30
8	Kimi Räikkönen	FIN	6	West McLaren Mercedes	McLaren MP4/19-Mercedes F0110P V10	M	61			+1 lap	1m 22.500s	39
9	Giancarlo Fisichella	I	11	Sauber Petronas	Sauber C23-Petronas 04 V10	B	61			+1 lap	1m 22.654s	60
10	Felipe Massa	BR	12	Sauber Petronas	Sauber C23-Petronas 04 V10	B	61			+1 lap	1m 22.895s	36
11	Olivier Panis	F	17	Panasonic Toyota Racing	Toyota TF104-RVX04 V10	M	61			+1 lap	1m 22.861s	59
12	David Coulthard	GB	5	West McLaren Mercedes	McLaren MP4/19-Mercedes F0110P V10	M	61			+1 lap	1m 22.951s	42
13	Mark Webber	AUS	14	Jaguar Racing	Jaguar R5-Cosworth CR6 V10	M	61			+1 lap	1m 22.931s	55
14	Christian Klien	A	15	Jaguar Racing	Jaguar R5-Cosworth CR6 V10	M	60			+2 laps	1m 23.647s	27
15	Zsolt Baumgartner	H	21	European Minardi Cosworth	Minardi PS04B-Cosworth CR3 V10	B	58			+4 laps	1m 26.075s	58
16	Takuma Sato	J	10	Lucky Strike BAR Honda	BAR 006-Honda RA004E V10	M	56	Engine		DNF	1m 21.929s	44
	Nick Heidfeld	D	18	Jordan Ford	Jordan EJ-14-Cosworth RS V10	B	48	Driveshaft			1m 23.381s	44
	Cristiano da Matta	BR	16	Panasonic Toyota Racing	Toyota TF104-RVX04 V10	M	32	Accident			1m 23.108s	25
	Gianmaria Bruni	I	20	European Minardi Cosworth	Minardi PS04B-Cosworth CR3 V10	B	22	Brake balance			1m 26.857s	11
	Giorgio Pantano	I	19	Jordan Ford	Jordan EJ-14-Cosworth RS V10	B	6	Steering hydraulics			1m 25.457s	6

All results and data © FOM 2004

Fastest lap: Michael Schumacher, on lap 10, 1m 20.411s, 137.230 mph/220.850 km/h (record).

Previous lap record: Michael Schumacher (Ferrari F2002-051 V10), 1m 22.491s, 133.769 mph/215.281 km/h (2003).

19th: GIANCARLO FISICHELLA Sauber-Petronas

17th: GIANMARIA BRUNI Minardi-Cosworth

15th: GIORGIO PANTANO Jordan-Cosworth

13th: OLIVIER PANIS Toyota

11th: DAVID COULTHARD McLaren-Mercedes

20th: KIMI RÄIKKÖNEN McLaren-Mercedes

18th: ZSOLT BAUMGARTNER Minardi-Cosworth

16th: NICK HEIDFELD Jordan-Cosworth

14th: CHRISTIAN KLIEN Jaguar-Cosworth

12th: FELIPE MASSA Sauber-Petronas

Grid order	1	2	3	4	5	6	7	8	9	10	11	12	13	14	15	16	17	18	19	20	21	22	23	24	25	26	27	28	29	30	31	32	33	34	35	36	37	38	39	40	41	42	43	44	45	46	47	4
9 BUTTON	9	9	9	9	9	9	9	9	1	1	1	1	1	1	1	1	1	1	1	1	1	1	1	1	1	1	1	1	1	1	1	1	1	1	1	1	1	1	1	1	1	1	1	1	1	1	1	1
1 M. SCHUMACHER	1	1	1	1	1	1	1	1	9	10	7	7	9	9	9	9	9	9	9	9	9	9	9	9	9	9	9	9	9	9	9	9	9	9	9	9	9	9	9	9	9	9	9	9	9	9	9	9
3 MONTOYA	3	3	3	3	3	3	3	3	10	7	8	9	3	3	3	3	3	3	3	3	3	3	3	3	7	7	7	7	3	3	3	3	3	3	3	3	3	4	7	7	8
2 BARRICHELLO	10	10	10	10	10	10	10	10	4	2	9	3	7	7	7	7	7	7	7	7	7	7	4	4	8	3	4	4	4	4	4	4	4	4	4	4	7	8	8	3
4 R. SCHUMACHER	4	4	4	4	4	4	4	2	8	3	4	4	4	4	4	4	4	4	4	4	2	2	3	3	4	7	7	7	7	7	7	7	7	7	7	8	3	3	4
8 ALONSO	2	2	2	2	2	2	2	7	9	4	2	2	2	2	2	2	2	2	2	8	8	4	4	2	2	2	2	2	2	2	2	2	2	2	2	3	4	4	7
10 SATO	7	7	7	7	7	7	7	3	2	8	8	8	8	8	8	8	8	8	3	3	3	3	8	8	8	8	8	8	8	8	8	8	8	8	8	2	2	2
14 WEBBER	14	14	14	14	14	14	8	17	4	10	10	10	10	10	10	10	10	10	10	10	10	10	10	10	10	10	10	10	10	10	10	10	10	10	10	10	10	10	10	10	1
7 TRULLI	8	8	8	8	8	8	14	3	11	11	11	11	11	11	11	11	6	12	12	12	17	17	6	6	6	6	6	6	6	6	6	6	6	6	6	6	6	6	6	6
16 DA MATTA	16	16	16	16	16	16	17	11	6	6	6	6	6	6	6	14	14	14	6	11	11	11	11	11	11	11	11	11	11	11	11	11	11	11	11
5 COULTHARD	17	12	12	12	12	12	11	6	18	18	18	18	14	14	14	16	17	11	11	12	12	12	17	17	12	12	12	12	12	12	12	12	12	12	1
12 MASSA	12	17	17	17	17	17	6	15	14	14	14	14	16	16	16	12	12	16	16	16	16	16	17	17	17	17	17	17	17	17
17 PANIS	19	19	19	19	19	19	16	18	16	16	16	16	17	17	17	17	11	5	5	5	5	5	5	5	5	5	5	5	14	14	14	14	14	14
15 KLIEN	11	11	11	11	11	6	18	14	16	16	16	17	17	17	17	6	6	16	14	14	14	14	5	5	5	5	5	5	14	14	14	14	14	14
19 PANTANO	6	6	6	6	6	15	12	17	12	17	17	18	18	18	18	18	18	18	18	18	18	18	18	18	18	18	18	18	18	18	18	18	18	1
18 HEIDFELD	15	15	15	15	15	18	16	16	20	20	5	5	5	5	5	5	5	5	15	15	15	15	15	15	15	15	15	15	15	15	15	15	15	15	15
20 BRUNI	18	18	18	18	18	20	20	20	5	5	15	21	21	21	21	21	21	21	21	21	21	21	21	21	21	21	21
21 BAUMGARTNER	20	20	20	20	20	21	21	15	21	21	21	21	21	21	21	21	21	21
11 FISICHELLA	21	21	21	21	21	5	5	5	21	21	20	20	20	20	20	20	20	20
6 RÄIKKÖNEN	5	5	5	5	5	5																							**Pit stop**

One lap behind leader

QUALIFYING

Bright and sunny (track 40–41°C, air 29°C)

Pos.	Driver	Lap time	Sector 1	Sector 2	Sector 3
1	Jenson Button	1m 19.753s	22.790s	26.826s	30.137s
2	Michael Schumacher	1m 20.011s	22.732s	26.649s	30.630s
3	Juan Pablo Montoya	1m 20.212s	22.972s	26.829s	30.411s
4	Rubens Barrichello	1m 20.451s	22.973s	26.803s	30.675s
5	Ralf Schumacher	1m 20.538s	23.303s	26.813s	30.422s
6	Fernando Alonso	1m 20.895s	23.288s	27.031s	30.576s
7	Takuma Sato	1m 20.913s	23.129s	27.081s	30.703s
8	Mark Webber	1m 20.921s	23.354s	26.855s	30.682s
9	Jarno Trulli	1m 21.034s	23.349s	27.098s	30.587s
10	Cristiano da Matta	1m 21.087s	23.522s	27.118s	30.447s
11	David Coulthard	1m 21.091s	23.294s	26.981s	30.816s
12	Felipe Massa	1m 21.532s	23.424s	27.394s	30.714s
13	Olivier Panis	1m 21.558s	23.633s	27.116s	30.809s
14	Christian Klien	1m 21.949s	23.649s	27.436s	30.864s
15	Giorgio Pantano	1m 23.352s	23.942s	27.818s	31.592s
16	Nick Heidfeld	1m 23.488s	23.789s	27.971s	31.728s
17	Gianmaria Bruni	1m 26.899s	24.992s	28.750s	33.157s
18	Zsolt Baumgartner	1m 46.299s	25.129s	28.716s	34.352s
19	Giancarlo Fisichella	No time	–	–	–
20	Kimi Räikkönen	No time	–	–	–

Chassis Log Book

	Driver	Chassis		Driver	Chassis
1	Michael Schumacher	F2004/234	11	Giancarlo Fisichella	C23/04
2	Rubens Barrichello	F2004/236	12	Felipe Massa	C23/03
	Spare	F2004/235		Spare	C23/01
3	Juan Pablo Montoya	FW26/05	14	Mark Webber	R5/03
4	Ralf Schumacher	FW26/07	15	Christian Klien	R5/01
	Spare	FW26/03		Björn Wirdheim	R5/02
				Spare	R5/02
5	David Coulthard	MP4/19-03			
6	Kimi Räikkönen	MP4/19-04	16	Cristiano da Matta	TF104/04
	Spare	MP4/19-01	17	Olivier Panis	TF104/03
				Ricardo Zonta	TF104/02
7	Jarno Trulli	R24/03		Spare	TF104/02
8	Fernando Alonso	R24/02			
	Spare	R24/01	18	Nick Heidfeld	EJ-14/03
			19	Giorgio Pantano	EJ-14/02
9	Jenson Button	006/05		Timo Glock	EJ-14/01
10	Takuma Sato	006/03		Spare	EJ-14/01
	Anthony Davidson	006/02			
	Spare	006/02	20	Gianmaria Bruni	PS04B/02
			21	Zsolt Baumgartner	PS04B/01
				Bas Leinders	PS04B/04
				Spare	PS04B/04

Photograph: Darren Heath

PRACTICE 1 (FRIDAY)

Bright and sunny (track 30–34°C, air 24–25°C)

Pos.	Driver	Laps	Time
1	Michael Schumacher	11	1m 20.084s
2	Rubens Barrichello	12	1m 21.443s
3	Ralf Schumacher	13	1m 22 250s
4	Anthony Davidson	20	1m 22.398s
5	Jenson Button	10	1m 22.448s
6	Juan Pablo Montoya	11	1m 22.796s
7	Jarno Trulli	11	1m 22.927s
8	Kimi Räikkönen	4	1m 23.054s
9	Fernando Alonso	13	1m 23.083s
10	Ricardo Zonta	20	1m 23.161s
11	David Coulthard	8	1m 23.197s
12	Mark Webber	11	1m 23.417s
13	Giancarlo Fisichella	9	1m 23.528s
14	Felipe Massa	13	1m 23.562s
15	Olivier Panis	13	1m 23.790s
16	Takuma Sato	11	1m 24.061s
17	Björn Wirdheim	29	1m 24.152s
18	Cristiano da Matta	12	1m 24.752s
19	Nick Heidfeld	12	1m 24.955s
20	Giorgio Pantano	12	1m 25.375s
21	Christian Klien	9	1m 25.679s
22	Timo Glock	14	1m 26.254s
23	Gianmaria Bruni	14	1m 27.933s
24	Zsolt Baumgartner	14	1m 29.312s
25	Bas Leinders	19	1m 29.414s

PRACTICE 2 (FRIDAY)

Bright and sunny (track 38–39°C, air 36°C)

Pos.	Driver	Laps	Time
1	Jenson Button	25	1m 20.966s
2	Takuma Sato	25	1m 21.159s
3	Michael Schumacher	23	1m 21.164s
4	Kimi Räikkönen	18	1m 21.586s
5	Jarno Trulli	25	1m 21.604s
6	Anthony Davidson	30	1m 21.643s
7	Juan Pablo Montoya	25	1m 21.661s
8	Fernando Alonso	25	1m 21.788s
9	David Coulthard	17	1m 21.795s
10	Ralf Schumacher	24	1m 22.057s
11	Rubens Barrichello	20	1m 22.096s
12	Mark Webber	28	1m 22.167s
13	Olivier Panis	22	1m 22.768s
14	Cristiano da Matta	23	1m 22.780s
15	Felipe Massa	27	1m 23.043s
16	Christian Klien	16	1m 23.211s
17	Giancarlo Fisichella	28	1m 23.335s
18	Björn Wirdheim	25	1m 23.470s
19	Ricardo Zonta	20	1m 23.500s
20	Nick Heidfeld	15	1m 23.866s
21	Giorgio Pantano	19	1m 24.091s
22	Gianmaria Bruni	16	1m 25.653s
23	Zsolt Baumgartner	10	1m 25.760s
24	Bas Leinders	22	1m 27.025s

PRACTICE 3 (SATURDAY)

Sunny and bright (track 38°C, air 23°C)

Pos.	Driver	Laps	Time
1	Michael Schumacher		1m 20.856s
2	Jenson Button		1m 21.165s
3	Rubens Barrichello		1m 21.583s
4	Juan Pablo Montoya		1m 21.764s
5	Ralf Schumacher		1m 21.864s
6	Fernando Alonso		1m 21.954s
7	Takuma Sato		1m 22.013s
8	David Coulthard		1m 22.051s
9	Kimi Räikkönen		1m 22.164s
10	Jarno Trulli		1m 22.462s
11	Mark Webber		1m 22.707s
12	Olivier Panis		1m 22.885s
13	Giancarlo Fisichella		1m 22.991s
14	Felipe Massa		1m 23.105s
15	Cristiano da Matta		1m 23.482s
16	Giorgio Pantano		1m 24.255s
17	Nick Heidfeld		1m 24.907s
18	Gianmaria Bruni		1m 26.783s
19	Zsolt Baumgartner		1m 27.539s
20	Christian Klien		No time

PRACTICE 4 (SATURDAY)

Sunny and bright (track 39°C, air 24°C)

Pos.	Driver	Laps	Time
1	Michael Schumacher	7	1m 20.125s
2	Jenson Button	15	1m 20.150s
3	Fernando Alonso	13	1m 20.844s
4	David Coulthard	10	1m 20.844s
5	Juan Pablo Montoya	7	1m 20.975s
6	Rubens Barrichello	10	1m 20.996s
7	Takuma Sato	14	1m 21.159s
8	Jarno Trulli	12	1m 21.198s
9	Kimi Räikkönen	14	1m 21.199s
10	Cristiano da Matta	13	1m 21.257s
11	Ralf Schumacher	10	1m 21.271s
12	Olivier Panis	12	1m 21.296s
13	Mark Webber	16	1m 21.393s
14	Giancarlo Fisichella	10	1m 22.022s
15	Felipe Massa	8	1m 22.077s
16	Christian Klien	8	1m 23.222s
17	Nick Heidfeld	13	1m 23.551s
18	Giorgio Pantano	7	1m 24.736s
19	Gianmaria Bruni	10	1m 26.199s
20	Zsolt Baumgartner	13	1m 27.451s

9th: JARNO TRULLI Renault

7th: TAKUMA SATO BAR-Honda

5th: RALF SCHUMACHER Williams-BMW

3rd: JUAN PABLO MONTOYA Williams-BMW

Pole: JENSON BUTTON BAR-Honda

10th: CRISTIANO DA MATTA Toyota

8th: MARK WEBBER Jaguar-Cosworth

6th: FERNANDO ALONSO Renault

4th: RUBENS BARRICHELLO Ferrari

2nd: MICHAEL SCHUMACHER Ferrari

49	50	51	52	53	54	55	56	57	58	59	60	61	62	
1	1	1	1	1	1	1	1	1	1	1	1	1	1	1
9	9	9	9	9	9	9	9	9	9	9	9	9	9	2
3	3	3	3	3	3	3	3	3	3	3	3	3	3	3
4	8	8	8	8	8	8	8	8	8	8	8	8	8	4
8	7	7	7	7	7	7	7	7	7	7	7	7	7	5
7	2	2	2	2	2	2	2	2	2	2	2	2	2	6
2	4	4	4	4	4	4	4	4	4	4	4	4	4	7
10	10	10	10	10	10	10	10	6	6	6	6	6	6	8
6	6	6	6	6	6	6	6	11	11	11	11	11		
11	11	11	11	11	11	11	11	12	12	12	12	12		
12	12	12	12	12	12	12	12	17	17	17	17	17		
17	17	17	17	17	17	17	17	5	5	5	5	5		
5	5	5	5	5	5	5	14	14	14	14	14			
14	14	14	14	14	14	14	15	15	15	15				
15	15	15	15	15	15	15	21	21						
21	21	21	21	21	21	21	21							

POINTS: DRIVERS

1	Michael Schumacher	40
2	Rubens Barrichello	24
3	Jenson Button	23
4	Juan Pablo Montoya	18
5	Fernando Alonso	16
6	Jarno Trulli	15
7	Ralf Schumacher	9
8 =	Takuma Sato	4
8 =	David Coulthard	4
10 =	Felipe Massa	1
10 =	Mark Webber	1
10 =	Kimi Räikkönen	1

POINTS: CONSTRUCTORS

1	Ferrari	64
2	Renault	31
3 =	BAR	27
3 =	Williams	27
5	McLaren	5
6 =	Sauber	1
6 =	Jaguar	1

Photograph: Darren Heath

FIA F1 WORLD CHAMPIONSHIP • ROUND 5

SPANISH GP
BARCELONA

Far left: Spanish hopes were high for local hero Fernando Alonso, but it was his teammate, Jarno Trulli (left), who bagged the champagne after leading at the start and eventually finishing third.

Below: A pensive Ron Dennis; disappointed with McLaren results in the season so far, but confident of better things to come.

Bottom: Five out of five for Schumacher.

Bottom left: Legends both: Emerson Fittipaldi and Michael Schumacher, winners of the Spanish Grand Prix.
Photographs: Darren Heath

DIARY

Ralf Schumacher reaches a deal to drive for Toyota in 2005, although no official word is yet forthcoming from the Japanese car maker.

Manchester unveils tentative plans to promote a Champ Car street race in 2005.

Alain Prost tests the Maserati MC12 supercar GT racer at Fiorano.

Former Arrows F1 team chief Tom Walkinshaw faces a £6.5 million bill following a High Court judgment relating to a £13 million overdraft facility granted by investment bank Morgan Grenfell, which held shares in the team.

CATALUNYA QUALIFYING

Jenson Button arrived in Barcelona aiming to sustain the momentum created by his brilliant pole position at Imola a fortnight earlier. On the face of it, one would have expected his BAR-Honda 006 to be the best of the Michelin runners around the Circuit de Catalunya, but in fact his challenge would be blunted by a simple driving error.

Slamming through the fast, uphill fifth-gear Turn Nine, the BAR's rear end momentarily skipped out of line, either due to a sudden gust of wind or Jenson trying to squeeze a tad too much from his chassis. This launched him on a wild ride over the kerb into the dusty outfield. At a stroke, his hopes for the weekend were wiped out and he had to be content with a 1m 17.575s best, a massive 2.553s away from Michael Schumacher's pole winning effort.

'My lap was very disappointing,' shrugged Button. 'It was going quite well early in the weekend, although I have been struggling a little bit with the set-up round here. Conditions changed a lot since pre-qualifying, as there's a lot more wind now, which is one of the reasons why I ended up having an excursion.'

Predictably, Michael Schumacher had no such problems as he breezed to pole position, his stunning 1m 15.022s best placing him 0.617s ahead of Juan Pablo Montoya's Williams FW26, which joined the world champion's Ferrari on the front row.

'Toward the end of the lap, I knew I had a very good first and second sector time, so in the final sector I made sure I was safe,' said Michael, 'especially as it is very easy to make a mistake at Turn Ten. But in the end, it was a very, very good lap. It was also a bit of a surprise, to be honest, but I am happy to take pole.'

For his part, Montoya was quick in pre-qualifying, but then opted to make a small front wing adjustment, which left him battling a touch too much oversteer. Despite this, he managed second-quickest time, but team-mate Ralf Schumacher (1m 16.293s) lost time in the second sector of the lap, ending up sixth.

Making up for Button's disappointment, Takuma Sato posted third-fastest time on 1m 15.809s, to line up ahead of Jarno Trulli's Renault R24 (1m 16.144s).

'It wasn't a perfect lap,' confessed the delighted Japanese driver. 'The first sector was good, then the car was a little twitchy in the second sector and I probably lost a little time in the last sector as a result.'

Trulli was well satisfied with his best qualifying performance so far of the season, but Fernando Alonso appeared to fall prey to the gusting crosswinds that had caught out Button, lining up the second Renault in eighth place on 1m 16.422s. Separating the two Renaults were Rubens Barrichello's fuel-heavy Ferrari (1m 16.272s), Ralf Schumacher's Williams and Olivier Panis's Toyota (1m 16.313s). Panis was in upbeat mood after a strong showing that contrasted dramatically with team-mate Cristiano da Matta's demeanour. The Brazilian had over-driven in a bid to compensate for excessive understeer and wound up in 11th place as a result.

Ninth on the grid on 1m 16.514s, Mark Webber was left mentally kicking himself after throwing away an even better qualifying position following a frustrating unforced error. 'My first two sectors were clean and I was going well until, unfortunately, I made a minor error in the final section and I lost a few tenths. But I'm confident that the car is in good shape and we should be challenging for points tomorrow.' By contrast, Christian Klien was a disappointed 16th after spinning into the gravel in Friday free practice.

McLaren's two revised-spec Mercedes V10s were scheduled to appear for the race, but only Kimi Räikkönen's was available, the sister unit earmarked for Coulthard having failed on the dyno. The Finn suffered a close call when his engine blew out all of its coolant prior to qualifying, but the problem was corrected without recourse to an engine change.

Subsequently, Räikkönen locked his brakes and ran wide in the final sector of the lap to end up 13th on 1m 17.445s, three places behind an equally disappointed Coulthard (1m 16.636s). The Scot had compensated for the missing 20bhp due to the lack of the upgraded engine by trimming his wings to the minimum settings he could get away with.

The Sauber drivers were running heavy fuel loads in line with a two-stop strategy, Giancarlo Fisichella (1m 17.444s) ending up 12th, while Felipe Massa (1m 17.866s) had to be content with 17th after making a mistake in Turn Seven. 'I lost everything there,' he shrugged. 'It was my fault completely.'

Jordan's Nick Heidfeld (1m 17.802s) and Giorgio Pantano (1m 20.607s) finished 15th and 19th, while the two Minardis of Gianmaria Bruni and Zsolt Baumgartner occupied 18th and 20th spots on the grid.

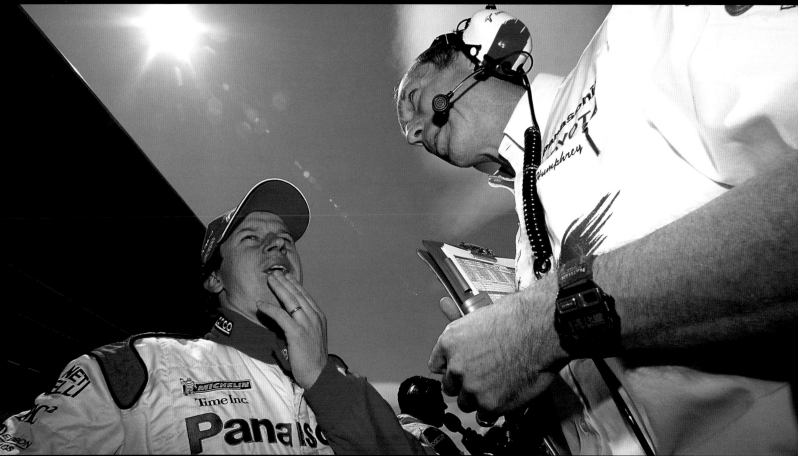

AS the starting lights went out at the Circuit de Catalunya, Michael Schumacher, one eye on his mirror, saw Jarno Trulli coming. From fourth place on the starting grid, the Italian deftly steered his Renault R24 between Michael's Ferrari and Juan Pablo Montoya's Williams FW26 to surge into an immediate lead. Schumacher conceded that, for a split second, he'd considered whether he should cut across in front of his light blue rival, but immediately realised that Trulli had made the perfect getaway and was practically alongside his Ferrari before he could muster a defensive reaction.

By the end of the opening lap, Trulli was 0.5s ahead of Schumacher, with Takuma Sato's BAR-Honda a brilliant third from the same row on the starting grid. Montoya, having been slightly wrong-footed by the speed of the Japanese driver's start, was back in fourth place ahead of Rubens Barrichello in the other Ferrari F2004 and local hero Fernando Alonso in the Renault R24.

'It was a very interesting start, but not what I was expecting,' said Schumacher later in the day. 'I did think about trying to close the door a bit on Trulli, but I did not feel it was fair and let him do what we was doing. Then, a couple of times, I did think about passing him, but it was too tight, so I opted to wait for the pit stops and let the strategy do the work.'

A critical indictment of the current state of F1, where a clever race strategy can yield a strong result without the need to force a risky overtaking manoeuvre on the circuit? Or a straightforward and uncomplicated assertion of Schumacher's and the Ferrari team's stunning ability? Either way, the German driver was merely stating the obvious.

At the end of lap nine, Trulli duly arrived in the pit lane for his first refuelling stop, the Renault R24 remaining stationary for just 5.9s before accelerating back into the fray. That left Schumacher leading from Sato, but the world champion was in for a 6.7s stop on lap ten, while the Japanese driver stopped next time around.

After that opening flurry of pit-lane activity, Rubens Barrichello's Ferrari – running with a heavier fuel load on a two-stop strategy – was propelled to the head of the pack, leading from Schumacher, Trulli, Giancarlo Fisichella's Sauber C23, which was also on a two-stopper, Sato, Massa, Alonso and Montoya, the Colombian having made his first stop at the same time as Trulli.

At the end of lap 17, Barrichello pitted for the first time, as did Fisichella from fifth place. This had the effect of restoring the status quo at the front of the pack, Rubens slipping back into the queue in third place. By lap 21, Michael Schumacher was 8.0s ahead of Trulli, and when the Renault driver made his second refuelling stop (5.3s) on lap 23, Michael piled on the pressure and stayed out until lap 25 before making his own second stop (8.0s). After that, he retained the lead ahead of Barrichello, with Trulli third after the running order settled down following Sato's second stop on lap 26.

'I had a great race after a difficult start,' Barrichello explained later. 'I was obviously on a two-stop strategy, which explains why I was happy to be fifth in qualifying with such a heavy fuel load. Even so, I was able to keep up a good pace in the early stages. We expected BAR to be quick, so there were two options on Saturday: to try and get pole or try something else. I was so frustrated with being stuck in traffic in the San Marino Grand Prix that I decided to gamble.' It worked out well for the Brazilian.

A shadow was briefly cast over Michael Schumacher's race prospects when his Ferrari's V10 engine began to sound a little ragged shortly before the half-distance mark. 'My [strategic] concern was where I would come out after the pit stops, but as almost everybody ran short first stints so it was not a problem,' he said. 'We first became aware of the broken exhaust just after the first stop.

'Ross [Brawn] came on the radio and said that there wasn't very much they could do, so we just hoped that it lasted. So I just did what I could to conserve it and just drove it home. I pre-

Above: Jarno Trulli storms his Renault R24 into a short-lived lead at the start, with Michael Schumacher heading the chase.

Left: Toyota driver Olivier Panis in debate with his engineer, Humphrey Corbett.
Photographs: Darren Heath

MOSLEY GETS TOUGH ON COST CUTTING

During the run-up to the Spanish Grand Prix, the FIA met with the F1 team principals in Monte Carlo in a bid to agree a radical package of technical changes designed to reduce expenditure and rein-in car performance on grounds of safety. Faced with the prospect of the sport's governing body imposing the rules – which include downsizing engines from 3-litre V10s to 2.4-litre V8s, banning traction control, having one tyre supplier and standardising some technical components – in 2008, the teams signalled their willingness to adopt most of the package in 2006.

The only significant sticking point was the proposal to change the engine rules. Both BMW and Mercedes argued persuasively that continuing the development of the current V10s to the point where they would last for two races was a cheaper option than developing new, smaller-capacity V8s.

Mosley gave them a month to demonstrate how they could produce a 50-per-cent saving in engine bills for the top seven works teams. He characterised the meeting as an upbeat and positive affair, claiming, 'I think really I couldn't have asked for more from the meeting.' After sober reflection, however, the teams were more cautious in their assessment. In particular, both David Richards (BAR) and Flavio Briatore (Renault) warned that there was still a lot to be decided and that a broad view had to prevail to ensure a healthy future for the sport.

'There's not a lot to be decided about what will happen in 2008,' admitted Richards. 'It's how we bring it forward from that date, that's the critical thing. That naturally gets embroiled in vested interests and the politics of the sport, and hopefully people will look at the bigger picture and take a view on things, that maybe the good health of F1 should be put ahead of their own personal interests.'

Briatore added, 'I don't think people care whether there is a 2.4-litre engine or a 3-litre engine in the cars. They want to watch a race. Our product is so expensive and we never take our customers into consideration. I mean, it is very much an engineering business, and we forget there are millions of people watching us. We forget the marketing issues, we forget the commercial issues. All these things have to be addressed.'

served the engine as much as I could, but there is only so much you can do.'

Michael's concern wasn't a possible engine failure, but the prospect of overheating rear suspension components within the tightly packaged rear bodywork, one of which had collapsed in similar circumstances at Monaco in 2000, causing his retirement. With sensors on the rear suspension monitoring any worrying heat build-up, his priority was to drive as normally as possible; backing off unduly might have aggravated the possibility of overheating, not reduced it.

As it was, Michael managed the tricky situation to excellent effect, crossing the finishing line 13.29s ahead of Barrichello who, in turn, was 19s in front of the marauding Renault R24s, which had both performed so strongly throughout the 66-lap chase.

Trulli drove brilliantly to finish third ahead of team-mate Fernando Alonso, the Spaniard's presence guaranteeing a capacity 100,000-strong crowd at the Circuit de Catalunya.

'I had a very good start,' said Trulli. 'It was right on the limit of a jump start, but it worked out very well. I was doing my pace at the beginning, quite good. The car was reacting well and I was keeping Michael behind me. He only took me when we pitted because he was quicker than me, as simple as that.'

Alonso added, 'Third and fourth is a great result for the team, particularly in terms of the championship, because we finished ahead of our main rivals. From my point of view, the race went well. I was stuck in the pack at the start, and it took the first two stints for me to get a clear track so I could begin running at my true pace. Everything went well from then on, although the car did not have very good grip today. Third and fourth is the best the team could have hoped for.'

Fifth place fell to Takuma Sato's BAR-Honda 006 after the best ever qualifying effort from a Japanese driver – he lined up third behind Schumacher and Juan Pablo Montoya's Williams-BMW. The rival Michael feared most in Spain, Jenson Button in the other BAR, was unexpectedly put out of the picture when the Brit ran wide on to the grass during qualifying, ending up 14th on the grid.

'I made a good start and it was very exciting to be so close to the front of the grid,' reflected Sato. 'Obviously, I am a little disappointed that we started from third and finished fifth, but both Jenson and I struggled with consistency [of handling] after each tyre change. It was a tough race, though.'

David Richards, the BAR team principal, added, 'Taku drove well this afternoon and is now gaining some real momentum, which I now see growing race by race.'

As for Button, he had battled back to eighth at the flag, setting the second-fastest race lap on his way to claiming a single championship point. 'I didn't get a very good start, and then I was a little disappointed with the first stint, as it just wasn't possible to over-

take,' he said. 'I struggled, to be honest. I lost so much time in the high-speed corners because when you're so close to the other cars, you lose a lot of downforce.'

Montoya faded after an early spurt, overheating brakes caused by the use of smaller cooling ducts eventually forcing him out, while team-mate Ralf Schumacher grappled with the problem and managed to squeeze home sixth.

'I knew this race would be difficult,' said Montoya. 'It's been like this every year, so we know this track is hard on the car. We did a good job yesterday in qualifying by putting the car on the front row of the grid, but then I lost two positions at the start.

'I started having brake problems in the very first part of the race, with the pedal going very long, but they then seemed to come back after the first pit stop, so I thought everything was okay. However, when Fisichella, who was ahead of me, pitted, and I was pushing hard to gain an advantage, the brakes stopped working again, so I had to retire.'

Behind Ralf Schumacher, Fisichella maximised the potential of his two-stop strategy to bring the Sauber C23 home seventh, adding another couple of points to the Hinwil team's total. 'My car was very good all the way through,' he enthused. 'The only problem I had was in lapped traffic, when I lost some time.'

Felipe Massa thought he could have kept up with his team-mate had it not been for flat-spotting his front tyres during his first stint. 'That gave me a lot of vibration and understeer,' he said. 'I could see Giancarlo, but he was going away from me. I changed the front wings [settings] slightly in my first stop and, on fresh rubber, the car was fine for the rest of the race. It felt great to beat the McLarens, and without that initial problem, I really think I could have been in the points.'

The two McLaren-Mercs ran reliably, which in itself was something of a minor step forward. Coulthard and Räikkönen wound up tenth and 11th, lapped by the winner, although they were not with-

out their problems. The Scot overshot slightly at his first fuel stop, and there was a slight problem with the refuelling nozzle during his second and third stops, while Räikkönen was delayed on his third stop when it was found necessary to top up his Mercedes V10's pneumatic valve gear reservoir, as the air pressure had dropped slightly.

'We just couldn't do better today, as it was clear we were not quick enough,' said Kimi. 'There is no point in me getting frustrated, as there is nothing I can do to change the situation, and I know the team is as motivated and focused as ever to make progress.' For the Finn and his team-mate, the long promised McLaren MP4/19B simply couldn't arrive soon enough.

In the Jaguar garage, there was a similar mood of acute disappointment after Mark Webber struggled home a lapped 12th, the marque's sole survivor after Christian Klien's retirement with 43 laps under his belt due to a throttle control problem.

'I suffered a slow start,' said Webber, 'which meant that by the first corner, I had already lost a few places. I tried to climb back up the grid, but during my first pit stop, we had a problem getting the left rear tyre changed, as I dropped the clutch too early. Subsequently, I just struggled with a lack of rear grip. It wasn't the race I'd hoped for.'

Webber at least managed to finish ahead of Cristiano da Matta in the only surviving Toyota TF104. The Brazilian driver reported that his car simply wasn't quick enough. Team-mate Olivier Panis collected a drive-through penalty for speeding in the pit lane before being stranded out on the circuit following a complete loss of hydraulic pressure.

Neither of the Jordans nor Minardis made the finish either, a stark reminder that funding levels and technical reliability are inextricably entwined in front-line F1. And that breaking Ferrari's cycle of domination would become progressively more difficult as the 2004 season unfolded in a seemingly unchallengeable scarlet blur.

Above: Rubens Barrichello did well on a two-stop strategy, which helped vault his Ferrari F2004 from fifth on the grid to second at the chequered flag.

Left: Ralf Schumacher struggled to take sixth place in his Williams-BMW FW26 after a careful run conserving his car's fading brakes.

Top left: FIA President Max Mosley signalled that the governing body intended to get even tougher on cost cutting during a meeting with the team principals in Monaco prior to the Spanish Grand Prix.
Photographs: Darren Heath

FIA F1 WORLD CHAMPIONSHIP • ROUND 5

GRAN PREMIO MARLBORO DE ESPAÑA

CATALUNYA 7–9 MAY 2004

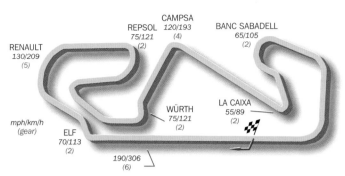

CATALUNYA CIRCUIT – BARCELONA

CAMPSA 120/193 (4)
REPSOL 75/121 (2)
BANC SABADELL 65/105 (2)
RENAULT 130/209 (5)
WÜRTH 75/121 (2)
LA CAIXA 55/89 (2)
mph/km/h (gear)
ELF 70/113 (2)
190/306 (6)

CIRCUIT LENGTH: 2.875 miles/4.627 km

RACE DISTANCE: 66 laps, 189.677 miles/305.256 km **RACE WEATHER:** Sunny (track 28–33°C, air 21–23°C)

Pos.	Driver	Nat.	No.	Entrant	Car/Engine	Tyres	Laps	Time/Retirement	Speed (mph/km/h)	Gap to leader	Fastest race lap	
1	Michael Schumacher	D	1	Scuderia Ferrari Marlboro	Ferrari F2004-052 V10	B	66	1h 27m 32.841s	129.994/209.205		1m 17.450s	12
2	Rubens Barrichello	BR	2	Scuderia Ferrari Marlboro	Ferrari F2004-052 V10	B	66	1h 27m 46.131s	129.666/208.677	+13.290s	1m 17.887s	16
3	Jarno Trulli	I	7	Mild Seven Renault F1 Team	Renault R24-RS4 V10	M	66	1h 28m 05.135s	129.199/207.926	+32.294s	1m 18.178s	12
4	Fernando Alonso	E	8	Mild Seven Renault F1 Team	Renault R24-RS4 V10	M	66	1h 28m 05.793s	129.183/207.900	+32.952s	1m 17.556s	27
5	Takuma Sato	J	10	Lucky Strike BAR Honda	BAR 006-Honda RA004E V10	M	66	1h 28m 15.168s	128.954/207.532	+42.327s	1m 17.678s	47
6	Ralf Schumacher	D	4	BMW WilliamsF1 Team	Williams FW26-BMW P84 V10	M	66	1h 28m 46.645s	128.192/206.306	+73.804s	1m 18.548s	27
7	Giancarlo Fisichella	I	11	Sauber Petronas	Sauber C23-Petronas 04 V10	B	66	1h 28m 49.949s	128.113/206.178	+77.108s	1m 19.062s	37
8	Jenson Button	GB	9	Lucky Strike BAR Honda	BAR 006-Honda RA004E V10	M	65			+1 lap	1m 17.495s	46
9	Felipe Massa	BR	12	Sauber Petronas	Sauber C23-Petronas 04 V10	B	65			+1 lap	1m 18.819s	43
10	David Coulthard	GB	5	West McLaren Mercedes	McLaren MP4/19-Mercedes F0110P V10	M	65			+1 lap	1m 19.175s	38
11	Kimi Räikkönen	FIN	6	West McLaren Mercedes	McLaren MP4/19-Mercedes F0110P V10	M	65			+1 lap	1m 18.842s	48
12	Mark Webber	AUS	14	Jaguar Racing	Jaguar R5-Cosworth CR6 V10	M	65			+1 lap	1m 18.617s	11
13	Cristiano da Matta	BR	16	Panasonic Toyota Racing	Toyota TF104-RVX04 V10	M	65			+1 lap	1m 19.112s	29
	Giorgio Pantano	I	19	Jordan Ford	Jordan EJ-14-Cosworth RS V10	B	51	Hydraulics			1m 19.896s	27
	Juan Pablo Montoya	COL	3	BMW WilliamsF1 Team	Williams FW26-BMW P84 V10	M	46	Brakes			1m 18.262s	28
	Christian Klien	A	15	Jaguar Racing	Jaguar R5-Cosworth CR6 V10	M	43	Throttle			1m 19.142s	18
	Olivier Panis	F	17	Panasonic Toyota Racing	Toyota TF104-RVX04 V10	M	33	Hydraulics			1m 19.199s	10
	Nick Heidfeld	D	18	Jordan Ford	Jordan EJ-14-Cosworth RS V10	B	33	Hydraulics			1m 18.971s	25
	Gianmaria Bruni	I	20	European Minardi Cosworth	Minardi PS04B-Cosworth CR3 V10	B	31	Brakes/spin			1m 22.323s	3
	Zsolt Baumgartner	H	21	European Minardi Cosworth	Minardi PS04B-Cosworth CR3 V10	B	17	Spin			1m 23.390s	8

Fastest lap: Michael Schumacher, on lap 12, 1m 17.450s, 133.638 mph/215.070 km/h (record for modified track layout).

Previous lap record: Rubens Barrichello (Ferrari F2003-GA-051 V10), 1m 20.143s, 132.023 mph/212.470 km/h (2003).

19th: GIORGIO PANTANO Jordan-Cosworth

17th: FELIPE MASSA Sauber-Petronas

15th: NICK HEIDFELD Jordan-Cosworth

13th: KIMI RÄIKKÖNEN McLaren-Mercedes

11th: CRISTIANO DA MATTA Toyota

20th: ZSOLT BAUMGARTNER Minardi-Cosworth

18th: GIANMARIA BRUNI Minardi-Cosworth

16th: CHRISTIAN KLIEN Jaguar-Cosworth

14th: JENSON BUTTON BAR-Honda

12th: GIANCARLO FISICHELLA Sauber-Petronas

Grid order	1	2	3	4	5	6	7	8	9	10	11	12	13	14	15	16	17	18	19	20	21	22	23	24	25	26	27	28	29	30	31	32	33	34	35	36	37	38	39	40	41	42	43	44	45	46	47	48	49	50
1 M. SCHUMACHER	7	7	7	7	7	7	7	1	1	2	2	2	2	2	2	1	1	1	1	1	1	1	1	1	1	1	1	1	1	1	1	1	1	1	1	1	1	1	1	1	1	1	1	1	1	1	1	1	1	1
3 MONTOYA	1	1	1	1	1	1	1	7	10	10	1	1	1	1	1	7	7	7	7	7	7	2	2	2	2	2	2	2	2	2	2	2	2	2	2	2	2	10	2	2	2	2	2							
10 SATO	10	10	10	10	10	10	10	10	2	1	7	7	7	7	7	2	2	2	2	2	10	10	10	7	7	7	7	7	7	7	7	7	7	7	7	8	10	2	10	7	7	7	7							
7 TRULLI	3	3	3	3	3	3	3	2	7	7	11	11	11	11	11	10	10	10	10	10	8	8	8	8	8	8	8	8	8	8	8	8	8	10	7	7	8	8	8	10	10	10	10							
2 BARRICHELLO	2	2	2	2	2	2	2	3	5	11	10	10	10	10	11	8	8	8	8	7	3	10	10	10	10	10	10	10	10	10	10	10	10	7	8	10	10	10	10											
4 R. SCHUMACHER	8	8	8	8	8	8	8	8	5	11	12	12	8	8	8	3	3	3	3	3	11	11	11	11	11	11	11	11	11	3	3	3	3	4	11	4	4	4	4											
17 PANIS	17	17	17	17	17	17	17	5	4	8	8	12	3	3	3	4	4	4	4	4	4	11	3	3	3	3	3	3	3	3	3	3	11	4	4	9	3	4	11	11	11	11								
8 ALONSO	5	5	5	5	5	5	5	4	11	9	3	3	12	12	12	11	11	11	11	11	6	6	6	4	4	4	4	4	4	4	4	9	9	9	3	11	9	9	9											
14 WEBBER	4	4	4	4	4	4	17	9	12	15	15	15	4	4	11	17	17	17	17	17	5	9	4	12	12	12	12	12	12	12	12	12	11	11	6	12	12	12	12											
5 COULTHARD	6	6	6	6	6	6	6	6	8	17	17	4	4	15	17	17	6	6	6	6	9	4	9	12	15	9	9	9	9	9	9	9	9	11	6	6	9	9	14	14	14									
16 DA MATTA	11	11	11	11	11	11	11	14	3	4	4	17	17	6	6	5	5	5	5	5	17	5	15	9	6	5	5	5	5	5	5	5	5	6	5	12	14	12	14	14	6	6	5							
11 FISICHELLA	14	14	14	14	14	14	14	14	14	9	9	9	9	9	5	9	9	9	9	9	12	15	9	6	5	5	5	5	5	5	5	12	14	14	14	6	6	6												
6 RÄIKKÖNEN	16	16	9	9	9	9	9	9	16	17	5	5	5	5	9	9	14	14	14	14	14	16	14	5	5	15	14	14	14	14	14	14	16	16	5	16	16	16												
9 BUTTON	9	9	16	16	16	16	16	8	19	9	9	9	9	15	14	14	16	16	16	16	15	5	17	14	14	14	6	16	16	16	16	16	5	5	16	19	19	19												
18 HEIDFELD	12	12	12	12	12	12	12	12	19	6	14	14	14	14	14	16	16	12	12	12	17	14	14	17	17	16	15	15	15	15	15	15	15	15	15	19	19	19												
15 KLIEN	19	19	19	19	19	19	19	19	15	14	16	16	16	16	16	18	18	18	18	15	15	14	16	16	15	15	19	19	19	19	19	19	19	19																
12 MASSA	15	15	15	15	15	15	15	17	16	18	18	18	18	18	15	15	15	15	15	18	19	18	18	18	18	18	18																							
20 BRUNI	18	18	18	18	18	18	18	18	18	18	18	18	18	18	18	19	19	19	19	19	18	19	19	19	19	19	19	19																						
19 PANTANO	20	20	20	20	21	21	21	21	21	21	21	20	20	20	20	20	20	20	20	20	20	20	20	20																										
21 BAUMGARTNER	21	21	21	21	20	20	20	20	20	20	20	21	21	21	21																																			

Pit stop
One lap behind leader

TIME SHEETS

QUALIFYING
Warm and sunny (track 32°C, air 31°C)

Pos.	Driver	Lap time	Sector 1	Sector 2	Sector 3
1	Michael Schumacher	1m 15.022s	21.789s	29.847s	23.386s
2	Juan Pablo Montoya	1m 15.639s	22.135s	29.972s	23.532s
3	Takuma Sato	1m 15.809s	21.869s	30.222s	23.718s
4	Jarno Trulli	1m 16.144s	22.257s	30.263s	23.624s
5	Rubens Barrichello	1m 16.272s	22.282s	30.432s	23.558s
6	Ralf Schumacher	1m 16.293s	22.187s	30.405s	23.701s
7	Olivier Panis	1m 16.313s	22.317s	30.274s	23.722s
8	Fernando Alonso	1m 16.422s	22.371s	30.459s	23.592s
9	Mark Webber	1m 16.514s	22.265s	30.359s	23.890s
10	David Coulthard	1m 16.636s	22.297s	30.673s	23.666s
11	Cristiano da Matta	1m 17.038s	22.584s	30.670s	23.784s
12	Giancarlo Fisichella	1m 17.444s	22.690s	30.835s	23.919s
13	Kimi Räikkönen	1m 17.445s	22.258s	30.796s	24.118s
14	Jenson Button	1m 17.575s	21.853s	31.666s	24.056s
15	Nick Heidfeld	1m 17.802s	22.565s	31.168s	24.069s
16	Christian Klien	1m 17.812s	22.847s	30.977s	23.988s
17	Felipe Massa	1m 17.866s	22.448s	31.377s	23.894s
18	Gianmaria Bruni	1m 19.817s	23.408s	31.922s	24.487s
19	Giorgio Pantano	1m 20.607s	22.611s	33.678s	24.318s
20	Zsolt Baumgartner	1m 21.470s	24.070s	32.396s	25.004s

CHASSIS LOG BOOK

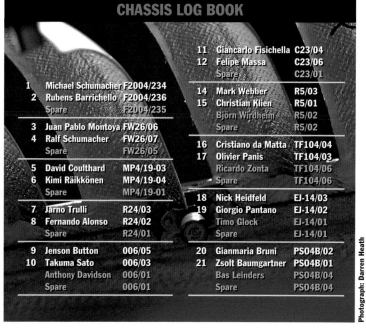

1	Michael Schumacher	F2004/234
2	Rubens Barrichello	F2004/236
	Spare	F2004/235
3	Juan Pablo Montoya	FW26/06
4	Ralf Schumacher	FW26/07
	Spare	FW26/05
5	David Coulthard	MP4/19-03
6	Kimi Räikkönen	MP4/19-04
	Spare	MP4/19-01
7	Jarno Trulli	R24/03
8	Fernando Alonso	R24/02
	Spare	R24/01
9	Jenson Button	006/05
10	Takuma Sato	006/03
	Anthony Davidson	006/01
	Spare	006/01
11	Giancarlo Fisichella	C23/04
12	Felipe Massa	C23/06
	Spare	C23/01
14	Mark Webber	R5/03
15	Christian Klien	R5/01
	Björn Wirdheim	R5/02
	Spare	R5/02
16	Cristiano da Matta	TF104/04
17	Olivier Panis	TF104/03
	Ricardo Zonta	TF104/06
	Spare	TF104/06
18	Nick Heidfeld	EJ-14/03
19	Giorgio Pantano	EJ-14/02
	Timo Glock	EJ-14/01
	Spare	EJ-14/01
20	Gianmaria Bruni	PS04B/02
21	Zsolt Baumgartner	PS04B/01
	Bas Leinders	PS04B/04
	Spare	PS04B/04

Photograph: Darren Heath

PRACTICE 1 (FRIDAY)
Light breeze, cloudy/sunny (track 53–27°C, air 16–20°C)

Pos.	Driver	Laps	Time
1	Michael Schumacher	8	1m 15.658s
2	Rubens Barrichello	8	1m 16.033s
3	Anthony Davidson	25	1m 16.616s
4	Ricardo Zonta	26	1m 16.639s
5	Jenson Button	6	1m 17.060s
6	Ralf Schumacher	12	1m 17.165s
7	Fernando Alonso	11	1m 17.429s
8	Takuma Sato	6	1m 17.481s
9	Olivier Panis	6	1m 17.489s
10	Kimi Räikkönen	5	1m 17.563s
11	Juan Pablo Montoya	10	1m 17.635s
12	Mark Webber	11	1m 17.763s
13	David Coulthard	7	1m 17.973s
14	Jarno Trulli	16	1m 18.341s
15	Cristiano da Matta	12	1m 18.362s
16	Björn Wirdheim	20	1m 18.603s
17	Christian Klien	14	1m 18.615s
18	Timo Glock	23	1m 18.655s
19	Felipe Massa	11	1m 18.760s
20	Giancarlo Fisichella	12	1m 18.886s
21	Nick Heidfeld	16	1m 19.198s
22	Giorgio Pantano	14	1m 19.925s
23	Gianmaria Bruni	16	1m 20.858s
24	Bas Leinders	21	1m 21.053s
25	Zsolt Baumgartner	17	1m 21.535s

PRACTICE 2 (FRIDAY)
Cloudy/light rain/sunny (track 33–27°C, air 21–19°C)

Pos.	Driver	Laps	Time
1	Jenson Button	19	1m 15.935s
2	Anthony Davidson	34	1m 16.188s
3	Ricardo Zonta	37	1m 16.360s
4	Ralf Schumacher	25	1m 16.433s
5	Fernando Alonso	20	1m 16.534s
6	Rubens Barrichello	28	1m 16.698s
7	Michael Schumacher	25	1m 16.729s
8	Jarno Trulli	20	1m 16.734s
9	Kimi Räikkönen	17	1m 16.798s
10	Cristiano da Matta	24	1m 16.833s
11	Olivier Panis	23	1m 16.925s
12	Juan Pablo Montoya	27	1m 17.067s
13	David Coulthard	16	1m 17.069s
14	Mark Webber	31	1m 17.178s
15	Timo Glock	31	1m 17.608s
16	Björn Wirdheim	21	1m 17.676s
17	Felipe Massa	22	1m 17.906s
18	Takuma Sato	4	1m 17.970s
19	Giancarlo Fisichella	24	1m 18.001s
20	Nick Heidfeld	23	1m 18.117s
21	Giorgio Pantano	21	1m 18.726s
22	Gianmaria Bruni	17	1m 19.149s
23	Zsolt Baumgartner	15	1m 20.313s
24	Bas Leinders	31	1m 22.189s
25	Christian Klien	2	No time

PRACTICE 3 (SATURDAY)
Warm and sunny (track 32–33°C, air 19–21°C)

Pos.	Driver	Laps	Time
1	Jenson Button	10	1m 15.984s
2	Jarno Trulli	8	1m 16.015s
3	Juan Pablo Montoya	4	1m 16.048s
4	Ralf Schumacher	7	1m 16.233s
5	Michael Schumacher	8	1m 16.519s
6	Takuma Sato	11	1m 16.685s
7	Olivier Panis	6	1m 16.721s
8	Rubens Barrichello	8	1m 16.795s
9	David Coulthard	8	1m 17.106s
10	Cristiano da Matta	8	1m 17.252s
11	Giancarlo Fisichella	6	1m 17.277s
12	Fernando Alonso	4	1m 17.294s
13	Kimi Räikkönen	8	1m 17.428s
14	Felipe Massa	7	1m 17.860s
15	Nick Heidfeld	13	1m 18.643s
16	Giorgio Pantano	10	1m 19.146s
17	Christian Klien	18	1m 19.851s
18	Zsolt Baumgartner	12	1m 19.949s
19	Gianmaria Bruni	3	No time
20	Mark Webber	2	No time

PRACTICE 4 (SATURDAY)
Warm and sunny (track 34–33°C, air 22–21°C)

Pos.	Driver	Laps	Time
1	Takuma Sato	13	1m 14.8376s
2	Michael Schumacher	11	1m 15.025s
3	Juan Pablo Montoya	13	1m 15.232s
4	Jarno Trulli	15	1m 15.457s
5	Rubens Barrichello	12	1m 15.540s
6	Jenson Button	11	1m 15.627s
7	David Coulthard	13	1m 15.768s
8	Fernando Alonso	12	1m 15.874s
9	Mark Webber	24	1m 15.895s
10	Cristiano da Matta	18	1m 15.895s
11	Kimi Räikkönen	7	1m 15.983s
12	Ralf Schumacher	17	1m 16.308s
13	Christian Klien	24	1m 16.648s
14	Nick Heidfeld	12	1m 16.746s
15	Giancarlo Fisichella	12	1m 17.145s
16	Felipe Massa	6	1m 17.282s
17	Giorgio Pantano	14	1m 17.665s
18	Olivier Panis	5	1m 18.392s
19	Zsolt Baumgartner	10	1m 20.449s
20	Gianmaria Bruni	6	1m 21.005s

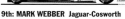

9th: MARK WEBBER Jaguar-Cosworth

7th: OLIVIER PANIS Toyota

5th: RUBENS BARRICHELLO Ferrari

3rd: TAKUMA SATO BAR-Honda

Pole: MICHAEL SCHUMACHER Ferrari

10th: DAVID COULTHARD McLaren-Mercedes

8th: FERNANDO ALONSO Renault

6th: RALF SCHUMACHER Williams-BMW

4th: JARNO TRULLI Renault

2nd: JUAN PABLO MONTOYA Williams-BMW

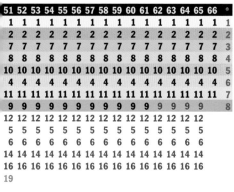

51	52	53	54	55	56	57	58	59	60	61	62	63	64	65	66	°
1	1	1	1	1	1	1	1	1	1	1	1	1	1	1	1	1
2	2	2	2	2	2	2	2	2	2	2	2	2	2	2	2	2
7	7	7	7	7	7	7	7	7	7	7	7	7	7	7	7	3
8	8	8	8	8	8	8	8	8	8	8	8	8	8	8	8	4
10	10	10	10	10	10	10	10	10	10	10	10	10	10	10	10	5
4	4	4	4	4	4	4	4	4	4	4	4	4	4	4	4	6
11	11	11	11	11	11	11	11	11	11	11	11	11	11	11	11	7
9	9	9	9	9	9	9	9	9	9	9	9	9	9	9	9	8
12	12	12	12	12	12	12	12	12	12	12	12	12	12			
5	5	5	5	5	5	5	5	5	5	5	5	5	5			
6	6	6	6	6	6	6	6	6	6	6	6	6	6			
14	14	14	14	14	14	14	14	14	14	14	14	14	14			
16	16	16	16	16	16	16	16	16	16	16	16	16	16			
19																

POINTS: DRIVERS

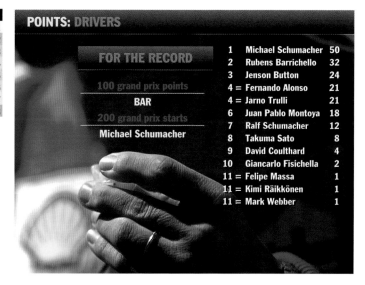

FOR THE RECORD

100 grand prix points

BAR

200 grand prix starts

Michael Schumacher

1	Michael Schumacher	50
2	Rubens Barrichello	32
3	Jenson Button	24
4 =	Fernando Alonso	21
4 =	Jarno Trulli	21
6	Juan Pablo Montoya	18
7	Ralf Schumacher	12
8	Takuma Sato	8
9	David Coulthard	4
10	Giancarlo Fisichella	2
11 =	Felipe Massa	1
11 =	Kimi Räikkönen	1
11 =	Mark Webber	1

POINTS: CONSTRUCTORS

1	Ferrari	82
2	Renault	42
3	BAR	32
4	Williams	30
5	McLaren	5
6	Sauber	3
7	Jaguar	1

Photographs: Darren Heath

Main photograph: After a dazzling lap to clinch pole position, Jarno Trulli hustles his Renault R24 through the Ste Devote at the head of the pack, taking a lead he would hold to the chequered flag.

Below: Trulli takes the applause, while Jenson Button looks suitably satisfied with a hard-won second place.
Photographs: Bryn Williams/crash.net

FIA F1 WORLD CHAMPIONSHIP • ROUND 6

MONACO GP
MONTE CARLO

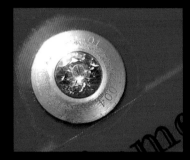

Producing a perfect qualifying lap on the streets of Monte Carlo has long been one of the greatest challenges facing any F1 driver. This is the track of tracks that takes no prisoners, but when three-times Monaco GP winner Sir Stirling Moss described Jarno Trulli's pole winning effort in the Renault R24 as 'stupefying – the perfect lap', the impish Italian from Pescara knew he'd achieved something very much out of the ordinary.

Shaving every barrier, but never putting a Michelin-shod wheel rim out of line, Trulli blitzed his way to the front of the grid with a 1m 13.985s best, edging out Ralf Schumacher's Williams-BMW FW26 by 0.360s on the time sheets. However, it would be Jenson Button's BAR-Honda 006 (1m 14.396s) that lined up alongside him on the front row, as Ralf had received a ten-place penalty following an engine change after Thursday free practice.

'It's wonderful to get my first pole here at Monaco,' said a delighted Trulli. 'It's the right place to do it from a strategy point of view and a fantastic reward for the whole team. My lap was fantastic. I wasn't particularly quick in the first sector, but the next two were nearly perfect. The car was very competitive in a race set-up, very consistent. We know that we are on the right strategy, so I am very optimistic for tomorrow.'

Trulli wound up 0.423s quicker than team-mate Fernando Alonso, who would start from third place on the grid. 'Even though I am fourth fastest today, I think I can run a very strong race,' said the Spaniard. 'The car is easy to drive here and very consistent on the long runs.'

Button was also very satisfied with his efforts. 'This is a race everyone wants to do well in, and to be in with the best chance of winning, or even [getting] on the podium, you have to be on the front row,' he enthused. 'We expected to be strong here, but I was struggling a little bit with set-up this morning. Thankfully, we were able to address this for the start of qualifying, although I was still unable to get the best out of sector three.'

Button's team-mate, Takuma Sato, had a much less positive time, winding up seventh on 1m 14.827s. 'It's a great shame, because I was on a really good lap until I had a moment in sector two coming off the kerb,' said the plucky Japanese driver. 'I wasn't able to pick up grip straight away, so I locked up into the chicane after the tunnel.'

Ralf Schumacher was understandably acutely disappointed that his potential front-row start had been parlayed into a place on row six, thanks to the application of what many in the paddock felt was a somewhat arbitrary rule that unfairly penalised a competitor for the frailty of his machinery.

'It's a bitter-sweet result,' shrugged Ralf Schumacher philosophically. ' but all in all, I am more pleased with my qualifying performance rather than depressed about the penalty. We got the best out of the car and I'm sure we'll have a competitive set-up for the race, although of course it's going to be very difficult from where we're starting on the grid.'

Ralf's disappointment may have been softened slightly by the fact that team-mate Juan Pablo Montoya lined up ninth after failing to improve on a 1m 15.039s best. 'My car felt much better in qualifying that in pre-qualifying,' said the Colombian, 'but I had a big moment at the last corner and lost some time there.'

Michael Schumacher was faced with the unfamiliar prospect of a second-row start after recording a 1m 14.516s best lap. 'The qualifying session was a little bit of a disappointment,' he acknowledged. 'That was the result of a difficult pre-qualifying, when I found the track to be very slippery. It was much worse that expected, as you can see from the fact that I was quicker in the morning. The result was that I was a long way off where we wanted to be.'

With Rubens Barrichello's Ferrari (1m 14.716s) winding up sixth on the grid, separated from Schumacher by Kimi Räikkönen's McLaren (1m 14.592s), it was an unusually modest day's work for Maranello. Räikkönen was well pleased with his efforts, but team-mate David Coulthard produced what might be termed a characteristically cautious qualifying lap to line up eighth on 1m 14.951s. 'At the last part of the swimming-pool section, things were not perfect, which lost me some momentum and consequently time,' he reflected.

Giancarlo Fisichella (1m 15.352s) did a good job to place his Sauber tenth ahead of Mark Webber's Jaguar R5 (1m 15.725s), the Australian coming back strongly after a hydraulic leak on his race chassis during the morning free practice session resulted in the team having to switch its engine into the spare car for qualifying. Team-mate Christian Klien (1m 15.919s) wound up 13th, just behind Olivier Panis's Toyota, after a troubled Thursday free practice, when an electronic glitch left him with no hydraulics, pitching him into the barrier at Massenet.

Main photograph: Cristiano da Matta scored a fine sixth place for Toyota, despite being slowed by a clutch problem and receiving a drive-through penalty for ignoring blue flags.
Photograph: Darren Heath

Inset, top: Billionaires playground: Roman Abramovic with Bernie Ecclestone.

Inset, above: Jaguar's diamond studded nose adornment went missing after Christian Klien kissed the barriers on the opening lap.
Photographs: Bryn Williams/crash.net

MICHAEL Schumacher's run of five straight grand prix wins since the start of the season came to a spectacular end at Monte Carlo, where his Ferrari F2004 was the victim of a freak collision while running in the lead at reduced speed behind the safety car on this most demanding of F1 circuits.

The world champion became involved in a controversial collision with Juan Pablo Montoya as he accelerated and braked hard to keep his tyres and brakes at working temperature while travelling at less than racing pace. By Schumacher's own admission, it had looked as though he might be hard pressed to win in Monaco, but such speculation became academic when he came three-wheeling out of the tunnel with his car's left front wheel resting on the top of its nose section.

As a result, the battle for victory came down to a tussle between two drivers each desperate to score his maiden grand prix win. And it was Jarno Trulli, in his 117th race, who finally edged out Jenson Button – in his 72nd – to score a remarkable success in a race of dramatically changing fortunes, which saw many of the fancied runners falling victim to the unyielding barriers that line the unique venue. At the chequered flag, Button's BAR-Honda 006 was 0.497s adrift in second place, Trulli having stoically fought off every challenge the British driver could muster. Both drivers had risen magnificently to the challenge of the classic track, starting side-by-side on the front row of the grid and never making a slip throughout the race.

Button had arrived in Monaco absolutely determined to make up for the slip at Barcelona that had cost him a chance of pole position and relegated him to eighth place at the end of the Spanish Grand Prix. Truth be told, there was nothing to choose between his BAR and Trulli's Renault on the sunlit streets of the principality, but the Italian just snatched pole after a scintillating lap on Saturday afternoon.

The first start was aborted when Olivier Panis stalled his Toyota TF104, which put him at the back of the grid for the restart. He promptly stalled again and had to be pushed into the pit lane, where he finally got away well behind the rest of the pack.

Trulli made a clean start to lead from pole position, with team-mate Fernando Alonso muscling ahead of Button to claim second spot going into Ste Devote. Takuma Sato produced a quite remarkable getaway, brushing wheels with Schumacher's Ferrari as he sprinted for the first turn. Out of the first corner, the Japanese driver was holding fourth place behind Button, and ahead of Räikkönen and Schumacher, but even at this early stage his BAR-Honda was trailing an ominous smoke haze, which appeared to have worsened by the time Trulli led Alonso through by 0.8s to complete the opening lap. Farther back, Christian Klien's Jaguar tangled with Zsolt Baumgartner's Minardi, dislodging the nose section on the Austrian's car, which caused it to slide into the barrier at the hairpin.

By the end of the second lap, Trulli, Alonso and Button were well ahead, Sato bottling up the rest of the field some 4.2s behind. It couldn't last, as the Japanese driver's Honda engine was clearly in trouble; eventually, it blew up spectacularly at Tabac mid-way around lap three.

Most of the runners successfully found a way through the smokescreen, but David Coulthard's McLaren slowed and was hit

from behind by Giancarlo Fisichella's Sauber C23, which flipped over the McLaren and landed upside-down on the edge of the circuit. The safety car was deployed immediately, but Fisichella scrambled out unhurt.

'I'm very disappointed today,' said the unflustered Italian with masterly understatement. 'I made a good start and was just driving gently, saving the tyres, when Sato's engine exploded. I had no vision at all.

'Barrichello and Montoya were in front, then suddenly there was a McLaren. I'm not sure why it was there, but the next thing I heard was a bang and I was upside-down. The car took all the impact and I stayed in the cockpit until all went quiet outside, just in case the accident wasn't finished.'

Honda attributed the engine failure to the delay on the grid for the restart, which just tipped its operating temperatures over the limit. Sato was extremely conciliatory about the whole episode. 'I immediately felt a loss of engine power and saw some smoke, then my race was over,' he explained. 'It was very unfortunate that the smoke caused the crash between Coulthard and Fisichella, and although there was nothing I could have done about it, I'm really pleased that no-one was hurt.'

The safety car was withdrawn at the end of lap seven and, as the pack accelerated up to race speed once more, Montoya scrambled his Williams ahead of Barrichello to take sixth place going into Ste Devote.

With 11 laps completed, only a second separated the two Renaults at the front of the field, while there was a 6.7s gap between Trulli and Michael Schumacher in fifth place. Button stopped for fuel (9.5s) on lap 18, but Trulli stayed out until lap 24 before making an 8.5s stop; Alonso came in next time around to refuel in 9.0s. This briefly elevated Michael Schumacher's Ferrari to the lead until he pitted on lap 26, getting back into the queue in third place, behind the Renault pair, but ahead of Button.

By lap 30, Trulli had edged some 2.7s ahead of Alonso, with Schumacher another 5.3s behind in third, but two laps later the whole group was covered by just 5.9s as the Ferrari ace continued chipping away. Trulli was clearly getting the upper hand in the

DIARY

Gianni Agnelli, driving force behind the Fiat empire and the man who master-minded the rescue of the cash strapped Maranello company in 1969, dies at the age of 82.

Jackie Stewart is re-elected president of the British Racing Drivers' Club, owner of Silverstone.

F1 teams confirm that they will support a demonstration run along London's Regent Street as a curtain raiser to the British Grand Prix.

The Queen formally opens the $500 million McLaren Technology Centre at Woking in the UK.

Inset, above far left: Klien skids into the barrier at the Loews hairpin on the opening lap.

Inset, above left: Giancarlo Fisichella emerged unscathed after flipping his Sauber over the back of David Coulthard's McLaren after Takuma Sato's BAR-Honda expired in a massive cloud of smoke.
Photographs: Bryn Williams/crash.net

Main photograph: Nick Heidfeld's luck changed at Monaco, as he bagged a couple of points by taking seventh place in his Jordan-Cosworth EJ-14.
Photograph: Darren Heath

Main photograph: Jenson Button drove with great determination to take second for BAR Honda, refusing to give up in the closing stages as he hurled his machine from barrier to barrier with masterly skill.

Right: Felipe Massa demonstrated great self-discipline in the Sauber C23, driving smoothly to an excellent fifth place, although lapped by the leaders.

Photographs: Darren Heath

battle with his team-mate, but Alonso's race ended on a deeply unsatisfactory note on lap 42. Unaccountably, he flew into the barrier after trying to lap Ralf Schumacher's Williams in the tunnel, getting off line on to the dust before losing control and seriously damaging his car in the impact.

'The reason for the crash is pretty simple,' said Fernando icily. 'I was lapping Ralf and he ignored the blue flags for the first seven corners. He slowed down to let me by at the entrance to the tunnel, then got back on the throttle and pushed me wide. There's no grip on the outside line and I lost control.'

Ralf, who had struggled with a transmission problem and been seriously short on gears – he had lost fifth shortly after the start – made no reference to the incident after his FW26 had ground to a halt after 69 laps when the gearbox packed up altogether.

'It's obviously a disappointing race, but these things seem to happen,' he said. 'Just after a few laps, I lost fifth gear, then sixth and seventh. By the last few laps, I had only fourth gear. I did the best I could, but it was obviously very hard to drive in those conditions, and I had to retire eventually with just a few laps to go.'

As the safety car was deployed to allow Alonso's crumpled Renault to be dragged to a place of safety, Michael Schumacher found himself at the head of the slow moving queue and became embroiled in a collision with Juan Pablo Montoya in the Williams FW26, which broke Schumacher's Ferrari's left front suspension.

Montoya survived to finish fourth. 'It was a good race for me,' grinned the Colombian. 'When you start in ninth at Monaco, you can't hope to finish fourth. With regards the contact with Michael in the tunnel, Michael braked very hard as he was warming up his brakes and I moved to the right side of the track to avoid him, but the gap narrowed and we touched.'

Michael, stony faced, walked straight to the Ferrari office after the collision, let off a bit of steam, and then composed his thoughts with characteristic discipline and diplomacy.

'Firstly, I must congratulate Jarno,' he said. 'Today, I don't think I could have really challenged him, but nevertheless when the accident with Montoya happened, I was leading the race. So the situation is that the race leader was knocked out of the race after being hit by a backmarker. I am sure there was no deliberate intention on his part, and I accept the stewards' decision that it was a racing incident.'

With the world champion out of the way, it seemed as though Button would be successful in his efforts to hunt down Trulli as they headed for the chequered flag. From 5.5s behind on lap 60, he trimmed the Renault driver's advantage to 4.1s on lap 65, 3.5s on lap 68, 1.6s on lap 71 and finally 0.5s on lap 74, with just three left to go.

From then on, it was a free-for-all between the two men, Jenson

later admitting that he had risked hitting the wall as he piled on the pressure, determined to force Trulli into making a mistake.

'It was a tough and incredibly exciting race for me, and I suspect everybody watching at home too,' said an elated Button, who could hardly have been prouder had he gained the top step of the rostrum. 'It felt great crossing the line in second place, but ever so slightly frustrating because I was only a second behind the winner. I didn't get a good start and Alonso was able to get by me, then the traffic was very bad because of the backmarkers and I was getting really frustrated, being stuck behind da Matta for three-and-a-half laps. After I broke free of them, I could really start catching Jarno. We had a great strategy today, but we just couldn't catch him.'

For Trulli, the weekend represented the realisation of a dream that had begun 117 races before, when he made his debut in a Minardi at the 1997 Australian Grand Prix. Although he had been tipped as one F1's most promising emergent stars, at one point his career seemed badly bogged down by a series of uncompetitive cars. Yet his self-belief and determination had finally paid off.

'It is hard to express what I am feeling right now,' he said. 'The team, the car, myself, we have all been improving bit by bit since the start of the season. Yesterday, I took my first pole position and said that all I needed now was a first win.

'To do so is a wonderful feeling. I believed in myself and the team, and hoped that maybe we could win here. To be honest, the way the race turned out really didn't help me: each time I built up a gap, the safety car came out, and I had quite a lot of trouble with traffic. But the car was perfect, the strategy correct and the pit stops were fantastic. I just want to thank everybody in the team, here at the track. They have worked so hard this year, and this is not just my win, it's theirs as well.'

Barrichello salvaged third for Ferrari, although he reckoned he was pretty fortunate to get his F2004 to the finish. 'Quite early in the race at Casino Square, the car hit the ground very hard, [and] I was locking the wheels and it felt as though I had a puncture,' he said. 'Then after my second pit, the car was still hitting the ground and was not turning in well. It felt like something was broken in the rear suspension, and all I could do was to drive slowly to carry the car home.'

Felipe Massa finished an excellent fifth, buoying up the Sauber team after Fisichella's spectacular early departure from the race. Da Matta was sixth ahead of Heidfeld and Panis, with Zsolt Baumgartner bringing up the rear in his Minardi. It was a bad day for Jaguar, Webber succumbing to electronic problems, while Kimi Räikkönen's McLaren was retired after yet another problem with its pneumatic valve gear. For Räikkönen and Coulthard, the upcoming MP4/19B simply couldn't be readied fast enough.

TENSION BETWEEN RALF AND WILLIAMS

Ralf Schumacher's relationship with the top BMW Williams team continued to deteriorate during the run-up to the Monaco Grand Prix, following a disappointing start to the season for the 28-year-old German driver.

The younger Schumacher made clear his belief that the Williams 'insider', who allegedly claimed that the German had been off form since the testing accident at Monza in September 2003, which caused him to miss the Italian Grand Prix, was in fact the team's technical director, Patrick Head. 'Patrick said that,' he claimed. 'If he had the kindness to show me that and explain it, then it would be good, not just spreading rumour for no reason. For me, it's nonsense and nothing else.'

He added, 'At the moment, both sides have reason to be looking at other options, to be honest. If we look at it, both drivers are not in a very good position for the championship, so it's not only the drivers. Both sides have reasons to be looking for other options.

'Both drivers expected to go for the championship this year with our package, and we aren't. But we are working hard to turn it around, and we should just be trying to get the best out of the car without blaming people for whatever reason.'

Ralf also dismissed the prospect of Jacques Villeneuve returning to the team, for which he had won the 1997 world championship.

'Certainly, Jacques would be good for Formula 1,' Schumacher said, 'but I'd just be very surprised if he came back to Williams. I remember the days when Frank and Patrick just blamed him for everything, and just hated him and wanted to fire him and said he was useless.'

FIA F1 WORLD CHAMPIONSHIP • ROUND 6

GRAND PRIX DE
MONTE CARLO
MONACO 21–23 MAY 2004

MONACO – MONTE CARLO GRAND PRIX CIRCUIT

GRAND HOTEL HAIRPIN 20/32 (1)
MIRABEAU 40/64 (2)
VIRAGE du PORTIER 45/72 (2)
STE DÉVOTE 50/81 (2)
MONTÉE de BEAU RIVAGE 160/258 (6)
CASINO
175/282 (6)
160/258 (6)
TUNNEL
NOUVELLE CHICANE 30/48 (2)
TABAC 95/153 (3)
mph/km/h (gear)
VIRAGE ANTHONY NOGHES 50/81 (2)
La RASCASSE 30/48 (2)

CIRCUIT LENGTH: 2.075 miles/3.340 km

Photograph: ???????

RACE DISTANCE: 77 laps, 159.804 miles/257.180 km **RACE WEATHER:** Dry and sunny (track 43°C, air 23°C)

Pos.	Driver	Nat.	No.	Entrant	Car/Engine	Tyres	Laps	Time/Retirement	Speed (mph/km/h)	Gap to leader	Fastest race lap
1	Jarno Trulli	I	7	Mild Seven Renault F1 Team	Renault R24-RS4 V10	M	77	1h 45m 46.601s	90.456/145.880		1m 14.870s 2
2	Jenson Button	GB	9	Lucky Strike BAR Honda	BAR 006-Honda RA004E V10	M	77	1h 45m 47.098s	90.639/145.869	+0.497s	1m 15.220s 40
3	Rubens Barrichello	BR	2	Scuderia Ferrari Marlboro	Ferrari F2004-052 V10	B	77	1h 47m 02.367s	89.576/144.159	+75.766s	1m 15.763s 16
4	Juan Pablo Montoya	COL	3	BMW WilliamsF1 Team	Williams FW26-BMW P84 V10	M	76			+1 lap	1m 15.395s 41
5	Felipe Massa	BR	12	Sauber Petronas	Sauber C23-Petronas 04 V10	B	76			+1 lap	1m 17.151s 23
6	Cristiano da Matta	BR	16	Panasonic Toyota Racing	Toyota TF104-RVX04 V10	M	76			+1 lap	1m 16.232s 22
7	Nick Heidfeld	D	18	Jordan Ford	Jordan EJ-14-Cosworth RS V10	B	75			+2 laps	1m 18.262s 35
8	Olivier Panis	F	17	Panasonic Toyota Racing	Toyota TF104-RVX04 V10	M	74			+3 laps	1m 16.494s 57
9	Zsolt Baumgartner	H	21	European Minardi Cosworth	Minardi PS04B-Cosworth CR3 V10	B	71			+6 laps	1m 21.886s 2
10	Ralf Schumacher	D	4	BMW WilliamsF1 Team	Williams FW26-BMW P84 V10	M	69	Engine		DNF	1m 17.588s 18
	Michael Schumacher	D	1	Scuderia Ferrari Marlboro	Ferrari F2004-052 V10	B	45	Accident			1m 14.439s 23
	Fernando Alonso	E	8	Mild Seven Renault F1 Team	Renault R24-RS4 V10	M	41	Accident			1m 15.226s 23
	Kimi Räikkönen	FIN	6	West McLaren Mercedes	McLaren MP4/19-Mercedes F0110P V10	M	27	Engine pneumatics			1m 16.203s 15
	Gianmaria Bruni	I	20	European Minardi Cosworth	Minardi PS04B-Cosworth CR3 V10	B	15	Gearbox			1m 21.592s 10
	Giorgio Pantano	I	19	Jordan Ford	Jordan EJ-14-Cosworth RS V10	B	12	Gearchange			1m 19.415s 10
	Mark Webber	AUS	14	Jaguar Racing	Jaguar R5-Cosworth CR6 V10	M	11	Electronics			1m 17.466s 11
	Takuma Sato	J	10	Lucky Strike BAR Honda	BAR 006-Honda RA004E V10	M	2	Engine			1m 21.368s 2
	David Coulthard	GB	5	West McLaren Mercedes	McLaren MP4/19-Mercedes F0110P V10	M	2	Collision			1m 20.560s 2
	Giancarlo Fisichella	I	11	Sauber Petronas	Sauber C23-Petronas 04 V10	B	2	Accident			1m 20.804 2
	Christian Klien	A	15	Jaguar Racing	Jaguar R5-Cosworth CR6 V10	M	0	Accident			

Fastest lap: Michael Schumacher, on lap 23, 1m 14.439s, 100.369 mph/161.528 km/h (record).

Previous lap record: Kimi Räikkönen (McLaren MP4/17D-Mercedes F0110M V10), 1m 14.545s, 100.226 mph/161.298 km/h (2003).

20th: GIANMARIA BRUNI Minardi-Cosworth

18th: GIORGIO PANTANO Jordan-Cosworth

16th: FELIPE MASSA Sauber-Petronas

14th: CHRISTIAN KLIEN Jaguar-Cosworth

12th: RALF SCHUMACHER Williams-BMW
Demoted after engine change

19th: ZSOLT BAUMGARTNER Minardi-Cosworth

17th: NICK HEIDFELD Jordan-Cosworth

15th: CRISTIANO DA MATTA Toyota

13th: OLIVIER PANIS Toyota

11th: MARK WEBBER Jaguar-Cosworth

Grid order	1	2	3	4	5	6	7	8	9	10	11	12	13	14	15	16	17	18	19	20	21	22	23	24	25	26	27	28	29	30	31	32	33	34	35	36	37	38	39	40	41	42	43	44	45	46	47	48	49	50	51	52	53	54	55	56	57	58	59	60
7 TRULLI	7	7	7	7	7	7	7	7	7	7	7	7	7	7	7	7	7	7	7	7	7	7	7	8	1	7	7	7	7	7	7	7	7	7	7	7	7	7	7	7	1	1	1	7	7	7	7	7	7	7	7	7	7	7	7	7	7	7	7	7
9 BUTTON	8	8	8	8	8	8	8	8	8	8	8	8	8	8	8	8	8	8	8	8	8	8	1	7	8	8	8	8	8	8	8	8	8	8	8	8	8	8	8	8	1	7	7	9	9	9	9	9	9	9	9	9	9	9	9	9	9	9	9	9
8 ALONSO	9	9	9	9	9	9	9	9	9	9	9	9	9	9	9	9	6	1	1	1	1	1	7	8	1	1	1	1	1	1	1	1	1	1	1	1	1	1	1	1	9	9	9	2	2	2	2	2	2	2	2	2	2	2	2	2	2	2	2	2
1 M. SCHUMACHER	10	10	6	6	6	6	6	6	6	6	6	6	6	6	6	6	1	2	16	16	16	9	9	9	9	9	9	9	9	9	9	9	9	9	9	9	9	9	9	9	2	2	2	3	3	3	3	3	3	3	3	3	3	3	3	3	3	3	3	3
6 RÄIKKÖNEN	6	6	1	1	1	1	1	1	1	1	1	1	1	1	1	1	2	16	9	6	6	6	6	6	2	2	2	2	2	2	2	2	2	2	2	2	3	3	3	16	16	16	16	16	12	12	12	12	12	12	12	12	12
2 BARRICHELLO	1	1	2	2	2	2	2	3	3	3	3	3	2	2	2	9	6	6	6	16	2	2	2	2	16	16	16	16	16	16	16	16	16	16	16	16	16	16	16	12	12	12	12	18	12	16	16	16	16	16	16	16	16	16
10 SATO	2	2	3	3	3	3	2	2	2	16	16	16	16	16	9	6	12	2	2	2	16	16	16	18	3	3	3	3	3	3	3	3	3	3	3	12	12	12	18	12	18	12	18	12	18	18	18	18	18	18	18
5 COULTHARD	5	5	14	14	14	14	14	14	14	14	16	12	12	2	18	18	18	18	18	18	3	18	12	12	12	12	12	18	18	18	18	4	4	4	4	4	4	4	4	4	4	4	4	4	4
3 MONTOYA	3	3	16	16	16	16	16	16	16	12	18	18	18	18	18	18	3	3	3	3	3	12	12	18	4	4	4	4	18	18	18	18	4	4	4	17	17	17	17	17	17	17	17	17	17
11 FISICHELLA	14	14	12	12	12	12	12	12	12	18	3	3	3	3	3	3	12	12	12	12	12	4	4	4	18	18	18	18	4	4	4	17	17	17	21	21	21	21	21	21	21	21	21
14 WEBBER	11	11	18	18	18	18	18	18	18	18	17	17	17	17	4	4	4	4	4	4	4	17	17	17	17	17	17	17	17	21	21	21
4 R. SCHUMACHER	16	16	19	19	19	19	19	19	19	17	4	4	4	4	17	17	17	17	17	21	21	21	21	21	21
17 PANIS	4	4	20	20	20	20	20	20	20	4	20	20	20	21	21	21	21	21	21
15 KLIEN	12	12	17	17	17	17	17	17	17	20	21	21	21
16 DA MATTA	18	18	21	21	21	21	21	21	4	4	21
12 MASSA	19	19	4	4	4	4	4	4	21	21
18 HEIDFELD	20	20
19 PANTANO	17	17
21 BAUMGARTNER	21	21
20 BRUNI		

Pit stop
One lap behind leader

TIME SHEETS

QUALIFYING

Warm and sunny (track 48°C, air 23°C)

Pos.	Driver	Lap time	Sector 1	Sector 2	Sector 3
1	Jarno Trulli	1m 13.985s	19.541s	36.711s	17.733s
2	Ralf Schumacher	1m 14.345s	19.515s	36.923s	17.907s
3	Jenson Button	1m 14.396s	19.487s	37.099s	17.810s
4	Fernando Alonso	1m 14.408s	19.502s	36.892s	18.014s
5	Michael Schumacher	1m 14.516s	19.430s	37.004s	18.082s
6	Kimi Räikkönen	1m 14.592s	19.692s	36.975s	17.925s
7	Rubens Barrichello	1m 14.716s	19.498s	37.184s	18.034s
8	Takuma Sato	1m 14.827s	19.360s	37.482s	17.985s
9	David Coulthard	1m 14.951s	19.733s	37.161s	18.057s
10	Juan Pablo Montoya	1m 15.039s	19.693s	37.240s	18.106s
11	Giancarlo Fisichella	1m 15.352s	19.890s	37.343s	18.119s
12	Mark Webber	1m 15.725s	20.083s	37.547s	18.095s
13	Olivier Panis	1m 15.859s	19.949s	37.671s	18.239s
14	Christian Klien	1m 15.919s	20.102s	37.495s	18.322s
15	Cristiano da Matta	1m 16.169s	20.102s	37.759s	18.308s
16	Felipe Massa	1m 16.248s	19.676s	38.094s	18.478s
17	Nick Heidfeld	1m 16.488s	20.099s	37.960s	18.429s
18	Giorgio Pantano	1m 17.443s	20.330s	38.517s	18.596s
19	Zsolt Baumgartner	1m 20.060s	21.032s	39.798s	19.230s
20	Gianmaria Bruni	1m 20.115s	21.083s	39.726s	19.306s

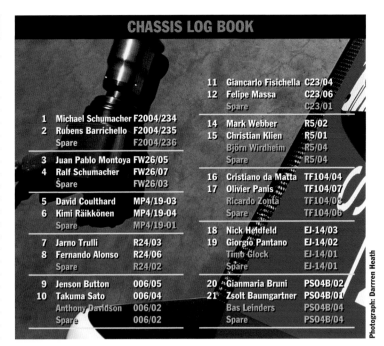

Photograph: Darrren Heath

CHASSIS LOG BOOK

1	Michael Schumacher	F2004/234
2	Rubens Barrichello	F2004/235
	Spare	F2004/236
3	Juan Pablo Montoya	FW26/05
4	Ralf Schumacher	FW26/07
	Spare	FW26/03
5	David Coulthard	MP4/19-03
6	Kimi Räikkönen	MP4/19-04
	Spare	MP4/19-01
7	Jarno Trulli	R24/03
8	Fernando Alonso	R24/06
	Spare	R24/02
9	Jenson Button	006/05
10	Takuma Sato	006/04
	Anthony Davidson	006/02
	Spare	006/02
11	Giancarlo Fisichella	C23/04
12	Felipe Massa	C23/06
	Spare	C23/01
14	Mark Webber	R5/02
15	Christian Klien	R5/01
	Björn Wirdheim	R5/04
	Spare	R5/04
16	Cristiano da Matta	TF104/04
17	Olivier Panis	TF104/07
	Ricardo Zonta	TF104/08
	Spare	TF104/06
18	Nick Heidfeld	EJ-14/03
19	Giorgio Pantano	EJ-14/02
	Timo Glock	EJ-14/01
	Spare	EJ-14/01
20	Gianmaria Bruni	PS04B/02
21	Zsolt Baumgartner	PS04B/01
	Bas Leinders	PS04B/04
	Spare	PS04B/04

PRACTICE 1 (THURSDAY)

Warm and cloudy (track 29°C, air 21°C)

Pos.	Driver	Laps	Time
1	Michael Schumacher	14	1m 16.502s
2	Takuma Sato	24	1m 17.279s
3	Jenson Button	19	1m 17.339s
4	Ricardo Zonta	28	1m 17.426s
5	David Coulthard	16	1m 17.524s
6	Fernando Alonso	22	1m 17.686s
7	Anthony Davidson	36	1m 17.791s
8	Jarno Trulli	24	1m 17.856s
9	Juan Pablo Montoya	16	1m 17.937s
10	Kimi Räikkönen	18	1m 17.952s
11	Giancarlo Fisichella	16	1m 18.338s
12	Rubens Barrichello	14	1m 18.621s
13	Cristiano da Matta	22	1m 18.889s
14	Olivier Panis	17	1m 19.218s
15	Mark Webber	8	1m 19.261s
16	Felipe Massa	16	1m 19.335s
17	Christian Klien	29	1m 19.487s
18	Giorgio Pantano	18	1m 20.528s
19	Timo Glock	15	1m 20.534s
20	Björn Wirdheim	18	1m 20.680s
21	Nick Heidfeld	17	1m 21.141s
22	Gianmaria Bruni	27	1m 21.201s
23	Zsolt Baumgartner	18	1m 22.203s
24	Bas Leinders	12	1m 23.361s
25	Ralf Schumacher	3	No time

PRACTICE 2 (THURSDAY)

Warm and cloudy (track 33°C, air 21°C)

Pos.	Driver	Laps	Time
1	Michael Schumacher	24	1m 14.741s
2	Anthony Davidson	32	1m 15.141s
3	Rubens Barrichello	27	1m 15.319s
4	Jarno Trulli	28	1m 15.472s
5	Kimi Räikkönen	14	1m 15.479s
6	Jenson Button	30	1m 15.520s
7	Takuma Sato	23	1m 15.664s
8	Ricardo Zonta	34	1m 15.690s
9	Fernando Alonso	28	1m 15.701s
10	Juan Pablo Montoya	29	1m 16.097s
11	David Coulthard	16	1m 16.229s
12	Ralf Schumacher	31	1m 16.556s
13	Cristiano da Matta	31	1m 16.743s
14	Giancarlo Fisichella	30	1m 16.748s
15	Olivier Panis	24	1m 17.007s
16	Giorgio Pantano	24	1m 17.309s
17	Felipe Massa	31	1m 17.422s
18	Timo Glock	28	1m 17.756s
19	Nick Heidfeld	18	1m 17.873s
20	Christian Klien	15	1m 17.988s
21	Gianmaria Bruni	24	1m 18.822s
22	Zsolt Baumgartner	19	1m 18.829s
23	Bas Leinders	25	1m 20.370s
24	Björn Wirdheim	2	No time

PRACTICE 3 (SATURDAY)

Warm and sunny (track 42°C, air 21°C)

Pos.	Driver	Laps	Time
1	Michael Schumacher	9	1m 15.751s
2	Rubens Barrichello	9	1m 15.770s
3	Mark Webber	19	1m 16.273s
4	Jenson Button	14	1m 16.358s
5	Jarno Trulli	8	1m 16.374s
6	Fernando Alonso	10	1m 16.386s
7	Kimi Räikkönen	15	1m 16.400s
8	Takuma Sato	15	1m 16.540s
9	Juan Pablo Montoya	13	1m 16.559s
10	David Coulthard	13	1m 16.756s
11	Ralf Schumacher	9	1m 16.863s
12	Giancarlo Fisichella	11	1m 17.209s
13	Cristiano da Matta	12	1m 17.409s
14	Giorgio Pantano	13	1m 18.117s
15	Olivier Panis	11	1m 18.299s
16	Christian Klien	21	1m 18.390s
17	Nick Heidfeld	12	1m 19.221s
18	Zsolt Baumgartner	6	1m 23.963s
19	Gianmaria Bruni	3	No time
20	Felipe Massa	2	No time

PRACTICE 4 (SATURDAY)

Warm and sunny (track 44C, air 22°C)

Pos.	Driver	Laps	Time
1	Michael Schumacher	16	1m 14.014s
2	Jarno trulli	19	1m 14.016s
3	Takuma Sato	22	1m 14.020s
4	Fernando Alonso	16	1m 14.138s
5	Juan Pablo Montoya	12	1m 14.212s
6	Jenson Button	15	1m 14.646s
7	David Coulthard	13	1m 14.670s
8	Ralf Schumacher	15	1m 14.752s
9	Kimi Räikkönen	18	1m 15.034s
10	Rubens Barrichello	17	1m 15.174s
11	Giancarlo Fisichella	14	1m 15.709s
12	Cristiano da Matta	25	1m 15.861s
13	Christian Klien	22	1m 16.101s
14	Felipe Massa	19	1m 16.332s
15	Nick Heidfeld	15	1m 16.385s
16	Olivier Panis	15	1m 16.431s
17	Giorgio Pantano	19	1m 16.700s
18	Mark Webber	4	1m 17.173s
19	Zsolt Baumgartner	12	1m 19.467s

10th: GIANCARLO FISICHELLA Sauber-Petronas

8th: DAVID COULTHARD McLaren-Mercedes

6th: RUBENS BARRICHELLO Ferrari

4th: MICHAEL SCHUMACHER Ferrari

2nd: JENSON BUTTON BAR-Honda

9th: JUAN PABLO MONTOYA Williams-BMW

7th: TAKUMA SATO BAR-Honda

5th: KIMI RÄIKKÖNEN McLaren-Mercedes

3rd: FERNANDO ALONSO Renault

Pole: JARNO TRULLI Renault

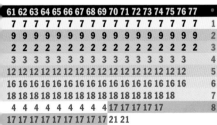

61	62	63	64	65	66	67	68	69	70	71	72	73	74	75	76	77	
7	7	7	7	7	7	7	7	7	7	7	7	7	7	7	7	7	1
9	9	9	9	9	9	9	9	9	9	9	9	9	9	9	9	9	2
2	2	2	2	2	2	2	2	2	2	2	2	2	2	2	2	2	3
3	3	3	3	3	3	3	3	3	3	3	3	3	3	3	3		4
12	12	12	12	12	12	12	12	12	12	12	12	12	12	12			5
16	16	16	16	16	16	16	16	16	16	16	16	16	16	16	16		6
18	18	18	18	18	18	18	18	18	18	18	18	18	18				7
4	4	4	4	4	4	4	4	4	17	17	17	17	17				8
17	17	17	17	17	17	17	17	17	21	21							
21	21	21	21	21	21	21	21	21									

FOR THE RECORD

First pole position

Jarno Trulli

First grand prix win

Jarno Trulli

POINTS: CONSTRUCTORS

1	Ferrari	88
2	Renault	52
3	BAR	40
4	Williams	35
5	Sauber	7
6	McLaren	5
7	Toyota	4
8	Jordan	2
9	Jaguar	1

POINTS: DRIVERS

1	Michael Schumacher	50
2	Rubens Barrichello	38
3	Jenson Button	32
4	Jarno Trulli	31
5	Juan Pablo Montoya	23
6	Fernando Alonso	21
7	Ralf Schumacher	12
8	Takuma Sato	8
9	Felipe Massa	5
10	David Coulthard	4
11	Cristiano da Matta	3
12 =	Giancarlo Fisichella	2
12 =	Nick Heidfeld	2
14 =	Olivier Panis	1
14 =	Kimi Räikkönen	1
14 =	Mark Webber	1

Photographs: Darrren Heath

Back in control on home ground.
Michael Schumacher once again stamped
his authority on the proceedings.
Photograph: Darren Heath

FIA F1 WORLD CHAMPIONSHIP • ROUND 7

EUROPEANGP
NÜRBURGRING

2004 FORMULA 1™ ALLIANZ (

NÜRBURGRING QUALIFYING

Michael Schumacher had a new chassis at his disposal following his retirement in Monaco, but he lost crucial track time with a hydraulic leak during Friday free practice. In no way did this affect his form on Saturday, however, when he made a brilliant effort to post the 60th pole position of his career on 1m 28.351s.

'I had the perfect lap, but I am surprised at the gap to the others,' he said, 'although I am not surprised to be on pole, as I expected to be very competitive. It was nice not to be first on the road in pre-qualifying [as a result of the Monaco retirement], as that helped in being able to run toward the end of the session.' Michael opted for the harder of the two Bridgestone tyre compounds on the basis of data gathered by Rubens Barrichello on Friday, when his own running had been limited by that hydraulic leak.

For his part, Barrichello made a few slight mistakes, which left him seventh (1m 29.353s) in the final order. Also the Brazilian had run with around 45 kg of extra fuel, which went a long way to explain the disparity in lap times between the two F2004s.

The privilege of joining Michael's Ferrari on the front row of the grid was reserved for Takuma Sato's BAR-Honda 006 (1m 28.986s). 'The track [conditions] had been changing a lot, but for me the conditions were similar to my pre-qualifying run, so I knew I had a good lap within my grasp,' said Sato. 'Michael's lap was stunning, but I didn't let it affect me. I just got on with the job and everything went well.'

By contrast, Jenson Button posted a 1m 29.245s, which could only earn him fifth place. 'I was disappointed with my lap because we could have done much better today,' he explained. 'I came into the weekend expecting to make the front row, but lack of grip has been a big problem, and that was the case in qualifying.'

Renault's Jarno Trulli had been sidelined by a wiring-loom problem at the end of Saturday free practice, and his R24 had only just been readied in time for his strong run to third on the grid with a 1m 29.135s lap, three places in front of team-mate Fernando Alonso (1m 29.313s), who was confident that he had a promising race set-up.

Trulli was obviously surprised at the result. 'It's hard to believe that I am here in third position,' he said in a hoarse whisper, his voice having suffered from all the post-Monaco interviews. 'It was a decent lap and the car was handling well, but I particularly want to thank my mechanics who did a fantastic job preparing the car after an electrical problem in free practice.'

David Coulthard suffered an engine failure in his McLaren-Mercedes on the slowing-down lap after his pre-qualifying run, but rather than use the spare MP4/19, he decided to stick with his original chassis, which meant changing the engine and starting from the back of the grid. Without that, the Scot would have been in line for a top-six slot together with Räikkönen, who displayed the car's much improved form by lining up fourth on 1m 29.137s. Even though there were no obvious changes to the car, the McLaren squad was in an upbeat mood, anticipating the testing debut of the revised MP4/19B, which was scheduled to roll out at Silverstone two days after the Nürburgring race.

For Williams, Juan Pablo Montoya (1m 29.354s) and Ralf Schumacher (1m 29.459s) lined up their FW26s in eighth and ninth places. On Friday, Montoya had freely confessed that he wasn't really on the same wavelength as his car. On Saturday, he had struggled with balance initially, and although the car had felt better in qualifying, he had still lacked speed and could only line up one place ahead of the similarly confused younger Schumacher. 'Nothing wrong,' said the Colombian with a mischievous twinkle in his eye. 'Just the usual – not enough downforce, not enough power.'

Toyota's Olivier Panis reported that he'd been balked briefly by Bas Leinders' Minardi on Friday, but he qualified a respectable tenth on Saturday (1m 29.697s). He said that the performance was the best he could have expected from the TF104 at that stage of its development. Cristiano da Matta admitted that he had lost time through Turns Four and Five, but the grip had improved as the rubber went down and he wound up 11th with a 1m 29.706s.

Mark Webber incurred a one-second penalty on his qualifying position after setting a fastest Friday sector time under waved yellow flags, which put him back to 14th on the grid after a great showing (1m 31.797s including the penalty) on a heavy fuel load. Christian Klien spun off on Friday, then improved his R5's handling balance on Saturday morning before gaining a respectable 12th on the grid on 1m 31.431s.

Sauber's Giancarlo Fisichella suffered an engine failure on Friday, while Felipe Massa experienced an electronics problem and stopped out on the circuit. On Saturday, Fisichella missed qualifying in a tactical bid to conserve tyres, starting on the back row. Massa wound up 16th after admitting to a mistake in Turn Seven, which cost him a couple of positions. 'Fisi' would more than make up for this disappointment come the race.

HEAD STANDS DOWN

Immediately after the Monaco Grand Prix, Patrick Head announced to the 500-strong WilliamsF1 workforce that he was standing down from his role as technical director and handing the reins to Sam Michael, the team's chief operations engineer.

The 57-year-old engineer had originally intended to retire from the F1 limelight at the end of the 2004 season, but the disappointing track performance of the new FW26 had prompted him to move aside earlier. It was announced that instead he would fill the position of director of engineering.

'The original plan was to move on at the end of 2004 when Williams was successful again, but it quickly became clear after the start of the season that the move would have to be made sooner,' said Head with a candour that was greeted with admiration and respect from all his colleagues.

Head, whose 30-per-cent stake in WilliamsF1 is believed to be worth over £50 million, made it clear that he was nowhere near ready to retire, and in any case would not turn his back on F1 until the team he had helped found in 1977 regained its competitive edge. 'I don't think any role that I take will be lesser,' he said. 'I suspect I will be working as hard, if not harder, but doing slightly different activities.'

Sam Michael, a 33-year-old Australian, is one of the sport's most highly regarded young engineers. A mechanical engineering graduate from the University of New South Wales, he entered F1 as a design engineer for the now defunct Lotus team in 1993, then moved to Jordan the following year. He switched to the Williams outfit in 2001.

IT was business as usual for Michael Schumacher in front of his home crowd, who had turned out for the European Grand Prix at the Nürburgring. The world champion and his Ferrari F2004 demonstrated with consummate ease that Jarno Trulli's victory at Monaco a week earlier had been no more that a minor deviation from what he intended to be an unchallenged romp to his seventh title crown.

After taking the chequered flag 17.98s ahead of team-mate Rubens Barrichello to score the 76th win of his career, Schumacher declined to shower champagne on the rostrum out of respect for Umberto Agnelli, the brother of the late Fiat patriarch Gianni Agnelli, who had died the previous week.

Jenson Button finished a strong third from fifth on the grid, consolidating third place in the drivers' world championship table on 38, two points ahead of Trulli. The Italian had outqualified his Renault team-mate, Fernando Alonso, for the fifth time in seven races.

Immediately prior to the start, however, it was the audacious Takuma Sato who sent a shudder through many of his rivals as he lined up his BAR-Honda 006 second on the grid alongside Schumacher's Ferrari.

Since Sato had jumped the start at Monaco and clipped the world champion's car as he did so, everybody was hoping that the Japanese driver would keep things under control for the sprint to the first corner at the Nürburgring, a tight and tricky right-hander that doubles back on itself before leading into an equally tight left-hander. But when it came to the start, Sato accelerated off the grid like a demon, plunging late into the braking area and forcing Trulli, who'd qualified third, to run wide on the exit.

'I made a good start, but the race was nearly over at the first corner,' Trulli complained. 'If I hadn't opened the door, Sato would have taken me out. I was third behind him and Michael when, two corners later, he made a mistake, so I took the inside line through Turn Four, but he closed the door.

'His right front wheel hit my front left and I nearly lost the car. In the confusion, I pressed the pit-lane speed limiter button and that cost me a number of positions.'

As if that wasn't enough, going into the first corner Juan Pablo Montoya locked up his Williams FW26 as he attempted to avoid an impending collision with Barrichello's Ferrari, but as he swerved

to the left, he tipped his own team-mate, Ralf Schumacher, into a spin that ended in his colliding with Cristiano da Matta. Both the younger Schumacher and his rival in the Toyota were out of the race on the spot, leaving Montoya to trail around to the pits for a replacement nose-cone. The Colombian resumed 18th and last, some 35s behind the rest of the pack.

Ralf Schumacher remained philosophical about his misfortune. 'Being taken out of the race at the first corner is definitely not what I was expecting,' he said with a hint of irony. 'It was a very unfortunate accident with Juan, who just braked a bit too late as he was trying to gain some places at the end of the straight.

'I am 100-per-cent sure Juan didn't do it on purpose. Therefore, I'm not going to blame him. It was a shame I hit da Matta too, but I was just a passenger in my car by that time. I'm sorry for Cristiano, but there was nothing I could do to avoid taking him out.'

The confusion played right into Michael Schumacher's hands. Having started the race with a very light fuel load, intending to sprint away in the opening stages before making an early first refuelling stop, he could hardly believe his luck when Ferrari technical director Ross Brawn told him over the radio that Kimi Räikkönen in the McLaren MP4/19 had taken advantage of the chaos to nip through into second place.

That news was a gift to Schumacher, as Räikkönen held up the tightly bunched pack consisting of Alonso, Sato, Barrichello, Button and Trulli. Schumacher was 2.4s ahead of the Finn at the end of the opening lap, but that advantage had stretched to an amazing 17s by the time he pulled into the pits for his first refuelling stop (8.3s) having completed only eight of the race's 60 laps.

Räikkönen made a 7.6s stop from second place at the end of lap nine, allowing Alonso ahead for one lap before he brought the Renault in for its first stop. The McLaren driver resumed the race, but pulled off immediately with engine failure. Sato then gloriously took the lead before coming in on lap 12, after which Barrichello headed the field until lap 15, when his first stop handed the lead back to Schumacher.

The race had settled down again by lap 17, with Schumacher leading from Sato, Barrichello and David Coulthard in the McLaren – running a long first stint of a two-stop refuelling

Above: Giancarlo Fisichella drove faultlessly to finish sixth.
Photograph: Darren Heath

Top left: Front-row man Takuma Sato with Michael Schumacher at the press conference.
Photograph: Bryn Williams/crash.net

Left: Patrick Head, standing aside to let a new generation of engineers have its head in the Williams team.
Photograph: Darren Heath

DIARY

Mika Häkkinen wins two Porsche Cup races at the Hamenlinna circuit in Finland, further fuelling speculation that he is considering a return to F1.

Buddy Rice wins the Indianapolis 500.

Former Indy winning team owner Doug Shierson dies from cancer aged 62.

Maserati MC12 GT racer faces threat unless all rival teams agree to changing the rule that effectively bans participation by works teams.

Jaguar F1 boss Tony Purnell deflects speculation that the team might be bought by Red Bull boss Dietrich Materschitz at the end of the season.

Above: Jenson Button earned another excellent podium finish, driving a strong race to third in the BAR-Honda.
Photograph: Darren Heath

strategy – ahead of Button and Mark Webber in the Jaguar R5.

Schumacher stopped again for fuel on laps 28 and 44, but never looked remotely like being challenged for the balance of the race. Barrichello, however, ran on a two-stop strategy in a bid to make up ground from his seventh place on the starting grid.

In fact, the outcome of Barrichello's battle for second with Sato looked very tightly balanced indeed. The Brazilian made his second refuelling stop on lap 38, dropping to third place behind the Japanese driver, who was then about 16s ahead. Sato had to stop again, but needed a lead of about 23s over the Ferrari to be able to refuel and have a chance of getting back out in front of his rival.

In the event, Sato was 21.2s in front of Barrichello when he followed Michael Schumacher into the pits at the end of lap 44, and Rubens just squeezed through into second as the Japanese driver came storming out of the pit lane. Fired up by the sight of the scarlet car immediately ahead, he aimed his BAR down the inside of the Ferrari going into lap 46 with an abandon that seemed as bold as it was over-ambitious.

Sato barged his way alongside the Ferrari, but although Barrichello swerved to the left to give him room, the two cars made contact. Sato pitted for a new nose section, but then his Honda engine blew up spectacularly, just as it had done at Monaco.

Sato was unabashed. 'I am extremely disappointed,' he said calmly.' Throughout the race, I was fighting all the time, and when I came out of my last pit stop on new tyres, I had a lot of grip and felt confident that I could challenge Rubens in the Ferrari, but I saw the opportunity to get past and unfortunately we touched.'

Barrichello was sanguine about this fleeting misfortune. 'I think Sato's move was a bit amateur,' he said. 'Luckily, I just saw his nose and moved over. After the incident, I lost part of my bargeboard, and it was lucky the race was in its final stages, as it affected the handling. It took me a couple of laps to assess what the car was doing, and then the team told me to push hard again, as Jenson was closing.'

The Brazilian duly kept control and led Button past the chequered flag by 4.54s, leaving Trulli and Alonso to storm home fourth and fifth in another strong result for Renault.

'Considering the problem I've had with poor grip throughout the weekend, third place is a great result for me,' said Button. 'Obviously this podium [finish] was slightly more lucky that the other four, but a podium nonetheless. It was a tough race and I had problems with traffic again.

'I had to get past David [Coulthard] because he was holding me up by two seconds a lap, but fortunately he made a mistake at the last corner and I was able to pass him on the outside. A little bit brave, maybe, but it paid off.'

Coulthard had started at the back of the grid after an engine failure in Saturday qualifying, and his McLaren-Mercedes briefly ran fourth ahead of Button before making the first of its two scheduled refuelling stops. The Scot didn't get to his second, as he suffered another engine failure on lap 26.

'After the first-lap problems, I was stuck behind Räikkönen, then behind slower cars after my first stop,' said Trulli. 'After that, I just pushed for the rest of the race in order to make up positions,

Below: Trouble in store for Ralf Schumacher after his Williams-BMW makes contact with team-mate Montoya.

Below centre: Ralf ends up in the gravel and takes out Cristiano da Matta.
Photographs: Peter Nygaard/GP Photo

and the car balance was good all the way through.' By contrast, Alonso was troubled by a vague feeling in his R24's steering.

Giancarlo Fisichella was well satisfied with sixth place, reporting that his Sauber C23 had been perfectly balanced throughout the race. Unfortunately, his team-mate, Felipe Massa, was not so happy, having suffered with a slight clutch problem at the start that had left him bottled up behind the Minardis, which cost him precious time. Also he had damaged his front wing, which had forced him to battle severe understeer for much of the race. He had ended up separated from his team-mate by Mark Webber (seventh) and the recovering Montoya (eighth).

'Seventh place was just what the doctor ordered,' grinned a satisfied Webber. 'My start was slightly slower than expected due to a clutch engagement problem, after which I'm pleased to say that our race strategy worked well, even allowing for the one-second penalty on our qualifying time.'

Completing the top ten was Nick Heidfeld's Jordan EJ-14. The young German had produced a good performance ahead of a rather disappointed Olivier Panis, whose Toyota had run eighth in the early stages, and Christian Klien in the other Jaguar. Giorgio Pantano counted himself lucky to have finished at all, having been troubled by a gearbox downshift glitch for the last 25 laps. Even so, he had been ahead of Bruni and Baumgartner at the chequered flag.

After the change of fortune at Monaco, Michael Schumacher was now firmly back on track. The day had shown just how formidable the Ferrari set-up really was, with no aspect of vulnerability that even its best prepared rivals could exploit.

Left: Schumacher and Barrichello in mutual congratulation mode after the latest Maranello 1-2.
Photograph: Bryn Williams/crash.net

Below: David Coulthard abandons his McLaren-Mercedes after its engine expired while the Scot was running ninth.
Photograph: Darren Heath

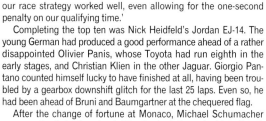

FIA F1 WORLD CHAMPIONSHIP • ROUND 7
ALLIANZ
GRAND PRIX OF EUROPE

Photograph: Darren Heath

NÜRBURGRING 28–30 MAY 2004

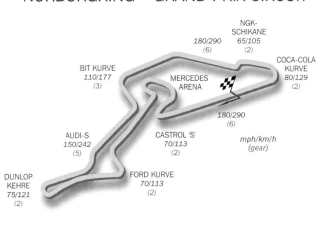

NÜRBURGRING – GRAND PRIX CIRCUIT

NGK-SCHIKANE 65/105 (2)
180/290 (6)
BIT KURVE 110/177 (3)
COCA-COLA KURVE 80/129 (2)
MERCEDES ARENA
180/290 (6)
AUDI-S 150/242 (5)
CASTROL 'S' 70/113 (2)
mph/km/h (gear)
DUNLOP KEHRE 75/121 (2)
FORD KURVE 70/113 (2)

CIRCUIT LENGTH: 3.199 miles/5.148 km

RACE DISTANCE: 60 laps, 191.398 miles/308.863 km RACE WEATHER: Dry and sunny (track 33–39°C, air 24°C)

Pos.	Driver	Nat.	No.	Entrant	Car/Engine	Tyres	Laps	Time/Retirement	Speed (mph/km/h)	Gap to leader	Fastest race lap	
1	Michael Schumacher	D	1	Scuderia Ferrari Marlboro	Ferrari F2004-052 V10	B	60	1h 32m 35.102s	124.373/200.159		1m 29.468s	7
2	Rubens Barrichello	BR	2	Scuderia Ferrari Marlboro	Ferrari F2004-052 V10	B	60	1h 32m 53.090s	123.971/199.513	+17.989s	1m 30.101s	14
3	Jenson Button	GB	9	Lucky Strike BAR Honda	BAR 006-Honda RA004E V10	M	60	1h 32m 57.634s	123.870/199.350	+22.533s	1m 30.457s	13
4	Jarno Trulli	I	7	Mild Seven Renault F1 Team	Renault R24-RS4 V10	M	60	1h 33m 28.774s	123.183/198.244	+53.673s	1m 31.131s	30
5	Fernando Alonso	E	8	Mild Seven Renault F1 Team	Renault R24-RS4 V10	M	60	1h 33m 36.088s	123.022/197.985	+60.987s	1m 31.065s	29
6	Giancarlo Fisichella	I	11	Sauber Petronas	Sauber C23-Petronas 04 V10	B	60	1h 33m 48.549s	122.750/197.547	+73.488s	1m 31.413s	23
7	Mark Webber	AUS	14	Jaguar Racing	Jaguar R5-Cosworth CR6 V10	M	60	1h 33m 51.307s	122.690/197.450	+76.206s	1m 31.893s	37
8	Juan Pablo Montoya	COL	3	BMW WilliamsF1 Team	Williams FW26-BMW P84 V10	M	59			+1 lap	1m 31.424s	43
9	Felipe Massa	BR	12	Sauber Petronas	Sauber C23-Petronas 04 V10	B	59			+1 lap	1m 32.729s	37
10	Nick Heidfeld	D	18	Jordan Ford	Jordan EJ-14-Cosworth RS V10	B	59			+1 lap	1m 32.121s	55
11	Olivier Panis	F	17	Panasonic Toyota Racing	Toyota TF104-RVX04 V10	M	59			+1 lap	1m 32.506s	12
12	Christian Klien	A	15	Jaguar Racing	Jaguar R5-Cosworth CR6 V10	M	59			+1 lap	1m 32.804s	14
13	Giorgio Pantano	I	19	Jordan Ford	Jordan EJ-14-Cosworth RS V10	B	58			+2 laps	1m 32.772s	27
14	Gianmaria Bruni	I	20	European Minardi Cosworth	Minardi PS04B-Cosworth CR3 V10	B	57			+3 laps	1m 35.555s	7
15	Zsolt Baumgartner	H	21	European Minardi Cosworth	Minardi PS04B-Cosworth CR3 V10	B	57			+3 laps	1m 34.666s	46
	Takuma Sato	J	10	Lucky Strike BAR Honda	BAR 006-Honda RA004E V10	M	47	Engine			1m 30.004s	11
	David Coulthard	GB	5	West McLaren Mercedes	McLaren MP4/19-Mercedes F0110P V10	M	25	Engine			1m 32.337s	14
	Kimi Räikkönen	FIN	6	West McLaren Mercedes	McLaren MP4/19-Mercedes F0110P V10	M	9	Engine			1m 31.670s	2
	Ralf Schumacher	D	4	BMW WilliamsF1 Team	Williams FW26-BMW P84 V10	M	0	Collision			–	
	Cristiano da Matta	BR	16	Panasonic Toyota Racing	Toyota TF104-RVX04 V10	M	0	Collision			–	

All results and data © FOM 2004

Fastest lap: Michael Schumacher, on lap 7, 1m 29.468s, 128.713 mph/207.144 km/h (record).

Previous lap record: Kimi Räikkönen (McLaren MP4/17D-Mercedes F0110M V10), 1m 32.621s, 124.331 mph/200.092 km/h (2003).

19th: GIANCARLO FISICHELLA Sauber-Petronas

17th: ZSOLT BAUMGARTNER Minardi-Cosworth

15th: GIORGIO PANTANO Jordan-Cosworth

13th: NICK HEIDFELD Jordan-Cosworth

11th: CRISTIANO DA MATTA Toyota

20th: GIANMARIA BRUNI Minardi-Cosworth

18th: DAVID COULTHARD McLaren-Mercedes

16th: FELIPE MASSA Sauber-Petronas

14th: MARK WEBBER Jaguar-Cosworth

12th: CHRISTIAN KLIEN Jaguar-Cosworth

Grid order	1	2	3	4	5	6	7	8	9	10	11	12	13	14	15	16	17	18	19	20	21	22	23	24	25	26	27	28	29	30	31	32	33	34	35	36	37	38	39	40	41	42	43	44	45	46	47
1 M. SCHUMACHER	1	1	1	1	1	1	1	8	10	10	2	2	2	2	1	1	1	1	1	1	1	1	1	1	1	1	1	1	1	1	1	1	1	1	1	1	1	1	1	1	1	1	1	1	1	1	1
10 SATO	6	6	6	6	6	6	6	6	10	2	2	10	1	1	1	10	10	10	10	10	10	10	10	10	10	10	2	2	2	2	2	2	2	2	2	2	2	10	10	10	10	10	10	2	2		
7 TRULLI	8	8	8	8	8	8	8	8	2	9	1	1	10	10	10	2	2	2	2	2	2	2	2	2	2	10	10	10	10	10	10	10	10	10	10	2	2	2	2	2	10	10					
6 RÄIKKÖNEN	10	10	10	10	10	10	10	10	9	8	9	5	5	5	5	5	5	5	9	9	9	9	9	7	7	8	9	9	9	9	9	9	9	9	9	9	9	9	9	9	9	9	9	9	9	9	
9 BUTTON	2	2	2	2	2	2	2	2	6	1	5	15	9	9	9	9	9	9	5	5	11	11	11	7	7	8	9	8	9	9	7	7	7	7	7	7	7	7	7	7	1	7	1				
8 ALONSO	9	9	9	9	9	9	9	9	1	17	15	9	15	15	15	14	14	14	11	11	7	7	7	11	11	9	7	7	8	8	8	8	8	8	8	8	8	11	11	8	8	8	1				
2 BARRICHELLO	7	7	7	7	7	7	7	7	5	18	18	18	14	14	11	11	11	7	7	8	8	8	5	11	11	11	11	11	11	11	11	11	11	11	11	11	11	8	11	11	11	12					
3 MONTOYA	17	17	17	17	17	17	17	17	15	5	8	8	8	11	11	15	7	7	8	7	17	5	14	14	14	14	14	14	14	14	14	14	14	3	3	3	14	14	14	14	14						
4 R. SCHUMACHER	5	5	5	5	5	5	5	5	18	19	14	14	18	7	7	8	8	17	7	5	14	14	18	18	18	18	3	3	3	3	3	3	3	14	14	14	3	3	3	3	3	2					
17 PANIS	15	15	15	15	15	15	15	15	19	14	11	11	7	8	8	12	3	3	14	17	18	18	15	3	3	3	12	12	12	12	12	12	12	12	18	18	18	18	18	18	1						
16 DA MATTA	18	18	18	18	18	18	18	18	14	11	7	7	8	12	12	14	14	3	18	15	15	12	3	15	12	15	15	15	18	18	18	18	17	12	12	12	12	12	12	12							
15 KLIEN	19	19	19	19	19	19	19	19	11	7	19	12	12	17	17	3	3	15	15	18	18	18	15	17	17	17	17	17	12	19	17	17	1														
18 HEIDFELD	14	14	14	14	14	14	14	14	7	12	12	17	17	3	3	15	15	18	18	18	15	12	17	12	15	18	18	18	15	17	17	17	17	17	17	17	15	15	15	15	15	15	19				
14 WEBBER	11	11	11	11	11	11	11	11	12	17	17	3	3	18	18	18	18	19	19	12	12	17	12	19	19	19	19	19	17	17	17	17	15	15	15	15	15	19	19	19	1						
19 PANTANO	3	20	20	20	12	12	12	12	3	3	3	19	19	19	19	19	12	12	12	3	3	17	20	20	20	20	20	20	20	20	20	20	20	21	20	20	20										
12 MASSA	20	21	12	12	20	20	20	20	20	20	20	21	21	20	20	20	20	20	20	20	20	21	21	21	21	21	21	21	21	21	21	21	21	20	21	21	21										
21 BAUMGARTNER	21	12	21	21	21	21	21	3	3	21	21	20	20	21	21	21	21	21	21																												
11 FISICHELLA	12	3	3	3	3	3	3	21	21																																						
20 BRUNI																																															
5 COULTHARD																																															

130

QUALIFYING

Sunny (track 35–34°C, air 22–21°C)

Pos.	Driver	Lap time	Sector 1	Sector 2	Sector 3
1	Michael Schumacher	1m 28.351s	28.940s	36.795s	22.616s
2	Takuma Sato	1m 28.986s	29.082s	37.086s	22.818s
3	Jarno Trulli	1m 29.135s	29.180s	37.139s	22.816s
4	Kimi Räikkönen	1m 29.137s	29.273s	37.254s	22.610s
5	Jenson Button	1m 29.245s	29.252s	37.226s	22.767s
6	Fernando Alonso	1m 29.313s	29.292s	37.206s	22.815s
7	Rubens Barrichello	1m 29.353s	29.225s	37.288s	22.840s
8	Juan Pablo Montoya	1m 29.354s	29.250s	37.217s	22.887s
9	Ralf Schumacher	1m 29.459s	29.410s	37.346s	22.703s
10	Olivier Panis	1m 29.697s	29.471s	37.350s	22.876s
11	Cristiano da Matta	1m 29.706s	29.416s	37.489s	22.801s
12	Christian Klien	1m 31.431s	29.971s	38.272s	23.188s
13	Nick Heidfeld	1m 31.604s	30.062s	38.355s	23.187s
14	Mark Webber	1m 31.797s	29.827s	37.637s	23.333s
15	Giorgio Pantano	1m 31.979s	30.089s	38.421s	23.469s
16	Felipe Massa	1m 31.982s	30.113s	38.447s	23.292s
17	Zsolt Baumgartner	1m 34.398s	30.459s	39.676s	23.887s
18	David Coulthard	No time	–	–	–
19	Giancarlo Fisichella	No time	–	–	–
20	Gianmaria Bruni	No time	–	–	–

	Driver	Chassis
1	Michael Schumacher	F2004/239
2	Rubens Barrichello	F2004/235
	Spare	F2004/236
3	Juan Pablo Montoya	FW26/06
4	Ralf Schumacher	FW26/07
	Spare	FW26/05
5	David Coulthard	MP4/19-05
6	Kimi Räikkönen	MP4/19-04
	Spare	MP4/19-01
7	Jarno Trulli	R24/03
8	Fernando Alonso	R24/06
	Spare	R24/02
9	Jenson Button	006/05
10	Takuma Sato	006/03
	Anthony Davidson	006/04
	Spare	006/04
11	Giancarlo Fisichella	C23/03
12	Felipe Massa	C23/06
	Spare	C23/01
14	Mark Webber	R5/04
15	Christian Klien	R5/01
	Björn Wirdheim	R5/05
	Spare	R5/05
16	Cristiano da Matta	TF104/04
17	Olivier Panis	TF104/07
	Ricardo Zonta	TF104/06
	Spare	TF104/06
18	Nick Heidfeld	EJ-14/03
19	Giorgio Pantano	EJ-14/02
	Timo Glock	EJ-14/01
	Spare	EJ-14/01
20	Gianmaria Bruni	PS04B/02
21	Zsolt Baumgartner	PS04B/01
	Bas Leinders	PS04B/04
	Spare	PS04B/04

Photograph: Darren Heath

PRACTICE 1 (FRIDAY)

Sunny (track 22–28°C, air 15–18°C)

Pos.	Driver	Laps	Time
1	Anthony Davidson	19	1m 29.477s
2	Michael Schumacher	14	1m 29.631s
3	Rubens Barrichello	12	1m 29.865s
4	Mark Webber	6	1m 31.448s
5	Ricardo Zonta	23	1m 31.587s
6	Kimi Räikkönen	4	1m 31.643s
7	Felipe Massa	9	1m 31.673s
8	Ralf Schumacher	14	1m 31.680s
9	Fernando Alonso	16	1m 31.768s
10	Jenson Button	11	1m 31.770s
11	Juan Pablo Montoya	10	1m 31.782s
12	Olivier Panis	10	1m 31.910s
13	David Coulthard	5	1m 32.301s
14	Takuma Sato	10	1m 32.500s
15	Jarno Trulli	15	1m 32.696s
16	Cristiano da Matta	15	1m 32.915s
17	Timo Glock	15	1m 33.925s
18	Nick Heidfeld	10	1m 33.971s
19	Christian Klien	11	1m 34.402s
20	Giorgio Pantano	15	1m 34.488s
21	Björn Wirdheim	9	1m 35.043s
22	Zsolt Baumgartner	13	1m 35.186s
23	Gianmaria Bruni	17	1m 35.455s
24	Bas Leinders	15	1m 37.609s
25	Giancarlo Fisichella	2	No time

PRACTICE 2 (FRIDAY)

Partly cloudy (track 28–26°C, air 18–17°C)

Pos.	Driver	Laps	Time
1	Kimi Räikkönen	18	1m 29.355s
2	Jenson Button	16	1m 29.618s
3	Ralf Schumacher	28	1m 29.677s
4	David Coulthard	17	1m 29.700s
5	Jarno Trulli	23	1m 29.919s
6	Rubens Barrichello	24	1m 29.943s
7	Anthony Davidson	32	1m 30.028s
8	Fernando Alonso	22	1m 30.163s
9	Michael Schumacher	9	1m 30.227s
10	Takuma Sato	17	1m 30.283s
11	Juan Pablo Montoya	20	1m 30.337s
12	Mark Webber	29	1m 30.466s
13	Olivier Panis	24	1m 30.497s
14	Cristiano da Matta	25	1m 30.531s
15	Ricardo Zonta	33	1m 30.949s
16	Giancarlo Fisichella	26	1m 30.974s
17	Björn Wirdheim	26	1m 31.780s
18	Timo Glock	29	1m 32.080s
19	Christian Klien	15	1m 32.217s
20	Felipe Massa	12	1m 32.310s
21	Gianmaria Bruni	19	1m 32.643s
22	Zsolt Baumgartner	18	1m 32.986s
23	Nick Heidfeld	20	1m 33.175s
24	Giorgio Pantano	17	1m 33.393s
25	Bas Leinders	19	1m 34.538s

PRACTICE 3 (SATURDAY)

Sunny, light wind (track 18–22°C, air 14–16°C)

Pos.	Driver	Laps	Time
1	Jenson Button		1m 29.495s
2	Ralf Schumacher		1m 30.192s
3	Takuma Sato		1m 30.261s
4	Juan Pablo Montoya		1m 30.369s
5	Michael Schumacher		1m 30.418s
6	Kimi Räikkönen		1m 30.532s
7	Jarno Trulli		1m 30.551s
8	Fernando Alonso		1m 30.600s
9	Rubens Barrichello		1m 30.681s
10	Olivier Panis		1m 31.248s
11	Cristiano da Matta		1m 31.814s
12	Giancarlo Fisichella		1m 31.816s
13	Felipe Massa		1m 32.206s
14	Mark Webber		1m 32.596s
15	Nick Heidfeld		1m 32.690s
16	Zsolt Baumgartner		1m 32.898s
17	Giorgio Pantano		1m 33.226s
18	Gianmaria Bruni		1m 33.499s
19	Christian Klien		1m 33.917s
20	David Coulthard		No time

PRACTICE 4 (SATURDAY)

Sunny, light wind (track 23–28°C, air 17–18°C)

Pos.	Driver	Laps	Time
1	Jenson Button		1m 28.827s
2	Michael Schumacher		1m 29.064s
3	Takuma Sato		1m 29.127s
4	Kimi Räikkönen		1m 29.354s
5	Rubens Barrichello		1m 29.545s
6	Fernando Alonso		1m 29.555s
7	David Coulthard		1m 29.955s
8	Ralf Schumacher		1m 30.176s
9	Olivier Panis		1m 30.277s
10	Cristiano da Matta		1m 30.316s
11	Giancarlo Fisichella		1m 30.519s
12	Mark Webber		1m 30.867s
13	Jarno trulli		1m 30.986s
14	Christian Klien		1m 31.061s
15	Felipe Massa		1m 31.504s
16	Nick Heidfeld		1m 31.956s
17	Zsolt Baumgartner		1m 32.753s
18	Gianmaria Bruni		1m 32.894s
19	Giorgio Pantano		1m 33.383s
20	Juan Pablo Montoya		No time

9th: RALF SCHUMACHER Williams-BMW

7th: RUBENS BARRICHELLO Ferrari

5th: JENSON BUTTON BAR-Honda

3rd: JARNO TRULLI Renault

Pole: MICHAEL SCHUMACHER Ferrari

10th: OLIVIER PANIS Toyota

8th: JUAN PABLO MONTOYA Williams-BMW

6th: FERNANDO ALONSO Renault

4th: KIMI RÄIKKÖNEN McLaren-Mercedes

2nd: TAKUMA SATO BAR-Honda

48	49	50	51	52	53	54	55	56	57	58	59	60	*
1	1	1	1	1	1	1	1	1	1	1	1	1	1
2	2	2	2	2	2	2	2	2	2	2	2	2	2
9	9	9	9	9	9	9	9	9	9	9	9	9	3
7	7	7	7	7	7	7	7	7	7	7	7	7	4
8	8	8	8	8	8	8	8	8	8	8	8	8	5
11	11	11	11	11	11	11	11	11	11	11	11	11	6
14	14	14	14	14	14	14	14	14	14	14	14	14	7
3	3	3	3	3	3	3	3	3	3	3	3	3	8
12	12	12	12	12	12	12	12	12	12	12	12		
18	18	18	18	18	18	18	18	18	18	18	18		
17	17	17	17	17	17	17	17	17	17	17	17		
15	15	15	15	15	15	15	15	15	15	15			
19	19	19	19	19	19	19	19	19	19	19			
20	20	20	20	20	20	20	20	20	20				
21	21	21	21	21	21	21	21	21					

Pit stop
One lap behind leader

First grand pix lap led

Takumo Sato

	Driver	Points
1	Michael Schumacher	60
2	Rubens Barrichello	46
3	Jenson Button	38
4	Jarno Trulli	36
5	Fernando Alonso	25
6	Juan Pablo Montoya	24
7	Ralf Schumacher	12
8	Takuma Sato	8
9 =	Felipe Massa	5
9 =	Giancarlo Fisichella	5
11	David Coulthard	4
12 =	Cristiano da Matta	3
12 =	Mark Webber	3
14	Nick Heidfeld	2
15 =	Olivier Panis	1
15 =	Kimi Räikkönen	1

	Constructor	Points
1	Ferrari	106
2	Renault	61
3	BAR	46
4	Williams	36
5	Sauber	10
6	McLaren	5
7	Toyota	4
8	Jaguar	3
9	Jordan	2

Photograph: Darren Heath

FIA F1 WORLD CHAMPIONSHIP • ROUND 8

CANADIANGP
MONTREAL

Main photograph: Victory number six for Michael Schumacher.

Inset: On the podium, but out of the points. After the celebrations, Ralf Schumacher found himself disqualified.
Photographs: Darren Heath

Main photograph: Michael Schumacher sweeps through the high-speed esses at the back of the Circuit Gilles Villeneuve, en route to his sixth win of the season.
Photograph: Darren Heath

Inset: Ralf Schumacher's second-place smile was short-lived. An infringement of brake cooling duct dimensions led to his disqualification.
Photograph: Bryn Williams/crash.net

MONTREAL QUALIFYING

Takuma Sato highlighted a day of dramatically contrasting fortunes for the BAR Honda team by setting fastest time in Friday practice for the Canadian Grand Prix. Earlier, his team-mate and test driver, Anthony Davidson, had walked away unhurt from a 130-mph accident that left his badly damaged car by the side of the track with wrecked suspension and bodywork.

Davidson, who had been evaluating tyres and chassis settings for the team's two race drivers, Sato and Jenson Button, had just set the fastest time in the first sector of his lap when his car spun out of control on the approach to a tight left-hand corner on the return leg of the circuit. The British driver's unscheduled off-track excursion came during a session that saw Michael Schumacher's Ferrari F2004 briefly brush one of the unyielding walls that line the track at the Circuit Gilles Villeneuve.

The following day, a superb effort at the wheel the Williams FW26

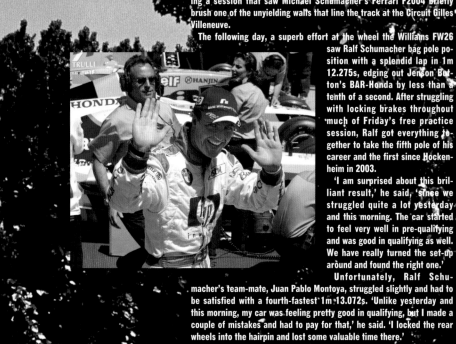

saw Ralf Schumacher bag pole position with a splendid lap in 1m 12.275s, edging out Jenson Button's BAR-Honda by less than a tenth of a second. After struggling with locking brakes throughout much of Friday's free practice session, Ralf got everything together to take the fifth pole of his career and the first since Hockenheim in 2003.

'I am surprised about this brilliant result,' he said, 'since we struggled quite a lot yesterday and this morning. The car started to feel very well in pre-qualifying and was good in qualifying as well. We have really turned the set-up around and found the right one.'

Unfortunately, Ralf Schumacher's team-mate, Juan Pablo Montoya, struggled slightly and had to be satisfied with a fourth-fastest 1m 13.072s. 'Unlike yesterday and this morning, my car was feeling pretty good in qualifying, but I made a couple of mistakes and had to pay for that,' he said. 'I locked the rear wheels into the hairpin and lost some valuable time there.'

The two Williams-BMWs were split by Button's BAR-Honda (1m 12.341s) and Jarno Trulli's Renault R24 (1m 13.023s). 'I'm pleased with my lap and front-row grid slot,' said Button, 'but not as pleased as if I'd held on to pole, but I'll settle for that. I lost a bit of time at the hairpin because I went in too deep and locked up the front right. There are a couple more tenths of a second in the car yet, so to be a second ahead of Michael is fantastic. A bit strange, but great nevertheless.'

For his part, Trulli was relishing the latest Renault V10 engine specification update, judging that his grid position put him in a strong position for the race. 'I had a good lap,' said the Italian, 'but I couldn't repeat my time from this morning. I think the hotter track conditions may have had something to do with it.'

Fernando Alonso qualified the other Renault fifth on 1m 13.308s. 'On my out-lap, I hit some debris from Sato's car [the BAR driver had missed the final chicane on his quick run and the high kerb had pitched him into a spin] and then made a small mistake at Turn Eight on the qualifying lap, and we found the car was damaged at the end of the run. I had a bit too much understeer to be really quick, but to be in the top five is enough to race well.'

Michael Schumacher (1m 13.355s) and Rubens Barrichello (1m 13.562s) lined up sixth and seventh, both F2004s running a heavy fuel load in a bid to make a two-stop strategy work on the technically punishing circuit.

'It will be a tight race,' said Schumacher. 'Last year, we had to overcome a few problems due to brake wear, but we did what we had to do. From a technical point of view, there are probably more demanding races on the calendar, but even so, I would always choose to race in Montreal.

'You need an interesting set-up for your car here. You need to be quick [on the straight], which means a low aerodynamic load [configuration], and the chicanes mean you need to have more downforce and good mechanics to be able to ride over the kerbs.'

After Sato's excellent Friday showing, everything went wrong in qualifying, and he dropped to 17th on 1m 17.004s, although in the end, he elected to start from the pit lane. 'It has been a difficult day for me,' shrugged the Japanese driver. 'In the morning session, we lost the first part of practice due to an oil pressure problem, and then lost part of the second, so we could not try all the variables on the car that we wanted to.

'However, the car felt great in pre-qualifying, and I started final qualifying feeling optimistic. But I missed the first part of the last chicane and hit the kerb. I'm very annoyed and I've certainly made life hard for myself.'

MICHAEL Schumacher conjured up his seventh win in the first eight races of the 2004 season in front of a capacity crowd at the Circuit Gilles Villeneuve. He had started from sixth place on the grid, which had given his over-optimistic rivals hope that the handicap would be a little too much even for the world champion to overcome.

Slowing up in the closing stages, Schumacher took the chequered flag only a second ahead of his brother Ralf's Williams-BMW FW26. The latter had started from pole position and set the pace so decisively in the opening stages of the race that it looked as though he might repeat his 2001 victory at the Montreal track, where he had beaten his older brother to score the first sibling 1-2 in F1 history.

Michael, however, ran a perfect two-stop strategy through the gruelling race, piling on the pressure with strategic precision whenever it was needed to emerge commandingly in control after the second round of refuelling stops.

Rubens Barrichello took third in the other Ferrari F2004, while Jenson Button in the BAR-Honda salvaged a low-key fourth, 0.7s ahead of Juan Pablo Montoya's Williams, after a disappointing race from second place on the grid.

'The race pace just wasn't there,' said Button. 'We came here looking for the win, but when it came to it, we weren't quick enough, not even as fast as the Williams, which was a surprise.'

Yet Button received an unexpected boost to his world championship ambitions when he was promoted from fourth to third place after both the Williams-BMWs and the Toyota F104s of Cristiano da Matta and Olivier Panis (originally eighth and tenth) were disqualified for having illegal front brake cooling ducts. Ralf Schumacher's consequent exclusion moved Rubens Barrichello up to second place behind Michael Schumacher to ensure a Ferrari 1-2 success.

At one point during the race, the crowd was treated to a wheel-to-wheel battle between the two Ferraris as Barrichello attempted to force his way ahead of Schumacher to take the lead.

'He pushed me very, very hard,' grinned Schumacher. 'He was very strong, during the second stint in particular, but we managed to keep ahead.'

Barrichello added that he had enjoyed every second of their battle. 'It was a great race and fun fighting him,' he said. 'The only chance I had was to overtake him on the race track or stay out slightly longer, but unfortunately I had a little bit less fuel than him [before the last stop] and then when I went out to the track again, I had a lot of fuel, but I cooked my brakes and there was no time to

cool them down. So Michael got another win, and I wish I could have had it.'

In qualifying, Button had appeared to be on course for pole position, but at the last moment Ralf Schumacher had pipped him by 0.066s, the first time the Williams-BMW driver had started at the front of the pack since 2003's French Grand Prix at Magny-Cours.

Sato had also marked himself out as a potential contender for pole position after setting second-fastest time in Friday free practice, but he had pushed too hard in qualifying, producing a neat 360-degree pirouette coming out of the final corner by the pits. He qualified 17th as a result, so BAR decided to start him from the pit lane, allowing his car to be fuelled for a long opening stint in the hope that he would be able to capitalise on any periods of running behind the safety car to make up crucial places. In the event, he had another erratic race, spinning in front of the Ferraris when they were running first and second, and then retiring with his third Honda engine failure in as many races.

At the start, Ralf Schumacher accelerated into an immediate lead from Button, but there was drama right behind them as Jarno Trulli's Renault R24, tipped as a strong contender after qualifying third, slowed abruptly and pulled over to the left, already out of the race with apparent suspension problems.

Meanwhile, Sato accelerated down the pit exit lane to be confronted by cars spinning in all directions after David Coulthard's McLaren was tapped by Christian Klien's Jaguar R5, which in turn was clipped by Mark Webber's Jaguar. As a consequence, the Australian driver was forced to pit for repairs at the end of the opening lap.

Ralf Schumacher completed the first lap 1.1s ahead of Button, with Fernando Alonso in the Renault third, then Montoya, Michael Schumacher and Kimi Räikkönen in the McLaren MP4/19 following in line astern. The younger Schumacher, displaying the poise and assurance he manages to demonstrate only intermittently, looked in complete control at the head of the pack, and by lap eight he had opened a decisive 3.2s advantage over his pursuers.

Button made his first refuelling stop from second place at the end of lap 13, leaving Ralf Schumacher with a 5.6s lead over Alonso; when Ralf came in at the end of lap 15 for fuel and tyres, the Spaniard took the lead before stopping himself on lap 17. Then Michael Schumacher surged ahead, setting a couple of really quick laps before making his first stop on lap 19.

From third place, Michael Schumacher maintained relentless pressure throughout the second stint of his race, putting himself

NO VILLENEUVE AT HOME GRAND PRIX

The downside for the Montreal fans was the fact that, for the first time since 1996, there was no Jacques Villeneuve for them to cheer on the track that had been named after his late father, Gilles, who had won the circuit's inaugural event for Ferrari in 1978.

This was an acutely ironic turn of events, considering the competitiveness of the BAR Honda team for whom Villeneuve had driven prior to being replaced by Takuma Sato at the final race of the 2003 season. Had he still been in the team, he might have had the opportunity to improve on his career-best second place in Canada, which he had achieved in his 1996 freshman season.

Villeneuve was not even present in his home city during the race weekend, but rumours that he would soon have a test drive with the Williams team refused to die, despite denials from both sides that anything concrete had been arranged.

Either way, the 33-year-old had made it clear that he was ready for action if and when the call came. 'I train every day in a very intensive way,' he said. 'Moreover, I've just bought two helmets and prepared two [helmet] visors, with two sets of white overalls – at my expense. One never knows what can happen, and if someone calls, I have the physical condition and the readiness to allow me to get into a car immediately.'

As circumstances would demonstrate later, Jacques hadn't made a bad investment.

Below: Christian Klien finished 13th after a lurid race in the Jaguar R5; he collided with team-mate Mark Webber and McLaren's David Coulthard at the first corner.
Photograph: Darren Heath

DIARY

Michael Schumacher and Tiger Woods named as the world's top earning sportsmen by Forbes' Celebrity 100 rich list, both checking in at around $80 million.

Red Bull again touted as a possible buyer for the Jaguar F1 team should Ford withdraw from the world championship.

Olivier Panis tipped as a possible candidate for a WilliamsF1 drive in 2005.

Bernie Ecclestone hires Michael Payne, director of global broadcast and media for the International Committee, as an advisor to his marketing programme for the world championship.

Above: Timo Glock found himself with two world championship points on his grand prix debut.

Right: Mark Webber readies himself before the start.

Below: Giancarlo Fisichella had another strong run to fourth place in Montreal, thanking his lucky stars for a poor start that helped him avoid the tangle between Klien and Coulthard.

Photographs: Darren Heath

in a position from which he could vault into the lead before the second round of refuelling stops.

For several laps, Barrichello hustled the world champion really hard, clearly wanting to get by while he was capable of running quicker, but despite several bold feints down the inside of his senior, he never quite managed to pull it off.

Ralf Schumacher was only 1.062s behind his brother at the finish. 'We had a strong car for the race,' said Michael. 'We thought we had no chance for pole position, so we went for a strategy which worked for the race and that worked out fantastic.'

Ralf made his second stop from the lead on lap 33, leaving the two Ferraris storming around absolutely nose-to-tail. Barrichello came in for his second stop on lap 44, but Michael stayed out until lap 47 for his, while Ralf waited until lap 48 for his third. That at least vaulted the younger Schumacher into second place, but there was nothing more he could do.

Following the disqualifications, Williams and Toyota confirmed that they would not appeal against the decision to exclude their cars. This was a blow for the Williams squad, which had seen Ralf Schumacher and Juan Pablo Montoya finish strongly in second and fifth places, narrowing the gap between the team and BAR to just three points in the battle for third place in the constructors' championship standings. That gap now opened to 16 points.

'The front brake ducts are not in accordance with the regula-

tions,' said Sam Michael, the Williams technical director. 'It was a mistake and unintentional. There was no performance gain and no gain on brake cooling because the inlet area was not bigger, but we accept the FIA's decision.'

Patrick Head, the Williams director of engineering, subsequently explained that in an effort to increase airflow through the front uprights, one of the team's aerodynamic staff had come up with a new cooling duct. This had been made by the composites department and fitted to the car for a Monza test, subsequently being used in Montreal.

'Throughout this entire process, nobody thought to say, "Perhaps we might check its dimensions,"' he noted dryly. 'I hardly think it's necessary to say that we now have systems in place to prevent it happening again.'

Giancarlo Fisichella ended up taking fourth place, albeit one lap down, after another strong run in his Sauber C23. 'I wasn't very quick off the line,' said 'Fisi', 'but that was a blessing after Coulthard and Klien tangled right in front of me in Turn One. I just managed to avoid both of them. After that, I just settled down and kept pushing hard. The car was a little inconsistent at various stages of the tyre wear, but five or six laps before each stop, it was very good and I was able to drive as if I was in a qualifying session.'

Kimi Räikkönen came out of the race with a fortunate fifth place. The Finn had made two unscheduled pit stops: the first was because of a drive-through penalty incurred for crossing the white line at the pit exit, while the second was to change his steering wheel due to an electrical problem. He'd already changed the wheel during his routine third refuelling stop.

Coulthard finished sixth in the revised order, but the biggest beneficiary of the disqualifications was Jordan, whose cars, driven by Timo Glock (standing in for Giorgio Pantano) and Nick Heidfeld, vaulted to seventh and eighth. Thus, Glock achieved the rare distinction of scoring championship points on his F1 debut.

'The start was really good,' said Glock, 'but I damaged my front wing early in the lap, which gave me a lot of understeer until my first pit stop, when I changed the wing. After the second stop, I was losing power or something, so I just concentrated on saving the engine. Towards the end, I had a coming together with Christian Klien, who was a lap down on me. I was expecting to pass him on the straight, but he moved over at a corner and we touched.'

That left Mark Webber's Jaguar in ninth place. Ironically, that appeared to benefit Williams, which was negotiating with Webber over the prospect of his switching to the team in 2005. It was believed that the Australian had a performance related clause in his Jaguar contract that would enable him to leave without penalty unless the team was in the top six in the constructors' table after the US Grand Prix, almost a mathematical impossibility.

Above: Jenson Button leads Fernando Alonso and Juan Pablo Montoya through the chicane. The Brit found himself elevated into third place following Ralf Schumacher's exclusion.
Photograph: Darren Heath

Photograph: Darren Heath

GRAND PRIX DU CANADA
MONTREAL 11–13 JUNE 2004

MONTREAL – CIRCUIT GILLES VILLENEUVE

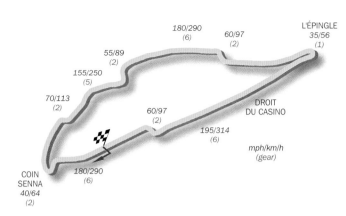

L'ÉPINGLE 35/56 (1)

180/290 (6) 60/97 (2)

55/89 (2)

155/250 (5)

70/113 (2)

60/97 (2) DROIT DU CASINO

195/314 (6)

mph/km/h (gear)

COIN SENNA 40/64 (2) 180/290 (6)

CIRCUIT LENGTH: 2.709 miles/4.361 km

RACE DISTANCE: 70 laps, 189.686 miles/305.270 km **RACE WEATHER:** Sunny (track 31–35°C, air 20–24°C)

Pos.	Driver	Nat.	No.	Entrant	Car/Engine	Tyres	Laps	Time/Retirement	Speed (mph/km/h)	Gap to leader	Fastest race lap	
1	Michael Schumacher	D	1	Scuderia Ferrari Marlboro	Ferrari F2004-052 V10	B	70	1h 28m 24.803s	128.726/207.165		1m 13.630s	18
2	Rubens Barrichello	BR	2	Scuderia Ferrari Marlboro	Ferrari F2004-052 V10	B	70	1h 28m 29.911s	128.602/206.966	+5.108s	1m 13.622s	68
3	Jenson Button	GB	9	Lucky Strike BAR Honda	BAR 006-Honda RA004E V10	M	70	1h 28m 45.212s	128.233/206.371	+20.409s	1m 14.246s	68
4	Giancarlo Fisichella	I	11	Sauber Petronas	Sauber C23-Petronas 04 V10	B	69			+1 lap	1m 15.078s	47
5	Kimi Räikkönen	FIN	6	West McLaren Mercedes	McLaren MP4/19-Mercedes F0110P V10	M	69			+1 lap	1m 14.752s	44
6	David Coulthard	GB	5	West McLaren Mercedes	McLaren MP4/19-Mercedes F0110P V10	M	69			+1 lap	1m 15.478s	55
7	Timo Glock	D	19	Jordan Ford	Jordan EJ-14-Cosworth RS V10	B	68			+2 laps	1m 16.300s	42
8	Nick Heidfeld	D	18	Jordan Ford	Jordan EJ-14-Cosworth RS V10	B	68			+2 laps	1m 15.890s	18
9	Christian Klien	A	15	Jaguar Racing	Jaguar R5-Cosworth CR6 V10	M	67			+3 laps	1m 15.731s	45
10	Zsolt Baumgartner	H	21	European Minardi Cosworth	Minardi PS04B-Cosworth CR3 V10	B	66			+4 laps	1m 17.516s	64
	Felipe Massa	BR	12	Sauber Petronas	Sauber C23-Petronas 04 V10	B	62	Accident			1m 15.560s	25
	Takuma Sato	J	10	Lucky Strike BAR Honda	BAR 006-Honda RA004E V10	M	48	Engine			1m 15.076s	25
	Fernando Alonso	E	8	Mild Seven Renault F1 Team	Renault R24-RS4 V10	M	44	Driveshaft			1m 14.179s	41
	Gianmaria Bruni	I	20	European Minardi Cosworth	Minardi PS04B-Cosworth CR3 V10	B	30	Gearbox			1m 18.025s	25
	Mark Webber	AUS	14	Jaguar Racing	Jaguar R5-Cosworth CR6 V10	M	6	Collision damage			1m 16.739s	6
	Jarno Trulli	I	7	Mild Seven Renault F1 Team	Renault R24-RS4 V10	M	0	Driveshaft			–	–
DQ	Ralf Schumacher	D	4	BMW WilliamsF1 Team	Williams FW26-BMW P84 V10	M	70				1m 14.040s	70
DQ	Juan Pablo Montoya	COL	3	BMW WilliamsF1 Team	Williams FW26-BMW P84 V10	M	70				1m 14.295s	69
DQ	Cristiano da Matta	BR	16	Panasonic Toyota Racing	Toyota TF104-RVX04 V10	M	69				1m 15.652s	39
DQ	Olivier Panis	F	17	Panasonic Toyota Racing	Toyota TF104-RVX04 V10	M	69				1m 16.045s	23

Fastest lap: Rubens Barrichello, on lap 68, 1m 13.622s, 132.505 mph/213.246 km/h.

Previous lap record: Juan Pablo Montoya (F1 Williams FW24-BMW V10), 1m 15.960s, 128.426 mph/206.682 km/h (2002).

19th: GIANMARIA BRUNI Minardi-Cosworth

17th: FELIPE MASSA Sauber-Petronas

15th: NICK HEIDFELD Jordan-Cosworth

13th: OLIVIER PANIS Toyota

11th: GIANCARLO FISICHELLA Sauber-Petro

20th: TAKUMA SATO BAR-Honda
Started from pit lane

18th: ZSOLT BAUMGARTNER Minardi-Cosworth

16th: TIMO GLOCK Jordan-Cosworth

14th: MARK WEBBER Jaguar-Cosworth

12th: CRISTIANO DA MATTA Toyota

Grid order	1	2	3	4	5	6	7	8	9	10	11	12	13	14	15	16	17	18	19	20	21	22	23	24	25	26	27	28	29	30	31	32	33	34	35	36	37	38	39	40	41	42	43	44	45	46	47	48	49	50	51	52	53	5
4 R. SCHUMACHER	4	4	4	4	4	4	4	4	4	4	4	4	8	8	1	1		4	4	4	4	4	4	4	4	4	4	4	4	4	1	1	1	1	1	1	1	1	1	1	1	1	1	4	1	1	1	1	1	1	1	1	1	5
9 BUTTON	9	9	9	9	9	9	9	9	9	9	9	8	8	1	1		2	4	9	9	9	9	9	9	9	9	9	9	9	9	1	1	2	2	2	2	2	2	2	2	2	4	4	1	9	4	4	4	4	4	4	4	4	4
7 TRULLI	8	8	8	8	8	8	8	8	8	8	8	1	1	2	2	4	9	1	1	1	1	1	1	1	1	1	1	1	1	1	2	2	4	4	4	4	4	4	4	4	4	8	9	9	9	3	2	2	2	2	2
3 MONTOYA	3	3	3	3	3	3	3	3	3	3	3	2	2	4	4	9	2	3	3	3	3	3	3	3	3	3	3	3	3	2	8	8	8	8	8	8	8	8	8	8	8	9	3	3	4	9	9	9	9			
8 ALONSO	1	1	1	1	1	1	1	1	1	1	1	16	16	9	9	3	3	2	2	2	2	2	2	2	2	2	8	9	9	9	9	9	9	9	9	9	9	9	2	2	2	2	3	3	3	3							
1 M. SCHUMACHER	6	6	6	6	6	6	2	2	2	2	2	9	9	16	16	8	8	8	8	8	8	8	8	8	3	3	3	3	3	3	3	3	3	3	3	11	11	11	11	6	6	6	6	6	6								
2 BARRICHELLO	2	2	2	2	2	2	6	6	6	6	3	3	17	17	17	11	11	11	11	6	6	6	6	6	11	11	11	11	11	11																								
6 RÄIKKÖNEN	16	16	16	16	16	16	16	16	16	17	17	17	17	7	6	18	11	6	6	6	12	16	16	16	16	16	16	16	16	16	16	16	16	16	16	16	16	11	16	16	16	16	16	16	16	16	1						
5 COULTHARD	17	17	17	17	17	17	17	17	17	6	6	6	6	6	18	11	6	12	12	12	12	11	11	11	11	11	11	11	11	11	16	5	5	5	5	5	5	5															
15 KLIEN	18	18	18	18	18	18	18	18	18	18	18	18	18	11	11	6	16	12	10	16	6	11	17	17	17	17	17	17	17	17	17	5	17	10	10	10	17	17	17	17													
11 FISICHELLA	19	19	11	11	11	11	11	11	11	11	11	11	11	11	16	16	16	16	17	17	5	5	5	5	10	10	10	10	10	10	5	17	17	10	17	17	17	19	19	19	19	1											
16 DA MATTA	11	11	19	19	5	5	5	5	5	19	19	19	19	19	12	12	10	17	17	5	10	10	10	10	10	5	5	5	5	5	5	10	10	19	19	19	12	12	12	12													
17 PANIS	15	5	5	5	19	19	19	19	12	12	10	10	12	12	10	10	5	5	10	10	19	19	19	19	19	19	14	19	12	12	12	12	12	18	15	15	15																
14 WEBBER	21	10	10	10	10	10	10	12	12	10	12	12	10	10	5	5	19	19	19	19	12	12	18	18	18	18	18	18	18	12	12	12	12	12	18	18	15	15	15	15	1												
18 HEIDFELD	10	15	15	15	15	15	12	10	10	15	15	15	15	15	19	19	19	20	20	18	18	18	12	12	12	12	12	18	18	18	18	18	18	15	15	15	21	21	21	21													
19 GLOCK		5	12	12	12	12	15	15	15	5	5	5	5	5	15	20	20	18	18	21	20	20	20	20	15	15	15	15	15	15	15	15	15	21	21	21																	
12 MASSA	20	21	21	21	21	21	21	20	20	20	20	20	20	20	20	15	15	21	21	20	21	15	15	15	20	21	21	21	21	21	21	21	21																				
21 BAUMGARTNER	12	20	20	20	20	20	20	21	21	21	21	21	21	21	21	21	21	15	15	15	15	21	21	21	21																												
20 BRUNI	14	14	14	14	14	14																																																
10 SATO																																																					

Pit stop

One lap behind leader

QUALIFYING

Sunny (track 34°C, air 23°C)

Pos.	Driver	Lap time	Sector 1	Sector 2	Sector 3
1	Ralf Schumacher	1m 12.275s	20.386s	23.022s	28.867s
2	Jenson Button	1m 12.341s	20.245s	23.033s	29.063s
3	Jarno Trulli	1m 13.023s	20.507s	23.517s	28.999s
4	Juan Pablo Montoya	1m 13.072s	20.500s	23.316s	29.256s
5	Fernando Alonso	1m 13.308s	20.530s	23.633s	29.115s
6	Michael Schumacher	1m 13.355s	20.592s	23.421s	29.342s
7	Rubens Barrichello	1m 13.562s	20.447s	23.882s	29.233s
8	Kimi Räikkönen	1m 13.595s	20.666s	23.445s	29.484s
9	David Coulthard	1m 13.681s	20.736s	23.724s	29.221s
10	Christian Klien	1m 14.532s	20.876s	23.673s	29.983s
11	Giancarlo Fisichella	1m 14.674s	21.032s	23.953s	29.689s
12	Cristiano da Matta	1m 14.851s	21.087s	23.852s	29.912s
13	Olivier Panis	1m 14.891s	21.029s	23.850s	30.012s
14	Mark Webber	1m 15.148s	20.916s	23.927s	30.305s
15	Nick Heidfeld	1m 15.321s	21.222s	24.098s	30.001s
16	Timo Glock	1m 16.323s	21.627s	24.467s	30.229s
17	Takuma Sato	1m 17.004s	20.136s	23.618s	31.055s
18	Zsolt Baumgartner	1m 17.064s	21.824s	24.571s	30.669s
19	Felipe Massa	No time	24.171s	25.606s	–
20	Gianmaria Bruni	No time	26.992s	32.188s	–

CHASSIS LOG BOOK

1	Michael Schumacher	F2004/239
2	Rubens Barrichello	F2004/235
	Spare	F2004/236
3	Juan Pablo Montoya	FW26/06
4	Ralf Schumacher	FW26/07
	Spare	FW26/03
5	David Coulthard	MP4/19-05
6	Kimi Räikkönen	MP4/19-04
	Spare	MP4/19-01
7	Jarno Trulli	R24/03
8	Fernando Alonso	R24/02
	Spare	R24/01
9	Jenson Button	006/05
10	Takuma Sato	006/03
	Anthony Davidson	006/04
	Spare	006/04
11	Giancarlo Fisichella	C23/03
12	Felipe Massa	C23/06
	Spare	C23/01
14	Mark Webber	R5/04
15	Christian Klien	R5/03
	Björn Wirdheim	R5/01
	Spare	R5/01
16	Cristiano da Matta	TF104/04
17	Olivier Panis	TF104/03
	Ricardo Zonta	TF104/07
	Spare	TF104/07
18	Nick Heidfeld	EJ-14/03
19	Timo Glock	EJ-14/02
	Spare	EJ-14/01
10	Gianmaria Bruni	PS04B/02
21	Zsolt Baumgartner	PS04B/01
	Bas Leinders	PS04B/03
	Spare	PS04B/03

Photograph: Darren Heath

PRACTICE 1 (FRIDAY)

Sunny (track 27–29°C, air 18–19°C)

Pos.	Driver	Laps	Time
1	Michael Schumacher	15	1m 14.013s
2	Rubens Barrichello	13	1m 14.291s
3	Anthony Davidson	19	1m 14.519s
4	Ricardo Zonta	23	1m 14.952s
5	Jarno Trulli	11	1m 15.428s
6	Fernando Alonso	14	1m 15.606s
7	Jenson Button	10	1m 15.905s
8	Juan Pablo Montoya	13	1m 15.928s
9	Ralf Schumacher	12	1m 15.948s
10	Olivier Panis	14	1m 15.997s
11	Giancarlo Fisichella	12	1m 16.240s
12	Cristiano da Matta	13	1m 16.475s
13	Kimi Räikkönen	7	1m 16.570s
14	Takuma Sato	13	1m 16.655s
15	Mark Webber	7	1m 16.820s
16	David Coulthard	8	1m 16.947s
17	Nick Heidfeld	17	1m 17.135s
18	Felipe Massa	6	1m 17.447s
19	Timo Glock	27	1m 17.890s
20	Christian Klien	23	1m 18.463s
21	Gianmaria Bruni	16	1m 18.828s
22	Zsolt Baumgartner	19	1m 18.959s
23	Bas Leinders	1	No time
24	Björn Wirdheim	3	No time

PRACTICE 2 (FRIDAY)

Sunny (track 33–36°C, air 21–23°C)

Pos.	Driver	Laps	Time
1	Takuma Sato	20	1m 14.086s
2	Fernando Alonso	29	1m 14.426s
3	Michael Schumacher	26	1m 14.535s
4	Kimi Räikkönen	19	1m 14.581s
5	Rubens Barrichello	31	1m 14.705s
6	Ricardo Zonta	33	1m 14.871s
7	Cristiano da Matta	30	1m 15.146s
8	Jenson Button	21	1m 15.152s
9	David Coulthard	19	1m 15.164s
10	Giancarlo Fisichella	28	1m 15.293s
11	Jarno Trulli	17	1m 15.492s
12	Anthony Davidson	21	1m 15.513s
13	Olivier Panis	28	1m 15.538s
14	Ralf Schumacher	22	1m 15.803s
15	Mark Webber	14	1m 15.926s
16	Felipe Massa	25	1m 16.119s
17	Gianmaria Bruni	22	1m 16.235s
18	Nick Heidfeld	23	1m 16.508s
19	Timo Glock	28	1m 16.524s
20	Juan Pablo Montoya	6	1m 16.564s
21	Christian Klien	27	1m 16.815s
22	Zsolt Baumgartner	17	1m 16.981s
23	Bas Leinders	23	1m 17.697s
24	Björn Wirdheim	18	1m 19.260s

PRACTICE 3 (SATURDAY)

Sunny (track 34°C, air 23°C)

Pos.	Driver	Laps	Time
1	Michael Schumacher	13	1m 13.865s
2	Fernando Alonso	9	1m 13.946s
3	Jenson Button	10	1m 14.047s
4	Rubens Barrichello	12	1m 14.284s
5	Jarno Trulli	11	1m 14.421s
6	Kimi Räikkönen	7	1m 14.584s
7	David Coulthard	7	1m 14.747s
8	Juan Pablo Montoya	17	1m 15.067s
9	Ralf Schumacher	134	1m 15.191s
10	Giancarlo Fisichella	10	1m 15.290s
11	Cristiano da Matta	13	1m 15.573s
12	Felipe Massa	16	1m 15.764s
13	Olivier Panis	13	1m 15.843s
14	Mark Webber	6	1m 15.854s
15	Christian Klien	10	1m 16.124s
16	Nick Heidfeld	15	1m 16.305s
17	Timo Glock	13	1m 16.928s
18	Gianmaria Bruni	15	1m 18.409s
19	Zsolt Baumgartner	15	1m 18.711s
20	Takuma Sato	4	No time

PRACTICE 4 (SATURDAY)

Sunny (track 35°C, air 24°C)

Pos.	Driver	Laps	Time
1	Jarno Trulli	13	1m 12.629s
2	Fernando Alonso	14	1m 12.901s
3	Jenson Button	14	1m 13.026s
4	Takuma Sato	11	1m 13.235s
5	Juan Pablo Montoya	14	1m 13.320s
6	Michael Schumacher	14	1m 13.420s
7	Kimi Räikkönen	14	1m 13.566s
8	David Coulthard	13	1m 13.686s
9	Rubens Barrichello	10	1m 13.904s
10	Christian Klien	20	1m 14.340s
11	Cristiano da Matta	24	1m 14.521s
12	Ralf Schumacher	16	1m 14.697s
13	Mark Webber	29	1m 14.835s
14	Giancarlo Fisichella	10	1m 14.902s
15	Olivier Panis	16	1m 14.916s
16	Felipe Massa	12	1m 15.332s
17	Nick Heidfeld	14	1m 15.987s
18	Timo Glock	17	1m 16.417s
19	Zsolt Baumgartner	17	1m 16.579s
20	Gianmaria Bruni	17	1m 16.825s

9th: DAVID COULTHARD McLaren-Mercedes

7th: RUBENS BARRICHELLO Ferrari

5th: FERNANDO ALONSO Renault

3rd: JARNO TRULLI Renault

Pole: RALF SCHUMACHER Williams-BMW

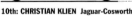

10th: CHRISTIAN KLIEN Jaguar-Cosworth

8th: KIMI RÄIKKÖNEN McLaren-Mercedes

6th: MICHAEL SCHUMACHER Ferrari

4th: JUAN PABLO MONTOYA Williams-BMW

2nd: JENSON BUTTON BAR-Honda

55	56	57	58	59	60	61	62	63	64	65	66	67	68	69	70	
1	1	1	1	1	1	1	1	1	1	1	1	1	1	1	1	1
4	4	4	4	4	4	4	4	4	4	4	4	4	4	4	4	2
2	2	2	2	2	2	2	2	2	2	2	2	2	2	2	2	3
9	9	9	9	9	9	9	9	9	9	9	9	9	9	9	9	4
3	3	3	3	3	3	3	3	3	3	3	3	3	3	3	3	5
6	6	6	6	6	11	11	11	11	11	11	11	11	11	11	11	6
11	11	11	11	11	6	6	6	6	6	6	6	6	6	6	6	7
16	16	16	16	16	16	16	16	16	16	16	16	16	16			8
5	5	5	5	5	5	5	5	5	5	5	5	5	5			
17	17	17	17	17	17	17	17	17	17	17	17	17	17			
19	19	19	19	19	19	19	19	19	19	19	19	19	19			
12	12	12	12	12	12	12	12	18	18	18	18	18	18			
18	18	18	18	18	18	18	18	15	15	15	15	15	15			
15	15	15	15	15	15	15	15	21	21	21	21					
21	21	21	21	21	21	21	21									

FOR THE RECORD

Fernando Alonso
100 laps led

Giancarlo Fisichella
150 grand prix points

Timo Glock
First grand prix start

Timo Glock
First grand prix point

POINTS: CONSTRUCTORS

1	Ferrari	122
2	Renault	61
3	BAR	51
4	Williams	48
5	Sauber	13
6	McLaren	7
7	Toyota	5
8	Jaguar	3
9	Jordan	2

POINTS: DRIVERS

1	Michael Schumacher	70
2	Rubens Barrichello	52
3	Jenson Button	43
4	Jarno Trulli	36
5	Juan Pablo Montoya	28
6	Fernando Alonso	25
7	Ralf Schumacher	20
8 =	Takuma Sato	8
8 =	Giancarlo Fisichella	8
10	Felipe Massa	4
11 =	Cristiano da Matta	4
11 =	David Coulthard	4
13 =	Kimi Räikkönen	3
13 =	Mark Webber	3
15	Nick Heidfeld	2
16	Olivier Panis	1

Photographs: Darren Heath

Above: Rubens Barrichello grabs the lead at the start of the US Grand Prix.

Right: Takuma Sato overcame a bad start to the weekend, having tangled with Felipe Massa's Sauber in Friday free practice, to line up third on the grid.
Photographs: Darren Heath

FIA F1 WORLD CHAMPIONSHIP • ROUND 9

UNITED STATESGP
INDIANAPOLIS

SAFETY AT ISSUE

Opinions were sharply divided in the Indianapolis paddock as to whether the US Grand Prix should have been stopped to facilitate the rescue of Ralf Schumacher, who had sat stunned in the cockpit of his wrecked Williams-BMW for around three minutes after a high-speed accident in front of the pits. Although the car carrying FIA medical delegate Sid Watkins had arrived within the time deemed acceptable under FIA regulations, leading members of the Grand Prix Drivers' Association expressed the view that the whole episode had been handled badly.

'What happened to Ralf was totally unacceptable,' said GPDA director Mark Webber. 'We have to speak to the FIA because two minutes is a long time if you are in trouble. We have to learn from it. It is easy now to make criticisms, but we have all got to sit down and make sensible decisions.

'Tyre failures on these cars are dangerous. The FIA knows that. They are not stupid, and we don't want to be trigger happy, but if you look at the worst cases, this would be right up there.'

David Coulthard added, 'Someone told me that Ralf was sitting there for two laps with no one with him, which I don't understand. Why the hell would that have been the case? According to Sid, he [Ralf] took 78 g and was knocked out for a while. I'm disappointed if he was sitting there for a few minutes, because that is real life or death stuff. That needs to be looked at.'

However, FIA President Max Mosley defended the procedures. 'In the worst kind of accident, when somebody's heart stops and they stop breathing, you need to get a resuscitation expert to them within two minutes,' he told F1 Racing magazine. 'I've read some criticism, based on the fact that the medical car took just over three minutes to get to the scene. That's true, because it's located at the pit-lane exit, and Ralf crashed near the end of the lap, but our accident and emergency cars are located so they can get a resuscitation expert to the scene within two minutes. And at Indianapolis, there was one there in one minute 39 seconds.'

Mosley also rejected criticism that the stewards had taken too long to black-flag Montoya after he had transgressed Article 85 of the FIA sporting regulations, seeking to change cars after leaving the grid within the prohibited 15s period immediately prior to the start. 'I don't believe we put Juan Pablo through any unnecessary risks, any more than he runs an unnecessary risk by doing so much testing,' he said.

The vexed issue of whether or not F1 cars should be racing at all on sections of track that make up Indy racing ovals was another matter altogether, an issue of concern that lingered long after Ralf Schumacher had returned to Europe for physiotherapy on his two cracked vertebrae.

Mark Blundell, who had survived a 190-mph trip into the wall following brake failure on his PacWest Reynard-Mercedes during the 1998 CART race at Rio de Janeiro, commented, 'Nothing is comparable to hitting concrete. None of the F1 boys has ever had anything until they hit concrete. I thought, "This is it, goodnight Vienna. I'm about to die."'

INDIANAPOLIS QUALIFYING

Ferrari was right on the pace again at Indianapolis, and Rubens Barrichello was brimming with confidence after his strong performance in Montreal the previous Sunday. Initially, both Ferrari drivers were troubled by localised blistering of the soft-option Bridgestone tyres, while Michael Schumacher dropped a left rear wheel over a kerb on Friday, pitching his F2004 into a spin.

On Saturday, Barrichello stole pole with a 1m 10.233s best, edging out the world champion by just over a tenth of a second. 'Before pre-qualifying, we made a small change to my car that was an improvement,' said the Brazilian. 'In the first sector, the car did not feel so good, but then it improved in the second sector, which is important, as it is the longest. Although I'm naturally a right-foot braker, I have been using my left also now, and like a footballer who can score with both feet has an advantage, it means my driving has improved.'

Schumacher conceded that he had nothing to complain about. 'Of course, I would like to have been first,' he grinned, 'but Rubens has done a better job than me and, to be honest, I expected to be farther back. I lost the lap in the second sector where the car was sliding about too much.'

BAR Honda's Takuma Sato had started the weekend on a wild note in Friday free practice, when he had tangled with Felipe Massa's Sauber under braking for Turn One, both cars spinning off, which led to the session being red-flagged. On Saturday, he was inside Schumacher's then-fastest time at the second split, but dropped to second at the end of the lap. He fell to third when Barrichello bagged pole.

Nevertheless, Sato's 1m 10.601s best was 0.2s quicker than team-mate Jenson Button, who joined him on the second row, the British driver had grappled with a touch too much oversteer after a late set-up change. 'When Taku did his first run, obviously he was running after me when the circuit was cleaner, and he had more wing than me, so we tried that setting and it was pretty awful actually. Loads of oversteer. In hindsight, I wish we'd left the car as it was.'

Both Renault drivers had complained of poor handing balance on Friday, Fernando Alonso having spun off after just three laps in the afternoon session. That had left Jarno Trulli to do most of the tyre evaluation work, despite suffering a suspected gearbox problem. Things were better on Saturday for Alonso, who managed a confident ninth, just 0.12s behind Juan Pablo Montoya's fifth-place Williams. Trulli

aborted his run due to another gearchange problem, which stemmed from an electronic glitch on the steering wheel, and was consigned to the back of the grid.

Williams's Ralf Schumacher had spun his FW26 twice in Friday free practice; he wound up sixth on the grid with a 1m 11.106s fastest lap after what he described as a 'decent qualifying, nothing special really.' Montoya was one place up on his German colleague, on 1m 11.062s. 'I'm a bit disappointed,' he said, 'because I believe there's more in the car than fifth position. Its balance certainly wasn't perfect.'

In the McLaren garage, there was a definite sense of excitement and anticipation as the team looked forward to the impending test debut of the new MP4/19B, which was due to run again at Jerez the week after the US race. In the meantime, it was just a question of getting the unloved original MP4/19 through the Indianapolis weekend as effectively as possible.

On Friday, David Coulthard had stopped out on the circuit with electrical problems. Then he got out of shape on his qualifying run to start 12th on 1m 12.026s. 'We didn't make any changes between sessions,' said the Scot, 'so I was a bit surprised when the car felt different. I got out of shape in the corners and used more traction control, which just soaks up the time.'

Thus, Coulthard ended up five places behind Kimi Räikkönen, who managed a 1m 11.137s and was much happier with the handling balance of his machine.

Having grappled initially with poor levels of grip in the Toyota TF104 during free practice, Olivier Panis (1m 11.167s) was very satisfied with his eventual eighth place in the line-up. He started the race confident that he could take another helping of world championship points. By contrast, Cristiano da Matta was disappointed not to have made it into the top ten and had to be satisfied with 11th on 1m 11.691s.

To boost Jaguar's efforts, Cosworth had brought along a development V10 for Mark Webber's car alone, a move that caused a degree of consternation among members of the Jordan team, who thought they had been assured parity of engine specification throughout the season. Mark spun off into the gravel on Saturday morning, but the subsequent light damage to the R5's nose and front suspension was easily repaired in time for qualifying. He satisfied himself with tenth place on 1m 11.286s, three spots ahead of team-mate Christian Klien (1m 12.170s), who was quite happy with the handling of his car on his first visit to Indy.

Top left: Olivier Panis celebrated his 150th grand prix with a strong run to fifth in the Toyota TF104.
Photograph: Peter Nygaard/GP Photo

Top right: Ferrari engineer Chris Dyer watches attentatively from the pit wall.

Above centre: Mark Webber checks screen data. The Australian's Jaguar R5 would retire with engine failure.

Above: Christian Klien's Jaguar and Felipe Massa's Sauber C23 went out on the opening lap.
Photographs: Darren Heath

Left: Cars are marshalled past the stricken Williams-BMW of Ralf Schumacher.

Inset, far left: Ralf Schumacher at the end of his big shunt.

Inset, left: The Mercedes pace car was on overtime.
Photographs: Bryn Williams/crash.net

MICHAEL Schumacher and Rubens Barrichello delivered another commanding 1-2 grand slam in the United States Grand Prix at Indianapolis, but the race was marred by a spectacular 180-mph accident that sent the world champion's brother, Ralf, slamming into the painfully unyielding retaining wall on the banked right-hander before the pits. The BMW Williams driver sustained injuries to his back that would keep him out of F1 for a full three months.

The younger Schumacher's massive shunt – the result of a punctured tyre caused by debris scattered on the track by an earlier accident – created controversy in the pit lane. Several drivers argued that the race should have been stopped, rather than continued at reduced pace behind the safety car, after the start/finish straight was left scattered with shards of razor-sharp material from the wrecked Williams-BMW FW26.

Ralf was hospitalised overnight for tests, and later flew back to Germany where he entered a private clinic for further treatment. His painful misfortune topped off another bad race for the Williams squad, coming just a week after its disqualifications in Montreal for running over-sized brake cooling ducts.

Ralf's team-mate, Juan Pablo Montoya, had experienced a problem with his FW26's external starter when he had lined up on the grid and had switched to the team's spare car, starting from the pit lane. Fifty-six laps had been completed before the stewards finally concluded that he had changed cars 2s into the 15s prohibition period before the formation lap, and he was black-flagged.

'I started from the pit lane and had a tough race, having to climb back up through the field,' said the Colombian. 'I managed to run as high as second at one point, but realistically we were on for a strong top-four position, but then I got the black flag.

'There was no arguing. We had broken the rules, but you would think they could have let us know about it quicker. For me and the team to have put in all that effort, only for it to be wasted, was really disappointing.'

At the beginning of the race, Barrichello made a copybook start from pole position, while Michael Schumacher neatly moved the other Ferrari to the left to prevent any chance of Takuma Sato coming through from the second row as the pack sprinted towards the first corner. Sato duly moved in behind Schumacher, but as they braked for the right-hander, Fernando Alonso's Renault R24 came blasting down the outside from ninth place on the grid, ran around the outside of Sato and grabbed third place after what was widely judged the most outstanding getaway of the season so far.

Farther back in the pack, a multiple collision eliminated Felipe Massa's Sauber C23, Christian Klien's Jaguar R5, Giorgio Pantano's Jordan EJ-14 and Gianmaria Bruni's Minardi PS04. All the drivers walked away, but the safety car had to be deployed to slow the field as track marshals swept up the widely scattered debris and tangled cars.

When the safety car was withdrawn at the start of lap six, Michael Schumacher was positioned perfectly at the exit of the final corner and leapfrogged ahead of Barrichello as they stormed down the start/finish straight. The world champion had made his move so early that some trackside observers mistakenly thought that his Ferrari had nosed ahead of its stablemate before they had actually crossed the start/finish line, which would have been against the rules.

At the end of lap six, Schumacher led Barrichello by 0.8s, but Alonso was right on their tail and looked likely to keep the Ferrari duo on their toes in a genuine contest for the lead. Unfortunately, approaching Turn One at 200 mph, the Spaniard's Renault suffered a failure of its right rear Michelin tyre, which pitched it sharply into the concrete retaining wall; the badly damaged car skidded to a halt in the corner's escape road.

This time, the wreckage was cleared up without recourse to the safety car, but a few moments later a flurry of waved yellow flags on the final banked corner before the pits was accompanied by a cloud of smoke and debris. Coming up to complete lap ten, Ralf Schumacher's Williams-BMW had spun at 180 mph and slammed backwards into the retaining wall before bouncing back into the middle of the track.

For the second time in the race, the safety car was deployed, and the FIA medical car carrying Professor Sid Watkins had to

Above: Kimi Räikkönen gets the all-clear to leave the McLaren pit. The Finn took sixth place, despite having twice to top up the engine's pneumatic valve reservoir.
Photograph: Darren Heath

DIARY

Former Ferrari F1 driver Stefan Johansson discusses the prospect of starting his own grand prix team with FIA officials.

F1 team owners object to Bernie Ecclestone's plans to expand the world championship to 20 races by 2006.

Both Williams test drivers Marc Gené and Antonio Pizzonia tipped as possible replacements for Ralf Schumacher if the German driver is sidelined on a long-term basis.

Danny Watts gives Lola its first F3 win for 11 years at Castle Combe, breaking an 11-year run of Dallara domination on the British championship scene.

complete a full lap before stopping alongside the wrecked Williams in which Schumacher was still sitting. He was clearly shaken, but was able to reassure his pit crew over the radio link that he was in one piece although winded and very bruised.

Michael Schumacher, leading the pack at a gentle pace behind the safety car, was understandably anxious about his brother's condition, but was quickly reassured over the radio link from the Ferrari pit.

'Ralf was going to get out of his car, but they told him to stay in there as a precaution until attention was summoned,' Michael Schumacher reflected later. 'The biggest concern I had was seeing Ralf sitting there for so long in the car. They kept telling me that they were informed that things weren't too bad, everything was looking alright, but, still, I mean…'

While the wrecked Williams and its attendant debris were being cleared up, most drivers took the opportunity to pit for fuel and tyres, but both BAR-Hondas stayed out. Consequently, when the field was unleashed again, at the end of lap 19, Sato and Jenson Button were running right behind Michael Schumacher's Ferrari, the Japanese driver keeping his brimming enthusiasm well under control on this occasion. He drove with an impressive poise and confidence as he shadowed and pressured the world champion for the next few laps.

At the end of lap 20, Schumacher's Ferrari came through 0.7s ahead of Sato and Button, with Montoya leading the pursuit from Kimi Räikkönen's McLaren MP4/19 and Barrichello's Ferrari F2004. Button pitted on lap 24 (6.7s), and Sato came in from second place on the following lap, leaving Montoya in the number-two slot, some 6.6s behind the leading Ferrari. At the end of lap 35, the Colombian made a 7.9s refuelling stop from second place, which left Barrichello 13.7s behind Schumacher. Trulli's Renault was next up, ahead of Olivier Panis's Toyota TF104 and the recovering Sato.

By this time, Button had gone, having retired after 26 laps following the loss of seventh gear due to a transmission oil leak. 'It was a pretty dramatic race, but my start wasn't very good and I lost two places to Alonso and Räikkönen,' said the Brit reflectively. 'After the first safety car [period], the car was working really well, but I was stuck behind Räikkönen. Then we had the second safety car, when Ralf had his big accident. Then we decided to stay out rather than pitting under the safety car, and I agree with the team it was the right thing to do.'

Barrichello had another eight laps' worth of fuel in his Ferrari's tank when Schumacher came in for his final stop at the end of lap 41; the Brazilian made the most of it, piling on the pressure before ducking in for his own final stop at the end of lap 50, a slick 7.9s affair that sent him back into the fray right on the world champion's tail. Had he not had a slow in-lap, worried by running over debris from a trackside board hit earlier by Giancarlo Fisichella's Sauber, Barrichello might well have resumed in the lead.

Armed with fresh tyres, the Brazilian strained every sinew to capitalise on his advantage, the two F2004s almost touching at one point as he tried to force his way ahead of Schumacher into Turn Four. But Michael hung on until the extra grip afforded by his team-mate's new Bridgestones faded and the Maranello equilibrium was duly restored.

Schumacher eventually took the chequered flag 2.95s ahead of Barrichello, but it had been a race of changing fortunes, and he was fully aware that the cards might well have fallen in his team-mate's favour.

'I think every time we put on new tyres after a couple of laps, when the tyres are pretty new, it moves a little bit and you can't really push that hard because we were marginal on blisters,' said Schumacher. 'You have to give the tyres a bit of time to wear down, and then you are able to push. And that was the phase, obviously, in the latter part, before the last pit stop, when he

Left: Jackie Stewart and Jaguar F1 team principal Tony Purnell.

Below: Lucky boy. Zsolt Baumgartner soldiered on to finish eighth and claim a single point for Minardi.
Photographs: Darren Heath

Bottom: Takuma Sato drove with measured assurance to claim a superb third place behind the Ferraris.
Photograph: Bryn Williams/crash.net

[Rubens] was going flat out and putting in good lap times, and I was in a struggle. And when he came out with new tyres, for one lap you can do it, as well for two, and then we get into this phase where Rubens was dropping back.'

Barrichello added with a grin, 'It is good to have a 1-2 again, but I am just disappointed because really, more than Canada, more than ever, I thought I had the win in my hands. I had a quick car, I was driving well and I was pushing like hell.'

Sato was gradually catching Jarno Trulli's Renault in the closing stages, and when Mark Webber's Jaguar blew its engine at the end of lap 61, going into the right-hander after the pits, the Japanese driver was able to nip past Trulli as he slithered across the infield on the Cosworth V10's scattered lubricant. It was a last-moment disappointment for the Italian, who had started from the back of the grid.

Fifth place fell to Olivier Panis after a strong run in the Toyota, a good reward for the popular Frenchman on his 150th GP outing. 'The team gave me a consistent and competitive car, and I drove a good race,' he said. 'I pushed so hard towards the end, and it was the perfect end to the weekend to finish just 37 seconds behind the winner.'

In sixth and seventh places were the McLarens of Räikkönen and David Coulthard, the Finn having been forced to make an extra stop to top up the pneumatic pressure on the Mercedes V10, while DC ran over debris that damaged a deflector vane; later, he made an unscheduled stop to remove a lump of polystyrene that had jammed beneath the car.

Finally, to underline the old adage that finishing in F1 is everything, Zsolt Baumgartner scored his first world championship point with eighth and last place in the Minardi, albeit three laps down on the winner. The Hungarian's quickest lap had been four seconds slower that the winning Ferrari's, but under the circumstances that didn't seem too dusty. Not bad at all, in fact.

FIA F1 WORLD CHAMPIONSHIP • ROUND 9

UNITED STATES GRAND PRIX
INDIANAPOLIS 18–20 JUNE 2004

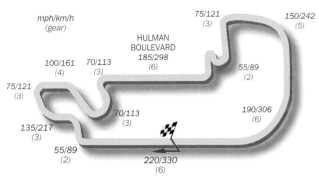

INDIANAPOLIS – GRAND PRIX CIRCUIT

mph/km/h
(gear)

75/121 (3) 150/242 (5)

HULMAN BOULEVARD
185/298 (6)

100/161 (4)   70/113 (3)

55/89 (2)

75/121 (3)

70/113 (3)

190/306 (6)

135/217 (3)

55/89 (2)   220/330 (6)

CIRCUIT LENGTH: 2.605 miles/4.192 km

RACE DISTANCE: 73 laps, 190.150 miles/306.016 km **RACE WEATHER:** Dry and sunny (track 45–49°C, air 24–25°C)

Pos.	Driver	Nat.	No.	Entrant	Car/Engine	Tyres	Laps	Time/Retirement	Speed (mph/km/h)	Gap to leader	Fastest race lap	
1	Michael Schumacher	D	1	Scuderia Ferrari Marlboro	Ferrari F2004-052 V10	B	73	1h 40m 29.914s	113.523/182.698		1m 10.412s	8
2	Rubens Barrichello	BR	2	Scuderia Ferrari Marlboro	Ferrari F2004-052 V10	B	73	1h 40m 32.864s	113.468/182.609	+2.950s	1m 10.399s	7
3	Takuma Sato	J	10	Lucky Strike BAR Honda	BAR 006-Honda RA004E V10	M	73	1h 40m 51.950s	113.110/182.033	+22.036s	1m 10.727s	47
4	Jarno Trulli	I	7	Mild Seven Renault F1 Team	Renault R24-RS4 V10	M	73	1h 41m 04.458s	112.877/181.658	+34.544s	1m 11.187s	45
5	Olivier Panis	F	17	Panasonic Toyota Racing	Toyota TF104-RVX04 V10	M	73	1h 41m 07.448s	112.821/181.568	+37.534s	1m 10.933s	46
6	Kimi Räikkönen	FIN	6	West McLaren Mercedes	McLaren MP4/19-Mercedes F0110P V10	M	72			+1 laps	1m 11.248s	59
7	David Coulthard	GB	5	West McLaren Mercedes	McLaren MP4/19-Mercedes F0110P V10	M	72			+1 laps	1m 12.155s	44
8	Zsolt Baumgartner	H	21	European Minardi Cosworth	Minardi PS04B-Cosworth CR3 V10	B	70			+3 laps	1m 14.097s	39
9	Giancarlo Fisichella	I	11	Sauber Petronas	Sauber C23-Petronas 04 V10	B	65			DNF	1m 12.129s	44
	Mark Webber	AUS	14	Jaguar Racing	Jaguar R5-Cosworth CR6 V10	M	60	Engine			1m 12.140s	46
	Nick Heidfeld	D	18	Jordan Ford	Jordan EJ-14-Cosworth RS V10	B	43	Engine			1m 13.095s	37
	Jenson Button	GB	9	Lucky Strike BAR Honda	BAR 006-Honda RA004E V10	M	26	Gearbox			1m 11.025s	22
	Cristiano da Matta	BR	16	Panasonic Toyota Racing	Toyota TF104-RVX04 V10	M	17	Gearbox			1m 12.872s	8
	Ralf Schumacher	D	4	BMW WilliamsF1 Team	Williams FW26-BMW P84 V10	M	9	Accident			1m 11.982s	8
	Fernando Alonso	E	8	Mild Seven Renault F1 Team	Renault R24-RS4 V10	M	8	Accident			1m 11.236s	8
	Christian Klien	A	15	Jaguar Racing	Jaguar R5-Cosworth CR6 V10	M	0	Accident				
	Felipe Massa	BR	12	Sauber Petronas	Sauber C23-Petronas 04 V10	B	0	Accident				
	Giorgio Pantano	I	19	Jordan Ford	Jordan EJ-14-Cosworth RS V10	B	0	Accident				
	Gianmaria Bruni	I	20	European Minardi Cosworth	Minardi PS04B-Cosworth CR3 V10	B	0	Accident				
DQ	Juan Pablo Montoya	COL	3	BMW WilliamsF1 Team	Williams FW26-BMW P84 V10	M	59	Black flag			1m 11.255s	37

Fastest lap: Rubens Barrichello, on lap 7, 1m 10.399s, 133.201 mph/214.366 km/h (record).

Previous lap record: Michael Schumacher (Ferrari F2003-GA 051 V10), 1m 11.473s, 131.199 mph/211.145 km/h (2003).

19th: ZSOLT BAUMGARTNER Minardi-Cosworth

17th: GIORGIO PANTANO Jordan-Cosworth

15th: FELIPE MASSA Sauber-Petronas

13th: CHRISTIAN KLIEN Jaguar-Cosworth

11th: CRISTIANO DA MATTA Toyota

20th: JARNO TRULLI Renault

18th: GIANMARIA BRUNI Minardi-Cosworth

16th: NICK HEIDFELD Jordan-Cosworth

14th: GIANCARLO FISICHELLA Sauber-Petronas

12th: DAVID COULTHARD McLaren-Mercedes

Grid order	1	2	3	4	5	6	7	8	9	10	11	12	13	14	15	16	17	18	19	20	21	22	23	24	25	26	27	28	29	30	31	32	33	34	35	36	37	38	39	40	41	42	43	44	45	46	47	48	49	50	51	52	53	54	55
2 BARRICHELLO	2	2	2	2	1	1	1	1	1	1	1	1	1	1	1	1	1	1	1	1	1	1	1	1	1	1	1	1	1	1	1	1	1	1	1	1	1	1	1	1	1	2	2	2	2	2	2	2	2	1	1	1	1	1	1
1 M. SCHUMACHER	1	1	1	1	2	2	2	2	10	10	10	10	10	10	10	10	10	10	10	10	10	10	10	3	3	3	3	3	3	3	3	3	2	2	2	2	2	1	7	7	1	1	1	1	2	2	2	2							
10 SATO	8	8	8	8	8	8	8	8	10	10	9	9	9	9	9	9	9	9	9	9	9	9	3	6	6	6	2	2	2	2	7	7	7	7	7	7	7	1	1	17	3	3	3	3	3	3	3	3							
9 BUTTON	10	10	10	10	10	10	10	10	6	6	14	14	14	14	14	3	3	3	3	3	3	6	2	2	2	7	7	7	7	17	17	17	10	10	10	10	17	3	7	7	7	7	7	7	7										
3 MONTOYA	6	6	6	6	6	6	6	9	9	3	3	3	3	6	6	6	6	6	2	17	17	17	17	3	10	10	10	10	17	17	17	3	10	17	17	17	10	10	10	10	10	10	10	10	10										
4 R. SCHUMACHER	9	9	9	9	9	9	9	4	17	2	6	6	6	2	2	2	2	7	17	17	6	10	10	10	10	3	3	3	3	3	10	17	17	17	17	17	17	17	17																
6 RÄIKKÖNEN	4	4	4	4	4	4	4	17	14	6	2	2	2	7	7	7	7	17	10	18	18	18	18	18	18	18	18	11	11	11	11	11	14	14	14	14	14	14	14																
17 PANIS	17	17	17	17	17	17	5	5	7	7	7	7	7	17	17	17	11	11	11	10	11	11	11	11	5	5	5	5	5	14	5	5	6	6	6	6																		
8 ALONSO	14	14	14	14	5	5	5	14	7	17	17	17	17	18	18	18	18	11	5	10	10	5	6	5	5	5	14	14	14	14	14	5	6	6	5	5	5																	
14 WEBBER	5	5	5	14	14	4	3	18	18	18	18	11	11	11	11	11	5	5	14	5	14	14	14	18	18	6	6	6	6	11	11	11	11	11	11																			
16 DA MATTA	7	7	7	7	7	7	18	11	11	11	11	5	5	5	5	14	14	14	21	21	21	6	6	18	18	18	21	21	21	21	21	21	21	21																				
5 COULTHARD	18	18	18	18	18	3	18	3	18	11	5	5	5	5	16	21	14	14	9	9	21	21	21	6	6	6	21	21	21	21	21																						
15 KLIEN	21	21	21	21	21	1	18	16	16	16	16	16	21	14	14	14	14																																				
11 FISICHELLA	3	3	3	3	11	11	11	21	21	21	21	21	21	14																																							
12 MASSA	11	11	11	11	11	21	21	16																																													
18 HEIDFELD	16	16	16	16	16	16	16																																														
19 PANTANO																																																					
20 BRUNI																																																					
21 BAUMGARTNER																																																					
7 TRULLI																																																					

Pit stop
One lap behind leader

TIME SHEETS

QUALIFYING

Sunny (track 36–41°C, air 24–25°C)

Pos.	Driver	Lap time	Sector 1	Sector 2	Sector 3
1	Rubens Barrichello	1m 10.233s	21.613s	29.039s	19.571s
2	Michael Schumacher	1m 10.400s	21.401s	29.483s	19.516s
3	Takuma Sato	1m 10.601s	21.774s	29.024s	19.803s
4	Jenson Button	1m 10.820s	21.789s	29.234s	19.797s
5	Juan Pablo Montoya	1m 11.062s	21.890s	2.390s	19.782s
6	Ralf Schumacher	1m 11.106s	21.850s	29.559s	19.697s
7	Kimi Räikkönen	1m 11.137s	22.188s	29.261s	19.688s
8	Olivier Panis	1m 11.167s	21.909s	29.379s	19.879s
9	Fernando Alonso	1m 11.185s	22.066s	29.247s	19.872s
10	Mark Webber	1m 11.286s	22.069s	29.350s	19.867s
11	Cristiano da Matta	1m 11.691s	22.224s	29.504s	19.963s
12	David Coulthard	1m 12.026s	22.286s	29.865s	19.845s
13	Christian Klien	1m 12.170s	22.294s	29.856s	20.020s
14	Giancarlo Fisichella	1m 12.470s	22.530s	29.979s	19.961s
15	Felipe Massa	1m 12.721s	22.514s	30.362s	19.845s
16	Nick Heidfeld	1m 13.147s	22.725s	30.162s	20.260s
17	Giorgio Pantano	1m 13.375s	22.744s	30.230s	20.401s
18	Gianmaria Bruni	1m 14.010s	22.998s	30.609s	20.403s
19	Zsolt Baumgartner	1m 14.812s	23.285s	30.646s	20.843s
20	Jarno Trulli	No time	–	–	–

PRACTICE 1 (FRIDAY)

Sunny, light cloud (track 37–41°C, air 27–29°C)

Pos.	Driver	Laps	Time
1	Rubens Barrichello	16	1m 11.354s
2	Michael Schumacher	16	1m 11.619s
3	Anthony Davidson	23	1m 11.693s
4	Juan Pablo Montoya	11	1m 12.008s
5	Ricardo Zonta	25	1m 12.366s
6	Björn Wirdheim	25	1m 12.424s
7	Jenson Button	14	1m 12.553s
8	Giancarlo Fisichella	12	1m 12.575s
9	Olivier Panis	16	1m 12.631s
10	Ralf Schumacher	14	1m 12.850s
11	Fernando Alonso	15	1m 12.989s
12	Kimi Räikkönen	8	1m 13.147s
13	Jarno Trulli	15	1m 13.351s
14	Felipe Massa	17	1m 13.371s
15	Takuma Sato	12	1m 13.532s
16	Cristiano da Matta	18	1m 13.555s
17	Mark Webber	10	1m 13.762s
18	David Coulthard	10	1m 13.916s
19	Christian Klien	26	1m 14.407s
20	Timo Glock	25	1m 15.017s
21	Nick Heidfeld	14	1m 15.020s
22	Bas Leinders	20	1m 15.028s
23	Giorgio Pantano	20	1m 15.260s
24	Gianmaria Bruni	9	1m 15.468s
25	Zsolt Baumgartner	16	1m 17.051s

PRACTICE 2 (FRIDAY)

Sunny, light cloud (track 38–43°C, air 28–32°C)

Pos.	Driver	Laps	Time
1	Rubens Barrichello	24	1m 10.365s
2	Anthony Davidson	42	1m 10.967s
3	Juan Pablo Montoya	29	1m 10.982s
4	Michael Schumacher	28	1m 11.036s
5	Jenson Button	19	1m 11.230s
6	Ralf Schumacher	30	1m 11.530s
7	Cristiano da Matta	35	1m 11.893s
8	Olivier Panis	30	1m 11.994s
9	Ricardo Zonta	42	1m 12.019s
10	Kimi Räikkönen	20	1m 12.197s
11	Mark Webber	33	1m 12.438s
12	Jarno Trulli	28	1m 12.441s
13	Giancarlo Fisichella	27	1m 12.537s
14	Takuma Sato	3	1m 12.601s
15	Björn Wirdheim	30	1m 12.761s
16	Christian Klien	31	1m 12.950s
17	Felipe Massa	32	1m 13.196s
18	Zsolt Baumgartner	18	1m 13.384s
19	Timo Glock	33	1m 13.446s
20	Fernando Alonso	3	1m 13.732s
21	Nick Heidfeld	18	1m 13.961s
22	Giorgio Pantano	20	1m 14.407s
23	Bas Leinders	21	1m 14.409s
24	Gianmaria Bruni	17	1m 14.428s
25	David Coulthard	2	No time

PRACTICE 3 (SATURDAY)

Sunny, light wind (track 27–28°C, air 22°C)

Pos.	Driver	Laps	Time
1	Rubens Barrichello	9	1m 10.911s
2	Jenson Button	9	1m 11.071s
3	Michael Schumacher	8	1m 11.207s
4	Fernando Alonso	12	1m 11.509s
5	Ralf Schumacher	14	1m 11.671s
6	Jarno Trulli	11	1m 11.723s
7	Takuma Sato	14	1m 11.989s
8	Cristiano da Matta	12	1m 12.001s
9	Kimi Räikkönen	7	1m 12.015s
10	Mark Webber	6	1m 12.128s
11	Christian Klien	6	1m 12.147s
12	Juan Pablo Montoya	8	1m 12.240s
13	Giancarlo Fisichella	10	1m 12.405s
14	Olivier Panis	14	1m 12.451s
15	David Coulthard	11	1m 12.584s
16	Felipe Massa	13	1m 12.911s
17	Gianmaria Bruni	12	1m 12.957s
18	Zsolt Baumgartner	12	1m 13.396s
19	Nick Heidfeld	11	1m 13.454s
20	Giorgio Pantano	12	1m 13.761s

PRACTICE 4 (SATURDAY)

Sunny, light wind (track 29–31°C, air 21°C)

Pos.	Driver	Laps	Time
1	Jenson Button	17	1m 10.056s
2	Michael Schumacher	16	1m 10.199s
3	Takuma Sato	23	1m 10.251s
4	Rubens Barrichello	16	1m 10.351s
5	Juan Pablo Montoya	13	1m 10.708s
6	Fernando Alonso	13	1m 10.749s
7	Cristiano da Matta	19	1m 10.802s
8	Ralf Schumacher	9	1m 10.820s
9	Jarno Trulli	13	1m 10.848s
10	Kimi Räikkönen	14	1m 11.222s
11	Olivier Panis	20	1m 11.242s
12	David Coulthard	13	1m 11.395s
13	Christian Klien	20	1m 11.992s
14	Nick Heidfeld	16	1m 12.524s
15	Mark Webber	14	1m 12.590s
16	Giorgio Pantano	9	1m 12.603s
17	Giancarlo Fisichella	10	1m 12.686s
18	Felipe Massa	9	1m 12.861s
19	Zsolt Baumgartner	13	1m 13.869s
20	Gianmaria Bruni	14	1m 13.915s

CHASSIS LOG BOOK

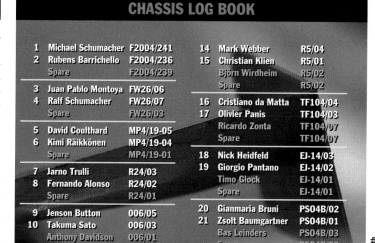

1	Michael Schumacher	F2004/241
2	Rubens Barrichello	F2004/236
	Spare	F2004/239
3	Juan Pablo Montoya	FW26/06
4	Ralf Schumacher	FW26/07
	Spare	FW26/03
5	David Coulthard	MP4/19-05
6	Kimi Räikkönen	MP4/19-04
	Spare	MP4/19-01
7	Jarno Trulli	R24/03
8	Fernando Alonso	R24/02
	Spare	R24/01
9	Jenson Button	006/05
10	Takuma Sato	006/03
	Anthony Davidson	006/01
	Spare	006/01
11	Giancarlo Fisichella	C23/04
12	Felipe Massa	C23/01
	Spare	C23/02
14	Mark Webber	R5/04
15	Christian Klien	R5/01
	Björn Wirdheim	R5/02
	Spare	R5/02
16	Cristiano da Matta	TF104/04
17	Olivier Panis	TF104/03
	Ricardo Zonta	TF104/07
	Spare	TF104/07
18	Nick Heidfeld	EJ-14/03
19	Giorgio Pantano	EJ-14/02
	Timo Glock	EJ-14/01
	Spare	EJ-14/01
20	Gianmaria Bruni	PS04B/02
21	Zsolt Baumgartner	PS04B/01
	Bas Leinders	PS04B/03
	Spare	PS04B/03

Photograph: Darren Heath

9th: FERNANDO ALONSO Renault

7th: KIMI RÄIKKÖNEN McLaren-Mercedes

5th: JUAN PABLO MONTOYA Williams-BMW
Started from pit lane

3rd: TAKUMA SATO BAR-Honda

Pole: RUBENS BARRICHELLO Ferrari

10th: MARK WEBBER Jaguar-Cosworth

8th: OLIVIER PANIS Toyota

6th: RALF SCHUMACHER Williams-BMW

4th: JENSON BUTTON BAR-Honda

2nd: MICHAEL SCHUMACHER Ferrari

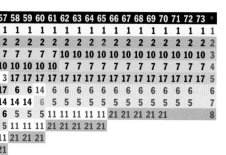

57	58	59	60	61	62	63	64	65	66	67	68	69	70	71	72	73	
1	1	1	1	1	1	1	1	1	1	1	1	1	1	1	1	1	1
2	2	2	2	2	2	2	2	2	2	2	2	2	2	2	2	2	2
7	7	7	7	10	10	10	10	10	10	10	10	10	10	10	10	10	3
10	10	10	10	10	7	7	7	7	7	7	7	7	7	7	7	7	4
3	17	17	17	17	17	17	17	17	17	17	17	17	17	17	17	17	5
17	6	6	14	6	6	6	6	6	6	6	6	6	6	6	6	6	6
14	14	14	6	5	5	5	5	5	5	5	5	5	5	5	5		7
6	5	5	5	11	11	11	11	11	21	21	21	21	21	21			8
5	11	11	11	21	21	21	21	21									
11	21	21	21														
21																	

FOR THE RECORD

150 grand prix starts
Olivier Panis

First grand prix point
Zsolt Baumgartner

POINTS: CONSTRUCTORS

1	Ferrari	142	6	Sauber	15
2	Renault	66	7	Toyota	8
3	BAR	58	8	Jordan	5
4	Williams	36	9	Jaguar	3
5	McLaren	17	10	Minardi	1

POINTS: DRIVERS

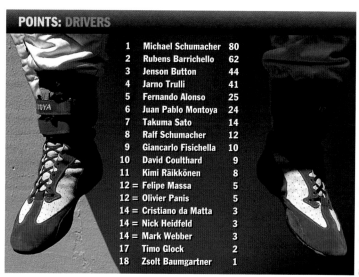

1	Michael Schumacher	80
2	Rubens Barrichello	62
3	Jenson Button	44
4	Jarno Trulli	41
5	Fernando Alonso	25
6	Juan Pablo Montoya	24
7	Takuma Sato	14
8	Ralf Schumacher	12
9	Giancarlo Fisichella	10
10	David Coulthard	9
11	Kimi Räikkönen	8
12 =	Felipe Massa	5
12 =	Olivier Panis	5
14 =	Cristiano da Matta	3
14 =	Nick Heidfeld	3
14 =	Mark Webber	3
17	Timo Glock	2
18	Zsolt Baumgartner	1

Photographs: Darren Heath

FRENCHGP
MAGNY-COURS

Main photograph: Fernando Alonso readies himself to take the start in his Renault R24 from pole position.
Photograph: Darren Heath

Inset, left: Aided by some shrewd pit-wall mathematics from the Ferrari squad, Michael Schumacher was switched to a creative four-stop refuelling strategy to pull off yet another stunning win in the French Grand Prix.
Photograph: Darren Heath

Inset, left: Alonso and Schumacher celebrate on the podium.
Photograph: Bryn Williams/crash.net

Fernando Alonso conjured up a brilliant pole winning effort on Renault's home turf, his 1m 13.698s best easing out Michael Schumacher's Ferrari F2004 by just 0.273s. However, the home team judged that the world champion's Bridgestone tyres were degrading at a slower rate than its own Michelins, giving reason to believe that Michael would be a formidable opponent when it came to the serious business of the race.

Even so, Alonso was upbeat and cheerful. 'It's nice to be here,' he trilled. 'The car has been quick all weekend, and pole position gives me a solid base for tomorrow's race. I did a very good lap. The car was understeering a bit too much at low speed, but it was very stable on the high-speed corners.'

By contrast, Jarno Trulli locked a wheel at Turn 13 and had to grapple with high-speed oversteer on his way to fifth (1m 14.070s) on the grid. Between the two Renaults lay Michael Schumacher's Ferrari, David Coulthard's new McLaren-Mercedes MP4/19B (1m 13.987s) and Jenson Button's BAR-Honda 006 (1m 13.995s).

Rubens Barrichello's F2004 had suffered a hydraulic glitch that had forced him to miss pre-qualifying, leaving the Brazilian to run first in the battle for grid positions. He fought lack of grip to qualify tenth on 1m 14.478s, while Schumacher admitted he was not quite fast enough through the third sector.

'I lost about one-tenth at Turn 13 because I was pushing too hard,' said Schumacher, 'but I lost the most time in the last two corners. But I'm still on the front row, so we will be in the fight tomorrow.'

The heavily revised McLaren MP4/19Bs were making their race debut, both Räikkönen and Coulthard reporting that the cars felt more stable and predictable under hard braking thanks to major aerodynamic, weight distribution and rear suspension changes. Coulthard was upbeat and cautiously optimistic after qualifying a strong third, but Räikkönen had pushed too hard, picking up excessive understeer at the first corner and lining up ninth with a 1m 14.346s best.

The Finn was angry at his slip. 'Unfortunately, I pushed too hard at the first corner,' he shrugged. 'I tried hard to compensate for this on the rest of the lap, which resulted in a few minor mistakes which cost me even more time. But I think it is obvious to everybody that the car shows potential.'

BAR Honda's Jenson Button had struggled with oversteer before pre-qualifying and had improved the balance with a slight set-up change. Even so, he confessed that he was frustrated with fourth on the grid. Takuma Sato was an undramatic seventh (1m 14.240s) after a trouble-free run.

'It was a reasonably good lap, but I'm disappointed we are outside the top three,' said Button. 'I was struggling with oversteer prior to pre-qualifying, so we made a change to the car. That didn't have the right effect, so we changed again for qualifying, and the balance was a lot better.'

For this race, the Williams-BMW FW26s had been fitted with smaller radiators and revised aerodynamics/bodywork; test driver Marc Gené

was standing in for the injured Ralf Schumacher alongside Juan Pablo Montoya. The Colombian had experienced a heavy shunt in Friday morning's wet free practice. The car had been rebuilt, but he struggled initially with set-up and was disappointed with sixth on the grid (1m 14.172s) after making a slip in the final sector. Gené ran a heavier fuel load to line-up eighth on 1m 14.275s, despite going wide on a pre-qualifying run.

Cristiano da Matta was pleased with the feel of his Toyota TF104, posting a satisfying 11th-fastest 1m 14.553s after managing to dial out a touch of pre-qualifying understeer in time for his second run. Olivier Panis (1m 15.130s) was left rather more disappointed at the prospects for his home grand prix after his car had bottomed out too much and then lost some grip in the final sector of the lap; he ended up 14th.

Jaguar enjoyed a generally promising qualifying session, Mark Webber winding up 12th on 1m 14.798s. He reported that the R5 felt particularly well balanced and that the grip levels were reassuringly high. He admitted that he may have lost a tenth of a second in the final sector, but generally his pace was encouraging. Christian Klien also had a worthwhile run to 13th, lapping just 0.3s slower than his team-mate.

The Sauber C23s came to Magny-Cours with a revised aerodynamic package, but Giancarlo Fisichella suffered a nasty off-track moment on Saturday morning when a front push-rod failed at the last corner, pitching him into the tyre barrier. The Italian switched to the spare car, which didn't have the complete new aero package, and wound up 15th on the grid with a 1m 16.177s, having run with a heavy fuel load in preparation for a two-stop strategy. Felipe Massa (1m 16.200s) was right behind, while the two Jordans and the Minardis brought up the rear, as was becoming the norm.

Photograph: Darren Heath

MOSLEY RESIGNS – FOR THE MOMENT

Max Mosley stunned the F1 community at the Circuit de Nevers by announcing that he would stand down as president of the FIA, motorsport's international governing body, at the end of October 2004, after 12 years presiding over the high-profile, media-driven sport. The shock decision by the 64-year-old former barrister caused speculation that the move could be a shrewd piece of political manoeuvring or a tacit acknowledgement by one of the sport's most senior powerbrokers that he was simply fed up with a business that has become increasing ungovernable.

Yet barely a week later, after a remarkable volte-face, it emerged that Mosley could stand again for the presidency of the FIA in 2005, and that he would be almost certain of winning another five-year term as the most powerful man in motorsport. It transpired that he had been begged to stay on barely a week after making his announcement.

'The reason I changed my mind was that I was being pressed from all sides, both from the sport and the non-sporting side of the FIA, to reconsider my decision,' Mosley said. 'Most of the support came from the so-called "Region One" of the FIA and its affiliated AIT [the motoring body that governs non-motorsport matters], which includes all of Europe outside the EU, plus Africa and the Middle East, a huge percentage of the 118 member countries of the FIA.'

In acceding to the request to stay, Mosley effectively undermined the efforts of Jacques Regis, the president of the French motorsport federation, and Robert Darbelnet, the president and chief executive of the AAA, America's largest automobile sporting organisation, and president of the AIT, to challenge him in 2005.

Mosley also made it clear that if he ran for election in 2005, it would be largely on his own terms. 'If I do, it will be very much on the basis of somebody dealing with the non-sporting side, and one, perhaps two individuals looking after the sport without me interfering on a day-to-day basis,' he said.

Mosley's plans to force through dramatic technical changes in F1, including smaller V8 engines and major restrictions on high-cost technology, were also apparently strengthened by this endorsement.

'It's been like having an enormous vote of confidence,' he said. 'The only hope any opposition might have had was if I couldn't carry the vote for these measures when it actually came to it, but they now realise that I can. The only way of challenging them is by a vote in the FIA or to go to arbitration and argue that the cars are not unacceptably fast and that no reasonable world council would have taken the decision to slow them down. And that would have had no chance of success.'

MICHAEL Schumacher and the Ferrari team continued their remorseless assault on the F1 record books at the French Grand Prix, which became the 79th victory of the six-times world champion's spectacular career. He finished 8.329s ahead of Fernando Alonso in the Renault R24, while team-mate Rubens Barrichello forced his Ferrari in front of Jarno Trulli's Renault within sight of the chequered flag to claim third.

Jenson Button ended up a disappointed fifth after a problem with his BAR-Honda's anti-stall mechanism lost him a crucial second at his final refuelling stop, preventing him from squeezing back out ahead of Trulli and Barrichello.

'We expected to do a lot better here, and fifth is not good enough,' said the Englishman. 'The race strategy was working well for us, but at the last pit stop the car went into anti-stall mode and cost me the time advantage that could have put us on the podium. We lost a possible third place so we really have to have solved these problems going into the British Grand Prix on Sunday.'

Admittedly, on this occasion, it looked as though Schumacher had a race on his hands when Alonso delighted the fans by planting his Renault R24 firmly on pole position and then led the first 32 laps of the race.

Realising that Schumacher faced a serious fight, Ferrari shifted up a gear and switched the world champion from a three- to a four-stop refuelling strategy. The reasoning was that a light fuel load would permit the searing sequence of quick laps that would be demanded of the driver to ensure that he came out of his final refuelling stop ahead of the French car.

Schumacher's challenge was clear-cut. In the ten laps preceding his fourth refuelling stop at the Circuit de Nevers, Michael would have to stretch his lead over Alonso to 10s to be sure of consolidating his advantage. He duly met the challenge, producing a series of laps in the 1m 15.5s bracket, while Alonso struggled to break the 1m 17s barrier.

For the Renault driver, it was a hugely disappointing result. He'd carried the battle to Schumacher more convincingly that anybody so far in 2004, apart from team-mate Jarno Trulli at Monaco, but he just couldn't close down the world champion's effort. Even so, he seemed bright and upbeat once the race was over.

'I have been waiting for this podium for a long time,' Alonso beamed. 'I could have had it at each of the last two races were it not for mechanical problems, so I am really happy to be here. I had a good race, fought as hard as possible, but I think Michael was just stronger today.'

Schumacher was running 0.6s behind Alonso when he made his first refuelling stop at the end of lap 11. The latter stayed out until lap 14 before coming in for the first time, but when he left the pits still 4s ahead of the world champion, the Ferrari team went on to red alert, bringing Michael in for his second stop on lap 29.

After taking the lead when Alonso made his second stop on lap 32, Schumacher came in again for a quick top-up on lap 42 before making the epic sprint to lap 58, stopping for the fourth time when he finally had the race in the bag.

Schumacher emerged from the pits some 8.2s ahead of Alonso, after which he stroked it easily home to the chequered flag.

'The strategy and the precision of the team in the pit stops were fantastic today,' said Schumacher. 'Before the start, I was not so optimistic, but it became clear that our Bridgestone tyres were very good at the end of their stints, which was not the case with the opposition's, so I was able to close the gap before the stops.

'Then, after the second stop, we decided to switch to a four-stop strategy. I had nothing to lose, and it was a case of no risk, no fun. I only accepted I could win five laps before my final pit stop, when the team told me I had enough of a gap to keep the lead.'

Maranello's technical director Ross Brawn gave team strategist Luca Baldisserri credit for coming up with the four-stop strategy. 'I just supported him on that,' he said. 'When we saw the way things were going, we opted to switch to a four-stop schedule for Michael and, taking into account the great performance of the Bridgestone tyre, it certainly worked.'

Ferrari's joy was further boosted when Rubens Barrichello dramatically forced his way past Jarno Trulli's Renault on the penultimate corner to take third.

At one point, the battle between Trulli and Barrichello, who was recovering from a tenth-place grid position caused by hydraulic problems in qualifying, seemed as though it would develop into a high-speed deadlock. The Brazilian's Ferrari was 5 mph faster than his opponent's Renault down the long back straight to the Adelaide hairpin, but Trulli made up 0.3s on his rival through the third sector of the lap. Barrichello generously admitted that if Trulli hadn't made a slight mistake on the last lap, he wouldn't have been close enough to try the move. But it worked to brilliant effect.

'I had a great race, and the other drivers were very fair on the track,' said Rubens. 'It was a shame I paid the penalty for my prequalifying problem, without which I could have had an even better race. I gave it all I had.

'As for Trulli, although I had better speed in Turn Three, it was

Above: Jarno Trulli finished fourth at Magny-Cours, having been overtaken only two corners from the chequered flag by a particularly determined Rubens Barrichello in his Ferrari.

Centre left: McLaren team manager Dave Ryan chats with Juan Pablo Montoya, the Colombian looking forward to switching to the Woking squad for 2005.
Photographs: Darren Heath

Bottom left: After a promising test programme, the new McLaren-Mercedes MP4/19B made its race debut at Magny-Cours, David Coulthard and Kimi Räikkönen finishing sixth and seventh.
Photograph: Bryn Williams/crash.net

Above: Jenson Button dropped from a possible third to fifth in his BAR-Honda 006 when the anti-stall mechanism caused a moment's hesitation from the V10 as he accelerated back into the race after his final refuelling stop.

Right: Cristiano da Matta and Nick Heidfeld contest the same piece of track.

Below far right: Marc Gené deputised for Ralf Schumacher, but had a disappointing race to tenth place.
Photographs: Peter Nygaard/GP Photo

Main photograph: Juan Pablo Montoya was lucky to come away from the French Grand Prix with a single championship point for eighth place after spinning from sixth to ninth early on.
Photograph: Darren Heath

DIARY

Speculation intensifies that the Jordan F1 team has acquired the services of Renault designer Mark Smith for the 2005 season.

McLaren declines to comment on rumours that its F1 technical director, Adrian Newey, might leave the team when his contract expires in 2005.

The prospect of a Turkish Grand Prix makes it likely that Bernie Ecclestone will try for 19 races on the F1 schedule in 2005.

difficult to follow him though the chicane and there he had better traction. But then, on the final lap, he slowed a bit too much at Turn 13 and I was able to get alongside him two turns later. It was risky, but it was worth it, even though I was being a bit careful not to damage the car, as it would have been a shame to get from tenth to fourth, then not finish. So I was trying 95 per cent, and when I saw I had a chance, I added another ten per cent, making it 105 per cent in total.'

For his part, Trulli was disappointed with his performance, and perhaps somewhat bemused by the rather unsympathetic tone adopted by some of his team colleagues to what was, after all, a minor slip when seen in the context of his 2004 season as a whole.

'I am gutted for myself and the team to have lost third place at the very end of the race,' he said. 'I made a fantastic start to get in front of Button and Coulthard, and the car seemed pretty competitive. Even so, I couldn't keep up with Fernando, as it seemed quite nervous to drive.

'The race was going to plan up until the last stint, when the car had less traction and was oversteering a lot. I defended against Rubens as much as possible, but on the last lap he passed me under braking. I tried to close the door, but couldn't.'

Behind Button, the new McLaren-Mercedes MP4/19Bs of David Coulthard and Kimi Räikkönen finished sixth and seventh on their race debuts, demonstrating much improved form compared with the unmodified car the two drivers had used since the start of the season. Revised aerodynamics and rear suspension geometry made them easier and more stable to drive, particularly under hard braking and when turning into the corners, and Coulthard and Räikkönen were actually edging steadily towards the battle for third place as they went into the closing stages of the race.

'At the start, I lost two positions to be fifth after the first corner,'

said Coulthard. 'This was a shame, as the race showed that both Kimi and I had the speed of the cars which were fighting for third. It was an encouraging race debut for the 19B, and I'm looking forward to my home grand prix at Silverstone next weekend and the rest of the season.'

Juan Pablo Montoya's FW26 added just a single point to the Williams tally for a disappointing eighth place. After a shunt on Friday, the Colombian had suffered with a bruised neck for the rest of the weekend, running sixth in the early stages of the race before clipping a kerb and spinning on lap 20. He dropped to eighth behind Räikkönen, but didn't have the speed to challenge in the closing stages. Gené suffered a clutch problem at the start, then touched Webber in Turn Three, eventually surviving to come home tenth.

'It was a very difficult race for me,' admitted Montoya, 'especially because of that intense pain in my neck which prevented me from being able to keep my head up. I didn't expect the pain to become so sharp in the race. Also, the balance of my car wasn't ideal, especially in the first part of the race, which caused me to make a few mistakes. I really hoped I could get much more than one single point today.'

Marc Gené's race as Ralf Schumacher's stand-in also delivered far less than the driver was expecting. 'I had problem with the clutch on the grid,' shrugged the Spaniard. 'I didn't want to jump the start, so I released it very slowly and lost three positions. Then Mark Webber and I touched on Turn Three and I nearly spun. Both my car and I just needed more speed today!'

While the Williams boys were disappointed with their lot, Jaguar drivers Mark Webber and Christian Klien were close to celebrating their measured and satisfyingly fast runs to ninth and 11th places in their R5s.

'Today's race was incredibly competitive, with most teams both reliable and fast,' said the Australian. 'The team has done an amazing job all weekend, and to see us finish both cars in ninth and 11th after only one retirement is a testament to all the hard work done at the track and back in the factory.'

Klien was similarly exuberant. 'The car was very well balanced for me and I got a good start,' he enthused. 'I certainly raced hard and was very pleased to be able to stay with my team-mate through most of the race.'

The Austrian had crossed the line comfortably ahead of the two Saubers of Giancarlo Fisichella and Felipe Massa, and the Toyotas of Cristiano da Matta and Olivier Panis. Fisichella had started out on a two-stop strategy, but after the race had begun was switched to a three-stopper, as the C23's pace was not fast enough and he was struggling for front-end grip. Massa had struggled with high levels of tyre degradation all afternoon.

It had been a tough afternoon for the Saubers and Toyotas. Their lack of performance was set dramatically in the context of contemporary F1's remarkable mechanical reliability, only three of the 20 starters failing to make it to the chequered flag.

GRAND PRIX DE FRANCE

MAGNY-COURS 2–4 JULY 2004

CIRCUIT DE NEVERS – MAGNY-COURS

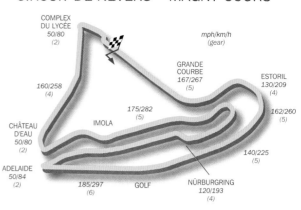

COMPLEX DU LYCÉE 50/80 (2)

mph/km/h (gear)

GRANDE COURBE 167/267 (5)

ESTORIL 130/209 (4)

160/258 (4)

175/282 (5)

162/260 (5)

CHÂTEAU D'EAU 50/80 (2)

IMOLA

140/225 (5)

ADELAIDE 50/84 (2)

185/297 (6)

GOLF

NÜRBURGRING 120/193 (4)

CIRCUIT LENGTH: 2.741 miles/4.411 km

Photograph: Darren Heath

RACE DISTANCE: 70 laps, 191.746 miles/308.586 km   RACE WEATHER: Sunny (track 38–41°C, air 27–32°C)

Pos.	Driver	Nat.	No.	Entrant	Car/Engine	Tyres	Laps	Time/Retirement	Speed (mph/km/h)	Gap to leader	Fastest race lap	
1	Michael Schumacher	D	1	Scuderia Ferrari Marlboro	Ferrari F2004-052 V10	B	70	1h 30m 18.133s	127.403/205.035		1m 15.377s	32
2	Fernando Alonso	E	8	Mild Seven Renault F1 Team	Renault R24-RS4 V10	M	70	1h 30m 26.462s	127.207/204.720	+8.329s	1m 15.551s	34
3	Rubens Barrichello	BR	2	Scuderia Ferrari Marlboro	Ferrari F2004-052 V10	B	70	1h 30m 49.755s	126.663/203.845	+31.622s	1m 16.035s	50
4	Jarno Trulli	I	7	Mild Seven Renault F1 Team	Renault R24-RS4 V10	M	70	1h 30m 50.215s	126.653/203.828	+32.082s	1m 16.248s	15
5	Jenson Button	GB	9	Lucky Strike BAR Honda	BAR 006-Honda RA004E V10	M	70	1h 30m 50.617s	126.643/203.813	+32.484s	1m 15.971s	50
6	David Coulthard	GB	5	West McLaren Mercedes	McLaren MP4/19B-Mercedes F0110P V10	M	70	1h 30m 53.653s	126.573/203.700	+35.520s	1m 16.303s	11
7	Kimi Räikkönen	FIN	6	West McLaren Mercedes	McLaren MP4/19B-Mercedes F0110P V10	M	70	1h 30m 54.363s	126.556/203.673	+36.230s	1m 15.791s	30
8	Juan Pablo Montoya	COL	3	BMW WilliamsF1 Team	Williams FW26-BMW P84 V10	M	70	1h 31m 01.552s	126.390/203.405	+43.419s	1m 16.140s	48
9	Mark Webber	AUS	14	Jaguar Racing	Jaguar R5-Cosworth CR6 V10	M	70	1h 31m 10.527s	126.182/203.071	+52.394s	1m 15.956s	53
10	Marc Gené	E	4	BMW WilliamsF1 Team	Williams FW26-BMW P84 V10	M	70	1h 31m 16.299s	126.049/202.857	+58.166s	1m 16.070s	56
11	Christian Klien	A	15	Jaguar Racing	Jaguar R5-Cosworth CR6 V10	M	69			+1 lap	1m 16.852s	37
12	Giancarlo Fisichella	I	11	Sauber Petronas	Sauber C23-Petronas 04 V10	B	69			+1 lap	1m 16.699s	22
13	Felipe Massa	BR	12	Sauber Petronas	Sauber C23-Petronas 04 V10	B	69			+1 lap	1m 17.388s	23
14	Cristiano da Matta	BR	16	Panasonic Toyota Racing	Toyota TF104-RVX04 V10	M	69			+1 lap	1m 16.937s	49
15	Olivier Panis	F	17	Panasonic Toyota Racing	Toyota TF104-RVX04 V10	M	68			+2 laps	1m 17.069s	53
16	Nick Heidfeld	D	18	Jordan Ford	Jordan EJ-14-Cosworth RS V10	B	68			+2 laps	1m 18.627s	26
17	Giorgio Pantano	I	19	Jordan Ford	Jordan EJ-14-Cosworth RS V10	B	67			+3 laps	1m 17.641s	15
18	Gianmaria Bruni	I	20	European Minardi Cosworth	Minardi PS04B-Cosworth CR3 V10	B	65			DNF	1m 18.932s	52
	Zsolt Baumgartner	H	21	European Minardi Cosworth	Minardi PS04B-Cosworth CR3 V10	B	31	Spun			1m 19.659s	13
	Takuma Sato	J	10	Lucky Strike BAR Honda	BAR 006-Honda RA004E V10	M	15	Engine			1m 16.809s	14

All results and data © FOM 2004

Fastest lap: Michael Schumacher, on lap 32, 1m 15.377s, 130.903 mph/210.669 km/h (record).

Previous lap record: Juan Pablo Montoya (Williams FW25-BMW P83 V10), 1m 15.512s, 130.669 mph/210.292 km/h (2003).

20th: ZSOLT BAUMGARTNER Minardi-Cosworth

18th: GIORGIO PANTANO Jordan-Cosworth

16th: FELIPE MASSA Sauber-Petronas

14th: OLIVIER PANIS Toyota

12th: MARK WEBBER Jaguar-Cosworth

19th: GIANMARIA BRUNI Minardi-Cosworth

17th: NICK HEIDFELD Jordan-Cosworth

15th: GIANCARLO FISICHELLA Sauber-Petronas

13th: CHRISTIAN KLIEN Jaguar-Cosworth

11th: CRISTIANO DA MATTA Toyota

Grid order	1	2	3	4	5	6	7	8	9	10	11	12	13	14	15	16	17	18	19	20	21	22	23	24	25	26	27	28	29	30	31	32	33	34	35	36	37	38	39	40	41	42	43	44	45	46	47	48	49	50	51	52	53	54
8 ALONSO	8	8	8	8	8	8	8	8	8	8	8	8	8	8	8	8	8	8	8	8	8	8	8	8	8	8	8	8	8	8	8	1	1	1	1	1	1	1	1	1	1	8	8	8	8	1	1	1	1	1	1	1	1	1
1 M. SCHUMACHER	1	1	1	1	1	1	1	1	1	1	1	7	7	9	1	1	1	1	1	1	1	1	1	1	1	1	1	1	1	7	7	1	8	8	8	8	8	8	8	8	1	1	1	1	8	8	8	8	8	8	8	8	8	8
5 COULTHARD	7	7	7	7	7	7	7	7	7	7	9	9	10	10	7	7	7	7	7	7	7	7	7	7	7	7	7	7	7	9	2	7	7	7	7	7	7	7	7	7	7	7	7	7	7	7	7	7	7	9	9	9	7	2
9 BUTTON	9	9	9	9	9	9	9	9	9	9	5	3	1	14	9	9	9	9	9	9	9	9	9	9	9	9	9	9	9	2	1	9	9	9	9	9	9	9	9	9	9	9	9	9	9	9	9	2	2	7	2			
7 TRULLI	5	5	5	5	5	5	5	5	5	3	10	14	7	5	5	5	5	5	5	5	5	5	5	5	5	5	5	5	1	9	2	2	2	2	2	2	2	2	2	2	2	2	2	2	2	2	3	7	9	5			
3 MONTOYA	3	3	3	3	3	3	3	3	3	3	2	1	7	9	15	3	2	2	2	2	2	2	2	2	2	2	2	2	3	14	14	5	5	5	5	5	5	5	5	5	5	5	5	5	5	3	14	5	9	5			
10 SATO	6	6	6	6	6	6	6	6	6	2	10	14	15	15	3	2	12	12	6	6	6	6	6	6	6	6	3	14	14	5	5	6	6	6	6	6	6	6	6	6	6	6	3	14	14	5	6	6						
4 GENÉ	10	10	10	2	2	2	2	2	2	6	1	15	5	5	2	12	6	6	12	3	3	3	3	3	3	3	14	5	4	4	15	15	3	3	3	3	3	3	3	3	3	14	5	5	6	4	4							
6 RÄIKKÖNEN	2	2	10	10	10	10	10	10	10	10	14	5	3	12	6	12	14	14	14	14	14	4	4	6	3	12	3	14	14	14	14	14	4	4	6	3	3	14	14	14	14	14	6	6	4	3	3							
2 BARRICHELLO	14	14	14	14	14	14	14	14	14	14	2	2	6	14	14	14	4	4	4	4	4	6	15	14	14	4	4	4	4	4	4	4	15	15	4	4	4	15	4	4	4	4	4	4	3	14	14							
16 DA MATTA	4	4	4	4	4	4	4	12	12	11	11	11	11	4	15	15	15	15	15	15	15	15	6	15	15	3	3	11	11	11	12	12	12	12	12	12	15	15	15	15	15	15	15	15	15	15	15							
14 WEBBER	16	16	16	16	16	16	16	16	16	16	11	6	6	6	14	4	4	4	15	16	16	16	16	16	16	16	12	12	12	12	12	12	11	11	11	11	11	11	11	11														
15 KLIEN	15	15	15	15	15	15	15	15	15	15	6	11	11	11	4	15	15	15	16	16	16	16	16	16	12	12	16	11	11	11	11	11	16	12	12	12	12	12	11	11														
17 PANIS	12	12	12	12	12	12	12	12	19	4	4	4	16	16	16	16	16	16	16	16	16	16	16	16	16	16	16	16	16	16	16	16	16	16	16	16	16	16	16															
11 FISICHELLA	19	19	11	11	11	11	11	11	11	18	18	16	18	18	18	18	17	17	17	17	17	17	17	17	17	17	17	17	18	18	17	17	17	17	17	17	17	17	17	17	17	17	17											
12 MASSA	11	11	19	19	19	19	19	19	4	19	18	18	18	18	18	17	18	18	18	18	18	18	18	18	18	18	18	17	17	18	18	18	18	18	18	18	18																	
18 HEIDFELD	18	18	18	18	18	18	18	18	18	16	16	18	17	17	17	17	20	20	20	20	20	20	20	20	20	20	19	19	19	19	19	19	19	19	19	19	19	19	19															
19 PANTANO	20	20	17	17	17	17	17	17	17	17	17	17	20	20	20	20	20	20	20	20	20	20	20	20	20	20	20	20	20	20	20	20	20	20	20	20	20	20																
20 BRUNI	21	17	20	20	20	20	20	20	20	20	20	20	21	21	21	21	21	21	21	21	21	21	21	21																														
21 BAUMGARTNER	17	21	21	21	21	21	21	21	21	21	21	21																																										

Pit stop

One lap behind leader

154

TIME SHEETS

QUALIFYING

Warm and sunny (track 33–39°C, air 22–24°C)

Pos.	Driver	Lap time	Sector 1	Sector 2	Sector 3
1	Fernando Alonso	1m 13.698s	24.017s	25.641s	24.040s
2	Michael Schumacher	1m 13.971s	23.816s	25.717s	24.438s
3	David Coulthard	1m 13.987s	23.975s	25.820s	24.280s
4	Jenson Button	1m 13.995s	24.069s	25.790s	24.136s
5	Jarno Trulli	1m 14.070s	24.052s	25.738s	24.136s
6	Juan Pablo Montoya	1m 14.172s	23.834s	25.752s	24.586s
7	Takuma Sato	1m 14.240s	23.992s	25.959s	24.289s
8	Marc Gené	1m 14.275s	23.976s	25.768s	24.531s
9	Kimi Räikkönen	1m 14.346s	24.291s	25.965s	24.090s
10	Rubens Barrichello	1m 14.478s	24.008s	25.836s	24.634s
11	Cristiano da Matta	1m 14.553s	24.189s	25.999s	24.365s
12	Mark Webber	1m 14.798s	24.288s	26.014s	24.496s
13	Christian Klien	1m 15.065s	24.354s	26.222s	24.489s
14	Olivier Panis	1m 15.130s	24.237s	26.153s	24.740s
15	Giancarlo Fisichella	1m 16.177s	24.728s	26.367s	25.082s
16	Felipe Massa	1m 16.200s	24.543s	26.530s	25.127s
17	Nick Heidfeld	1m 16.807s	24.701s	26.832s	25.274s
18	Giorgio Pantano	1m 17.462s	25.141s	26.899s	25.422s
19	Gianmaria Bruni	1m 17.913s	25.124s	27.131s	25.658s
20	Zsolt Baumngartner	1m 18.247s	25.064s	27.272s	25.911s

CHASSIS LOG BOOK

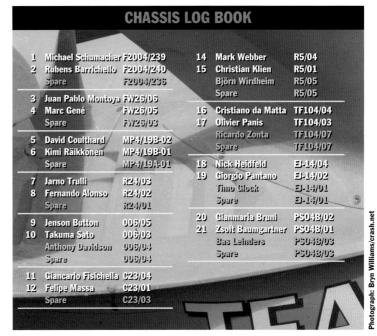

	Driver	Chassis		Driver	Chassis
1	Michael Schumacher	F2004/239	14	Mark Webber	R5/04
2	Rubens Barrichello	F2004/240	15	Christian Klien	R5/01
	Spare	F2004/236		Björn Wirdheim	R5/05
				Spare	R5/05
3	Juan Pablo Montoya	FW26/06			
4	Marc Gené	FW26/05	16	Cristiano da Matta	TF104/04
	Spare	FW26/03	17	Olivier Panis	TF104/03
				Ricardo Zonta	TF104/07
5	David Coulthard	MP4/19B-02		Spare	TF104/07
6	Kimi Räikkönen	MP4/19B-01			
	Spare	MP4/19A-01	18	Nick Heidfeld	EJ-14/04
			19	Giorgio Pantano	EJ-14/02
7	Jarno Trulli	R24/03		Timo Glock	EJ-14/01
8	Fernando Alonso	R24/02		Spare	EJ-14/01
	Spare	R24/01			
			20	Gianmaria Bruni	PS04B/02
9	Jenson Button	006/05	21	Zsolt Baumgartner	PS04B/01
10	Takuma Sato	006/03		Bas Leinders	PS04B/03
	Anthony Davidson	006/04		Spare	PS04B/03
	Spare	006/04			
11	Giancarlo Fisichella	C23/04			
12	Felipe Massa	C23/01			
	Spare	C23/03			

Photograph: Bryn Williams/crash.net

PRACTICE 1 (FRIDAY)

Sun and showers (track 29–30°C, air 22–23°C)

Pos.	Driver	Laps	Time
1	Rubens Barrichello	4	1m 15.487s
2	Michael Schumacher	4	1m 15.713s
3	Marc Gené	14	1m 19.348s
4	Timo Glock	17	1m 19.428s
5	Giorgio Pantano	12	1m 19.466s
6	Nick Heidfeld	12	1m 20.531s
7	Gianmaria Bruni	13	1m 21.203s
8	Bas Leinders	11	1m 22.267s
9	Anthony Davidson	17	1m 26.552s
10	Cristiano da Matta	5	1m 26.757s
11	Olivier Panis	4	1m 27.449s
12	Jenson Button	5	1m 28.317s
13	Ricardo Zonta	18	1m 29.085s
14	Christian Klien	8	1m 29.626s
15	Zsolt Baumgartner	12	1m 29.877s
16	Takuma Sato	10	1m 30.092s
17	Björn Wirdheim	17	1m 30.204s
18	Jarno Trulli	4	1m 39.392s
19	Felipe Massa	3	No time
20	Fernando Alonso	3	No time
21	Giancarlo Fisichella	1	No time
22	David Coulthard	1	No time
23	Juan Pablo Montoya	3	No time
24	Kimi Räikkönen	1	No time
25	Mark Webber	1	No time

PRACTICE 2 (FRIDAY)

Sun and showers (track 26–29°C, air 20–22°C)

Pos.	Driver	Laps	Time
1	Cristiano da Matta	12	1m 15.518s
2	Jarno Trulli	9	1m 16.206s
3	Anthony Davidson	17	1m 16.231s
4	Jenson Button	8	1m 16.397s
5	Michael Schumacher	7	1m 16.397s
6	Fernando Alonso	10	1m 16.454s
7	David Coulthard	8	1m 16.464s
8	Mark Webber	14	1m 16.745s
9	Kimi Räikkönen	10	1m 16.794s
10	Rubens Barrichello	5	1m 17.094s
11	Olivier Panis	10	1m 17.303s
12	Giancarlo Fisichella	13	1m 17.324s
13	Juan Pablo Montoya	5	1m 17.556s
14	Marc Gené	17	1m 17.688s
15	Ricardo Zonta	15	1m 17.735s
16	Christian Klien	10	1m 17.936s
17	Takuma Sato	11	1m 17.967s
18	Felipe Massa	7	1m 18.614s
19	Giorgio Pantano	10	1m 18.711s
20	Björn Wirdheim	16	1m 19.179s
21	Nick Heidfeld	12	1m 19.270s
22	Gianmaria Bruni	10	1m 19.349s
23	Timo Glock	25	1m 19.490s
24	Zsolt Baumgartner	13	1m 19.636s
25	Bas Leinders	16	1m 19.914s

PRACTICE 3 (SATURDAY)

Warm and sunny (track 33–35°C, air 22–23°C)

Pos.	Driver	Laps	Time
1	Michael Schumacher	12	1m 14.944s
2	David Coulthard	11	1m 15.402s
3	Jarno Trulli	11	1m 15.423s
4	Fernando Alonso	15	1m 15.434s
5	Olivier Panis	14	1m 15.478s
6	Rubens Barrichello	14	1m 15.500s
7	Juan Pablo Montoya	16	1m 15.529s
8	Mark Webber	8	1m 15.907s
9	Giancarlo Fisichella	11	1m 15.910s
10	Jenson Button	15	1m 16.304s
11	Cristiano da Matta	17	1m 16.384s
12	Takuma Sato	16	1m 16.569s
13	Marc Gené	18	1m 16.608s
14	Felipe Massa	14	1m 16.619s
15	Christian Klien	27	1m 16.669s
16	Gianmaria Bruni	15	1m 17.174s
17	Giorgio Pantano	19	1m 17.399s
18	Zsolt Baumgartner	14	1m 17.731s
19	Nick Heidfeld	16	1m 17.846s
20	Kimi Räikkönen	1	No time

PRACTICE 4 (SATURDAY)

Warm and sunny (track 34–37°C, air 22–23°C)

Pos.	Driver	Laps	Time
1	Kimi Räikkönen	18	1m 14.513s
2	Jenson Button	14	1m 14.568s
3	Michael Schumacher	14	1m 14.571s
4	Takuma Sato	18	1m 14.711s
5	Rubens Barrichello	12	1m 14.817s
6	Olivier Panis	23	1m 14.883s
7	Cristiano da Matta	22	1m 14.885s
8	David Coulthard	7	1m 14.977s
9	Jarno Trulli	12	1m 15.033s
10	Fernando Alonso	15	1m 15.096s
11	Marc Gené	10	1m 15.179s
12	Mark Webber	24	1m 15.350s
13	Christian Klien	22	1m 15.449s
14	Felipe Massa	19	1m 16.062s
15	Giancarlo Fisichella	9	1m 16.161s
16	Zsolt Baumgartner	15	1m 16.861s
17	Giorgio Pantano	12	1m 17.104s
18	Nick Heidfeld	15	1m 17.162s
19	Gianmaria Bruni	8	1m 19.401s
20	Juan Pablo Montoya	8	1m 21.458s

10th: RUBENS BARRICHELLO Ferrari

8th: MARC GENÉ Williams-BMW

6th: JUAN PABLO MONTOYA Williams-BMW

4th: JENSON BUTTON BAR-Honda

2nd: MICHAEL SCHUMACHER Ferrari

9th: KIMI RÄIKKÖNEN McLaren-Mercedes

7th: TAKUMA SATO BAR-Honda

5th: JARNO TRULLI Renault

3rd: DAVID COULTHARD McLaren-Mercedes

Pole: FERNANDO ALONSO Renault

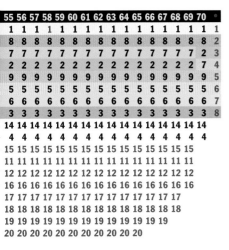

55	56	57	58	59	60	61	62	63	64	65	66	67	68	69	70	
1	1	1	1	1	1	1	1	1	1	1	1	1	1	1	1	1
8	8	8	8	8	8	8	8	8	8	8	8	8	8	8	8	2
7	7	7	7	7	7	7	7	7	7	7	7	7	7	2	3	
2	2	2	2	2	2	2	2	2	2	2	2	2	2	7	4	
9	9	9	9	9	9	9	9	9	9	9	9	9	9	9	5	
5	5	5	5	5	5	5	5	5	5	5	5	5	5	5	6	
6	6	6	6	6	6	6	6	6	6	6	6	6	6	7		
3	3	3	3	3	3	3	3	3	3	3	3	3	3	3	8	
14	14	14	14	14	14	14	14	14	14	14	14	14	14	14		
4	4	4	4	4	4	4	4	4	4	4	4	4	4	4		
15	15	15	15	15	15	15	15	15	15	15	15	15	15	15		
11	11	11	11	11	11	11	11	11	11	11	11	11	11	11		
12	12	12	12	12	12	12	12	12	12	12	12	12	12	12		
16	16	16	16	16	16	16	16	16	16	16	16	16	16			
17	17	17	17	17	17	17	17	17	17	17	17	17	17			
18	18	18	18	18	18	18	18	18	18	18	18	18	18			
19	19	19	19	19	19	19	19	19	19	19	19	19	19			
20	20	20	20	20	20	20	20	20	20	20						

FOR THE RECORD

400 grand prix points

Rubens Barrichello

POINTS: CONSTRUCTORS

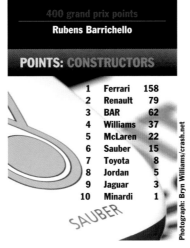

1	Ferrari	158
2	Renault	79
3	BAR	62
4	Williams	37
5	McLaren	22
6	Sauber	15
7	Toyota	8
8	Jordan	5
9	Jaguar	3
10	Minardi	1

Photograph: Bryn Williams/crash.net

POINTS: DRIVERS

1	Michael Schumacher	90
2	Rubens Barrichello	68
3	Jenson Button	48
4	Jarno Trulli	46
5	Fernando Alonso	33
6	Juan Pablo Montoya	25
7	Takuma Sato	14
8 =	Ralf Schumacher	12
8 =	David Coulthard	12
10 =	Giancarlo Fisichella	10
10 =	Kimi Räikkönen	10
12 =	Felipe Massa	5
12 =	Olivier Panis	5
14 =	Cristiano da Matta	3
14 =	Mark Webber	3
14 =	Nick Heidfeld	3
17	Timo Glock	2
18	Zsolt Baumgartner	1

Photograph: Darren Heath

155

BRITISH GP
SILVERSTONE

Back in contention. Kimi Räikkönen qualified the new McLaren MP4/19B on pole at Silverstone and really hassled Michael Schumacher's winning Ferrari.
Photograph: Darren Heath

The anomalies of the qualifying system were again thrown into dramatic relief on a weekend when a new format had been scheduled to be introduced. However, a difference of opinion between the FIA and the teams had led to it being shelved at the last minute, much to Bernie Ecclestone's understandable annoyance.

Rain was expected late in qualifying, which meant that many of the quick contenders deliberately fumbled pre-qualifying to be able to run sooner rather than later in the battle for grid position, the running order being the reverse of the times in the first session.

Thus we were treated to the absurd sight of Schumacher deliberately spinning his Ferrari to lose time, such an obviously bungled display that it looked as though some Formula Ford novice had been let loose in the best F1 car on earth.

You might be tempted to conclude that the paying spectators deserved more than this circus act. It wasn't just the Ferrari boys, one should emphasise, who were involved in this myopic idiocy, which happily backfired, allowing local hero Button's BAR to edge out Schumacher's F2004 to take a fine third in the starting order.

At the end of the day, Kimi Räikkönen qualified his McLaren brilliantly on pole with a 1m 18.233s best, just 0.072s ahead of 2003 Silverstone winner Rubens Barrichello. 'We ran the MP4/19B for the first time during a test here at Silverstone six weeks ago and now it has started to show its real potential,' said the Finn. 'The balance has been good throughout and we should have a strong car for tomorrow's race.'

Barrichello and Schumacher both coyly confessed that they'd deliberately lost time in pre-qualifying for strategic reasons. 'I am happy with my second place,' Barrichello admitted, 'although my car started to slide in the final sector, which is where I lost pole.' Schumacher also had a good lap, but was a touch disappointed that his 1m 18.710s best left him fourth behind Button's BAR (1m 18.580s).

'The car has been handling much better than yesterday,' said Button. 'We're not 100 per cent happy with it after all the positive testing we've done with it here, but I think strategy-wise we're in good shape for the race.' His BAR team-mate, Takuma Sato, wound up eighth on 1m 19.688s, reasonably happy with his time considering the race strategy he had in mind.

Fifth and sixth in the qualifying order were Renault duo Jarno Trulli (1m 18.715s) and Fernando Alonso (1m 18.811s), but the latter's engine-change penalty dropped him to 16th and allowed David Coulthard's McLaren to move up to the outside of row three on the grid on 1m 19.148s.

'It was not an easy qualifying due to the wind conditions,' said Coulthard. 'I lost a lot of time through Becketts and as a result I was not quick through the middle sector. I was a little disappointed with my performance.'

Juan Pablo Montoya was similarly affected by the crosswind, his Williams-BMW FW26 managing a 1m 19.378s, which placed him seventh on the grid. He was almost a full second quicker than the 12th-placed Marc Gené in the other Williams, the Spaniard having struggled badly in the gusty conditions.

Jaguar had been hoping for a strong showing in its own backyard, and Mark Webber duly delivered, his 1m 20.004s best earning him ninth place in the final line-up after Alonso's penalty had been factored into the equation. 'The car is feeling pretty good round here,' he reported. 'There was a small amount of oversteer on a couple of corners, but generally my lap was good and error-free.' His team-mate, Christian Klien, managed a 1m 21.559s, which placed him 13th.

Felipe Massa bagged 11th (tenth) with a 1m 20.202s, having been balked by Olivier Panis's Toyota as the Japanese car ran a very slow cooling off lap. Panis had his time disallowed as a penalty for this unfathomable transgression, being placed 17th in the final order ahead of both Minardis, which had engine changes, and the Sauber of Giancarlo Fisichella, who had elected not to make a qualifying run after incurring a ten-place penalty on Friday for an engine failure. It made more strategic sense in Sauber's view for him to stay in the pits and start at the back of the grid.

In the Minardi garage, there was much sadness following the death on Friday evening of the team's hugely popular sporting director, John Walton. He'd suffered a couple of heart attacks the previous Tuesday evening in London and was greatly missed.

STEWART AND ECCLESTONE IN SILVERSTONE SPAT

The personal animosity between Bernie Ecclestone and Sir Jackie Stewart boiled over again on the eve of the British Grand Prix, the former triple world champion accusing the F1 commercial rights holder of going back on previous assurances about the future of the Silverstone race.

Ecclestone denied that he had confirmed the race would be safe for 2005 and 2006, then added to the provocation by imposing an arbitrary deadline of 30 September for the appointment of a promoter for the 2005 race.

'We are dismayed at Bernie Ecclestone's latest threat to the future of the British Grand Prix at Silverstone,' thundered Stewart in response. 'His deadline of 30 September, as stated in the press, has never been mentioned in all our discussions with Formula One Management and with the British government.

'We are surprised at Mr Ecclestone's backtracking on the FOA's assurances of the security of the 2005/06 Grand Prix. Mr Ecclestone instigated the discussions with regard to a promoter of his choice being appointed by FOA and the BRDC to run these races, and these discussions continued.'

Earlier, it had appeared that Silverstone's prospects of retaining the British Grand Prix beyond 2006 had been strengthened when the BRDC reached an agreement with the Interpublic Group to take back the lease and the running of the track. That move brought to an end the disastrous foray into British motorsport by the world's second-largest advertising company, Interpublic, which was thought to have spent in excess of £285 million since 1999 when it bought into Brands Hatch Leisure, the company that owned the contract to run the British Grand Prix.

Earlier in 2004, Interpublic had agreed to pay £66 million to Ecclestone to escape from a contract to promote Britain's round of the world championship until 2015. The latest deal with the BRDC appeared to have cleared the decks for negotiations with Ecclestone over how Silverstone should be upgraded to ensure the future of the British Grand Prix beyond 2006.

Originally, it had been intended that a new pits and paddock complex would be built in time for the 2005 race, but Ecclestone granted a postponement until 2007 to give the club enough time to develop a totally new plan of campaign.

'The payment will give the BRDC security in the medium term, which will enable the club carefully to evaluate its future options and therefore determine its own destiny,' said Alexander Hooton, the BRDC's chief executive.

However, London's mayor, Ken Livingstone, claimed that he had made a £20 million offer to Ecclestone to run a London Grand Prix as early as 2007. 'We are serious about this,' he said. 'I told Bernie that if he wants to put on a grand prix in the centre of London, we could clear the way. We have discussed it with the Palace, with the Royal Parks Agency and with the police. Everyone recognises this is a huge plus for London.'

Nigel Mansell, who came out of retirement at 50 to demonstrate a Jordan-Ford in the Regent Street parade on the Tuesday afternoon prior to the Silverstone race, said such an event would be 'the best grand prix in the world. They could barrier the roads off to make it safe. It would be absolutely sensational.'

Jackie Stewart, however, cautioned that the event was unlikely. 'If there is to be an additional grand prix in London, the financial viability must be carefully evaluated,' he said, 'especially in relation to the cost to the British taxpayer.'

DIARY

Speculation intensifies that all is not well in the relationship between Jarno Trulli and the Renault team.

Williams announces that Antonio Pizzonia will replace Marc Gené as stand-in for Ralf Schumacher in German Grand Prix.

F3000 pacemaker Vitantonio Liuzzi linked with possible Sauber F1 test.

Jacques Villeneuve confirms he is still intending to return to F1 during the 2004 season.

Above: New hero. Jenson Button signs for his fans.

Top left: Old hero. Nigel Mansell drove a Jordan-Ford along Regent Street on the Tuesday prior to the British Grand Prix as part of a spectacular F1 demonstration through the streets of London's West End, watched by more than 20,000 fans.
Photographs: Darren Heath

KIMI Räikkönen made Michael Schumacher work hard for his victory in the British Grand Prix at Silverstone, but although the Ferrari driver finished the 60-lap race with a strong spurt to reinforce the message that he remained F1's undisputed pacemaker, the Finn signalled that the McLaren Mercedes team was set for a renaissance by taking the chequered flag just 2.1s adrift. It was only Räikkönen's second race at the wheel of the promising McLaren MP4/19B, which had made its debut in France just a week earlier.

'Although we didn't win today, it was an exciting race, and second is a great result for the entire team,' said Räikkönen. 'I made a very good start and was able to push throughout the race. Unfortunately, I had a bit of traffic after my pit stops, but that's racing. I struggled with the [handling] balance at the rear with my last set of tyres, and as a result it wasn't possible to attack harder and press Michael in my last stint.'

Rubens Barrichello's Ferrari F2004 finished third, while Jenson Button's hopes of home victory followed Tim Henman's Wimbledon tennis aspirations out of the window as he trailed home a rather dispirited fourth, a particular disappointment considering he had pipped Schumacher's Ferrari in qualifying to take third on the grid.

'We came into this race expecting a lot more than we've been able to deliver,' said Button, whose BAR-Honda 006 never quite yielded its expected pace. 'Today's race performance was nowhere near our testing performance earlier in the year. We struggled with a lack of grip compared to the Ferraris, and it was like we were in a different race in terms of the way our car was handling. Somehow, we've managed to drop behind a bit, which is very disappointing in front of our home crowd.'

Räikkönen had started the season widely tipped as a world championship contender, but the disastrously uncompetitive McLaren MP4/19 had wiped out his chances during the first half of the year. At Silverstone, however, armed with the promising new 'B' version of the car, he started strongly from pole position and came slamming through to lead the opening lap by 3.5s from Rubens Barrichello's Ferrari. This reflected the fact that he was

driving a lighter car with the intention of refuelling three times, unlike Barrichello and Schumacher who were scheduled to make two stops. The Ferrari pair had qualified second and fourth respectively on Saturday afternoon.

Initially, the race settled down with Räikkönen leading from Barrichello, followed by Jenson Button's BAR-Honda in third and Schumacher's Ferrari in fourth. Then there was a slight gap to Jarno Trulli's Renault, David Coulthard's McLaren-Mercedes, Juan Pablo Montoya's Williams-BMW and the other BAR-Honda of Takuma Sato.

Räikkönen made his first refuelling stop in 7.9s at the end of lap 11, relinquishing the lead to Schumacher, who stayed out until lap 15 before refuelling for the first time, just squeezing back into the chase 1.3s ahead of the Finn. From then on, Michael drove just quickly enough to keep the McLaren driver at bay, and although Räikkönen closed right up on to his tail in the tight infield section, once the Ferrari got out on to the long straights, the extra power beneath Schumacher's right foot settled the matter in decisive fashion.

On lap 28, Räikkönen made his second stop from his position a few yards behind the Ferrari's rear wing. Then, on lap 37, Schumacher came in for the second time, again rejoining the fray less than a second ahead of the McLaren. By now, it had become clear that Räikkönen would be hard pressed to keep in touch with the leaders on his three-stop schedule, but after Jarno Trulli crashed heavily in his Renault with 20 laps to run, the safety car was deployed to slow the field, which had the effect of evening-out the fuel-consumption strategies when the cars were unleashed for the final 15 laps. Trulli's accident was later identified as having been caused by a suspension breakage; he was fortunate to have escaped with no more than a shaking.

'The important thing is that Jarno wasn't injured,' said Pat Symonds, Renault's executive director of engineering. 'Up to that point, Jarno didn't seem to have the speed we expected, although we don't know why at this stage.'

Trulli had quickly extricated himself from the crumpled car and walked to the trackside doctor before being taken to the circuit

Above: Kimi Räikkönen exploited every ounce of potential from the McLaren-Mercedes MP4/19B to bag pole position and take the race to Schumacher's Ferrari, finishing a strong second after an epic chase.
Photograph: Darren Heath

medical centre for a precautionary check-up. 'It was a big accident,' he said, 'but I gave the marshals the thumbs-up straight away. Everything happened very quickly, but I think it was a rear suspension failure. Even before the crash, though, things were not going well. I was very [fuel] heavy in the first two stints, but even taking that into account, I was struggling to be quick. The car was tricky to drive, and I had trouble holding position.'

All in all, it was a bad day for the Enstone based team, as Jarno's team-mate, Fernando Alonso, had incurred an engine-change penalty, which had dropped him from sixth to 16th on the grid. He had a hard race climbing back to tenth at the chequered flag, crossing the line just 1.1s behind Mark Webber's eighth-placed Jaguar R5 and 0.8s adrift of Massa's Sauber in ninth.

'I think we could have done better today,' said Alonso, 'but we missed the opportunity to pit just after Jarno's accident. We only had two corners in which to react, but we didn't manage it. Otherwise, I could have been in the points. Having said that, when you start from the back, you know that it will be a hard race. I was held up by traffic in every stint, first behind Heidfeld, then Webber, then da Matta. I only did a few laps on my own, but when I did, I was very quick and the car balance was very good. But today circumstances prevented us from making the most of our speed.'

Michael Schumacher could hardly suppress a sense of de-

lighted disbelief as he reflected on a race that, in effect, had come to him and his Ferrari as reward for the world champion's matchless ability to determine the best point to push his hardest.

'I am amazed how the race went,' said Schumacher. 'I thought I had a good strategy, which to a certain extent we sacrificed qualifying for the race, but I never expected it to pay out so early. I was not worried by Kimi's pace at the start because I knew my strategy, and even if he had been ahead after my second stop, I would not have worried because he had to come in again. I did not want to overdo it and just left the potential of the car to do the work.'

Barrichello, who had won at Silverstone in 2003, was clearly disappointed that his race had yielded only third place; his personal aspiration had been considerably higher. 'After the start, it was clear that Kimi's tyres had warmed up quicker, and I found it really difficult to match his pace,' said the Brazilian. 'Then I caught him up again and was able to pull away from Button. But after the first pit stop, the car felt heavy and I struggled again.'

Behind Button, Juan Pablo Montoya came home fifth in the Williams-BMW, while Giancarlo Fisichella drove a tremendous race in his Sauber C23, bagging sixth place after being relegated to the back of the grid following an unscheduled engine change during practice.

Montoya had mixed feelings about the race. He was broadly

Below: Juan Pablo Montoya just managed to keep Giancarlo Fisichella's Sauber at bay in the battle for fifth place.

Below centre: Mark Webber took the final championship point of the afternoon with eighth place in his Jaguar R5.

Bottom: Minardi stripped its cars of sponsorship identification on race day, instead carrying a tribute to John Walton, its popular sporting director who had died on the Friday of the British Grand Prix weekend following a heart attack.
Photographs: Darren Heath

satisfied with fifth, but he didn't really have the pace. 'Although the car is not quick enough, it worked pretty well,' he reflected. 'I believe we got the best out of it today. At the start, I made a mistake, releasing the clutch too quickly, and that cost me a place to Sato. Then I tried to keep pushing, but it was not possible to catch those in front. When the safety car came out [for the Trulli shunt], the team did a great job by calling me in, and I had a perfect pit stop. However, back on the track, the backmarkers were frustrating and I lost a lot of time.'

Both Fisichella and his team-mate, Felipe Massa, had been extremely enthusiastic about the aerodynamic effect of a revised engine cover, but the former's engine problems cost the team dear.

'After his engine problems put us to the back of the grid, we started Giancarlo on a two-stop strategy with a long first stint,' said Peter Sauber. 'Felipe was held up by a Toyota [on its slowing-down lap] in qualifying and was then stuck all race behind a Jaguar. Then Giancarlo's engine began losing air pressure, and the consequent long pit stop to deal with it cost us fifth place.'

Seventh was David Coulthard, the Scot having been unable to extract the sort of speed from his McLaren that Räikkönen had delivered so splendidly. Even so, he admitted that the MP4/19B was a great improvement. The suggestion that it might have come a bit late in the day to resuscitate his reputation was left unsaid.

FOSTER'S
BRITISH GRAND PRIX
SILVERSTONE 9–11 JULY 2004

Photograph: Darren Heath

SILVERSTONE – GRAND PRIX CIRCUIT

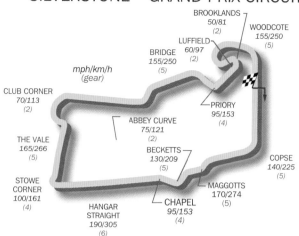

mph/km/h (gear)

BROOKLANDS 50/81 (2)
WOODCOTE 155/250 (5)
LUFFIELD 60/97 (2)
BRIDGE 155/250 (5)
CLUB CORNER 70/113 (2)
PRIORY 95/153 (4)
ABBEY CURVE 75/121 (2)
THE VALE 165/266 (5)
BECKETTS 130/209 (5)
COPSE 140/225 (5)
STOWE CORNER 100/161 (4)
MAGGOTTS 170/274 (5)
CHAPEL 95/153 (4)
HANGAR STRAIGHT 190/305 (6)

RACE DISTANCE: 60 laps, 191.746 miles/308.586 km **RACE WEATHER:** Overcast (track 25°C, air 18–20°C)

Pos.	Driver	Nat.	No.	Entrant	Car/Engine	Tyres	Laps	Time/Retirement	Speed (mph/km/h)	Gap to leader	Fastest race lap	
1	Michael Schumacher	D	1	Scuderia Ferrari Marlboro	Ferrari F2004-052 V10	B	60	1h 24m 42.700s	135.709/218.403		1m 18.739s	14
2	Kimi Räikkönen	FIN	6	West McLaren Mercedes	McLaren MP4/19B-Mercedes F0110P V10	M	60	1h 24m 44.830s	135.652/218.311	+2.130s	1m 19.554s	10
3	Rubens Barrichello	BR	2	Scuderia Ferrari Marlboro	Ferrari F2004-052 V10	B	60	1h 24m 45.814s	135.626/218.269	+3.114s	1m 19.296s	8
4	Jenson Button	GB	9	Lucky Strike BAR Honda	BAR 006-Honda RA004E V10	M	60	1h 24m 53.383s	135.425/217.945	+10.683s	1m 19.488s	10
5	Juan Pablo Montoya	COL	3	BMW WilliamsF1 Team	Williams FW26-BMW P84 V10	M	60	1h 24m 54.873s	135.385/217.881	+12.173s	1m 19.968s	26
6	Giancarlo Fisichella	I	11	Sauber Petronas	Sauber C23-Petronas 04 V10	B	60	1h 24m 55.588s	135.365/217.850	+12.888s	1m 19.813s	22
7	David Coulthard	GB	5	West McLaren Mercedes	McLaren MP4/19B-Mercedes F0110P V10	M	60	1h 25m 02.368s	135.186/217.561	+19.688s	1m 20.547s	25
8	Mark Webber	AUS	14	Jaguar Racing	Jaguar R5-Cosworth CR6 V10	M	60	1h 25m 06.401s	135.079/217.389	+23.701s	1m 20.768s	11
9	Felipe Massa	BR	12	Sauber Petronas	Sauber C23-Petronas 04 V10	B	60	1h 25m 06.723s	135.070/217.375	+24.023s	1m 20.484s	58
10	Fernando Alonso	E	8	Mild Seven Renault F1 Team	Renault R24-RS4 V10	M	60	1h 25m 07.535s	135.049/217.341	+24.835s	1m 20.442s	39
11	Takuma Sato	J	10	Lucky Strike BAR Honda	BAR 006-Honda RA004E V10	M	60	1h 25m 16.436s	134.814/216.963	+33.736s	1m 20.790s	12
12	Marc Gené	E	4	BMW WilliamsF1 Team	Williams FW26-BMW P84 V10	M	60	1h 25m 17.003s	134.799/216.939	+34.303s	1m 20.434s	58
13	Cristiano da Matta	BR	16	Panasonic Toyota Racing	Toyota TF104-RVX04 V10	M	59			+1 lap	1m 20.768s	35
14	Christian Klien	A	15	Jaguar Racing	Jaguar R5-Cosworth CR6 V10	M	59			+1 lap	1m 20.956s	10
15	Nick Heidfeld	D	18	Jordan Ford	Jordan EJ-14-Cosworth RS V10	B	59			+1 lap	1m 21.720s	17
16	Gianmaria Bruni	I	20	European Minardi Cosworth	Minardi PS04B-Cosworth CR3 V10	B	56			+3 laps	1m 24.296s	33
	Giorgio Pantano	I	19	Jordan Ford	Jordan EJ-14-Cosworth RS V10	B	47	Spin			1m 22.146s	13
	Jarno Trulli	I	7	Mild Seven Renault F1 Team	Renault R24-RS4 V10	M	39	Accident			1m 20.655s	34
	Zsolt Baumgartner	H	21	European Minardi Cosworth	Minardi PS04B-Cosworth CR3 V10	B	29	Engine			1m 24.317s	12
	Olivier Panis	F	17	Panasonic Toyota Racing	Toyota TF104-RVX04 V10	M	16	Accident			1m 23.131s	4

All results and data © FOM 2004

Fastest lap: Michael Schumacher, on lap 14, 1m 18.739s, 146.052 mph/235.049 km/h (record).

Previous lap record: Rubens Barrichello (Ferrari F2003-GA 051 V10), 1m 15.512s, 130.669 mph/210.292 km/h (2003).

19th: ZSOLT BAUMGARTNER Minardi-Cosworth
Took penalty following engine change

17th: OLIVIER PANIS Toyota
Time disallowed

15th: NICK HEIDFELD Jordan-Cosworth

13th: CHRISTIAN KLIEN Jaguar-Cosworth

11th: MARC GENÉ Williams-BMW

20th: GIANCARLO FISICHELLA Sauber-Petronas

18th: GIANMARIA BRUNI Minardi-Cosworth
Took penalty following engine change

16th: FERNANDO ALONSO Renault
Demoted following engine change

14th: GIORGIANO PANTANO Jordan-Cosworth

12th: CRISTIANO DA MATTA Toyota

Grid order	1	2	3	4	5	6	7	8	9	10	11	12	13	14	15	16	17	18	19	20	21	22	23	24	25	26	27	28	29	30	31	32	33	34	35	36	37	38	39	40	41	42	43	44	45	46	47
6 RÄIKKÖNEN	6	6	6	6	6	6	6	6	6	6	1	1	1	1	1	1	1	1	1	1	1	1	1	1	1	1	1	1	1	1	1	1	1	1	1	1	1	1	1	1	1	1	1	1	1	1	1
2 BARRICHELLO	2	2	2	2	2	2	2	9	9	1	7	10	6	6	6	6	6	6	6	6	6	6	6	6	6	6	6	6	6	6	6	6	6	6	6	6	6	6	6	6	6	6	6	6	6	6	6
9 BUTTON	9	9	9	9	9	9	9	2	1	9	10	6	10	14	9	9	9	9	9	9	9	9	9	9	9	2	3	2	2	2	2	2	2	2	2	2	2	2	2	2	2	2	2	2	2	2	2
1 M. SCHUMACHER	1	1	1	1	1	1	1	1	7	7	6	7	14	12	14	2	2	2	2	2	2	2	2	2	2	9	9	9	9	9	9	9	9	9	9	9	9	9	9	9	9	9	9	9	9	9	9
7 TRULLI	7	7	7	7	7	7	7	7	5	5	10	14	14	12	9	2	11	11	11	11	11	11	11	3	3	3	5	7	11	11	11	11	11	11	11	11	11	3	3	3	3	3	3	3	3		
5 COULTHARD	5	5	5	5	5	5	5	5	10	3	12	12	9	2	12	3	3	3	3	3	3	3	3	9	7	11	3	3	3	3	3	3	3	11	11	11	11	11	11	11	11	11					
3 MONTOYA	10	10	3	3	3	3	3	3	5	14	9	9	2	10	11	5	5	5	5	5	5	7	7	7	11	3	14	14	14	14	12	12	5	5	5	5	5	5	5	5	5	5	5	5	5	5	5
10 SATO	3	3	10	10	10	10	10	10	14	12	2	2	16	11	3	7	7	7	7	7	11	11	11	11	3	14	12	12	12	12	14	5	7	8	8	14	14	14	14	14	14						
14 WEBBER	14	14	14	14	14	14	14	14	2	16	16	15	16	5	18	14	14	14	14	14	14	14	14	12	7	5	5	5	5	7	8	14	14	12	12	12	12	12									
12 MASSA	12	12	12	12	12	12	12	12	2	16	15	15	11	15	7	14	8	8	8	8	2	12	12	12	5	5	10	10	10	7	7	8	14	12	12	8	8	8	8	8	8	8					
4 GENÉ	4	4	4	4	4	4	4	4	16	15	11	11	3	18	4	8	12	12	10	10	10	10	10	10	10	10	7	7	16	14	12	4	4	10	10	10	10	10									
16 DA MATTA	16	16	16	8	8	8	8	16	16	15	11	3	18	8	4	12	10	12	4	4	16	16	16	16	16	8	16	4	4	10	10	4	10	4	4	4	4	4									
15 KLIEN	19	8	8	16	16	16	16	8	15	11	19	5	5	7	4	12	10	10	10	16	16	16	16	16	8	4	10	16	16	16	16	16	16	16													
19 PANTANO	8	19	19	19	15	15	15	15	11	19	18	8	10	10	10	8	5	15	15	15	15	15	15	15	15	15	10	16	15	15	15	15	15	15													
18 HEIDFELD	15	15	15	15	19	11	11	11	19	18	18	18	8	16	16	16	15	4	4	4	4	4	4	4	4	10	18	15	18	18	18	18	18	18													
8 ALONSO	18	11	11	11	11	19	19	19	8	8	8	19	4	4	5	15	4	18	18	18	18	18	18	18	18	18	19	19	19	19	19	19	19	19													
17 PANIS	11	18	18	18	18	18	18	17	4	4	4	4	19	19	19	19	19	19	19	19	19	19	19	20	20	20	20	20	20	20	20																
20 BRUNI	17	17	17	17	17	17	17	18	17	17	17	17	17	17	20	20	20	20	20	20	20	20	20																								
21 BAUMGARTNER	20	20	20	20	20	20	20	20	20	20	21	21	21	20	20	20	21	21	21																												
11 FISICHELLA	21	21	21	21	21	21	21	21	20	20	20	21	20																																		

QUALIFYING

Sunny/overcast (track 31°C, air 20°C)

Pos.	Driver	Lap time	Sector 1	Sector 2	Sector 3
1	Kimi Räikkönen	1m 18.233s	25.050s	33.517s	19.666s
2	Rubens Barrichello	1m 18.305s	24.611s	33.686s	20.008s
3	Jenson Button	1m 18.580s	24.944s	33.680s	19.956s
4	Michael Schumacher	1m 18.710s	24.888s	33.832s	19.990s
5	Jarno Trulli	1m 18.715s	25.141s	33.797s	19.777s
6	Fernando Alonso	1m 18.811s	24.991s	33.866s	19.954s
7	David Coulthard	1m 19.148s	25.203s	33.857s	20.088s
8	Juan Pablo Montoya	1m 19.378s	25.264s	33.745s	20.369s
9	Takuma Sato	1m 19.688s	25.368s	34.235s	20.085s
10	Mark Webber	1m 20.004s	25.279s	34.334s	20.391s
11	Felipe Massa	1m 20.202	25.374s	34.595s	20.233s
12	Olivier Panis	1m 20.335s	25.573s	34.625s	20.137s
13	Marc Gené	1m 20.335s	25.373s	34.559s	20.403s
14	Cristiano da Matta	1m 20.545s	25.428s	34.850s	20.267s
15	Christian Klien	1m 21.559s	25.724s	35.112s	20.675s
16	Giorgio Pantano	1m 22.458s	26.101s	35.635s	20.722s
17	Nick Heidfeld	1m 22.677s	26.210s	35.243s	21.224s
18	Gianmaria Bruni	1m 23.437s	26.551s	35.930s	20.956s
19	Zsolt Baumgartner	1m 24.117s	26.733s	36.72s	21.112s
20	Giancarlo Fisichella	No time	–	–	–

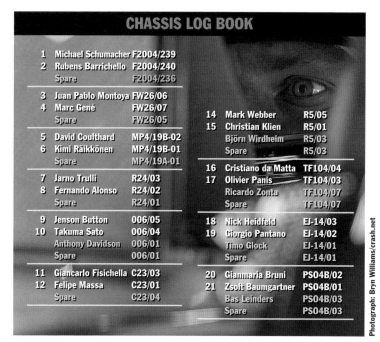

1	Michael Schumacher	F2004/239
2	Rubens Barrichello	F2004/240
	Spare	F2004/236
3	Juan Pablo Montoya	FW26/06
4	Marc Gené	FW26/07
	Spare	FW26/05
5	David Coulthard	MP4/19B-02
6	Kimi Räikkönen	MP4/19B-01
	Spare	MP4/19A-01
7	Jarno Trulli	R24/03
8	Fernando Alonso	R24/02
	Spare	R24/01
9	Jenson Button	006/05
10	Takuma Sato	006/04
	Anthony Davidson	006/01
	Spare	006/01
11	Giancarlo Fisichella	C23/03
12	Felipe Massa	C23/01
	Spare	C23/04
14	Mark Webber	R5/05
15	Christian Klien	R5/01
	Björn Wirdheim	R5/03
	Spare	R5/03
16	Cristiano da Matta	TF104/04
17	Olivier Panis	TF104/03
	Ricardo Zonta	TF104/07
	Spare	TF104/07
18	Nick Heidfeld	EJ-14/03
19	Giorgio Pantano	EJ-14/02
	Timo Glock	EJ-14/01
	Spare	EJ-14/01
20	Gianmaria Bruni	PS04B/02
21	Zsolt Baumgartner	PS04B/01
	Bas Leinders	PS04B/03
	Spare	PS04B/03

Photograph: Bryn Williams/crash.net

PRACTICE 1 (FRIDAY)

Cloudy (track 22–24°C, air 17°C)

Pos.	Driver	Laps	Time
1	Rubens Barrichello	16	1m 19.138s
2	Michael Schumacher	25	1m 19.214s
3	Juan Pablo Montoya	13	1m 19.502s
4	Marc Gené	14	1m 19.687s
5	Anthony Davidson	23	1m 19.748s
6	David Coulthard	6	1m 20.021s
7	Felipe Massa	17	1m 20.430s
8	Giancarlo Fisichella	10	1m 20.446s
9	Kimi Räikkönen	5	1m 20.633s
10	Jenson Button	8	1m 20.866s
11	Ricardo Zonta	27	1m 21.095s
12	Björn Wirdheim	24	1m 21.277s
13	Takuma Sato	13	1m 21.285s
14	Mark Webber	6	1m 21.520s
15	Jarno Trulli	13	1m 21.792s
16	Fernando Alonso	5	1m 22.003s
17	Christian Klien	11	1m 22.279s
18	Cristiano da Matta	16	1m 22.466s
19	Olivier Panis	15	1m 22.520s
20	Giorgio Pantano	20	1m 22.664s
21	Nick Heidfeld	20	1m 22.716s
22	Timo Glock	23	1m 23.149s
23	Gianmaria Bruni	19	1m 23.663s
24	Zsolt Baumgartner	20	1m 23.715s
25	Bas Leinders	18	1m 24.887s

PRACTICE 2 (FRIDAY)

Cloudy (track 23–24°C, air 17–18°C)

Pos.	Driver	Laps	Time
1	Kimi Räikkönen	16	1m 18.655s
2	Giancarlo Fisichella	20	1m 18.660s
3	Michael Schumacher	14	1m 19.162s
4	David Coulthard	17	1m 19.287s
5	Jenson Button	19	1m 19.401s
6	Rubens Barrichello	22	1m 19.473s
7	Marc Gené	20	1m 19.540s
8	Jarno Trulli	21	1m 19.601s
9	Takuma Sato	13	1m 19.611s
10	Felipe Massa	23	1m 19.676s
11	Juan Pablo Montoya	20	1m 19.746s
12	Fernando Alonso	30	1m 19.874s
13	Ricardo Zonta	35	1m 20.095s
14	Olivier Panis	25	1m 20.489s
15	Cristiano da Matta	19	1m 20.829s
16	Anthony Davidson	14	1m 20.861s
17	Christian Klien	30	1m 21.073s
18	Mark Webber	27	1m 21.352s
19	Björn Wirdheim	33	1m 21.353s
20	Nick Heidfeld	13	1m 22.365s
21	Timo Glock	24	1m 22.500s
22	Gianmaria Bruni	25	1m 22.516s
23	Giorgio Pantano	14	1m 22.586s
24	Bas Leinders	20	1m 22.792s
25	Zsolt Baumgartner	23	1m 23.436s

PRACTICE 3 (SATURDAY)

Overcast (track 25°C, air 16°C)

Pos.	Driver	Laps	Time
1	Kimi Räikkönen	5	1m 19.315s
2	Jenson Button	6	1m 19.468s
3	Michael Schumacher	11	1m 19.571s
4	Rubens Barrichello	8	1m 19.585s
5	Juan Pablo Montoya	10	1m 19.699s
6	Jarno Trulli	5	1m 19.966s
7	David Coulthard	5	1m 19.979s
8	Takuma Sato	6	1m 20.177s
9	Fernando Alonso	13	1m 20.482s
10	Marc Gené	13	1m 20.552s
11	Felipe Massa	6	1m 20.685s
12	Giancarlo Fisichella	9	1m 20.759s
13	Cristiano da Matta	11	1m 21.017s
14	Mark Webber	5	1m 21.295s
15	Olivier Panis	15	1m 21.416s
16	Christian Klien	6	1m 21.706s
17	Giorgio Pantano	11	1m 21.984s
18	Nick Heidfeld	12	1m 22.503s

PRACTICE 4 (SATURDAY)

Overcast (track 26°C, air 18°C)

Pos.	Driver	Laps	Time
1	Kimi Räikkönen	14	1m 18.280s
2	Jenson Button	12	1m 18.414s
3	Rubens Barrichello	13	1m 18.623s
4	Jarno Trulli	14	1m 18.694s
5	Marc Gené	10	1m 18.832s
6	Juan Pablo Montoya	11	1m 18.912s
7	David Coulthard	11	1m 18.919s
8	Michael Schumacher	8	1m 18.951s
9	Fernando Alonso	12	1m 19.169s
10	Giancarlo Fisichella	10	1m 19.895s
11	Cristiano da Matta	19	1m 20.183s
12	Felipe Massa	6	1m 20.281s
13	Mark Webber	23	1m 20.310s
14	Olivier Panis	16	1m 20.531s
15	Nick Heidfeld	12	1m 20.726s
16	Takuma Sato	8	1m 20.837s
17	Christian Klien	18	1m 20.913s
18	Zsolt Baumgartner	15	1m 21.980s
19	Giorgio Pantano	11	1m 22.014s
20	Gianmaria Bruni	12	1m 23.941s

9th: MARK WEBBER Jaguar-Cosworth

7th: JUAN PABLO MONTOYA Williams-BMW

5th: JARNO TRULLI Renault

3rd: JENSON BUTTON BAR-Honda

Pole: KIMI RÄIKKÖNEN McLaren-Mercedes

10th: FELIPE MASSA Sauber-Petronas

8th: TAKUMA SATO BAR-Honda

6th: DAVID COULTHARD McLaren-Mercedes

4th: MICHAEL SCHUMACHER Ferrari

2nd: RUBENS BARRICHELLO Ferrari

48	49	50	51	52	53	54	55	56	57	58	59	60	
1	1	1	1	1	1	1	1	1	1	1	1	1	1
6	6	6	6	6	6	6	6	6	6	6	6	6	2
2	2	2	2	2	2	2	2	2	2	2	2	2	3
9	9	9	9	9	9	9	9	9	9	9	9	9	4
3	3	3	3	3	3	3	3	3	3	3	3	3	5
11	11	11	11	11	11	11	11	11	11	11	11	11	6
5	5	5	5	5	5	5	5	5	5	5	5	5	7
14	14	14	14	14	14	14	14	14	14	14	14	14	8
12	12	12	12	12	12	12	12	12	12	12	12	12	
8	8	8	8	8	8	8	8	8	8	8	8	8	
10	10	10	10	10	10	10	10	10	10	10	10	10	
4	4	4	4	4	4	4	4	4	4	4	4	4	
16	16	16	16	16	16	16	16	16	16	16	16		
15	15	15	15	15	15	15	15	15	15	15	15		
18	18	18	18	18	18	18	18	18	18	18	18		
20	20	20	20	20	20	20	20	20					

Pit stop
One lap behind leader

1	Ferrari	174
2	Renault	79
3	BAR	67
4	Williams	41
5	McLaren	32
6	Sauber	18
7	Toyota	8
8	Jordan	5
9	Jaguar	4
10	Minardi	1

1	Michael Schumacher	100
2	Rubens Barrichello	74
3	Jenson Button	53
4	Jarno Trulli	46
5	Fernando Alonso	33
6	Juan Pablo Montoya	29
7	Kimi Räikkönen	18
8 =	Takuma Sato	14
8 =	David Coulthard	14

Photographs: Darren Heath

FIA F1 WORLD CHAMPIONSHIP • ROUND 12

GERMANGP

HOCKENHEIM

Another tremendous drive from Jenson Button saw him climb through to second place from 13th on the grid after taking a ten-place penalty for an engine change.
Photograph: Darren Heath

HOCKENHEIM QUALIFYING

Ferrari arrived fresh from an intensive Jerez tyre test confident that the team's Bridgestone rubber would perform well in the torrid conditions anticipated for Michael Schumacher's home race, and with no worries about a repeat of 2003's dramatic drop-off in performance. The world champion duly bagged his 61st career pole position, while Rubens Barrichello hinted that he was running a heavier fuel load after lining up eighth.

'To be honest, I'm not so surprised to be on pole, but I am surprised at the gap to the others,' Schumacher said, reflecting on his 1m 13.306s best, 0.9s quicker that his team-mate. 'Running in the midfield in the second session was not much of a disadvantage, and the circuit did not seem to pick up more speed toward the end.'

In the BMW Williams squad, Antonio Pizzonia replaced Marc Gené as Ralf Schumacher's stand-in, but after a promising Jerez test, the young Brazilian marked his return to the F1 race grid by taking things too cautiously in qualifying, winding up a very disappointed 11th on 1m 14.556s. New aero parts on the FW26 helped Juan Pablo Montoya to bag second on the grid with a 1m 13.668s, despite admitting to a slight mistake coming into the stadium section.

McLaren started the weekend on an upbeat and positive note. Buoyed by a successful test with the MP4/19B at Silverstone, Kimi Räikkönen sustained the team's promising British GP momentum by qualifying a strong third on 1m 13.690s. David Coulthard had been frustrated by brake balance problems during Friday free practice, but was much more confident with his car in qualifying, lining up fourth, just over 0.1s away from his team-mate.

'I'm much happier with the balance of my car, as we have taken a significant step forward since yesterday,' said Coulthard. 'My qualifying lap was good, and I think I could have been even a little faster, but as our pace has been pretty consistent, we should have a strong race tomorrow. I think we have a good strategy.'

The Renault R24s displayed excellent handling balance on both new and scrubbed tyres, Fernando Alonso successfully dialling out a touch of understeer in time for qualifying, which saw him post sixth-fastest time on 1m 13.874s after struggling slightly in Friday free practice. Jarno Trulli was also much happier with his car's handling balance on the second day and took seventh on the grid with a 1m 14.134s best after a trouble-free run.

For BAR, however, there was a measure of disappointment when the team was prohibited from running its front torque transfer system for the balance of the season following a ruling by FIA technical delegate Charlie Whiting. The system had been designed to shift torque loads between the front wheels under braking and prevent them from locking in that situation.

'We are not going to debate this matter in public,' said BAR team principal David Richards, 'but it is something we want clarification on, because the consequences of what has been suggested have major implications on other areas of the car.'

As if that wasn't disappointing enough, Jenson Button suffered an engine failure that demoted him ten places from an excellent third (1m 13.674s) in qualifying, much to the team's acute frustration. Takuma Sato badly damaged the right-hand suspension of his BAR-Honda when he spun coming out of the right-hander into the stadium straight during Saturday free practice, losing valuable preparation time and winding up an unhappy ninth (subsequently eighth following Button's demotion) on the grid with a 1m 14.287s.

Toyota had two new TF104Bs on hand for Olivier Panis and Cristiano da Matta, although test driver Ricardo Zonta continued to use one of the original-spec cars. Panis had struggled initially to find the right balance, but set-up changes made on Friday night improved things, and he was moderately content with ninth on the grid on 1m 14.368s, by contrast with da Matta who trailed in 15th place, unable to better 1m 15.454s.

All three of the Jaguar drivers had lost a lot of time on Friday while their brake cooling ducts were changed, but Mark Webber and Christian Klien had picked up the pace again on Saturday, working on handling balance during the free practice session. Webber wound up 11th on 1m 14.802s, having continued to struggle with slight handling difficulties, and reported that his lap was not perfect, although he had been impressed with the revised aero package being used for the race. Klien was satisfied with 12th spot on 1m 15.011s, despite having made one slight mistake

Both Sauber drivers clearly aimed for the two-stop strategy that had served them so well in recent races, Giancarlo Fisichella (1m 15.395s) just pipping Felipe Massa (1m 15.616s) to line up 14th and 16th. Fisichella reported that his Bridgestones seemed very consistent and stable in race conditions, and both drivers confirmed that the handling balance of their cars was very good.

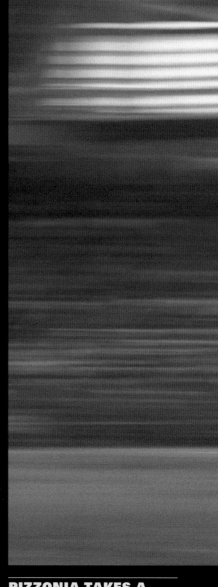

PIZZONIA TAKES A POP AT JAGUAR

Antonio Pizzonia settled a few outstanding scores with the Jaguar team at Hockenheim as he settled into his new role as stand-in for the injured Ralf Schumacher in the BMW Williams team. Twelve months almost to the day after he had been replaced by Justin Wilson following a strong performance in the 2003 British Grand Prix at Silverstone, the 23-year-old Brazilian celebrated his return to the F1 starting grid by accusing the underfinanced British team of favouring his one-time team-mate, Mark Webber, with better equipment.

'They didn't have a lot of money, and it was easier to develop one car rather than two,' said Pizzonia. 'We're talking here about engine [specification], bits of suspension and the number of revs I could use. I used to get some parts [fitted to the car] one or two races later, some of which I knew about, but most of which I didn't.'

Pizzonia did admit, however, that he overdrove the Jaguar in a desperate attempt to be competitive, which also had an adverse effect on his performance. 'In the end, I was just putting a bit too much pressure on myself,' he said. 'Now I'm back in F1 with Williams, I feel more respected as a racing driver and a human being.'

Pizzonia's enduring prowess as a Williams test driver had earned him a rare second chance to make an impact in the usually unforgiving F1 eco-system. He shrugged off the views of those in the paddock who wondered whether he was like an actor who relished the dress rehearsals only to suffer stage fright on the opening night.

'This is not going to be my first grand prix,' he said, 'and I know the Williams FW26 really well and have covered a great deal of mileage in this car. I am a lot more involved in the team than I was at Jaguar and feel that I have grown up a lot, both in and out of the car.'

JENSON Button hadn't expected to be battling for second place in the German Grand Prix any more than he had anticipated having to drive one-handed for the last 20 laps around the Hockenheim circuit. He had been forced to hold his helmet steady after its neck strap had worked loose and threatened to strangle him as the 180-mph airflow lifted it from his head. It was undoubtedly the most formidable performance of his career.

In reality, Button's problem wasn't quite as bad as it may have looked to television viewers, but it added a suitably dramatic flourish to the best race of the 24-year-old's career. He stormed across the finishing line just 8.38s behind the inevitably dominant Michael Schumacher in the Ferrari F2004, consolidating his third place in the world championship with six of the season's 18 races left to run.

Happily, the race also went a long way toward placating those critics of contemporary F1 racing who had been chorusing that the sport offered insufficient genuine overtaking out on the circuit. On this occasion, the entire 66-lap event was punctuated by lurid passing moves and wheel-to-wheel moments.

'Toward the end of the race, my helmet strap started to work loose and my helmet was lifting down the straights, which was pulling the strap tight against my throat and choking me,' said Button as he climbed the steps to the rostrum. 'I had to drive one-handed for most of the time. I couldn't breathe very well, and it was just more worrying than anything else. I was just slightly pulling it down to get more air in.'

While Button was struggling out on the circuit, in the pits the BAR engineers were busy examining his spare helmet on the assumption that their driver's problem was a loose visor. They thought that they could probably tape it down at the final refuelling stop, but when Button explained the actual cause of his difficulty, all they could do was keep their fingers crossed that all would be well.

'This was without doubt the best race of my F1 career,' said Button, who had qualified superbly with third-fastest time, but had been awarded a ten-place penalty for an engine change during Friday practice and actually had lined up in 13th place on the grid.

'I'm just so thrilled to finish second when I thought the best I could hope for was maybe fifth, at best. The car felt fantastic, the engine was great and the teamwork from the boys was incredible.

'I made a good start, but had a terrible first lap and didn't gain anything, but then the team did a fantastic job in the first pit stop. I had a great fight with Fernando [Alonso], who had incredible traction out of Turn Three where I was losing out to him, then on the

straight I could get close to him again. I tried a few times to get past him and nothing seemed to work, but then I finally got him down the inside and held on to it.'

More crucially, Button's performance nailed once and for all the lie that he couldn't overtake. He had made up a place by the end of the opening lap and, thanks to running a remarkably long and quick opening stint to lap 14 before his first refuelling stop, he came out of the first round of pit visits in fifth.

By running longer on each of his three stints, Button not only enjoyed three short spells in the lead, but also leap-frogged ahead of McLaren driver David Coulthard on his third stop to take fourth; he came out of the pits right on the tail of Fernando Alonso's third-placed Renault.

Earlier, the BAR driver had got alongside Alonso coming out of the hairpin, but could not quite manage to get the jump on the Spanish star, who is certainly no soft touch. After that final refuelling stop, the task became slightly easier because the Renault had picked up tyre debris, but Button was hampered by that loose helmet strap. On lap 51, he tried again, jinking out to the left as he came through the fast right-hander before the second-gear, 75-mph, left-hand Turn Eight, situated in the lee of the huge Mercedes grandstand. He sliced through on the inside and Alonso had no answer. The deed was done. *F1 Racing* magazine readers would later choose that move on the Renault driver as the overtaking manoeuvre of the year.

Juan Pablo Montoya's Williams-BMW FW26 had qualified on the front row a fraction slower than Schumacher's pole-position Ferrari F2004, but any hope of the Colombian carrying the fight to the world champion evaporated at the start, when he made a painfully slow getaway and found himself engulfed by the rest of the pack.

By the end of the opening lap, Schumacher's Ferrari was already a second ahead of Alonso's Renault, but Kimi Räikkönen forced the McLaren-Mercedes MP4/19B into second place next time around and gallantly kept the Ferrari in sight through the first series of scheduled refuelling stops, which began on lap nine. At the tail of the field, Rubens Barrichello brought his Ferrari in for a replacement nose section after hitting the back of Coulthard's McLaren at the hairpin, a slip that wiped out the Brazilian's race hopes and consigned him to a distant 12th place at the end of the afternoon.

Having run a longer opening stint in a bid to vault through the pack from his lowly grid position, Button found himself leading at the end of lap 13 just as Räikkönen's McLaren spun out of control

Above: Michael Schumacher gave the home crowd exactly what it wanted with another home win at Hockenheim.

Facing page: Antonio Pizzonia took over from Marc Gené as Ralf Schumacher's BMW Williams stand-in.
Photographs: Darren Heath

DIARY

Mark Webber formally signs for BMW Williams for 2005.

Giancarlo Fisichella to switch to Renault as Jarno Trulli announces he will leave the French squad at the end of 2004.

Dario Franchitti wins IRL Milwaukee race at the wheel of his Andretti Green Dallara-Honda.

Bobby Rahal admits he is talking to Prodrive about the prospect of running an Aston Martin DBR9 GT racer at Le Mans and in the USA in 2005.

DTM ace Gary Paffett tipped for possible Sauber F1 test.

in front of the pits, slamming off the road into the tyre barrier at over 150 mph after its rear wing failed dramatically. Mindful of the need to protect David Coulthard's sister car, within a lap-and-a-half of Räikkönen's accident, the McLaren pit-wall crew accessed the team's component data base at the factory in Woking in an attempt to discover whether the other MP4/19B might be at risk.

'These components had covered thousands of miles and we had to assume that this was an isolated failure,' said McLaren CEO Martin Whitmarsh after confirming the decision that the Scot could continue. 'We must assume that this was either a quality-control problem or the component has somehow become damaged. We were comfortable with our decision to let David continue.'

Meanwhile, Schumacher was having a challenging time at the front of the pack. 'It was a tough race, as I was under pressure first from Kimi, then from Jenson and Fernando,' he admitted. 'I was able to keep the gap, but not really extend it. The team's pit work was superb. I did feel under pressure because Jenson was very quick, and at one stage I was not sure if he was only planning to stop twice, or what pace he would be able to run at once he got past Fernando.'

In the closing stages of the race, the pressure on Button eased a little as Alonso fell away slightly in third place, troubled by a sudden handling imbalance that later was attributed to debris lodged beneath the car; a similar problem afflicted his team-mate, Jarno Trulli.

'I don't know what happened to the car during the final stint,' said Alonso. 'At first, I thought it was a problem with the front wing, then the suspension, but whatever the cause, the result was obvious. I just had no front grip at all. I radioed to the team that I was coming into the pits, but they told me to stay out.'

Alonso's problem raised Coulthard's hope that he might be able to close in and challenge for the final place on the podium. However, after his McLaren had been hit on the opening lap by Barrichello's Ferrari, the Scot had been left to grapple with unpredictable handling due to a damaged diffuser and rear wing end-plate.

'In addition, I picked up some debris from Kimi's accident, which broke the deflector on my front wing,' said Coulthard after battling home fourth. 'The team worked hard in the pit stops to try and dial out the understeer, but the problems continued. I was looking forward to mounting a real challenge for the podium today, but it just wasn't possible.'

In any event, on lap 58, Alonso clipped a kerb quite hard, dislodging what turned out to be another competitor's bargeboard, which had been jammed beneath his Renault. This immediately restored his car's handling, allowing him to hang on ahead of Coulthard until the end of the race.

Jarno Trulli shared Alonso's problems. He drove strongly in the first stint, but then ran over some debris from Räikkönen's accident and soon began to struggle with inconsistent handling.

'Unfortunately, his [Alonso's] problem happened earlier in the race and the other competitors were much closer,' said Trulli. 'I lost front grip, the car was understeering and would not turn into any of the corners. Then we changed the nose and front wing [at his second stop] and everything was okay again.'

Trailing Coulthard, Montoya crossed the line 23.05s behind the winner, Schumacher, a far cry from his flag-to-flag victory of 2003. 'What a bad start I had,' reflected the Colombian. 'The clutch didn't bite soon enough on the start, and then I just had so much wheelspin that the car didn't go anywhere. I had no grip at all and lost a cool five positions.

'I also had some blistering problems on my rear tyres, and it came to the point where driving the car was very, very hard since it was pointy and unpredictable. I'm obviously a bit disappointed, because when you start from second, you expect a podium finish.'

In sixth place, Mark Webber had a great race in the Jaguar R5, making an aero change at the final stop to dial out oversteer. He reported that the R5 felt really good throughout. Christian Klien also looked convincing, fending off Trulli's Renault in the closing stages to finish tenth.

Just 0.8s behind Webber as he took the flag was Antonio Pizzonia in the other Williams-BMW. The young Brazilian had turned in

an excellent performance, which yielded a personal fastest race lap, just 0.1s away from Montoya's best.

Takuma Sato came home eighth to take the final point in the other BAR-Honda. 'During the race, I experienced two separate problems with the HANS device slipping out from under the shoulder strap, which means a loss of support,' he said. He also survived a quick 360-degree spin coming into the stadium section in the closing stages.

Sauber's Giancarlo Fisichella was boxed in at the start, losing crucial track space, and at the second scheduled stop, the mechanics were unable to change his left rear tyre due to a jammed wheel nut. As a result, he missed out on a point by one place. Felipe Massa was slowed by a badly blistering second set of tyres, and he complained of poor stability after struggling home 13th.

Although Schumacher delivered the result required by the adoring masses who thronged the Hockenheim grandstands in his support, Button was the darling of the day. But as he quaffed champagne with David Richards and the rest of the BAR crew after stepping down from the podium, he was harbouring a secret. A secret that would hit the headlines a week later to become the most controversial event of the 2004 season.

Below left: With the exception of Michael Schumacher's first place, Michelin cleaned up the rest of the points on offer.

Bottom: Mark Webber drove a strong race for Jaguar. Here he leads Juan Pablo Montoya, who eventually won the battle for fifth place.
Photographs: Darren Heath

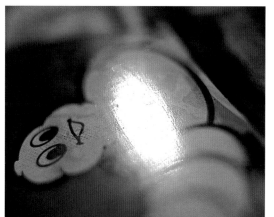

Photograph: Darren Heath

FIA F1 WORLD CHAMPIONSHIP • ROUND 12
GRÖSSER MOBIL 1 PREIS VON
DEUTSCHLAND

HOCKENHEIM

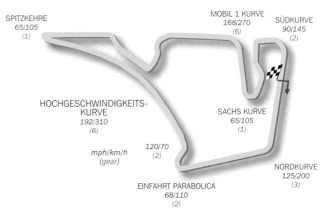

SPITZKEHRE
65/105
(1)

MOBIL 1 KURVE
168/270
(6)

SÜDKURVE
90/145
(2)

HOCHGESCHWINDIGKEITS-
KURVE
192/310
(6)

SACHS KURVE
65/105
(1)

mph/km/h
(gear)

120/70
(2)

NORDKURVE
125/200
(3)

EINFAHRT PARABOLICA
68/110
(2)

CIRCUIT LENGTH: 2.842 miles/4.574 km

HOCKENHEIM 23–25 JULY 2004

RACE DISTANCE: 66 laps, 187.582 miles/301.884 km RACE WEATHER: Hot and sunny (track 39–41°C, air 27–28°C)

Pos.	Driver	Nat.	No.	Entrant	Car/Engine	Tyres	Laps	Time/Retirement	Speed (mph/km/h)	Gap to leader	Fastest race lap	
1	Michael Schumacher	D	1	Scuderia Ferrari Marlboro	Ferrari F2004-052 V10	B	66	1h 23m 54.848s	134.124/215.852		1m 13.783s	5
2	Jenson Button	GB	9	Lucky Strike BAR Honda	BAR 006-Honda RA004E V10	M	66	1h 24m 03.236s	133.901/215.493	+8.388s	1m 14.117s	11
3	Fernando Alonso	E	8	Mild Seven Renault F1 Team	Renault R24-RS4 V10	M	66	1h 24m 11.199s	133.690/215.153	+16.351s	1m 14.265s	8
4	David Coulthard	GB	5	West McLaren Mercedes	McLaren MP4/19B-Mercedes F0110P V10	M	66	1h 24m 14.079s	133.613/215.030	+19.231s	1m 14.558s	8
5	Juan Pablo Montoya	COL	3	BMW WilliamsF1 Team	Williams FW26-BMW P84 V10	M	66	1h 24m 17.903s	133.513/214.868	+23.055s	1m 14.446s	10
6	Mark Webber	AUS	14	Jaguar Racing	Jaguar R5-Cosworth CR6 V10	M	66	1h 24m 35.956s	133.037/214.103	+41.108s	1m 14.883s	65
7	Antonio Pizzonia	E	4	BMW WilliamsF1 Team	Williams FW26-BMW P84 V10	M	66	1h 24m 36.804s	133.015/214.068	+41.956s	1m 14.586s	65
8	Takuma Sato	J	10	Lucky Strike BAR Honda	BAR 006-Honda RA004E V10	M	66	1h 24m 41.690s	132.887/213.862	+46.842s	1m 14.585s	29
9	Giancarlo Fisichella	I	11	Sauber Petronas	Sauber C23-Petronas 04 V10	B	66	1h 25m 01.950s	132.360/213.013	+67.102s	1m 15.635s	39
10	Christian Klien	A	15	Jaguar Racing	Jaguar R5-Cosworth CR6 V10	M	66	1h 25m 03.426s	132.321/212.951	+68.578s	1m 15.045s	33
11	Jarno Trulli	I	7	Mild Seven Renault F1 Team	Renault R24-RS4 V10	M	66	1h 25m 05.106s	132.278/212.881	+70.258s	1m 14.386s	9
12	Rubens Barrichello	BR	2	Scuderia Ferrari Marlboro	Ferrari F2004-052 V10	B	66	1h 25m 08.100s	132.200/212.756	+73.252s	1m 14.963s	59
13	Felipe Massa	BR	12	Sauber Petronas	Sauber C23-Petronas 04 V10	B	65			+1 lap	1m 16.248s	61
14	Olivier Panis	F	17	Panasonic Toyota Racing	Toyota TF104B-RVX04 V10	M	65			+1 lap	1m 14.247s	59
15	Giorgio Pantano	I	19	Jordan Ford	Jordan EJ-14-Cosworth RS V10	B	63			+3 laps	1m 16.058s	63
16	Zsolt Baumgartner	H	21	European Minardi Cosworth	Minardi PS04B-Cosworth CR3 V10	B	62			+4 laps	1m 18.760s	18
17	Gianmaria Bruni	I	20	European Minardi Cosworth	Minardi PS04B-Cosworth CR3 V10	B	62			+4 laps	1m 18.372s	52
	Nick Heidfeld	D	18	Jordan Ford	Jordan EJ-14-Cosworth RS V10	B	42	Handling problem			1m 16.903s	20
	Cristiano da Matta	BR	16	Panasonic Toyota Racing	Toyota TF104B-RVX04 V10	M	38	Tyre failure			1m 15.145s	20
	Kimi Räikkönen	FIN	6	West McLaren Mercedes	McLaren MP4/19B-Mercedes F0110P V10	M	13	Accident			1m 13.780s	10

Fastest lap: Kimi Räikkönen, on lap 10, 1m 13.780s, 138.679 mph/223.182 km/h (record).

Previous lap record: Juan Pablo Montoya (Williams FW25-BMW P83 V10), 1m 14.917s, 136.574 mph/219.795 km/h (2003).

19th: GIANMARIA BRUNI Minardi-Cosworth

17th: GIORGIO PANTANO Jordan-Cosworth

15th: CRISTIANO DA MATTA Toyota

13th: JENSON BUTTON BAR-Honda
Demoted following engine change

11th: MARK WEBBER Jaguar-Cosworth

20th: ZSOLT BAUMGARTNER Minardi-Cosworth

18th: NICK HEIDFELD Jordan-Cosworth

16th: FELIPE MASSA Sauber-Petronas

14th: GIANCARLO FISICHELLA Sauber-Petronas

12th: CHRISTIAN KLIEN Jaguar-Cosworth

Grid order	1	2	3	4	5	6	7	8	9	10	11	12	13	14	15	16	17	18	19	20	21	22	23	24	25	26	27	28	29	30	31	32	33	34	35	36	37	38	39	40	41	42	43	44	45	46	47	48	49	50	51	52
1 SCHUMACHER	1	1	1	1	1	1	1	1	1	6	9	9	9	9	1	1	1	1	1	1	1	1	1	1	1	1	1	1	8	9	9	9	9	9	1	1	1	1	1	1	1	1	1	1	1	1	9	9	9	1	1
3 MONTOYA	8	6	6	6	6	6	6	6	6	3	14	1	1	8	8	8	8	8	8	8	8	8	8	8	9	1	1	1	1	8	8	8	8	8	8	8	8	9	1	1	1	8	9
6 RÄIKKÖNEN	6	8	8	8	8	8	8	7	7	14	1	6	8	5	5	5	5	5	5	5	5	5	5	9	1	8	8	8	8	9	9	9	9	9	9	9	9	8	8	8	8	9	8
5 COULTHARD	7	7	7	7	7	7	7	8	3	9	6	8	5	3	3	3	3	3	9	9	9	9	9	5	5	5	5	5	5	5	5	5	5	5	5	5	5	3	5	5	5	5
8 ALONSO	5	5	5	5	5	5	5	5	5	1	15	15	3	9	9	9	9	9	3	3	3	3	3	14	14	15	3	3	3	3	3	3	3	3	3	3	3	3	3	3	3	3
7 TRULLI	14	14	14	3	3	3	3	3	14	15	8	5	7	7	7	7	7	7	7	7	7	7	7	10	14	15	3	15	14	14	14	14	14	14	14	14	14	10	10	10	14	14	14
2 BARRICHELLO	3	3	3	14	14	14	14	14	14	9	8	5	3	11	14	14	14	14	14	14	14	7	7	10	10	14	10	3	10	10	10	10	10	10	10	10	10	4	15	14	10	10	10
10 SATO	4	4	4	4	4	4	4	4	10	10	7	7	14	11	11	11	11	11	10	14	14	14	7	7	10	14	10	11	11	11	11	11	11	11	11	11	4	2	14	15	4	4	4
17 PANIS	10	10	10	10	10	10	10	9	15	5	3	11	12	12	12	2	10	12	12	4	4	4	4	4	17	11	11	4	4	4	4	4	4	4	4	4	11	2	15	4	4	2	2
4 PIZZONIA	15	15	15	9	9	9	9	4	8	11	11	14	4	4	10	10	12	12	11	12	15	15	15	17	11	4	15	15	15	15	15	15	15	15	15	2	2	15	14	11	11	11	11
14 WEBBER	16	9	9	15	15	15	15	15	16	19	12	12	10	10	4	4	4	4	15	15	17	17	10	12	2	2	2	2	2	2	2	2	2	15	7	11	2	15	15	15
15 KLIEN	9	16	16	16	16	16	16	16	11	12	4	15	15	15	15	15	2	11	11	11	11	12	12	12	16	16	16	16	7	7	7	7	7	17	17	17	7	7	7	7
9 BUTTON	11	11	11	11	11	11	11	11	9	4	10	10	18	18	2	2	2	2	16	2	12	16	16	16	7	7	7	7	7	12	12	12	12	7	7	12	12	17	7	7	12	12
11 FISICHELLA	19	19	19	19	19	19	19	19	12	10	18	18	16	16	2	18	16	16	16	17	11	2	2	16	7	7	7	7	12	17	17	17	17	12	12	12	17	17	17
16 DA MATTA	12	12	12	12	12	12	12	12	17	16	16	2	2	16	16	17	17	11	16	16	16	6	17	17	17	17	17	18	19	19	19	19	19	19	19	19
12 MASSA	18	18	18	18	18	18	17	17	17	4	18	2	17	17	17	18	18	18	18	18	18	18	18	18	18	18	18	18	18	21	21	21	21	21	21	21
19 PANTANO	21	21	17	17	17	17	18	18	16	17	17	21	19	19	19	19	19	19	19	19	19	19	19	19	19	21	21	20	20	20	20	20	20
18 HEIDFELD	20	17	21	21	21	21	21	2	2	2	21	20	20	20	21	21	21	21	21	21	21	21	21	21	21	21	21	20	20	20
20 BRUNI	17	20	20	20	20	2	2	2	21	21	19	20	19	19	21	20	20	20	20	20	20	20	20	20	20	20	20	20	20	20
21 BAUMGARTNER	2	2	2	2	2	20	20	20	20	20	20	19

Pit stop
One lap behind leader

TIME SHEETS

QUALIFYING

Sunny with cloud (track: 34°C, air 27–26°C)

Pos.	Driver	Lap time	Sector 1	Sector 2	Sector 3
1	Michael Schumacher	1m 13.306s	16.348s	34.457s	22.501s
2	Juan Pablo Montoya	1m 13.668s	16.168s	34.582s	22.918s
3	Jenson Button	1m 13.674s	16.153s	34.713s	22.808s
4	Kimi Räikkönen	1m 13.690s	16.153s	34.704s	22.823s
5	David Coulthard	1m 13.821s	16.113s	34.665s	23.043s
6	Fernando Alonso	1m 13.874s	16.355s	34.402s	23.117s
7	Jarno Trulli	1m 14.134s	16.297s	34.854s	22.983s
8	Rubens Barrichello	1m 14.278s	16.366s	34.790s	23.122s
9	Takuma Sato	1m 14.287s	16.604s	34.786s	22.897s
10	Olivier Panis	1m 14.368s	16.365s	35.001s	23.002s
11	Antonio Pizzonia	1m 14.556s	16.438s	34.937s	23.181s
12	Mark Webber	1m 14.802s	16.605s	34.948s	23.249s
13	Christian Klien	1m 15.011s	16.753s	34.926s	23.332s
14	Giancarlo Fisichella	1m 15.395s	16.534s	35.424s	23.437s
15	Cristiano da Matta	1m 15.454s	16.723s	35.383s	23.348s
16	Felipe Massa	1m 15.616s	16.677s	35.498s	23.441s
17	Giorgio Pantano	1m 16.192s	16.695s	35.588s	23.909s
18	Nick Heidfeld	1m 16.310s	16.912s	35.618s	23.780s
19	Gianmaria Bruni	1m 18.055s	17.293s	36.430s	24.322
20	Zsolt Baumgartner	1m 18.400s	17.197s	36.567s	24.636s

CHASSIS LOG BOOK

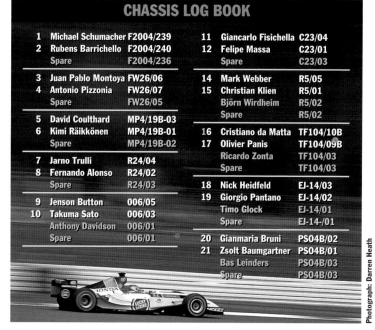

1	Michael Schumacher	F2004/239
2	Rubens Barrichello	F2004/240
	Spare	F2004/236
3	Juan Pablo Montoya	FW26/06
4	Antonio Pizzonia	FW26/07
	Spare	FW26/05
5	David Coulthard	MP4/19B-03
6	Kimi Räikkönen	MP4/19B-01
	Spare	MP4/19B-02
7	Jarno Trulli	R24/04
8	Fernando Alonso	R24/02
	Spare	R24/03
9	Jenson Button	006/05
10	Takuma Sato	006/03
	Anthony Davidson	006/01
	Spare	006/01

11	Giancarlo Fisichella	C23/04
12	Felipe Massa	C23/01
	Spare	C23/03
14	Mark Webber	R5/05
15	Christian Klien	R5/01
	Björn Wirdheim	R5/02
	Spare	R5/02
16	Cristiano da Matta	TF104/10B
17	Olivier Panis	TF104/09B
	Ricardo Zonta	TF104/03
	Spare	TF104/03
18	Nick Heidfeld	EJ-14/03
19	Giorgio Pantano	EJ-14/02
	Timo Glock	EJ-14/01
	Spare	EJ-14-/01
20	Gianmaria Bruni	PS04B/02
21	Zsolt Baumgartner	PS04B/01
	Bas Leinders	PS04B/03
	Spare	PS04B/03

Photograph: Darren Heath

PRACTICE 1 (FRIDAY)

Sunny (track 36–41°C, air 29–31°C)

Pos.	Driver	Laps	Time
1	Anthony Davidson	32	1m 15.756s
2	Michael Schumacher	11	1m 15.864s
3	Kimi Räikkönen	8	1m 16.318s
4	Ricardo Zonta	36	1m 16.340s
5	Giancarlo Fisichella	11	1m 16.451s
6	Olivier Panis	20	1m 16.484s
7	Rubens Barrichello	16	1m 16.493s
8	Jenson Button	12	1m 16.544s
9	Juan Pablo Montoya	14	1m 16.795s
10	Antonio Pizzonia	14	1m 16.845s
11	David Coulthard	8	1m 16.916s
12	Cristiano da Matta	21	1m 17.111s
13	Fernando Alonso	11	1m 17.142s
14	Felipe Massa	18	1m 17.361s
15	Jarno Trulli	14	1m 17.487s
16	Takuma Sato	14	1m 17.526s
17	Björn Wirdheim	20	1m 17.714s
18	Nick Heidfeld	15	1m 18.257s
19	Timo Glock	17	1m 18.768s
20	Christian Klien	9	1m 18.810s
21	Gianmaria Bruni	17	1m 19.088s
22	Bas Leinders	14	1m 19.270s
23	Zsolt Baumgartner	13	1m 19.959s
24	Giorgio Pantano	17	1m 20.029s
25	Mark Webber	1	No time

PRACTICE 2 (FRIDAY)

Sunny, scattered cloud (track 43–46°C, air 31–34°C)

Pos.	Driver	Laps	Time
1	Michael Schumacher	27	1m 15.001s
2	Kimi Räikkönen	18	1m 15.045s
3	Juan Pablo Montoya	25	1m 15.167s
4	Jenson Button	23	1m 15.379s
5	Antonio Pizzonia	25	1m 15.470s
6	Anthony Davidson	33	1m 15.576s
7	Takuma Sato	21	1m 15.657s
8	Fernando Alonso	30	1m 15.677s
9	Rubens Barrichello	19	1m 15.738s
10	Ricardo Zonta	38	1m 16.200s
11	David Coulthard	18	1m 16.265s
12	Björn Wirdheim	28	1m 16.342s
13	Mark Webber	27	1m 16.514s
14	Jarno Trulli	32	1m 16.660s
15	Christian Klien	31	1m 16.854s
16	Felipe Massa	30	1m 16.865s
17	Giancarlo Fisichella	26	1m 17.026s
18	Cristiano da Matta	26	1m 17.300s
19	Olivier Panis	23	1m 17.419s
20	Timo Glock	25	1m 17.724s
21	Giorgio Pantano	24	1m 17.869s
22	Zsolt Baumgartner	21	1m 18.098s
23	Bas Leinders	17	1m 18.224s
24	Nick Heidfeld	23	1m 18.243s
25	Gianmaria Bruni	25	1m 18.309s

PRACTICE 3 (SATURDAY)

Overcast (track 24–26°C, air 22–23°C)

Pos.	Driver	Laps	Time
1	Michael Schumacher	11	1m 15.066s
2	Juan Pablo Montoya	5	1m 15.277s
3	Rubens Barrichello	10	1m 15.354s
4	Kimi Räikkönen	6	1m 15.626s
5	Jenson Button	10	1m 15.839s
6	Olivier Panis	7	1m 15.882s
7	David Coulthard	7	1m 15.919s
8	Antonio Pizzonia	12	1m 16.151s
9	Giancarlo Fisichella	9	1m 16.232s
10	Jarno Trulli	5	1m 16.334s
11	Cristiano da Matta	8	1m 16.457s
12	Fernando Alonso	5	1m 16.462s
13	Felipe Massa	8	1m 16.532s
14	Christian Klien	5	1m 16.650s
15	Mark Webber	7	1m 16.961s
16	Nick Heidfeld	10	1m 17.369s
17	Gianmaria Bruni	11	1m 18.198s
18	Giorgio Pantano	4	1m 18.914s
19	Zsolt Baumgartner	9	1m 21.288s
20	Takuma Sato	4	No time

PRACTICE 4 (SATURDAY)

Overcast (track 27–28°C, air 23–24°C)

Pos.	Driver	Laps	Time
1	Jenson Button	15	1m 13.676s
2	Juan Pablo Montoya	11	1m 13.976s
3	David Coulthard	11	1m 14.064s
4	Kimi Räikkönen	14	1m 14.100s
5	Fernando Alonso	12	1m 14.320s
6	Rubens Barrichello	12	1m 14.393s
7	Michael Schumacher	14	1m 14.459s
8	Jarno Trulli	15	1m 14.468s
9	Antonio Pizzonia	10	1m 14.766s
10	Cristiano da Matta	19	1m 14.791s
11	Olivier Panis	16	1m 14.953s
12	Mark Webber	25	1m 15.000s
13	Christian Klien	20	1m 15.481s
14	Giancarlo Fisichella	10	1m 15.572s
15	Felipe Massa	10	1m 15.588s
16	Nick Heidfeld	16	1m 16.832s
17	Gianmaria Bruni	13	1m 18.227s
18	Zsolt Baumgartner	15	1m 18.691s

9th: OLIVIER PANIS Toyota

7th: RUBENS BARRICHELLO Ferrari

5th: FERNANDO ALONSO Renault

3rd: KIMI RÄIKKÖNEN Mclaren-Mercedes

Pole: MICHAEL SCHUMACHER Ferrari

10th: ANTONIO PIZZONIA Williams-BMW

8th: TAKUMA SATO BAR-Honda

6th: JARNO TRULLI Renault

4th: DAVID COULTHARD McLaren-Mercedes

2nd: JUAN PABLO MONTOYA Williams-BMW

53	54	55	56	57	58	59	60	61	62	63	64	65	66	
1	1	1	1	1	1	1	1	1	1	1	1	1	1	1
9	9	9	9	9	9	9	9	9	9	9	9	9	9	2
8	8	8	8	8	8	8	8	8	8	8	8	8	8	3
5	5	5	5	5	5	5	5	5	5	5	5	5	5	4
3	3	3	3	3	3	3	3	3	3	3	3	3	3	5
14	14	14	14	14	14	14	14	14	14	14	14	14	14	6
10	10	10	10	10	10	10	10	4	4	4	4	4	4	7
4	4	4	4	4	4	4	10	10	10	10	10	10	10	8
2	2	2	2	2	2	2	2	2	2	2	2	11	
11	11	11	11	11	11	11	11	11	11	11	11	11	15	
15	15	15	15	15	15	15	15	15	15	15	15	15	7	
7	7	7	7	7	7	7	7	7	7	7	7	7	2	
12	12	12	12	12	12	12	12	12	12	12	12	12		
17	17	17	17	17	17	17	17	17	17	17	17	17		
19	19	19	19	19	19	19	19	19	19	19				
21	21	21	21	21	21	21	21	21	21					
20	20	20	20	20	20	20	20	20	20					

POINTS: CONSTRUCTORS

1	Ferrari	184
2	Renault	85
3	BAR	76
4	Williams	47
5	McLaren	37
6	Sauber	18
7	Toyota	8
8	Jaguar	7
9	Jordan	5
10	Minardi	1

POINTS: DRIVERS

1	Michael Schumacher	110
2	Rubens Barrichello	74
3	Jenson Button	61
4	Jarno Trulli	46
5	Fernando Alonso	39
6	Juan Pablo Montoya	33
7	David Coulthard	19
8	Kimi Räikkönen	18
9	Takuma Sato	15

10	Giancarlo Fisichella	13
11	Ralf Schumacher	12
12	Mark Webber	7
13 =	Felipe Massa	5
13 =	Olivier Panis	5
15 =	Cristiano da Matta	3
15 =	Nick Heidfeld	3
17 =	Timo Glock	2
17 =	Antonio Pizzonia	2
19	Zsolt Baumgartner	1

FOR THE RECORD

1st grand prix point
Antonio Pizzonia

Photographs: Darren Heath

Main photograph and inset: Still breaking records. Michael Schumacher took his 12th win of the season as Ferrari wrapped up the constructors' championship.
Photographs: Darren Heath

HUNGARIAN GP

HUNGARORING

HUNGARORING QUALIFYING

Two key elements of the F1 mix had changed in the run-up to the Hungarian Grand Prix. Bridgestone had made considerable progress on Ferrari's behalf, most specifically with a new soft-compound tyre that played to the strength of the well-balanced F2004 chassis. Also a new rule had been introduced for the race, intended by the FIA to eliminate any possibility of teams running flexible rear wings.

The new rule did not affect the Ferrari team's performance one jot. Michael Schumacher expertly threw pole position 0.177s away from the grasp of team-mate Rubens Barrichello with a best lap of 1m 19.146s. That effectively ensured that the outcome of the race was a foregone conclusion. Yet Schumacher confessed that he was not unduly surprised at the way the grid order had shaped up.

'No, not really, honestly. I guess that's what you should have expected with the exception of the McLarens,' he commented. 'I expected them to be a little faster, but maybe they are running on a different strategy. But, in general, you have to expect the BARs to be quick and the Renaults to be quick.'

Barrichello also radiated confidence. 'It's a little bit disappointing not to have pole because this morning, although the track [conditions] was different from when Michael was out, it really was a good lap this morning [in pre-qualifying],' he said. 'But in qualifying, I missed out a little bit toward the end of the lap, but even so I'm happy. The lap wasn't too bad.'

The BAR-Hondas of Takuma Sato (1m 19.693s) and Jenson Button (1m 19.700s) lined up third and fourth on the second row of the grid. 'We expected to be strong here after Germany,' said an ebullient Sato, 'and this has proved to be the case. I think the weather has taken everybody by surprise, and the last few runners of the afternoon – including myself – were lucky that the rain held off until after the session.'

Button speculated that he may not have generated enough heat in the tyres on his out-lap, compromising his qualifying run. 'I would have been happier to be on the front row,' he mused, 'but the Bridgestones have been working better than any of us expected.'

Fernando Alonso lined up fifth in his Renault R24 after posting a 1m 19.996s best, but Jarno Trulli's run was spoiled by a rain shower, which dampened the second sector of his lap. He wound up ninth on 1m 20.411s.

Of the Williams drivers, Antonio Pizzonia (1m 20.170s) just pipped Juan Pablo Montoya (1m 20.199s) for sixth place on the grid, a particularly satisfying performance by the young Brazilian. Both FW26s ran with conventional nose sections in place of the distinctive 'walrus tusk' configuration used since the start of the season. These had only been subjected to wind-tunnel testing rather than any circuit running prior to the race, but the signs were promising.

'I'm fairly pleased with my qualifying lap, even if I didn't have much luck because it started to rain a bit when I was in the last sector and that slowed me slightly,' said Pizzonia. 'My car felt better in the final qualifying than in pre-qualifying, and also the track conditions improved from one session to another.'

Montoya was confident about his car's race set-up, but didn't hold out much hope of success on the tortuous little circuit given his seventh-place starting position.

Giancarlo Fisichella did a good job to qualify his Sauber eighth on 1m 20.324s, but Felipe Massa was very despondent to wind up 20th and last following an engine failure on Friday. Rather than taking the ten-place penalty, he decided to save a set of tyres and not take part in qualifying.

'Of all the circuits we visit, this one, together with Monaco, is the most difficult on which to overtake, and therefore the worst on which to have an engine problem that loses you grid positions,' shrugged the Brazilian.

On the face of it, gambling on the harder Michelin tyre compound made perfect sense for the McLaren team, but when the conditions turned unexpectedly cool on Saturday, Kimi Räikkönen (1m 20.570s) and David Coulthard (1m 20.897s) ended up languishing in tenth and 12th places, split by Mark Webber's Jaguar R5 (1m 20.730s).

'I think we have been too conservative with our tyre choice and are paying the price,' shrugged Coulthard.

'It's hard to judge where the car is on the circuit and we are sliding around a bit,' a team insider remarked wryly. 'Blame it on a false sense of security.'

Farther back, the usual suspects filled the last few rows of the grid, the Toyota squad being particularly frustrated over the lack of form displayed by the TF104B on the high-downforce track; Olivier Panis (1m 21.068s) and new boy Ricardo Zonta (1m 21.135s) lined up 13th and 15th.

'We are all disappointed with the outcome of today's qualifying session,' said the team's technical director, Mike Gascoyne. 'I don't think our grid positions reflect our true performance level. This morning, the balance on the car was pretty good, but in qualifying the cars just seemed to lack grip.'

DIARY

Williams strongly denies that its one-time chief designer, Adrian Newey, is to rejoin the team from McLaren in 2005.

The FIA and Ferrari dismiss allegations of collusion in connection with the framing of the 2005 F1 technical regulations.

Former Tyrrell F1 driver and 1985 Indianapolis winner Danny Sullivan announces that he will retire from racing at the end of the season.

Adrian Fernandez wins the Kentucky IRL race by 0.01s from Buddy Rice.

MICHAEL Schumacher and Rubens Barrichello hung Ferrari's rivals out to dry yet again in the Hungarian Grand Prix at Budapest, clinching the Maranello team's 14th constructors' championship title since the contest was inaugurated in 1958.

Despite all the upbeat predictions from BAR Honda, BMW Williams and McLaren Mercedes, they simply couldn't come close to challenging the superbly reliable F2004s, which cruised to their seventh 1-2 of the season. That feat was achieved despite some nerve-racking leaks from the Italian team's refuelling rigs after the first round of scheduled stops.

It was Schumacher's seventh straight win of 2004, a record not bettered in the 51 years since Alberto Ascari bagged nine consecutive victories – also for Ferrari – across the 1952 and '53 seasons. It gave the German driver a total of 82 grand prix wins, matching the combined career totals of Alain Prost and Nigel Mansell. Moreover, he had achieved a one-season record of 12 wins and his fifth grand slam: achieving pole position, setting fastest lap, leading every lap and winning the race. That record had been bettered only by the late Jim Clark, who had produced eight such dominant performances.

'This [constructors'] title means more than winning 12 races in a season,' said Schumacher. 'To win here compared to last year shows why we have won the title so early. The win might have looked easy from the outside, but I was flat out most of the way until the final pit stop. In the early stages, Rubens was pushing very hard and anything could have happened.'

Certainly, it was a dramatic contrast to 2003's race, when Schumacher had been lapped by Alonso's victorious Renault after a particularly uncompetitive performance from the Ferrari team and its Bridgestone rubber.

'We could judge our performance against the opposition's performance at Jerez,' said Schumacher, 'so we knew pretty well what we could do here. I didn't [quite] have Rubens on my neck, but he was only four or five seconds behind at the first stops, but it's so easy to run wide and lose time here that you have to keep pushing all the time. It's so much more predictable a car to drive than last year's.'

Jenson Button and the BAR Honda team may have dreamed of a maiden victory in the Hungarian Grand Prix, but when the chips were down, the Michelin-shod BARs could not live with the dominant Italian machines. Button, seeking the tranquillity of his BAR 006's cockpit as a refuge from the storm of speculation over his future F1 career (see sidebar), had qualified in fourth place behind the two Ferraris and his team-mate, Takuma Sato. When the starting lights went out, however, Schumacher and Barrichello's confident sprint toward the first corner indicated that they would brook no opposition; they surged away into the distance, never to be challenged throughout the 70-lap procession.

Barrichello just managed to scramble into the first corner in second place. 'I actually had a good start and I think that the rain yesterday cleaned our side [of the track] a little bit, so I had a good start. It was difficult to know where Michael was going to brake because I had to defend myself and even try to overtake him if I could. After that, we were just running at our own pace.'

From his impressive third on the grid, Takuma Sato's bubbling enthusiasm got the best of him, his BAR running wide into the first corner, a slip that cost him dear. By the end of the opening lap, he was back in eighth place behind the two Ferraris, Fernando Alonso's Renault R24, Juan Pablo Montoya's Williams-BMW, Button's BAR, Jarno Trulli's Renault and the McLaren MP4/19B of Kimi Räikkönen.

'I had a difficult start,' said Sato with masterly understatement. 'I got off the line reasonably okay, but at Turn One I was outside Alonso, put a wheel off-line and into the dusty area. I lost traction, and several cars managed to get by me over the next few corners as I lost momentum, so it was a tough opening lap.'

As if that wasn't enough first-corner action, Ricardo Zonta, who'd been drafted into the Toyota squad as a replacement for the dismissed Cristiano da Matta, was pitched into a spin by Giorgio Pantano's Jordan, the Japanese car clipping Mark Webber's Jaguar R5 as it pirouetted out of line. All three continued.

Alonso came in from third place for his first refuelling stop at the end of lap ten, followed next time around by Barrichello, Montoya, Button and Trulli from the leading bunch. Schumacher

Below: Ross Brawn reflects on another Ferrari world championship secured.
Photograph: Darren Heath

www.jensonbutton.com

brought his Ferrari in at the end of lap 12, accelerating smoothly back into the contest at the head of the field. The Ferrari mechanics were left pondering a potentially serious problem, however, having discovered a leak from Barrichello's refuelling rig, which raised concerns that the Brazilian's car might not have been fully fuelled at its first stop.

A quick calculation revealed those concerns to be misplaced. As a precautionary move, however, the couplings on both rigs were changed and both Ferraris were fuelled from Schumacher's allotted rig for their remaining two stops apiece.

Alonso, having benefited from a brilliant start that had catapulted him from fifth to third, thereafter enjoyed a lonely race to finish behind the Ferraris. It was a good drive, but a far cry from his dominant 2003 performance, which produced the surreal sight of his Renault actually lapping Schumacher's Ferrari as it trailed in eighth place.

'At the start, I got a little bit balked by Sato,' said the Spaniard. 'He tried to close the door a bit, and I had to lift off a bit; probably because of that, I lost second place, because I arrived quite close to Rubens, but not enough. After that, the race was quite calm.

There was nothing in front and nothing behind. I was just controlling the gaps.

'I don't think much would have changed if I'd got ahead of Rubens at the first corner. On the pit stops, the Ferraris were much faster than us, and I think that even if I had run second in the early laps, he would have overtaken me. But it *would* have been more interesting if I had run second in the early stages.'

Alonso's team-mate, Jarno Trulli, pulled up with a sudden loss of power after battling acute understeer on his second set of tyres. It was another disappointing result for the Italian driver.

Montoya was content with fourth; a strong start had seen him gain three places through the first couple of corners. 'After my first pit stop, I lost quite a bit of time behind Webber, and this prevented me from getting closer to Alonso, but I don't think I could have caught the Renault today,' he admitted.

Button could do little more than hang on gamely to finish fifth. 'I'm a little bit disappointed because we came here expecting better things,' said the Englishman, who remained at the centre of a continuing row over whether or not he would be able to quit the BAR squad and join Mark Webber at Williams in 2005.

BUTTON'S MOVE TRIGGERS CONTROVERSY

Jenson Button looked ever so slightly sheepish when he walked into the BAR Honda pit for the first time during the Hungarian Grand Prix weekend. He had not seen his mechanics since announcing a fortnight earlier that he would be leaving the team at the end of the season to join the BMW Williams squad.

Button's management was seeking to extricate the 24-year-old from his BAR deal by claiming that the option the team had recently exercised to secure his services for 2005 and beyond was invalid. His manager, John Byfield, was questioning Honda's long-term commitment to supplying engines to the BAR squad only weeks after the Japanese car company had reaffirmed its determination to power the team to continued F1 success.

The breach between Button and the BAR team came just after he had finished second in the German Grand Prix in July, when Byfield had sent a brief fax to David Richards, advising him that the driver would not be staying in 2005 and would be switching to Williams.

Byfield claimed that Honda's failure to give BAR the necessary assurances in the manner specified over the issue of continued engine supply gave Button a perfectly legitimate escape route. However, it was believed that the real reason the driver had sought a way of leaving the team stemmed from a disagreement over points-related bonus payments of around $1.8 million following a change in FIA rules at the start of 2003, which awarded points for the first eight finishing positions rather than the top six, as had previously been the case.

'There is absolutely no question, we have a valid contract with Jenson,' said BAR boss David Richards after Byfield had communicated Button's decision. 'If anything, I feel sorry for Jenson at the present moment for being so misled. Both myself and Geoff Willis, our technical director, have been attempting to call him for the last 24 hours, but without any success. This is a quite extraordinary situation.'

Williams, which had given Button his F1 chance in 2000, remained confident that its new contract with the British driver was valid and that he would be available to rejoin them for 2005.

'There has been a long-term relationship between the Williams team and Jenson,' said Frank Williams. 'We have maintained that relationship until the present day, and I am delighted that one of the most talented drivers in F1 has accepted the opportunity to return to the team.'

Button added, 'I am pleased that I had the option to rejoin the BMW Williams team where my Formula 1 career started. For the meantime, the 2004 season has my full focus and attention.

'Beyond this, I have every confidence that the massive investment in resources and the depth of talent at Williams and BMW provide the best platform for my future ambitions to be a world champion.'

The dispute was referred to the FIA Contracts Recognition Board for adjudication, as provided under the terms of the Concorde Agreement. However, an official verdict would be more that two months coming.

laps after each pit stop, but this cleared up after five or six laps. 'I did my best, really pushed and didn't make any mistakes,' said 'Fisi', whose performance made up for the disappointing retirement of team-mate Felipe Massa after 21 laps with a worryingly 'long' brake pedal that couldn't be sorted out, prompting the team to err on the side of caution and withdraw him from the race.

McLaren had a disappointing weekend. The team had opted to use the harder Michelin tyre for qualifying, only to encounter uncharacteristically cool conditions that left Kimi Räikkönen and David Coulthard trailing in tenth and 12th places. Räikkönen was the first retirement – with an electrical problem in his car's injection system – while Coulthard came home ninth, struggling to keep his car under control on the wrong tyre choice.

'There was not a lot I could do on the track, as we started so far back,' shrugged the Scot. 'It's almost impossible to overtake on this track, so I think we will just forget about this weekend and look forward to the Belgian GP in two weeks' time.'

Mark Webber brought his Jaguar R5 home tenth, frustrated that a spin had cost him any real chance of challenging Coulthard, while Olivier Panis piloted the sole surviving Toyota to 11th place after Zonta had first blistered his tyres and then stopped with an electronics problem. Nick Heidfeld's Jordan, Christian Klien's Jaguar and the two Minardis completed the list of finishers.

For Schumacher, it had been another great day and yet one more example of his passion for the sport that had not shown even the slightest signs of dimming. 'It's a great atmosphere we have in the team, and the good thing about Formula 1 is that it is always going forward,' he reflected almost poignantly. 'It just keeps going, and I like to enjoy it as long as it does. One day, it will finish, and we all know that.'

Below: Toyota test driver Ricardo Zonta was back in F1 at Budapest, at the expense of Cristiano da Matta.
Photograph: Darren Heath

'I think we might not have put the best condition of tyres on at the first stop, so we lost a lot of time.' explained Button. 'I had a lot of oversteer, which made it very difficult to drive and that's why Jarno was able to get so close to me. Once I made the decision to put a set of conditioned [scrubbed] tyres on, then the handling balance was much better.'

With Sato following Button home in sixth place, members of the BAR team could at least console themselves that they had moved to within eight points of Renault in the battle for second place in the constructors' championship.

Antonio Pizzonia came home seventh after a difficult run, just 1.1s behind Sato. 'The handling of my car was pretty difficult, especially in the beginning, but we made some changes in the pit stops and the situation improved,' he said. 'For most of the race, I was behind Sato, trying to get close enough to pass him, but I never had the right opportunity to do so. We nearly got him at the last pit stop, but I had traffic in the pit lane.'

Eighth place fell to Giancarlo Fisichella's Sauber C23. The Italian reported that his car had good race pace and balance, the sole problem being predictable Bridgestone tyre graining two or three

Above: Another driver to receive a second chance, Antonio Pizzonia claimed seventh for Williams for the second race running.

Right: Olivier Panis struggled home in a lowly 11th for Toyota
Photographs: Darren Heath

Photograph: Darren Heath

FIA F1 WORLD CHAMPIONSHIP • ROUND 13

MARLBORO
MAGYAR NAGYDIJ

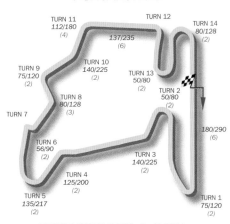

HUNGARORING

TURN 11 112/180 (4)
TURN 12 137/235 (6)
TURN 14 80/128 (2)
TURN 9 75/120 (2)
TURN 10 140/225 (2)
TURN 13 50/80 (2)
TURN 2 50/80 (2)
TURN 8 80/128 (3)
TURN 7
TURN 6 56/90 (2)
TURN 3 140/225 (2)
180/290 (6)
TURN 4 125/200 (2)
TURN 5 135/217 (2)
TURN 1 75/120 (2)

CIRCUIT LENGTH: 2.722miles/4.381 km

RACE DISTANCE: 70 laps, 190.551 miles/306.663 km   RACE WEATHER: Sunny/cloudy (track 35–39°C, air 26–27°C)

Pos.	Driver	Nat.	No.	Entrant	Car/Engine	Tyres	Laps	Time/Retirement	Speed (mph/km/h)	Gap to leader	Fastest race lap	
1	Michael Schumacher	D	1	Scuderia Ferrari Marlboro	Ferrari F2004-052 V10	B	70	1h 35m 26.131s	119.799/192.798		1m 19.071s	29
2	Rubens Barrichello	BR	2	Scuderia Ferrari Marlboro	Ferrari F2004-052 V10	B	70	1h 35m 30.827s	119.701/192.640	+4.696s	1m 19.213s	29
3	Fernando Alonso	E	8	Mild Seven Renault F1 Team	Renault R24-RS4 V10	M	70	1h 36m 10.730s	118.872/191.307	+44.599s	1m 20.275s	49
4	Juan Pablo Montoya	COL	3	BMW WilliamsF1 Team	Williams FW26-BMW P84 V10	M	70	1h 36m 28.744s	118.503/190.712	+62.613s	1m 20.715s	49
5	Jenson Button	GB	9	Lucky Strike BAR Honda	BAR 006-Honda RA004E V10	M	70	1h 36m 33.570s	118.404/190.553	+67.439s	1m 20.425s	47
6	Takuma Sato	J	10	Lucky Strike BAR Honda	BAR 006-Honda RA004E V10	M	69			+1 lap	1m 21.030s	10
7	Antonio Pizzonia	E	4	BMW WilliamsF1 Team	Williams FW26-BMW P84 V10	M	69			+1 lap	1m 20.501s	48
8	Giancarlo Fisichella	I	11	Sauber Petronas	Sauber C23-Petronas 04 V10	B	69			+1 lap	1m 21.022s	53
9	David Coulthard	GB	5	West McLaren Mercedes	McLaren MP4/19B-Mercedes F0110P V10	M	69			+1 lap	1m 21.134s	67
10	Mark Webber	AUS	14	Jaguar Racing	Jaguar R5-Cosworth CR6 V10	M	69			+1 lap	1m 20.825s	45
11	Olivier Panis	F	17	Panasonic Toyota Racing	Toyota TF104B-RVX04 V10	M	69			+1 lap	1m 21.310s	50
12	Nick Heidfeld	D	18	Jordan Ford	Jordan EJ-14-Cosworth RS V10	B	68			+2 laps	1m 21.518s	68
13	Christian Klien	A	15	Jaguar Racing	Jaguar R5-Cosworth CR6 V10	M	68			+2 laps	1m 22.530s	45
14	Gianmaria Bruni	I	20	European Minardi Cosworth	Minardi PS04B-Cosworth CR3 V10	B	66			+4 laps	1m 24.601s	65
15	Zsolt Baumgartner	H	21	European Minardi Cosworth	Minardi PS04B-Cosworth CR3 V10	B	65			+5 laps	1m 24.855s	63
	Giorgio Pantano	I	19	Jordan Ford	Jordan EJ-14-Cosworth RS V10	B	48	Gearbox			1m 22.927s	43
	Jarno Trulli	I	7	Mild Seven Renault F1 Team	Renault R24-RS4 V10	M	41	Engine			1m 20.705s	10
	Ricardo Zonta	BR	16	Panasonic Toyota Racing	Toyota TF104B-RVX04 V10	M	31	Electronics			1m 22.525s	13
	Felipe Massa	BR	12	Sauber Petronas	Sauber C23-Petronas 04 V10	B	21	Brakes			1m 21.856s	14
	Kimi Räikkönen	FIN	6	West McLaren Mercedes	McLaren MP4/19B- Mercedes F0110P V10	M	13	Electrical			1m 21.678s	6

All results and data © FOM 2004

Fastest lap: Michael Schumacher, on lap 29, 1m 19.071s, 123.939 mph/199.461 km/h (record).

Previous lap record: Juan Pablo Montoya (Williams FW25-BMW P83 V10), 1m 22.095s, 119.374 mph/192.114 km/h (2003).

19th: GIANMARIA BRUNI Minardi-Cosworth

17th: GIORGIO PANTANO Jordan-Cosworth

15th: CRISTIANO DA MATTA Toyota

13th: OLIVIER PANIS Toyota

11th: MARK WEBBER Jaguar-Cosworth

20th: FELIPE MASSA Sauber-Petronas

18th: ZSOLT BAUMGARTNER Minardi-Cosworth

16th: NICK HEIDFELD Jordan-Cosworth

14th: CHRISTIAN KLIEN Jaguar-Cosworth

12th: DAVID COULTHARD McLaren-Mercedes

Grid order	1	2	3	4	5	6	7	8	9	10	11	12	13	14	15	16	17	18	19	20	21	22	23	24	25	26	27	28	29	30	31	32	33	34	35	36	37	38	39	40	41	42	43	44	45	46	47	48	49	50	51	52	53	54
1 SCHUMACHER	1	1	1	1	1	1	1	1	1	1	1	1	1	1	1	1	1	1	1	1	1	1	1	1	1	1	1	1	1	1	1	1	1	1	1	1	1	1	1	1	1	1	1	1	1	1	1	1	1	1	1	1	1	1
2 BARRICHELLO	2	2	2	2	2	2	2	2	2	2	2	2	2	2	2	2	2	2	2	2	2	2	2	2	2	2	2	2	2	2	2	2	2	2	2	2	2	2	2	2	2	2	2	2	2	2	2	2	2	2	2	2	2	2
10 SATO	8	8	8	8	8	8	8	8	8	3	10	4	8	8	8	8	8	8	8	8	8	8	8	8	8	8	8	8	8	3	8	8	8	8	8	8	8	8	8	8	8	8	8	8	8	8	8	8	8	8	8	3	8	8
9 BUTTON	3	3	3	3	3	3	3	3	3	9	4	8	4	14			3	3	3	3	3	3	3	3	3	3	3	3	3	8	4	4	3	3	3	3	3	3	3	3	3	3	3	3	3	3	3	3	3	8	3	3		
8 ALONSO	9	9	9	9	9	9	9	9	9	7	8	14	14	3	14	9	9	9	9	9	9	9	9	9	9	9	9	9	9	7		3	9	9	9	9	9	9	9	9	9	4	9	9	9	9								
4 PIZZONIA	7	7	7	7	7	7	7	7	7	10	14	3	9	9			7	7	7	7	7	7	7	7	7	7	7	7	7	14	3	9	10	10	10	10	10	10	10	10	10	10	10	4	4	9	10	10	10	10				
3 MONTOYA	6	6	6	6	6	6	6	6	6	10	4	3	9	9	7	7	10	10	10	10	10	10	10	10	10	10	10	10	4	4	9	10	4	4	4	4	4	4	4	4	4	4	4	10	10	10	4	4	4					
11 FISICHELLA	10	10	10	10	10	10	10	10	10	11	8	9	7	7	10	10	4	4	4	4	4	4	4	4	4	4	4	4	11	11	10	7	7	7	7	7	7	7	7	7	7	11	11	11	11	11	11	11	11	5	5	11	11	
7 TRULLI	11	11	11	11	11	11	11	11	11	4	5	7	18	10	4	4	11	11	11	11	11	11	11	11	11	11	10	10	5	5	11	11	11	11	11	11	11	11	11	5	5	5	5	5	5	5	5	11	11					
6 RÄIKKÖNEN	4	4	4	4	4	4	4	4	4	5	14	18	10	18	11	11	5	5	5	5	5	5	5	5	5	5	5	5	11	11	5	5	5	5	5	5	5	5	5	14	14	14	14	14	17	17	17	17	14	14	14			
14 WEBBER	5	5	5	5	5	5	5	5	5	6	17	15	5	5	14	14	14	14	14	14	14	14	14	14	14	14	14	14	14	14	14	14	14	14	14	14	14	14	14	17	17	17	17	17	14	14	14	14	17	17	17	17	18	
5 COULTHARD	14	14	14	14	14	14	14	14	14	18	12	11	11	15	18	18	18	18	18	18	18	18	18	18	18	18	18	17	17	17	14	14	14	14	14	17	17	17	17	18	18	18	18	18	18	18	18	18	18	18	18	18	18	18
17 PANIS	18	18	18	18	18	18	18	18	18	17	6	5	18	17	17	17	17	17	17	17	17	17	17	17	17	17	18	15	15	15	18	18	18	18	18	18	15	15	15	15	15	15	15	15	15	15	15	15	15	15	15	15	15	15
15 KLIEN	15	15	15	15	15	15	15	15	15	12	15	19	17	12	12	16	16	16	16	16	16	16	16	19	19	15	15	19	19	19	19	19	19	19	19	19	19	19	19	19	20	20	20	20	20	20	20	20	20	20	20	20		
16 ZONTA	17	17	17	17	17	17	17	17	17	15	19	12	16	16	16	16	19	19	19	19	19	18	18	18	19	19	19	19	19	19	19	19	19	20	20	20	20	20	20	20	21	21	21	21	21	21								
18 HEIDFELD	19	19	19	19	19	12	12	12	12	11	12	16	16	16	16	15	15	15	15	15	15	16	16	16	16	16	21	20	20	20	20	20	20	20	20	21	21	21	21	21	21													
19 PANTANO	12	12	12	16	12	19	19	19	19	11	5	16	19	19	15	15	15	12	12	20	20	20	20	20	20	20	20	21	21	21	21	21	21	21	21	21																		
21 BAUMGARTNER	20	20	20	16	16	16	16	16	16	16	6	21	21	20	20	20	20	20	20	21	21	21	21	21	21	21	21	21																										
20 BRUNI	16	16	16	20	20	20	20	20	20	20	20	20	21	20	20	20	21	21	21	21	21	21																																
12 MASSA	21	21	21	21	21	21	21	21	21	21	21	20																																										

Pit stop
One lap behind leader

178

TIME SHEETS

QUALIFYING

Cloudy and windy/ (track 32–29°C, air 25–24°C)

Pos.	Driver	Lap time	Sector 1	Sector 2	Sector 3
1	Michael Schumacher	1m 19.146s	28.269	28.346	22.531
2	Rubens Barrichello	1m 19.323s	28.172	22.558	22.593
3	Takuma Sato	1m 19.693s	28.409	28.502	22.782
4	Jenson Button	1m 19.700s	28.716	28.582	22.402
5	Fernando Alonso	1m 19.996s	28.595	28.869	22.532
6	Antonio Pizzonia	1m 20.170s	28.403	29.137	22.630
7	Juan Pablo Montoya	1m 20.199s	28.460	29.165	22.574
8	Giancarlo Fisichella	1m 20.324s	28.635	28.970	22.719
9	Jarno Trulli	1m 20.411s	28.519	29.112	22.780
10	Kimi Räikkönen	1m 20.570s	28.568	29.254	22.748
11	Mark Webber	1m 20.730s	29.097	28.912	22.721
12	David Coulthard	1m 20.897s	28.521	29.501	22.875
13	Olivier Panis	1m 21.068s	28.894	29.201	22.973
14	Christian Klien	1m 21.118s	28.794	29.310	23.014
15	Ricardo Zonta	1m 21.135s	28.965	29.394	22.830
16	Nick Heidfeld	1m 22.180s	29.056	29.800	23.324
17	Giorgio Pantano	1m 22.356s	29.185	29.494	23.677
18	Zsolt Baumgartner	1m 24.329s	29.353	30.888	24.088
19	Gianmaria Bruni	1m 24.679s	29.724	31.069	23.886
20	Felipe Massa	No time	–	–	–

PRACTICE 1 (FRIDAY)

Sunny and windy (track 34–36°C, air 25–27C)

Pos.	Driver	Laps	Time
1	Michael Schumacher	10	1m 21.552s
2	Rubens Barrichello	11	1m 21.938s
3	Anthony Davidson	24	1m 21.951s
4	Kimi Räikkönen	5	1m 23.24s
5	David Coulthard	8	1m 23.100s
6	Juan Pablo Montoya	8	1m 23.753s
7	Olivier Panis	8	1m 23.827s
8	Ryan Briscoe	20	1m 24.108s
9	Jarno Trulli	13	1m 24.124s
10	Jenson Button	14	1m 24.140s
11	Fernando Alonso	13	1m 24.191s
12	Giancarlo Fisichella	13	1m 24.198s
13	Ricardo Zonta	14	1m 24.236s
14	Björn Wirdheim	23	1m 24.265s
15	Giorgio Pantano	15	1m 24.353s
16	Antonio Pizzonia	13	1m 24.381s
17	Nick Heidfeld	13	1m 24.462s
18	Timo Glock	22	1m 24.843s
19	Takuma Sato	13	1m 25.071s
20	Felipe Massa	17	1m 25.218s
21	Christian Klien	10	1m 25.834s
22	Bas Leinders	18	1m 26.074s
23	Zsolt Baumgartner	11	1m 28.296s
24	Gianmaria Bruni	12	1m 28.893s
25	Mark Webber	4	No time

PRACTICE 2 (FRIDAY)

Overcast and windy (track 35–34°C, air 26°C)

Pos.	Driver	Laps	Time
1	Kimi Räikkönen	20	1m 20.884s
2	Michael Schumacher	30	1m 21.009s
3	Juan Pablo Montoya	24	1m 21.185s
4	David Coulthard	19	1m 21.203s
5	Olivier Panis	23	1m 21.352s
6	Takuma Sato	22	1m 21.364s
7	Antonio Pizzonia	26	1m 21.574s
8	Jenson Button	19	1m 21.685s
9	Rubens Barrichello	19	1m 21.712s
10	Fernando Alonso	22	1m 21.948s
11	Mark Webber	33	1m 21.999s
12	Anthony Davidson	34	1m 22.356s
13	Björn Wirdheim	23	1m 22.559s
14	Nick Heidfeld	19	1m 22.651s
15	Timo Glock	21	1m 22.697s
16	Giancarlo Fisichella	23	1m 22.743s
17	Jarno Trulli	28	1m 22.788s
18	Ricardo Zonta	28	1m 22.808s
19	Giorgio Pantano	22	1m 22.937s
20	Christian Klien	30	1m 23.003s
21	Ryan Briscoe	22	1m 23.170s
22	Felipe Massa	20	1m 23.188s
23	Bas Leinders	17	1m 25.339s
24	Zsolt Baumgartner	16	1m 25.450s
25	Gianmaria Bruni	4	1m 26.365s

PRACTICE 3 (SATURDAY)

Overcast/sunny (track 21–22°C, air 19–20°C)

Pos.	Driver	Laps	Time
1	Michael Schumacher	10	1m 20.216s
2	Antonio Pizzonia	14	1m 20.482s
3	Juan Pablo Montoya	15	1m 20.696s
4	Jenson Button	11	1m 20.731s
5	Rubens Barrichello	12	1m 20.830s
6	Jarno Trulli	10	1m 21.257s
7	Fernando Alonso	8	1m 21.392s
8	David Coulthard	8	1m 21.555s
9	Felipe Massa	6	1m 21.593s
10	Kimi Räikkönen	8	1m 21.825s
11	Olivier Panis	15	1m 21.838s
12	Ricardo Zonta	17	1m 21.927s
13	Giancarlo Fisichella	9	1m 22.013s
14	Mark Webber	9	1m 22.068s
15	Christian Klien	6	1m 22.421s
16	Giorgio Pantano	11	1m 22.709s
17	Gianmaria Bruni	14	1m 23.112s
18	Nick Heidfeld	13	1m 23.242s
19	Zsolt Baumgartner	14	1m 24.233s
20	Takuma Sato	4	No time

PRACTICE 4 (SATURDAY)

Overcast/sunny (track 26–28°C, air 22–24°C)

Pos.	Driver	Laps	Time
1	Jenson Button	15	1m 19.556s
2	Michael Schumacher	18	1m 19.747s
3	Rubens Barrichello	10	1m 19.768s
4	Antonio Pizzonia	11	1m 19.913s
5	Jarno Trulli	10	1m 20.130s
6	Takuma Sato	20	1m 20.363s
7	Fernando Alonso	12	1m 20.363s
8	Juan Pablo Montoya	15	1m 20.480s
9	Ricardo Zonta	18	1m 20.606s
10	Kimi Räikkönen	13	1m 20.614s
11	Olivier Panis	12	1m 20.689s
12	David Coulthard	13	1m 20.914s
13	Mark Webber	24	1m 21.112s
14	Giancarlo Fisichella	12	1m 21.165s
15	Christian Klien	22	1m 21.390s
16	Nick Heidfeld	14	1m 21.712s
17	Felipe Massa	4	1m 21.989s
18	Giorgio Pantano	12	1m 23.083s
19	Gianmaria Bruni	14	1m 23.979s
20	Zsolt Baumgartner	13	1m 24.522s

CHASSIS LOG BOOK

1	Michael Schumacher	F2004/239
2	Rubens Barrichello	F2004/240
	Spare	F2004/236
3	Juan Pablo Montoya	FW26/06
4	Antonio Pizzonia	FW26/07
	Spare	FW26/05
5	David Coulthard	MP4/19B-03
6	Kimi Räikkönen	MP4/19B-01
	Spare	MP4/19B-02
7	Jarno Trulli	R24/04
8	Fernando Alonso	R24/02
	Spare	R24/03
9	Jenson Button	006/05
10	Takuma Sato	006/06
	Anthony Davidson	006/04
	Spare	006/04
11	Giancarlo Fisichella	C23/04
12	Felipe Massa	C23/01
	Spare	C23/02
14	Mark Webber	R5/05
15	Christian Klien	R5/01
	Björn Wirdheim	R5/02
	Spare	R5/02
16	Ricardo Zonta	TF104/10B
17	Olivier Panis	TF104/09B
	Ryan Briscoe	TF104/07
	Spare	TF104/07
18	Nick Heidfeld	EJ-14/03
19	Giorgio Pantano	EJ-14/02
	Timo Glock	EJ-14/01
	Spare	EJ-14/01
20	Gianmaria Bruni	PS04B/01
21	Zsolt Baumgartner	PS04B/02
	Bas Leinders	PS04B/03
	Spare	PS04B/03

Photograph: Darren Heath

9th: JARNO TRULLI Renault

7th: JUAN PABLO MONTOYA Williams-BMW

5th: FERNANDO ALONSO Renault

3rd: TAKUMA SATO BAR-Honda

Pole: MICHAEL SCHUMACHER Ferrari

10th: KIMI RÄIKKÖNEN McLaren-Mercedes

8th: GIANCARLO FISICHELLA Sauber-Petronas

6th: ANTONIO PIZZONIA Williams-BMW

4th: JENSON BUTTON BAR-Honda

2nd: RUBENS BARRICHELLO Ferrari

55	56	57	58	59	60	61	62	63	64	65	66	67	68	69	70	
1	1	1	1	1	1	1	1	1	1	1	1	1	1	1	1	1
2	2	2	2	2	2	2	2	2	2	2	2	2	2	2	2	2
8	8	8	8	8	8	8	8	8	8	8	8	8	8	8	8	3
3	3	3	3	3	3	3	3	3	3	3	3	3	3	3	3	4
9	9	9	9	9	9	9	9	9	9	9	9	9	9	9	9	5
10	10	10	10	10	10	10	10	10	10	10	10	10	10	10	10	6
4	4	4	4	4	4	4	4	4	4	4	4	4	4	4	4	7
11	11	11	11	11	11	11	11	11	11	11	11	11	11	11	11	8
5	5	5	5	5	5	5	5	5	5	5	5	5				
14	14	14	14	14	14	14	14	14	14	14	14	14	14			
17	17	17	17	17	17	17	17	17	17	17	17	17	17			
18	18	18	18	18	18	18	18	18	18	18	18	18	18			
15	15	15	15	15	15	15	15	15	15	15	15	15				
20	20	20	20	20	20	20	20	20	20	20	20					
21	21	21	21	21	21	21	21	21	21							

FOR THE RECORD

12 wins in a season

Michael Schumacher

200 grand prix points

Juan Pablo Montoya

100 grand prix points

Fernando Alonso

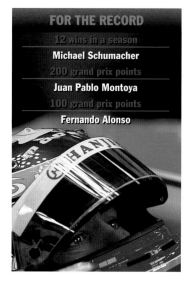

POINTS: CONSTRUCTORS

1	Ferrari	202
2	Renault	91
3	BAR	83
4	Williams	54
5	McLaren	37
6	Sauber	19
7	Toyota	8
8	Jaguar	7
9	Jordan	5
10	Minardi	1

POINTS: DRIVERS

1	Michael Schumacher	120
2	Rubens Barrichello	82
3	Jenson Button	65
4	Jarno Trulli	46
5	Fernando Alonso	45
6	Juan Pablo Montoya	38
7	David Coulthard	19
8 =	Kimi Räikkönen	18
8 =	Takuma Sato	18
10	Giancarlo Fisichella	14
11	Ralf Schumacher	12
12	Mark Webber	7
13 =	Felipe Massa	5
13 =	Olivier Panis	5
15	Antonio Pizzonia	4
16 =	Cristiano da Matta	3
16 =	Nick Heidfeld	3
18	Timo Glock	2
19	Zsolt Baumgartner	1

Photographs: Darren Heath

BELGIANGP
SPA-FRANCORCHAMPS

Main photograph and inset: After a season of major disappointments, it all came right for Kimi Räikkönen at Spa. He beat Michael Schumacher in a straight fight.
Photographs: Darren Heath

Right: Juan Pablo Montoya poses with his Williams-BMW.

Photograph: Bryn Williams/crash.net

Below: Jarno Trulli mastered the conditions to snatch pole for Renault on Michelin intermediate rubber.

Photograph: Daren Heath

SPA-FRANCORCHAMPS QUALIFYING

Qualifying proved to be a cliffhanger on a soaking track surface, Jarno Trulli getting the best out of the Michelin intermediates on his Renault R24 to post a 1m 56.232s and edge out Michael Schumacher's Ferrari F2004, which was running Bridgestone's full wet rubber, by less than 0.1s. It was Jarno's second ever pole, following on from Monaco earlier in the year, but Michael's performance in the terrible conditions was absolutely electrifying, and he seemed well on course to take his customary position at the front of the grid before losing 0.4s at the 'bus stop'.

By contrast with Schumacher, Rubens Barrichello's initially strong performance was spoiled when he got into an oversteering slide at the reprofiled 'bus stop' chicane and dropped to sixth on 1m 58.175s.

'Everything went quite well, except there was a bit more rain when the last group of five cars went out,' said the Brazilian. 'The last corner caught me out, even though I was feeling the tyres were losing a bit of their performance, so I was being careful.'

The return to Spa after an absence of two years, while welcomed by all in the paddock, was tempered in some small degree by the fact that the fast swerves from Blanchimont to the 'bus stop' chicane before the pits had been opened out with wider run-off areas, which had involved felling hundreds of trees. The chicane itself had been altered significantly, eliminating any realistic prospect of overtaking manoeuvres, and the greater levels of tyre grip achieved since the last race in 2002 meant that Blanchimont and Eau Rouge were flat out as a matter of routine. 'Blanchimont is even flat out in the wet in top gear, no problem,' said Juan Pablo Montoya.

Fernando Alonso also ran intermediates, but the rain intensified during his qualifying run, and he had a couple of lurid moments on his way to third on the grid with a best of 1m 56.686s. Räikkönen had been fastest on Friday, and he had followed that up with third in pre-qualifying, only to mess up his qualifying effort with a big mistake at the 'bus stop' chicane during heavy rain, which dropped him to tenth on the grid on 1m 59.635s. Coulthard did a good job on intermediates, despite also being hampered by worsening track conditions, and ended up a strong fourth on 1m 57.990s.

'Unfortunately, it started raining heavily during my run,' said Räikkönen. 'I made a mistake in the last chicane, which cost me some time. However, from our performance yesterday in the dry, I think we should be looking okay in the race when the weather hopefully will be dry again.' As it turned out, the Finn was right on the money.

Sauber's Giancarlo Fisichella switched from wet Bridgestones to extreme-wets just before his qualifying run, ending up a fine fifth (1m 58.040s); nevertheless, he believed that the change had cost him slight track performance. Felipe Massa finished the day eighth, the Brazilian also having used extreme-wets to post a 1m 59.008s, although he complained about excessive wheelspin in what he described as 'extraordinary conditions', which prevailed throughout the session.

For BMW Williams, Juan Pablo Montoya (1m 59.681s) was caught out just as the track appeared to be drying when a burst of heavy rain scuppered his chances after he'd opted for intermediate Michelin rubber, dropping him to 11th in the final line-up. Meanwhile, Antonio Pizzonia had slid off the road in Saturday free practice, damaging his FW26's left front suspension; he followed that up with a disappointing 14th-place qualifying lap on 2m 01.447s.

For Jenson Button and the BAR Honda crew, a 2m 00.237s best could only earn him 12th on the grid after the team failed to switch him to intermediates as the track became patchily dry. 'We made the wrong tyre choice due to the standing water that was on the track, and this cost us in our performance today,' said Button. Takuma Sato also found that his extreme-wet tyres overheated excessively in the conditions, losing a lot of grip by the end of his lap and leaving him 15th on 2m 01.813s.

Toyota's Olivier Panis qualified well to line up ninth on 1m 59.552s, making up for the disappointment on Friday when the team's third driver, Ryan Briscoe, suffered a punctured tyre and crashed heavily going down to Eau Rouge. He was taken to hospital for a precautionary scan of his arm, but thankfully was uninjured.

DIARY

Michael Scumacher confirms he will race on at least to the end of his current contract in 2006.

Anthony Davidson expresses hopes for a race drive with either BAR or Williams in 2005.

COURT CHALLENGE FOR ECCLESTONE

Bernie Ecclestone's control of F1 racing's lucrative commercial rights looked set to be challenged further by the three banks that had funded his fortune when it emerged that they were planning another action in the London High Court.

Bayersiche Landesbank, Lehman Brothers and J.P. Morgan Chase were ready to claim that manoeuvring through offshore companies had enabled Ecclestone to deprive them of voting control of Formula One Administration and Formula One Management. According to that highly respected source The Economist, the two key operating companies command around $800 million of commercial rights, most of which is not shared among the competing teams. The banks' legal action came at a time when the teams were intensifying their claim for a bigger share of the commercial-rights pie.

The three banks had originally funded the $2.1 billion acquisition of a 75-per-cent stake in SLEC, the company that controls F1 commercial rights through FOM and FOA, by the German Kirch media group, which subsequently went bust.

The car companies' plans for a separate championship under the GPWC banner had been shelved in December 2003, when they had signed a Memorandum of Understanding with Ecclestone that was seen as a first step toward rectifying the unfair distribution of the commercial-rights income. But they judged that Ecclestone had failed to deliver on that MOU and were intensifying the pressure again.

For 2004, the ten teams received 47 per cent of the TV money under the terms of the Concorde Agreement, sharing around $375 million between them, but they had no share of the race promoters' fees, which vary between $14 and $20 million per event. Nor did the teams share in the lucrative income stream from trackside advertising, title sponsorship and corporate entertainment – estimated at over $400 million – which was collected by Allsport Management, a Swiss based company run by Ecclestone's pal, Paddy McNally. The memorandum of understanding proposed that Allsport should become part of the SLEC group as soon as possible, and agreed that the teams should receive significantly more money, calculated on all the revenues from the commercial rights.

KIMI Räikkönen stormed to the second victory of his F1 career at Spa-Francorchamps, exercising great tactical acuity to hold off Michael Schumacher's Ferrari after a performance that emphasised his sheer flair and the impressive competitive level of the McLaren-Mercedes MP4/19B. By any standards, it was a truly epic race on one of the best circuits in the world, which had the crowds on tenterhooks right up to the moment when the Flying Finn breezed past the chequered flag, 3.1s ahead of his German rival.

It was also a race full of spectacular action. From the first corner, it was clear that a healthy slice of mayhem was on the menu after Rubens Barrichello's Ferrari clipped Mark Webber's Jaguar, and Felipe Massa's Sauber tagged Räikkönen's McLaren hard enough to badly deform its right-hand water radiator. 'It was surprising that it was sufficiently durable to last the distance,' said McLaren MD Martin Whitmarsh after the race.

'I locked up at La Source at the start and didn't see Kimi until we touched,' explained Massa. 'Then Sato [actually it was Button] really hit the back of my car. I pitted for a new rear wing, but stopped again a lap later because the car was vibrating really badly.'

Thankfully, Räikkönen survived. He had qualified tenth, one place ahead of Juan Pablo Montoya's Williams FW26, and the pair threaded their way through the carnage to complete the opening lap fifth and sixth. On the exit of Eau Rouge, Gianmaria Bruni's Minardi was speared by Giorgio Pantano's Jordan, causing the safety car to be deployed for the first of three occasions that afternoon.

Meanwhile, Jenson Button's BAR-Honda 006 lost its nose wings in the mêlée surrounding Massa's Sauber. He came in for a replacement at the end of the opening lap, at the same time being fuelled for a long stint that saw him pit from an eventual second place on lap 21, eight to ten laps later than most of his rival front-runners.

'I got a bad start when I was hit by Pizzonia, and went wide and into the back of Massa at Turn One,' explained Button. 'I lost my front wing and had to pit at the end of the opening lap. After that, the car was running reasonably well, we had a good fuel load and I was pretty pleased with the balance of the car.'

Räikkönen overtook Michael Schumacher after the restart following the first safety-car period going into the Eau Rouge corner at the beginning of lap five. A lap later, the Finn passed his team-mate, David Coulthard, to take third.

On lap ten, early leader Jarno Trulli brought his Renault into the pits, allowing Räikkönen to move into second position. Two laps later, Fernando Alonso's R24 retired from the lead position, and the Finn went ahead. This was a bitter disappointment for the Renault squad. Alonso had been pulling away in the lead when he spun on the entry to Les Combes on lap 12. Although he restarted, he spun again at Turn Eight (Rivage) and retired from the race due to engine oil leaking on to the rear tyres.

'To retire from the lead of a race is never good, especially at this stage of the season,' said Alonso. 'We looked competitive compared to Räikkönen and the other cars, and I was just beginning to run at my full pace when the car spun. I'm just disappointed because it was a good chance for a strong result today.'

Trulli finished the day similarly disillusioned. He'd run strongly up to his first refuelling stop, but therafter simply couldn't reproduce his early pace, lack of rear grip really shaking his confidence through the high-speed corners. He would wind up ninth. 'I am very upset with this performance,' he shrugged. 'But right now, I just want to understand what happened.'

Race leader Räikkönen came into the pits on lap 13 for his first scheduled refuelling stop and rejoined the race in fourth position. On lap 17, he was back in the lead, coming into the pits for his second planned stop on lap 29; he resumed in second position for one lap. After Michael Schumacher's second stop, the McLaren driver took the lead once more.

Below: While David Coulthard and Michael Schumacher give each other plenty of room, Rubens Barrichello is rammed by Mark Webber, and Felipe Massa and Kimi Räikkönen skirmish.
Photograph: Bryn Williams/crash.net

Top: Felipe Massa survived his first-corner collision with Räikkönen and went on to take fourth place.

Above: Antonio Pizzonia saw a potential podium place disappear when the gearbox of his Williams failed.
Photographs: Darren Heath

The safety car was deployed again between laps 30 and 34, and laps 40 and 41. After the last restart, on lap 42, Räikkönen delivered the fastest lap in the race (1m 45.108s); he crossed the finishing line after 44 laps as the winner. By contrast, David Coulthard's MP4/19B suffered a right rear tyre failure on lap 12. The Scot drove very slowly back to the pits for a new tyre and resumed the race in last position. After the second safety-car period, he took eighth place on lap 37.

Unfortunately, Jenson Button's strong recovery counted for nothing, as eventually he crashed out in spectacular style at 190 mph going into Les Combes; his right rear Michelin had blown out, pitching him straight into Zsolt Baumgartner's Minardi, which he had been lapping at the time. Thankfully, both drivers emerged unharmed. It was a mixed day for the French tyre company, other failures sidelining David Coulthard's McLaren and Montoya's Williams in worrying contrast to the success with Räikkönen.

'Three teams had problems with their right rears, which is unusual because that tyre has an easy life around Spa,' said Michelin competitions director Pierre Dupasquier. 'We will obviously put all the failed tyres under microscopic examination, but it was clear that there was a deep cut on the inside sidewall of Coulthard's car, which might have been caused by him straying too far over a kerb.'

While Räikkönen grappled with an intermittent gearbox down-change problem, which gave him a few worrying moments when the rear wheels locked, Montoya claimed the distinction of possibly the best overtaking move of the year. He forced his way inside Schumacher's Ferrari to take fifth early in the race at the chicane before the pits.

Later, Montoya tried a similar move on Jarno Trulli's Renault R24, which had led commandingly from pole in the opening stages. On this occasion, however, there wasn't enough room and the Colombian pitched Trulli into a spin, wiping him out as serious contender.

As Coulthard attempted to overtake Christian Klien on lap 39, he touched the back of the Jaguar, losing his front wing, which forced him to make an extra pit stop for a replacement. In the last three laps, after the third safety-car period, he improved from tenth to seventh position.

This was a crucial moment for Räikkönen. Having dealt with Coulthard, the Finn slowed the pace of the final pre-restart formation lap as much as he dared, knowing that the Ferraris' now-cool Bridgestone rubber would take a little time to come up to working temperature when the pack was unleashed for the final three-lap sprint to the flag. And he did the job brilliantly.

'Kimi's fastest lap on the penultimate lap of the race was absolutely sensational,' said McLaren team principal Ron Dennis. Nobody disagreed with him

Barrichello's run to third place after making an early pit stop to change a damaged rear wing was another splendid performance that almost was overshadowed by the rest of the excitement.

Talking of that first stop, he commented, 'There is a magic feeling because Ross [Brawn] was talking to me as if we were talking face-to-face in a living room and saying "Keep it going, we are just changing your wing, we think we can do it before the safety car comes by, and then you can go and try again." I [went back into the race] five or more seconds behind the last car, but I kept on going.'

Antonio Pizzonia was extremely disappointed to lose out on a possible podium finish after his Williams FW26 succumbed to a gearbox problem while running third. Teammate Juan Pablo Montoya suffered a tyre failure that damaged the rear wing and suspension; all in all, a disappointing day for the team.

Felipe Massa and Giancarlo Fisichella ran well after their early problems to take fourth and fifth for Sauber, while Klien survived to come home sixth ahead of the recovering Coulthard. Olivier Panis's Toyota, the disappointed Trulli, and Ricardo Zonta's Toyota completed the list of finishers ahead of Nick Heidfeld's Jordan.

When it was all over, Michael Schumacher looked slightly overawed, almost wistful, as he trooped down from the victory rostrum in company with Räikkönen and Barrichello. It had been the most important second place of his life, securing his all-time record world championship, an achievement that almost certainly will never be approached at any time in the future.

'It was an eventful day, honestly, with all the safety cars and the conditions we had at that moment,' he mused reflectively. 'It was a tough one, and considering where I had

Left: 700 grands prix for Ferrari, and another world championship in 2004.

Below: The safety car was deployed soon after the start.
Photographs: Darren Heath

dropped back to, and where I finished now, I think I should only be happy anyway.

'We clinched the championship, we had a tough fight, Kimi drove a superb race. I think all three of us should be very happy to be here at the moment, if you imagine what had happened to Rubens and still he managed to come back to third position, so it is a great day for all of us, and I'm just so delighted and happy.'

He added, 'I would have honestly and obviously rather finished the championship with a victory, but today simply we weren't strong enough at the right moments, and that's the way it is. We have won so many races this year, it was clear that at some stage somebody else would win, and today it happened. The better man won and we're quite happy with what we achieved.'

Schumacher is not a competitor who wears his heart on his sleeve, and he dodged any questions about the emotions of the moment. 'I'm just so proud to have achieved this with the team which is made up of so many extraordinary people,' he said. 'What I feel today is difficult to put into words, but it doesn't feel anything like what I felt at winning the fifth or sixth championship. It's very special to me to have achieved this seventh championship here at Spa, which means so much to me, and to have clinched the title in Ferrari's 700th grand prix makes it particularly special.'

Ferrari's sporting director, Jean Todt, also praised Schumacher's remarkable level of achievement. 'In Budapest, we won the constructors' championship, and here Michael has clinched the drivers',' he said. 'This team is writing a unique chapter in the history of Ferrari. It was an incredible and action packed race.'

Left: Christian Klien and David Coulthard exchange views after the race
Photograph: Bryn Williams/crash.net

Below: Only second place for Michael, but clinching the championship was more than adequate compensation.
Photograph: Darren Heath

FORMULA 1
BELGIAN GRAND PRIX

SPA-FRANCORCHAMPS 27–29 AUGUST 2004

OFOSTER'S

Photograph: Darren Heath

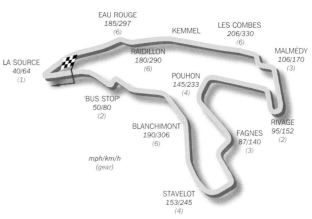

SPA-FRANCORCHAMPS

EAU ROUGE
185/297
(6)

KEMMEL

LES COMBES
206/330
(6)

RAIDILLON
180/290
(6)

MALMÉDY
106/170
(3)

LA SOURCE
40/64
(1)

POUHON
145/233
(4)

'BUS STOP
50/80
(2)

BLANCHIMONT
190/306
(6)

RIVAGE
95/152
(2)

FAGNES
87/140
(3)

mph/km/h
(gear)

STAVELOT
153/245
(4)

CIRCUIT LENGTH: 4.333 miles/6.973 km

RACE DISTANCE: 44 laps, 190.715 miles/306.927 km **RACE WEATHER:** Overcast and dry (track 19–25°C, air 19–21°C)

Pos.	Driver	Nat.	No.	Entrant	Car/Engine	Tyres	Laps	Time/Retirement	Speed (mph/km/h)	Gap to leader	Fastest race lap	
1	Kimi Räikkönen	FIN	6	West McLaren Mercedes	McLaren MP4/19B-Mercedes F0110P V10	M	44	1h 32m 35.274s	123.589/198.898		1m 45.108s	42
2	Michael Schumacher	D	1	Scuderia Ferrari Marlboro	Ferrari F2004-052 V10	B	44	1h 32m 38.406s	123.520/198.786	+3.132s	1m 45.503s	28
3	Rubens Barrichello	BR	2	Scuderia Ferrari Marlboro	Ferrari F2004-052 V10	B	44	1h 32m 39.645s	123.492/198.742	+4.371s	1m 45.666s	43
4	Felipe Massa	BR	12	Sauber Petronas	Sauber C23-Petronas 04 V10	B	44	1h 32m 47.778s	123.306/198.452	+12.504s	1m 47.624s	29
5	Giancarlo Fisichella	I	11	Sauber Petronas	Sauber C23-Petronas 04 V10	B	44	1h 32m 49.378s	123.277/198.395	+14.104s	1m 46.758s	11
6	Christian Klien	A	15	Jaguar Racing	Jaguar R5-Cosworth CR6 V10	M	44	1h 32m 49.888s	123.265/198.376	+14.614s	1m 47.509s	11
7	David Coulthard	GB	5	West McLaren Mercedes	McLaren MP4/19B-Mercedes F0110P V10	M	44	1h 32m 53.244s	123.191/198.257	+17.970s	1m 46.579s	11
8	Olivier Panis	F	17	Panasonic Toyota Racing	Toyota TF104B-RVX04 V10	M	44	1h 32m 53.967s	123.175/198.231	+18.693s	1m 47.765s	29
9	Jarno Trulli	I	7	Mild Seven Renault F1 Team	Renault R24-RS4 V10	M	44	1h 32m 57.967s	123.100/198.110	+22.115s	1m 45.898s	9
10	Ricardo Zonta	BR	16	Panasonic Toyota Racing	Toyota TF104B-RVX04 V10	M	41			DNF	1m 47.576s	26
11	Nick Heidfeld	D	18	Jordan Ford	Jordan EJ-14-Cosworth RS V10	B	40			+4 laps	1m 50.471s	40
	Juan Pablo Montoya	COL	3	BMW WilliamsF1 Team	Williams FW26-BMW P84 V10	M	37	Puncture/ Suspension			1m 46.547s	36
	Antonio Pizzonia	E	4	BMW WilliamsF1 Team	Williams FW26-BMW P84 V10	M	31	Gearbox			1m 46.740s	26
	Jenson Button	GB	9	Lucky Strike BAR Honda	BAR 006-Honda RA004E V10	M	29	Accident			1m 47.151s	26
	Zsolt Baumgartner	H	21	European Minardi Cosworth	Minardi PS04B-Cosworth CR3 V10	B	28	Accident			1m 51.031s	25
	Fernando Alonso	E	8	Mild Seven Renault F1 Team	Renault R24-RS4 V10	M	11	Accident			1m 45.870s	9
	Mark Webber	AUS	14	Jaguar Racing	Jaguar R5-Cosworth CR6 V10	M	0	Accident				
	Takuma Sato	J	10	Lucky Strike BAR Honda	BAR 006-Honda RA004E V10	M	0	Accident				
	Gianmaria Bruni	I	20	European Minardi Cosworth	Minardi PS04B-Cosworth CR3 V10	B	0	Accident				
	Giorgio Pantano	I	19	Jordan Ford	Jordan EJ-14-Cosworth RS V10	B	0	Accident				

All results and data © FOM 2004

Fastest lap: Kimi Räikkönen, on lap 42, 1m 45.108s, 148.465 mph/238.931 km/h (record for modified track layout).

Previous lap record: Michael Schumacher (Ferrari F2002-051 V10), 1m 47.176s, 145.329 mph/233.884 km/h (2002).

20th: RICARDO ZONTA Toyota

18th: ZSOLT BAUMGARTNER Minardi-Cosworth

16th: NICK HEIDFELD Jordan-Cosworth

14th: ANTONIO PIZZONIA Williams-BMW

12th: JENSON BUTTON BAR-Honda

19th: GIORGIO PANTANO Jordan-Cosworth

17th: GIANMARIA BRUNI Minardi-Cosworth

15th: TAKUMA SATO BAR-Honda

13th: CHRISTIAN KLIEN Jaguar-Cosworth

11th: JUAN PABLO MONTOYA Williams-BMW

Grid order	1	2	3	4	5	6	7	8	9	10	11	12	13	14	15	16	17	18	19	20	21	22	23	24	25	26	27	28	29	30	31	32	33	34	35	36
7 TRULLI	7	7	7	7	7	7	7	7	7	8	8	6	3	1	4	6	6	6	6	6	6	6	6	6	6	6	6	6	1	6	6	6	6	6		
1 M. SCHUMACHER	8	8	8	8	8	8	8	8	6	6	3	3	1	4	1	9	9	9	9	9	1	1	1	1	1	1	1	6	1	1	1	1	1	1		
8 ALONSO	5	5	5	5	5	6	6	6	5	5	1	1	4	3	6	4	1	1	9	4	4	4	4	4	4	4	4	4	3	3	3	3				
5 COULTHARD	1	1	1	1	6	5	5	5	5	3	3	11	11	6	6	9	7	7	7	4	3	3	3	3	3	3	9	3	3	2	2	2	2	2		
11 FISICHELLA	6	6	6	6	3	3	3	3	7	1	4	4	11	9	7	1	12	3	3	2	9	9	9	9	9	3	16	2	16	16	16	16	16			
2 BARRICHELLO	3	3	3	3	1	1	1	1	1	11	9	9	9	7	12	12	3	4	11	11	11	11	11	11	11	16	16	16	12	16	12	12	12	12	12	
14 WEBBER	11	11	11	11	11	11	11	11	11	4	7	7	7	16	3	3	4	11	2	2	9	2	16	16	16	12	12	2	12	11	11	11	11	11		
12 MASSA	4	4	4	4	4	4	4	4	4	9	16	16	12	11	11	11	12	7	16	16	12	12	12	17	17	17	17	11	17	17	17	15	15			
17 PANIS	15	15	15	15	15	15	15	15	9	9	7	12	12	12	11	16	17	17	2	16	16	12	12	17	17	2	2	11	11	15	15	15	17			
6 RÄIKKÖNEN	16	16	16	16	9	9	9	9	16	16	17	17	17	17	2	17	15	12	17	17	2	2	2	15	15	11	15	15	7	7	7	5	17			
3 MONTOYA	9	9	9	9	16	16	16	15	12	12	2	2	2	2	15	15	17	12	17	7	15	15	15	15	11	11	15	7	7	5	5	7	7			
9 BUTTON	12	21	21	21	12	12	12	12	12	17	12	15	15	15	15	16	16	17	15	15	7	7	7	7	7	7	5	5	18	18	18	18	18			
15 KLIEN	21	17	17	17	21	21	17	17	2	2	21	21	21	21	21	21	5	5	5	5	5	5	5	5	5	5	5	18	18							
4 PIZZONIA	2	18	18	18	17	18	2	2	15	15	18	18	18	18	5	5	21	21	21	21	21	21	21	21	18											
10 SATO	18	12	12	12	18	18	2	18	18	18	5	5	5	5	18	18	18	18	18	18	18	18	18													
18 HEIDFELD	17	2	2	2	2	2	21	21	21	21																										
20 BRUNI																																				
21 BAUMGARTNER																																				
19 PANTANO																																				
16 ZONTA																																				

TIME SHEETS

QUALIFYING

Wet and cool (track 19–22°C, air 17–19°C)

Pos.	Driver	Lap time	Sector 1	Sector 2	Sector 3
1	Jarno Trulli	1m 56.232s	31.253s	52.739s	32.240s
2	Michael Schumacher	1m 56.304s	31.249s	52.396s	32.659s
3	Fernando Alonso	1m 56.686s	31.091s	53.428s	32.167s
4	David Coulthard	1m 57.990s	31,217s	54.458s	32.239s
5	Giancarlo Fisichella	1m 58.040s	31.708s	53.010s	33.322s
6	Rubens Barrichello	1m 58.175s	31.280s	52.233s	34.562s
7	Mark Webber	1m 58.729s	31.832s	53.784s	33.113s
8	Felipe Massa	1m 59.008s	31.818s	53.554s	33.393s
9	Olivier Panis	1m 59.552s	31.879s	54.325s	33.348s
10	Kimi Räikkönen*	1m 59.635s	–	–	–
11	Juan Pablo Montoya	1m 59.681s	31.521s	55.613s	32.547s
12	Jenson Button	2m 00.237s	31.332s	55.897s	33.008s
13	Christian Klien	2m 01.246s	32.545s	54.877s	33.791s
14	Antonio Pizzonia	2m 01.447s	31.706s	56.143s	33.301s
15	Takuma Sato	2m 01.813s	31.574s	56.136s	33.162s
16	Nick Heidfeld	2m 02.645s	32.652s	55.546s	34.447s
17	Gianmaria Bruni	2m 02.651s	32.833s	55.674s	34.144s
18	Zsolt Baumgartner	2m 03.303s	32.533s	56.969s	33.801s
19	Giorgio Pantano	2m 03.833s	32.486s	56.527s	34.820s
20	Ricardo Zonta	2m 03.895s	32.733s	56.806s	33.853s

* Räikkönen's car failed to register sector times.

PRACTICE 1 (FRIDAY)

Overcast (track 18–19°C, air 16–17°C)

Pos.	Driver	Laps	Time
1	Anthony Davidson	12	1m 45.104s
2	Michael Schumacher	10	1m 45.408s
3	Rubens Barrichello	8	1m 45.605s
4	Björn Wirdheim	20	1m 46.658s
5	Kimi Räikkönen	6	1m 46.674s
6	Fernando Alonso	10	1m 45.679s
7	Mark Webber	16	1m 45.782s
8	Christian Klien	18	1m 45.809s
9	Antonio Pizzonia	10	1m 47.083s
10	Ryan Briscoe	21	1m 47.506s
11	Jenson Button	6	1m 47.511s
12	Juan Pablo Montoya	13	1m 47.560s
13	Takuma Sato	5	1m 47.618s
14	Giancarlo Fisichella	12	1m 47.648s
15	David Coulthard	6	1m 47.650s
16	Felipe Massa	11	1m 47.765s
17	Jarno Trulli	9	1m 47.829s
18	Ricardo Zonta	12	1m 48.642s
19	Olivier Panis	10	1m 48.834s
20	Giorgio Pantano	9	1m 50.165s
21	Bas Leinders	13	1m 50.311s
22	Timo Glock	19	1m 50.317s
23	Gianmaria Bruni	12	1m 50.531s
24	Nick Heidfeld	10	1m 50.805s
25	Zsolt Baumgartner	10	1m 50.950s

PRACTICE 2 (FRIDAY)

Sunny/cloudy (track 23–22°C, air 18–19°C)

Pos.	Driver	Laps	Time
1	Kimi Räikkönen	14	1m 44.701s
2	Jenson Button	15	1m 45.015s
3	Michael Schumacher	16	1m 45.137s
4	Anthony Davidson	25	1m 45.437s
5	Takuma Sato	20	1m 45.451s
6	David Coulthard	13	1m 45.507s
7	Antonio Pizzonia	14	1m 45.559s
8	Rubens Barrichello	20	1m 45.625s
9	Fernando Alonso	20	1m 45.658s
10	Juan Pablo Montoya	17	1m 45.678s
11	Felipe Massa	20	1m 45.960s
12	Giancarlo Fisichella	19	1m 45.978s
13	Mark Webber	10	1m 46.471s
14	Olivier Panis	17	1m 46.528s
15	Ricardo Zonta	20	1m 46.902s
16	Jarno Trulli	21	1m 46.912s
17	Björn Wirdheim	23	1m 47.265s
18	Christian Klien	8	1m 47.370s
19	Ryan Briscoe	9	1m 47.634s
20	Zsolt Baumgartner	16	1m 48.687s
21	Nick Heidfeld	18	1m 48.803s
22	Timo Glock	21	1m 48.817s
23	Giorgio Pantano	17	1m 48.962s
24	Bas Leinders	16	1m 49.480s
25	Gianmaria Bruni	16	1m 49.742s

PRACTICE 3 (SATURDAY)

Session cancelled due to fog.

PRACTICE 4 (SATURDAY)

Wet and cool (track 19–21°C, air 17–18°C)

Pos.	Driver	Laps	Time
1	Rubens Barrichello		1m 57.085s
2	Michael Schumacher		1m 57.906s
3	Kimi Räikkönen		1m 57.975s
4	Giancarlo Fisichella		1m 58.138s
5	David Coulthard		1m 58.434s
6	Felipe Massa		1m 58.864s
7	Jenson Button		1m 59.182s
8	Jarno Trulli		1m 59.519s
9	Takuma Sato		2m 00.088s
10	Fernando Alonso		2m 01.475s
11	Ricardo Zonta		2m 02.175s
12	Christian Klien		2m 02.411s
13	Mark Webber		2m 02.501s
14	Juan Pablo Montoya		2m 02.559s
15	Olivier Panis		2m 02.592s
16	Nick Heidfeld		2m 03.556s
17	Giorgio Pantano		2m 04.131s
18	Gianmaria Bruni		2m 05.485s
19	Antonio Pizzonia		2m 07.337s
20	Zsolt Baumgartner		2m 09.428s

*Session reduced to 15 minutes due to fog.

CHASSIS LOG BOOK

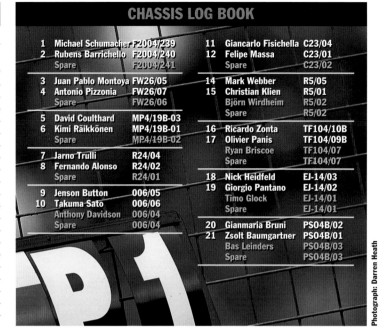

1	Michael Schumacher	F2004/239
2	Rubens Barrichello	F2004/240
	Spare	F2004/241
3	Juan Pablo Montoya	FW26/05
4	Antonio Pizzonia	FW26/07
	Spare	FW26/06
5	David Coulthard	MP4/19B-03
6	Kimi Räikkönen	MP4/19B-01
	Spare	MP4/19B-02
7	Jarno Trulli	R24/04
8	Fernando Alonso	R24/02
	Spare	R24/01
9	Jenson Button	006/05
10	Takuma Sato	006/06
	Anthony Davidson	006/04
	Spare	006/04
11	Giancarlo Fisichella	C23/04
12	Felipe Massa	C23/01
	Spare	C23/02
14	Mark Webber	R5/05
15	Christian Klien	R5/01
	Björn Wirdheim	R5/02
	Spare	R5/02
16	Ricardo Zonta	TF104/10B
17	Olivier Panis	TF104/09B
	Ryan Briscoe	TF104/07
	Spare	TF104/07
18	Nick Heidfeld	EJ-14/03
19	Giorgio Pantano	EJ-14/02
	Timo Glock	EJ-14/01
	Spare	EJ-14/01
20	Gianmaria Bruni	PS04B/02
21	Zsolt Baumgartner	PS04B/01
	Bas Leinders	PS04B/03
	Spare	PS04B/03

FOR THE RECORD

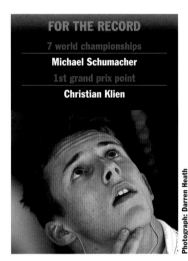

7 world championships

Michael Schumacher

1st grand prix point

Christian Klien

10th: KIMI RÄIKKÖNEN McLaren-Mercedes

8th: FELIPE MASSA Sauber-Petronas

6th: RUBENS BARRICHELLO Ferrari

4th: DAVID COULTHARD McLaren-Mercedes

2nd: MICHAEL SCHUMACHER Ferrari

9th: OLIVIER PANIS Toyota

7th: MARK WEBBER Jaguar-Cosworth

5th: GIANCARLO FISICHELLA Sauber-Petronas

3rd: FERNANDO ALONSO Renault

Pole: JARNO TRULLI Renault

37	38	39	40	41	42	43	44	
6	6	6	6	6	6	6	6	1
1	1	1	1	1	1	1	1	2
2	2	2	2	2	2	2	2	3
16	16	16	16	16	12	12	12	4
12	12	12	12	12	11	11	11	5
11	11	11	11	11	15	15	15	6
15	15	15	15	15	17	5	5	7
5	5	17	17	17	5	17	17	8
17	17	7	7	7	7	7	7	
7	7	5	5	5				
3	18	18	18					
18								

Pit stop
One lap behind leader

POINTS: CONSTRUCTORS

1	Ferrari	216
2	Renault	91
3	BAR	83
4	Williams	54
5	McLaren	49
6	Sauber	28
7	Jaguar	10
8	Toyota	9
9	Jordan	5
10	Minardi	1

POINTS: DRIVERS

1	Michael Schumacher	128
2	Rubens Barrichello	88
3	Jenson Button	65
4	Jarno Trulli	46
5	Fernando Alonso	45
6	Juan Pablo Montoya	38
7	Kimi Räikkönen	28
8	David Coulthard	21
9 =	Takuma Sato	18
9 =	Giancarlo Fisichella	18
11	Ralf Schumacher	12
12	Felipe Massa	10
13	Mark Webber	7
14	Olivier Panis	6
15	Antonio Pizzonia	4
16 =	Christian Klien	3
16 =	Cristiano da Matta	3
16 =	Nick Heidfeld	3
19	Timo Glock	2
20	Zsolt Baumgartner	1

Rubens Barrichello stepped out of Michael
Schumacher's shadow at Monza to score
his first win of 2004.
Photograph: Darren Heath

ITALIANGP
MONZA

MONZA QUALIFYING

Rubens Barrichello simply blitzed his way to pole position at Monza. 'That was a seriously impressive lap by Rubens,' said technical director Ross Brawn admiringly of the Brazilian's 1m 20.089s lap. 'It was almost as perfect as it gets.'

The Ferrari number two ran fractionally more wing than team-mate Michael Schumacher, who went a touch too deep into the tricky Parabolica right-hander on his qualifying run and had to settle for third on the grid, behind chirpy Juan Pablo Montoya. The Colombian squeezed his Williams-BMW FW26 on to the outside of the front row with a 1m 20.620s best.

'I am so happy with this result,' enthused Barrichello. 'The car was really good, and I got the most out of it. It felt better through the Lesmos than it did in the last section, and even if you can never do a perfect lap, I think it was pretty near the limit. I won here in 2002 and I like Monza. All the support we get gives me a boost.'

The previous week's testing had finished on a fraught note for Maranello. Michael Schumacher's F2004 had suffered a 190-mph tyre failure on the start-line straight and slammed tail-first into the concrete pit wall with such an impact that its engine and gearbox had been written off. Happily for the mechanics, the remainder of the car had been repairable, while Schumacher had survived unharmed. His best qualifying lap was 1m 20.637s.

Antonio Pizzonia wound up eighth in the other Williams on 1m 20.888s. 'After a good pre-qualifying, I had a slightly less successful final qualifying lap,' he said, 'but I am still happy because I know I have quite a good race car. Unfortunately, I made a small mistake in the middle sector which cost me probably a few positions, but still I know we have a consistent pace for the race and a good strategy.'

Fernando Alonso (1m 20.645s) grappled understeer in his Renault at the second chicane and the Lesmos to grab a confident fourth place on the grid; he reported that his car was handling extremely well in the other fast corners. Jarno Trulli (1m 21.027s) opted for a more conservative race strategy, lining up ninth, although he was unhappy with his car's rather nervous feel on the limit. Unbeknown to the majority of outsiders, this would be Trulli's final race for Renault.

'I am really pleased with my qualifying performance,' he said. 'I pushed to the limit and managed to put in a good lap. I still do not feel consistently comfortable with the car, and it was nervous and difficult to drive on the lap, so I took a lot of risks and they paid off.'

Takuma Sato (1m 20.715s) produced an outstanding performance to qualify fifth on an all-BAR third row, the Japanese driver making the most of the team's testing data from the previous week. Jenson Button was satisfied with his car's handling in pre-qualifying, but had too much oversteer when it came to the battle for grid positions, settling for sixth on 1m 20.786s.

Kimi Räikkönen had arrived at Monza on the crest of a wave after his victory at Spa, but he admitted that he had entered Parabolica a touch too fast on his qualifying lap. The result was seventh on the grid with a 1m 20.877s. David Coulthard felt confident about his MP4/19B's handling, but lost a crucial fraction through the Ascari chicane, which dropped him to tenth in the final order on 1m 21.049s.

Toyota's Ricardo Zonta made up for his Spa disappointment with a decent 11th place on 1m 21.520s, but Olivier Panis was less happy because his car had needed a gearbox change just before pre-qualifying. He judged 13th (1m 21.841s) a good grid position under the circumstances. Unfortunately, he would not last a lap in the race, spinning off on the first lap after hitting Pizzonia.

Mark Webber (1m 21.602s) was content to have split the Toyotas in 12th place after an enjoyable qualifying session, while Christian Klien (1m 21.989s) made some valuable overnight chassis changes and lined up 14th after a slight mistake at the Variante Ascari on his qualifying bid.

David Coulthard spins the tyres on his McLaren; the Scot finished sixth at Monza after a busy race.
Photograph: Darren Heath

Right: Antonio Pizzonia took another seventh place for Williams.

Below: Jenson Button had a strong run to third place after believing at one point he was in with a chance of victory.

Below right: Michelin's Dupasquier, still trying to find a way to beat Ferrari.

Below far right: Michael Schumacher sported a special Italian version of his helmet in red, white and green.

Bottom: Giancarlo Fisichella overcame early difficulties to claim eighth place and the final point on offer.
Photographs: Darren Heath

Photograph: Darren Heath

FERRARI grand slams have become a central element of recent F1 history, but few have been as impressive or, quite frankly, unexpected as the dominant performance of Rubens Barrichello and Michael Schumacher in the 2004 Italian Grand Prix at Monza, a race made tantalisingly unpredictable by a rain shower shortly before the start. Of even greater significance, however, was the blinding speed displayed by both Ferrari F2004s, almost as if they'd gone into 'fast forward' mode in a spurt of breathtaking pace that strongly suggested to most of their rivals that this was the first time in the season that the Italian cars had demonstrated their true capabilities. It was a demoralising scene.

The Ferrari drivers had started on completely different strategies, so it seemed unlikely that the race would go the team's way. On a wet track that was drying after a spell of heavy rain, Barrichello started from pole position on intermediate Bridgestone tyres, leaving Schumacher to gamble on the use of dry-weather rubber from his third place on the grid.

By any standards, it was a brilliant victory for Barrichello, who had confounded onlookers by snatching the initiative with a series of blisteringly fast laps two-thirds of the way through the race. They had enabled him to dodge into the pits for a third refuelling stop and still emerge ahead of Button, who, for much of the race, had looked favourite to score the win.

'I have had a few wins,' said Rubens as he celebrated his eighth career victory, 'but this is the first time I won twice at the same race, and it is just as magic as the last time at Monza [in 2002].

'Some people say Formula 1 is boring, but there was nothing boring about this race. It is an unbelievable feeling. This has been the best season ever, and all that was missing for me was a win.

'I knew that the track was going to dry probably earlier than I thought. It was actually dangerous, because in those circumstances the Michelin runners could have come diving up the inside, so for me, starting from pole, it was difficult to judge where to brake. So I just went flat out, and it worked.'

And he did go flat out! At the end of the opening lap, Ferrari's number two appeared out of Parabolica apparently all alone and slammed across the start line a breathtaking 6.9s ahead of Fernando Alonso's Renault. Third was Juan Pablo Montoya's Williams FW26, ahead of Kimi Räikkönen's McLaren and the BAR-Hondas of Jenson Button and Takuma Sato.

Michael Schumacher, struggling for grip on his dry Bridgestones, was tipped into a spin and completed the first lap in 15th place. 'At the first chicane [on the opening lap], I could not stop the car in time, and at the second chicane, I got into a nice four-wheel slide, but Jenson was outside me. We touched and it spun me round,' explained the world champion. 'It was very frustrating waiting for the cars to go past before I could start again. But the car worked fantastically well. As for my tyre choice at the start, I knew that really there was no right choice, so when I saw that Rubens had gone for the rain tyre, I decided to go the other way, so that at least one Ferrari got it right.'

By the end of lap two, Barrichello was 8.8s ahead of Alonso, with Schumacher in the other Ferrari up to 14th, but 26.3s down on the leader. On lap three, the Brazilian's lead was down to 6.6s, while Button moved ahead of Montoya to take third up lap four. By now, the track was beginning to dry out. Then Barrichello came in for his first stop (6.9s) at the end of lap five; he switched to dry rubber at the same time. That left Alonso leading by 5.9s from Button, but when the Spaniard made his first refuelling stop at the end of lap ten, the BAR driver went ahead. The Brit held the lead through his own first stop on lap 14, and as the afternoon unfolded, it really began to look as though the 24-year-old was finally poised on the verge of his maiden grand prix success.

By lap 21, Button was just ahead of Alonso, with Montoya and Barrichello in third and fourth, the quartet covered by just 5.3s. That blanket came down to 4.1s on lap 23, then to 3.4s on lap 24, Button just hanging on ahead of Alonso by 1.2s. The latter driver kept up the pressure, trimming Button's advantage to just 0.9s by lap 27, but then the Renault team leader pitted – together with Montoya – at the end of lap 33, while Button stayed out for another lap before making his second stop.

That left Schumacher and Barrichello 1-2 in their Ferraris, but the world champion came in on lap 36, leaving his number two in front of Button and Alonso. Unfortunately, the Spaniard's prospects went straight out of the window when he spun the Renault at the second chicane on lap 41 and was unable to continue.

'Jenson overtook me at the first round of pit stops, but I was keeping up with him,' explained Alonso. 'My spin occurred when I took too much kerb in the second chicane and lost control of the rear end of the car, but after that I was surprised that the marshals decided not to push me as the rules allow them to. But that's life.'

At this stage, Button began to realise that he had a good chance of taking his first win, but as the track dried, he was progressively flattened by the Ferraris. 'Their performance in the dry was staggering,' he said after finishing third. 'The pace of those two guys was untouchable. My car was stronger on low fuel loads toward the end of each run, but there was just no chance to race the Ferraris.'

Barrichello's pace between laps 36 and 46 was simply shattering, adding 14s to a 10s lead and enabling him to dive in for his final stop without losing his advantage over Button, who lost second to Michael Schumacher just moments later. Revving their V10s really hard, the two Ferrari drivers proved that the F2004 was pretty well 2s a lap faster than anything else on the track. Barrichello's win emphasised just how big a gap the likes of McLaren, Williams and BAR had to bridge to have a realistic hope of racing for victory in 2005.

Schumacher closed right up to Barrichello in the closing stages of the race, but the world champion abided by the Maranello house rule that the leading driver at the final round of refuelling stops must not be challenged by his partner.

As usual, Schumacher was generous in his praise of Barrichello, and rightly so. 'Rubens really deserves this win, as he drove a great race after a fantastic qualifying,' he said. 'It's good to see him up here on the top of the podium again.' Jean Todt added, 'I was particularly pleased for Rubens, as this win was the icing on the cake, a stupendous win in a great season. Winning this way in front of our fans and our staff is really a very emotional moment.'

Takuma Sato expressed himself well-satisfied with his fourth place: 'It was a very spectacular race. We started in damp conditions with half the circuit still wet, so I think everyone seemed to struggle a bit in the early stages. I lost quite a few places on the exit to the first chicane, but once the conditions improved, I was able to get back on the pace.'

Behind Sato, Juan Pablo Montoya finished a disappointing fifth from second on the grid, while David Coulthard took sixth ahead of Antonio Pizzonia, despite the Brazilian running into the back of his rival in the closing stages. Coulthard had started from the pit lane with his McLaren's tanks brim-full, allowing him to switch to dry rubber and pursue a one-stop strategy from the outset.

Montoya was philosophical about his misfortune. 'I didn't have enough grip at the start and I lost one position to Alonso,' he explained. 'My car was pretty good in both the first and the second stints, when we were close to the cars in front and quite competitive. However, in the last stint, the car became very difficult to drive, and I dropped from third to sixth because of a gearbox problem.'

Pizzonia was happy with seventh. 'My race was basically compromised on the very first lap, when I got hit from behind and spun off,' said the Brazilian. 'I dropped to 19th place and basically spent the rest of the afternoon climbing back to seventh behind Coulthard. He had more speed than me on the straight, and I had a good opportunity with a couple of laps to go when David made a mistake in the last corner and I got very close to him coming out of the Parabolica, but we both locked up and hit each other going into the first chicane, luckily with no consequences for either of us.'

Completing the list of point scorers was Giancarlo Fisichella in the Sauber C23 in eighth place. 'A point was what I expected, but also not what I expected, given the unusual circumstances at the start of the race,' grinned the Italian. 'I was always confident that we could score, but to begin with, I lost vital time through the combination of low downforce, high fuel load and dry tyres. But once the track began to dry, I felt more confident, and was able to start pushing hard and have a very good race.

'At the end, I saw Pizzonia and Coulthard collide, and hoped momentarily that I might get even more, but I am satisfied with a point for eighth today.'

Kimi Räikkönen's hopes of repeating his Belgian Grand Prix victory were thwarted by a water leak that damaged the engine of his car.

ECCLESTONE SLAMS 'SELFISH' FERRARI

Bernie Ecclestone accused the Ferrari team of being 'selfish' in blocking proposed changes to the F1 regulations intended to inject a degree of unpredictability into the sport, which had been dominated for five seasons by its number-one driver, Michael Schumacher.

Speaking at Monza, Ecclestone also reiterated his belief that the famous Italian team had learned nothing from the embarrassment caused to F1 as a whole after the 2002 Austrian Grand Prix, when Rubens Barrichello had been instructed to relinquish victory to Schumacher almost on the finishing line.

'They have a policy to win the world championship,' he said. 'They don't want to take any risks, but what's a little bit bad is the selfishness of the team over not wanting to compromise over the regulations to make the racing a little more challenging.

'The one-by-one qualifying, for example, has been a complete disaster, and Ferrari haven't done anything to help, as they won't agree to change anything. They are terribly selfish like that.'

Although personally a fan of Schumacher, Ecclestone expressed doubt that the German driver would have enjoyed as much success had Ayrton Senna not been killed in 1994. 'Don't get me wrong, I'm a Schumacher fan,' he said. 'But would he have won as many championships as he has done if Senna had not left us? I very much doubt it. Of course, Ayrton never had the luxuries Michael has had. Michael has never had anybody in his team who has been able, or been in a position, to challenge him, and he's certainly in the best team there is.'

Ecclestone's remarks came shortly after an attack on him by Ferrari's chairman, Luca di Montezemolo, over the vexed issue of the continuing inequitable division of F1's commercial-rights revenue. 'Such an expensive sport cannot survive if we do not increase revenues,' said Montezemolo. 'A certain era is finished, and we have to look at something new which is totally acceptable to the players who at the moment get only 47 per cent of the money from the TV rights, and nothing from the tickets, advertising and other sources of income. It is not possible any more. We said these things three years ago, but unfortunately somebody [Ecclestone] has not understood.'

GRAN PREMIO VODAFONE D'ITALIA

MONZA 10–12 SEPTEMBER 2004

Photograph: Darren Heath

MONZA – GRAND PRIX CIRCUIT

PRIMA VARIANTE 71/115 (2)

CURVA GRANDE 181/290 (5)

218/350 (6)

CURVA PARABOLICA 155/250 (4)

RETTILINEO PARABOLICA 205/330 (6)

VARIANTE ASCARI 100/161 (3)

CURVA DEL VIALONE 90/145 (3)

SECONDA VARIANTE 70/113 (2)

CURVA DEL SERRAGLIO 205/330 (6)

mph/km/h (gear)

CURVA DI LESMOS 100/161 (3)

CIRCUIT LENGTH: 3.600 miles/5.793 km

RACE DISTANCE: 53 laps, 190.587 miles/306.720 km RACE WEATHER: Rain/sunny/overcast/sunny (track 29–35°C, air 24–27°C)

Pos.	Driver	Nat.	No.	Entrant	Car/Engine	Tyres	Laps	Time/Retirement	Speed (mph/km/h)	Gap to leader	Fastest race lap	
1	Rubens Barrichello	BR	2	Scuderia Ferrari Marlboro	Ferrari F2004-052 V10	B	53	1h 15m 18.448s	151.847/244.374		1m 21.046s	41
2	Michael Schumacher	D	1	Scuderia Ferrari Marlboro	Ferrari F2004-052 V10	B	53	1h 15m 19.795s	151.801/244.301	+1.347s	1m 21.361s	35
3	Jenson Button	GB	9	Lucky Strike BAR Honda	BAR 006-Honda RA004E V10	M	53	1h 15m 28.645s	1151.585/243.823	+10.197s	1m 22.671s	35
4	Takuma Sato	J	10	Lucky Strike BAR Honda	BAR 006-Honda RA004E V10	M	53	1h 15m 33.818s	151.332/243.545	+15.370s	1m 22.660s	32
5	Juan Pablo Montoya	COL	3	BMW WilliamsF1 Team	Williams FW26-BMW P84 V10	M	53	1h 15m 50.800s	150.767/242.636	+32.352s	1m 22.929s	32
6	David Coulthard	GB	5	West McLaren Mercedes	McLaren MP4/19B-Mercedes F0110P V10	M	53	1h 15m 51.887s	150.731/242.578	+33.439s	1m 22.889s	24
7	Antonio Pizzonia	E	4	BMW WilliamsF1 Team	Williams FW26-BMW P84 V10	M	53	1h 15m 52.200s	150.721/242.562	+33.752s	1m 22.246s	32
8	Giancarlo Fisichella	I	11	Sauber Petronas	Sauber C23-Petronas 04 V10	B	53	1h 15m 53.879s	150.665/242.472	+35.431s	1m 22.615s	51
9	Mark Webber	AUS	14	Jaguar Racing	Jaguar R5-Cosworth CR6 V10	M	53	1h 16m 15.209s	149.962/241.342	+56.761s	1m 23.090s	53
10	Jarno Trulli	I	7	Mild Seven Renault F1 Team	Renault R24-RS4 V10	M	53	1h 16m 24.764s	149.650/240.839	+66.316s	1m 22.855s	52
11	Ricardo Zonta	BR	16	Panasonic Toyota Racing	Toyota TF104B-RVX04 V10	M	53	1h 16m 40.979s	149.123/239.990	+82.531s	1m 23.410s	52
12	Felipe Massa	BR	12	Sauber Petronas	Sauber C23-Petronas 04 V10	B	52			+1 lap	1m 22.941s	50
13	Christian Klien	A	15	Jaguar Racing	Jaguar R5-Cosworth CR6 V10	M	52			+1 lap	1m 23.432s	29
14	Nick Heidfeld	D	18	Jordan Ford	Jordan EJ-14-Cosworth RS V10	B	52			+1 lap	1m 24.166s	23
15	Zsolt Baumgartner	H	21	European Minardi Cosworth	Minardi PS04B-Cosworth CR3 V10	B	50			+3 laps	1m 26.356s	31
	Fernando Alonso	E	8	Mild Seven Renault F1 Team	Renault R24-RS4 V10	M	40	Spun			1m 22.881s	31
	Giorgio Pantano	I	19	Jordan Ford	Jordan EJ-14-Cosworth RS V10	B	33	Spun			1m 24.061s	13
	Gianmaria Bruni	I	20	European Minardi Cosworth	Minardi PS04B-Cosworth CR3 V10	B	29	Pit fire			1m 26.371s	24
	Kimi Räikkönen	FIN	6	West McLaren Mercedes	McLaren MP4/19B-Mercedes F0110P V10	M	13	Engine			1m 23.365s	11
	Olivier Panis	F	17	Panasonic Toyota Racing	Toyota TF104B-RVX04 V10	M	0					

All results and data © FOM 2004

Fastest lap: Rubens Barrichello, on lap 41, 1m 21.046s, 159.891 mph/257.320 km/h (record).

Previous lap record: Michael Schumacher (Ferrari F2003-GA-051 V10), 1m 21.832s, 158.355 mph/254.848 km/h (2003).

19th: ZSOLT BAUMGARTNER Minardi-Cosworth

17th: GIORGIO PANTANO Jordan-Cosworth

15th: GIANCARLO FISICHELLA Sauber-Petronas

13th: OLIVIER PANIS Toyota

11th: RICARDO ZONTA Toyota

20th: NICK HEIDFELD Jordan-Cosworth

18th: GIANMARIA BRUNI Minardi-Cosworth

16th: FELIPE MASSA Sauber-Petronas

14th: CHRISTIAN KLIEN Jaguar-Cosworth

12th: MARK WEBBER Jaguar-Cosworth

Grid order	1	2	3	4	5	6	7	8	9	10	11	12	13	14	15	16	17	18	19	20	21	22	23	24	25	26	27	28	29	30	31	32	33	34	35	36	37	38	39	40	4
2 BARRICHELLO	2	2	2	2	8	8	8	8	8	8	9	9	9	9	9	9	9	9	9	9	9	9	9	9	9	9	9	9	9	9	9	9	9	9	9	9	1	1	2	2	2
3 MONTOYA	8	8	8	8	9	9	9	9	9	9	3	3	3	8	8	8	8	8	8	8	8	8	8	8	8	8	8	8	8	8	8	8	8	1	2	2	9	9	9	9	9
1 M. SCHUMACHER	3	3	3	9	2	3	3	3	3	6	6	10	1	3	3	3	3	3	3	3	3	3	3	3	3	3	3	3	3	3	3	3	3	2	9	9	8	8	8	8	2
8 ALONSO	6	9	9	3	3	6	6	6	6	10	10	6	3	1	2	2	2	2	2	2	2	2	2	2	2	2	2	2	2	10	10	10	10	4	8	8	1	1	1	1	10
10 SATO	9	6	6	6	10	10	10	10	14	14	8	4	4	11	11	10	10	10	10	10	10	10	10	10	10	10	1	1	1	8	4	10	10	10	10	10
9 BUTTON	10	12	12	10	10	15	15	15	15	15	15	8	1	2	2	11	10	10	11	5	5	5	5	5	1	1	1	2	2	2	2	3	3	11	3	3	3	3	5
6 RÄIKKÖNEN	12	10	10	12	7	7	14	14	14	8	1	4	11	11	10	5	5	5	1	1	1	1	4	4	4	4	4	4	10	10	3	11	5	5	5	5
4 PIZZONIA	7	15	7	7	15	14	7	7	7	7	7	2	10	10	5	14	14	14	4	4	4	4	11	11	11	11	11	11	11	11	5	5	4	4	1
7 TRULLI	15	7	15	15	14	2	2	2	2	1	2	11	5	14	1	1	1	4	14	11	11	11	14	14	14	14	14	14	5	5	5	4	11	11	11	11
5 COULTHARD	16	14	14	14	12	11	11	11	1	2	16	19	1	4	4	11	11	14	14	14	14	5	5	5	5	5	7	7	14	14	14	14	14
16 ZONTA	14	20	20	20	11	1	1	11	4	11	5	14	15	14	15	15	15	15	15	15	15	15	15	7	16	14	7	7	7	7	7	7	7
14 WEBBER	20	16	11	11	1	4	4	4	4	11	16	19	15	7	7	7	7	7	7	7	7	7	15	16	14	15	15	16	16	16	16	16	16
17 PANIS	11	11	5	5	4	16	16	16	16	16	14	7	18	18	18	7	7	7	16	16	16	16	16	12	16	16	16	15	12	15	12
15 KLIEN	19	1	16	1	4	5	5	5	5	5	19	16	16	16	16	16	18	19	19	19	19	12	15	12	12	12	12	12	15	12	15
11 FISICHELLA	1	19	1	16	16	19	19	19	19	15	7	16	19	19	19	19	19	19	18	18	18	18	18	18	18
12 MASSA	5	5	19	19	20	20	21	21	21	18	18	1	1	12	12	12	18	18	18	18	18	18	18	21	21	21	21	21	21
19 PANTANO	21	21	4	4	19	21	18	18	18	21	21	21	21	21	21	21	21	21	21	21	21	21
20 BRUNI	18	18	21	21	21	18	12	12	20	20	12	12	12	20	20	20	20	20	20	20	20
21 BAUMGARTNER	4	4	18	18	18	12	20	20	12	12	20	20	20
18 HEIDFELD																																									

TIME SHEETS

QUALIFYING

Sunny/overcast (track 33–36°C, air 26–27°C)

Pos.	Driver	Lap time	Sector 1	Sector 2	Sector 3
1	Rubens Barrichello	1m 20.089s	26.017s	27.150s	26.992s
2	Juan Pablo Montoya	1m 20.620s	25.987s	27.669s	26.964s
3	Michael Schumacher	1m 20.637s	25.927s	27.363s	27.347s
4	Fernando Alonso	1m 20.645s	26.094s	27.592s	26.959s
5	Takuma Sato	1m 20.715s	26.239s	27.430s	27.046s
6	Jenson Button	1m 20.786s	26.158s	27.549s	27.079s
7	Kimi Räikkönen	1m 20.877s	25.964s	27.724s	27.189s
8	Antonio Pizzonia	1m 20.888s	26.035s	27.846s	27.007s
9	Jarno Trulli	1m 21.027s	26.006s	27.631s	27.347s
10	David Coulthard	1m 21.049s	26.053s	27.649s	27.390s
11	Ricardo Zonta	1m 21.520s	26.489s	27.746s	27.285s
12	Mark Webber	1m 21.602s	26.560s	27.899s	27.143s
13	Olivier Panis	1m 21.841s	26.569s	27.790s	27.482s
14	Christian Klien	1m 21.989s	26.612s	28.000s	27.377s
15	Giancarlo Fisichella	1m 22.239s	26.350s	28.281s	27.608s
16	Felipe Massa	1m 22.287s	26.995s	27.950s	27.342s
17	Nick Heidfeld	1m 22.301s	26.682s	28.054s	27.565s
18	Giorgio Pantano	1m 23.239s	26.619s	28.471s	28.149s
19	Zsolt Baumgartner	1m 24.808s	26.860s	29.196s	28.752s
20	Gianmaria Bruni	1m 24.940s	27.127s	29.109s	28.704s

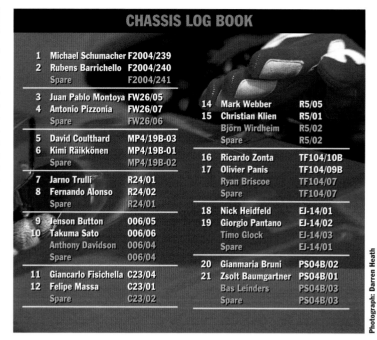

Photograph: Darren Heath

CHASSIS LOG BOOK

1	Michael Schumacher	F2004/239
2	Rubens Barrichello	F2004/240
	Spare	F2004/241
3	Juan Pablo Montoya	FW26/05
4	Antonio Pizzonia	FW26/07
	Spare	FW26/06
5	David Coulthard	MP4/19B-03
6	Kimi Räikkönen	MP4/19B-01
	Spare	MP4/19B-02
7	Jarno Trulli	R24/01
8	Fernando Alonso	R24/02
	Spare	R24/01
9	Jenson Button	006/05
10	Takuma Sato	006/06
	Anthony Davidson	006/04
	Spare	006/04
11	Giancarlo Fisichella	C23/04
12	Felipe Massa	C23/01
	Spare	C23/02
14	Mark Webber	R5/05
15	Christian Klien	R5/01
	Björn Wirdheim	R5/02
	Spare	R5/02
16	Ricardo Zonta	TF104/10B
17	Olivier Panis	TF104/09B
	Ryan Briscoe	TF104/07
	Spare	TF104/07
18	Nick Heidfeld	EJ-14/01
19	Giorgio Pantano	EJ-14/02
	Timo Glock	EJ-14/03
	Spare	EJ-14/01
20	Gianmaria Bruni	PS04B/02
21	Zsolt Baumgartner	PS04B/01
	Bas Leinders	PS04B/03
	Spare	PS04B/03

PRACTICE 1 (FRIDAY)

Sunny (track 29–35°C, air 24–27°C)

Pos.	Driver	Laps	Time
1	Michael Schumacher	10	1m 20.526s
2	Rubens Barrichello	4	1m 20.861s
3	Anthony Davidson	25	1m 20.902s
4	Kimi Räikkönen	5	1m 21.637s
5	Fernando Alonso	10	1m 21.778s
6	Jenson Button	5	1m 21.904s
7	Jarno Trulli	11	1m 22.052s
8	Björn Wirdheim	24	1m 22.065s
9	Antonio Pizzonia	9	1m 22.159s
10	Juan Pablo Montoya	9	1m 22.232s
11	Takuma Sato	8	1m 22.245s
12	David Coulthard	5	1m 22.248s
13	Felipe Massa	13	1m 22.259s
14	Giancarlo Fisichella	11	1m 22.460s
15	Olivier Panis	8	1m 22.487s
16	Ricardo Zonta	10	1m 22.507s
17	Ryan Briscoe	21	1m 22.815s
18	Mark Webber	7	1m 23.071s
19	Timo Glock	28	1m 23.333s
20	Bas Leinders	16	1m 23.696s
21	Christian Klien	7	1m 23.723s
22	Nick Heidfeld	11	1m 24.000s
23	Giorgio Pantano	10	1m 24.412s
24	Gianmaria Bruni	11	1m 26.062s
25	Zsolt Baumgartner	13	1m 26.161s

PRACTICE 2 (FRIDAY)

Sunny (track 37–38°C, air 27–28°C)

Pos.	Driver	Laps	Time
1	Kimi Räikkönen	13	1m 20.846s
2	Rubens Barrichello	21	1m 20.899s
3	Michael Schumacher	20	1m 21.080s
4	Jenson Button	16	1m 21.124s
5	Antonio Pizzonia	18	1m 21.264s
6	Takuma Sato	20	1m 21.313s
7	Juan Pablo Montoya	17	1m 21.419s
8	Anthony Davidson	37	1m 21.544s
9	Fernando Alonso	18	1m 21.630s
10	David Coulthard	12	1m 22.052s
11	Jarno Trulli	19	1m 22.191s
12	Ryan Briscoe	35	1m 22.197s
13	Felipe Massa	18	1m 22.258s
14	Ricardo Zonta	22	1m 22.298s
15	Giancarlo Fisichella	12	1m 22.302s
16	Timo Glock	17	1m 22.332s
17	Mark Webber	24	1m 22.392s
18	Olivier Panis	15	1m 22.813s
19	Björn Wirdheim	26	1m 22.914s
20	Christian Klien	25	1m 23.199s
21	Giorgio Pantano	17	1m 23.818s
22	Bas Leinders	19	1m 24.045s
23	Zsolt Baumgartner	17	1m 24.063s
24	Gianmaria Bruni	23	1m 24.225s
25	Nick Heidfeld	2	No time

PRACTICE 3 (SATURDAY)

Overcast/sunny (track 23–24°C, air 21–22°C)

Pos.	Driver	Laps	Time
1	Juan Pablo Montoya	6	1m 21.700s
2	Fernando Alonso	9	1m 21.705s
3	Antonio Pizzonia	8	1m 21.723s
4	Rubens Barrichello	9	1m 21.855s
5	Takuma Sato	7	1m 21.867s
6	Michael Schumacher	7	1m 21.962s
7	Kimi Räikkönen	5	1m 22.018s
8	Jenson Button	9	1m 22.062s
9	David Coulthard	6	1m 22.097s
10	Felipe Massa	6	1m 22.284s
11	Giancarlo Fisichella	5	1m 22.369s
12	Jarno Trulli	9	1m 22.774s
13	Mark Webber	7	1m 22.784s
14	Ricardo Zonta	9	1m 22.867s
15	Olivier Panis	9	1m 23.103s
16	Christian Klien	8	1m 23.332s
17	Gianmaria Bruni	14	1m 24.411s
18	Giorgio Pantano	11	1m 24.526s
19	Nick Heidfeld	12	1m 24.669s
20	Zsolt Baumgartner	10	1m 26.114s

PRACTICE 4 (SATURDAY)

Overcast/sunny (track 26–31°C, air 22–24°C)

Pos.	Driver	Laps	Time
1	Rubens Barrichello	11	1m 20.555s
2	Juan Pablo Montoya	11	1m 20.653s
3	Jenson Button	13	1m 20.734s
4	Fernando Alonso	11	1m 20.773s
5	Takuma Sato	11	1m 20.805s
6	Kimi Räikkönen	11	1m 20.856s
7	Michael Schumacher	10	1m 20.898s
8	Antonio Pizzonia	10	1m 20.921s
9	David Coulthard	11	1m 21.058s
10	Jarno Trulli	8	1m 21.506s
11	Felipe Massa	14	1m 21.859s
12	Olivier Panis	18	1m 21.889s
13	Giancarlo Fisichella	9	1m 21.929s
14	Ricardo Zonta	20	1m 22.114s
15	Christian Klien	18	1m 22.230s
16	Mark Webber	15	1m 22.490s
17	Nick Heidfeld	13	1m 23.146s
18	Gianmaria Bruni	14	1m 23.794s
19	Giorgio Pantano	2	No time
20	Zsolt Baumgartner	2	No time

9th: JARNO TRULLI Renault

7th: KIMI RÄIKKÖNEN McLaren-Mercedes

5th: TAKUMA SATO BAR-Honda

3rd: MICHAEL SCHUMACHER Ferrari

Pole: RUBENS BARRICHELLO Ferrari

10th: DAVID COULTHARD McLaren-Mercedes

8th: ANTONIO PIZZONIA Williams-BMW

6th: JENSON BUTTON BAR-Honda

4th: FERNANDO ALONSO Renault

2nd: JUAN PABLO MONTOYA Williams-BMW

42	43	44	45	46	47	48	49	50	51	52	53	
2	2	2	2	2	2	2	2	2	2	2	2	1
9	1	1	1	1	1	1	1	1	1	1	1	2
1	9	9	9	9	9	9	9	9	9	9	9	3
10	10	10	10	10	10	10	10	10	10	10	10	4
3	3	3	3	3	3	3	3	3	3	3	3	5
5	5	5	5	5	5	5	5	5	5	5	5	6
4	4	4	4	4	4	4	4	4	4	4	4	7
11	11	11	11	11	11	11	11	11	11	11	11	8
14	14	14	14	14	14	14	14	14	14	14	14	
7	7	7	7	7	7	7	7	7	7	7	7	
16	16	16	16	16	16	16	16	16	16	16	16	
12	12	12	12	12	12	12	12	12	12	12		
15	15	15	15	15	15	15	15	15	15	15		
18	18	18	18	18	18	18	18	18	18	18		
21	21	21	21	21	21	21	21	21				

Pit stop

One lap behind leader

FOR THE RECORD

700 grand prix starts

Ferrari

15 races led in a season

Michael Schumacher

Most points in a season

Ferrari

POINTS: CONSTRUCTORS

1	Ferrari	234
2	BAR	94
3	Renault	91
4	Williams	60
5	McLaren	52
6	Sauber	29
7	Jaguar	10
8	Toyota	9
9	Jordan	5
10	Minardi	1

POINTS: DRIVERS

1	Michael Schumacher	136
2	Rubens Barrichello	98
3	Jenson Button	71
4	Jarno Trulli	46
5	Fernando Alonso	45
6	Juan Pablo Montoya	42
7	Kimi Räikkönen	28
8	David Coulthard	24
9	Takuma Sato	23
10	Giancarlo Fisichella	19
11	Ralf Schumacher	12
12	Felipe Massa	10
13	Mark Webber	7
14 =	Olivier Panis	6
14 =	Antonio Pizzonia	6
16 =	Christian Klien	3
16 =	Cristiano da Matta	3
16 =	Nick Heidfeld	3
19	Timo Glock	2
20	Zsolt Baumgartner	1

Photographs: Darren Heath

FIA F1 WORLD CHAMPIONSHIP • ROUND 16

CHINESE GP
SHANGHAI

Left: Rubens Barrichello speeds past the gigantic main grandstand.
Photograph: Darren Heath

Below: To boldly go where no Formula 1 car has gone before...
Photograph: Bryn Williams/crash.net

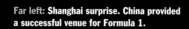

Far left: Shanghai surprise. China provided a successful venue for Formula 1.

Left: Getting better all the time. Two wins on the bounce for Barrichello.
Photographs: Bryn Williams/crash.net

197

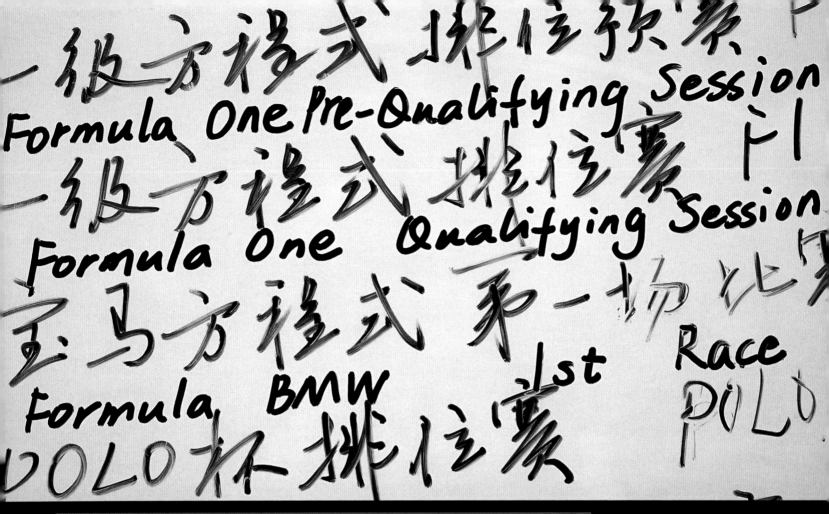

一级方程式 排位预赛

Formula One Pre-Qualifying Session

一级方程式 排位赛 F1

Formula One Qualifying Session

宝马方程式 第一场比赛

Formula BMW 1st Race

POLO杯 排位赛

POLO

Above: Schedule in two languages.

SHANGHAI QUALIFYING

The Shanghai facility was like nothing we'd ever seen before, but even the magnificent pit buildings paled into insignificance compared to the remarkable sight that befell us at the end of qualifying. As last runner Michael Schumacher embarked on his quest for yet another pole, the Ferrari suddenly snapped out of line at the first corner. In an instant, the red car was sailing backwards across the run-off area, sending up a cloud of dust. The reality soon hit home. Michael would be starting from the back – and we would have a race!

These days, teams have access to such good simulation facilities that they arrive at a new track with a very good idea of things like ratios and set-up, but Friday practice always fills in the blanks. Shanghai, with its interesting mix of corners, proved to be a fascinating challenge. The fact that the green track surface changed constantly made life even more interesting.

'I think it's probably a little bit quicker than we were expecting,' noted Toyota technical director Mike Gascoyne after the first day of practice. 'It's always difficult to know what kerbs you're going to use, and this sort of thing. The grip seems quite reasonable, although it's very smooth and new. We decided to run with lower wing levels than perhaps we were initially simulating, because of the grip. You need good aero efficiency, good engine power, good change of direction. And you need to be fairly easy on the tyres.'

Bearing in mind the technical nature of the circuit, it was no real surprise that circumstances favoured Ferrari. Monza winner Rubens Barrichello was first out on a dirty track in pre-qualifying, setting a bench mark of 1m 33.787s, which was smashed immediately by Schumacher's 1m 33.185s.

Despite the track improving, no one went faster than the world champion, and only Kimi Räikkönen bettered Barrichello. Meanwhile, the Michelin teams were given plenty of food for thought when Giancarlo Fisichella and Felipe Massa lined up fourth and fifth. Either the Saubers were running very light, or Bridgestone had found something special.

Having ensured the prime last spot, Schumacher seemed content to wait and see what the others could come up with. The track certainly appeared to get quicker as qualifying proper unfolded. Of the serious contenders, the returning Ralf Schumacher held top spot for a while on 1m 34.891s, until Jenson Button upped the ante with a 1m 34.295s. He still held pole when the last three cars came out.

He didn't have it for long, for Barrichello went quickest with a 1m 34.012s. Räikkönen came close to usurping the Brazilian on 1m 34.178s, despite a wobble at the last corner. That left Michael Schumacher. Surely he wouldn't have too much trouble wrapping things up? His trip into the gravel came as a shock to everyone; standing on the pit wall, Luca di Montezemolo suddenly had nowhere to hide.

As the world champion crawled back to the pits, the speculation began. The consensus was that he must have experienced some kind of technical glitch, but some suggested that he'd gone off deliberately to

give himself more of a challenge on Sunday. It sounded a little far-fetched, but then the German had indulged in a spurious spin in pre-qualifying at Silverstone, albeit only to gain a more favourable track position for the run that counted. In the end, he had to admit that he'd got it wrong.

'I was shocked when I saw Michael spinning,' said Barrichello. 'It's not very often that you see Michael doing such a mistake. So, when I saw it, I stayed 20 seconds without words because I didn't know what to say, really.'

Once he'd recovered his composure, Barrichello was delighted to have the pole, while Räikkönen's second was a boost for McLaren and further proof that the MP4/19B was consistently quick. But the happiest man in the place appeared to be Button, looking a little unfamiliar in the 555 overalls custom made for the race. Although he was only third, the team made it pretty clear that he was on a good strategy and had outperformed any predictions.

Sauber again looked good, with Massa fourth on 1m 34.759s, and Fisichella seventh on 1m 34.951s and, as it turned out, harder tyres. The pair were split by Schumacher Jr – clearly suffering no after-effects from his lay-off – and Fernando Alonso, although this was not a track that suited Renault. Olivier Panis gave Toyota some encouragement with eighth.

Takuma Sato was a disappointed ninth fastest for BAR; a Friday engine failure had already doomed him to the unfashionable end of the grid. He was running a very heavy load, but nevertheless was expected to do rather better.

Of the rest, David Coulthard was a disappointed tenth after making a mistake, while a handling problem put troubled Juan Pablo Montoya a lacklustre 11th. Just days after Ford had announced the sale of Jaguar and Cosworth, Mark Webber was 12th, ahead of the returning Jacques Villeneuve in the second Renault. With Giorgio Pantano now terminally out of favour, Timo Glock made his first appearance for Jordan since Canada and took 17th, only two places behind team-mate Nick Heidfeld. All in this group gained a spot when Sato was moved back.

Despite the tricky nature of the track, the only man other than Michael to screw up completely in qualifying was Minardi's Gianmaria Bruni, who spun at the exit of the first right-hander. That made the world champion's mistake look even more astounding. Could he make amends on Sunday?

Below: Kimi Räikkönen provided the sternest challenge to Barrichello.
Photographs: Darren Heath

Bottom: The BAR team sported 555 branding in Friday practice on Anthony Davidson's car.
Photograph: Bryn Williams/crash.net

FTER Monza in 2004, we'd all come to believe that Michael Schumacher could give the rest a head start and still make the podium; in Shanghai, a scrappy race and arguably his least convincing performance in years proved that he is, after all, human. Not only did he mess up in qualifying, but also he failed to make much progress through the field after starting from the pit lane. Moreover, a collision, a spin and a puncture (that's three separate events!) dropped him back down the order.

It was an entertaining race, which was good news for the packed stands of local fans – many of them wealthy paddock club guests – who were experiencing the sport for the first time. And what a venue it was too. Malaysia and Bahrain had merely been the appetisers for what will surely stand as Herrman Tilke's finest creation, as it is unlikely that any other government will give the German architect such resources for future projects.

On the whole, the locals proved extremely hospitable, and cosmopolitan Shanghai had far more to offer than many expected. The only downside was the appalling traffic. Indeed, on Sunday morning, four members of the Williams marketing team were lucky to escape with minor injuries after their van was T-boned outside the circuit. It was their good fortune that FIA doctors Sid Watkins and Gary Hartstein were by chance next on the scene.

The prospect of Schumacher starting from the back of the grid was exciting, but Ferrari robbed us of the chance of seeing a mega first lap from the great man. Ross Brawn had decided on a change of tactics by starting him from the pit lane with a fresh engine and extra fuel. To avoid a penalty should the start be aborted, the fuelling process couldn't begin until the lights came on, costing him further valuable seconds.

Pole man Rubens Barrichello had to hang on to his advantage at the start, for it was known that the Bridgestones would go through a difficult graining stage. With Fernando Alonso back in sixth, the driver with the best chance of ousting him was Kimi Räikkönen, but when the lights went out, Barrichello slotted neatly in front of the McLaren. Alonso was the man on the move, however, barging his way up to third, while Felipe Massa also found a way past Jenson Button.

It looked a bit messy farther back, but against expectations the entire field made it through the first right-left-left complex without drama. All eyes were on the Ferrari pit, however. After waiting to take on his extra fuel, Schumacher was more than 3.7s adrift of Gianmaria Bruni's Minardi at the end of the first lap, and it was already obvious that, even for him, it was going to be a long slog.

Button lost valuable time behind Massa in the first couple of laps, before usurping him on the third. At that point, he was 5.7s behind the leader, but Barrichello was going through the expected graining stage and had Räikkönen right on his tail. Had the

McLaren-Mercedes got ahead, the Finn would have been able to open up a gap.

Button impressed with a good move on Alonso that put him in third on lap seven. The leaders were out of reach, but a good strategy could still bounce him ahead. Massa signalled the start of the pit-stop sequence when he dropped out of fifth on lap ten. Räikkönen was still right with Barrichello and had a genuine chance of getting ahead if he could run a lap or two later. He couldn't, for when the Brazilian's Ferrari dived into the pits on lap 12, the McLaren followed. The status quo was resumed as they rejoined.

Alonso dropped out of second place on lap 13, and Button came in a lap later. He'd only gone two laps farther on this stint, but a longer stop confirmed what the team had more or less admitted after qualifying – Jenson was going for two stops, while his main rivals were on three. Now we really had a race to watch.

Meanwhile, there had been some great action farther down the field. Jacques Villeneuve hadn't had a great first lap, but became embroiled in a fight with Juan Pablo Montoya, who had been badly delayed when Panis failed to get off the line cleanly. Sato made respectable progress, indicating the amount of fuel he was carrying by stopping on lap 18.

Schumacher had picked his way through the stragglers, but his ultra-heavy load – he was fuelled for 20 laps – didn't do him any favours in traffic. Nor did a collision with Christian Klien at the hairpin, which sidelined the Jaguar, or a spectacular spin at the corner leading on to the back straight. Michael had just got into fifth when he finally pitted, but everyone else had stopped once, and the real picture was revealed when he dropped straight back to 14th.

Although Räikkönen stayed with Barrichello after the first round of stops, he was frustrated at again being unable to take advantage of the Bridgestone's early dip in performance. The second stops would give him a chance to jump the Ferrari, but he was the first to blink, pitting on lap 27 for a very short stop. Barrichello stayed out for two more laps and, on near empty tanks, had no problem remaining in front.

In fact, McLaren had gambled on an ultra-quick stop and a short third stint to put Räikkönen ahead. It was worth a shot, but the plan didn't work, and he remained stuck behind the Ferrari. The Finn came in again for his third stop on lap 36, after just nine laps. One lap earlier, Button had made his second and final stop, and when the McLaren emerged still behind the BAR, it was obvious that the gamble had handed second to the Englishman.

Button's charge in the middle of the race had been impressive to watch, and at one point it seemed that his two-stop effort might eventually topple Barrichello. The Brazilian continued to bang in the times, however, and after Button's stop he ran seven critical laps on low fuel before finally coming in. With a heavy load on

DIARY

Richard Lyons bids for Jordan F1 drive in Japanese Grand Prix.

Birmingham City Council considers reviving Super Prix road race, which was held from 1986 to 1990.

Patrick Carpentier announces he will move from Champ Car to the Indy Racing League in 2005.

Silverstone to host rounds of WTCC and FIA GT series in 2005.

Below: **Not-so-champion. Michael Schumacher had a rare 'off' weekend.**
Photograph: Darren Heath

board, Button had no answer, and when Barrichello emerged from his last stop on lap 42, he was an incredible 8.2s up the road.

'When the gap started getting bigger by about one-and-a-half seconds a lap, I thought we might be in trouble then!,' said Button. 'When it got to 27s on the pit board, I thought I'm going to push as hard as I can, but it's going to be very difficult to be in front when Rubens comes out of the pits.'

Over the remaining 14 laps, Barrichello backed off to such an extent that the Ferrari pit began to get a little nervous, but he insisted everything was under control. He crossed the line with Button right behind him, while Räikkönen was just 1s adrift of the BAR. A little artificial it may have been, but it kept the locals on their toes.

'Rubens drove fantastically well,' said Ross Brawn. 'When he had to, he was very quick, and he looked after the car when he didn't have to be quick. He drove hard and drove well in the beginning of the race. In the third stint, we needed to make sure we had the gap, and we knew we had the gap within a few laps of Rubens' pit stop, if nothing goes wrong. So then we asked him to look after the equipment. He looked after it very well. It got a little bit close at the end, but he seemed to feel he had it under control.'

'I always push very hard toward the end,' said Button, who put in yet another impressive performance. 'But I had to push 100 per cent to try and keep Kimi behind. It's also a circuit where you don't breathe for about 20 seconds, because you've got the left, you've got the right, the quick two corners and the two lefts. After that, you're breathing pretty heavily! It was a tough race, but it was great to get home on the podium. I thought we had the chance of a win, and when I was at the end of my second stint, I was putting in some good lap times. But it didn't come off.'

Alonso had a relatively unspectacular run to fourth, some 32s

behind the winner, while Montoya overcame the handicap of his hampered getaway and plugged away to fifth. Takuma Sato took sixth, using his strategy to good effect and earning BAR three more crucial points in the battle for second with Renault. The remaining points were taken by Sauber twins Giancarlo Fisichella and Massa, the latter fading after looking strong in the early laps.

David Coulthard finished ninth, having lost time in a clash with Ralf Schumacher at the hairpin on lap 38. At least he was able to continue after a quick stop, while the German arrived back at his garage to find the crew awaiting his team-mate. Confusion ensued, and despite having a healthy car, the younger Schumacher opted not to continue. That didn't go down too well and spoiled what had been an otherwise solid return.

Mark Webber completed the top ten, having had Villeneuve in his mirrors for much of the race. And then, in a lapped 12th place, came Michael Schumacher. In the middle of the race, the Ferrari star had actually spent time behind his old pal Villeneuve, before a left rear puncture on lap 35 effectively finished any chance he'd had of even making it into the points. He still had to make a third and final fuel stop as late as lap 47.

'He [Schumacher] wasn't making the progress through the traffic we'd hoped,' said Ross Brawn. 'I think with the heavy fuel load we gave him, it wasn't so easy. But I think maybe points could have been a possibility, but with the spin and the puncture we had, that went out of the window. I think he was just driving for pride then. I see he did the fastest lap at the end of the race.

'He's saved up all his worst bits to the end, when they didn't matter. I've said before that he's not put a foot wrong this year. He had a spin in very difficult conditions in Monza, and he had a couple of spins here this weekend. It's not bad for a whole season.'

VILLENEUVE RETURNS

Jacques Villeneuve was back in the F1 paddock in China, almost a full year after his final grand prix with BAR at Indianapolis, and inevitably he was the focus of media attention. The Canadian's sudden return to the limelight was the culmination of an extraordinary series of events in the days following the Italian Grand Prix.

Earlier in the year, the chances of Villeneuve ever racing an F1 car again had seemed remote. However, the dawn of 'Buttongate' in the middle of August seemed to throw the 1997 world champion a lifeline. If Button really was going, then why couldn't Villeneuve return to replace him?

That's what the man himself thought, and he immediately began campaigning to get his old job back. At first, it seemed like a joke, but some folk in the BAR, BAT and Honda camps genuinely thought it would be a good idea. The problem was that Villeneuve had not only spent the previous winter rubbishing David Richards, but had also made a point of snubbing his former boss in a nightclub on the Sunday night of the Monaco Grand Prix. Rebuilding the bridges was never going to be easy, but, to his credit, Villeneuve made what was probably the most difficult phone call of his life.

Although publicly Richards claimed that he would be willing to forget the past and consider the former BAR driver, Villeneuve soon realised that, even if the Button seat were to become available, his chances of getting the drive would be slim. However, a visit to the Sauber factory, a couple of days after the Hungarian Grand Prix, opened his eyes to another

option; encouraged by the Swiss team's positive reception, he began to consider a drive with the Hinwil outfit for 2005.

That was on the verge of being confirmed when, out of the blue, a more immediate opportunity arose. The relationship between Flavio Briatore and Jarno Trulli had reached breaking point at Monza. With the encouragement of Bernie Ecclestone, Briatore began to look for a way to get the Canadian into the Renault for the last three races, at Trulli's expense.

Things moved very quickly on the Monday and Tuesday. At one point, Giancarlo Fisichella was set to join Renault three races early, leaving the Sauber seat for Villeneuve. The drama was resolved when the latter showed up for a seat fitting at Enstone on Tuesday evening. After two frantic days of testing at Silverstone, he was on the plane to Shanghai.

It was never going to be easy. Villeneuve had tried to keep fit with the aid of loyal trainer Erwin Gollner, but nothing can fully replicate driving an F1 car on a weekly basis. He also found that in the year he'd been away, grip levels had risen to such a degree that pushing to the limit was more taxing than he had expected.

Consider too that Villeneuve hardly knew the car, which was notoriously difficult to drive, he had no experience of Michelin tyres, he was on a track that neither he nor his team were familiar with, and he was up against an extremely motivated team-mate in Fernando Alonso. Nevertheless, he compared favourably with the Spaniard in practice, but fell back in qualifying. Unfortunately, a large group of cars filled the time

gap, so it looked worse than it was.

'I was disappointed with the starting position,' said Villeneuve. 'I was okay with the lap time compared to Fernando, but in a small amount of lap time there were a lot of cars, and that was frustrating. I had a hard time all weekend with new tyres. In first qualy, they worked well, and in second qualy I wasn't happy somehow. I also didn't want to go off, because there's no point starting at the back. Physically, it's gone up in level by quite a lot, the tyre grip, downforce, everything. The g-forces that are pulled are a lot higher.'

In the race, Villeneuve spent some of the time in company with old rivals like Michael Schumacher and Juan Pablo Montoya; the latter actually put a big hole in the Renault's sidepod. But despite rubbing wheels with the big names, he finished only 11th, having spent much of the race chasing Mark Webber. It was hardly an improvement on what Trulli had achieved in the previous couple of races.

'I'm not happy with the position in the end, of course. The start went well, the Renault's really great at the start, but then I didn't get into the rhythm quick enough and lost the positions again in the first two laps. Once I got in the rhythm, I was stuck behind Webber. I was just going faster and faster. I could fight until the end, and that made it fun. But we didn't score any points, so that's a little bit annoying.'

Villeneuve's reputation had not been well served by the hurried comeback, but future boss Peter Sauber insisted that he was unconcerned.

FORMULA 1 SINOPEC
CHINESE GRAND PRIX
SHANGHAI 24–26 SEPTEMBER 2004

Photograph: Darrn Heath

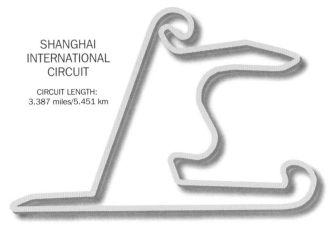

SHANGHAI
INTERNATIONAL
CIRCUIT

CIRCUIT LENGTH:
3.387 miles/5.451 km

RACE DISTANCE: 56 laps, 189.559 miles/305.066 km **RACE WEATHER:** Sunny/cloudy (track 36–34°C, air 28–26°C)

Pos.	Driver	Nat.	No.	Entrant	Car/Engine	Tyres	Laps	Time/Retirement	Speed (mph/km/h)	Gap to leader	Fastest race lap	
1	Rubens Barrichello	BR	2	Scuderia Ferrari Marlboro	Ferrari F2004-052 V10	B	56	1h 29m 12.420s	127.496/205.185		1m 32.455s	28
2	Jenson Button	GB	9	Lucky Strike BAR Honda	BAR 006-Honda RA004E V10	M	56	1h 29m 13.455s	127.471/205.145	+1.035s	1m 32.935s	33
3	Kimi Räikkönen	FIN	6	West McLaren Mercedes	McLaren MP4/19B-Mercedes F0110P V10	M	56	1h 29m 13.889s	127.460/205.128	+1.469s	1m 32.876s	53
4	Fernando Alonso	E	8	Mild Seven Renault F1 Team	Renault R24-RS4 V10	M	56	1h 29m 44.930s	126.540/203.946	+32.510s	1m 33.625s	55
5	Juan Pablo Montoya	COL	3	BMW WilliamsF1 Team	Williams FW26-BMW P84 V10	M	56	1h 29m 57.613s	126.428/203.467	+45.193s	1m 33.108s	34
6	Takuma Sato	J	10	Lucky Strike BAR Honda	BAR 006-Honda RA004E V10	M	56	1h 30m 07.211s	126.204/203.106	+54.791s	1m 33.533s	36
7	Giancarlo Fisichella	I	11	Sauber Petronas	Sauber C23-Petronas 04 V10	B	56	1h 30m 17.884s	125.955/202.705	+65.464s	1m 33.520s	25
8	Felipe Massa	BR	12	Sauber Petronas	Sauber C23-Petronas 04 V10	B	56	1h 30m 32.500s	125.616/202.160	+80.080s	1m 33.483s	43
9	David Coulthard	GB	5	West McLaren Mercedes	McLaren MP4/19B-Mercedes F0110P V10	M	56	1h 30m 33.039s	125.604/202.140	+80.619s	1m 33.727s	26
10	Mark Webber	AUS	14	Jaguar Racing	Jaguar R5-Cosworth CR6 V10	M	55			+1 lap	1m 34.893s	32
11	Jacques Villeneuve	CDN	7	Mild Seven Renault F1 Team	Renault R24-RS4 V10	M	55			+1 lap	1m 34.950s	55
12	Michael Schumacher	D	1	Scuderia Ferrari Marlboro	Ferrari F2004-052 V10	B	55			+1 lap	1m 32.238s	55
13	Nick Heidfeld	D	18	Jordan Ford	Jordan EJ-14-Cosworth RS V10	B	55			+1 lap	1m 34.717s	55
14	Olivier Panis	F	17	Panasonic Toyota Racing	Toyota TF104B-RVX04 V10	M	55			+1 lap	1m 34.603s	51
15	Timo Glock	D	19	Jordan Ford	Jordan EJ-14-Cosworth RS V10	B	55			+1 lap	1m 34.931s	54
16	Zsolt Baumgartner	H	21	European Minardi Cosworth	Minardi PS04B-Cosworth CR3 V10	B	53			+3 laps	1m 37.578s	51
	Gianmaria Bruni	I	20	European Minardi Cosworth	Minardi PS04B-Cosworth CR3 V10	B	38	Lost front wheel			1m 37.377s	23
	Ralf Schumacher	D	4	BMW WilliamsF1 Team	Williams FW26-BMW P84 V10	M	37	Puncture			1m 33.546s	31
	Ricardo Zonta	BR	16	Panasonic Toyota Racing	Toyota TF104B-RVX04 V10	M	35	Gearbox			1m 34.269s	24
	Christian Klien	A	15	Jaguar Racing	Jaguar R5-Cosworth CR6 V10	M	11	Collision damage			1m 36.888s	10

All results and data © FOM 2004

Fastest lap: Michael Schumacher, on lap 55, 1m 32.238s, 132.196 mph/212.749 km/h (record for new track).

19th: MICHAEL SCHUMACHER Ferrari
Started from pit lane

17th: TIMO GLOCK Jordan-Cosworth

15th: NICK HEIDFELD Jordan-Cosworth

13th: JACQUES VILLENEUVE Renault

11th: JUAN PABLO MONTOYA Williams-BMW

20th: GIANMARIA BRUNI Minardi-Cosworth

18th: ZSOLT BAUMGARTNER Minardi-Cosworth

16th: CHRISTIAN KLIEN Jaguar-Cosworth

14th: RICARDO ZONTA Toyota

12th: MARK WEBBER Jaguar-Cosworth

Grid order	1	2	3	4	5	6	7	8	9	10	11	12	13	14	15	16	17	18	19	20	21	22	23	24	25	26	27	28	29	30	31	32	33	34	35	36	37	38	39	40	41	42	43
2 BARRICHELLO	2	2	2	2	2	2	2	2	2	2	2	9	9	4	2	2	2	2	2	2	2	2	2	2	2	2	2	2	2	9	9	9	9	9	9	2	2	2	2	2	2	2	2
6 RÄIKKÖNEN	6	6	6	6	6	6	6	6	6	6	9	8	4	2	6	6	6	6	6	6	6	6	6	6	6	6	6	9	9	2	2	2	2	2	6	9	9	9	9	9	9	9	9
9 BUTTON	8	8	8	8	8	8	9	9	9	9	6	4	2	6	9	9	9	9	9	9	9	9	9	9	9	9	6	6	6	6	6	6	6	6	4	4	10	10	10	10	6	6	6
12 MASSA	12	12	9	9	9	9	8	8	8	8	8	2	6	10	10	10	8	8	8	8	8	8	8	8	8	8	8	8	8	8	8	8	8	8	10	10	10	10	11	11	11	11	8
4 R. SCHUMACHER	9	9	12	12	11	11	11	11	11	11	4	6	14	3	8	8	4	4	4	4	4	4	4	4	4	4	4	4	4	4	8	10	3	3	3	3	8	8	8	8	12
8 ALONSO	11	11	11	11	4	4	4	4	4	4	11	14	14	3	10	8	4	4	1	1	11	11	11	11	11	11	5	10	10	10	10	3	8	8	8	8	12	12	12	12	3
11 FISICHELLA	4	4	4	4	12	5	5	5	5	5	5	7	7	10	8	18	18	1	11	11	5	5	5	5	5	11	3	3	3	3	3	8	4	4	5	11	3	3	3	10
17 PANIS	5	5	5	5	12	16	16	16	16	16	3	3	8	14	4	1	11	5	16	16	16	16	12	12	10	3	5	5	5	11	12	10	10	10	11
5 COULTHARD	16	16	16	16	16	12	12	12	14	14	10	7	14	5	16	12	12	12	16	0	3	11	11	11	11	11	11	11	11	11	5	5	5	5	5
3 MONTOYA	14	14	14	14	14	14	14	14	12	7	18	1	11	1	11	5	10	10	10	10	3	14	7	7	7	7	14	14	12	4	14	14	14	14	14
14 WEBBER	7	7	7	7	7	7	7	3	1	18	18	5	16	12	10	10	3	3	3	14	7	7	7	7	7	7	12	18	14	7	7	7	7	7
7 VILLENEUVE	3	3	3	3	3	3	3	3	3	10	19	19	11	1	16	3	3	14	14	14	7	1	1	1	1	1	8	14	7	17	17	1	1	1
16 ZONTA	18	18	10	10	10	10	10	10	10	11	11	5	16	3	14	14	7	7	7	1	16	16	16	16	16	16	7	7	7	17	1	1	18	18	18
18 HEIDFELD	10	10	18	18	18	18	18	18	1	5	5	12	14	14	7	7	1	1	1	16	12	12	12	12	12	12	12	1	17	1	18	18	17	17	17
15 KLIEN	15	15	15	15	15	15	15	15	19	16	16	16	19	7	18	18	18	18	18	18	18	18	18	18	18	18	18	19	1	19	19	19	19	19
19 GLOCK	19	19	17	17	17	17	17	17	1	15	12	12	12	7	19	19	19	19	19	19	19	19	19	19	19	19	19	17	19	16	19	20	21	21	21
20 BRUNI	17	17	19	19	19	19	19	19	12	17	17	17	7	19	19	19	19	19	19	17	17	17	17	17	17	17	19	21	21	21
10 SATO	21	21	1	1	1	19	1	19	19	17	1	21	21	21	21	21	21	21	21	20	21	21	21	21	21	21	21	20
21 BAUMGARTNER	20	20	21	21	21	21	21	21	21	20	20	20	20	20	20	20	20	20	20	20	20	20	20	20
1 M. SCHUMACHER	1	1	20	20	20	20	20	20	20	20	20

QUALIFYING

Sunny (track 39–40°C, air 29°C)

Pos.	Driver	Lap time	Sector 1	Sector 2	Sector 3
1	Rubens Barrichello	1m 34.012s	24.733s	27.777s	41.502s
2	Kimi Räikkönen	1m 34.178s	24.909s	27.949s	41.320s
3	Jenson Button	1m 34.295s	24.907s	28.076s	41.312s
4	Felipe Massa	1m 34.759s	24.697s	28.322s	41.730s
5	Ralf Schumacher	1m 34.891s	25.058s	28.248s	41.585s
6	Fernando Alonso	1m 34.917s	25.085s	28.097s	41.735s
7	Giancarlo Fisichella	1m 34.951s	24.985s	28.245s	41.721s
8	Olivier Panis	1m 34.975s	25.108s	28.168s	41.699s
9	Takuma Sato	1m 34.993s	24.904s	28.231s	41.858s
10	David Coulthard	1m 35.029s	24.932s	28.446s	41.651s
11	Juan Pablo Montoya	1m 35.245s	25.036s	28.407s	41.802s
12	Mark Webber	1m 35.286s	24.898s	28.473s	41.915s
13	Jacques Villeneuve	1m 35.384s	25.220s	28.425s	41.739s
14	Ricardo Zonta	1m 35.410s	25.154s	28.157s	42.099s
15	Nick Heidfeld	1m 36.507s	25.278s	28.844s	42.385s
16	Christian Klien	1m 36.535s	25.336s	28.799s	42.400s
17	Timo Glock	1m 37.140s	25.184s	28.983s	42.973s
18	Zsolt Baumgartner	1m 40.240s	26.166s	30.351s	43.691s
19	Michael Schumacher	No time	42.030s	34.522s	46.658s
20	Gianmaria Bruni	No time	36.897s	32.242s	44.567s

1	Michael Schumacher	F2004/239
2	Rubens Barrichello	F2004/240
	Spare	F2004/241
3	Juan Pablo Montoya	FW26/05
4	Ralf Schumaher	FW26/07
	Spare	FW26/06
5	David Coulthard	MP4/19B-03
6	Kimi Räikkönen	MP4/19B-01
	Spare	MP4/19B-02
7	Jacques Villeneuve	R24/08
8	Fernando Alonso	R24/07
	Spare	R24/03
9	Jenson Button	006/05
10	Takuma Sato	006/06
	Anthony Davidson	006/04
	Spare	006/04
11	Giancarlo Fisichella	C23/04
12	Felipe Massa	C23/03
	Spare	C23/02

14	Mark Webber	R5/05
15	Christian Klien	R5/06B
	Björn Wirdheim	R5/02
	Spare	R5/02
16	Ricardo Zonta	TF104/10B
17	Olivier Panis	TF104/09B
	Ryan Briscoe	TF104/11B
	Spare	TF104/11B
18	Nick Heidfeld	EJ-14/01
19	Timo Glock	EJ-14/02
	Robert Doornbos	EJ-14/03
	Spare	EJ-14/03
20	Gianmaria Bruni	PS04B/02
21	Zsolt Baumgartner	PS04B/04
	Bas Leinders	????
	Spare	????

Photograph: Darren Heath

PRACTICE 1 (FRIDAY)

Sunny, scattered clouds (track 37–35°C, air 27–26°C)

Pos.	Driver	Laps	Time
1	Anthony Davidson	22	1m 35.369s
2	Ralf Schumacher	13	1m 35.455s
3	Juan Pablo Montoya	13	1m 35.761s
4	Felipe Massa	12	1m 36.086s
5	Ryan Briscoe	21	1m 36.394s
6	Jenson Button	11	1m 36.475s
7	Rubens Barrichello	14	1m 36.660s
8	Fernando Alonso	15	1m 36.884s
9	Giancarlo Fisichella	9	1m 36.944s
10	Ricardo Zonta	16	1m 36.970s
11	Kimi Räikkönen	5	1m 37.102s
12	Björn Wirdheim	19	1m 37.142s
13	Olivier Panis	14	1m 37.191s
14	Jacques Villeneuve	20	1m 37.240s
15	Michael Schumacher	11	1m 37.300s
16	Takuma Sato	9	1m 37.438s
17	Timo Glock	15	1m 37.587s
18	David Coulthard	5	1m 37.976s
19	Nick Heidfeld	14	1m 38.132s
20	Christian Klien	15	1m 38.504s
21	Mark Webber	11	1m 38.761s
22	Gianmaria Bruni	13	1m 38.805s
23	Robert Doornbos	23	1m 39.244s
24	Bas Leinders	15	1m 39.529s
25	Zsolt Baumgartner	12	1m 42.795s

PRACTICE 2 (FRIDAY)

Sunny/cloudy (track 35–34°C, air 26–27°C)

Pos.	Driver	Laps	Time
1	Anthony Davidson	22	1m 33.289s
2	Jenson Button	19	1m 34.174s
3	Kimi Räikkönen	16	1m 34.289s
4	David Coulthard	15	1m 34.362s
5	Rubens Barrichello	21	1m 34.448s
6	Giancarlo Fisichella	23	1m 34.680s
7	Ralf Schumacher	23	1m 34.714s
8	Michael Schumacher	25	1m 34.776s
9	Ricardo Zonta	23	1m 34.868s
10	Olivier Panis	25	1m 34.870s
11	Ryan Briscoe	29	1m 34.881s
12	Felipe Massa	23	1m 34.959s
13	Fernando Alonso	27	1m 35.514s
14	Juan Pablo Montoya	22	1m 35.646s
15	Jacques Villeneuve	25	1m 35.851s
16	Mark Webber	22	1m 35.886s
17	Björn Wirdheim	19	1m 36.363s
18	Nick Heidfeld	19	1m 36.630s
19	Zsolt Baumgartner	15	1m 37.076s
20	Chrisitan Klien	25	1m 37.111s
21	Gianmaria Bruni	19	1m 37.431s
22	Timo Glock	15	1m 37.728s
23	Bas Leinders	18	1m 38.522s
24	Robert Doornbos	15	1m 39.051s
25	Takuma Sato	1	No time

PRACTICE 3 (SATURDAY)

Sunny, light wind (track 29–31°C, air 26–27°C)

Pos.	Driver	Laps	Time
1	Ralf Schumacher	7	1m 34.380s
2	Juan Pablo Montoya	7	1m 34.679s
3	Michael Schumacher	9	1m 34.844s
4	Rubens Barrichello	8	1m 34.854s
5	Giancarlo Fisichella	14	1m 35.049s
6	Kimi Räikkönen	5	1m 35.532s
7	Ricardo Zonta	8	1m 35.597s
8	Jenson Button	9	1m 35.660s
9	David Coulthard	5	1m 35.930s
10	Jacques Villeneuve	9	1m 35.965s
11	Mark Webber	6	1m 36.002s
12	Takuma Sato	13	1m 36.226s
13	Fernando Alonso	8	1m 36.243s
14	Felipe Massa	18	1m 36.539s
15	Olivier Panis	6	1m 36.623s
16	Christian Klien	4	1m 37.160s
17	Nick Heidfeld	10	1m 37.166s
18	Gianmaria Bruni	12	1m 37.533s
19	Zsolt Baumgartner	13	1m 37.552s
20	Timo Glock	11	1m 38.128s

PRACTICE 4 (SATURDAY)

Sunny (track 33–37°C, air 27–28°C)

Pos.	Driver	Laps	Time
1	Michael Schumacher	13	1m 33.448s
2	Rubens Barrichello	12	1m 33.796s
3	Kimi Räikkönen	11	1m 34.042s
4	Jenson Button	15	1m 34.233s
5	Giancarlo Fisichella	10	1m 34.286s
6	Nick Heidfeld	12	1m 34.404s
7	Juan Pablo Montoya	12	1m 34.458s
8	David Coulthard	10	1m 34.470s
9	Ricardo Zonta	19	1m 34.518s
10	Felipe Massa	12	1m 34.607s
11	Fernando Alonso	12	1m 34.627s
12	Ralf Schumacher	9	1m 34.769s
13	Takuma Sato	16	1m 35.155s
14	Olivier Panis	14	1m 35.211s
15	Jacques Villeneuve	12	1m 35.309s
16	Mark Webber	20	1m 35.354s
17	Christian Klien	17	1m 35.869s
18	Gianmaria Bruni	10	1m 36.748s
19	Timo Glock	14	1m 37.158s
20	Zsolt Baumgartner	9	1m 38.014s

9th: TAKUMA SATO BAR-Honda

7th: GIANCARLO FISICHELLA Sauber-Petronas

5th: RALF SCHUMACHER Williams-BMW

3rd: JENSON BUTTON BAR-Honda

Pole: RUBENS BARRICHELLO Ferrari

10th: DAVID COULTHARD McLaren-Mercedes

8th: OLIVIER PANIS Toyota

6th: FERNANDO ALONSO Renault

4th: FELIPE MASSA Sauber-Petronas

2nd: KIMI RÄIKKÖNEN McLaren-Mercedes

44	45	46	47	48	49	50	51	52	53	54	55	56	
2	2	2	2	2	2	2	2	2	2	2	2	2	1
9	9	9	9	9	9	9	9	9	9	9	9	9	2
6	6	6	6	6	6	6	6	6	6	6	6	6	3
8	8	8	8	8	8	8	8	8	8	8	8	4	4
12	3	3	3	3	3	3	3	3	3	3	3	3	5
3	10	10	10	10	10	10	10	10	10	10	10	10	6
10	11	11	11	11	11	11	11	11	11	11	11	11	7
11	12	12	12	12	12	12	12	12	12	12	12	12	8
5	5	5	5	5	5	5	5	5	5	5	5	5	
14	14	14	14	14	14	14	14	14	14	14	14		
7	7	7	7	7	7	7	7	7	7	7	7		
1	1	1	1	1	1	1	1	1	1	1	1		
18	18	18	18	18	18	18	18	18	18	18	18		
17	17	17	17	17	17	17	17	17	17	17	17		
19	19	19	19	19	19	19	19	19	19	19	19		
21	21	21	21	21	21	21	21	21	21				

Pit stop
One lap behind leader

POINTS: CONSTRUCTORS

1	Ferrari	244
2	BAR	105
3	Renault	96
4	Williams	64
5	McLaren	58
6	Sauber	32
7	Jaguar	10
8	Toyota	9
9	Jordan	5
10	Minardi	1

FOR THE RECORD

10 driver fastest laps in a season

Michael Schumacher

POINTS: DRIVERS

1	Michael Schumacher	136
2	Rubens Barrichello	108
3	Jenson Button	79
4	Fernando Alonso	50
5 =	Jarno Trulli	46
5 =	Juan Pablo Montoya	46
7	Kimi Räikkönen	34
8	Takuma Sato	26
9	David Coulthard	24
10	Giancarlo Fisichella	21
11	Ralf Schumacher	12
12	Felipe Massa	11
13	Mark Webber	7
14 =	Olivier Panis	6
14 =	Antonio Pizzonia	6
16 =	Christian Klien	3
16 =	Cristiano da Matta	3
16 =	Nick Heidfeld	3
19	Timo Glock	2
20	Zsolt Baumgartner	1

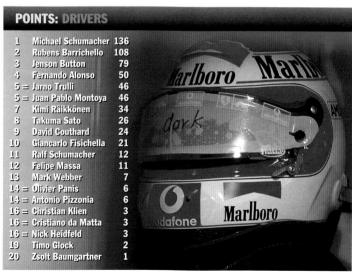

Photographs: Darren Heath

Above: The stands were packed with a sea of enthusiastic Takuma Sato fans.
Photograph: Darren Heath

Right: Back on top. Michael Schumacher reasserted his authority after three races without a win.
Photograph: Bryn Williams/crash.net

FIA F1 WORLD CHAMPIONSHIP • ROUND 17

JAPANESEGP
SUZUKA

Right: Ralf Schumacher took advantage of his late qualifying run to plant his Williams-BMW on the front row.
Photograph: Bryn Williams/crash.net

Above: Batten down the hatches. The Renault crew removes the pit-wall shelter.
Photograph: Bryn Williams/crash.net

Below: Olivier Panis, at his final grand prix of 2004, splashes through the murk during practice.
Photograph: Darren Heath

SUZUKA QUALIFYING

Usually at 1 pm on the Saturday of a race weekend, members of the grand prix circus are working at fever pitch as qualifying kicks off and the moment of truth arrives. At Suzuka, however, things were very different. The paddock resembled a post-apocalypse sci-fi movie: instead of the usual hustle and bustle, only a few hardy souls moved around in the driving rain.

Over in the Circuit Hotel, there was an unusual sight. After a morning spent in the bowling alley, Michael Schumacher, Rubens Barrichello, David Coulthard, Mark Webber, Olivier Panis, Giancarlo Fisichella, Felipe Massa, Christian Klien and Alex Wurz adjourned to the restaurant for a very unusual communal lunch. Later they would hire a local sports hall and enjoy an indoor football tournament, during which an off-duty Ross Brawn – usually pretty busy on Saturday afternoons – took a couple of spectacular tumbles.

Meanwhile, in the nearby city of Yokkaichi, mechanics and engineers from nearly every team wandered the streets, desperately trying to kill time. McDonald's proved an impromptu meeting point.

Yes folks, Suzuka was a strange weekend. The threat of a typhoon wrecking the circuit caused the unprecedented cancellation of a whole day's action, and led to the most intimate bonding session between a group of drivers since the infamous 1982 strike at Kyalami. The condensed schedule set up the most exciting qualifying session of the year, and became a fascinating experiment in how qualifying might be run in the future.

The action kicked off at 9 am on Sunday morning and, allowing for the second runs, that left barely three hours until the cars had to form up on the grid. With only stop-start wet running on Friday behind them, everyone had to wing it. And since the track was wet but drying at the start of the first session, circumstances provided a lifeline to those who had struggled in China and thus had earned the later pre-qualifying slots.

That first session was pure entertainment, as each driver had to find his own limits on the slippery track. Shanghai points scorers Rubens Barrichello, Jenson Button, Kimi Räikkönen, Fernando Alonso and Juan Pablo Montoya were the first to go out, and all suffered badly.

So who gained? After his awful race in Shanghai, Michael Schumacher was 12th in line, and having learned from what he'd seen, he went quickest. No serious contenders followed him until brother Ralf in 18th, but the Williams driver could manage only second fastest. The 20th and last out was Toyota newcomer Jarno Trulli, who made his point in great style by going top.

The track continued to dry through the second runs to the extent that grooved tyres became standard, but conditions were still marginal, and those who went early were still stuffed. After Montoya, Alonso and Räikkönen had shot their bolts, Button, running ninth, went fastest on 1m 35.157s. Barrichello appeared two slots later and seemed certain to take pole, only to slide frustratingly wide at the chicane.

'I knew I had to come with something special,' said Barrichello, 'and that was something special on my side because we know that our tyres are very good at any stage, but on damp conditions, are tough. At that time, the track was still very wet for me. I couldn't give up, I had to try.'

Then a spectacular 1m 34.897s from local hero Takuma Sato bumped Button down to second. Only five cars remained – who could beat the BAR driver? Not Olivier Panis, who hadn't even completed one flying lap in the wet on Friday. Then Mark Webber – who had put in a great first run – went fastest on 1m 34.571s. The Jaguar driver didn't stay on top for long, however, for Ralf Schumacher moved the target by going fastest on 1m 34.032s.

Now, all eyes were on Schumacher Sr. Barrichello had shown that it wasn't easy on Bridgestone's dry tyres, but despite a wobble at the start of his lap, the world champion easily stole pole on 1m 33.542s. Only Trulli remained, but this time it was asking a little much to beat the Ferrari star. The Italian had to settle for sixth.

With so much uncertainty, and so much potential for an upset, it seemed incredible that Michael Schumacher had actually benefited from his misery in China to take pole. It was clear that, barring a first-lap upset, nobody would be able to stop him.

'Looking back to China,' he admitted, 'I should be thankful for not having been so good because that's obviously made it possible for me to be where I am now.'

Ralf Schumacher's premature withdrawal in Shanghai had also played into his hands, much to the frustration of team-mate Montoya. Farther back, however, it was a grid that promised much, as Webber had claimed an opportunistic third ahead of Sato, Button, Trulli, Fisichella, Coulthard, Jacques Villeneuve and Panis.

The real victims of the weather were outside the top ten, Alonso, Räikkönen and Montoya filling 11th to 13th, while a frustrated Barrichello was back in 15th, aware that a hat-trick was unlikely. Massa, who had gone off at Spoon, dropped to the back, while Zsolt Baumgartner also fell off the road.

The teams may have been put under intense pressure in preparation for the race, but the change of schedule gave everyone food for thought. 'I think it was good,' said Flavio Briatore. 'There was nothing wrong with it, and the spectators enjoyed it. Normally, you arrive at 8 am and there's nothing to do. Friday should be a test day, and we should cancel some other tests. This is the way to go.'

'I thought it worked very well,' said an intrigued Max Mosley. 'It was nice for the public and it's a good start to the day. I'm sure all the teams are talking about it, and maybe we'll get feedback over the next few days.

IN the days leading up to Suzuka, there had been much talk of bad weather, so it was no surprise when Friday proved to be soaking wet. As the paddock began to appreciate that an impending typhoon was going to be rather more than just a heavy shower, it became obvious that, for once, the sport would have to give way to nature.

By 6 pm on Friday, it had been announced that the venue would be closed on Saturday, giving everyone an unexpected day off prior to qualifying on Sunday morning. In the event, the typhoon missed Suzuka by some 40 miles, but the damage it inflicted on Tokyo late on Saturday afternoon proved that the authorities had made a wise decision.

The situation created a highly unusual qualifying session that could have generated the most interesting grid of the year. Ironically, it favoured those who'd had bad races in China, and that meant none other than Michael Schumacher, who started from pole ahead of brother Ralf.

Of course, everyone was desperately short of dry set-up information, but in such circumstances there's one team you bet money on to have got its sums right. Not only that, but the world champion is usually in a class of his own at Suzuka, and with many of his most likely challengers way down the order, including team-mate Rubens Barrichello, the result seemed a foregone conclusion.

With the sun shining and the stands packed with Takuma Sato fans, Michael made a perfect start to slot in ahead of Ralf. Concerns about surprise third qualifier Mark Webber serving as a mobile chicane were allayed when the Jaguar stumbled off the line, and the BARs of Sato and Jenson Button surged past. Then the Brit swept around the outside of his team-mate into Turn One to claim third, causing Sato to edge on to the kerbs and lift briefly. It had been a forceful move from Button; in fact, he was heavier than Sato and was on two, rather than three, stops; by getting in front,

he'd made it impossible for the local hero to outrace him.

Running in tandem, the BARs could do nothing about the leaders. After just five laps, Michael Schumacher was 2.7s ahead of his brother, and a massive 9.1s clear of Button. Sato, Jarno Trulli (showing well on his first Toyota outing), Webber, David Coulthard and Giancarlo Fisichella completed an unlikely top eight, while Jacques Villeneuve led the tight-knit following group as Fernando Alonso, Kimi Räikkönen, Juan Pablo Montoya and Barrichello struggled to make up ground from their lowly qualifying positions.

Coulthard was enjoying his best run for some time, although he was not entirely happy: 'It was frustrating, because I was slow in a straight line. I passed Webber a couple of times on the straight, and then he pulled in front of me before braking. It's disappointing when that happens.'

On lap seven, Button let Sato into third, and finally the Japanese driver was able to make use of his lighter load, although he didn't pull very far ahead. Meanwhile, Ralf Schumacher's respectable pace was explained in part when he kicked off the pit-stop sequence as early as lap nine, leaving Sato in second. The local ace was a massive 18.5s down on the leader when he came in on lap 12. Michael Schumacher followed a lap later, and was so far ahead of Button (who had yet to stop) that he was able to resume still in front. Quick laps as his tank emptied had also left early stopper Ralf Schumacher – who got caught in traffic – far behind. As far as a lead battle was concerned, this race was going to be a dead loss.

'I didn't really have any tough competition,' Michael Schumacher admitted later, with considerable understatement. 'Although in the beginning of the race, we weren't sure if Ralf was on two stops and so on. So you had to fight until the pit stops were settled down, and then we could sort of control the race.'

Button pitted for the first time on lap 15, resuming in fourth just behind Sato. But he'd taken on more fuel, and since he had only

DIARY

Red Bull continues negotiations for the acquisition of the Jaguar F1 team.

Richard Lyons fails in bid to secure a Jordan F1 drive.

Ron Dennis admits it is possible that David Coulthard may have a future role within the McLaren empire.

Below: Under sunny skies, Michael Schumacher grabs the advantage at the start of the Japanese Grand Prix, ahead of younger brother Ralf on his penultimate outing for Williams.
Photograph: Darren Heath

one stop to come to the two of his team-mate, he was well set. Meanwhile, Webber was out of the picture, the Aussie being unable to continue after scalding hot radiator air found its way into the cockpit.

There was plenty to watch farther back as the big names edged toward the points and almost tripped over each other in the process. Barrichello spent a long time behind Montoya, until at the end of lap 22, he finally swept past on the pit straight. He managed to take Trulli as well in a tight move at Turn One.

'I was stuck behind Villeneuve, who was going so slow, and then I lost time behind Trulli and Montoya,' explained Barrichello. 'Juan is a difficult one. He goes to overtake everyone, but it's so damn difficult to pass him. He doesn't want to be overtaken! He was out of shape so many times. He made sure he wouldn't make it easy. I had to keep on trying. At least, I made it through and, on the same straight, I made it past Trulli as well. I don't think he was expecting me, but luckily we didn't touch, because it was very close.'

Out in front, Michael Schumacher was on a demonstration run; memories of his awful day in China were erased completely. He pitted for the second time on lap 26 and comfortably retained his lead.

Despite so many quick cars being mired in the pack, the race passed with surprisingly few incidents until the end of lap 38. Barrichello had reeled in fifth-placed Coulthard at such a rate that at the first opportunity, he felt justified in making a lunge down the inside into the chicane. The Scot didn't think the Ferrari was close enough to even try and turned in as usual.

'I came quite quickly out of 130R and basically I was able to go for the inside,' said the Ferrari driver. 'I think the last time he looked behind was 130R, because he thought there would have been no possibility. But I was coming very fast, and I would have made it stick. I was only a car-and-a-half, a car actually, behind him. I went to the inside, and I got him by surprise.'

'It was like the Senna/Prost incident a few years ago,' commented Coulthard. 'It's all very well if you can get your car in the inside, but there's a corner! If I wasn't there, he wouldn't have made the corner. He wanted to catch me by surprise. He knew it was optimistic, and it didn't work out.'

The result was heavy wheel-on-wheel contact, and after bouncing across the dirt, both cars crawled into the pits to retire. It was a bitter disappointment for Coulthard, who had outrun his team-mate and desperately needed a good result.

When their crippled number-two car appeared in the pit lane, the Ferrari guys had to act quickly, since Michael Schumacher was expected to make his final stop on lap 39. At that stage, his lead on brother Ralf had grown to 23.1s, but over the remaining 14 laps, he allowed his advantage to drop to a still very comfortable 14s. His 13th win of the year may have been just another for the world champion, but Suzuka is the race that Bridgestone prizes above all others.

'It was obviously a very different and strange Sunday for us,' said Schumacher. 'It was exciting in one way because there was no free practice on Saturday, and it was straight into qualifying this morning. In a way, I like it because it suits my style, but on the other side, it put a lot of pressure to all the mechanics and everybody in the team. But anyway, we got it, we got the pole position and the win, and Rubens got the fastest lap. That proves how good we were, and we did it for Bridgestone.'

It was evident that Ralf Schumacher was back on form on only the second outing since his accident, and his petulant retirement in China was also forgotten. 'We maybe pitted a little earlier than we needed to considering the pace we were able to go,' he opined. 'But it still worked out. It was pretty hard because I had some traffic in the race, but luckily they had to pit a bit earlier and then I could pull out the gap I needed again.'

Sato made his third and final stop on lap 41, allowing Button to slip into third place. In the late stages, the on-board camera showed 'Taku' supporting his helmet with his hand, the result of aggravating a neck injury. 'It was a tough one, but I did my best,' he said. 'I struggled a little bit for grip. We took different strategies, but at the end of the day, it was a great result for the team.'

Honda would have preferred to see its man please the huge crowd by taking the podium slot, but the 3-4 result all but guaranteed BAR second place in the constructors' championship.

It was small comfort on a bad day for Renault that Alonso was able to take advantage of the Barrichello/Coulthard incident to follow the BARs home. 'To be fifth after starting 11th was the maximum for today,' he said. 'I was constantly pushing.'

A two-stop strategy saw Räikkönen jump up the order in the late stages, the McLaren driver finishing just 2s shy of Alonso, while Montoya and Fisichella completed the points scorers. Massa enjoyed himself by charging from the back of the grid to ninth, the Brazilian just getting ahead of his future team-mate. Villeneuve found the going even tougher than he'd expected, severe understeer leaving him drained by the flag.

Villeneuve did at least beat the man he had replaced at Renault, Trulli fading after a strong early stint. Christian Klien took a lacklustre 12th for Jaguar, only just outpacing Nick Heidfeld's Jordan, while a disappointing 14th went to Olivier Panis on his final outing for Toyota. It was not the way the Frenchman would have wanted to bow out.

In the end, the mixed-up qualifying that had promised so much had served only to make life easier for Michael Schumacher. His team-mate was left to rue the mishap that had condemned him to the lower reaches of the grid. 'On the very same track as Michael, I was able to have a good car and go as fast as him,' said Barrichello. 'If I had started from pole or the front row, it would have been a completely different story. The fastest lap here will say that I had the car and chances to win the race.'

Facing page, top: Takuma Sato just missed out on a podium place in his home grand prix.

Facing page, bottom: Jacques Villeneuve again failed to make much of an impression in the Renault.

Below: Jarno Trulli made his debut for Toyota, but the race delivered less than he had expected.

Photographs: Darren Heath

TRULLI AT TOYOTA

It seems inconceivable that a man who took two pole positions in 2004 and beat all comers to win the Monaco GP should be regarded as liability, but following a series of disappointing outings, Jarno Trulli was ousted from Renault after the Monza race.

The frustrated Italian had claimed that he found the car undrivable, while others were convinced that Flavio Briatore's estranged protégé had been underperforming deliberately after losing his drive for 2005. That seemed unlikely given Trulli's straightforward nature, and the damage that his reputation suffered.

At least he had a soft landing. While the deal hadn't been announced, he had already signed for Toyota, and soon saw the benefits of escaping from his miserable situation at Renault. Just four days after Monza, Trulli was in the TF104B at Silverstone, although lack of time to make him comfortable meant that the test was inconclusive. Subsequently, he skipped China, but after a proper run at Jerez, the team announced that he would take part in the last two races, replacing Ricardo Zonta in Japan, and the retiring Olivier Panis in Brazil.

At Suzuka, Trulli impressed his new team and did much to restore his reputation in the paddock by setting the fastest time in first qualifying. As a replacement driver, he had the advantage of being last out on a drying track. Nevertheless, it was an impressive achievement given his overall lack of time in the car. He was sixth in final qualifying and ran well in the early laps, but his pace faded in the race – as had been expected – when the tyre performance dropped off a few laps into each stint. Eventually, he finished 11th.

'He doesn't know the car like everyone else and hasn't been driving it all year,' said technical director Mike Gascoyne. 'We sent the bloke out in the wet for his first ever lap on intermediates. Okay, he had the conditions in his favour, but I still think it was a pretty impressive effort. It was a good lift for the whole team when you've got someone doing that.'

Trulli admitted that Japan had been his most enjoyable grand prix meeting for several months, and he was more than happy to be in an environment where he felt wanted. During the first part of the race, he had run well ahead of the Renaults, but he denied that he had had any thoughts about proving a point to his former team.

'It was just a race weekend, and I did my job,' he said. 'I'm not here to prove anything, I was here because I've been asked to come. I know a lot of people are into this matter, but I didn't know anything, and anyway I finished behind both Renaults, and I didn't really care. I'm here to look after me and my team, and I believe I've done my best.'

Trulli was well aware that, if nothing else, he had earned himself a valuable head start on future team-mate Ralf Schumacher: 'After three days testing in Jerez, we said, "Okay, let's take the risk." It's part of our job. Sitting at home wouldn't have helped, while here I finished the race, showed some good performance and did some good things. I met a lot of people from the team and got to know them, and it was good experience. I've gained a lot of time.'

While Suzuka was a fresh start for Trulli, it was also the end of the line for team-mate Panis, one race earlier than he had intended. After a decade in the sport, the Frenchman endured a low-key outing, finishing 14th. It was a sad way to end a career that, at times, had promised so much more.

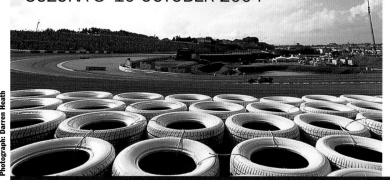

FIA F1 WORLD CHAMPIONSHIP • ROUND 17

FUJI TELEVISION
JAPANESE GRAND PRIX
SUZUKA 8–10 OCTOBER 2004

Photograph: Darren Heath

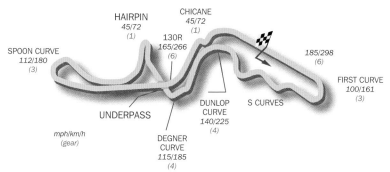

SUZUKA RACING CIRCUIT

HAIRPIN 45/72 (1)

CHICANE 45/72 (1)

130R 165/266 (6)

185/298 (6)

SPOON CURVE 112/180 (3)

FIRST CURVE 100/161 (3)

UNDERPASS

DUNLOP CURVE 140/225 (4)

S CURVES

mph/km/h (gear)

DEGNER CURVE 115/185 (4)

CIRCUIT LENGTH: 3.617 miles/5.821 km

RACE DISTANCE: 53 laps, 191.117 miles/307.573 km   RACE WEATHER: Sunny and dry (track 32–34°C, air 28°C)

Pos.	Driver	Nat.	No.	Entrant	Car/Engine	Tyres	Laps	Time/Retirement	Speed (mph/km/h)	Gap to leader	Fastest race lap	
1	Michael Schumacher	D	1	Scuderia Ferrari Marlboro	Ferrari F2004-052 V10	B	53	1h 24m 26.985s	135.784/218.524		1m 32.796s	41
2	Ralf Schumacher	D	4	BMW WilliamsF1 Team	Williams FW26-BMW P84 V10	M	53	1h 24m 41.083s	135.408/217.918	+14.098s	1m 33.467s	23
3	Jenson Button	GB	9	Lucky Strike BAR Honda	BAR 006-Honda RA004E V10	M	53	1h 24m 46.647s	135.260/217.680	+19.662s	1m 33.819s	33
4	Takuma Sato	J	10	Lucky Strike BAR Honda	BAR 006-Honda RA004E V10	M	53	1h 24m 58.766s	134.938/217.162	+31.781s	1m 33.742s	28
5	Fernando Alonso	E	8	Mild Seven Renault F1 Team	Renault R24-RS4 V10	M	53	1h 25m 04.752s	134.780/216.908	+37.767s	1m 34.279s	29
6	Kimi Räikkönen	FIN	6	West McLaren Mercedes	McLaren MP4/19B-Mercedes F0110P V10	M	53	1h 25m 06.347s	134.738/216.840	+39.362s	1m 33.920s	35
7	Juan Pablo Montoya	COL	3	BMW WilliamsF1 Team	Williams FW26-BMW P84 V10	M	53	1h 25m 22.332s	134.317/216.163	+55.347s	1m 33.779s	30
8	Giancarlo Fisichella	I	11	Sauber Petronas	Sauber C23-Petronas 04 V10	B	53	1h 25m 23.261s	134.293/216.124	+56.276s	1m 33.850s	44
9	Felipe Massa	BR	12	Sauber Petronas	Sauber C23-Petronas 04 V10	B	53	1h 25m 56.641s	134.666/216.725	+89.656s	1m 33.64s	40
10	Jacques Villeneuve	CDN	7	Mild Seven Renault F1 Team	Renault R24-RS4 V10	M	52			+1 lap	1m 35.290s	28
11	Jarno Trulli	I	16	Panasonic Toyota Racing	Toyota TF104B- RVX04 V10	M	52			+1 lap	1m 34.626s	52
12	Christian Klien	A	15	Jaguar Racing	Jaguar R5-Cosworth CR6 V10	M	52			+1 lap	1m 35.261s	32
13	Nick Heidfeld	D	18	Jordan Ford	Jordan EJ-14-Cosworth RS V10	B	52			+1 lap	1m 35.524s	25
14	Olivier Panis	F	17	Panasonic Toyota Racing	Toyota TF104B-RVX04 V10	M	51			+2laps	1m 34.438s	11
15	Timo Glock	D	19	Jordan Ford	Jordan EJ-14-Cosworth RS V10	B	51			+2laps	1m 36.667s	14
16	Gianmaria Bruni	I	20	European Minardi Cosworth	Minardi PS04B-Cosworth CR3 V10	B	50			+3 laps	1m 39.352s	27
	Zsolt Baumgartner	H	21	European Minardi Cosworth	Minardi PS04B-Cosworth CR3 V10	B	41	Spun off			1m 39.434s	26
	David Coulthard	GB	5	West McLaren Mercedes	McLaren MP4/19B-Mercedes F0110P V10	M	38	Collision with RB			1m 33.917s	14
	Rubens Barrichello	BR	2	Scuderia Ferrari Marlboro	Ferrari F2004-052 V10	B	38	Collision with DC			1m 32.730s	30
	Mark Webber	AUS	14	Jaguar Racing	Jaguar R5-Cosworth CR6 V10	M	20	Cockpit overheating			1m 34.229s	13

All results and data © FOM 2004

Fastest lap: Rubens Barrichello, on lap 30, 1m 32.730s, 140.082 mph/225.441 km/h (record for new track).

Previous lap record: Ralf Schumacher (Williams FW25-BMW P83 V10), 1m 33.069s, 139.069 mph/223.805 km/h (2003).

19th: FELIPE MASSA Sauber-Petronas

17th: TIMO GLOCK Jordan-Cosworth

15th: RUBENS BARRICHELLO Ferrari

13th: JUAN PABLO MONTOYA Williams-BMW

11th: FERNANDO ALONSO Renault

20th: ZSOLT BAUMGARTNER Minardi-Cosworth

18th: GIANMARIA BRUNI Minardi-Cosworth

16th: NICK HEIDFELD Jordan-Cosworth

14th: CHRISTIAN KLIEN Jaguar-Cosworth

12th: KIMI RÄIKKÖNEN McLaren-Mercedes

Grid order	1	2	3	4	5	6	7	8	9	10	11	12	13	14	15	16	17	18	19	20	21	22	23	24	25	26	27	28	29	30	31	32	33	34	35	36	37	38	39	40	4
1 M. SCHUMACHER	1	1	1	1	1	1	1	1	1	1	1	1	1	1	1	1	1	1	1	1	1	1	1	1	1	1	1	1	1	1	1	1	1	1	1	1	1	1	1	1	1
4 R. SCHUMACHER	4	4	4	4	4	4	4	4	10	10	9	9	9	9	4	4	4	4	4	4	4	4	10	10	9	9	9	9	9	9	9	9	9	4	4	4	4	10			
14 WEBBER	9	9	9	9	9	9	10	10	9	9	10	5	5	5	10	10	10	10	10	10	10	10	9	9	5	5	5	5	4	4	4	4	10	10	10	10	4	1			
10 SATO	10	10	10	10	10	10	9	9	16	16	5	8	4	4	9	9	9	9	9	9	9	9	5	5	4	4	4	4	5	8	10	10	9	9	9	9	9	9			
9 BUTTON	16	16	16	16	16	16	16	16	5	5	8	4	8	10	5	5	5	5	5	5	5	4	4	8	8	8	8	8	10	5	5	5	5	8	8	8					
16 TRULLI	14	14	14	14	14	14	14	14	11	4	10	10	7	8	8	8	8	8	8	8	8	8	10	10	10	10	10	6	6	2	2	3	3	3							
11 FISICHELLA	5	5	5	5	5	5	5	5	11	8	16	7	7	15	16	16	16	16	16	16	16	2	2	2	2	2	6	6	6	8	5	11	11								
5 COULTHARD	7	7	11	11	11	11	11	11	8	4	11	6	8	15	14	3	3	3	2	16	16	11	11	3	3	2	2	2	2	8	8	3	11	6	6						
7 VILLENEUVE	11	11	7	7	7	7	8	8	4	14	7	15	15	16	14	3	2	2	3	11	11	3	3	11	6	7	7	7	3	3	11	6	7	7							
17 PANIS	8	8	8	8	8	7	7	7	6	16	16	11	2	11	11	11	11	3	3	16	7	7	7	3	3	3	11	11	11	6	2	12	12	1							
8 ALONSO	6	6	6	6	6	6	3	3	6	2	11	11	14	2	11	6	6	6	6	6	6	12	7	11	11	11	11	11	7	16	16	12	12	16	16	1					
6 RÄIKKÖNEN	3	3	3	3	3	3	6	6	2	18	14	14	3	11	6	7	7	12	12	12	12	12	16	16	16	16	16	16	16	12	18	16	12	16	16	1					
3 MONTOYA	2	17	17	17	2	2	2	2	2	3	15	3	3	2	6	7	12	12	12	12	7	16	16	12	12	12	12	7	7	7	15	18	18	1							
15 KLIEN	17	2	2	2	17	12	12	12	12	14	2	2	6	7	12	18	18	18	18	18	15	15	15	15	15	15	7	7	7	15	18	18	1								
2 BARRICHELLO	18	18	18	18	18	12	17	18	18	3	17	12	12	17	15	15	15	15	15	15	15	15	15	15	15	15	15	15	15	19	19	19	1								
18 HEIDFELD	15	15	15	12	12	18	18	17	15	17	17	17	17	19	17	17	17	17	17	17	17	17	17	17	17	17	17	17	17	17	17	20	20	2							
19 GLOCK	19	19	12	15	15	15	15	15	19	12	18	18	14	19	19	17	19	19	19	19	19	19	19	19	19	19	19	19	19	19	21	21	2								
20 BRUNI	12	12	19	19	19	19	19	20	20	19	14	14	20	20	20	20	20	20	20	20	20	20	20	20	20	20	20	20	20	20											
12 MASSA	20	20	20	20	20	20	20	20	21	21	21	21	20	20	20	21	21	21	21	21	21	21	21	21	21	21	21	21	21												
21 BAUMGARTNER	21	21	21	21	21	21	21	21	20	20	20	20	21	21	21																										

QUALIFYING (SUNDAY MORNING)
Wet, drying (track 23–30°C, air 24–26°C)

Pos.	Driver	Lap time	Sector 1	Sector 2	Sector 3
1	Michael Schumacher	1m 33.542s	31.677s	41.741s	20.124s
2	Ralf Schumacher	1m 34.032s	31.889s	41.536s	20.607s
3	Mark Webber	1m 34.571s	32.215s	42.035s	20.321s
4	Takuma Sato	1m 34.897s	32.141s	42.009s	20.747s
5	Jenson Button	1m 35.157s	32.632s	41.722s	20.803s
6	Jarno Trulli	1m 35.213s	32.514s	42.267s	20.432s
7	Giancarlo Fisichella	1m 36.136s	32.839s	42.292s	21.005s
8	David Coulthard	1m 36.156s	33.159s	42.593s	20.404s
9	Jacques Villeneuve	1m 36.274s	32.805s	42.657s	20.812s
10	Olivier Panis	1m 36.420s	32.393s	42.884s	21.143s
11	Fernando Alonso	1m 36.663s	33.602s	42.181s	20.880s
12	Kimi Räikkönen	1m 36.820s	33.532s	42.308s	20.980s
13	Juan Pablo Montoya	1m 37.653s	33.872s	42.545s	21.236s
14	Christian Klien	1m 38.258s	34.259s	42.819s	21.180s
15	Rubens Barrichello	1m 38.637s	32.980s	42.116s	22.690s
16	Nick Heidfeld	1m 41.953s	35.062s	45.030s	21.861s
17	Timo Glock	1m 43.533s	35.177s	46.429s	21.520s
18	Gianmaria Bruni	1m 48.069s	37.613s	46.985s	21.890s
19	Felipe Massa	No time	34.386s	45.860s	22.849s
20	Zsolt Baumgartner	No time	–	–	–

PRACTICE 1 (FRIDAY)
Heavy rain (track 17–18°C, air 18–19°C)

Pos.	Driver	Laps	Time
1	Michael Schumacher	5	1m 47.906s
2	Giancarlo Fisichella	8	1m 48.362s
3	Rubens Barrichello	4	1m 49.846s
4	Jenson Button	5	1m 49.937s
5	Nick Heidfeld	7	1m 51.438s
6	Kimi Räikkönen	5	1m 51.530s
7	Timo Glock	8	1m 52.602s
8	Juan Pablo Montoya	4	1m 53.517s
9	Robert Doornbos	10	1m 53.603s
10	Fernando Alonso	4	1m 54.012s
11	Bas Leinders	10	1m 55.455s
12	Ralf Schumacher	5	1m 55.632s
13	Jacques Villeneuve	5	1m 57.547s
14	Jarno Trulli	10	1m 58.351s
15	Anthony Davidson	4	2m 00.712s
16	Gianmaria Bruni	5	2m 02.825s
17	Zsolt Baumgartner	7	2m 03.955s
18	Olivier Panis	1	No time
19	Felipe Massa	3	No time
20	Mark Webber	2	No time
21	Christian Klien	3	No time
22	Takuma Sato	1	No time
23	David Coulthard	3	No time

PRACTICE 2 (FRIDAY)
Heavy rain (track 16–17°C, air 17–18°C)

Pos.	Driver	Laps	Time
1	Michael Schumacher	5	1m 45.388s
2	Giancarlo Fisichella	4	1m 46.102s
3	Kimi Räikkönen	5	1m 46.749s
4	Rubens Barrichello	5	1m 46.874s
5	David Coulthard	7	1m 48.033s
6	Timo Glock	8	1m 49.277s
7	Nick Heidfeld	4	1m 49.286s
8	Takuma Sato	6	1m 49.370s
9	Anthony Davidson	12	1m 49.598s
10	Jacques Villeneuve	8	1m 49.672s
11	Fernando Alonso	7	1m 49.712s
12	Ralf Schumacher	4	1m 49.736s
13	Juan Pablo Montoya	3	1m 50.060s
14	Jarno Trulli	7	1m 50.386s
15	Mark Webber	9	1m 50.666s
16	Robert Doornbos	11	1m 51.007s
17	Christian Klien	9	1m 52.232s
18	Bas Leinders	8	1m 52.942s
19	Gianmaria Bruni	6	1m 53.194s
20	Jenson Button	3	1m 53.482s
21	Zsolt Baumgartner	8	1m 54.703s
22	Felipe Massa	2	No time
23	Olivier Panis	1	No time

PRACTICE 3 (SATURDAY)
CANCELLED

PRACTICE 4 (SATURDAY)
CANCELLED

1	Michael Schumacher	F2004/241
2	Rubens Barrichello	F2004/240
	Spare	F2004/239
3	Juan Pablo Montoya	FW26/05
4	Ralf Schumaher	FW26/07
	Spare	FW26/06
5	David Coulthard	MP4/19B-03
6	Kimi Räikkönen	MP4/19B-01
	Spare	MP4/19B-02
7	Jacques Villeneuve	R24/08
8	Fernando Alonso	R24/07
	Spare	R24/03
9	Jenson Button	006/05
10	Takuma Sato	006/06
	Anthony Davidson	006/04
	Spare	006/04
11	Giancarlo Fisichella	C23/04
12	Felipe Massa	C23/03
	Spare	C23/02
14	Mark Webber	R5/6B
15	Christian Klien	R5/1
	Björn Wirdheim	R5/2
	Spare	R5/2
16	Jarno Trulli	TF104/10B
17	Olivier Panis	TF104/09B
	Spare	TF104/11B
18	Nick Heidfeld	EJ-14/03
19	Timo Glock	EJ-14/02
	Robert Doornbos	EJ-14/01
	Spare	EJ-14/01
20	Gianmaria Bruni	PS04B/02
21	Zsolt Baumgartner	PS04B/04
	Bas Leinders	PS04B/03
	Spare	PS04B/03

9th: JACQUES VILLENEUVE Renault

7th: GIANCARLO FISICHELLA Sauber-Petronas

5th: JENSON BUTTON BAR-Honda

3rd: MARK WEBBER Jaguar-Cosworth

Pole: MICHAEL SCHUMACHER Ferrari

10th: OLIVIER PANIS Toyota

8th: DAVID COULTHARD McLaren-Mercedes

6th: JARNO TRULLI Toyota

4th: TAKUMA SATO BAR-Honda

2nd: RALF SCHUMACHER Williams-BMW

42	43	44	45	46	47	48	49	50	51	52	53	
1	1	1	1	1	1	1	1	1	1	1	1	1
4	4	4	4	4	4	4	4	4	4	4	4	2
9	9	9	9	9	9	9	9	9	9	9	9	3
10	10	10	10	10	10	10	10	10	10	10	10	4
8	8	8	8	8	8	8	8	8	8	8	8	5
6	6	6	6	6	6	6	6	6	6	6	6	6
3	3	3	3	3	3	3	3	3	3	3	3	7
11	11	11	11	11	11	11	11	11	11	11	11	8
7	7	7	7	7	7	7	12	12	12	12	12	
12	12	12	12	12	12	12	7	7	7	7		
16	16	16	16	16	16	16	16	16	16	16		
15	15	15	15	15	15	15	15	15	15	15		
18	18	18	18	18	18	18	18	18	18	18		
17	17	17	17	17	17	17	17	17	17			
19	19	19	19	19	19	19	19	19	19			
20	20	20	20	20	20	20	20	20				

Pit stop
One lap behind leader

FOR THE RECORD

one hundred grands prix
B·A·R

100 grand prix starts
BAR

50 grand prix starts
Fernando Alonso
Toyota

POINTS: CONSTRUCTORS

1	Ferrari	254
2	BAR	116
3	Renault	100
4	Williams	74
5	McLaren	61
6	Sauber	33
7	Jaguar	10
8	Toyota	9
9	Jordan	5
10	Minardi	1

POINTS: DRIVERS

1	Michael Schumacher	146
2	Rubens Barrichello	108
3	Jenson Button	85
4	Fernando Alonso	54
5	Juan Pablo Montoya	48
6	Jarno Trulli	46
7	Kimi Räikkönen	37
8	Takuma Sato	31
9	David Coulthard	24
10	Giancarlo Fisichella	22
11	Ralf Schumacher	20
12	Felipe Massa	11
13	Mark Webber	7
14 =	Olivier Panis	6
14 =	Antonio Pizzonia	6
16 =	Christian Klien	3
16 =	Cristiano da Matta	3
16 =	Nick Heidfeld	3
19	Timo Glock	2
20	Zsolt Baumgartner	1

Rubens Barrichello and Kimi Räikkönen
take the lead at the start of the
Brazilian GP, while (right) Juan Pablo
Montoya and Felipe Massa try to
outdrag each other.
Photograph: Darren Heath

FIA F1 WORLD CHAMPIONSHIP • ROUND 18
BRAZILIANGP
INTERLAGOS

Right: Interlagos was David Coulthard's final grand prix for McLaren.

Centre right: Schumacher's badly rumpled Ferrari after its shunt in practice.

Far right: Paul Stoddart, Ian Phillips and Bernie Ecclestone brew up some more F1 political moves.

Below: Felipe Massa drove impressively for Sauber in his home grand prix.

Photographs: Darren Heath

COST CUTTING PLANS IRK FERRARI

Embarrassingly, Ferrari team principal Jean Todt was put on the spot at Interlagos when he was ambushed by the other nine F1 teams, who announced that they had agreed to a package of plans that would drastically reduce the sport's costs from the start of the 2005 season.

During two days of highly charged debate, the penny finally seemed to have dropped that the sport simply couldn't continue spending at its current rate. Even supposedly well-heeled teams, such as McLaren Mercedes and BMW Williams, joined in the call, but Ferrari declined to sign.

The agreement included the proposal that F1 commercial rights holder Bernie Ecclestone negotiate with both Michelin and Bridgestone a substantial reduction, if not a total ban, on tyre testing. It was suggested that car testing be limited to ten days each year, with two free practice sessions lasting for two hours on the Friday at future grands prix. This would complement the already agreed revised 2005 format of two qualifying sessions, one on Saturday and the other on Sunday morning.

The official communiqué concluded, 'While the above measures represent a significant step forward we, the undersigned teams, feel this is only the first move towards achieving the goal of reducing the necessity to spend enormous sums of money in order to be competitive in F1. Such a course of action will ensure the continuing long-term health and prosperity of the sport and its participants.'

The document had even been signed by Peter Sauber, despite the fact that the Swiss team principal was closely aligned with the Ferrari team through his long-standing engine supply contract.

Cleverly, the proposals had been linked with Bernie Ecclestone's desire to see a 19-race calendar. Furthermore, if the cost cutting rules were introduced, there would be no problem in the teams attending the French and British grands prix, both of which generate financial difficulties.

Todt made it clear, however, that Ferrari would not be intimidated into signing. He indicated his willingness to prepare a more global proposal that would lean in the direction of cutting costs, although a series of measures – one engine to last two weekends for example – had been approved already by the F1 Commission for 2005.

A Ferrari insider commented, 'Regarding Mr Ecclestone's manoeuvre to put Ferrari in a corner and to make GPWC split, I have to say – off the record – that he did not succeed. The link between the fate of Silverstone and Magny-Cours and the cost cutting is clearly specious, and used as an excuse to divert the attention of the public opinion far away from his own responsibilities.'

By that, the Ferrari man was referring to the fact that there had been no mention of Ecclestone carving off a bigger share of the commercial-rights cake for the teams. Not yet, at least.

INTERLAGOS QUALIFYING

In China a month earlier, qualifying (and hence the race) had been turned on its head when Michael Schumacher had spun off on the very last run. In Brazil, the upset happened rather earlier, for even before the session started, we knew that the world champion would be taking a ten-place penalty.

In the closing minutes of Saturday morning's second timed practice session, Schumacher's Ferrari had bobbled on the bumps at the tricky right-hander behind the pits. As he applied opposite lock, the car had flicked suddenly in the opposite direction and spun across the asphalt run-off at an awkward angle. He was unable to avoid a heavy right rear impact with the tyre wall; the car bounced up into the air and landed hard, then an oil fire briefly ignited at the rear.

The session was stopped, and the driver's grim expression as he examined the wreckage – captured by the roll-bar TV camera – told the story. When the car arrived back in the pits, Ross Brawn took one look at the crushed exhausts and coating of extinguisher dust, and made the inevitable call. Not only would Michael have to transfer to the spare chassis, he would require a fresh V10 as well. And that, of course, meant a penalty.

As a result, a lot of people went into the afternoon session thinking that they had a serious chance, no one more so than Rubens Barrichello. Even better, following his shunt in Japan, he had the third-to-last slot in pre-qualifying and, thus, was pretty well set.

Michael Schumacher had the double disadvantage of being first out in a car he hadn't yet run. Nevertheless, his time survived assaults from brother Ralf, Jenson Button, Takuma Sato, Fernando Alonso and Kimi Räikkönen before it was finally beaten by seventh runner Juan Pablo Montoya. Then Felipe Massa caused an upset by taking second for Sauber, but everyone was waiting for his countryman, Barrichello. Sure enough, Rubinho delighted the partisan crowds by going quicker than Montoya on 1m 09.822s, securing the last slot in qualifying proper.

When it mattered, Mark Webber, Alonso and Button took turns to hold the top spot before Räikkönen nabbed it with a 1m 10.892s, despite a couple of oversteering moments. David Coulthard, Sato and Ralf Schumacher couldn't beat the Finn's time. And then came Michael Schumacher.

The world champion was caught between a rock and a hard place,

saddled with the penalty, but nevertheless forced to run with an unwieldy, high fuel load. It would be the only means by which he could make his way through the pack, whether he started 11th or 20th. It was not a tidy run, and he managed only fifth on 1m 11.386s. In reality, of course, that was 15th, and there were still three drivers to come.

Massa was the first of them, and he stunned everyone by slipping into second on 1m 10.922s, between Räikkönen and Button. Then Montoya went ahead of the Finn to secure top spot with 1m 10.850s, despite admitting to being a little conservative on the brakes for the first turn.

That left only Barrichello to carry the hopes and dreams of his fellow Paulistas. It was pure theatre and, as in 2003, he didn't disappoint the fans, putting in a storming lap to guarantee pole with 1m 10.646s.

'As I went across the line and saw that I was on pole, my legs were very numb,' he said afterwards. 'It was immense pressure, because if you make a mistake now, they would probably come down out of the grandstands and kill you!'

With Montoya, Räikkönen, Massa and Button lined up behind the Ferrari, there was a different car in each of the top five spots, although it seemed more than likely that the Sauber driver had run a low fuel load and wouldn't be a serious contender. However, the first two appeared to be genuine threats, while Button, who had made a mistake in S2, could not be ignored. There was a feeling in the Michelin camp that Ferrari and Bridgestone really could be beaten.

'It's going to be exciting,' said the Colombian. 'Hopefully, I can get a good start and we can keep up with them. Normally, they're very quick, but my car has been feeling good here and we should be really strong.'

Sato and Ralf Schumacher were sixth and seventh; after Michael Schumacher had dropped back from his eighth place, Alonso, Trulli and Fisichella completed an intriguing top ten. Webber was 11th on Jaguar's final outing, while Coulthard and Villeneuve had little to cheer about in 12th and 13th. Back after missing Suzuka, a troubled Ricardo Zonta could manage only 14th in the second Toyota.

Michael Schumacher eventually tumbled down to 18th, ahead of only the two Minardi drivers, who followed their normal routine and changed engines. Incredibly, Zsolt Baumgartner had actually gone faster than Barrichello's 2003 pole time of 19 months earlier. Such is progress.

THERE was a palpable sense of anticipation at Interlagos on Sunday morning, and the long queues outside the main gates told their own story. Rubens Barrichello was on pole and, thanks to his huge 'off' in practice, Michael Schumacher was down in 18th. During a decade of frustration at his home event, Barrichello had earned only a humble fourth place back in 1994. Would this be the year when everything finally fell into place for him?

A look at some of the names lined up immediately behind Barrichello suggested that it wouldn't be easy, and there was another joker in the pack. All weekend, there had been talk of rain on Sunday. Only a little drizzle fell from the grey skies during the morning, but with impeccable timing, the rain arrived properly just a few minutes before the cars headed out to the start. It continued to fall as the cars sat on the grid, albeit only lightly. Nevertheless, the conditions were the very definition of marginal. It meant that, as in Monza, life would be very difficult for the Bridgestone runners.

When the blankets finally came off, intermediates were the tyres of choice. Only three drivers had opted for grooved rubber, namely Renault drivers Fernando Alonso (in eighth) and Jacques Villeneuve (13th), plus McLaren's David Coulthard (12th). As the rain was beginning to peter out, it became clear that everyone else would have to follow suit pretty soon. The big question was how much time would the three gamblers lose in the critical opening laps? Early stops also meant that the issue of who was carrying a heavier fuel load would become academic.

There was drama even before the lights, Button arriving with clouds of smoke pouring from the back of his BAR and providing an unwelcome distraction for Ralf Schumacher, who was immediately behind. Barrichello appeared to get away well from pole, while fellow front-row occupant Juan Pablo Montoya spun his wheels helplessly and failed in his attempt to block Kimi Räikkönen from charging through into second. Then Montoya found himself edged out by Felipe Massa at Turn One.

Barrichello ran a little wide through the complex, and at the left-hander on the exit, Räikkönen jinked to the inside and accelerated

past into the lead, showing the superior grip of the Michelins. It was great stuff as the field slithered its way around the greasy track. Montoya tried desperately to get back past Massa, but Button managed to jump both of the Latin Americans and grab third in a bold move down the inside.

At the end of the lap, Räikkönen, Barrichello, Button, Massa, Montoya, Takuma Sato, Ralf Schumacher and Jarno Trulli filled the points positions. Michael Schumacher was already up to tenth, while the three starters on grooved tyres appeared to be in trouble; Alonso, Villeneuve and Coulthard were running 15th, 16th and 17th, ahead of spinner Giancarlo Fisichella and the two Minardis.

Both Massa and Montoya got ahead of Button on the second lap, but the Brit fought back past the Brazilian going into Turn One. There was even more drama behind when the world champion lost it at the right-hand part of the complex, the Ferrari looping lazily around. Incredibly, after Italy and China, this was his third spin in four races, and it dropped him down to 17th. Surely, even he couldn't do much from there.

Everything closed up at the front as Barrichello's tyres briefly began to work better. Taking advantage of a lighter fuel load, he charged past Räikkönen at the start of the fourth lap, while Montoya kept a close watch. The Colombian's tyres also seemed to be better than the Finn's: 'I started to find that I had a bit more grip than the other people, and I started using that grip and it worked to my advantage.'

Meanwhile, after apparently overcoming his smoky start, Button pulled off and parked, the victim of an engine failure. It was not how he or the team wanted to end their great season, especially after days of distracting debate about BAR's victory at the Contracts Recognition Board.

As early as lap four, Ralf Schumacher signalled the start of a rush for dry tyres, and soon the pits were full of chaotic activity. Räikkönen, Montoya, Sato, Trulli and Michael Schumacher were in on the next lap; the first two indulged in a spectacular drag race out of the pit lane. The Finn won the battle, but the Colombian the war, sweeping past on the run to the fast left-hander at the end of

Above: Kimi Räikkönen pushed Montoya all the way, but eventually had to settle for second place.
Photograph: Darren Heath

DIARY

FIA Contracts Recognition Board rules that Jenson Button's BAR contract for 2005 is valid and takes precedence over any contract with Williams.

Eddie Jordan close to concluding Toyota engine supply deal for 2005.

Renault confirms that it remains committed to F1 at least until 2007.

David Coulthard states that he is the only logical choice to take the vacant seat at Williams alongside Mark Webber in 2005.

Below: Fernando Alonso and Ralf Schumacher scrap for fourth place.
Photograph: Darren Heath

Bottom: Montoya and Barrichello on the podium at Interlagos.
Photograph: Bryn Williams/crash.net

the back straight. 'I managed to pass Kimi coming out of the pits,' said Montoya, 'and I think that was the race decided.'

Later, McLaren received a $10,000 fine for releasing the Finn in a dangerous manner.

Next time around, leader Barrichello ducked into the pits, followed by Christian Klien, Mark Webber, Ricardo Zonta, Timo Glock and Zsolt Baumgartner. The two Jaguars arrived almost together, and there were farcical scenes as the Aussie waited for his team-mate to be serviced. It was an embarrassing start to Jaguar's last outing, but worse was to come

Massa led for two laps before coming in on lap seven, while Nick Heidfeld, Fisichella and Gianmaria Bruni were the last to pit, a lap after that.

It was time to take stock. What about the three guys who had been on dry tyres from the start? The tactic had worked, at least for Alonso, who found himself in a handy lead, ahead of Montoya, Räikkönen, the younger Schumacher, Sato and Barrichello. The later stop had clearly cost the Ferrari driver, and he was struggling to get his dry tyres to work in the still tricky conditions.

'If it is wet, we are the best. If it is dry, we are the best,' he rued. 'In these conditions, we just have to improve a bit, but that is how the race was.'

Running seventh and eighth, Villeneuve and Coulthard had not made as much of the circumstances as Alonso. It remained to be seen how the strategy would unfold for the Spaniard, however, as he was out of sync on stops and would need fuel sometime soon.

In fact, he ran as late as lap 18, and during that time, the gap to Montoya – who was obviously running with a much heavier load – dropped from only 7.9s to 6.7s. Meanwhile, Räikkönen had fallen a crucial 4s behind the Williams driver, but was under no threat from Ralf Schumacher. Sato and Barrichello had also fallen away. After his stop, Alonso was sixth, chased by the recovering Michael Schumacher.

The start of lap 24 brought disaster for Jaguar as Webber went down the inside of Klien, who failed to see his team-mate. The Austrian turned in, and the two green cars made heavy contact. Webber went out on the spot, while the unfortunate Klien had to stop for a new nose-piece. It seemed an appropriately ridiculous end to the Jaguar adventure.

Ralf Schumacher began the second round of stops when he came in on lap 26. Sato and Barrichello followed a lap later, while leader Montoya came in on lap 28. Räikkönen stayed out for one more lap, resuming some 6.4s behind the Colombian after taking on more fuel.

When everything had settled down, Alonso was up to third. By now, it had become obvious that he was going to get by on two stops compared to the three of his rivals. Ralf Schumacher, Barrichello, Sato, Michael Schumacher and Villeneuve completed the top eight.

The rest of the race was all about the two leaders, and even a little mistake when spots of rain fell around lap 30 failed to spoil Montoya's progress. Räikkönen narrowed the gap to 4.6s, but it

had grown to 5.8s when Montoya pitted for the final time on lap 50. The Finn had five more laps of fuel on board, and a chance to bang in some faster laps and steal the lead. It was asking a lot, however, and he didn't quite make it. When he came out of the pits after stopping on lap 55, Montoya remained tantalisingly out of reach; the gap was 1.4s as they crossed the line at the end of that lap.

Räikkönen pushed hard to the flag, cutting the margin to as low as 0.569s on lap 59, but there was never a hint of an opportunity to get by. This was only the fourth victory of Montoya's F1 career, and it was the perfect way to say goodbye to Williams.

'It's awesome to finish the season like that,' he grinned. 'It really pumps me up for next year, and I'm looking forward to working with Kimi.'

'I got close, but not close enough to do anything,' said the McLaren driver.

Watching his future driver beat his current star was a strange experience for Ron Dennis: 'We came here to win, and to be quite honest I'm disappointed that we didn't, because I think we had a chance. Really, the weather, more than anything, made life difficult for everybody, but Juan Pablo drove a very good race, and he deserved to win.'

The final stops might not have helped Räikkönen, but they did boost Barrichello. He managed to jump not only Ralf Schumacher, but also Alonso to take third place, the local hero eventually crossing the line 24s behind the winner. It was not what he had wanted, but at least this was his first visit to the Interlagos podium.

Barrichello was a similar margin ahead of a remarkable little group of four cars that ran nose to tail through the final stint. The opportunistic Alonso had not been the fastest of this lot, but he had held on to fourth, a good reward for his tyre gamble. Sato had been behind him until Ralf Schumacher had passed the BAR to claim fifth just three laps from the end. The Japanese driver had held on to sixth, despite the close attentions of Michael Schumacher, who had to settle for a humble seventh. Some way behind this lot, Massa took the final point, although he had deserved more.

Despite his first-lap spin, Fisichella was right with his team-mate at the flag in ninth. Villeneuve was much happier with his race, but another tenth wasn't much to shout about, and he'd been left far behind by Alonso. Coulthard was equally frustrated by 11th on his final McLaren outing.

'It wasn't so much of a gamble,' said Dennis, 'because Alonso was on grooved tyres, and it proved to be the right decision for him. Obviously, at the end of the day, it didn't work for David; it wasn't the best race for him, but he brought the car home in one piece.'

A low-key day for Toyota saw Trulli and Zonta finish 12th and 13th, ahead of the disgraced Klien, Glock, Baumgartner and Bruni. Apart from Button and Webber, the only other retirement was Heidfeld, the victim of a driveshaft failure on lap 16.

It had been an intriguing race, and for only the third time in 2004, Ferrari had been beaten. Both Williams and McLaren had appeared to gain momentum at the end of the season. Could they carry it into the next?

Above: Montoya ended his Williams career with a well-taken victory.
Photograph: Darren Heath

GRAND PREMIO DO BRASIL

Photograph: Darren Heath

INTERLAGOS 22–24 OCTOBER 2004

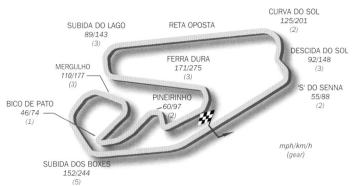

INTERLAGOS, SÃO PAULO
AUTODROMO CARLOS PACE

SUBIDA DO LAGO
89/143
(3)

RETA OPOSTA

CURVA DO SOL
125/201
(2)

MERGULHO
110/177
(3)

FERRA DURA
171/275
(3)

DESCIDA DO SOL
92/148
(3)

BICO DE PATO
46/74
(1)

PINEIRINHO
60/97
(2)

'S' DO SENNA
55/88
(2)

SUBIDA DOS BOXES
152/244
(5)

mph/km/h
(gear)

CIRCUIT LENGTH: 2.677 miles/4.309 km

RACE DISTANCE: 71 laps, 190.083 miles/305.909 km RACE WEATHER: Light rain, drying, overcast (track 26–28°C, air 24–25°C)

Pos.	Driver	Nat.	No.	Entrant	Car/Engine	Tyres	Laps	Time/Retirement	Speed (mph/km/h)	Gap to leader	Fastest race lap	
1	Juan Pablo Montoya	COL	3	BMW WilliamsF1 Team	Williams FW26-BMW P84 V10	M	71	1h 28m 01.451s	129.566/208.516		1m 11.473s	49
2	Kimi Räikkönen	FIN	6	West McLaren Mercedes	McLaren MP4/19B-Mercedes F0110P V10	M	71	1h 28m 02.473s	129.541/208.476	+1.022s	1m 11.562s	52
3	Rubens Barrichello	BR	2	Scuderia Ferrari Malboro	Ferrari F2004-052 V10	B	71	1h 28m 25.550s	128.977/207.569	+24.099s	1m 11.672s	22
4	Fernando Alonso	E	8	Mild Seven Renault F1 Team	Renault R24-RS4 V10	M	71	1h 28m 50.359s	128.367/206.603	+48.908s	1m 12.118s	42
5	Ralf Schumacher	D	4	BMW WilliamsF1 Team	Williams FW26-BMW P84 V10	M	71	1h 28m 51.191s	128.357/206.571	+49.740s	1m 11.764s	23
6	Takuma Sato	J	10	Lucky Strike BAR Honda	BAR 006-Honda RA004E V10	M	71	1h 28m 51.699s	128.345/206.551	+50.248s	1m 11.941s	51
7	Michael Schumacher	D	1	Scuderia Ferrari Malboro	Ferrari F2004-052 V10	B	71	1h 28m 52.077s	128.336/206.537	+50.626s	1m 11.763s	49
8	Felipe Massa	BR	12	Sauber Petronas	Sauber C23-Petronas 04 V10	B	71	1h 29m 03.761s	128.055/206.085	+62.310s	1m 12.066s	68
9	Giancarlo Fisichella	I	11	Sauber Petronas	Sauber C23-Petronas 04 V10	B	71	1h 29m 05.293s	128.018/206.026	+63.842s	1m 11.877s	69
10	Jacques Villeneuve	CDN	7	Mild Seven Renault F1 Team	Renault R24-RS4 V10	M	70			+1 lap	1m 12.210s	68
11	David Coulthard	GB	5	West McLaren Mercedes	McLaren MP4/19B-Mercedes F0110P V10	M	70			+1 lap	1m 12.522s	40
12	Jarno Trulli	I	16	Panasonic Toyota Racing	Toyota TF104B-RVX04 V10	M	70			+1 lap	1m 12.435s	65
13	Ricardo Zonta	BR	17	Panasonic Toyota Racing	Toyota TF104B-RVX04 V10	M	70			+1 lap	1m 12.961s	69
14	Christian Klien	A	15	Jaguar Racing	Jaguar R5-Cosworth CR6 V10	M	69			+2 laps	1m 12.891s	49
15	Timo Glock	D	19	Jordan Ford	Jordan EJ-14-Cosworth RS V10	B	69			+2 laps	1m 13.905s	68
16	Zsolt Baumgartner	H	21	European Minardi Cosworth	Minardi PS04B-Cosworth CR3 V10	B	67			+4 laps	1m 14.743s	45
17	Gianmaria Bruni	I	20	European Minardi Cosworth	Minardi PS04B-Cosworth CR3 V10	B	67			+4 laps	1m 14.756s	50
	Mark Webber	AUS	14	Jaguar Racing	Jaguar R5-Cosworth CR6 V10	M	23	Collision			1m 13.197s	20
	Nick Heidfeld	D	18	Jordan Ford	Jordan EJ-14-Cosworth RS V10	B	15	Transmission			1m 15.855s	11
	Jenson Button	GB	9	Lucky Strike BAR Honda	BAR 006-Honda RA004E V10	M	3	Engine			1m 24.440s	2

All results and data © FOM 2004

Fastest lap: Juan Pablo Montoya, on lap 49, 1m 11.473s, 134.861 mph/217.038 km/h (record).

Previous lap record: Michael Schumacher (F1 Ferrari F2000 V10), 1m 14.755s, 128.940 mph/207.509 km/h (2000).

20th: ZSOLT BAUMGARTNER Minardi-Cosworth

18th: MICHAEL SCHUMACHER Ferrari
Demoted due to engine change.

16th: NICK HEIDFELD Jordan-Cosworth

14th: RICARDO ZONTA Toyota

12th: DAVID COULTHARD McLaren-Mercedes

19th: GIANMARIA BRUNI Minardi-Cosworth

17th: TIMO GLOCK Jordan-Cosworth

15th: CHRISTIAN KLIEN Jaguar-Cosworth

13th: JACQUES VILLENEUVE Renault

11th: MARK WEBBER Jaguar-Cosworth

Grid order	1	2	3	4	5	6	7	8	9	10	11	12	13	14	15	16	17	18	19	20	21	22	23	24	25	26	27	28	29	30	31	32	33	34	35	36	37	38	39	40	41	42	43	44	45	46	47	48	49	50	51	52	53	54	55
2 BARRICHELLO	6	6	6	2	2	12	12	8	8	8	8	8	8	8	8	8	8	3	3	3	3	3	3	3	3	3	3	6	3	3	3	3	3	3	3	3	3	3	3	3	3	3	3	3	3	3	3	3	3	6	6	6	6	6	
3 MONTOYA	2	2	2	6	12	2	8	3	3	3	3	3	3	3	3	3	3	6	6	6	6	6	6	6	6	6	6	3	6	6	6	6	6	6	6	6	6	6	6	6	6	6	6	6	6	6	6	6	6	3	3	3	3	3	
6 RÄIKKÖNEN	9	3	3	3	6	8	3	6	6	6	6	6	6	6	6	6	4	4	4	4	4	4	4	10	8	8	8	8	8	8	8	8	8	8	8	8	8	8	8	8	8	4	2	2	10	10	10	10	10	2					
12 MASSA	12	12	12	12	3	15	6	4	4	4	4	4	4	4	4	4	10	10	10	10	10	10	10	2	4	4	4	4	4	4	4	4	4	4	4	4	4	4	4	4	4	2	4	10	1	2	2	2	2	8					
9 BUTTON	3	9	10	10	15	18	10	10	10	10	10	10	10	10	10	10	2	2	2	2	2	2	2	8	1	10	10	10	10	2	2	2	2	2	2	2	2	2	2	2	2	8	10	1	2	4	8	8	8	10					
10 SATO	10	10	4	16	10	14	4	2	2	2	2	2	2	2	2	2	8	8	8	8	8	8	8	1	10	2	2	2	2	10	10	10	10	10	10	10	10	10	10	10	10	1	8	8	8	8	4	4	4	4					
4 R. SCHUMACHER	4	4	16	15	14	11	11	7	7	7	7	7	7	7	7	7	1	1	1	1	1	1	4	12	12	12	12	11	11	1	1	1	1	1	1	1	1	1	1	1	1	10	1	8	4	1	1	1	1	1					
8 ALONSO	16	16	9	17	16	17	10	5	12	5	5	5	5	1	1	1	1	1	7	12	12	12	12	12	12	12	11	11	11	11	11	12	1	7	7	7	7	7	7	7	7	12	12	12	12	12	12	11	11	12					
16 TRULLI	15	15	15	14	17	3	2	18	5	1	1	1	5	12	12	12	12	17	16	16	16	16	16	16	1	1	1	1	7	5	5	5	5	5	12	12	12	12	12	11	11	11	11	11	11	11	11	12	12	11					
11 FISICHELLA	1	1	17	4	18	6	7	12	1	12	12	12	12	17	17	17	17	16	15	15	15	15	11	11	11	11	7	7	7	7	5	12	12	12	12	12	12	11	11	11	11	7	7	7	7	7	7	7	7	7					
14 WEBBER	17	17	18	18	4	16	11	16	16	17	17	17	16	16	16	16	16	15	15	14	7	7	7	7	5	12	11	11	11	11	11	5	16	16	16	16	5	5	5	5	5	5	5	5											
5 COULTHARD	18	18	14	1	11	1	16	11	16	16	16	16	15	15	15	15	14	7	7	7	17	17	17	17	17	17	17	17	17	17	17	16	5	5	5	17	17	17	17	16	16	16	16	16											
7 VILLENEUVE	14	14	1	11	1	19	1	1	15	15	15	15	14	14	14	14	11	11	17	17	17	17	17	17	17	17	15	15	15	15	16	16	16	16	17	17	16	16	16	17	17	17	17	17											
17 ZONTA	19	19	11	19	19	16	17	17	14	14	14	14	11	11	11	11	7	7	14	15	15	15	15	15	15	15	16	16	16	16	15	15	15	15	15	15	15	15	15	15	15	15	15	15											
15 KLIEN	8	11	19	8	4	7	15	15	19	19	11	11	11	11	5	5	5	5	5	5	5	5	5	15	19	19	19	19	19	19	19	19	19	19	19	19	19	19	19	19	19	19	19	19											
18 HEIDFELD	7	20	8	20	20	5	20	14	11	11	19	19	19	19	19	19	19	19	19	21	20	20	20	20	20	21	21	21	21	21	21	21	21	21	21	21	21	20	21	21	21	21	21	21											
19 GLOCK	5	8	20	7	7	1	14	19	18	18	18	18	18	18	21	20	20	21	20	20	21	21	21	21	20	20	20	20	20	20	20	20	20	20	20	20	20	21	20	20	20	20	20	20											
1 M. SCHUMACHER	11	7	21	21	5	20	19	20	21	21	21	21	21	21	20	20	20	20	20	20																																			
20 BRUNI	20	5	5	5	21	21	21	21	20	20	20	20	20	20																																									
21 BAUMGARTNER	21	21	21	7																																																			

Pit stop
One lap behind leader

TIME SHEETS

QUALIFYING

Sunny (track 30–50°C, air 27–30°C)

Pos.	Driver	Lap time	Sector 1	Sector 2	Sector 3
1	Rubens Barrichello	1m 10.646s	17.883s	36.071s	16.692s
2	Juan Pablo Montoya	1m 10.850s	18.082s	36.154s	16.614s
3	Kimi Räikkönen	1m 10.892s	18.043s	36.185s	16.644s
4	Felipe Massa	1m 10.922s	17.908s	36.226s	16.761s
5	Jenson Button	1m 11.092s	17.938s	36.216s	16.929s
6	Takuma Sato	1m 11.120s	18.102s	36.166s	16.852s
7	Ralf Schumacher	1m 11.131s	18.322s	36.200s	16.609s
8	Michael Schumacher	1m 11.386s	18.048s	36.449s	16.889s
9	Fernando Alonso	1m 11.454s	18.169s	36.478s	16.807s
10	Jarno Trulli	1m 11.483s	18.189s	36.323s	16.939s
11	Giancarlo Fisichella	1m 11.571s	18.107s	36.563s	16.901s
12	Mark Webber	1m 11.665s	18.259s	36.337s	17.069s
13	David Coulthard	1m 11.750s	18.229s	36.619s	16.902s
14	Jacques Villeneuve	1m 11.836s	18.259s	36.698s	16.879s
15	Ricardo Zonta	1m 11.974s	18.346s	36.761s	16.867s
16	Christian Klien	1m 12.211s	18.333s	36.775s	17.103s
17	Nick Heidfeld	1m 12.829s	18.393s	37.049s	17.387s
18	Timo Glock	1m 13.502s	18.514s	37.597s	17.391s
19	Zsolt Baumgartner	1m 13.550s	18.522s	37.824s	17.204s
20	Gianmaria Bruni	No time	–	–	–

PRACTICE 1 (FRIDAY)

Sunny (track 34–38°C, air 25–27°C)

Pos.	Driver	Laps	Time
1	Juan Pablo Montoya	11	1m 12.547s
2	Ryan Briscoe	25	1m 12.614s
3	Ralf Schumacher	12	1m 12.873s
4	Kimi Räikkönen	4	1m 13.150s
5	Anthony Davidson	22	1m 13.232s
6	David Coulthard	6	1m 13.277s
7	Jarno Trulli	15	1m 13.512s
8	Takuma Sato	10	1m 13.839s
9	Rubens Barrichello	13	1m 13.855s
10	Fernando Alonso	12	1m 13.990s
11	Michael Schumacher	13	1m 14.042s
12	Giancarlo Fisichella	14	1m 14.118s
13	Mark Webber	9	1m 14.147s
14	Jenson Button	13	1m 14.187s
15	Ricardo Zonta	14	1m 14.207s
16	Felipe Massa	13	1m 14.479s
17	Jacques Villeneuve	13	1m 14.585s
18	Robert Doornbos	27	1m 14.966s
19	Björn Wirdheim	24	1m 15.065s
20	Nick Heidfeld	12	1m 15.414s
21	Christian Klien	15	1m 15.476s
22	Zsolt Baumgartner	12	1m 15.490s
23	Timo Glock	18	1m 15.647s
24	Gianmaria Bruni	13	1m 16.406s
25	Bas Leinders	1	No time

PRACTICE 2 (FRIDAY)

Sunny, cloudy, windy (track 34–35°C, air 24–25°C)

Pos.	Driver	Laps	Time
1	Rubens Barrichello	25	1m 11.166s
2	Michael Schumacher	28	1m 11.334s
3	Kimi Räikkönen	20	1m 11.526s
4	Jenson Button	24	1m 11.731s
5	Anthon Davidson	31	1m 11.920s
6	Takuma Sato	23	1m 11.988s
7	Fernando Alonso	30	1m 12.005s
8	Felipe Massa	24	1m 12.183s
9	Ryan Briscoe	34	1m 12.209s
10	Ralf Schumacher	26	1m 12.235s
11	Juan Pablo Montoya	24	1m 12.280s
12	Jacques Villeneuve	31	1m 12.316s
13	Robert Doornbos	27	1m 12.345s
14	Ricardo Zonta	30	1m 12.347s
15	David Coulthard	24	1m 12.430s
16	Takuma Sato	36	1m 12.545s
17	Giancarlo Fisichella	29	1m 12.631s
18	Mark Webber	35	1m 12.816s
19	Nick Heidfeld	24	1m 13.114s
20	Gianmaria Bruni	31	1m 13.467s
21	Christian Klien	32	1m 13.509s
22	Timo Glock	24	1m 13.966s
23	Zsolt Baumgartner	25	1m 13.979s
24	Björn Wirdheim	28	1m 14.303s
25	Bas Leinders	10	1m 14.754s

PRACTICE 3 (SATURDAY)

Sunny (track 38–39°C, air 26–27°C)

Pos.	Driver	Laps	Time
1	Jenson Button	9	1m 11.466s
2	Takuma Sato	11	1m 11.580s
3	Kimi Räikkönen	7	1m 11.591s
4	Rubens Barrichello	6	1m 11.641s
5	Ralf Schumacher	8	1m 11.714s
6	Michael Schumacher	9	1m 11.740s
7	Giancarlo Fisichella	6	1m 11.985s
8	Felipe Massa	5	1m 12.064s
9	David Coulthard	7	1m 12.085s
10	Juan Pablo Montoya	7	1m 12.208s
11	Jarno Trulli	5	1m 12.263s
12	Mark Webber	8	1m 12.356s
13	Fernando Alonso	8	1m 12.563s
14	Christian Klien	8	1m 12.612s
15	Ricardo Zonta	10	1m 13.025s
16	Nick Heidfeld	8	1m 13.327s
17	Zsolt Baumgartner	10	1m 14.284s
18	Gianmaria Bruni	11	1m 14.336s
19	Timo Glock	11	1m 14.805s
20	Jacques Villeneuve	2	No time

PRACTICE 4 (SATURDAY)

Sunny (track 39–43°C, air 28–30°C)

Pos.	Driver	Laps	Time
1	Rubens Barrichello	15	1m 10.229s
2	Michael Schumacher	15	1m 10.352s
3	Kimi Räikkönen	15	1m 10.385s
4	David Coulthard	11	1m 10.413s
5	Jenson Button	16	1m 10.480s
6	Fernando Alonso	11	1m 10.683s
7	Ralf Schumacher	9	1m 10.997s
8	Takuma Sato	18	1m 11.127s
9	Mark Webber	23	1m 11.130s
10	Felipe Massa	10	1m 11.142s
11	Juan Pablo Montoya	12	1m 11.157s
12	Jacques Villeneuve	18	1m 11.321s
13	Giancarlo Fisichella	5	1m 11.425s
14	Ricardo Zonta	16	1m 11.688s
15	Jarno Trulli	15	1m 11.711s
16	Christian Klien	21	1m 12.248s
17	Nick Heidfeld	12	1m 12.299s
18	Zsolt Baumgartner	17	1m 12.990s
19	Timo Glock	17	1m 13.818s
20	Gianmaria Bruni	16	1m 14.411s

CHASSIS LOG BOOK

No.	Driver	Chassis
1	Michael Schumacher	F2004/241
2	Rubens Barrichello	F2004/240
	Spare	F2004/239
3	Juan Pablo Montoya	FW26/05
4	Ralf Schumaher	FW26/07
	Spare	FW26/06
5	David Coulthard	MP4/19B-03
6	Kimi Räikkönen	MP4/19B-01
	Spare	MP4/19B-02
7	Jacques Villeneuve	R24/08
8	Fernando Alonso	R24/07
	Spare	R24/03
9	Jenson Button	006/05
10	Takuma Sato	006/06
	Anthony Davidson	006/04
	Spare	006/04
11	Giancarlo Fisichella	C23/04
12	Felipe Massa	C23/01
	Spare	C23/02
14	Mark Webber	R5/6B
15	Christian Klien	R5/1
	Björn Wirdheim	R5/5
	Spare	R5/5
16	Jarno Trulli	TF104/10B
17	Olivier Panis	TF104/09B
	Ryan Briscoe	TF104/11B
	Spare	TF104/11B
18	Nick Heidfeld	EJ-14/01
19	Timo Glock	EJ-14/02
	Robert Doornbos	EJ-14/03
	Spare	EJ-14/03
20	Gianmaria Bruni	PS04B/02
21	Zsolt Baumgartner	PS04B/04
	Bas Leinders	PS04B/03
	Spare	PS04B/03

10th: GIANCARLO FISICHELLA Sauber-Petronas

8th: FERNANDO ALONSO Renault

6th: TAKUMA SATO BAR-Honda

4th: FELIPE MASSA Sauber-Petronas

2nd: JUAN PABLO MONTOYA Williams-BMW

9th: JARNO TRULLI Toyota

7th: RALF SCHUMACHER Williams-BMW

5th: JENSON BUTTON BAR-Honda

3rd: KIMI RÄIKKÖNEN McLaren-Mercedes

Pole: RUBENS BARRICHELLO Ferrari

56	57	58	59	60	61	62	63	64	65	66	67	68	69	70	71	
3	3	3	3	3	3	3	3	3	3	3	3	3	3	3	3	1
6	6	6	6	6	6	6	6	6	6	6	6	6	6	6	6	2
2	2	2	2	2	2	2	2	2	2	2	2	2	2	2	2	3
8	8	8	8	8	8	8	8	8	8	8	8	8	8	8	8	4
10	10	10	10	10	10	10	10	10	10	10	10	4	4	4		5
4	4	4	4	4	4	4	4	4	4	4	10	10	10			6
1	1	1	1	1	1	1	1	1	1	1	1	1	1	1	1	7
12	12	12	12	12	12	12	12	12	12	12	12	12	12	12	12	8
11	11	11	11	11	11	11	11	11	11	11	11	11	11	11	11	
7	7	7	7	7	7	7	7	7	7	7	7	7	7			
5	5	5	5	5	5	5	5	5	5	5	5	5				
16	16	16	16	16	16	16	16	16	16	16	16	16				
17	17	17	17	17	17	17	17	17	17	17	17	17				
15	15	15	15	15	15	15	15	15	15	15	15					
19	19	19	19	19	19	19	19	19	19	19	19					
21	21	21	21	21	21	21	21	21	21	21	21					
20	20	20	20	20	20	20	20	20	20	20	20					

FOR THE RECORD

50 grand prix starts
Mark Webber

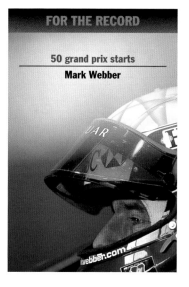

POINTS: CONSTRUCTORS

1	Ferrari	262
2	BAR	119
3	Renault	105
4	Williams	88
5	McLaren	69
6	Sauber	34
7	Jaguar	10
8	Toyota	9
9	Jordan	5
10	Minardi	1

POINTS: DRIVERS

1	Michael Schumacher	148
2	Rubens Barrichello	114
3	Jenson Button	85
4	Fernando Alonso	59
5	Juan Pablo Montoya	58
6	Jarno Trulli	46
7	Kimi Räikkönen	45
8	Takuma Sato	34
9 =	Ralf Schumacher	24
9 =	David Coulthard	24
11	Giancarlo Fisichella	22
12	Felipe Massa	12
13	Mark Webber	7
14 =	Olivier Panis	6
14 =	Antonio Pizzonia	6
16 =	Christian Klien	3
16 =	Cristiano da Matta	3
16 =	Nick Heidfeld	3
19	Timo Glock	2
20	Zsolt Baumgartner	1

DRIVERS' POINTS TABLE

Compiled by EMMA HENRY

Place	Driver	Nationality	Date of birth	Car	Australia	Malaysia	Bahrain	San Marino	Spain	Monaco	Europe	Canada	USA	France	Britain	Germany	Hungary	Belgium	Italy	China	Japan	Brazil	Points total
1	Michael Schumacher	D	3/1/69	Ferrari	1pf	1p	1pf	1f	1pf	Rf	1pf	1	1	1f	1f	1p	1pf	2	2	12f	1p	7	148
2	Rubens Barrichello	BR	23/5/72	Ferrari	2	4	2	6	2	3	2	2f	2pf	3	3	12	2	3	1pf	1p	Rf	3p	114
3	Jenson Button	GB	19/1/80	BAR-Honda	6	3	3	2p	8	2	3	3	R	5	4	2	5	R	3	2	3	R	85
4	Fernando Alonso	E	29/7/81	Renault	3	7	6	4	4	R	5	R	R	2p	10	3	3	R	R	4	5	4	59
5	Juan Pablo Montoya	COL	20/9/75	Williams-BMW	5	2f	13	3	R	4	8	DQ	DQ	8	5	5	4	R	5	5	7	1f	58
6	Jarno Trulli	I	13/7/74	Renault	7	5	4	5	3	1p	4	R	4	4	R	11	R	9p	10	–	–	–	46
				Toyota	–	–	–	–	–	–	–	–	–	–	–	–	–	–	–	–	11	12	
7	Kimi Räikkönen	FIN	17/10/79	McLaren-Mercedes	R	R	R	8	11	R	R	5	6	7	2p	Rf	R	1f	R	3	6	2	45
8	Takuma Sato	J	28/1/77	BAR-Honda	9	15*	5	16*	5	R	R	R	3	R	11	8	6	R	4	6	4	6	34
9 =	Ralf Schumacher	D	30/6/75	Williams-BMW	4	R	7	7	6	10*	R	DQp	R	–	–	–	–	–	–	R	2	5	23
9 =	David Coulthard	GB	27/3/71	McLaren-Mercedes	8	6	R	12	10	R	R	6	7	6	7	4	9	7	6	9	R	11	23
11	Giancarlo Fisichella	I	14/1/73	Sauber-Petronas	10	11	11	9	7	R	6	4	9*	12	6	9	8	5	8	7	8	9	22
12	Felipe Massa	BR	25/4/81	Sauber-Petronas	R	8	12	10	9	5	9	R	R	13	9	13	R	4	12	8	9	8	12
13	Mark Webber	AUS	27/8/76	Jaguar-Cosworth	R	R	8	13	12	R	7	R	R	9	8	6	10	R	9	10	R	R	7
14 =	Olivier Panis	F	2/9/66	Toyota	13	12	9	11	R	8	11	DQ	5	15	R	14	11	8	R	14	14	–	6
14 =	Antonio Pizzonia	BR	11/9/80	Williams-BMW	–	–	–	–	–	–	–	–	–	–	–	7	7	R	7	–	–	–	6
16 =	Christian Klien	A	7/2/83	Jaguar-Cosworth	11	10	14	14	R	R	12	9	R	11	14	10	13	6	13	R	12	14	3
16 =	Cristiano da Matta	BR	19/9/73	Toyota	12	9	10	R	13	6	R	DQ	R	14	13	R	–	–	–	–	–	–	3
16 =	Nick Heidfeld	D	10/5/77	Jordan-Ford Cosworth	R	R	15	R	R	7	10	8	R	16	15	R	12	11	14	13	13	R	3
19	Timo Glock	D	10/3/82	Jordan-Ford Cosworth	–	–	–	–	–	–	–	7	–	–	–	–	–	–	–	15	15	15	2
20	Zsolt Baumgartner	H	1/1/81	Minardi-Cosworth	R	16	R	15	R	9	15	10	8	R	R	16	15	R	15	16	R	16	1
21 =	Jacques Villeneuve	CDN	9/4/71	Renault	–	–	–	–	–	–	–	–	–	–	–	–	–	–	–	11	10	10	0
21 =	Ricardo Zonta	BR	23/3/76	Toyota	–	–	–	–	–	–	–	–	–	–	–	–	R	10*	11	R	–	13	0
21 =	Marc Gené	E	29/3/74	Williams-BMW	–	–	–	–	–	–	–	–	–	10	12	–	–	–	–	–	–	–	0
21 =	Giorgio Pantano	I	4/2/79	Jordan-Ford Cosworth	14	13	16	R	R	R	13	–	R	17	R	15	R	R	R	–	–	–	0
21 =	Gianmaria Bruni	I	30/5/81	Minardi-Cosworth	NC	14	17	R	R	R	14	R	R	18	16	17	14	R	R	R	16	17	0

The following drivers took part in Friday Private Testing at grand prix meetings:

Ryan Briscoe	AUS	Toyota	b. 24/9/81
Anthony Davidson	GB	BAR-Honda	b. 18/4/79
Robert Doornbos	NL	Jordan-Ford Cosworth	b. 23/9/81
Timo Glock	D	Jordan-Ford Cosworth	b. 10/3/82
Bas Leinders	B	Minardi-Cosworth	b. 16/7/75
Björn Wirdheim	S	Jaguar-Cosworth	b. 4/4/80
Ricardo Zonta	BR	Toyota	b. 23/3/76

KEY

p	pole position	*	classified, but not running at the finish
f	fastest lap		
R	retired	NC	not classified
DQ	disqualified		

POINTS & PERCENTAGES
Compiled by DAVID HAYHOE

GRID POSITIONS: 2004

Pos.	Driver	Starts	Best	Worst	Average
1	Michael Schumacher	18	1	20	3.94
2	Rubens Barrichello	18	1	15	5.50
3	Jenson Button	18	1	14	5.50
4	Juan Pablo Montoya	18	2	13	5.61
5	Ralf Schumacher	12	1	12	6.00
6	Jarno Trulli	17	1	20	6.71
7	Fernando Alonso	18	1	19	7.56
8=	Takuma Sato	18	2	20	8.22
8=	Kimi Räikkönen	18	1	20	8.22
10	David Coulthard	18	3	20	9.39
11=	Antonio Pizzonia	4	6	14	9.50
11=	Marc Gené	2	8	11	9.50
13	Mark Webber	18	2	14	9.72
14	Jacques Villeneuve	3	9	13	11.33
15	Olivier Panis	17	7	18	11.59
16	Cristiano da Matta	12	9	15	11.67
17	Giancarlo Fisichella	18	5	20	12.33
18	Felipe Massa	18	4	20	13.39
19	Christian Klien	18	10	19	13.67
20	Ricardo Zonta	5	11	20	14.60
21	Nick Heidfeld	18	13	20	16.00
22	Timo Glock	4	16	17	16.50
23	Giorgio Pantano	14	14	19	16.79
24	Gianmaria Bruni	18	16	20	18.28
25	Zsolt Baumgartner	18	17	20	18.72

Additionally, Ryan Briscoe, Anthony Davidson, Robert Doornbos, Timo Glock, Bas Leinders, Björn Wirdheim and Ricardo Zonta tested at grand prix meetings, but did not participate in qualifying.

CAREER PERFORMANCES: 2004 DRIVERS

Driver	Nationality	Races	Championships	Wins	2nd places	3rd places	4th places	5th places	6th places	7th places	8th places	Pole positions	Fastest laps	Points
Fernando Alonso	E	51	–	1	2	5	7	3	2	2	1	3	1	114
Rubens Barrichello	BR	196	–	9	24	24	15	13	5	6	3	13	15	451
Zsolt Baumgartner	H	20	–	–	–	–	–	–	–	1	–	–	–	1
Gianmaria Bruni	I	18	–	–	–	–	–	–	–	–	–	–	–	–
Jenson Button	GB	84	–	–	4	6	6	10	4	5	6	1	–	130
David Coulthard	GB	175	–	13	26	21	9	16	11	11	2	12	18	475
Cristiano da Matta	BR	28	–	–	–	–	–	3	2	–	–	–	–	13
Giancarlo Fisichella	I	141	–	1	5	4	6	9	7	11	10	1	1	116
Marc Gené	E	36	–	–	–	–	1	1	–	3	–	–	–	5
Timo Glock	D	4	–	–	–	–	–	–	–	1	–	–	–	2
Nick Heidfeld	D	84	–	–	1	2	2	7	5	5	–	–	–	28
Christian Klien	A	18	–	–	–	–	–	–	1	–	–	–	–	3
Felipe Massa	BR	34	–	–	–	–	1	2	2	2	4	–	–	16
Juan Pablo Montoya	COL	68	–	4	13	6	8	6	1	2	3	11	11	221
Olivier Panis	F	158	–	1	3	1	4	8	8	11	11	–	–	76
Giorgio Pantano	I	14	–	–	–	–	–	–	–	–	–	–	–	–
Antonia Pizzonia	BR	15	–	–	–	–	–	–	–	3	–	–	–	6
Kimi Räikkönen	FIN	68	–	2	10	6	6	2	4	4	2	3	6	169
Takuma Sato	J	36	–	–	–	1	2	3	4	–	2	–	–	39
Michael Schumacher	D	213	7	83	36	18	9	7	5	3	3	63	66	1186
Ralf Schumacher	D	127	–	6	6	12	16	16	6	7	2	5	7	259
Jarno Trulli	I	130	–	1	1	2	11	9	8	7	8	2	–	117
Jacques Villeneuve	CDN	133	1	11	5	7	9	6	8	8	8	13	9	219
Mark Webber	AUS	50	–	–	–	–	–	1	4	5	3	–	–	26
Ricardo Zonta	BR	36	–	–	–	–	–	–	3	1	3	–	–	31

Drivers beginning the formation lap are deemed to have made a start. Also, where races have been subject to a restart, those retiring during the initial race are included as having started.

UNLAPPED: 2004

Number of cars on same lap as leader

Grand Prix	Starters	at 1/4 distance	at 1/2 distance	at 3/4 distance	at full distance
Australia	20	16	9	5	6
Malaysia	20	18	14	8	7
Bahrain	20	18	15	12	7
San Marino	20	17	11	7	7
Spain	20	18	13	9	7
Monaco	20	12	7	3	3
Europe	20	15	13	8	7
Canada	20	16	11	7	5
USA	20	13	10	8	5
France	20	17	14	11	10
Britain	20	18	15	12	12
Germany	20	16	15	12	12
Hungary	20	17	8	5	5
Belgium	20	16	13	11	9
Italy	20	17	15	11	11
China	20	18	16	12	9
Japan	20	19	15	10	9
Brazil	20	16	13	9	9

LAP LEADERS: 2004

Grand Prix	Michael Schumacher	Rubens Barrichello	Jarno Trulli	Fernando Alonso	Jenson Button	Juan Pablo Montoya	Kimi Räikkönen	Ralf Schumacher	Felipe Massa	Takuma Sato	Antonio Pizzonia	Total
Australia	58	–	–	–	–	–	–	–	–	–	–	58
Malaysia	52	1	–	–	–	3	–	–	–	–	–	56
Bahrain	50	6	–	–	1	–	–	–	–	–	–	57
San Marino	54	–	–	–	8	–	–	–	–	–	–	62
Spain	51	7	8	–	–	–	–	–	–	–	–	66
Monaco	4	–	72	1	–	–	–	–	–	–	–	77
Europe	53	4	–	1	–	–	–	2	–	–	–	60
Canada	39	–	–	2	–	–	29	–	–	–	–	70
USA	59	14	–	–	–	–	–	–	–	–	–	73
France	34	–	36	–	–	–	–	–	–	–	–	70
Britain	49	–	–	–	–	–	11	–	–	–	–	66
Germany	53	–	–	1	11	–	1	–	–	–	–	70
Hungary	70	–	–	–	–	–	–	–	–	–	–	44
Belgium	2	–	9	2	–	1	29	–	–	–	1	53
Italy	2	21	–	6	24	–	–	–	–	–	–	56
China	–	47	–	–	8	–	–	1	–	–	–	53
Japan	53	–	–	–	–	–	–	–	–	–	–	53
Brazil	–	2	–	11	–	47	9	–	2	–	–	71
Total	683	102	89	60	52	51	50	30	2	2	1	1122
Per cent	60.9	9.1	7.9	5.3	4.6	4.5	4.5	2.7	0.2	0.2	0.1	100

RETIREMENTS: 2004

Number of cars that retired

Grand Prix	Starters	at 1/4 distance	at 1/2 distance	at 3/4 distance	at full distance	% of finishers
Australia	20	2	3	4	5	75.0
Malaysia	20	–	2	4	5	75.0
Bahrain	20	1	1	1	3	85.0
San Marino	20	1	2	3	5	75.0
Spain	20	–	4	6	7	65.0
Monaco	20	7	8	10	11	45.0
Europe	20	3	4	4	5	75.0
Canada	20	2	3	5	6	70.0
USA	20	7	8	9	12	40.0
France	20	1	2	2	3	85.0
Britain	20	–	2	3	4	80.0
Germany	20	1	1	3	3	85.0
Hungary	20	1	1	3	3	85.0
Belgium	20	5	5	8	10	50.0
Italy	20	1	1	4	5	75.0
China	20	1	1	4	4	80.0
Japan	20	–	1	3	4	80.0
Brazil	20	2	3	3	3	85.0

Main photograph: Vitantonio Liuzzi speeds across the line to take the win in the season's finale at Monza.

Below: Setting the tone. Arden team-mates Liuzzi (left) and Robert Doornbos share the podium at Imola.
Photographs: LAT Photographic

F3000 REVIEW by SIMON ARRON

DEMOLITION MAN

Above: Liuzzi, an emphatic F3000 champion.

Top: Robert Doornbos partnered Liuzzi at Arden International.

Photographs: LAT Photographic

VITANTONIO Liuzzi gave an apologetic cough and giggled. 'I'm sorry,' he said. 'It's just that I have got used to...' His voice tailed off and he shrugged, still grinning broadly, before switching to a different seat. The Italian had just strolled into the Budapest press conference room and helped himself to the race winner's chair. It took a gentle tap on the shoulder to remind him that he had actually finished second. It was an understandable error – and it was just about the only mistake the 23-year-old made during the most comprehensive demolition job in the 20-season history of the FIA Formula 3000 Championship.

Liuzzi began the campaign with a reputation to endorse. He had been highly fancied to win the 2002 German F3 title, only to sink without trace, for reasons that have never been satisfactorily explained. Backer Red Bull kept faith, however, and fast-tracked him to the following season's FIA F3000 series, from which he emerged as the outstanding rookie. There were little touches that hinted at his capacity for the extraordinary – taking pole position by more than 0.5s in Budapest, for instance, even though his only previous experience of the track amounted to half a dozen laps on a scooter – but victory remained elusive.

That was then. Twelve months on, as his Budapest *faux pas* illustrated, he had more or less forgotten how it felt not to win. After joining defending champion team Arden International ahead of the 2004 season, his track record was extraordinary: ten starts, nine pole positions, seven victories and two second places. Only at the Nürburgring – traditionally a miserable hunting ground for Arden – did he fail to score, the victim of a broken wheel sustained during the first-lap scramble, when he failed to get away from pole with his customary briskness.

Liuzzi's team played a critical part in his success. Mid-race tyre stops, tried at the end of 2003, became a mandatory feature of the championship – and Arden, guided by the level-headed engineering savvy of Mick Cook, got through the whole season with barely a fumble. That gave Liuzzi an extra weapon: if he was leading, he paced himself accordingly; if he was chasing, he'd remain patient and wait for the tyre stops, confident that his crew would gain him time and – more often than not – track position.

Arden boss Christian Horner, who was planning to take his organisation into F1 on the back of three consecutive titles in the FIA F3000 Championship for Teams, was bowled over by

Liuzzi's strength in depth. 'Tonio seems to tick all the right boxes,' he said. 'He has tremendous natural speed, superb car control and an intelligent racing brain.

'That was particularly evident at Silverstone, where his car had an imbalance during the second half of the race. He focused on looking after his front tyres and didn't worry about his lead shrinking. He made sure the car was still in decent shape during the final stages – and that left him with enough performance in reserve when it mattered.

'He also has a fantastic ability to get on with the job on cold tyres during his out-laps in the middle of races. He is willing to listen, is very self-analytical and has been an absolute pleasure to work with.'

There were those who felt that Liuzzi's mildly off-key performances – finishing second – in the back-to-back wet races at Budapest and Spa hinted at a possible weakness, but Horner disagreed. 'In Hungary,' he said, 'Tonio was driving with an eye on the championship. His twin objectives were to finish and to beat Enrico Toccacelo, his main title rival. Victory wasn't essential. He was on a similar mission in Belgium, where he was ultimately slowed by a wet set-up on a drying track – although he beat all the others who were in the same boat.'

Liuzzi got to hear about this shred of doubt, and it amused him greatly. 'Yeah, someone told me,' he said at Monza. 'I spend a couple of races driving tactically, because I want to make sure of the title, and apparently that means I can't drive in the wet.

'You know, I have never wanted a wet race so much as I do this weekend, just to show what's possible now that the title is settled and the pressure is off.'

He didn't get the adverse weather he craved, but he did sign off with another flawless, dominant performance.

Liuzzi wasn't short of serious rivals. The most consistent – for the first three-quarters of the season, at least – was the aforementioned Toccacelo. Driving for the revitalised BCN team, which blossomed under the direction of newly appointed British engineer Nick Wasyliw, the experienced Italian was invariably within a whisker of Liuzzi in terms of pure speed, but his pit crew was no match for Arden's, and at least two potential victories disappeared in a cascade of wheel nuts during mandatory tyre stops.

One win, a string of second places and an iniquitous scoring system kept Toccacelo in the title hunt for longer than seemed

reasonable, but this was still a laudable, mature campaign from someone who once performed more like a trainee Exocet than a racing driver.

The marriage between perennial front-runner Patrick Friesacher and multiple title winner Super Nova ought to have been the catalyst for a title challenge, but the Austrian didn't settle in his new environment and – after a fitful start to the season – he returned to the more familiar surroundings of Coloni Motorsport.

Subsequently, Friesacher's performances improved, although his pace was sometimes compromised because now and again he allowed his ambition to stray beyond the laws of physics. His aggressive streak was admirable, but occasionally you wondered whether four seasons at this level have allowed a touch of desperation to creep in. His magisterial victory in Budapest underlined his potential when the chemistry was right.

Arden number two, Robert Doornbos, was the only other winner. The Dutchman had an encouraging rookie season and benefited from a close friendship – on and off the track – with team-mate Liuzzi. Accepting that his primary goal was to learn, he proved an adept scholar. A podium finish on his debut was a bonus, but by the end of the season, he had become sufficiently quick and consistent to receive champagne showers on a regular basis.

At a sodden Spa, Doornbos gambled on reattaching his rear anti-roll bar, when everybody else on the grid decided not to do so, and sailed away to win by more than half a minute. Bright and articulate, he peaked at exactly the right time, finally giving the Dutch fans someone other than Jos Verstappen to focus on.

Although Doornbos was the season's best rookie, he wasn't the only newcomer to catch the eye. Argentine duo José Maria Lopez (CMS Performance) and Esteban Guerrieri (BCN) both showed a terrific turn of speed. Renault backed Lopez justified some of his pre-season hype, but for all his raw pace, he struggled to shake off a habit of clattering into things.

In sharp contrast, relatively little was expected of Guerrieri. He was a last-minute signing and had only managed to test for about ten minutes pre-season, but despite stepping up directly from Formula Renault 2000, he adapted quickly and showed astute racecraft. Like Toccacelo, however, Guerrieri suffered at the hands of an eager, but sometimes ham-fisted, pit crew. The two compatriots eventually finished level on points – but Guerrieri was the more impressive.

New team Ma-Con Engineering became a regular front-runner thanks to the guile of veteran Tomas Enge, who had made a record 55 FIA F3000 starts by the end of the season. The Czech might have managed more than a trio of podium finishes but for a series of collisions with Frenchman Yannick Schroeder (Durango), who was an occasional front-runner until financial restraints forced him to do his annual disappearing trick.

Scholarly Italian Raffaele Giammaria (AEZ) suffered the season's biggest accident, during pre-season testing in Barcelona, but he returned to the track a few weeks later to notch up a podium finish. He might not have much of a reputation, but he's a canny, dependable racer.

There were flashes of promise from others – including British F3 champion Alan van der Merwe (Super Nova), Jeffrey van Hooydonk (with Coloni, at the start of the season), Ernesto Viso (who joined Durango mid-season) and Matteo Grassotto (AEZ) – but only nine drivers made a podium appearance, and three of those only managed it once. This is a level playing field that is designed to filter the cream to the top, and the statistics suggest the formula is effective.

On other levels, however, there is still work to be done. Liuzzi's reward for obliterating his rivals included a one-day trial with Sauber, which came with a promise – or so he thought – of a 2005 race seat if all went well. It was only when he arrived at Jerez, on the eve of the test, that he learned the Swiss team had just finalised a two-year contract with Jacques Villeneuve.

The sport remains a flawed meritocracy. The new Renault endorsed GP2 Series, which is due to replace the FIA F3000 Championship in 2005, needs to address that situation as a matter of urgency.

Top: **Argentine rookie José Maria Lopez was quick, but prone to error.**

Above centre: **Driving for BCN, Enrico Toccacelo was Liuzzi's main rival.**

Above left: **Esteban Guerrieri was another newcomer to make a good impression.**

Above: **Tomas Enge returned to the series with Ma-Con Engineering, but failed to notch a win.**

Left: **Patrick Friesacher pulled off a great win at the Hungaroring.**
Photographs: LAT Photographic

HEIRS APPARENT?

FORMULA 3 REVIEW
by ANDREW VAN DE BURGT

Far left: James Rossiter's programme benefited from the backing of the British Racing Drivers' Club.

Left: Adam Carroll was another strong challenger to Nelson Piquet in the British F3 series.

Photographs: LAT Photographic

AHEAD of the 2004 F3 season, the talk had been of two sons of former F1 world champions trying to make names for themselves in their own right. But while Nelson Angelo Piquet duly wrapped up the British F3 title, 22-year-old Briton Jamie Green stole Nico Rosberg's thunder in the Euroseries.

In 2003, Green had been the runner-up in Britain, finishing ahead of Piquet, although the Brazilian had made most of the headlines. When Green's British team, Carlin Motorsport, had opted not to run in the Pau Grand Prix race, he had found a seat with the French ASM outfit. The Brit had impressed team boss Frédéric Vasseur greatly in his pre-race test, and his podium finish in the race had put him high on the Mercedes-Benz powered team's wanted list for 2004.

It was a bold move for Green to commit to ASM and the Euroseries. It meant having to live in France and race on a host of tracks he'd never driven before. But it proved emphatically the right decision.

With ASM favourite Alexandre Premat and the rejuvenated Eric Salignon as Green's team-mates, ASM had the strongest driver line-up in the championship. The team also had the best prepared cars, making it a formidable outfit. Premat continued where he had left off in 2003, driving with total commitment and muscling the Dallara around the track. His style made him one of most enjoyable drivers to watch, but it was hard on his car and tyres. In contrast, Green was smooth and precise. He was also incredibly quick. Despite his lack of track knowledge, he racked up six pole positions – more than anyone else. He also managed seven wins, including a stunning pair of back-to-back victories at Brno, where he was in a different league to the opposition.

Green took the championship lead after the second round at Estoril and was never headed for the rest of the season. In large part, this was due to his fabulous consistency – he barely made a mistake all year and scored points in all but two of the races. One of these was at Magny-Cours, where he was spun out at the Adelaide hairpin on the first lap. While most of his rivals were making heavy weather of overtaking at the French Grand Prix venue, Green scythed through the field, rising from last to ninth.

Having endured a miserable season in British F3 during 2003, which culminated with him being released from the Renault driver development programme, Salignon needed to rebuild his stock. Returning to a French team gave him a psychological boost, while the performance of the ASM car allowed him to demonstrate his talent on the track. Salignon occupied the middle ground between Premat's aggression and Green's deftness, and there were times when he had the legs of both of them. That was particularly true at Zandvoort in Holland. In the Marlboro Masters, the highest-profile, non-championship F3 race in Europe, he was cruising to a comfortable win when he spun with the flag almost in sight. He atoned, however, with a dominant win in the Euroseries round at the same track and looked set to take the runner-up spot behind Green in the championship until his season was cut short by a road accident. Although his injuries were limited to minor burns and damaged vertebrae, he was forced to skip the final two rounds and slipped to sixth in the standings.

Rosberg began his season in most impressive fashion, winning both races at the Hockenheim season opener. After that, however, his championship charge became derailed. At the next race, he collided with a car that had stalled ahead of him on the grid – and that would not be the last time that his race was effectively over on the first lap. He did win again, at the Nürburgring, and there were times when he showed he had inherited his father's doggedness.

Premat picked up Salignon's gift in the Marlboro Masters, but he also gave away wins. At Pau, he was unstoppable. He cruised to victory in the first race and was doing the same in the second when he collided with a stranded car and a marshal recovering it. Yellow flags had been waved ahead of the trouble spot, so Premat had the book thrown at him, losing his earlier win for the offence.

Green and Nicolas Lapierre were the beneficiaries. Lapierre, winner of the end-of-season F3 classic at Macau in 2003, also collected a pair of wins in the final round of the season at Hockenheim, ending the season third in the points, the top Opel powered driver.

McLaren protégé Lewis Hamilton had also starred in the Far East races at the end of 2003, taking pole in Korea. A move to the Euroseries was a big step up for the reigning British Formula Renault champ, especially as it would also be the first year in the series for his Manor Motorsport team. Pre-season testing suggested that the combination would be a front-runner from the off, but the balance of the car was better suited to the cooler winter conditions, and with testing strictly controlled, it took the team until mid-season to really find its feet. Still, Hamilton drove with great verve to victory at Norisring.

Hamilton's graduation to the Euroseries was primarily due to McLaren's links with Mercedes-Benz, whose engines Manor ran in 2004. It illustrated how the series has become the premier F3 championship. Yet while the strength in depth of the British series may have suffered as a result, the competition at the front was as fierce as ever. Although Piquet did what was expected of him by taking the title, he didn't have things all his own way, and had to deal with determined challenges from Adam Carroll and James Rossiter.

From the outset, it looked as though Piquet had been studying his dad's 1987 F1 title winning season as he racked up podium finishes without taking a race win. But as Nelson Sr had demonstrated at Williams, consistency pays, and Nelsinho's steady start laid the foundation for his championship.

While money had never been an issue for the Brazilian, for Adam Carroll it had been a constant struggle. For 2004, however, his manager, John Sweeney, and P1 Motorsport team boss Roly Vincini found a full budget, and he responded magnificently. He also led the British charge when Europe's two main championships collided at the Marlboro Masters. But ultimately he lacked Piquet's consistency.

James Rossiter's Fortec team was the sensation of the early part of the season, and the Brit raced into an early championship lead. Like Carroll, however, he could not sustain the fight with Piquet.

In total, ten drivers won races in the British series. All three of Carlin Motorsport's drivers – Clivio Piccione, Danilo Dirani and Alvaro Parente – stood on the top step of the podium, but none of them managed to string a sequence of results together to mount a championship challenge. Ernesto Viso won at Knockhill before switching to F3000. Lucas di Grassi picked up two wins; Aussie Fortec driver Marcus Marshall made the right tyre choice to win on slicks at a damp Silverstone; and history was made at Castle Combe in June, when Danny Watts ended Dallara's 11-year unbeaten streak by taking victory in the Promotecme Lola-Dome. It was a popular win for the team, which had struggled to find the necessary budget, but the success was never repeated.

The Lola-Dome made a brief appearance in the Euroseries, Coloni Motorsport entering two cars in the opening two rounds. But when Christian Montanari's sponsor pulled out, the team reverted to the Italian series with Toni Vilander. The Finn was an instant front-runner and ended the season tied at the top of the standings with Matteo Cressoni. But the title went to the Ombra Racing driver, as Vilander had not entered enough races to be eligible.

In Japan, reigning German F3 Cup champion Joao Paulo de Oliveira was a regular front-runner, but a heavy crash at Mine, which forced him to sit out the race, handed the title to Inging's Ronny Quintarelli.

In Germany, Bastian Kolmsee won the title for HS when Finn Timo Lienemann spun out of the final round. Sud-Am honours went to Brazilian Xandinho Negrão, who was signed to join Carlin in the British series for 2005. In Spain, Racing Engineering's Borja Garcia overcame Portuguese veteran Manuel Giao.

For 2005, the Spanish series will be opened up to contemporary machinery, having run 1999-spec cars for four seasons. The teams there will have plenty of choice, as by the end of the season it had been announced that Lola and Dome had parted company and would each be trying to challenge Dallara's dominant position. With Mygale and Ligier also building cars to the 2005 regulations, the Italian constructor faces its toughest test yet.

Above centre: McLaren Mercedes protégé Lewis Hamilton picked up the F3 pace impressively.

Above: Danny Watts celebrates his win with the Lola.

Facing page, main photograph: Jamie Green takes the Euroseries title at Zandvoort.

Insets: Heirs apparent? Piquet (top) took the British F3 championship, while Nico Rosberg (bottom) shone in the Euroseries.

Photographs: LAT Photographic

DOMINANT
PERFORMANCE

SPORTS & GT REVIEW **by GARY WATKINS**

THE 72nd running of the Le Mans 24 Hours was trumpeted as an all-out battle between a flotilla of Audi R8s. It mattered not that this was the first time in years that no factory teams were gunning for outright victory; the prospect of four identical privately entered cars slugging it out more than made up for that. Nor did it matter, as it turned out, that two of those Audis were removed from the equation in a bizarre incident before the race was a couple of hours old. The remaining pair put on an amazing race, fighting tooth and nail on the way to the closest competitive finish at La Sarthe since 1969.

That was the year when Jacky Ickx took the first of his six victories, a tally equalled in 2004 by Tom Kristensen. The Dane and his team-mates in the Japanese Goh squad, Rinaldo Capello and Seiji Ara, battled it out with Audi Sport UK Team Veloqx drivers Johnny Herbert, Jamie Davies and Guy Smith nearly all the way through a race that remained open almost to the end. The two examples of Audi's all-conquering prototype were never separated by more than two complete laps, and the gap was more usually less than one lap of the renowned 8.48-mile Circuit de la Sarthe.

Both cars suffered technical problems along the way, but it was the Veloqx entry that lost most time in the pits. A stop for the 'British' Audi to effect repairs to the suspension shortly after the 15-hour mark cost the car 7m. That reversed the fortunes of the two R8s and ultimately decided the destination of the victory laurels.

The result would surely have been different had one or more of the other Audis been in the thick of the fight at the end. While Veloqx had its suspension problems, the Goh team suffered braking issues early on, was required to cure a misfire in the night, and even suffered a spectacular flash fire in the pits during the closing stages. It is inconceivable that one of the ultra-reliable R8s would have run through the race without problem but for *that* incident at the end of the second hour.

Allan McNish aboard the other Veloqx Audi and Champion driver JJ Lehto were running in together, in second and third positions, when they arrived at the near-flat right-hander at the start of the Porsche Curves. Neither driver came close to making the corner thanks to a mixture of oil and water put down by a backmarker.

Lehto explained that there wasn't a lot that they could have done to keep their respective cars out of the tyre wall. 'There were no oil flags, no nothing,' said the Finn, who was partnered with Emanuele Pirro and Marco Werner. 'Allan and me were first on to it. It was like being on an ice rink.'

The two R8s ended up wedged in the tyres, side by side. Both somehow made it back to the pits where they were repaired, with the loss of nine laps for the Champion entry and 19 for Veloqx. Lehto and his partners would take the final place on the podium, but the more badly damaged car could make it only as high as fifth in the hands of Frank Biela and Pierre Kaffer after McNish was diagnosed with mild concussion and was unable to take any further part in the proceedings.

McNish and Lehto weren't the first Audi drivers to need help to get out of the gravel, however. Capello had gone off at the Dunlop Chicane on lap eight, losing the best part of three minutes. That meant the Japanese entry was forced to play a game of catch up. But so evenly matched were the leading Audi crews that it was almost impossible for the Goh drivers to make inroads into the advantage held by Veloqx. The leader lost time with a 30s stop-go penalty for overtaking under a yellow flag, but things equalled out when Kristensen began to suffer engine problems and was forced to make an unscheduled stop for the ignition coil to be replaced.

The pendulum swung in favour of Goh at the beginning of the 16th hour. A worsening understeer problem that had been costing the Veloqx car time was investigated when Herbert came in to hand over to Davies. A seized rose joint in the left rear suspension was diagnosed, and the team set about changing the pushrod. Two laps were lost, turning a one-lap advantage into a one-lap deficit.

Goh had a couple of hiccups on the run to the finish. First, Kristensen picked up two slow punctures that required unscheduled stops, then Capello lost a minute due to the fire. That brought the race alive, but 30-year-old Ara, who completed the race for Goh, had enough in hand to hang on for a 40s victory.

The battle for GTS honours should have provided another thriller, but the needle match between the factory Chevrolet team and the Prodrive Ferrari squad never quite materialised. Both had looked set for victory at different times, but the American operation eventually came out on top after an incident packed race.

The Chevy Corvette C5-R, driven by Oliver Gavin, Olivier Beretta and Jan Magnussen, led for much of the first quarter of the race, before Magnussen was tipped into the barriers by a faster car. That handed a clear advantage to the number-one Prodrive 550 Maranello driven by Tomas Enge, Alain Menu and Peter Kox, an advantage that was extended to five laps after a vibration on the Gavin Corvette caused yet further delay.

Then the tables turned in Chevrolet's favour when the leading

Facing page, top: **Arms aloft, Tom Kristensen celebrates his sixth victory at Le Mans.**

Facing page, centre left and right: **In a race of fluctuating fortunes, Johnny Herbert, Guy Smith and Jamie Davies were forced to settle for second place with the Audi Sport UK Team Veloqx entry.**

Facing page, bottom: **The victorious Japanese Goh Audi handled by Tom Kristensen, Rinaldo Capello and Seiji Ara.**

Above: **The Racing for Holland Dome-Judd of Tom Coronal, Justin Wilson and Ralph Firman was fast, but gearbox maladies and a shunt put the car out of the running.**
Photographs: LAT Photographic

Above: The GTS class winner was the Chevrolet Corvette of Oliver Gavin, Jan Magnussen and Olivier Beretta.

Right: Allan McNish and Pierre Kaffer celebrate their win at Silverstone in the Euro GT series.

Far right: JJ Lehto and Marco Werner won the American Le Mans Series in their Champion Racing Audi.

Below right: Evenly matched. The Veloqx Audis of Kaffer (8) and Herbert (88) lead the field at Spa. The cars notched two wins apiece in the four-round Euroseries.

Centre far right: Mika Salo and Andrea Bertolini in the controversial Maserati MC12, which took a win at Oschersleben.

Bottom far right: Fabrizio Gollin and Luca Cappellari driving the Scuderia Italia Ferrari took the honours in the FIA GT Championship.

Photographs: LAT Photographic

Ferrari hit problems of its own just after quarter-distance. A wheel bearing failure resulted in significant body damage that required a series of pit stops, eventually dropping the car to third in class behind the second Corvette driven by Ron Fellows, Johnny O'Connell and Max Papis.

The White Lightning/Petersen Motorsport Porsche squad claimed GT honours at the end of a good day for American teams. Sascha Maassen took pole position in the factory blessed 911 GT3-RS, and he and team-mates Patrick Long and Jörg Bergmeister had a clear lead when they ran into gearbox problems during the night.

Four laps were lost, and even though the car was the fastest in the 'baby' category for much of the event, race honours looked to be going the way of the similar Freisinger Porsche driven by Stephane Ortelli, Roman Dumas and Ralf Kelleners. Late engine problems for the German team, however, allowed the US squad to retain its GT class crown.

The new Le Mans Endurance Series was dominated by Audi, and the Veloqx team in particular. Its two R8s won all four rounds, the driver pairings of Herbert/Davies and McNish/Kaffer taking two victories apiece. The title went to the former after the latter retired from the season closing Spa race. Kaffer had misjudged the speed of a slower car, which precipitated a fiery accident that handed the end-of-season crown to Herbert and Davies on a plate.

Audi continued its domination of the American Le Mans Series; this time, the Audi North American backed Champion Racing squad took the honours. JJ Lehto and Marco Werner were dominant enough to have wrapped up the title with two rounds to go. Veloqx took the season opener at Sebring, courtesy of McNish, Kaffer and Biela, while the Dyson team's Lola-MGs proved that they were fast with a string of pole positions. However, they had neither the consistency of pace nor the reliability to claim more than one victory.

It was also a case of *déjà vu* in the European based FIA GT Championship. The Scuderia Italia Ferrari team again claimed the drivers' crown with Fabrizio Gollin and Luca Cappellari, and notched up the teams' title for good measure. The Italian squad's Ferrari 550 Maranello was no longer the fastest car in the championship, though. That title passed to the Saleen S7R, which was finally honed into a winning car by Konrad Motorsport. The German outfit was boosted by the arrival of former DTM touring car drivers Uwe Alzen and Michael Bartels, who instilled a new level of professionalism into the team.

The new – and controversial – Maserati MC12 was also a race winner. Initially, the car had been denied permission to take part in the series, but this ruling was reversed so that its performance could be assessed, provided it ran a narrower rear wing. That wasn't enough to stop ex-F1 driver Mika Salo and Maserati test driver Andrea Bertolini from giving the car a maiden win at Oschersleben in Germany in September.

The future of the Maserati wasn't clear as the season closed, although it appeared that the car would have its wings clipped under new rules for 2005. It had already been announced that the Audi R8 would have to race with new restrictions in Europe in 2005. These were intended to give the advantage to a new breed of prototypes that began to be phased in from the start of the 2004 season. Yet, as the season drew to a close, no one was betting against one of the most successful sports cars of all time taking another victory in the Le Mans 24 Hours.

FUTURE PERFECT

TOURING CARS REVIEW by CHARLES BRADLEY

Above: Rough and tumble. Yvan Muller's Vauxhall comes under attack from Jason Plato's SEAT during a typically rumbustious BTCC battle.
Photograph: LAT Photographic

AS the 2004 season came to a close, the touring car world appeared to be on the cusp of something really big. The sport's governing body, the FIA, had given the green light to a World Touring Car Championship for 2005, the first tin-top series to carry that name since 1987. The WTCC will be run to the FIA's own Super 2000 2-litre regulations and has been launched at a time when the category from which it was spawned, the European Touring Car Championship, is attracting more manufacturer interest than ever.

In the ETCC in 2004, Alfa Romeo and BMW battled for the title, with SEAT not far behind. Toe-in-the-water efforts from Ford and Peugeot looked likely to lead to bigger things, while American giant Chevrolet will join the party in 2005 following the rebranding of the Daewoo range, aided by two-time British champion Alain Menu. The timing for the step up to world status appears perfect.

On the track, the 2004 ETCC was decided by the narrowest of margins. BMW drivers Andy Priaulx of England and Dirk Muller of Germany finished the season on equal points – 111 – but Andy took the title for having won more races than Dirk during the year, five to three. It was an amazing result for Priaulx, a former British hillclimb champion, who conquered not only the works Schnitzer-run BMWs of Dirk and Jörg Muller, but also the three- and sometimes four-strong factory Autodelta Alfa Romeo force too.

Priaulx's sole BMW Team Great Britain entry, run by the Belgian based team RBM, was often on the receiving end of the rough-house tactics that prevail in the ETCC, and entered the Dubai finale as very much the second favourite. He qualified on pole, however, and finished second in both races to outgoing champion Gabriele Tarquini of Alfa. In contrast, Dirk Muller suffered a nightmare. He was hit by a privateer Alfa in the opening race, causing a puncture and removing any chance of scoring points, then he just fell short of the third place he needed in the final race, despite a charging drive from the back of the grid.

Alfa's Tarquini scored more race wins (six) than anyone else, but disastrous weekends at Brno and Oschersleben stymied his title defence; he could only take third in the championship ahead of Jörg Muller (BMW), and Alfa team-mates Fabrizio Giovanardi and the impressive (but wild) rookie Augusto Farfus. Alfa will look back on the season as one when it dropped the ball somewhat, and will be keen to atone in 2005.

British champion James Thompson made some guest appearances for Alfa, winning at Donington and taking two podiums in Dubai. SEAT also won its first ETCC event, when former BTCC champ Rickard Rydell triumphed on BMW's home turf at Oschersleben. In truth, however, the Spanish marque's campaign was

slightly disappointing, failing to match BMW and Alfa for pace in most races. Jordi Gené was its best placed championship finisher in eighth.

Former Champ Car hero Alex Zanardi made a full-time return to racing, but his BMW – specially adapted to cope with his prosthetic legs – failed to match the pace of his colleagues' cars due to its extra weight. Nevertheless, the fact he was racing at all was heartwarming and demonstrated that his enthusiasm for the sport remained undimmed.

The championship outcome was almost as close in Britain, where the BTCC continued its steady recovery and the racing was as good as ever. A new television package meant that half of the races were broadcast live terrestrially, but on the flipside it lost manufacturer support from MG and Honda. Proton will follow suit in 2005, but its absence won't be noticed by many, as its three-year programme failed to deliver anything like the expected results.

As in the past two seasons, the title chase was fought out by the works Vauxhall drivers, James Thompson (who won in 2002) and 2003 champ Yvan Muller. It came down to a final-round showdown at Donington Park and went right to the last race of the season. Despite winning that, Muller was powerless to stop Thompson's march to the title, as the Briton had scored the point for setting fastest lap. That was all that separated them after no fewer than 30 rounds. It was the final bow for the old-shape Astra coupé, which had won the title for four years running, and also Thompson's last BTCC campaign – for a while at least – as he was preparing for the brave new world of the WTCC.

The best of the rest was returning former champion Jason Plato, who spearheaded SEAT's inaugural BTCC campaign with its ETCC-spec Toledo. His TV presenter role meant that his off-track personality was as strong as his uncompromising reputation on it. He made no apologies for exploiting the new race formats, often aiming for a tenth-place finish in the first race (even if it meant slowing to a crawl) to give him pole for the reverse-grid second race (as well as a ballast reduction). If he won that, it meant pole for race three as well!

In fact, Plato won more races than anyone else, but his overall points tally was always going to suffer, so he finished third. It suited SEAT's aim of winning races rather than going for the title, but a different approach can be expected for 2005. BTCC organisers did a good job of balancing the SEAT's base weight, which changed a couple of times mid-season, as the Toledo mixed it with the pure BTCC-bred machinery. Plato's rookie team-mate, Rob Huff, also scored a win with the car.

After losing its factory support over the winter, WSR bravely

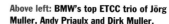

ploughed on with its MG ZS programme in the Independents' class. Anthony Reid and Colin Turkington were both overall race winners, and Reid looked set to join the championship fight until a disastrous weekend at Brands Hatch blunted his mid-season charge.

Honda also withdrew its full support, but former works team Arena fielded Tom Chilton, while Team Dynamics ran Matt Neal and Dan Eaves in Independents' Cup Civic Type-Rs. All three won races, but none had the consistency required to challenge the big boys on a regular basis.

The new race formats for 2004 proved a success, despite the occasional 'go slow' for the coveted tenth spot, which gave pole position for the reverse grid of the second race. Nobody seemed unduly concerned about the loss of pit stops, and the high energy of the short and sharp races seemed to reflect the genre perfectly. Thompson's departure from the series, however, meant the loss of another star name; the days of big players such as Menu, Rydell and Laurent Aiello seem unlikely to be repeated in the short term.

Meanwhile, the German DTM series continued to attract some of the biggest names and crowds; its events at Hockenheim significantly outsold the German Grand Prix in terms of tickets sold. On the subject of beating F1, the series also raced in China, on a temporary street circuit in downtown Shanghai, two months before the inaugural Chinese Grand Prix. The event almost ended in disaster, however, when a manhole cover worked loose and caused chaos. A four-hour delay while all 72 covers were welded shut meant that the single race held took place almost at dusk!

The series had changed tack for 2004, the emphasis being on four-door saloons rather than coupés. Audi made a full-on factory effort for the first time and won the title, but owed much to the Abt Sportsline team, which had scooped the crown in 2002 as a privateer effort.

It was Abt's 26-year-old Swedish protégé Mattias Ekstrom who romped to the title, keeping the challenge of Merc's young guns, Gary Paffett and Christijan Albers, at arm's length. Since joining the series in 2001, Ekstrom had looked a potential champion; he just needed the machinery to prove it.

Audi pulled a neat stunt at the opening round, when aerodynamic packages are frozen, by blindsiding the opposition with a stack of exterior wings on its rear corners and flanks. In all, there were 16 of the 'winglets', which knocked a good 5 mph off its top speed when compared to its rivals, but were worth their weight in gold in terms of extra downforce. The boys in Ingolstadt had got their sums right, as although the extra drag meant that the car struggled at Norisring and Hockenheim, the pay-off at circuits such as Oschersleben, Zandvoort and Brno gave it the edge.

Although Ekstrom's record of finishing every race in the points (and no lower than fifth) was exemplary, perhaps the most flourishing talent to emerge was Paffett. The Briton won his first ever DTM race in the works AMG Mercedes ranks, and followed up the Hockenheim success with wins at Lausitz, Norisring, Nürburgring and Shanghai. Unfortunately, two of those didn't count for points. Shanghai was a non-championship event, a toe-in-the-water exercise that could lead to an end-of-season winter championship in far-flung destinations in future, but it was his disqualification after winning at Lausitz that really hurt.

It was the drive of the season, Paffett fighting his way up from seventh on the grid to pass the likes of Ekstrom, Albers and Jean Alesi to score a sensational win. However, his car ran out of fuel on the slowing-down lap, and the stewards disqualified him because his C-class did not contain the requisite 1.5 litres of fuel mandated by the rulebook for testing. Of course, the scrutineers didn't really *need* that volume of fuel sample, just like they didn't *need* to point out that Paffett got out of his car outside the *parc fermé* – by a matter of metres – which also broke the rules. It was a decision that smacked of pettiness, although fortunately the 12-point reverse to Ekstrom that weekend didn't directly affect the outcome of the championship.

The best of the rest was Mercedes' Albers, who was the model of consistency in the first half of the season, including a sensational win at Estoril, where he passed Ekstrom and Paffett in one brilliant round-the-outside move at the first corner. A brake related retirement at the Nürburgring led him to take a more aggressive approach to the rest of the season, but brain fade at Oschersleben, where he drove over the white line at the pit exit, and a collision with Audi's Martin Tomczyk at Brno put paid to his title hopes. An opportunity squandered.

Sports car superstar Tom Kristensen joined the series with Audi and took a narrow win over team-mate Tomczyk at Oschersleben. He finished fourth in the championship, and his arrival raised the standard of drivers even further.

The DTM's third manufacturer, Opel, suffered another year to forget. Its new Vectra failed to make the best of its tyres, which meant

the one-lap Super Pole qualifying format worked against it. An aerodynamic imbalance, which caused the car to bottom-out at the front end, made it susceptible to locking wheels under braking.

Timo Scheider was Opel's best placed driver in the championship, and he should have scored its first podium in the second round at Estoril, but his throttle cable snagged, causing an off-track excursion. That left veteran Manuel Reuter to make the only Opel appearance in the top three at Oschersleben, but only after he had barged Paffett off the track late on.

One of the big news stories of the year was ex-F1 star Heinz-Harald Frentzen's first year in the DTM, which proved difficult. Only at Brno did he score a couple of points, and at some circuits he looked strangely out of his depth for someone with a handful of GP wins to his name.

The other notable Opel incident of 2004 was Peter Dumbreck's 120-mph head-on smash at Zandvoort, from which the Scot walked away, proving that the DTM boasts some of the safest cars in the world.

Meanwhile, also in Germany, the V8 STAR series had finally been put out of its misery in 2004, the spec silhouette series having been cancelled after three years of failing to establish itself. As on the race-track, only the strongest survive.

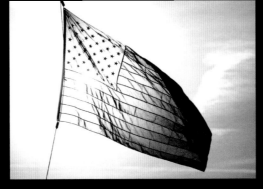

THAT'S ENTERTAINMENT

US RACING REVIEW by GORDON KIRBY

Below: Brian France, who introduced the 'Chase for the Championship'.

Bottom: Packs of cars running in close proximity on fast ovals such as Talledega is the essence of NASCAR.
Photographs: LAT Photographic

IN recent years, AUTOCOURSE has chronicled NASCAR's irresistible emergence as the goliath of American motor racing. Many observers will tell you that NASCAR's great success in the American sports marketplace is a remarkable, recent phenomenon, prompted by the rise of the all-sports cable TV network, ESPN. Truth be told, however, it's been going on for 40 or more years, since the Daytona Speedway was opened in 1959 in fact.

Thirty-one years ago, I wrote my first American season review for AUTOCOURSE; the piece opened with a photo of NASCAR Grand National cars in action and a homily to NASCAR's good management, stable rules package and money making methods with the focus on entertainment. In the previous year's AUTOCOURSE, my predecessor, Pete Lyons, lamented the demise of the unlimited race car in both CanAm and Indycars as the SCCA and USAC failed to cope with the onrush of new technology.

'One might suspect,' Lyons wrote, 'that...the motor racing world had run its course of fascination for The Machine. There seems to be a genuine interest in manipulating the machinery to produce better racing. The idea is almost this simple: settle on a design, freeze it, and get on out to the speedway. It appears full strength in NASCAR which if regarded as Show Biz is certainly the most successful motor sporting operation.'

Three decades later, many media pundits continue to wonder what NASCAR's success is all about. They offer many theories, but studiously ignore the real reason fuelling stock car racing's boom. Most have forgotten, or never really knew, that the key to NASCAR's strength is very tight management of the technical rules, and similar control of the manufacturers' spending and influence, essential areas in which every other sanctioning body around the world has failed completely.

In 2003, Brian France took over as NASCAR's CEO from his father, Bill France Jr, who had run NASCAR since 1972. Bill Jr had inherited the reins from his legendary father, Bill Sr, who had founded NASCAR in 1949 and run the organisation with an iron fist. He had also built the Daytona Speedway, the first modern, high-banked superspeedway in America.

It's an open question whether Brian France can fill the giant shoes of his father and grandfather, but he's just beginning his reign at the helm of a behemoth, whose major-league status even his visionary grandfather could not have imagined.

This past year, France introduced a controversial new point system, which only history will be able to judge. The invention of the 'Chase for the Championship', a play-off among the top ten in points over the final ten of 36 races, drew a lot of criticism from fans, press, drivers and teams alike, who reckoned it detracted from the hard slog of the traditional year-long championship battle. But 'The Chase' generated a huge amount of media coverage at a time when the NFL football season and baseball's World Series would normally dominate America's airwaves and sports pages.

Junior is The Man

Without doubt, the most visible racing driver in America today is Dale Earnhardt Jr. Following the death of his father at Daytona in 2001, he assumed a role of mythic proportions, despite not having won a single championship. Dale Jr is on the celebrity/entertainment/lifestyle pages as often as he's in the sports pages. Comparing his fifth win in the race to his father's record of ten wins on the Alabama superspeedway, Junior said, 'This don't mean shit compared to what Daddy did here.' He was fined $25,000 and docked 25 points, losing critical ground in a close battle for the championship with primary rival Kurt Busch. And, of course, the incident and NASCAR's response created many more stories and sound bites.

Earnhardt also made racing's other big media splash of the year when he crashed a Corvette sports car on his out-lap of a morning warm-up for an American Le Mans series race at Sears Point (excuse me, that's Infineon Raceway) in July. Before he could clamber out, the Corvette caught fire. Although the fire looked much more damaging than it actually was, Junior was not wearing fireproof underwear and received second-degree burns to his legs, so he had to have relief drivers ready for the next two races.

For most of the year, Hendrick Chevrolet team-mates Jeff Gordon and Jimmie Johnson sat atop the point standings. After the first 26 races, prior to the newly concocted championship play-off over the final ten races, Gordon and Johnson were 1-2, sharing nine wins between them. Johnson was four-time champion Gordon's protégé, and his car was co-owned by Gordon as part of Hendrick's four-car team. But neither Gordon nor Johnson fared well in the opening races of the championship chase.

Kurt Busch surged to the front by winning the first of the play-off races, chased by Earnhardt and Gordon. The 26-year-old Busch had started racing at NASCAR's top level in 2001 with Jack Roush's five-car Ford team. He had won four races in 2002 and finished third in the championship. He had won four more races in 2003, but tumbled to 11th in the points with a

Top left: Kurt Busch celebrates winning the Nextel Cup.

Above far left: Champion Busch waves the number 97 flag as he parades his Rousch Racing Ford.

Top: Dale Earnhardt Jr is helped away from the charred wreck of his Corvette at Sears Point.

Above left: Happily, Earnhardt was soon back in winning action.

Above: Jimmie Johnson finished the season just eight points shy of the championhip in the closest ever title finish.
Photographs: LAT Photographic

poor close to the season. In 2004, it was different, as Busch came on strong in the closing months of the long season. To clinch the championship at the final round by the scant margin of just eight points

In his sixth year in Cup cars, Earnhardt, 29, enjoyed his best season to date aboard his DEI (Dale Earnhardt Incorporated) Chevrolet. Junior was more competitive across the board on all types of track in 2004, and he won six races, but only wound up a somewhat disappointing fifth in the championship.

Veteran Mark Martin had one of his better years for some time, finishing fourth in the championship ahead of both 2003 champion Matt Kenseth and 2002 champ Tony Stewart. Near the end of the year, Martin announced that he would cut back at the end of 2005, when he planned to run only selected Busch (NASCAR's second division) races. Former champions Terry Labonte and Rusty Wallace made similar announcements of reduced involvement; NASCAR's current old guard is passing into history.

For all NASCAR's immense success, today's American motor sport landscape is a Lilliputian world. Looking around at the shortage of multiple champions and nationally- or internationally-known legends like America enjoyed in great numbers through the 1960s, '70s, '80s and '90s, it's fair to say that four-time NASCAR champion Jeff Gordon is the only great driver racing in America today. There are no other high-profile multiple champions active in stock cars, or Indy or Champ cars, a shocking comparison to the days of yore, when there were many legends racing in both stock cars and Indy cars. Of course, one could make the same argument about F1 today.

A sad example of this situation in 2004 was the obscure status of two great American racing teams. First, consider Chip Ganassi's IRL and NASCAR teams, neither of which was much north of nowhere during the season. Ganassi's four-time CART champion and one-time IRL champion team fell to the back of the grid as Toyota's IRL engine was outpowered by Honda and, to a lesser degree, Chevrolet. Scott Dixon, 2003 champion and touted early in the year for a Williams F1 seat, had a disastrous season, struggling for speed in most races and finishing a dismal tenth in points. Team-mate Darren Manning fared no better and was 11th in the championship. Ganassi's NASCAR team, now five years old, also produced poor results. Drivers Jamie McMurray, Sterling Marlin and Casey Mears finished 11th, 21st and 22nd in the big show.

In roughly similar straights was Penske Racing. Although Penske's IRL and NASCAR outfits enjoyed their occasional weekends in the sun in 2004, overall the team that once had defined America's engagement in global motor sport was reduced to being just another bit player in the domestic oval racing scene.

It was one thing for Ganassi's teams to suffer this humiliation, but quite another for Penske. For many years, Penske's entries helped raise the level of preparation and presentation around the world in F1 and international sports car racing, but in the 21st century they have become merely part of the furniture of America's weekly oval racing show. Indeed, Penske's drivers, Ryan Newman and Rusty Wallace, made it into seventh and 18th respectively in NASCAR's championship, while his Indy drivers, Helio Castroneves and Sam Hornish Jr, fared slightly better, finishing fourth and seventh in the IRL series.

Kanaan wins for Honda

Brazilian ace Tony Kanaan beat Andretti-Green team-mate Dan Wheldon to the IRL championship; both drivers had Honda engines. Kanaan had won the Indy Lights championship in 1997 and raced in CART from 1998 to 2002. The 29-year-old was the man to beat in the IRL in 2004, winning three races and wrapping up the title with one race to go. Incredibly, he finished every one of the season's 3,305 laps, a first-time achievement in the sport's history.

Brit Wheldon was also a front-runner in many races, similarly winning three times on his way to second in the championship. Andretti-Green fielded four cars in 2004, Dario Franchitti and Bryan Herta being the other drivers. Franchitti won two races, having bounced back after missing most of the races in 2003 because of a back injury.

Buddy Rice finished third in the championship, and won the Indy 500 for Bobby Rahal's team and Honda. The Japanese manufacturer swept the year, dominating after the pre-Indy switch from 3.5-litre to 3.0-litre engines and soundly trouncing arch rival Toyota. Like Rahal's team, Adrian Fernandez also switched to the IRL in 2004 because of his financial ties to Honda. He came through to win three races, helping Honda to dominate over Toyota and Chevrolet. Penske's Sam Hornish and Helio Castroneves were the only non-Honda drivers to win races, and each did so only once: Hornish in the season opener, Castroneves in the finale.

As has been reported in past editions of AUTOCOURSE, Indy or Champ car racing has been seriously damaged in recent years by a civil war that started in 1996. That was the year Indianapolis Motor Speedway President Tony George created his own Indy Racing League (IRL) series in opposition to the existing Championship Auto Racing Teams (CART) Indy Car World Series.

George had inherited the Speedway in 1990 and immediately started arguing with the CART team owners about control of the sport. He finally decided to take the Indy 500 out of the CART championship and start his own, ovals-only series, explaining that he was going to cut costs and restrict technology, as well as bring in more American drivers from the country's grass-roots dirt-track ranks.

Sadly, none of those goals has been achieved. Instead, open-wheel racing in the United States has been decimated over the past nine years, and many people have been driven out of business. Now it is virtually impossible to sell any worthwhile sponsorship for any form of American open-wheel racing, and young American drivers find it very difficult to move up the ladder.

To give some perspective to the dilemma Indy car racing faces today, consider that in 1967 there were 87 entries for the Indy 500, including naturally aspirated Offenhausers, supercharged Offies, turbo Offies, stock-block Fords, turbo Fords and a Granatelli turbine. It was the height of the technical revolution at Indianapolis and the zenith of the race's history. In fact, 12 active F1 drivers were entered that year, and six of them failed to qualify! In 1995, the last year that CART's teams and drivers raced at Indianapolis, there were no fewer than 104 entries, of which 96 driver/car combinations made practice runs

Right: Dan Wheldon made his mark with three wins and a second place in the IRL championship.

Below left: Fight to the finish. Jimmie Johnson (48) and Jeff Gordon slug it out at Homestead in the battle for second spot in the Nextel Cup.

Below: Michael Andretti ran an awesomely strong four-car squad in the IRL. With Honda power, his drivers took victories in eight of the 14 rounds.

Below right: Dario Franchitti bounced back from his injury problems with two wins.

Photographs: LAT Photographic

Above: Adrian Fernandez snatches the win, but Tony Kanaan clinches the IRL championship in a thrilling finish at the Calfornia Speedway.

Left: Guitar man. Left-hander Kanaan wields his Les Paul à la Jimi Hendrix after his win at Nashville.

Below: Penske's Helio Castroneves had a tough season, which was brightened by a win in the season's finale at Fort Worth.
Photographs: LAT Photographic

and 71 made qualifying runs. The 2004 race witnessed the smallest field at Indianapolis since 1947, and the IRL struggled to pull together a full complement of 33 cars. In fact, not one driver failed to qualify or was 'bumped' from the field.

The crowds and TV ratings for the IRL have also declined. Even at Indianapolis in the past two years, there were plenty of empty seats, and the 500's TV ratings have fallen from a high of 14 in 1992 to below five in 2004. The last time the Indy 500 out-drew the Daytona 500 was in 1995, and in 2004 Daytona's TV audience was four times bigger than Indy's. Most IRL races pull crowds that are anywhere from a quarter to a tenth the size of NASCAR crowds at the same tracks.

In the wake of the CART/IRL split, CART went through a series of management changes as the team owner driven organisation struggled unsuccessfully to find any kind of useful leadership. Torn apart by self-interest, they agreed to what turned out to be an ill-advised stock-market flotation in 1998. During this time, there was also an endlessly unresolved argument about engine rules, as well as a storm in 2001 over Honda and Ford Cosworth cheating the pop-off valve. That led to the defection of Toyota and Honda, and eventually most of CART's top teams, to the IRL. The result was the CART bankruptcy proceedings of 2003.

Sad to say, the team owners who deserted CART for the IRL failed to provide the necessary leadership when they had the opportunity during their CART years. They failed to develop a business plan and a technical philosophy; they failed to manage the rules correctly, and to build and develop good relationships with the manufacturers. The IRL has inherited the same problems, and since most IRL teams are funded primarily by

Toyota, Honda or Chevrolet, the question is what will happen at the end of 2006, when Toyota is likely to depart the IRL for a full-time commitment to NASCAR?

Will Honda pull out of the IRL and join Toyota in NASCAR, or continue to supply IRL engines without serious team subsidies as it has done in recent years? The betting inside the industry is that Honda ultimately will follow Toyota's lead and make the move to NASCAR.

Retired three-time Indy 500 winner Bobby Unser commented, 'If all that happens, and I'm one of those who believe that is what's going to happen, then Tony's got a big problem on his hands. You think you've seen short fields at Indianapolis the last few years? Well brother, you ain't seen nothin' yet.'

Brilliant Bourdais

CART's assets were purchased in 2003 by Open-Wheel Racing Series (OWRS), a consortium of three team owners, Gerald Forsythe, Kevin Kalkhoven and Paul Gentilozzi. They have re-branded the series as the Champ Car World Series and refer to the cars as Champ Cars, reflecting the 100-year history of American national championship racing. The new owners worked hard to rebuild the series through 2004, and put together a very promising commercial platform for 2005 and beyond. There's a new, three-year TV package with CBS and Speedchannel, series sponsorship from AOL, expanded support from McDonald's, sponsor of champion Sébastien Bourdais's car, as Champ Car's fast food restaurant, and additional associate sponsorship for five years from Ford, as Ford America, Canada,

Far left: Buddy Rice and Bobby Rahal pose with the Borg-Warner Trophy after the Indy 500.

Below left: No fluke. Rice backed up his Brickyard win with another two victories during the 2004 IRL season.

Left: Paul Tracy opened the Champ Car season with a win at Long Beach, but the reigning title holder was overshadowed by Sébastien Bourdais (below). The young Frenchman was sensationally fast for Newman/Haas Racing.

Photographs: LAT Photographic

Mexico and South America will focus on the Champ Car World Series now that the company has pulled out of F1.

Champ Car's greatest strength lies in its venues and tremendous fan base. In 2003, amid serious political and financial troubles, the Champ Car World Series still drew almost 2.7 million people to its total of 17 races, averaging 158,000 per race. That was second only to NASCAR's average crowd of 176,000, and way ahead of the IRL's 2003 average of 63,500, which falls to around 45,000 without the Indy 500. Clearly, the fans remained faithful to the diverse mix of race-tracks, primarily street circuits and road courses, that comprise one of the world's most challenging and respected racing series. Paul Newman, co-owner of Newman/Haas Racing, said, 'The fans are the greatest strength that Champ Car has. The fans are unbelievably passionate and committed. I talked to a lot of them at Long Beach this year, and their enthusiasm gave me a lot of heart. They really believe in the series.'

For sure, Champ Car must develop a better organisation than we've seen in the past, with improved methods of operating, promoting and marketing. But clearly, the most important factor in making a successful racing series is having the sanctioning body squarely in the driver's seat, writing and enforcing sensible, technically interesting rules and enjoying good relationships with the manufacturers competing in the series. NASCAR and Ferrari aside, the history of automobile racing series and manufacturers is that they come and go. The manufacturers take part, inflating the technical and financial stakes. Then they leave, deflating them. The same essential failures killed CanAm, the original TransAm, Formula 5000, IMSA and CART, and it's very clear that if either the IRL or Champ Car are to achieve long-term success, they will have to be effective in these key areas, where so many others have failed.

The Champ Car World Series rose from CART's ashes to put on a good first year. The championship was all about Newman/Haas, as Sébastien Bourdais and Bruno Junqueira finished 1-2 after dominating the second half of the season in particular. In his second year in America, Bourdais emerged as a serious talent – cool, smooth, analytical and blindingly fast. He won seven of 14 races in 2004 and was on the front row in all bar three races. Team-mate Junqueira was always close to Bourdais, but had to play second fiddle to the brilliant Frenchman, winning just one race as Newman/Haas dominated on the way to the team's fifth Champ Car title.

Defending champion Paul Tracy won the season opener in Long Beach, but didn't win again until Vancouver at the end of July. Things just didn't go Tracy's way in 2004 and he wound up fourth in the championship, behind Forsythe team-mate Patrick Carpentier, who won at Laguna Seca in September and inexplicably decided to move to the IRL in 2005 with Eddie Cheever's team. Others winning races were Ryan Hunter-Reay and Alex Tagliani. Hunter-Reay scored a dominant victory on the Milwaukee Mile oval in June, leading all the way, while Tagliani finally won his first Champ Car race at Elkhart Lake in August. This was also the first Champ Car win for Paul Gentilozzi's Rocketsports team. Top rookie was 22-year-old A.J. Allmendinger, who battled for rookie of the year honours with F1 refugee Justin Wilson. Toyota/Atlantic champion in 2003, Allmendinger frequently ran near the front and showed himself to be a tough racer, finishing seventh in the championship.

Jon Fogarty turned down an IRL ride with Bobby Rahal's team to return to Toyota/Atlantic in 2004. The 29-year-old had won the Atlantic title in 2002, and returned to the series after trying unsuccessfully to break into Champ Cars. He proved to be the man to beat in Atlantic, winning six races, and surely deserves a proper Champ Car ride. Scotsman Ryan Dalziel was Fogarty's primary challenger, while 18-year-old Canadian Andrew Ranger was rookie of the year.

America's inaugural Formula BMW championship was won by 19-year-old German Andreas Wirth, who beat 17-year-old Canadian James Hinchcliffe to the title. The IRL's Infiniti Pro Series was won by Brazilian Thiago Medeiros.

The American Le Mans sports car championship was taken by JJ Lehto aboard Champion Racing's Audi R8, while the rival GrandAm sports car series went to Max Papis and Scott Pruett aboard Chip Ganassi's Toyota powered car. Paul Gentilozzi gained his fourth TransAm championship, equalling Mark Donohue's long-standing record of 29 wins scored during the TransAm's heyday back in 1968–71.

Facing page: Bourdais and Paul Tracy head the field into Turn One at the Molson Indy Toronto.

Above: Bruno Junqueira gets out of shape in his Newman-Haas Lola at Laguna Seca.

Left: Paul Gentilozzi returned to the TransAm Championship on a full-time basis and wrapped up his fourth title.
Photographs: LAT Photographic

Above: Chip Ganassi's championship winning Toyota leads the GrandAm cars at the start of the September round at Homestead-Miami Speedway.

Left: Jon Fogarty returned to Atlantic competition in an attempt to break into Champ Cars.
Photographs: LAT Photographic

MAJOR RESULTS

OTHER CHAMPIONSHIP RACING SERIES WORLDWIDE

Compiled by DAVID HAYHOE

International Formula 3000 Championship

All cars are Lola B2/50-Zytek Judd KV.

FIA INTERNATIONAL FORMULA 3000 CHAMPIONSHIP, Autodromo Enzo e Dino Ferrari, Imola, Italy, 24 April. Round 1. 31 laps of the 3.065-mile/4.933-km circuit, 94.856 miles/152.656 km.
1 Vitantonio Liuzzi, I, 52m 46.960s, 107.826 mph/173.530 km/h; **2** Enrico Toccacelo, I, 52m 55.813s; **3** Robert Doornbos, NL, 53m 18.048s; **4** Raffaele Giammaria, I, 53m 20.465s; **5** Tomas Enge, CZ, 53m 21.475s; **6** Jeffrey van Hooydonk, B, 53m 31.021s; **7** Yannick Schroeder, F, 53m 32.782s; **8** Alan van der Merwe, ZA, 53m 32.997s; **9** Patrick Friesacher, A, 53m 33.321s; **10** Tony Schmidt, D, 53m 46.118s; **11** Jan Heylen, B, 54m 01.951s; **12** Mathias Lauda, A, 54m 14.103s; **13** Rodrigo Ribeiro, BR, 54m 26.160s; **14** Ferdinando Monfardini, I, 30 laps; **15** Nico Verdonck, B, 30; **16** José Maria Lopez, RA, 17 (DNF); **17** Esteban Guerrieri, RA, 10 (DNF); **18** Can Artam, TR, 3 (DNF).
Fastest lap: Lopez, 1m 39.847s, 110.517 mph/177.860 km/h.

FIA INTERNATIONAL FORMULA 3000 CHAMPIONSHIP, Circuit de Catalunya, Montmeló, Barcelona, Spain, 8 May. Round 2. 33 laps of the 2.875-mile/4.627-km circuit, 94.800 miles/152.566 km.
1 Vitantonio Liuzzi, I, 53m 22.107s, 106.580 mph/171.524 km/h; **2** Enrico Toccacelo, I, 53m 33.771s; **3** Raffaele Giammaria, I, 54m 11.121s; **4** Patrick Friesacher, A, 54m 14.702s; **5** Esteban Guerrieri, RA, 54m 15.084s; **6** José Maria Lopez, RA, 54m 18.155s; **7** Mathias Lauda, A, 54m 27.402s; **8** Rodrigo Ribeiro, BR, 54m 39.624s; **9** Nico Verdonck, B, 54m 40.281s; **10** Can Artam, TR, 54m 48.919s; **11** Jan Heylen, B, 54m 52.653s; **12** Alan van der Merwe, ZA, 32 laps; **13** Ferdinando Monfardini, I, 32; **14** Robert Doornbos, NL, 30; **15** Jeffrey van Hooydonk, B, 28 (DNF); **16** Tomas Enge, CZ, 18 (DNF); **17** Yannick Schroeder, F, 18 (DNF).
Fastest lap: Liuzzi, 1m 34.233s, 109.837 mph/176.766 km/h.

FIA INTERNATIONAL FORMULA 3000 CHAMPIONSHIP, Monte Carlo Street Circuit, Monaco, 22 May. Round 3. 45 laps of the 2.075-mile/3.340-km circuit, 93.392 miles/150.300 km.
1 Vitantonio Liuzzi, I, 1h 08m 07.431s, 82.255 mph/132.377 km/h; **2** Enrico Toccacelo, I, 1h 08m 10.281s; **3** José Maria Lopez, RA, 1h 08m 18.347s; **4** Raffaele Giammaria, I, 1h 08m 36.283s; **5** Patrick Friesacher, A, 1h 08m 36.704s; **6** Robert Doornbos, NL, 1h 08m 53.284s; **7** Jeffrey van Hooydonk, B, 1h 08m 53.635s; **8** Jan Heylen, B, 1h 09m 11.600s; **9** Alan van der Merwe, ZA, 1h 09m 12.470s; **10** Yannick Schroeder, F, 44 laps; **11** Tony Schmidt, D, 44; **12** Nico Verdonck, B, 44; **13** Ferdinando Monfardini, I, 44; **14** Tomas Enge, CZ, 44; **15** Rodrigo Ribeiro, BR, 30 (DNF); **16** Mathias Lauda, A, 18 (DNF); **17** Can Artam, TR, 1 (DNF); **18** Esteban Guerrieri, RA, 0 (DNF).
Fastest lap: Enge, 1m 26.911s, 85.966 mph/138.348 km/h.

FIA INTERNATIONAL FORMULA 3000 CHAMPIONSHIP, Nürburgring Grand Prix Circuit, Nürburg/Eifel, Germany, 29 May. Round 4. 30 laps of the 3.199-mile/5.148-km circuit, 95.954 miles/154.423 km.
1 Enrico Toccacelo, I, 56m 22.535s, 102.123 mph/164.351 km/h; **2** Robert Doornbos, NL, 56m 32.492s; **3** Yannick Schroeder, F, 56m 33.118s; **4** Esteban Guerrieri, RA, 56m 34.765s; **5** José Maria Lopez, RA, 56m 34.910s; **6** Raffaele Giammaria, I, 56m 35.317s; **7** Tomas Enge, CZ, 56m 37.497s; **8** Jeffrey van Hooydonk, B, 56m 52.921s; **9** Jan Heylen, B, 56m 53.897s; **10** Mathias Lauda, A, 57m 01.739s; **11** Vitantonio Liuzzi, I, 57m 02.083s; **12** Nico Verdonck, B, 57m 04.577s; **13** Can Artam, TR, 57m 49.083s; **14** Tony Schmidt, D, 57m 49.226s; **15** Ferdinando Monfardini, I, 57m 52.372s; **16** Rodrigo Ribeiro, BR, 29 laps; **17** Alan van der Merwe, ZA, 18 (DNF); **18** Patrick Friesacher, A, 15 (DNF).
Fastest lap: Lopez, 1m 49.453s, 105.212 mph/169.322 km/h.

FIA INTERNATIONAL FORMULA 3000 CHAMPIONSHIP, Circuit de Nevers, Magny-Cours, France, 3 July. Round 5. 35 laps of the 2.741-mile/4.411-km circuit, 95.815 miles/154.199 km.
1 Vitantonio Liuzzi, I, 56m 18.071s, 102.110 mph/164.329 km/h; **2** Tomas Enge, CZ, 56m 24.569s; **3** Patrick Friesacher, A, 56m 40.144s; **4** Yannick Schroeder, F, 56m 40.442s; **5** Robert Doornbos, NL, 56m 42.487s; **6** Esteban Guerrieri, RA, 56m 55.547s; **7** Tony Schmidt, D, 56m 56.241s; **8** Ernesto Viso, YV, 56m 57.602s; **9** Alan van der Merwe, ZA, 57m 07.240s; **10** Ferdinando Monfardini, I, 57m 13.780s; **11** Nico Verdonck, B, 57m 14.182s; **12** Enrico Toccacelo, I, 57m 18.397s; **13** Jeffrey van Hooydonk, B, 57m 40.657s; **14** Raffaele Giammaria, I, 32 laps (DNF); **15** José Maria Lopez, RA, 22 (DNF); **16** Can Artam, TR, 22 (DNF); **17** Mathias Lauda, A, 1 (DNF).
Fastest lap: Liuzzi, 1m 31.791s, 107.496 mph/172.997 km/h.

FIA INTERNATIONAL FORMULA 3000 CHAMPIONSHIP, Silverstone Grand Prix Circuit, Towcester, Northamptonshire, Great Britain, 10 July. Round 6. 30 laps of the 3.194-mile/5.141-km circuit, 95.769 miles/154.125 km.
1 Vitantonio Liuzzi, I, 50m 22.548s, 114.065 mph/183.570 km/h; **2** Enrico Toccacelo, I, 50m 23.636s; **3** Tomas Enge, CZ, 50m 25.536s; **4** José Maria Lopez, RA, 50m 41.440s; **5** Patrick Friesacher, A, 50m 44.317s; **6** Raffaele Giammaria, I, 50m 49.450s; **7** Tony Schmidt, D, 50m 58.473s; **8** Alan van der Merwe, ZA, 51m 04.878s; **9** Ferdinando Monfardini, I, 51m 07.916s; **10** Robert Doornbos, NL, 51m 09.789s; **11** Ernesto Viso, YV, 51m 10.002s; **12** Nico Verdonck, B, 51m 27.362s; **13** Mathias Lauda, A, 51m 28.205s; **14** Yannick Schroeder, F, 51m 29.802s; **15** Esteban Guerrieri, RA, 51m 47.748s; **16** Jeffrey van Hooydonk, B, 5 laps (DNF); **17** Olivier Tielemans, NL, 1 (DNF).
Fastest lap: Enge, 1m 38.384s, 116.890 mph/188.116 km/h.

FIA INTERNATIONAL FORMULA 3000 CHAMPIONSHIP, Hockenheimring Grand Prix Circuit, Heidelberg, Germany, 24 July. Round 7. 33 laps of the 2.842-mile/4.574-km circuit, 93.791 miles/150.942 km.
1 Vitantonio Liuzzi, I, 51m 01.849s, 110.276 mph/177.472 km/h; **2** Enrico Toccacelo, I, 51m 08.548s; **3** Esteban Guerrieri, RA, 51m 14.562s; **4** Robert Doornbos, NL, 51m 16.970s; **5** Tony Schmidt, D, 51m 17.348s; **6** José Maria Lopez, RA, 51m 28.201s; **7** Ernesto Viso, YV, 52m 11.472s; **8** Nico Verdonck, B, 52m 26.269s; **9** Jeffrey van Hooydonk, B, 52m 27.528s; **10** Can Artam, TR, 52m 34.089s; **11** Alan van der Merwe, ZA, 32 laps (DNF); **12** Olivier Tielemans, NL, 32; **13** Mathias Lauda, A, 23 (DNF); **14** Yannick Schroeder, F, 1 (DNF); **15** Raffaele Giammaria, I, 1 (DNF); **16** Tomas Enge, CZ, 0 (DNF); **17** Ferdinando Monfardini, I, 0 (DNF).
Fastest lap: Toccacelo, 1m 30.591s, 112.944 mph/181.766 km/h.

FIA INTERNATIONAL FORMULA 3000 CHAMPIONSHIP, Hungaroring, Mogyorod, Budapest, Hungary, 14 August. Round 8. 35 laps of the 2.722-mile/4.381-km circuit, 95.274 miles/153.328 km.
1 Patrick Friesacher, A, 1h 08m 38.544s, 83.278 mph/134.023 km/h; **2** Vitantonio Liuzzi, I, 1h 08m 41.057s; **3** Enrico Toccacelo, I, 1h 08m 58.732s; **4** Tomas Enge, CZ, 1h 09m 00.087s; **5** Esteban Guerrieri, RA, 1h 09m 20.903s; **6** Ernesto Viso, YV, 1h 09m 27.095s; **7** Robert Doornbos, NL, 1h 09m 40.000s; **8** José Maria Lopez, RA, 1h 09m 56.536s; **9** Jeffrey van Hooydonk, B, 1h 10m 11.910s; **10** Raffaele Giammaria, I, 1h 10m 14.137s; **11** Tony Schmidt, D, 34 laps; **12** Nico Verdonck, B, 34; **13** Ferdinando Monfardini, I, 34; **14** Can Artam, TR, 34; **15** Olivier Tielemans, NL, 33; **16** Mathias Lauda, A, 31 (DNF); **17** Chanoch Nissany, IS, 23 DNF); **18** Yannick Schroeder, F, 13 (DNF).
Fastest lap: Enge, 1m 37.927s, 100.075 mph/161.055 km/h.

FIA INTERNATIONAL FORMULA 3000 CHAMPIONSHIP, Circuit de Spa-Francorchamps, Stavelot, Belgium, 28 August. Round 9. 22 laps of the 4.335-mile/6.976-km circuit, 95.353 miles/153.455 km.
1 Robert Doornbos, NL, 58m 14.019s, 98.245 mph/158.110 km/h; **2** Vitantonio Liuzzi, I, 58m 41.896s; **3** José Maria Lopez, RA, 58m 43.338s; **4** Tomas Enge, CZ, 58m 52.387s; **5** Patrick Friesacher, A, 58m 52.513s; **6** Tony Schmidt, D, 58m 10.895s; **7** Esteban Guerrieri, RA, 59m 12.640s; **8** Matteo Grassotto, I, 59m 20.889s; **9** Jeffrey van Hooydonk, B, 59m 23.781s; **10** Ernesto Viso, YV, 59m 51.372s; **11** Nico Verdonck, B, 59m 52.550s; **12** Enrico Toccacelo, I, 59m 58.310s; **13** Can Artam, TR, 1h 00m 09.155s; **14** Mathias Lauda, A, 1h 00m 13.467s; **15** Matteo Meneghello, I, 1h 00m 31.162s; **16** Ferdinando Monfardini, I, 21 laps; **17** Chanoch Nissany, IS, 7 (DNF); **18** Olivier Tielemans, NL, 6 (DNF).
Fastest lap: Doornbos, 2m 29.524s, 104.364 mph/167.957 km/h.

FIA INTERNATIONAL FORMULA 3000 CHAMPIONSHIP, Autodromo Nazionale di Monza, Milan, Italy, 11 September. Round 10. 26 laps of the 3.600-mile/5.793-km circuit, 93.398 miles/150.309 km.
1 Vitantonio Liuzzi, I, 44m 20.747s, 126.368 mph/203.369 km/h; **2** Tomas Enge, CZ, 44m 30.159s; **3** Robert Doornbos, NL, 44m 36.227s; **4** Raffaele Giammaria, I, 44m 44.193s; **5** Esteban Guerrieri, RA, 44m 44.435s; **6** Mathias Lauda, A, 45m 06.299s; **7** Jeffrey van Hooydonk, B, 45m 06.532s; **8** Ernesto Viso, YV, 45m 28.607s; **9** Can Artam, TR, 46m 43.393s; **10** Tony Schmidt, D, 25 laps (DNF); **11** Olivier Tielemans, NL, 25; **12** Chanoch Nissany, IS, 25; **13** Patrick Friesacher, A, 17 (DNF); **14** Ferdinando Monfardini, I, 17 (DNF); **15** José Maria Lopez, RA, 2 (DNF); **16** Matteo Grassotto, I, 2 (DNF); **17** Enrico Toccacelo, I, 0 (DNF); **18** Michele Rugolo, I, 0 (DNF).
Fastest lap: Liuzzi, 1m 39.775s, 129.878 mph/209.018 km/h.

Final championship points

Drivers
1 Vitantonio Liuzzi, I, 86; **2** Enrico Toccacelo, I, 56; **3** Robert Doornbos, NL, 44; **4** Tomas Enge, CZ, 38; **5** Patrick Friesacher, A, 33; **6=** José Maria Lopez, RA, 28; **6=** Esteban Guerrieri, RA, 28; **8** Raffaele Giammaria, I, 27; **9** Yannick Schroeder, F, 13; **10** Tony Schmidt, D, 11; **11** Jeffrey van Hooydonk, B, 8; **12** Ernesto Viso, YV, 7; **13** Mathias Lauda, A, 5; **14** Alan van der Merwe, ZA, 2; **15=** Nico Verdonck, B, 1; **15=** Jan Heylen, B, 1; **15=** Rodrigo Ribeiro, BR, 1; **15=** Matteo Grassotto, I, 1.

Teams
1 Arden International, 130; **2** BCN Competicion, 84; **3** Ma-Con Engineering, 49; **4** CMS Performance, 33; **5** Coloni Motorsport, 30; **6** AEZ I.E. Engineering, 23; **7** Durango Formula, 21; **8** Super Nova Racing, 13; **9** Team Astromega, 7.

Superfund Euro 3000 Series

All cars are Lola B99/50-Zytek Judd KV.

SUPERFUND EURO 3000, Automotodrom Brno Masaryk Circuit, Brno, Czech Republic, 2 May. Round 1. 25 laps of the 3.357-mile/5.403-km circuit, 83.932 miles/135.075 km.
1 Fabrizio del Monte, I, 48m 16.727s, 104.309 mph/167.869 km/h; **2** Norbert Siedler, A, 48m 32.458s, **3** Nicky Pastorelli, NL, 48m 42.696s; **4** Bernhard Auinger, A, 48m 45.820s; **5** 'Babalus', I, 48m 50.151s; **6** Christiano Tuka Rocha, BR, 48m 51.197s; **7** Jonny Reid, NZ, 49m 06.151s; **8** Sven Heidfeld, D, 49m 09.994s; **9** Fausto Ippoliti, I, 49m 10.072s; **10** Giacomo Ricci, I, 49m 13.692s.

SUPERFUND EURO 3000, Autódromo Fernanda Pires da Silva, Alcabideche, Estoril, Portugal, 30 May. Round 2. 36 laps of the 2.599-mile/4.183-km circuit, 93.571 miles/150.588 km.
1 Fabrizio del Monte, I, 56m 37.594s, 99.145 mph/159.559 km/h; **2** Nicky Pastorelli, NL, 56m 38.295s; **3** Bernhard Auinger, A, 56m 44.812s; **4** Norbert Siedler, A, 56m 56.747s; **5** Maxime Hodencq, B, 57m 12.382s; **6** Fausto Ippoliti, I, 57m 32.954s; **7** Giacomo Ricci, I, 57m 59.079s; **8** Tor Graves, GB, 58m 04.948s; **9** Rafael Sarandenses, E, 35 laps; **10** Allam Khodair, BR, 33.
Fastest lap: Siedeler, 1m 32.163s, 101.528 mph/163.393 km/h.

SUPERFUND EURO 3000, Circuito Permanente de Jerez, Jerez de la Frontera, Spain, 6 June. Round 3. 34 laps of the 2.751-mile/4.428-km circuit, 93.549 miles/150.552 km.
1 Fabrizio del Monte, I, 59m 35.497s, 94.190 mph/151.584 km/h; **2** Mathias Lauda, A, 59m 38.091s; **3** Jonny Reid, NZ, 59m 39.754s; **4** 'Babalus', I, 59m 48.551s; **5** Fausto Ippoliti, I, 59m 53.203s; **6** Nicky Pastorelli, NL, 59m 53.734s; **7** Bernhard Auinger, A, 59m 55.866s; **8** Maxime Hodencq, B, 33 laps (DNF)*; **9** Allam Khodair, BR, 32 (DNF); **10** Loic Deman, B, 24 (DNF).
* excluded.
Fastest lap: del Monte, 1m 36.869s, 102.253 mph/164.560 km/h.

SUPERFUND EURO 3000, Autodromo Nazionale di Monza, Milan, Italy, 27 June. Round 4. 26 laps of the 3.600-mile/5.793-km circuit, 93.590 miles/150.618 km.
1 Nicky Pastorelli, NL, 44m 38.955s, 125.767 mph/202.402 km/h; **2** Christiano Tuka Rocha, BR, 44m 41.909s; **3** Fabrizio del Monte, I, 45m 07.806s; **4** Fausto Ippoliti, I, 45m 09.798s; **5** 'Babalus', I, 45m 12.111s; **6** Maxime Hodencq, B, 45m 25.372s; **7** Norbert Siedler, A, 45m 45.648s; **8** Giacomo Ricci, I, 45m 51.925s; **9** Mathias Lauda, A, 22 laps (DNF); **10** Bernhard Auinger, A, 15 (DNF).
Fastest lap: Rocha, 1m 41.882s, 127.192 mph/204.696 km/h.

SUPERFUND EURO 3000, Circuit de Spa-Francorchamps, Stavelot, Belgium, 18 July. Round 5. 22 laps of the 4.335-mile/6.976-km circuit, 95.363 miles/153.472 km.
1 Bernhard Auinger, A, 48m 09.141s, 118.827 mph/191.233 km/h; **2** Nicky Pastorelli, NL, 48m 09.793s; **3** Fabrizio del Monte, I, 48m 18.902s; **4** Alex Lloyd, GB, 48m 19.314s; **5** Norbert Siedler, A, 48m 26.370s; **6** Jonny Reid, NZ, 48m 31.142s; **7** Fausto Ippoliti, I, 48m 35.479s; **8** Maxime Hodencq, B, 48m 54.782s; **9** Allam Khodair, BR, 48m 57.078s; **10** Tor Graves, GB, 49m 19.274s.
Fastest lap: Pastorelli, 2m 09.944s, 120.089 mph/193.265 km/h.

DONINGTON PARK GOLD CUP, Donington Park National Circuit, Castle Donington, Derbyshire, Great Britain, 29 August. Round 6. 43 laps of the 1.957-mile/3.149-km circuit, 84.138 miles/135.407 km.
1 Jonny Reid, NZ, 52m 27.738s, 96.227 mph/154.862 km/h; **2** Norbert Siedler, A, 52m 34.217s; **3** Christiano Tuka Rocha, BR, 52m 46.195s; **4** Bernhard Auinger, A, 53m 06.417s; **5** Nicky Pastorelli, NL, 53m 08.445s; **6** Fausto Ippoliti, I, 53m 22.925s; **7** Mathias Lauda, A, 53m 29.222s; **8** Jean de Pourtales, F, 53m 38.344s; **9** Loic Deman, B, 42 laps; **10** Tor Graves, 21 (DNF).
Fastest lap: Alex Lloyd, GB, 1m 00.751s, 115.951 mph/186.604 km/h.

SUPERFUND EURO 3000, Circuit de Dijon-Prenois, Fontaine-les-Dijon, France, 12 September. Round 7. 40 laps of the 2.361-mile/3.800-km circuit, 94.448 miles/152.000 km.
1 Alex Lloyd, GB, 47m 53.396s, 118.332 mph/190.437 km/h; **2** Jonny Reid, NZ, 48m 03.414s; **3** Fabrizio del Monte, I, 48m 15.425s; **4** Nicky Pastorelli, NL, 48m 26.930s; **5** Fausto Ippoliti, I, 48m 44.463s; **6** Bernhard Auinger, A, 49m 01.353s; **7** Jean de Pourtales, F, 39 laps; **8** Tor Graves, GB, 39; **9** Allam Khodair, BR, 21 (DNF); **10** Maxime Hodencq, B, 1 (DNF).

SUPERFUND EURO 3000, Omloop van Zolder, Hasselt, Belgium, 19 September. Round 8. 38 laps of the 2.471-mile/3.977-km circuit, 93.905 miles/151.126 km.
1 Norbert Siedler, A, 56m 34.171s, 99.600 mph/160.291 km/h; **2** Jonny Reid, NZ, 56m 40.420s; **3** Christiano Tuka Rocha, BR, 56m 46.898s; **4** Mathias Lauda, A, 5m 06.630s; **5** Fabrizio del Monte, I, 57m 07.978s; **6** Fausto Ippoliti, I, 57m 09.155s; **7** Matteo Meneghello, I, 57m 34.064s; **8** Tor Graves, GB, 57m 41.297s; **9** Loic Deman, B, 57m 48.766s; **10** Jean de Pourtales, F, 21 laps (DNF).
Fastest lap: Seidler, 1m 24.793s, 104.918 mph/168.849 km/h.

SUPERFUND 3000, Nürburgring Sprint Circuit, Nürburg/Eifel, Germany, 30/31 October. 2 x 42 laps of the 2.255-mile/3.629-km circuit.
Round 9 (94.708 miles/152.418 km).
1 Norbert Siedler, A, 58m 46.799s, 96.674 mph/155.582 km/h; **2** Jonny Reid, NZ, 58m 47.332s; **3** Nicky Pastorelli, NL, 58m 47.891s; **4** Fausto Ippoliti, I, 59m 08.100s; **5** Bernhard Auinger, A, 59m 08.483s; **6** Fabrizio del Monte, I, 59m 25.693s; **7** Mathias Lauda, A, 59m 32.164s; **8** Maxime Hodencq, B, 59m 45.804s; **9** Loic Deman, B, 59m 57.593s; **10** Luca Filippi, I, 40 laps.
Fastest lap: Auinger, 1m 22.064s, 98.921 mph/159.198 km/h.

Round 10 (94.708 miles/152.418 km).
1 Nicky Pastorelli, NL, 1h 01m 50.452s, 91.889 mph/147.881 km/h; **2** Alex Lloyd, GB, 1h 01m 53.275s; **3** Fausto Ippoliti, I, 1h 01m 58.505s; **4** Bernhard Auinger, A, 1h 01m 59.166s; **5** Jonny Reid, NZ, 1h 02m 01.659s; **6** Allam Khodair, BR, 1h 02m 24.996s; **7** Jean de Pourtales, F, 1h 02m 34.234s; **8** Mathias Lauda, A, 25 laps (DNF); **9** Maxime Hodencq, B, 19 (DNF); **10** Gianni Giudici, I, 7 (DNF).
Fastest lap: Pastorelli, 1m 21.218s, 99.951 mph/160.856 km/h.

Final championship points

1 Nicky Pastorelli, NL, 46; **2** Fabrizio del Monte, I, 45; **3** Norbert Siedler, A, 37; **4** Jonny Reid, NZ, 35; **5** Bernhard Auinger, A, 26; **6** Alex Lloyd, GB, 19; **7** Fausto Ippoliti, I, 17; **8** Christiano Tuka Rocha, BR, 15; **9** Mathias Lauda, A, 9; **10** 'Babalus', I, 7; **11** Maxime Hodencq, B, 3; **12** Allam Khodair, BR, 1.

BRDC British Formula 3 Championship

BRDC BRITISH FORMULA 3 CHAMPIONSHIP, Donington Park National Circuit, Castle Donington, Derbyshire, Great Britain, 4 April. 20 and 23 laps of the 1.9573-mile/3.150-km circuit.
Round 1 (39.146 miles/62.999 km).
1 Adam Carroll, GB (Dallara F304-Mugen Honda), 21m 37.231s, 108.636 mph/174.832 km/h; **2** Nelson Angelo Piquet, BR (Dallara F304-Mugen Honda), 21m 55.178s; **3** James Rossiter, GB (Dallara F304-Opel), 22m 02.477s; **4** Danilo Dirani, BR (Dallara F304-Mugen Honda), 22m 04.382s; **5** Ernesto Viso, YV (Dallara F304-Mugen Honda), 22m 04.578s; **6** Andrew Thompson, GB (Dallara F304-Renault), 22m 04.859s; **7** Fairuz Fauzy, MAL (Dallara F304-Opel), 22m 10.008s; **8** Alvaro Parente, P (Dallara F304-Mugen Honda), 22m 10.988s; **9** Marko Asmer, EST (Dallara F304-Renault), 22m 14.507s; **10** Lucas di Grassi, BR (Dallara F304-Renault), 22m 15.428s.
Scholarship class winner: Ryan Lewis, GB (Dallara F301-Mugen Honda), 22m 40.785s (15th).
Fastest lap: Carroll, 1m 04.067s, 109.983 mph/177.000 km/h.

Round 2 (45.018 miles/72.449 km).
1 Clivio Piccione, MC (Dallara F304-Mugen Honda), 31m 34.165s, 85.560 mph/137.696 km/h; **2** Nelson Angelo Piquet, BR (Dallara F304-Mugen Honda), 31m 37.087s; **3** Will Davison, AUS (Dallara F304-Opel), 31m 39.019s; **4** Will Power, AUS (Dallara F304-Mugen Honda), 31m 48.662s; **5** Ernesto Viso, YV (Dallara F304-Mugen Honda), 31m 49.355s; **6** Andrew Thompson, GB (Dallara F304-Renault), 31m 51.133s; **7** Marko Asmer, EST (Dallara F304-Renault), 31m 55.807s; **8** James Rossiter, GB (Dallara F304-Opel), 31m 56.109s; **9** Lucas di Grassi, BR (Dallara F304-Renault), 32m 10.462s; **10** Alvaro Parente, P (Dallara F304-Mugen Honda), 32m 23.159s.
Scholarship class winner: Lewis, 32m 40.371s (12th).
Fastest lap: Piquet, 1m 11.705s, 98.268 mph/158.147 km/h.

BRDC BRITISH FORMULA 3 CHAMPIONSHIP, Silverstone International Circuit, Towcester, Northamptonshire, Great Britain, 18 April. 18 laps of the 2.249-mile/3.619-km circuit.
Round 3 (40.482 miles/65.149 km).
1 James Rossiter, GB (Dallara F304-Opel), 26m 44.355s, 90.837 mph/146.188 km/h; **2** Will Power, AUS (Dallara F304-Mugen Honda), 26m 47.162s; **3** Nelson Angelo Piquet, BR (Dallara F304-Mugen Honda), 26m 47.836s; **4** Adam Carroll, GB (Dallara F304-Mugen Honda), 26m 58.232s; **5** Danny Watts, GB (Lola-Dome F106/04-Mugen Honda), 26m 59.523s; **6** Clivio Piccione, MC (Dallara F304-Mugen Honda), 27m 07.498s; **7** Ernesto Viso, YV (Dallara F304-Mugen Honda), 27m 09.910s; **8** Alvaro Parente, P (Dallara F304-Mugen Honda), 27m 10.238s; **9** Marko Asmer, EST (Dallara F304-Renault), 27m 12.030s; **10** Will Davison, AUS (Dallara F304-Opel), 27m 13.349s.
Scholarship class winner: Ryan Lewis, GB (Dallara F301-Mugen Honda), 27m 38.550s (15th).
Fastest lap: Piquet, 1m 27.511s, 92.519 mph/148.894 km/h.

Round 4 cancelled due to torrential rain. Race postponed to 5 June at Snetterton.

BRDC BRITISH FORMULA 3 CHAMPIONSHIP, Croft Circuit, Croft-on-Tees, North Yorkshire, Great Britain, 2 May. 18 and 20 laps of the 2.127-mile/3.423-km circuit.
Round 5 (38.286 miles/61.615 km).
1 Danilo Dirani, BR (Dallara F304-Mugen Honda), 22m 41.872s, 101.206 mph/162.875 km/h; **2** James Rossiter, GB (Dallara F304-Opel), 22m 47.100s; **3** Will Davison, AUS (Dallara F304-Opel), 22m 53.684s; **4** Marko Asmer, EST (Dallara F304-Renault), 22m 57.770s; **5** Nelson Angelo Piquet, BR (Dallara F304-Mugen Honda), 23m 00.149s; **6** Lucas di Grassi, BR (Dallara F304-Renault), 23m 04.904s; **7** Danny Watts, GB (Lola-Dome F106/04-Mugen Honda), 23m 05.497s; **8** Karun Chandhok, IND (Dallara F304-Mugen Honda), 23m 06.160s; **9** Clivio Piccione, MC (Dallara F304-Mugen Honda), 23m 06.795s; **10** Andrew Thompson, GB (Dallara F304-Renault), 23m 07.174s.
Scholarship class winner: Ryan Lewis, GB (Dallara F301-Opel), 23m 17.317s (13th).
Fastest lap: Dirani, 1m 14.726s, 102.470 mph/164.910 km/h.

Round 6 (42.540 miles/68.461 km).
1 Danilo Dirani, BR (Dallara F304-Mugen Honda), 27m 49.559s, 91.727 mph/147.621 km/h; **2** Will Davison, AUS (Dallara F304-Opel), 27m 53.373s; **3** Lucas di Grassi, BR (Dallara F304-Renault), 27m 55.146s; **4** Clivio Piccione, MC (Dallara F304-Mugen Honda), 27m 56.046s; **5** Karun Chandhok, IND (Dallara F304-Mugen Honda), 27m 57.699s; **6** Marko Asmer, EST (Dallara F304-Renault), 27m 58.926s; **7** Andrew Thompson, GB (Dallara F304-Renault), 27m 59.551s; **8** Fairuz Fauzy, MAL (Dallara F304-Opel), 28m 03.180s; **9** Danny Watts, GB (Lola-Dome F106/04-Mugen Honda), 28m 03.726s; **10** Alvaro Parente, P (Dallara F304-Mugen Honda), 28m 04.231s.
Scholarship class winner: Barton Mawer, AUS (Dallara F301-Opel), 28m 24.507s (12th).
Fastest lap: Dirani, 1m 15.701s, 101.151 mph/162.786 km/h.

BRDC BRITISH FORMULA 3 CHAMPIONSHIP, Knockhill Racing Circuit, By Dunfermline, Fife, Scotland, Great Britain, 16 May. 25 and 28 laps of the 1.2986-mile/2.090-km circuit.
Round 7 (32.465 miles/52.247 km).
1 Ernesto Viso, YV (Dallara F304-Mugen Honda), 20m 05.507s, 96.950 mph/156.026 km/h; **2** Will Power, AUS (Dallara F304-Mugen Honda), 20m 07.301s; **3** James Rossiter, GB (Dallara F304-Opel), 20m 07.835s; **4** Adam Carroll, GB (Dallara F304-Mugen Honda), 20m 14.309s; **5** Clivio Piccione, MC (Dallara F304-Mugen Honda), 20m 14.798s; **6** Karun Chandhok, IND (Dallara F304-Mugen Honda), 20m 15.900s; **7** Danilo Dirani, BR (Dallara F304-Mugen Honda), 20m 16.607s; **8** Alvaro Parente, P (Dallara F304-Mugen Honda), 20m 18.186s; **9** Andrew Thompson, GB (Dallara F304-Renault), 20m 22.790s; **10** Nelson Angelo Piquet, BR (Dallara F304-Mugen Honda), 20m 23.088s.
Scholarship class winner: Barton Mawer, AUS (Dallara F301-Opel), 20m 46.720s (14th).
Fastest lap: Rossiter, 47.645s, 98.121 mph/157.910 km/h.

Round 8 (36.361 miles/58.517 km).
1 James Rossiter, GB (Dallara F304-Opel), 26m 27.461s, 82.458 mph/132.704 km/h; **2** Will Power, AUS (Dallara F304-Mugen Honda), 26m 28.459s; **3** Nelson Angelo Piquet, BR (Dallara F304-Mugen Honda), 26m 29.079s; **4** Lucas di Grassi, BR (Dallara F304-Renault), 26m 35.196s; **5** Karun Chandhok, IND (Dallara F304-Mugen Honda), 26m 35.713s; **6** Ernesto

Viso, YV (Dallara F304-Mugen Honda), 26m 36.204s; 7 Will Davison, AUS (Dallara F304-Opel), 26m 37.225s; 8 Alvaro Parente, P (Dallara F304-Mugen Honda), 26m 37.535s; 9 Danilo Dirani, BR (Dallara F304-Mugen Honda), 26m 38.323s; 10 Andrew Thompson, GB (Dallara F304-Renault), 26m 43.646s.
Scholarship class winner: Ryan Lewis, GB (Dallara F301-Mugen Honda), 26m 52.856s (14th).
Fastest lap: Piquet, 47.535s, 98.348 mph/158.275 km/h.

BRDC BRITISH FORMULA 3 CHAMPIONSHIP, Snetterton Circuit, Norfolk, Great Britain, 5/6 June. 23, 22 and 20 laps of the 1.952-mile/3.141-km circuit.
Round 4 (44.896 miles/72.253 km). Postponed from 18 April.
1 Nelson Angelo Piquet, BR (Dallara F304-Mugen Honda), 26m 49.593s, 100.414 mph/161.601 km/h; 2 Adam Carroll, GB (Dallara F304-Mugen Honda), 26m 51.500s; 3 Lucas di Grassi, BR (Dallara F304-Renault), 26m 53.043s; 4 Danilo Dirani, BR (Dallara F304-Mugen Honda), 26m 54.737s; 5 Danny Watts, GB (Lola-Dome F106/04-Mugen Honda), 26m 55.311s; 6 Alvaro Parente, P (Dallara F304-Mugen Honda), 26m 57.039s; 7 Fairuz Fauzy, MAL (Dallara F304-Opel), 26m 58.862s; 8 Clivio Piccione, MC (Dallara F304-Mugen Honda), 26m 59.676s; 9 Andrew Thompson, GB (Dallara F304-Renault), 27m 00.271s.10 Will Power, AUS (Dallara F304-Mugen Honda), 27m 06.799s.
Scholarship class winner: Ryan Lewis, GB (Dallara F301-Mugen Honda), 27m 12.609s (15th).
Fastest lap: Piquet, 1m 02.202s, 112.974 mph/181.814 km/h.

Round 9 (42.944 miles/69.112 km).
1 Nelson Angelo Piquet, BR (Dallara F304-Mugen Honda), 25m 01.173s, 102.985 mph/165.738 km/h; 2 Adam Carroll, GB (Dallara F304-Mugen Honda), 25m 01.773s; 3 Will Power, AUS (Dallara F304-Mugen Honda), 25m 04.857s; 4 Danilo Dirani, BR (Dallara F304-Mugen Honda), 25m 05.531s; 5 Ernesto Viso, YV (Dallara F304-Mugen Honda), 25m 11.478s; 6 Danny Watts, GB (Lola-Dome F106/04-Mugen Honda), 25m 11.854s; 7 Fairuz Fauzy, MAL (Dallara F304-Opel), 25m 13.137s; 8 Will Davison, AUS (Dallara F304-Opel), 25m 13.843s; 9 Clivio Piccione, MC (Dallara F304-Mugen Honda), 25m 14.356s; 10 James Walker, GB (Dallara F304-Renault), 25m 17.864s.
Scholarship class winner: Lewis, 25m 22.764s (12th).
Fastest lap: Piquet, 1m 02.750s, 111.987 mph/180.226 km/h.

Round 10 (39.040 miles/62.829 km).
1 Adam Carroll, GB (Dallara F304-Mugen Honda), 21m 05.660s, 111.044 mph/178.708 km/h; 2 James Rossiter, GB (Dallara F304-Opel), 21m 06.025s; 3 Will Power, AUS (Dallara F304-Mugen Honda), 21m 07.973s; 4 Nelson Angelo Piquet, BR (Dallara F304-Mugen Honda), 21m 08.452s; 5 Danny Watts, GB (Lola-Dome F106/04-Mugen Honda), 21m 14.826s; 6 Fairuz Fauzy, MAL (Dallara F304-Opel), 21m 16.743s; 7 Lucas di Grassi, BR (Dallara F304-Renault), 21m 26.592s; 8 Alvaro Parente, P (Dallara F304-Mugen Honda), 21m 26.826s; 9 Ernesto Viso, YV (Dallara F304-Mugen Honda), 21m 27.270s; 10 Will Davison, AUS (Dallara F304-Opel), 21m 27.814s.
Scholarship class winner: Lewis, 21m 38.702s (17th).
Fastest lap: Piquet, 1m 02.657s, 112.153 mph/180.494 km/h.

BRDC BRITISH FORMULA 3 CHAMPIONSHIP, Castle Combe Circuit, Wiltshire, Great Britain, 20 June. 2 x 20 laps of the 1.850-mile/2.977-km circuit.
Round 11 (37.000 miles/59.546 km).
1 Danny Watts, GB (Lola-Dome F106/04-Mugen Honda), 20m 08.642s, 110.206 mph/177.360 km/h; 2 Clivio Piccione, MC (Dallara F304-Mugen Honda), 20m 11.106s; 3 Adam Carroll, GB (Dallara F304-Mugen Honda), 20m 13.924s; 4 Ernesto Viso, YV (Dallara F304-Mugen Honda), 20m 14.392s; 5 Alvaro Parente, P (Dallara F304-Mugen Honda), 20m 15.835s; 6 Will Power, AUS (Dallara F304-Mugen Honda), 20m 16.747s; 7 Nelson Angelo Piquet, BR (Dallara F304-Mugen Honda), 20m 16.973s; 8 James Rossiter, GB (Dallara F304-Opel), 20m 19.874s; 9 Lucas di Grassi, BR (Dallara F304-Renault), 20m 24.026s; 10 Andrew Thompson, GB (Dallara F304-Renault), 20m 27.548s.
Scholarship class winner: Ryan Lewis, GB (Dallara F301-Mugen Honda), 21m 00.992s (15th).
Fastest lap: Rossiter, 59.561, 111.818 mph/179.954 km/h.

Round 12 (37.000 miles/59.546 km).
1 Alvaro Parente, P (Dallara F304-Mugen Honda), 27m 55.095s, 79.518 mph/127.972 km/h; 2 Adam Carroll, GB (Dallara F304-Mugen Honda), 27m 56.071s; 3 Danny Watts, GB (Lola-Dome F106/04-Mugen Honda), 27m 57.137s; 4 Clivio Piccione, MC (Dallara F304-Mugen Honda), 27m 57.605s; 5 James Rossiter, GB (Dallara F304-Opel), 27m 58.969s; 6 Fairuz Fauzy, MAL (Dallara F304-Opel), 27m 59.616s; 7 Marko Asmer, EST (Dallara F304-Renault), 28m 01.922s; 8 Lucas di Grassi, BR (Dallara F304-Renault), 28m 03.482s; 9 Karun Chandhok, IND (Dallara F304-Mugen Honda), 28m 04.738s; 10 Ryan Lewis, GB (Dallara F301-Mugen Honda), 28m 05.228s (1st Scholarship class).
Fastest lap: Asmer, 1m 09.976s, 95.175 mph/153.170 km/h.

BRDC BRITISH FORMULA 3 CHAMPIONSHIP, Donington Park Grand Prix Circuit, Castle Donington, Derbyshire, Great Britain, 27 June. 2 x 18 laps of the 2.500-mile/4.023-km circuit.
Round 13 (45.000 miles/72.420 km).
1 Adam Carroll, GB (Dallara F304-Mugen Honda), 29m 40.608s, 90.980 mph/146.418 km/h; 2 Clivio Piccione, MC (Dallara F304-Mugen Honda), 29m 52.767s; 3 James Rossiter, GB (Dallara F304-Opel), 29m 55.075s; 4 Karun Chandhok, IND (Dallara F304-Mugen Honda), 29m 56.287s; 5 Danilo Dirani, BR (Dallara F304-Mugen Honda), 30m 01.468s; 6 Nelson Angelo Piquet, BR (Dallara F304-Mugen Honda), 30m 01.977s; 7 Alvaro Parente, P (Dallara F304-Mugen Honda), 30m 06.185s; 8 Ryan Lewis, GB (Dallara F301-Mugen Honda), 30m 11.570s (1st Scholarship class); 9 Stephen Jelley, GB (Dallara F301-Opel), 30m 21.239s; 10 Ronayne O'Mahoney, IRL (Dallara F301-Opel), 30m 52.727s.
Fastest lap: Piquet, 1m 37.128s, 92.661 mph/149.124 km/h.

Round 14 (45.000 miles/72.420 km).
1 Clivio Piccione, MC (Dallara F304-Mugen Honda), 26m 22.638s, 102.361 mph/164.734 km/h; 2 Alvaro Parente, P (Dallara F304-Mugen Honda), 26m 25.517s; 3 Nelson Angelo Piquet, BR (Dallara F304-Mugen Honda), 26m 32.049s; 4 Marko Asmer, EST (Dallara F304-Renault), 26m 35.641s; 5 James Walker, GB (Dallara F304-Renault), 26m 38.381s; 6 James Rossiter, GB (Dallara F304-Opel), 26m 39.646s; 7 Adam Carroll, GB (Dallara F304-Mugen Honda), 26m 39.714s; 8 Danny Watts, GB (Lola-Dome F106/04-Mugen Honda), 26m 39.880s; 9 Danilo Dirani, BR (Dallara F304-Mugen Honda), 26m 48.311s; 10 Will Power, AUS (Dallara F304-Mugen Honda), 27m 00.518s.
Scholarship class winner: Jelley, 27m 13.966s (13th).
Fastest lap: Dirani, 1m 26.260s, 104.336 mph/167.912 km/h.

BRDC BRITISH FORMULA 3 CHAMPIONSHIP, Oulton Park International Circuit, Tarporley, Cheshire, Great Britain, 18 July. 2 x 14 laps of the 2.692-mile/4.332-km circuit.
Round 15 (37.688 miles/60.653 km).
1 Nelson Angelo Piquet, BR (Dallara F304-Mugen Honda), 21m 26.263s, 105.481 mph/169.756 km/h; 2 Fairuz Fauzy, MAL (Dallara F304-Mugen Honda), 21m 32.544s; 3 Alvaro Parente, P (Dallara F304-Mugen Honda), 21m 35.873s; 4 Adam Carroll, GB (Dallara F304-Mugen Honda), 21m 37.617s; 5 James Rossiter, GB (Dallara F304-Opel), 21m 38.084s; 6 Danny Watts, GB (Lola-Dome F106/04-Mugen Honda), 21m 39.295s; 7 Andrew Thompson, GB (Dallara F304-Renault), 21m 51.870s; 8 Clivio Piccione, MC (Dallara F304-Mugen Honda), 21m 54.101s; 9 Marcus Marshall, AUS (Dallara F304-Opel), 21m 54.799s; 10 James Walker, GB (Dallara F304-Renault), 21m 55.981s.
Scholarship class winner: Ryan Lewis, GB (Dallara F301-Mugen Honda), 22m 00.068s (13th).
Fastest lap: Piquet, 1m 30.580s, 106.991 mph/172.185 km/h.

Round 16 (37.688 miles/60.653 km).
1 Nelson Angelo Piquet, BR (Dallara F304-Mugen Honda), 21m 11.118s, 106.738 mph/171.778 km/h; 2 Lucas di Grassi, BR (Dallara F304-Renault), 21m 23.098s; 3 James Rossiter, GB (Dallara F304-Opel), 21m 23.582s; 4 Alvaro Parente, P (Dallara F304-Mugen Honda), 21m 24.832s; 5 Danilo Dirani, BR (Dallara F304-Mugen Honda), 21m 26.525s; 6 Marko Asmer, EST (Dallara F304-Renault), 21m 27.189s; 7 Fairuz Fauzy, MAL (Dallara F304-Mugen Honda), 21m 31.229s; 8 Adam Carroll, GB (Dallara F304-Mugen Honda), 21m 32.257s; 9 Danny Watts, GB (Lola-Dome F106/04-Mugen Honda), 21m 36.563s; 10 Andrew Thompson, GB (Dallara F304-Renault), 21m 41.437s.
Scholarship class winner: Stephen Jelley, GB (Dallara F301-Opel), 21m 50.773s (11th).
Fastest lap: Piquet, 1m 29.929s, 107.765 mph/173.431 km/h.

BRDC BRITISH FORMULA 3 CHAMPIONSHIP, Silverstone Grand Prix Circuit, Towcester, Northamptonshire, Great Britain, 15 August. 2 x 15 laps of the 3.194-mile/5.140-km circuit.
Round 17 (47.910 miles/77.104 km).
1 Nelson Angelo Piquet, BR (Dallara F304-Mugen Honda), 26m 14.820s, 109.521 mph/176.257 km/h; 2 James Rossiter, GB (Dallara F304-Opel), 26m 15.535s; 3 Danny Watts, GB (Lola-Dome F106/04-Mugen Honda), 26m 23.130s; 4 Will Power, AUS (Dallara F304-Mugen Honda), 26m 25.865s; 5 Adam Carroll, GB (Dallara F304-Mugen Honda), 26m 28.870s; 6 Marko Asmer, EST (Dallara F304-Renault), 26m 33.335s; 7 Rob Austin, GB (Dallara F304-Opel), 26m 36.077s; 8 Fairuz Fauzy, MAL (Dallara F304-Mugen Honda), 26m 38.298s; 9 Alvaro Parente, P (Dallara F304-Mugen Honda), 26m 39.733s; 10 Clivio Piccione, MC (Dallara F304-Mugen Honda), 26m 46.426s.
Scholarship class winner: Vasilije Calasan, F (Dallara F301-Mugen Honda), 27m 23.728s (16th).
Fastest lap: Piquet, 1m 44.170s, 110.381 mph/177.641 km/h.

Round 18 (47.910 miles/77.104 km).
1 Marcus Marshall, AUS (Dallara F304-Opel), 28m 23.542s, 101.246 mph/162.939 km/h; 2 Alvaro Parente, P (Dallara F304-Mugen Honda), 28m 24.513s; 3 Danilo Dirani, BR (Dallara F304-Mugen Honda), 28m 33.614s; 4 Nelson Angelo Piquet, BR (Dallara F304-Mugen Honda), 29m 10.876s; 5 Rob Austin, GB (Dallara F304-Opel), 29m 12.471s; 6 Will Power, AUS (Dallara F304-Mugen Honda), 29m 15.137s; 7 James Rossiter, GB (Dallara F304-Opel), 29m 16.054s; 8 Danny Watts, GB (Lola-Dome F106/04-Mugen Honda), 29m 22.644s; 9 Vasilije Calasan, F (Dallara F301-Mugen Honda), 29m 30.108s (1st Scholarship class); 10 Marko Asmer, EST (Dallara F304-Renault), 29m 31.050s.
Fastest lap: Carroll, 1m 45.478s, 109.012 mph/175.438 km/h.

BRDC BRITISH FORMULA 3 CHAMPIONSHIP, Thruxton Circuit, Andover, Hampshire, Great Britain, 30 August. 2 x 16 laps of the 2.356-mile/3.792-km circuit.
Round 19 (37.696 miles/60.666 km).
1 Lucas di Grassi, BR (Dallara F304-Renault), 18m 12.975s, 124.162 mph/199.819 km/h; 2 James Rossiter, GB (Dallara F304-Opel), 18m 13.604s; 3 Adam Carroll, GB (Dallara F304-Mugen Honda), 18m 13.974s; 4 Clivio Piccione, MC (Dallara F304-Mugen Honda), 18m 14.754s; 5 Marko Asmer, EST (Dallara F304-Renault), 18m 18.670s; 6 Danny Watts, GB (Lola-Dome F106/04-Mugen Honda), 18m 26.401s; 7 Alvaro Parente, P (Dallara F304-Mugen Honda), 18m 26.772s; 8 Danilo Dirani, BR (Dallara F304-Mugen Honda), 18m 27.993s; 9 Andrew Thompson, GB (Dallara F304-Renault), 18m 28.965s; 10 Will Power, AUS (Dallara F304-Mugen Honda), 18m 32.664s.
Scholarship class winner: Ryan Lewis, GB (Dallara F301-Mugen Honda), 18m 37.646s (12th).
Fastest lap: Rob Austin, GB (Dallara F304-Opel), 1m 07.570s, 125.523 mph/202.010 km/h.

Round 20 (37.696 miles/60.666 km).
1 Lucas di Grassi, BR (Dallara F304-Renault), 18m 09.582s, 124.548 mph/200.441 km/h; 2 Nelson Angelo Piquet, BR (Dallara F304-Mugen Honda), 18m 10.254s; 3 Rob Austin, GB (Dallara F304-Opel), 18m 13.093s; 4 James Rossiter, GB (Dallara F304-Opel), 18m 13.541s; 5 Alvaro Parente, P (Dallara F304-Mugen Honda), 18m 15.077s; 6 Clivio Piccione, MC (Dallara F304-Mugen Honda), 18m 15.916s; 7 Adam Carroll, GB (Dallara F304-Mugen Honda), 18m 19.254s; 8 Danny Watts, GB (Lola-Dome F106/04-Mugen Honda), 18m 21.470s; 9 Marko Asmer, EST (Dallara F304-Renault), 18m 21.998s; 10 Andrew Thompson, GB (Dallara F304-Renault), 18m 27.469s.
Scholarship class winner: Stephen Jelley, GB (Dallara F301-Opel), 18m 39.667s (15th).
Fastest lap: Piquet, 1m 07.437s, 125.771 mph/202.408 km/h.

BRDC BRITISH FORMULA 3 CHAMPIONSHIP, Circuit de Spa-Francorchamps, Stavelot, Belgium, 12 September. 2 x 11 laps of the 4.316-mile/6.946-km circuit.
Round 21 (47.476 miles/76.406 km).
1 Adam Carroll, GB (Dallara F304-Mugen Honda), 30m 06.595s, 94.606 mph/152.254 km/h; 2 Clivio Piccione, MC (Dallara F304-Mugen Honda), 30m 07.326s; 3 Danilo Dirani, BR (Dallara F304-Mugen Honda), 30m 12.034s; 4 Danny Watts, GB (Lola-Dome F106/04-Mugen Honda), 30m 13.079s; 5 Marko Asmer, EST (Dallara F304-Renault), 30m 14.312s; 6 Nelson Angelo Piquet, BR (Dallara F304-Mugen Honda), 30m 14.773s; 7 Lucas di Grassi, BR (Dallara F304-Renault), 30m 16.858s; 8 Will Power, AUS (Dallara F304-Mugen Honda), 30m 19.278s; 9 Greg Franchi, B (Dallara F304-Opel), 30m 20.086s; 10 Alvaro Parente, P (Dallara F304-Mugen Honda), 30m 23.063s.
Scholarship class winner: Ryan Lewis, GB (Dallara F301-Mugen Honda), 30m 47.906s (15th).
Fastest lap: Carroll, 2m 16.618s, 113.731 mph/183.033 km/h.

Round 22 (47.476 miles/76.406 km).
1 Adam Carroll, GB (Dallara F304-Mugen Honda), 25m 10.015s, 113.188 mph/182.158 km/h; 2 Clivio Piccione, MC (Dallara F304-Mugen Honda), 25m 10.776s; 3 Danilo Dirani, BR (Dallara F304-Mugen Honda), 25m 17.616s; 4 Nelson Angelo Piquet, BR (Dallara F304-Mugen Honda), 25m 18.013s; 5 Danny Watts, GB (Lola-Dome F106/04-Mugen Honda), 25m 19.106s; 6 Lucas di Grassi, BR (Dallara F304-Renault), 25m 22.451s; 7 Marko Asmer, EST (Dallara F304-Renault), 25m 23.110s; 8 Alvaro Parente, P (Dallara F304-Mugen Honda), 25m 24.732s; 9 Will Power, AUS (Dallara F304-Mugen Honda), 25m 26.491s; 10 Nicolas Lapierre, F (Dallara F304-Opel), 25m 28.358s.
Scholarship class winner: Lewis, 25m 50.082s (16th).
Fastest lap: James Rossiter, GB (Dallara F304-Opel), 2m 16.254s, 114.035 mph/183.522 km/h.

BRDC BRITISH FORMULA 3 CHAMPIONSHIP, Brands Hatch Indy Circuit, West Kingsdown, Dartford, Kent, Great Britain, 3 October. 2 x 28 laps of the 1.2262-mile/1.973-km circuit.
Round 23 (34.334 miles/55.255 km).
1 James Rossiter, GB (Dallara F304-Opel), 22m 20.713s, 92.190 mph/148.366 km/h; 2 Nelson Angelo Piquet, BR (Dallara F304-Mugen Honda), 22m 21.416s; 3 Danny Watts, GB (Lola-Dome F106/04-Mugen Honda), 22m 33.351s; 4 Danilo Dirani, BR (Dallara F304-Mugen Honda), 22m 35.397s; 5 Marko Asmer, EST (Dallara F304-Renault), 22m 35.888s; 6 Rob Austin, GB (Dallara F304-Opel), 22m 35.933s; 7 James Walker, GB (Dallara F304-Renault), 22m 36.181s; 8 Alvaro Parente, P (Dallara F304-Mugen Honda), 22m 44.166s; 9 Adam Carroll, GB (Dallara F304-Mugen Honda), 22m 44.469s; 10 Andrew Thompson, GB (Dallara F304-Renault), 22m 49.243s.
Scholarship class winner: Ryan Lewis, GB (Dallara F301-Mugen Honda), 23m 07.283s (12th).
Fastest lap: Austin, 46.463s, 95.007 mph/152.899 km/h.

Round 24 (34.334 miles/55.255 km).
1 Nelson Angelo Piquet, BR (Dallara F304-Mugen Honda), 22m 00.574s, 93.596 mph/150.629 km/h; 2 James Rossiter, GB (Dallara F304-Opel), 22m 10.270s; 3 Lucas di Grassi, BR (Dallara F304-Renault), 22m 10.592s; 4 Adam Carroll, GB (Dallara F304-Mugen Honda), 22m 10.881s; 5 Alvaro Parente, P (Dallara F304-Mugen Honda), 22m 11.860s; 6 Danny Watts, GB (Lola-Dome F106/04-Mugen Honda), 22m 14.173s; 7 Andrew Thompson, GB (Dallara F304-Renault), 22m 14.548s; 8 Marko Asmer, EST (Dallara F304-Renault), 22m 16.779s; 9 Will Power, AUS (Dallara F304-Mugen Honda), 22m 18.950s; 10 James Walker, GB (Dallara F304-Renault), 22m 20.453s.
Scholarship class winner: Lewis, 22m 35.015s (14th).
Fastest lap: Asmer, 46.315s, 95.311 mph/153.388 km/h.

Final championship points

1 Nelson Angelo Piquet, BR, 282; 2 Adam Carroll, GB, 233; 3 James Rossiter, GB, 228; 4 Clivio Piccione, MC, 161; 5 Danilo Dirani, BR, 146; 6 Danny Watts, GB, 139; 7 Alvaro Parente, P, 137; 8 Lucas di Grassi, BR, 130; 9 Will Power, AUS, 111; 10 Marko Asmer, EST, 87; 11 Ernesto Viso, YV, 66; 12 Fairuz Fauzy, MAL, 49; 13 Will Davison, AUS, 48; 14 Karun Chandhok, IND, 37; 15 Andrew Thompson, GB, 36; 16 Rob Austin, GB, 32; 17 Marcus Marshall, AUS, 24; 18 James Walker, GB, 20; 19 Alexandre Negrao, BR, 1.

Scholarship Class
1 Ryan Lewis, GB, 423; 2 Stephen Jelley, GB, 266; 3 Vasilije Calasan, F, 212; 4 Barton Mawer, AUS, 134; 5 Ronayne O'Mahoney, IRL, 121.

Formula 3 Euro Series

FORMULA 3 EURO SERIES, Hockenheimring Grand Prix Circuit, Heidelberg, Germany, 17/18 April. 2 x 18 laps of the 2.842-mile/4.574-km circuit.
Round 1 (51.159 miles/82.332 km).
1 Nico Rosberg, FIN (Dallara F303-Opel), 28m 50.559s, 106.423 mph/171.271 km/h; 2 Alexandre Prémat, F (Dallara F302-Mercedes Benz), 28m 51.673s; 3 Franck Perera, F (Dallara F304-Opel), 28m 56.125s; 4 Jamie Green, GB (Dallara F302-Mercedes Benz), 28m 56.962s; 5 Eric Salignon, F (Dallara F303-Mercedes Benz), 28m 57.656s; 6 Robert Kubica, PL (Dallara F302-Mercedes Benz), 29m 04.519s; 7 Bruno Spengler, CDN (Dallara F302-Mercedes Benz), 29m 05.633s; 8 Nicolas Lapierre, F (Dallara F304-Opel), 29m 06.563s; 9 Giedo van der Garde, NL (Dallara F302-Opel), 29m 12.274s; 10 Maximilian Götz, D (Dallara F303-TOM'S Toyota), 29m 13.928s.
Fastest lap: Prémat, 1m 34.979s, 107.726 mph/173.369 km/h.

Round 2 (51.159 miles/82.332 km).
1 Nico Rosberg, FIN (Dallara F303-Opel), 28m 31.991s, 107.577 mph/173.129 km/h; 2 Jamie Green, GB (Dallara F302-Mercedes Benz), 28m 32.874s; 3 Alexandre Prémat, F (Dallara F302-Mercedes Benz), 28m 40.322s; 4 Giedo van der Garde, NL (Dallara F302-Opel), 28m 43.898s; 5 Eric Salignon, F (Dallara F303-Mercedes Benz), 28m 44.510s; 6 Lewis Hamilton, GB (Dallara F302-Mercedes Benz), 28m 44.980s; 7 Robert Kubica, PL (Dallara F302-Mercedes Benz), 28m 46.701s; 8 Alexandros Margaritis, GR (Dallara F303-Opel), 28m 49.286s; 9 Daniel la Rosa, I (Dallara F304-Opel), 28m 50.853s; 10 Charles Zwolsman, NL (Dallara F302-Mercedes Benz), 28m 55.547s.
Fastest lap: Green, 1m 33.754s, 109.134 mph/175.634 km/h.

FORMULA 3 EURO SERIES, Autódromo Fernanda Pires da Silva, Alcabideche, Estoril, Portugal, 1/2 May. 2 x 19 laps of the 2.703-mile/4.350-km circuit.
Round 3 (51.356 miles/82.650 km).
1 Alexandre Prémat, F (Dallara F302-Mercedes Benz), 30m 12.123s, 102.026 mph/164.194 km/h; 2 Jamie Green, GB (Dallara F302-Mercedes Benz), 30m 15.559s; 3 Nicolas Lapierre, F (Dallara F304-Opel), 30m 27.245s; 4 Dennis Furchheim, D (Dallara F304-Opel), 30m 34.062s; 5 Loic Duval, F (Dallara F302-Opel), 30m 36.016s; 6 Alexandros Margaritis, GR (Dallara F303-Opel), 30m 39.741s; 7 Tom Kimber-Smith, GB (Dallara F303-Mercedes Benz), 30m 40.484s; 8 Franck Perera, F (Dallara F304-Opel), 30m 40.964s; 9 Robert Kubica, PL (Dallara F302-Mercedes Benz), 30m 41.125s; 10 Bruno Spengler, CDN (Dallara F302-Mercedes Benz), 30m 41.621s.
Fastest lap: Green, 1m 34.556s, 102.909 mph/165.616 km/h.

Round 4 (51.356 miles/82.650 km).
1 Eric Salignon, F (Dallara F303-Mercedes Benz), 30m 03.472s, 102.515 mph/164.982 km/h; 2 Jamie Green, GB (Dallara F302-Mercedes Benz), 30m 10.059s; 3 Nicolas Lapierre, F (Dallara F304-Opel), 30m 10.689s; 4 Nico Rosberg, FIN (Dallara F303-Opel), 30m 11.296s; 5 Roberto Streit, BR (Dallara F304-Opel), 30m 14.395s; 6 Giedo van der Garde, NL (Dallara F302-Opel), 30m 20.786s; 7 Franck Perera, F (Dallara F304-Opel), 30m 21.341s; 8 Alexandre Prémat, F (Dallara F302-Mercedes Benz), 30m 24.077s; 9 Lewis Hamilton, GB (Dallara F302-Mercedes Benz), 30m 24.653s; 10 Bruno Spengler, CDN (Dallara F302-Mercedes Benz), 30m 26.353s.
Fastest lap: Salignon, 1m 34.067s, 99.477 mph/166.477 km/h.

FORMULA 3 EURO SERIES, Autodromo Adria International Raceway, Adria, Italy, 15/16 May. 2 x 26 laps of the 1.679-mile/2.702-km circuit.
Round 5 (43.653 miles/70.252 km).
1 Jamie Green, GB (Dallara F302-Mercedes Benz), 31m 04.084s, 84.304 mph/135.674 km/h; 2 Katsuyuki Hiranaka, J (Dallara F304-Opel), 31m 11.024s; 3 Giedo van der Garde, NL (Dallara F302-Opel), 31m 14.635s; 4 Adrian Sutil, D (Dallara F303-Mercedes Benz), 31m 17.393s; 5 Nico Rosberg, FIN (Dallara F303-Opel), 31m 17.875s; 6 Alexandros Margaritis, GR (Dallara F303-Opel), 31m 25.774s; 7 Bruno Spengler, CDN (Dallara F302-Mercedes Benz), 31m 27.116s; 8 Alexandre Prémat, F (Dallara F302-Mercedes Benz), 31m 27.741s; 9 Tom Kimber-Smith, GB (Dallara F303-Mercedes Benz), 31m 29.030s; 10 Maximilian Götz, D (Dallara F303-TOM'S Toyota), 31m 31.336s.
Fastest lap: Rosberg, 1m 11.039s, 85.083 mph/136.928 km/h.

Round 6 (43.653 miles/70.252 km).
1 Eric Salignon, F (Dallara F303-Mercedes Benz), 31m 10.846s, 83.999 mph/135.183 km/h; 2 Franck Perera, F (Dallara F304-Opel), 31m 12.476s; 3 Daniel la Rosa, I (Dallara F304-Opel), 31m 14.791s; 4 Nicolas Lapierre, F (Dallara F304-Opel), 31m 15.816s; 5 Lewis Hamilton, GB (Dallara F302-Mercedes Benz), 31m 17.291s; 6 Giedo van der Garde, NL (Dallara F302-Opel), 31m 17.694s; 7 Adrian Sutil, D (Dallara F303-Mercedes Benz), 31m 20.334s; 8 Jamie Green, GB (Dallara F302-Mercedes Benz), 31m 29.584s,9 Alexandros Margaritis, GR (Dallara F303-Opel), 31m 33.453s; 10 Robert Kath, D (Dallara F303-Opel), 31m 35.003s.
Fastest lap: Spengler, 1m 11.029s, 85.095 mph/136.947 km/h.

64th GRAND PRIX DE PAU, FIA FORMULA 3 EUROPE CUP, Circuit de Pau Ville, France. 30/31 May. 19 and 22 laps of the 1.715-mile/2.760-km circuit.
Round 7 (32.585 miles/52.440 km).
1 Jamie Green, GB (Dallara F302-Mercedes Benz), 30m 02.398s, 65.083 mph/104.740 km/h; 2 Nicolas Lapierre, F (Dallara F304-Opel), 30m 26.984s; 3 Robert Kubica, PL (Dallara F302-Mercedes Benz), 30m 29.711s; 4 Lewis Hamilton, GB (Dallara F302-Mercedes Benz), 30m 36.095s; 5 Franck Perera, F (Dallara F304-Opel), 30m 46.534s; 6 Bruno Spengler, CDN (Dallara F302-Mercedes Benz), 30m 51.995s; 7 Loic Duval, F (Dallara F302-Opel), 30m 52.031s; 8 Roberto Streit, BR (Dallara F304-Opel), 30m 53.541s; 9 Katsuyuki Hiranaka, J (Dallara F304-Opel), 30m 54.608s; 10 Charles Zwolsman, NL (Dallara F302-Mercedes Benz), 31m 21.237s.
Fastest lap: Green, 1m 28.433s, 69.815 mph/112.356 km/h.

Round 8 (37.730 miles/60.720 km).
1 Nicolas Lapierre, F (Dallara F304-Opel), 30m 47.121s, 73.534 mph/118.342 km/h; 2 Robert Kubica, PL (Dallara F302-Mercedes Benz), 30m 51.293s; 3 Jamie Green, GB (Dallara F302-Mercedes Benz), 30m 51.775s; 4 Eric Salignon, F (Dallara F303-Mercedes Benz), 30m 57.381s; 5 Roberto Streit, BR (Dallara F304-Opel), 30m 59.953s; 6 Franck Perera, F (Dallara F304-Opel), 31m 00.120s; 7 Lewis Hamilton, GB (Dallara F302-Mercedes Benz), 31m 01.658s; 8 Katsuyuki Hiranaka, J (Dallara F304-Opel), 31m 08.089s; 9 Maximilian Götz, D (Dallara F303-TOM'S Toyota), 31m 08.260s; 10 Tom Kimber-Smith, GB (Dallara F303-Mercedes Benz), 31m 14.203s.
Fastest lap: Lapierre, 1m 12.412s, 85.261 mph/137.215 km/h.

FORMULA 3 EURO SERIES, Norisring, Nürnberg, Germany, 26/27 June. 2 x 35 laps of the 1.429-mile/2.300-km circuit.
Round 9 (50.020 miles/80.500 km).
1 Lewis Hamilton, GB (Dallara F302-Mercedes Benz), 29m 08.759s, 102.972 mph/165.718 km/h; 2 Loic Duval, F (Dallara F302-Opel), 29m 10.805s; 3 Franck Perera, F (Dallara F304-Opel), 29m 12.631s; 4 Nico Rosberg, FIN (Dallara F303-Opel), 29m 14.973s; 5 Roberto Streit, BR (Dallara F304-Opel), 29m 16.352s; 6 Jamie Green, GB (Dallara F302-Mercedes Benz), 29m 22.044s; 7 Eric Salignon, F (Dallara F303-Mercedes Benz), 29m 31.707s; 8 Bruno Spengler, CDN (Dallara F302-Mercedes Benz), 29m 33.172s; 9 Katsuyuki Hiranaka, J (Dallara F304-Opel), 29m 34.190s; 10 Daniel la Rosa, I (Dallara F304-Opel), 29m 35.989s.
Fastest lap: Alexandre Prémat, F (Dallara F302-Mercedes Benz), 49.316s, 104.326 mph/167.897 km/h.

Round 10 (50.020 miles/80.500 km).
1 Alexandre Prémat, F (Dallara F302-Mercedes Benz), 29m 09.469s, 102.930 mph/165.650 km/h; 2 Jamie Green, GB (Dallara F302-Mercedes Benz), 29m 09.956s; 3 Lewis Hamilton, GB (Dallara F302-Mercedes Benz), 29m 10.220s; 4 Robert Kubica, PL (Dallara F302-Mercedes Benz), 29m 15.201s; 5 Nicolas Lapierre, F (Dallara F304-Opel), 29m 15.972s; 6 Bruno Spengler, CDN (Dallara F302-Mercedes Benz), 29m 19.010s; 7 Roberto Streit, BR (Dallara F304-Opel), 29m 19.904s; 8 Loic Duval, F (Dallara F302-Opel), 29m 20.516s; 9 Eric Salignon, F (Dallara F303-Mercedes Benz), 29m 21.230s; 10 Maximilian Götz, D (Dallara F303-TOM's Toyota), 29m 28.160s.
Fastest lap: Hamilton, 49.324s, 104.309 mph/167.870 km/h.

FORMULA 3 EURO SERIES, Circuit de Nevers, Magny-Cours, France, 3/4 July. 2 x 18 laps of the 2.741-mile/4.411-km circuit.
Round 11 (49.336 miles/79.398 km).
1 Jamie Green, GB (Dallara F302-Mercedes Benz), 30m 59.788s, 95.499 mph/153.691 km/h; 2 Eric Salignon, F (Dallara F303-Mercedes Benz), 31m 02.495s; 3 Loic Duval, F (Dallara F302-Opel), 31m 07.559s; 4 Alexandros Margaritis, GR (Dallara F303-Opel), 31m 09.652s; 5 Bruno Spengler, CDN (Dallara F302-Mercedes Benz), 31m 10.275s; 6 Nico Rosberg, FIN (Dallara F303-Opel), 31m 10.753s; 7 Roberto Streit, BR (Dallara F304-Opel), 31m 12.600s; 8 Nicolas Lapierre, F (Dallara F304-Opel), 31m 14.354s; 9 Robert Kubica, PL (Dallara F302-Mercedes Benz), 31m 14.895s; 10 Franck Perera, F (Dallara F304-Opel), 31m 16.031s.
Fastest lap: Green, 1m 36.996, 101.727 mph/163.714 km/h.

Round 12 (49.336 miles/79.398 km).
1 Alexandre Prémat, F (Dallara F302-Mercedes Benz), 28m 57.534s, 102.219 mph/164.505 km/h; 2 Nico Rosberg, FIN (Dallara F303-Opel), 28m 58.328s; 3 Bruno Spengler, CDN (Dallara F302-Mercedes Benz), 29m 02.686s; 4 Nicolas Lapierre, F (Dallara F304-Opel), 29m 05.309s; 5 Robert Kubica, PL (Dallara F302-Mercedes Benz), 29m 13.246s; 6 Charles Zwolsman, NL (Dallara F302-Mercedes Benz), 29m 17.692s; 7 Giedo van der Garde, NL (Dallara F302-Opel), 29m 19.537s; 8 Franck Perera, F (Dallara F304-Opel), 29m 21.444s; 9 Jamie Green, GB (Dallara F302-Mercedes Benz), 29m 22.020s; 10 Roberto Streit, BR (Dallara F304-Opel), 29m 30.127s.
Fastest lap: Lewis Hamilton, GB (Dallara F302-Mercedes Benz), 1m 35.917s, 102.872 mph/165.556 km/h.

FORMULA 3 EURO SERIES, Nürburgring Sprint Circuit, Nürburg/Eifel, Germany, 31 July/1 August. 2 x 22 laps of the 2.255-mile/3.629-km circuit.
Round 13 (49.609 miles/79.838 km).
1 Nico Rosberg, FIN (Dallara F303-Opel), 30m 54.367s, 96.309

mph/154.995 km/h; **2** Jamie Green, GB (Dallara F302-Mercedes Benz), 30m 59.442s; **3** Lewis Hamilton, GB (Dallara F302-Mercedes Benz), 31m 07.388s; **4** Daniel la Rosa, I (Dallara F304-Opel), 31m 08.840s; **5** Robert Kubica, PL (Dallara F302-Mercedes Benz), 31m 09.336s; **6** Alexandre Prémat, F (Dallara F302-Mercedes Benz), 31m 12.094s; **7** Giedo van der Garde, NL (Dallara F302-Opel), 31m 16.320s; **8** Nicolas Lapierre, F (Dallara F304-Opel), 31m 16.710s; **9** Bruno Spengler, CDN (Dallara F302-Mercedes Benz), 31m 18.880s; **10** Franck Perera, F (Dallara F304-Opel), 31m 20.189s.
Fastest lap: Rosberg, 1m 23.356s, 97.388 mph/156.730 km/h.

Round 14 (49.609 miles/79.838 km).
1 Jamie Green, GB (Dallara F302-Mercedes Benz), 30m 50.736s, 96.498 mph/155.299 km/h; **2** Robert Kubica, PL (Dallara F302-Mercedes Benz), 30m 51.582s; **3** Nico Rosberg, FIN (Dallara F303-Opel), 30m 53.808s; **4** Lewis Hamilton, GB (Dallara F302-Mercedes Benz), 30m 55.247s; **5** Alexandre Prémat, F (Dallara F302-Mercedes Benz), 31m 05.172s; **6** Nicolas Lapierre, F (Dallara F304-Opel), 31m 06.902s; **7** Bruno Spengler, CDN (Dallara F302-Mercedes Benz), 31m 07.982s; **8** Franck Perera, F (Dallara F304-Opel), 31m 08.638s; **9** Hannes Neuhauser, A (Dallara F303-Opel), 31m 11.429s; **10** Charles Zwolsman, NL (Dallara F302-Mercedes Benz), 31m 17.400s.
Fastest lap: Green, 1m 23.415s, 97.319 mph/156.619 km/h.

FORMULA 3 EURO SERIES, Circuit Park Zandvoort, Netherlands, 4/5 September. 14 and 19 laps of the 2.677-mile/4.30749-km circuit.
Round 15 (37.472 miles/60.305 km).
1 Eric Salignon, F (Dallara F303-Mercedes Benz), 28m 58.299s, 77.604 mph/124.891 km/h; **2** Nicolas Lapierre, F (Dallara F304-Opel), 28m 58.785s; **3** Lewis Hamilton, GB (Dallara F302-Mercedes Benz), 28m 59.102s; **4** Giedo van der Garde, NL (Dallara F302-Opel), 28m 59.597s; **5** Alexandre Prémat, F (Dallara F302-Mercedes Benz), 28m 59.643s; **6** Franck Perera, F (Dallara F304-Opel), 29m 00.777s; **7** Daniel la Rosa, I (Dallara F304-Opel), 29m 01.571s; **8** Robert Kubica, PL (Dallara F302-Mercedes Benz), 29m 02.178s; **9** Maximilian Götz, D (Dallara F303-TOM's Toyota), 29m 03.824s; **10** Katsuyuki Hiranaka, J (Dallara F304-Opel), 29m 05.672s.
Fastest lap: Salignon, 1m 33.203s, 103.383 mph/166.378 km/h.

Round 16 (50.854 miles/81.842 km).
1 Jamie Green, GB (Dallara F302-Mercedes Benz), 29m 59.938s, 101.712 mph/163.690 km/h; **2** Eric Salignon, F (Dallara F303-Mercedes Benz), 30m 00.145s; **3** Alexandre Prémat, F (Dallara F302-Mercedes Benz), 30m 07.793s; **4** Nicolas Lapierre, F (Dallara F304-Opel), 30m 10.795s; **5** Robert Kubica, PL (Dallara F302-Mercedes Benz), 30m 11.597s; **6** Lewis Hamilton, GB (Dallara F302-Mercedes Benz), 30m 17.312s; **7** Daniel la Rosa, I (Dallara F304-Opel), 30m 18.109s; **8** Giedo van der Garde, NL (Dallara F302-Opel), 30m 19.225s; **9** Franck Perera, F (Dallara F304-Opel), 30m 22.318s; **10** Alexandros Margaritis, GR (Dallara F303-Opel), 30m 25.506s.
Fastest lap: Salignon, 1m 33.723s, 102.809 mph/165.455 km/h.

FORMULA 3 EURO SERIES, Automotodrom Brno Masaryk Circuit, Brno, Czech Republic, 18/19 September. 2 x 15 laps of the 3.355-mile/5.400-km circuit.
Round 17 (50.331 miles/81.000 km).
1 Jamie Green, GB (Dallara F302-Mercedes Benz), 28m 31.884s, 105.844 mph/170.339 km/h; **2** Alexandre Prémat, F (Dallara F302-Mercedes Benz), 28m 37.370s; **3** Franck Perera, F (Dallara F304-Opel), 28m 50.968s; **4** Nico Rosberg, FIN (Dallara F303-Opel), 28m 53.342s; **5** Giedo van der Garde, NL (Dallara F302-Opel), 28m 54.784s; **6** Roberto Streit, BR (Dallara F304-Opel), 28m 55.423s; **7** Lewis Hamilton, GB (Dallara F302-Mercedes Benz), 28m 55.778s; **8** Loic Duval, F (Dallara F302-Opel), 28m 57.122s; **9** Nicolas Lapierre, F (Dallara F304-Opel), 28m 58.438s; **10** Robert Kubica, PL (Dallara F302-Mercedes Benz), 28m 59.002s.
Fastest lap: Green, 1m 53.176s, 106.732 mph/171.768 km/h.

Round 18 (50.331 miles/81.000 km).
1 Jamie Green, GB (Dallara F302-Mercedes Benz), 28m 20.149s, 106.574 mph/171.514; **2** Alexandre Prémat, F (Dallara F302-Mercedes Benz), 28m 27.966s; **3** Giedo van der Garde, NL (Dallara F302-Opel), 28m 39.343s; **4** Lewis Hamilton, GB (Dallara F302-Mercedes Benz), 28m 45.195s; **5** Bruno Spengler, CDN (Dallara F302-Mercedes Benz), 28m 47.900s; **6** Franck Perera, F (Dallara F304-Opel), 28m 48.620s; **7** Roberto Streit, BR (Dallara F304-Opel), 28m 49.918s; **8** Robert Kubica, PL (Dallara F302-Mercedes Benz), 28m 50.271s; **9** Andreas Zuber, A (Dallara F303-Opel), 28m 54.598s; **10** Charles Zwolsman, NL (Dallara F302-Mercedes Benz), 28m 56.839s.
Fastest lap: Green, 1m 52.395s, 107.473 mph/172.961.

FORMULA 3 EURO SERIES, Hockenheimring Grand Prix Circuit, Heidelberg, Germany, 2/3 October. 2 x 18 laps of the 2.842-mile/4.574-km circuit.
Round 19 (51.159 miles/82.332 km).
1 Nicolas Lapierre, F (Dallara F304-Opel), 28m 59.962s, 105.848 mph/170.346 km/h; **2** Lewis Hamilton, GB (Dallara F302-Mercedes Benz), 29m 04.162s; **3** Charles Zwolsman, NL (Dallara F302-Mercedes Benz), 29m 09.832s; **4** Robert Kubica, PL (Dallara F302-Mercedes Benz), 29m 11.217s; **5** Franck Perera, F (Dallara F304-Opel), 29m 13.825s; **6** Maximilian Götz, D (Dallara F303-Mercedes Benz), 29m 17.382s; **7** Alexandros Margaritis, GR (Dallara F303-Opel), 29m 18.003s; **8** Nico Rosberg, FIN (Dallara F303-Opel), 29m 24.651s; **9** Philipp Baron, A (Dallara F302-Mugen Honda), 29m 29.221s; **10** Jamie Green, GB (Dallara F302-Mercedes Benz), 29m 30.555s.
Fastest lap: Alexandre Prémat, F (Dallara F302-Mercedes Benz), 1m 35.629s, 106.994 mph/172.190 km/h.

Round 20 (51.159 miles/82.332 km).
1 Nicolas Lapierre, F (Dallara F304-Opel), 28m 40.437s, 107.049 mph/172.279 km/h; **2** Jamie Green, GB (Dallara F302-Mercedes Benz), 28m 41.172s; **3** Roberto Streit, BR (Dallara F304-Opel), 28m 46.395s; **4** Alexandre Prémat, F (Dallara F302-Mercedes Benz), 28m 50.594s; **5** Alexandros Margaritis, GR (Dallara F303-Opel), 28m 51.520s; **6** Lewis Hamilton, GB (Dallara F302-Mercedes Benz), 28m 53.531s; **7** Robert Kubica, PL (Dallara F302-Mercedes Benz), 28m 54.757s; **8** Nico Rosberg, FIN (Dallara F303-Opel), 28m 55.601s; **9** Bruno Spengler, CDN (Dallara F302-Mercedes Benz), 29m 03.324s; **10** Andreas Zuber, A (Dallara F303-Opel), 29m 08.834s.
Fastest lap: Lapierre, 1m 34.683s, 108.063 mph/173.911 km/h.

Final championship points

1 Jamie Green, GB, 139; **2** Alexandre Prémat, F, 88; **3** Nicolas Lapierre, F, 85; **4** Nico Rosberg, FIN, 70; **5** Lewis Hamilton, GB, 68; **6** Eric Salignon, F, 64; **7** Robert Kubica, PL, 53; **8** Franck Perera, F, 48; **9** Giedo van der Garde, NL, 37; **10** Roberto Streit, BR, 28; **11** Bruno Spengler, CDN, 27; **12** Loic Duval, F, 22; **13** Alexandros Margaritis, GR, 18; **14** Daniel la Rosa, I, 15; **15=** Katsuyuki Hiranaka, J, 9; **15=** Adrian Sutil, D, 9; **15=** Charles Zwolsman, NL, 9; **18=** Dennis Furchheim, D, 5; **18=** Tom Kimber-Smith, GB, 5.

Rookie Cup
1 Frank Perera, 147; **2** Giedo van der Garde, 130; **3** Roberto Streit, 116.

Recaro F3-Cup

RECARO F3-CUP, Hockenheimring Grand Prix Circuit, Heidelberg, Germany, 24/25 April. 2 x 16 laps of the 2.842-mile/4.574-km circuit.
Round 1 (45.474 miles/73.184 km).
1 Jan Seyffarth, D (Dallara F302-Renault), 26m 08.360s, 104.382 mph/167.986 km/h; **2** Tomas Kostka, CZ (Dallara F302-Opel), 26m 14.097s; **3** Timo Lienemann, D (Dallara F302-Opel), 26m 14.668s; **4** Bastian Kolmsee, D (Dallara F302-Opel), 26m 15.150s; **5** Michael Devaney, IRL (Dallara F302-Opel), 26m 15.505s; **6** Franz Schmöller, D (Dallara F302-Opel), 26m 24.423s; **7** Thomas Holzer, D (Dallara F302-Opel), 26m 25.717s; **8** Ho-Pin Tung, CN (Dallara F302-Opel), 26m 32.902s; **9** Marcel Leipert, D (Dallara F302-Opel), 26m 34.196s; **10** Marcus Steinel, D (Dallara F302-Opel), 26m 35.231s.
Fastest lap: Schmöller, 1m 36.926s, 105.562 mph/169.886 km/h.

Round 2 (45.474 miles/73.184 km).
1 Jan Seyffarth, D (Dallara F302-Renault), 26m 03.332s, 104.717 mph/168.526 km/h; **2** Tomas Kostka, CZ (Dallara F302-Opel), 26m 08.116s; **3** Franz Schmöller, D (Dallara F302-Opel), 26m 09.558s; **4** Timo Lienemann, D (Dallara F302-Opel), 26m 10.159s; **5** Michael Devaney, IRL (Dallara F302-Opel), 26m 11.731s; **6** Ho-Pin Tung, CN (Dallara F302-Opel), 26m 12.980s; **7** Bastian Kolmsee, D (Dallara F302-Opel), 26m 13.425s; **8** Thomas Holzer, D (Dallara F302-Opel), 26m 18.903s; **9** Marcel Leipert, D (Dallara F302-Opel), 26m 20.983s; **10** Marcus Steinel, D (Dallara F302-Opel), 26m 40.234s.
Fastest lap: Seyffarth, 1m 36.515s, 106.012 mph/170.610 km/h.

RECARO F3-CUP, Motopark Oschersleben, Germany, 8/9 May. 2 x 19 laps of the 2.279-mile/3.667-km circuit.
Round 3 (43.293 miles/69.673 km).
1 Michael Devaney, IRL (Dallara F302-Opel), 26m 15.669s, 98.913 mph/159.185 km/h; **2** Thomas Holzer, D (Dallara F302-Opel), 26m 20.042s; **3** Timo Lienemann, D (Dallara F302-Opel), 26m 20.788s; **4** Filip Salaquarda, CZ (Dallara F303-Opel), 26m 42.465s; **5** Marcel Leipert, D (Dallara F302-Opel), 26m 43.254s; **6** Franz Schmöller, D (Dallara F302-Opel), 26m 43.317s; **7** Jan Seyffarth, D (Dallara F302-Renault), 26m 44.121s; **8** Marcus Steinel, D (Dallara F302-Opel), 26m 49.683s; **9** Jochen Nerpel, D (Dallara F302-Opel), 26m 50.140s; **10** Maro Engel, D (Dallara F302-Renault), 26m 54.985s.
Fastest lap: Devaney, 1m 21.756s, 100.333 mph/161.471 km/h.

Round 4 (43.293 miles/69.673 km).
1 Bastian Kolmsee, D (Dallara F302-Opel), 26m 11.396s, 99.182 mph/159.618 km/h; **2** Ho-Pin Tung, CN (Dallara F302-Opel), 26m 22.517s; **3** Jan Seyffarth, D (Dallara F302-Renault), 26m 22.893s; **4** Michael Devaney, IRL (Dallara F302-Opel), 26m 23.735s; **5** Marcel Leipert, D (Dallara F302-Opel), 26m 28.152s; **6** Maro Engel, D (Dallara F302-Renault), 26m 28.582s; **7** Jochen Nerpel, D (Dallara F302-Opel), 26m 30.609s; **8** Timo Lienemann, D (Dallara F302-Opel), 26m 30.920s; **9** Thomas Holzer, D (Dallara F302-Opel), 27m 17.438s; **10** Claudio Consiglio, I (Dallara F301-Opel), 27m 19.147s.
Fastest lap: Kolmsee, 1m 21.341s, 100.845 mph/162.295 km/h.

RECARO F3-CUP, Circuit van Drenthe, Assen, Netherlands, 22/23 May. 14 and 20 laps of the 2.412-mile/3.881-km circuit.
Round 5 (33.762 miles/54.334 km).
1 Michael Devaney, IRL (Dallara F302-Opel), 26m 19.662s, 76.942 mph/123.825 km/h; **2** Bastian Kolmsee, D (Dallara F302-Opel), 26m 21.130s; **3** Marcel Leipert, D (Dallara F302-Opel), 26m 51.753s; **4** Timo Lienemann, D (Dallara F302-Opel), 27m 07.065s; **5** Franz Schmöller, D (Dallara F302-Opel), 27m 15.869s; **6** Jochen Nerpel, D (Dallara F302-Opel), 27m 21.945s; **7** Frank Brendecke, D (Dallara F302-Opel), **13** laps; **8** Thomas Holzer, D (Dallara F302-Opel), 12; **9** Luca Iannaccone, I (Dallara F399-Opel), 12; **10** Claudio Consiglio, I (Dallara F301-Opel), **5** (DNF).
Fastest lap: Kolmsee, 1m 28.791s, 97.775 mph/157.354 km/h.

Round 6 (48.231 miles/77.620 km).
1 Timo Lienemann, D (Dallara F302-Opel), 25m 37.302s, 112.945 mph/181.768 km/h; **2** Bastian Kolmsee, D (Dallara F302-Opel), 25m 40.975s; **3** Franz Schmöller, D (Dallara F302-Opel), 25m 44.366s; **4** Ho-Pin Tung, CN (Dallara F302-Opel), 25m 49.161s; **5** Michael Devaney, IRL (Dallara F302-Opel), 25m 49.317s; **6** Marcel Leipert, D (Dallara F302-Opel), 25m 56.131s; **7** Jochen Nerpel, D (Dallara F302-Opel), 25m 56.388s; **8** Thomas Holzer, D (Dallara F302-Opel), 25m 59.500s; **9** Frank Brendecke, D (Dallara F302-Opel), 26m 36.058s; **10** Luca Iannaccone, I (Dallara F399-Opel), **19** laps.
Fastest lap: Holzer, 1m 15.928s, 114.339 mph/184.011 km/h.

RECARO F3-CUP, EuroSpeedway Lausitz, Klettwitz, Dresden, Germany, 3/4 July, 15 and 14 laps of the 2.817-mile/4.534-km circuit.
Round 7 (42.259 miles/68.010 km).
1 Thomas Holzer, D (Dallara F302-Opel), 25m 27.527s, 99.595 mph/160.283 km/h; **2** Bastian Kolmsee, D (Dallara F302-Opel), 25m 31.330s; **3** Timo Lienemann, D (Dallara F302-Opel), 25m 32.140s; **4** Jochen Nerpel, D (Dallara F302-Opel), 25m 34.263s; **5** Filip Salaquarda, CZ (Dallara F303-Opel), 25m 36.824s; **6** Franz Schmöller, D (Dallara F302-Opel), 25m 37.569s; **7** Jan Seyffarth, D (Dallara F302-Renault), 25m 40.611s; **8** Christopher Brück, D (Dallara F303-Opel), 25m 41.097s; **9** Jan Heylen, B (Dallara F302-Opel), 25m 45.198s; **10** Marcel Leipert, D (Dallara F302-Opel), 25m 50.662s.
Fastest lap: Heylen, 1m 40.460s, 100.958 mph/162.477 km/h.

Round 8 (39.442 miles/63.476 km).
1 Jochen Nerpel, D (Dallara F302-Opel), 25m 24.124s, 93.163 mph/149.931 km/h; **2** Jan Heylen, B (Dallara F302-Opel), 25m 26.289s; **3** Timo Lienemann, D (Dallara F302-Opel), 25m 27.542s; **4** Michael Devaney, IRL (Dallara F302-Opel), 25m 28.693s; **5** Bastian Kolmsee, D (Dallara F302-Opel), 25m 29.303s; **6** Ho-Pin Tung, CN (Dallara F302-Opel), 25m 30.42s; **7** Franz Schmöller, D (Dallara F302-Opel), 25m 30.865s; **8** Filip Salaquarda, CZ (Dallara F303-Opel), 25m 36.302s; **9** Marcel Leipert, D (Dallara F302-Opel), 25m 36.723s; **10** Jan Seyffarth, D (Dallara F302-Renault), 25m 43.100s.
Fastest lap: Heylen, 1m 40.197s, 101.223 mph/162.903 km/h.

RECARO F3-CUP, Nürburgring Sprint Circuit, Nürburg/Eifel, Germany, 10/11 July. 14 and 18 laps of the 2.255-mile/3.629-km circuit.
Round 9 (31.569 miles/50.806 km).
1 Jan Heylen, B (Dallara F302-Opel), 25m 39.606s, 73.817 mph/118.798 km/h; **2** Bastian Kolmsee, D (Dallara F302-Opel), 25m 49.838s; **3** Ho-Pin Tung, CN (Dallara F302-Opel), 25m 58.602s; **4** Thomas Holzer, D (Dallara F302-Opel), 26m 08.720s; **5** Timo Lienemann, D (Dallara F302-Opel), 26m 08.833s; **6** Jan Seyffarth, D (Dallara F302-Renault), 26m 15.718s; **7** Markus Mann, D (Dallara F302-Opel), 26m 35.901s; **8** Marcel Leipert, D (Dallara F302-Opel), 26m 47.214s; **9** Marcus Steinel, D (Dallara F302-Opel), 26m 57.020s; **10** Franz Schmöller, D (Dallara F302-Opel), 26m 58.671s.
Fastest lap: Heylen, 1m 39.203s, 81.831 mph/131.694 km/h.

Round 10 (40.589 miles/65.322 km).
1 Jan Heylen, B (Dallara F302-Opel), 25m 18.354s, 96.237 mph/154.878 km/h; **2** Timo Lienemann, D (Dallara F302-Opel), 25m 20.722s; **3** Bastian Kolmsee, D (Dallara F302-Opel), 25m 24.653s; **4** Ho-Pin Tung, CN (Dallara F302-Opel), 25m 30.314s; **5** Filip Salaquarda, CZ (Dallara F303-Opel), 25m 36.347s; **6** Michael Devaney, IRL (Dallara F302-Opel), 25m 38.622s; **7** Marcel Leipert, D (Dallara F302-Opel), 25m 42.797s; **8** Markus Mann, D (Dallara F302-Opel), 25m 47.757s; **9** Franz Schmöller, D (Dallara F302-Opel), 25m 49.303s; **10** Marcus Steinel, D (Dallara F302-Opel), 25m 49.692s.
Fastest lap: Heylen, 1m 23.099s, 97.689 mph/157.215 km.

RECARO F3-CUP, Sachsenring, Oberlungwitz, Germany, 14/15 August. 20 and 19 laps of the 2.265-mile/3.645-km circuit.
Round 11 (45.298 miles/72.900 km).
1 Bastian Kolmsee, D (Dallara F302-Opel), 26m 14.724s, 103.556 mph/166.658 km/h; **2** Michael Devaney, IRL (Dallara F302-Opel), 26m 25.109s; **3** Jan Seyffarth, D (Dallara F302-Renault), 26m 29.566s; **4** Franz Schmöller, D (Dallara F302-Opel), 26m 31.626s; **5** Ho-Pin Tung, CN (Dallara F302-Opel), 26m 33.029s; **6** Thomas Holzer, D (Dallara F302-Opel), 26m 33.491s; **7** Jochen Nerpel, D (Dallara F302-Opel), 26m 41.108s; **8** Marcel Leipert, D (Dallara F302-Opel), 26m 44.758s; **9** Yari Benedetti, I (Dallara F301-Opel), 26m 45.643s; **10** Marcus Steinel, D (Dallara F302-Opel), 27m 16.146s.
Fastest lap: Kolmsee, 1m 18.149s, 104.334 mph/167.910 km/h.

Round 12 (43.033 miles/69.255 km).
1 Timo Lienemann, D (Dallara F302-Opel), 25m 02.940s, 103.077 mph/165.887 km/h; **2** Jan Heylen, B (Dallara F302-Opel), 25m 04.551s; **3** Bastian Kolmsee, D (Dallara F302-Opel), 25m 08.077s; **4** Thomas Holzer, D (Dallara F302-Opel), 25m 08.560s; **5** Michael Devaney, IRL (Dallara F302-Opel), 25m 10.573s; **6** Jochen Nerpel, D (Dallara F302-Opel), 25m 13.943s; **7** Franz Schmöller, D (Dallara F302-Opel), 25m 14.370s; **8** Jan Seyffarth, D (Dallara F302-Renault), 25m 20.697s; **9** Filip Salaquarda, CZ (Dallara F303-Opel), 25m 30.548s; **10** Yari Benedetti, I (Dallara F301-Opel), 25m 28.427s.
Fastest lap: Holzer, 1m 18.415s, 103.981 mph/167.340 km/h.

RECARO F3-CUP, Nürburgring Sprint Circuit, Nürburg/Eifel, Germany, 28/29 August. 15 and 17 laps of the 2.248-mile/3.618-km circuit.
Round 13 (33.722 miles/54.270 km).
1 Jan Heylen, B (Dallara F302-Opel), 25m 14.605s, 80.152 mph/128.992 km/h; **2** Jan Seyffarth, D (Dallara F302-Renault), 25m 24.775s; **3** Ho-Pin Tung, CN (Dallara F302-Opel), 25m 25.441s; **4** Timo Lienemann, D (Dallara F302-Opel), 25m 29.482s; **5** Franz Schmöller, D (Dallara F302-Opel), 25m 38.790s; **6** Michael Devaney, IRL (Dallara F302-Opel), 25m 39.670s; **7** Thomas Holzer, D (Dallara F302-Opel), 25m 42.671s; **8** Marcus Steinel, D (Dallara F302-Opel), 25m 56.516s; **9** Marcel Leipert, D (Dallara F302-Opel), 25m 56.750s; **10** Yari Benedetti, I (Dallara F301-Opel), 25m 57.571s.
Fastest lap: Heylen, 1m 38.845s, 81.878 mph/131.770 km/h.

Round 14 (38.218 miles/61.506 km).
1 Jan Heylen, B (Dallara F302-Opel), 26m 11.476s, 87.551 mph/140.900 km/h; **2** Timo Lienemann, D (Dallara F302-Opel), 26m 16.650s; **3** Michael Devaney, IRL (Dallara F302-Opel), 26m 18.129s; **4** Jochen Nerpel, D (Dallara F302-Opel), 26m 23.284s; **5** Franz Schmöller, D (Dallara F302-Opel), 26m 26.387s; **6** Filip Salaquarda, CZ (Dallara F303-Opel), 26m 30.476s; **7** Thomas Holzer, D (Dallara F302-Opel), 26m 31.119s; **8** Marcel Leipert, D (Dallara F302-Opel), 26m 45.696s; **9** Franco Coscia, RA (Dallara F302-Opel), 26m 55.445s; **10** Marcus Steinel, D (Dallara F302-Opel), 26m 57.291s.
Fastest lap: Heylen, 1m 22.903s, 97.623 mph/157.109 km/h.

RECARO F3-CUP, EuroSpeedway Lausitz, Klettwitz, Dresden, Germany, 11/12 September. 2 x 15 laps of the 2.817-mile/4.534-km circuit.
Round 15 (42.259 miles/68.010 km).
1 Jan Heylen, B (Dallara F302-Opel), 25m 11.122s, 100.676 mph/162.023 km/h; **2** Timo Lienemann, D (Dallara F302-Opel), 25m 14.472s; **3** Bastian Kolmsee, D (Dallara F302-Opel), 25m 16.113s; **4** Franz Schmöller, D (Dallara F302-Opel), 25m 22.302s; **5** Jochen Nerpel, D (Dallara F302-Opel), 25m 28.331s; **6** Michael Devaney, IRL (Dallara F302-Opel), 25m 29.777s; **7** Thomas Holzer, D (Dallara F302-Opel), 25m 30.511s; **8** Yari Benedetti, I (Dallara F301-Opel), 25m 34.471s; **9** Filip Salaquarda, CZ (Dallara F303-Opel), 25m 36.670s; **10** Jan Seyffarth, D (Dallara F302-Renault), 25m 42.019s.
Fastest lap: Heylen, 1m 39.666s, 101.763 mph/163.771 km/h.

Round 16 (42.259 miles/68.010 km).
1 Jan Heylen, B (Dallara F302-Opel), 25m 14.992s, 100.419 mph/161.609 km/h; **2** Timo Lienemann, D (Dallara F302-Opel), 25m 15.157s; **3** Thomas Holzer, D (Dallara F302-Opel), 25m 19.343s; **4** Bastian Kolmsee, D (Dallara F302-Opel), 25m 20.552s; **5** Michael Devaney, IRL (Dallara F302-Opel), 25m 25.065s; **6** Ho-Pin Tung, CN (Dallara F302-Opel), 25m 29.891s; **7** Franz Schmöller, D (Dallara F302-Opel), 25m 31.309s; **8** Jochen Nerpel, D (Dallara F302-Opel), 25m 33.712s; **9** Marcel Leipert, D (Dallara F302-Opel), 25m 44.676s; **10** Jan Seyffarth, D (Dallara F302-Renault), 25m 44.904s.
Fastest lap: Heylen, 1m 39.518s, 101.914 mph/164.015 km/h.

RECARO F3-CUP, Motopark Oschersleben, Germany, 9/10 October. 2 x 19 laps of the 2.279-mile/3.667-km circuit.
Round 17 (43.293 miles/69.673 km).
1 Bastian Kolmsee, D (Dallara F302-Opel), 26m 02.795s, 99.728 mph/160.496 km/h; **2** Ho-Pin Tung, CN (Dallara F302-Opel), 26m 05.112s; **3** Michael Devaney, IRL (Dallara F302-Opel), 26m 20.268s; **4** Timo Lienemann, D (Dallara F302-Opel), 26m 20.544s; **5** Jan Heylen, B (Dallara F302-Opel), 26m 21.012s; **6** Thomas Holzer, D (Dallara F302-Opel), 26m 21.630s; **7** Franz Schmöller, D (Dallara F302-Opel), 26m 25.766s; **8** Jochen Nerpel, D (Dallara F302-Opel), 26m 28.243s; **9** Marcel Leipert, D (Dallara F302-Opel), 26m 28.665s; **10** Peter Elkmann, D (Dallara F302-Opel), 26m 45.659s.
Fastest lap: Tung, 1m 21.674s, 100.434 mph/161.633 km/h.

Round 18 (43.293 miles/69.673 km).
1 Bastian Kolmsee, D (Dallara F302-Opel), 25m 42.123s, 101.065 mph/162.648 km/h; **2** Michael Devaney, IRL (Dallara F302-Opel), 25m 56.816s; **3** Thomas Holzer, D (Dallara F302-Opel), 26m 04.221s; **4** Franz Schmöller, D (Dallara F302-Opel), 26m 05.551s; **5** Ho-Pin Tung, CN (Dallara F302-Opel), 26m 06.182s; **6** Marcel Leipert, D (Dallara F302-Opel), 26m 17.530s; **7** Jan Seyffarth, D (Dallara F302-Renault), 26m 19.324s; **8** Filip Salaquarda, CZ (Dallara F303-Opel), 26m 20.397s; **9** Jochen Nerpel, D (Dallara F302-Opel), 26m 21.581s; **10** Yari Benedetti, I (Dallara F31-Opel), 26m 22.291s.
Fastest lap: Kolmsee, 1m 20.283s, 102.174 mph/164.433 km/h.

Final championship points

1 Bastian Kolmsee, D, 217; **2** Timo Lienemann, D, 208; **3** Jan Heylen, B, 181; **4** Michael Devaney, IRL, 175; **5** Thomas Holzer, D, 121; **6** Franz Schmöller, D, 115; **7** Ho-Pin Tung, CN, 111; **8** Jan Seyffarth, D, 106; **9** Jochen Nerpel, D, 82; **10** Marcel Leipert, D, 66; **11** Filip Salaquarda, CZ, 42; **12** Tomas Kostka, CZ, 36; **13** Marcus Steinel, D, 13; **14** Yari Benedetti, I, 8; **15=** Maro Engel, D, 7; **15=** Markus Mann, D, 7; **17** Frank Brendecke, D, 6; **18=** Luca Iannaccone, I, 3; **18=** Christopher Brück, D, 3; **20** Franco Coscia, RA, 2; **21=** Claudio Consiglio, I, 1; **21=** Peter Elkmann, D, 1.

Rookie Cup
1= Bastian Kolmsee, 100; **1=** Timo Lienemann, 100; **3** Michael Devaney, 58.

Italian Formula 3 Championship

ITALIAN FORMULA 3 CHAMPIONSHIP, Autodromo Adria International Raceway, Adria, Italy, 4 April. Round 1. 28 laps of the 1.679-mile/2.702-km circuit, 47.010 miles/75.656 km.
1 Matteo Cressoni, I (Dallara F304-Mugen Honda), 38m 05.000s, 74.065 mph/119.195 km/h; **2** Alessandro 'Alex' Ciompi, I (Dallara F304-Opel), 38m 05.805s; **3** Michele Rugolo, I (Dallara F304-Opel), 38m 07.395s; **4** Andrea Tiso, I (Dallara F304-Opel), 38m 14.468s; **5** Giovanni Berton, I (Dallara F303-Opel), 38m 16.671s; **6** Davide Rigon, I (Dallara F302-Opel), 38m 17.142s; **7** Davide Mazzoleni, I (Dallara F304-Mugen Honda), 38m 18.254s; **8** Omar Galeffi, I (Dallara F302-Opel), 38m 19.528s; **9** Maurizio Ceresoli, I (Dallara F303-Opel), 38m 26.356s; **10** Paolo Meloni, RSM (Dallara F303-Renault), 38m 26.704s.
Fastest lap: Ciompi, 1m 12.640s, 83.208 mph/133.910 km/h.

ITALIAN FORMULA 3 CHAMPIONSHIP, Autodromo Mario Umberto Borzacchini, Magione, Perugia, Italy, 2 May. Round 2. Round 2. 30 laps of the 1.558-mile/2.507-km circuit, 46.733 miles/75.210 km.
1 Stefano Gattuso, I (Dallara F304-Mugen Honda), 35m 04.774s, 79.933 mph/128.639 km/h; **2** Davide Mazzoleni, I (Dallara F304-Mugen Honda), 35m 06.210s; **3** Andrea Tiso, I (Dallara F304-Opel), 35m 06.578s; **4** Alessandro 'Alex' Ciompi, I (Dallara F304-Opel), 35m 07.928s; **5** Omar Galeffi, I (Dallara F302-Opel), 35m 32.328s; **6** Maurizio Ceresoli, I (Dallara F303-Opel), 35m 33.896s; **7** Paolo Meloni, RSM (Dallara F303-Renault), 35m 53.303s; **8** Michele Rugolo, I (Dallara F302-Opel), 15 laps; **9** Matteo Cressoni, I (Dallara F304-Mugen Honda), 0 (DNF); **10** Davide Rigon, I (Dallara F302-Opel), 0 (DNF).
Fastest lap: Rugolo, 1m 08.624s, 81.721 mph/131.517 km/h.

48th PREMIO PEGUSA, Autodromo di Pergusa, Enna-Pergusa, Sicily, 30 May. Round 3. 18 laps of the 3.076-mile/4.950-km circuit, 55.364 miles/89.100 km.
1 Matteo Cressoni, I (Dallara F304-Mugen Honda), 37m 50.297s, 87.791 mph/141.285 km/h; **2** Alessandro 'Alex' Ciompi, I (Dallara F304-Opel), 37m 54.598s; **3** Omar Galeffi, I (Dallara F302-Opel), 37m 59.631s; **4** Stefano Gattuso, I (Dallara F304-Mugen Honda), 38m 05.900s; **5** Andrea Tiso, I (Dallara F304-Opel), 38m 23.927s; **6** Davide Mazzoleni, I (Dallara F304-Mugen Honda), 17 laps; **7** Maurizio Ceresoli, I (Dallara F303-Opel), 9 (DNF); **8** Davide di Benedetto, I (Dallara F304-Mugen Honda), 8 (DNF); **9** Michele Rugolo, I (Dallara F302-Opel); **10** Davide Rigon, I (Dallara F302-Opel).
Fastest lap: Gattuso, 1m 38.301s, 112.642 mph/181.280 km/h.

ITALIAN FORMULA 3 CHAMPIONSHIP, Autodromo Internazionale del Mugello, Scarperia, Firenze (Florence), Italy, 11 July. 2 x 12 laps of the 3.259-mile/5.245-km circuit.
Round 4 (39.109 miles/62.940 km).
1 Toni Vilander, FIN (Lola-Dome F106/03-Mugen Honda), 21m 38.731s, 108.408 mph/174.466 km/h; **2** Michele Rugolo, I (Dallara F302-Opel), 21m 52.157s; **3** Matteo Cressoni, I (Dallara F304-Mugen Honda), 21m 53.452s; **4** Davide Rigon, I (Dallara F302-Opel), 21m 55.496s; **5** Stefano Gattuso, I (Dallara F304-Mugen Honda), 21m 57.264s; **6** Davide di Benedetto, I (Dallara F304-Mugen Honda), 21m 58.398s; **7** Alessandro 'Alex' Ciompi, I (Dallara F304-Opel), 22m 09.128s; **8** Andrea Tiso, I (Dallara F304-Opel), 22m 12.184s; **9** Maurizio Ceresoli, I (Dallara F303-Opel), 22m 50.793s; **10** Paolo Meloni, RSM (Dallara F303-Renault), 8 laps.
Fastest lap: Vilander, 1m 46.763s, 109.895 mph/176.859 km/h.

Round 5 (39.109 miles/62.940 km).
1 Toni Vilander, FIN (Lola-Dome F106/03-Mugen Honda), 21m 49.932s, 107.481 mph/172.974 km/h; **2** Matteo Cressoni, I (Dallara F304-Mugen Honda), 21m 59.545s; **3** Davide di Benedetto, I (Dallara F304-Mugen Honda), 22m 00.374s; **4** Stefano Gattuso, I (Dallara F304-Mugen Honda), 22m 11.696s; **5** Davide Rigon, I (Dallara F302-Opel), 22m 13.396s; **6** Alessandro 'Alex' Ciompi, I (Dallara F304-Opel), 22m 13.621s; **7** Michele Rugolo, I (Dallara F302-Opel), 22m 15.022s; **8** Andrea Tiso, I (Dallara F304-Opel), 22m 35.026s; **9** Maurizio Ceresoli, I (Dallara F303-Opel), 22m 36.077s; **10** Paolo Meloni, RSM (Dallara F303-Renault), 0 (DNF)
Fastest lap: Vilander, 1m 48.064s, 108.572 mph/174.730 km/h.

ITALIAN FORMULA 3 CHAMPIONSHIP, Autodromo Internazionale Enzo e Dino Ferrari, Imola, Italy, 1 August. 2 x 13 laps of the 3.065-mile/4.933-km circuit.
Round 6 (39.848 miles/64.129 km).
1 Toni Vilander, FIN (Lola-Dome F106/03-Mugen Honda), 23m 24.089s, 102.168 mph/164.423 km/h; **2** Matteo Cressoni, I (Dallara F304-Mugen Honda), 23m 31.650s; **3** Michele Rugolo, I (Dallara F302-Opel), 23m 39.748s; **4** Davide di Benedetto, I (Dallara F304-Mugen Honda), 23m 42.886s; **5** Stefano Gattuso, I (Dallara F304-Mugen Honda), 23m 47.697s; **6** Alessandro 'Alex' Ciompi, I (Dallara F304-Opel), 23m 48.698s; **7** Davide Rigon, I (Dallara F302-Opel), 23m 51.919s; **8** Maurizio Ceresoli, I (Dallara F303-Opel), 24m 13.110s; **9** Andrea Tiso, I (Dallara F304-Opel), 24m 31.336s; **10** Giampiero Negrotti, I (Dallara F303-Opel), 25m 05.022s.
Fastest lap: Vilander, 1m 47.271s, 102.868 mph/165.551 km/h.

Round 7 (39.848 miles/64.129 km).
1 Toni Vilander, FIN (Lola-Dome F106/03-Mugen Honda), 23m 44.338s, 100.715 mph/162.085 km/h; **2** Matteo Cressoni, I

(Dallara F304-Mugen Honda), 23m 47.218s; **3** Alessandro 'Alex' Ciompi, I (Dallara F304-Opel), 23m 52.032s; **4** Davide di Benedetto, I (Dallara F304-Mugen Honda), 23m 53.031s; **5** Michele Rugolo, I (Dallara F302-Opel), 23m 53.489s; **6** Stefano Gattuso, I (Dallara F304-Mugen Honda), 24m 00.194s; **7** Davide Rigon, I (Dallara F302-Opel), 24m 02.382s; **8** Andrea Tiso, I (Dallara F304-Opel), 24m 04.261s; **9** Maurizio Ceresoli, I (Dallara F303-Opel), 24m 38.609s; **10** Giampiero Negrotti, I (Dallara F303-Opel), 25m 16.570s.
Fastest lap: Vilander, 1m 48.722s, 101.496 mph/163.341 km/h.

43rd TROFEO AUTOMOBILE CLUB PARMA, Autodromo Riccardo Paletti, Varano dei Melegari, Parma, Italy, 5 September. Round 8. 32 laps of the 1.476-mile/2.375-km circuit, 47.224 miles/76.000 km.
1 Toni Vilander, FIN (Lola-Dome F106/03-Mugen Honda), 34m 24.317s, 82.355 mph/132.538 km/h; **2** Matteo Cressoni, I (Dallara F304-Mugen Honda), 34m 28.433s; **3** Michele Rugolo, I (Dallara F302-Opel), 34m 32.296s; **4** Andrea Tiso, I (Dallara F304-Opel), 34m 36.501s; **5** Alessandro 'Alex' Ciompi, I (Dallara F304-Opel), 34m 47.935s; **6** Davide di Benedetto, I (Dallara F304-Mugen Honda), 34m 52.767s; **7** Stefano Gattuso, I (Dallara F304-Mugen Honda), 34m 55.117s; **8** Maurizio Ceresoli, I (Dallara F303-Opel), 35m 15.811s; **9** Francesco Dracone, I (Dallara F303-Mugen Honda), 30 laps; **10** Paolo Nocera, I (Dallara F304-Mugen Honda), 11 (DNF).
Fastest lap: Vilander, 1m 03.900s, 83.141 mph/133.803 km/h.

ITALIAN FORMULA 3 CHAMPIONSHIP, Autodromo Nazionale di Monza, Milan, Italy, 26 September. 2 x 12 laps of the 3.600-mile/5.793-km circuit.
Round 9 (43.195 miles/69.516 km).
1 Marco Bonanomi, I (Dallara F302-Mugen Honda), 22m 03.324s, 117.509 mph/189.113 km/h; **2** Daniel la Rosa, I (Dallara F302-Mugen Honda), 22m 11.205s; **3** Michele Rugolo, I (Dallara F302-Opel), 22m 11.280s; **4** Stefano Gattuso, I (Dallara F304-Mugen Honda), 22m 18.697s; **5** Davide di Benedetto, I (Dallara F304-Mugen Honda), 22m 23.726s; **6** Maurizio Ceresoli, I (Dallara F303-Opel), 22m 44.764s; **7** Paolo Nocera, I (Dallara F302-Opel), **11** laps; **8** Francesco Dracone, I (Dallara F303-Mugen Honda), 11; **9** Andrea Tiso, I (Dallara F304-Opel), 7; **10** Davide Mazzoleni, I (Dallara F304-Mugen Honda), 6.
Fastest lap: Rugolo, 1m 49.138s, 118.736 mph/191.087 km/h.

Round 10 (43.195 miles/69.516 km).
1 Marco Bonanomi, I (Dallara F302-Mugen Honda), 22m 02.210s, 117.608 mph/189.272 km/h; **2** Daniel la Rosa, I (Dallara F302-Mugen Honda), 22m 03.675s; **3** Matteo Cressoni, I (Dallara F304-Mugen Honda), 22m 04.225s; **4** Toni Vilander, FIN (Lola-Dome F106/03-Mugen Honda), 22m 18.217s; **5** Davide Mazzoleni, I (Dallara F304-Mugen Honda), 22m 19.579s; **6** Andrea Tiso, I (Dallara F304-Opel), 22m 23.578s; **7** Stefano Gattuso, I (Dallara F304-Mugen Honda), 22m 27.565s; **8** Alessandro 'Alex' Ciompi, I (Lola-Dome F106/03-Opel), 22m 29.085s; **9** Maurizio Ceresoli, I (Dallara F303-Opel), 22m 31.661s; **10** Davide di Benedetto, I (Dallara F304-Mugen Honda), 22m 37.374s.
Fastest lap: la Rosa, 1m 49.588s, 118.248 mph/190.302 km/h.

ITALIAN FORMULA 3 CHAMPIONSHIP, Autodromo di Vallelunga, Campagnano di Roma, Italy, 10 October. 2 x 20 laps of the 2.015-mile/3.243-km circuit.
Round 11 (40.302 miles/64.860 km).
1 Marco Bonanomi, I (Dallara F304-Mugen Honda), 23m 30.159s, 102.887 mph/165.581 km/h; **2** Alessandro 'Alex' Ciompi, I (Dallara F304-Opel), 23m 32.192s; **3** Stefano Gattuso, I (Dallara F304-Mugen Honda), 23m 33.831s; **4** Matteo Cressoni, I (Dallara F304-Mugen Honda), 23m 34.482s; **5** Paolo Nocera, I (Dallara F302-Opel), 23m 39.299s; **6** Michele Rugolo, I (Dallara F302-Opel), 23m 40.124s; **7** Andrea Tiso, I (Dallara F304-Opel), 23m 40.502s; **8** Maurizio Ceresoli, I (Dallara F303-Opel), 23m 46.425s; **9** Toni Vilander, FIN (Lola-Dome F106/03-Opel), 4 laps; **10** D Valsecchi, I (Dallara F304-Mugen Honda), 0 (DNF).
Fastest lap: Ciompi, 1m 09.791s, 103.944 mph/167.282 km/h.

Round 12 (40.302 miles/64.860 km).
1 Toni Vilander, FIN (Lola-Dome F106/03-Opel), 23m 41.299s, 102.081 mph/164.284 km/h; **2** Michele Rugolo, I (Dallara F302-Opel), 23m 42.423s; **3** Paolo Nocera, I (Dallara F302-Opel), 23m 53.896s; **4** Marco Bonanomi, I (Dallara F304-Mugen Honda), 23m 54.134s; **5** Andrea Tiso, I (Dallara F304-Opel), 23m 55.043s; **6** Alessandro 'Alex' Ciompi, I (Dallara F304-Opel), 23m 55.795s; **7** Stefano Gattuso, I (Dallara F304-Mugen Honda), 23m 57.861s; **8** Matteo Cressoni, I (Dallara F304-Mugen Honda), 23m 58.440s; **9** Maurizio Ceresoli, I (Dallara F303-Opel), 24m 09.316s.
Fastest lap: Vilander, 1m 09.388s, 104.548 mph/168.254 km/h.

ITALIAN FORMULA 3 CHAMPIONSHIP, Autodromo Internazionale di Misano, Misano Adriatico, Rimini, Italy, 24 October. 2 x 16 laps of the 2.523-mile/4.060-km circuit.
Round 13 (40.364 miles/64.960 km).
1 Michele Rugolo, I (Dallara F302-Opel), 23m 36.402s, 102.592 mph/165.106 km/h; **2** Alessandro 'Alex' Ciompi, I (Lola-Dome F106/03-Opel), 23m 37.478s; **3** Lopez Barda, MC (Dallara F302-Mugen Honda), 23m 44.039s; **4** Stefano Gattuso, I (Dallara F304-Mugen Honda), 23m 48.467s; **5** Marco Bonanomi, I (Dallara F304-Mugen Honda), 23m 49.071s; **6** Andrea Tiso, I (Dallara F304-Opel), 23m 50.988s; **7** Maurizio Ceresoli, I (Dallara F303-Opel), 23m 56.800s; **8** Paolo Nocera, I (Dallara F302-Opel), 24m 06.074s; **9** Toni Vilander, FIN (Lola-Dome F106/03-Opel), 14 laps (DNF); **10** Matteo Cressoni, I (Dallara F304-Mugen Honda), 0 (DNF).
Fastest lap: Rugolo, 1m 27.443s, 103.862 mph/167.149 km/h.

Round 14 (40.364 miles/64.960 km).
1 Alessandro 'Alex' Ciompi, I (Lola-Dome F106/03-Opel), 23m 37.988s, 102.477 mph/164.921 km/h; **2** Michele Rugolo, I (Dallara F302-Opel), 23m 45.431s; **3** Maurizio Ceresoli, I (Dallara F303-Opel), 23m 53.236s; **4** Andrea Tiso, I (Dallara F304-Opel), 23m 53.524s; **5** Matteo Cressoni, I (Dallara F304-Mugen Honda), 23m 54.261s; **6** Marco Bonanomi, I (Dallara F304-Mugen Honda), 23m 55.003s; **7** Stefano Gattuso, I (Dallara F304-Mugen Honda), 23m 57.352s; **8** Toni Vilander, FIN (Lola-Dome F106/03-Opel), 15 laps; **9** Lopez Barda, MC (Dallara F302-Mugen Honda), 7 (DNF); **10** Paolo Nocera, I (Dallara F302-Opel), 6 (DNF).
Fastest lap: Ciompi, 1m 27.407s, 103.904 mph/167.218 km/h.

Final championship points

1 Matteo Cressoni, I, 146; **2** Alessandro 'Alex' Ciompi, I, 139; **3** Michele Rugolo, I, 135; **4** Stefano Gattuso, I, 112; **5** Andrea Tiso, I, 85; **6** Maurizio Ceresoli, I, 49.

Drivers ineligible for the final table, as they had not competed in the requisite number of races: Toni Vilander, FIN, 146; Marco Bonanomi, I, 86; Davide di Benedetto, I, 53; Davide Mazzoleni, I, 33; Davide Rigon, I, 32; Daniel la Rosa, I, 31; Paolo Nocera, I, 28; Omar Galeffi, I, 23; Lopez Barda, MC, 12; Giovanni Berton, I, 8; Paolo Meloni, RSM, 6; Francesco Dracone, I, 5; Giampiero Negrotti, I, 2.

Major Non-Championship Formula 3

2003

The following races were run after AUTOCOURSE 2003–2004 went to press.

FIA F3 WORLD CUP, 50th MACAU GP, Circuito Da Guia, Macau, 16 November. 10 and 15 laps of the 3.801-mile/6.120-km circuit.
Leg 1 (38.028 miles/61.200 km).
1 James Courtney, AUS (Dallara F302-TOM'S Toyota), 25m 43.212s, 88.711 mph/142.767 km/h; **2** Nicolas Lapierre, F (Dallara F302-Renault), 25m 47.819s; **3** Richard Antinucci, USA (Dallara F302-Renault), 25m 52.268s; **4** Fabio Carbone, BR (Dallara F302-Renault), 25m 54.363s; **5** Lewis Hamilton, GB (Dallara F302-Mugen Honda), 25m 56.524s; **6** Robert Kubica, PL (Dallara F302-Opel), 25m 57.404s; **7** Fairuz Fauzy, MAL (Dallara F302-Mugen Honda), 25m 58.352s; **8** Andrew Thompson, GB (Dallara F302-Renault), 26m 07.281s; **9** Ronnie Quintareli, I (Dallara F302-Opel), 26m 08.167s; **10** Katsuyuki Hiranaka, J (Dallara F303-Opel), 26m 08.376s.
Fastest lap: Courtney, 2m 13.381s, 102.639 mph/165.181 km/h.

Leg 2 (57.042 miles/91.800 km).
1 Nicolas Lapierre, F (Dallara F302-Renault), 37m 00.778s, 92.468 mph/148.813 km/h; **2** Fabio Carbone, BR (Dallara F302-Renault), 37m 06.194s; **3** Katsuyuki Hiranaka, J (Dallara F303-Opel), 37m 16.160s; **4** Ronnie Quintareli, I (Dallara F302-Opel), 37m 17.389s; **5** Pierre Kaffer, D (Dallara F303-TOM'S Toyota), 37m 17.444s; **6** Paolo Montin, I (Dallara F303-Nissan), 37m 22.889s; **7** Ryan Briscoe, AUS (Dallara F303-Opel), 37m 28.427s; **8** Nelson Angelo Piquet, BR (Dallara F302-Renault), 37m 42.245s; **9** César Campanico, P (Dallara F302-Renault), 37m 46.524s; **10** Danny Watts, GB (Dallara F302-Mugen Honda), 37m 46.643s.
Fastest lap: Courtney, 2m 12.937s, 102.981 mph/165.733 km/h.

Combined result (95.070 miles/153.000 km).
1 Nicolas Lapierre, F (Dallara F302-Renault), 1h 02m 48.597s, 90.817 mph/146.155 km/h; **2** Fabio Carbone, BR (Dallara F302-Renault), 25 laps; **3** Katsuyuki Hiranaka, J (Dallara F303-Opel), 25; **4** Ronnie Quintareli, I (Dallara F302-Opel), 25; **5** Ryan Briscoe, AUS (Dallara F303-Opel), 25; **6** Hiroki Yoshimoto, J (Dallara F302-Opel), 25; **7** Michael Ho, PRC (Dallara F302-TOM'S Toyota), 25; **8** Rob Austin, GB (Dallara F302-Opel), 25; **9** Fairuz Fauzy, MAL (Dallara F302-Mugen Honda), 25; **10** Pedro Barral, E (Dallara F302-Opel), 24.

INTERNATIONAL F3 KOREA SUPER PRIX, Changwon City Raceway, South Korea, 23 November. 24 and 23 laps of the -1.873-mile/3.014-km circuit.
Leg 1 (44.948 miles/72.336 km).
1 Richard Antinucci, USA (Dallara F302-Renault), 28m 37.027s, 94.239 mph/151.663 km/h; **2** Nelson Angelo Piquet, BR (Dallara F303-Renault), 28m 38.678s; **3** Robert Doornbos, NL (Dallara F302-Opel), 28m 39.956s; **4** James Courtney, AUS (Dallara F302-TOM'S Toyota), 28m 41.523s; **5** Tatsuya Kataoka, J (Dallara F303-TOM'S Toyota), 28m 45.311s; **6** Robert Kubica, J (Dallara F302-Opel), 28m 46.410s; **7** Fabio Carbone, BR (Dallara F302-Renault), 28m 54.419s; **8** César Campanico, P (Dallara F302-Renault), 28m 57.787s; **9** Nicolas Lapierre, F (Dallara F302-Renault), 28m 59.281s; **10** Danny Watts, GB (Dallara F302-Mugen Honda), 29m 03.560s.
Fastest lap: Piquet, 1m 10.350s, 95.837 mph/154.235 km/h.

Leg 2 (43.075 miles/69.322 km).
1 Richard Antinucci, USA (Dallara F302-Renault), 27m 25.208s, 94.255 mph/151.689 km/h; **2** Robert Doornbos, NL (Dallara F302-Opel), 27m 27.190s; **3** Nelson Angelo Piquet, BR (Dallara F303-Renault), 27m 27.681s; **4** James Courtney, AUS (Dallara F302-TOM'S Toyota), 27m 28.209s; **5** Tatsuya Kataoka, J (Dallara F303-TOM'S Toyota), 27m 33.689s; **6** Robert Kubica, J (Dallara F302-Opel), 27m 34.312s; **7** César Campanico, P (Dallara F302-Renault), 27m 43.499s; **8** Fabio Carbone, BR (Dallara F302-Renault), 27m 46.417s; **9** Danny Watts, GB (Dallara F302-Mugen Honda), 27m 46.997s; **10** Alvaro Parente, P (Dallara F302-Mugen Honda), 27m 50.881s.
Fastest lap: Courtney, 1m 10.647s, 95.434 mph/153.586 km/h.

Combined result (88.022 miles/141.658 km).
1 Richard Antinucci, USA (Dallara F302-Renault), 56m 02.235s, 94.247 mph/151.676 km/h; **2** Robert Doornbos, NL (Dallara F302-Opel); **3** Nelson Angelo Piquet, BR (Dallara F303-Renault); **4** James Courtney, AUS (Dallara F302-TOM'S Toyota); **5** Tatsuya Kataoka, J (Dallara F303-TOM'S Toyota); **6** Robert Kubica, J (Dallara F302-Opel); **7** César Campanico, P (Dallara F302-Renault); **8** Fabio Carbone, BR (Dallara F302-Renault); **9** Danny Watts, GB (Dallara F302-Mugen Honda); **10** Alvaro Parente, P (Dallara F302-Mugen Honda).

2004

14th MARLBORO MASTERS OF FORMULA 3, Circuit Park Zandvoort, Netherlands, 8 August. 25 laps of the 2.677-mile/4.30749-km circuit, 66.914 miles/107.687 km.
1 Alexandre Prémat, F (Dallara F303-Mercedes Benz), 43m 20.751s, 92.623 mph/149.062 km/h; **2** Eric Salignon, F (Dallara F303-Mercedes Benz), 43m 22.881s; **3** Adam Carroll, GB (Dallara F304-Mugen Honda), 43m 24.856s; **4** James Rossiter, GB (Dallara F304-Opel), 43m 30.085s; **5** Lucas di Grassi, BR (Dallara F304-Renault), 43m 34.021s; **6** Nico Rosberg, FIN (Dallara F303-Opel), 43m 35.008s; **7** Lewis Hamilton, GB (Dallara F302-Mercedes Benz), 43m 35.854s; **8** Nelson Angelo Piquet, BR (Dallara F304-Mugen Honda), 43m 39.654s; **9** Jamie Green, GB (Dallara F302-Mercedes Benz), 43m 42.046s; **10** Danny Watts, GB (Lola-Dome F106/04-Mugen Honda), 43m 42.258s.
Fastest lap: Salignon, 1m 34.220s, 102.267 mph/164.583 km/h.

Results of the Macau race will be given in AUTOCOURSE 2005–2006.

FIA GT Championship

FIA GT CHAMPIONSHIP, Autodromo Nazionale di Monza, Milan, Italy, 28 March. Round 3. 87 laps of the -mile/5.793-km circuit, 313.165 miles/503.991 km.
1 Fabrizio Gollin/Luca Cappellari, I/I (Ferrari 550 Maranello), 2h 39m 50.695s, 117.551 mph/189.180 km/h; **2** Matteo Bobbi/Gabriele Gardel, I/CH (Ferrari 550 Maranello), 2h 40m 35.485s; **3** Philipp Peter/Fabio Babini, A/I (Ferrari 575 M Maranello), 2h 41m 16.516s; **4** Emanuele Naspetti/Mike Hezemans, I/NL (Ferrari 575 M Maranello), 86 laps; **5** Stefano Livio/Enzo Calderari/Lilian Bryner, I/CH/CH (Ferrari 550 Maranello), 85; **6** Christophe Bouchut/Marc Goossens/Arjan van der Zwaan, F/B/NL (Chrysler Viper GTS-R), 84; **7** Stéphane Ortelli/Emmanuel Collard, MC/F (Porsche 996 GT3-RSR), 84 (1st NGT class); **8** Christian Pescatori/Fabrizio de Simone, I/I (Ferrari 360 Modena), 84; **9** Bert Longin/Ian Khan/Christophe Pillon, B/GB/CH (Ferrari 575 M Maranello), 83; **10** Chris Goodwin/Miguel Ramos, GB/P (Saleen S7-R), 81.
Fastest lap: Michael Bartels/Uwe Alzen, D/D (Saleen S7-R), 1m 44.708s, 123.759 mph/199.171 km/h.

FIA GT CHAMPIONSHIP, Circuit de la Comunitat Valenciana Ricardo Tormo, Cheste, Valencia, Spain, 18 April. Round 2. 112 laps of the 2.489-mile/4.005-km circuit, 278.722 miles/448.560 km.
1 Fabrizio Gollin/Luca Cappellari, I/I (Ferrari 550 Maranello), 3h 01m 01.276s, 92.383 mph/148.676 km/h; **2** Matteo Bobbi/Gabriele Gardel, I/CH (Ferrari 550 Maranello), 3h 01m 25.096s; **3** Peter Kox/Oliver Gavin, NL/GB (Lamborghini Murcielago), 3h 02m 03.139s; **4** Karl Wendlinger/Toto Wolff/Robert Lechner, A/A/A (Ferrari 575 M Maranello), 3h 02m 21.356s; **5** Jamie Campbell-Walter/Jamie Derbyshire, GB/GB (Lister Storm), 111 laps; **6** Thomas Erdos/Mike Newton, BR/GB (Saleen S7-R), 111; **7** Sascha Maassen/Lucas Luhr, D/D (Porsche 996 GT3-RSR), 110 (1st NGT class); **8** Bert Longin/Ian Khan/Thomas Bleiner, B/GB/A (Ferrari 575 M Maranello), 110; **9** Antoine Gosse/Andrea Garbagnati/Stéphane Daoudi, F/I/F (Ferrari 575 M Maranello), 108; **10** Christian Pescatori/Fabrizio de Simone, I/I (Ferrari 360 Modena), 107.
Fastest lap: Michael Bartels/Uwe Alzen, D/D (Saleen S7-R), 1m 32.241s, 97.125 mph/156.308 km/h.

FIA GT CHAMPIONSHIP, Circuit de Nevers, Magny-Cours, France, 2 May. Round 3. 105 laps of the 2.741-mile/4.411-km circuit, 287.791 miles/463.155 km.
1 Michael Bartels/Uwe Alzen, D/D (Saleen S7-R), 3h 00m 13.044s, 95.815 mph/154.199 km/h; **2** Karl Wendlinger/Toto Wolff/Robert Lechner, A/A/A (Ferrari 575 M Maranello), 3h 00m 51.274s; **3** Fabrizio Gollin/Luca Cappellari, I/I (Ferrari 550 Maranello), 3h 01m 17.082s; **4** Matteo Bobbi/Gabriele Gardel, I/CH (Ferrari 550 Maranello), 3h 01m 33.235s; **5** Walter Lechner Jr./Toni Seiler/Franz Konrad, A/CH/D (Saleen S7-R), 3h 02m 06.676s; **6** Philipp Peter/Fabio Babini, A/I (Ferrari 575 M Maranello), 104 laps; **7** Jamie Campbell-Walter/Jamie Derbyshire, GB/GB (Lister Storm), 103; **8** Sascha Maassen/Lucas Luhr, D/D (Porsche 996 GT3-RSR), 103 (1st NGT class); **9** Stéphane Ortelli/Emmanuel Collard, MC/F (Porsche 996 GT3-RSR), 102; **10** Christophe Bouchut/Bertil Roos/Arjan van der Zwaan, F/S/NL (Chrysler Viper GTS-R), 101.
Fastest lap: Bartels/Alzen, 1m 39.093s, 99.574 mph/160.249 km/h.

FIA GT CHAMPIONSHIP, Hockenheimring Grand Prix Circuit, Heidelberg, Germany, 16 May. Round 4. 105 laps of the 2.842-mile/4.574-km circuit, 298.426 miles/480.270 km.
1 Matteo Bobbi/Gabriele Gardel, I/CH (Ferrari 550 Maranello), 3h 01m 27.749s, 98.674 mph/158.800 km/h; **2** Fabrizio Gollin/Luca Cappellari, I/I (Ferrari 550 Maranello), 3h 01m 30.812s; **3** Stefano Livio/Enzo Calderari/Lilian Bryner, I/CH/CH (Ferrari 550 Maranello), 3h 01m 35.825s; **4** Jamie Campbell-Walter/Jamie Derbyshire, GB/GB (Lister Storm), 3h 01m 40.940s; **5** Emanuele Naspetti/Mike Hezemans, I/NL (Ferrari 575 M Maranello), 3h 01m 59.460s; **6** Philipp Peter/Fabio Babini, A/I (Ferrari 575 M Maranello), 3h 02m 22.441s; **7** Christophe Bouchut/Henrik Roos/Arjan van der Zwaan, F/S/NL (Chrysler Viper GTS-R), 104 laps; **8** Sascha Maassen/Lucas Luhr, D/D (Porsche 996 GT3-RSR), 103 (1st NGT class); **9** Stéphane Ortelli/Emmanuel Collard, MC/F (Porsche 996 GT3-RSR), 103; **10** Christian Pescatori/Fabrizio de Simone, I/I (Ferrari 360 Modena), 103.
Fastest lap: Karl Wendlinger/Toto Wolff/Robert Lechner, A/A/A (Ferrari 575 M Maranello), 1m 38.151s, 104.245 mph/167.766 km/h.

FIA GT CHAMPIONSHIP, Automotodrom Brno Masaryk Circuit, Brno, Czech Republic, 30 May. Round 5. 87 laps of the 3.357-mile/5.403-km circuit, 292.082 miles/470.061 km.
1 Michael Bartels/Uwe Alzen, D/D (Saleen S7-R), 3h 00m 13.766s, 97.237 mph/156.488 km/h; **2** Karl Wendlinger/Jaime Melo Jr., A/BR (Ferrari 575 M Maranello), 3h 00m 43.209s; **3** Fabrizio Gollin/Luca Cappellari, I/I (Ferrari 550 Maranello), 3h 00m 52.167s; **4** Philipp Peter/Fabio Babini, A/I (Ferrari 575 M Maranello), 86 laps; **5** Jamie Campbell-Walter/Jamie Derbyshire, GB/GB (Lister Storm), 86 laps; **6** Toni Seiler/Franz Konrad/Harald Becker, CH/D/D (Saleen S7-R), 86; **7** Stefano Livio/Enzo Calderari/Lilian Bryner, I/CH/CH (Ferrari 550 Maranello), 85; **8** Bert Longin/Ian Khan/Robert Lechner, B/GB/A (Ferrari 575 M Maranello), 85; **9** Arjan van der Zwaan/Stephane Lemert/Henrik Roos, NL/B/S (Chrysler Viper GTS-R), 85; **10** Christian Pescatori/Fabrizio de Simone, I/I (Ferrari 360 Modena), 85 (1st NGT class).
Fastest lap: Alzen, 1m 59.417s, 101.210 mph/162.881 km/h.

LG SUPER RACING WEEKEND, Donington Park Grand Prix Circuit, Castle Donington, Derbyshire, Great Britain, 27 June. Round 6. 117 laps of the 2.500-mile/4.023-km circuit, 292.474 miles/470.691 km.
1 Michael Bartels/Uwe Alzen, D/D (Saleen S7-R), 3h 00m 20.491s, 97.307 mph/156.600 km/h; **2** Philipp Peter/Fabio Babini, A/I (Ferrari 575 M Maranello), 3h 00m 40.318s; **3** Matteo Bobbi/Gabriele Gardel, I/CH (Ferrari 550 Maranello), 3h 00m 46.601s; **4** Fabrizio Gollin/Luca Cappellari, I/I (Ferrari 550 Maranello), 3h 01m 43.788s; **5** Karl Wendlinger/Jaime Melo Jr., A/BR (Ferrari 575 M Maranello), 3h 05m 13.775s; **6** Emanuele Naspetti/Gianni Morbidelli, I/I (Ferrari 575 M Maranello), 116 laps; **7** Stefano Livio/Enzo Calderari/Lilian Bryner, I/CH/CH (Ferrari 550 Maranello), 116; **8** Thomas Erdos/Mike Newton, BR/GB (Saleen S7-R), 116; **9** Chris Goodwin/Miguel Ramos, GB/P (Saleen S7-R), 115; **10** Stéphane Ortelli/Emmanuel Collard, MC/F (Porsche 996 GT3-RSR), 114 (1st NGT class).
Fastest lap: Bartels/Alzen, 1m 28.906s, 101.221 mph/162.900 km/h.

FIA GT CHAMPIONSHIP, Circuit de Spa-Francorchamps, Stavelot, Belgium, 31 July-1 August. Round 7. 558 laps of the 4.335-mile/6.976-km circuit, 2418.754 miles/3892.608 km.
1 Fabrizio Gollin/Luca Cappellari/Enzo Calderari/Lilian Bryner, I/I/CH/CH (Ferrari 550 Maranello), 24h 01m 56.535s, 100.646 mph/161.974 km/h; **2** Philipp Peter/Fabio Babini/Mika Salo/Vincent Vosse, A/I/FIN/B (Ferrari 575 M Maranello), 557 laps; **3** Stéphane Ortelli/Romain Dumas/Emmanuel Collard, MC/F/F (Porsche 996 GT3-RSR), 545 (1st NGT class); **4** Jorg Bergmeister/Timo Bernhard/Alexei Vasiliev, D/D/RUS (Porsche 996 GT3-RSR), 543; **5** Sascha Maassen/Lucas Luhr/Marc Lieb, D/D/D (Porsche 996 GT3-RSR), 528; **6** Jorg Muller/Dirk Muller/Hans-Joachim Stuck, D/D/D (BMW M3 GTR), 525; **7** Matteo Bobbi/Gabriele Gardel/Stefano Livio/Miguel Angel de Castro, I/CH/I/E (Ferrari 550 Maranello), 524; **8** Mike Jordan/David Jones/Godfrey Jones, GB/GB/GB (Porsche 996 GT3-RSR), 521; **9** Gerold Ried/Christian Ried/Horst Felbermayr/Horst Felbermayr Jr., D/D/A/A (Porsche 996 GT3-RSR), 513 (1st NGT class); **10** Vanina Ickx/Jean-François Hemroulle/Peter Wyss, B/B/CH (Porsche 996 GT3 Cup), 507.
Fastest lap: Emanuele Naspetti/Gianni Morbidelli/Didier Defourny/Frederic Bouvy, I/I/B/B (Ferrari 575 M Maranello), 2m 18.111s, 112.988 mph/181.836 km/h.

FIA GT CHAMPIONSHIP, Autodromo Enzo e Dino Ferrari, Imola, Italy, 5 September. Round 8. 97 laps of the 3.065-mile/4.933-km circuit, 297.327 miles/478.501 km.
1 Michael Bartels/Uwe Alzen, D/D (Saleen S7-R), 3h 01m 26.436s, 98.322 mph/158.234 km/h; **2** Andrea Bertolini/Mika Salo, I/FIN (Maserati MC12), 3h 02m 09.579s; **3** Johnny Herbert/Fabrizio de Simone, GB/I (Maserati MC12), 3h 02m 48.962s; **4** Fabrizio Gollin/Luca Cappellari, I/I (Ferrari 550 Maranello), 96 laps; **5** Stefano Livio/Enzo Calderari/Lilian Bryner, I/CH/CH (Ferrari 550 Maranello), 96; **6** Matteo Bobbi/Gabriele Gardel, I/CH (Ferrari 550 Maranello), 95; **7** Philipp Peter/Fabio Babini, A/I (Ferrari 575 M Maranello), 95; **8** Emanuele Naspetti/Gianni Morbidelli, I/I (Ferrari 575 M Maranello), 95; **9** Sascha Maassen/Lucas Luhr, D/D (Porsche 996 GT3-RSR), 94 (1st NGT class); **10** Karl Wendlinger/Jaime Melo Jr., A/BR (Ferrari 575 M Maranello), 94.
Fastest lap: Bartels/Alzen, 1m 47.399s, 102.746 mph/165.353 km/h.

FIA GT CHAMPIONSHIP, Motopark Oschersleben, Germany, 19 September. Round 9. 118 laps of the 2.279-mile/3.667-km circuit, 268.871 miles/432.706 km.
1 Andrea Bertolini/Mika Salo, I/FIN (Maserati MC12), 3h 00m 27.405s, 89.397 mph/143.870 km/h; **2** Fabrizio Gollin/Luca Cappellari, I/I (Ferrari 550 Maranello), 117 laps; **3** Chris Goodwin/José-Pedro Fontes, GB/P (Saleen S7-R), 117; **4** Karl Wendlinger/Tarso Marques, A/BR (Ferrari 575 M Maranello), 117; **5** Matteo Bobbi/Gabriele Gardel, I/CH (Ferrari 550 Maranello), 116; **6** Stefano Livio/Enzo Calderari/Lilian Bryner, I/CH/CH (Ferrari 550 Maranello), 116; **7** Thomas Erdos/Mike Newton, BR/GB (Saleen S7-R), 116 (1st NGT class); **8** Johnny Herbert/Fabrizio de Simone, GB/I (Maserati MC12), 116; **9** Sascha Maassen/Lucas Luhr, D/D (Porsche 996 GT3-RSR), 116; **10** Stéphane Ortelli/Emmanuel Collard, MC/F (Porsche 996 GT3-RSR), 115.
Fastest lap: Michael Bartels/Uwe Alzen, D/D (Saleen S7-R), 1m 24.701s, 96.845 mph/155.856 km/h.

FIA GT CHAMPIONSHIP, Dubai Circuit, United Arab Emirates, 10 October. Round 10. 88 laps of the 3.352-mile/5.394-km circuit, 294.948 miles/474.672 km.
1 Matteo Bobbi/Gabriele Gardel, I/CH (Ferrari 550 Maranello), 3h 00m 10.909s, 98.217 mph/158.064 km/h; **2** Johnny Herbert/Fabrizio de Simone, GB/I (Maserati MC12), 3h 00m 53.356s; **3** Thomas Biagi/Enzo Calderari/Lilian Bryner, I/CH/CH (Ferrari 550 Maranello), 3h 01m 43.222s; **4** Michael Bartels/Uwe Alzen, D/D (Saleen S7-R), 3h 02m 10.149s; **5** Fabrizio Gollin/Luca Cappellari, I/I (Ferrari 550 Maranello), 87 laps; **6** Gianni Morbidelli/Fabio Babini, I/I (Ferrari 575 M Maranello), 86; **7** Sascha Maassen/Lucas Luhr, D/D (Porsche 996 GT3-RSR), 86; **8** Stéphane Ortelli/Emmanuel Collard, MC/F (Porsche 996 GT3-RSR), 85; **9** Thomas Erdos/Mike Newton, BR/GB (Saleen S7-R), 85; **10** Christian Pescatori/Jaime Melo Jr., I/BR (Ferrari 360 Modena), 85.
Fastest lap: Bobbi/Gardel, 1m 56.936s, 103.185 mph/166.060 km/h.

Provisional championship points

GT Class
Drivers
1= Fabrizio Gollin, I, 85; 1= Luca Cappellari, I, 85; 3= Matteo Bobbi, I, 68.5; 3= Gabriele Gardel, CH, 68.5; 5= Enzo Calderari, CH, 50; 5= Lilian Bryner, CH, 50; 5= Fabio Babini, I, 50; **8** Karl Wendlinger, A, 46.5; **9** Philipp Peter, A, 46; **10=** Uwe Alzen, D, 44; **10=** Michael Bartels, D, 44; **12** Stefano Livio, I, 36.5; **13** Jaime Melo Jr., BR, 20; **14** Emanuele Naspetti, I, 18; **15=** Mika Salo, FIN, 17; **15=** Vincent Vosse, B, 17; **17=** Jamie Campbell-Walter, GB, 16; **17=** Jamie Derbyshire, GB, 16; **19=** Mike Newton, GB, 14; **19=** Thomas Erdos, BR, 14; **19=** Robert Lechner, A, 14; **22** Bert Longin, B, 13.5; **23=** Chris Goodwin, GB, 13; **23=** Toto Wolff, A, 13; **23=** Gianni Morbidelli, I, 13; **26** Miguel Angel de Castro, E, 12.5; **27** Mike Hezemans, NL, 9; **28=** José-Pedro Fontes, P, 8; **28=** Thomas Biagi, I, 8; **30=** Alex Müller, D, 7.5; **30=** Pierre-Yves Corthals, F, 7.5.

Teams
1 BMS Scuderia Italia, 153.5; **2** G.P.C. Giesse Squadra Corse, 68; **3** JMB Racing, 56; **4** Vitaphone Racing Team, 44; **5** Care Racing Development, 32.

N-GT Class
Drivers
1= Stéphane Ortelli, MC, 90; 1= Emmanuel Collard, F, 90; 3= Sascha Maazen, D, 85.5; 3= Lucas Luhr, D, 85.5; 5= Christian Pescatori, I, 48; 5= Alexei Vasiliev, RUS, 48; 7= Gerold Ried, D, 40; 7= Christian Ried, D, 40; **9** Fabrizio de Simone, I, 36; **10** Nikolaj Fomenko, RUS, 26.

Teams
1 Freisinger Yukos Motorsport, 138; **2** Freisinger Motorsport, 85.5; **3** G.P.C. Giesse Squadra Corse, 52; **4** Proton Competition, 41; **5** Gruppe M Europe, 16.5.

Result of the Zhuhai race will be given in AUTOCOURSE 2005–2006.

Other Sports Car Race

72nd 24 HEURES DU MANS, Circuit International Du Mans, Les Raineries, Le Mans, France, 12-13 June. 379 laps of the 8.482-mile/13.650-km circuit, 3214.571 miles/5173.350 km.
1 Rinaldo Capello/Seiji Ara/Tom Kristensen, I/J/DK (Audi R8), 24h 00m 55.345s, 133.855 mph/215.418 km/h (1st LM1 class); **2** Jamie Davies/Johnny Herbert/Guy Smith, GB/GB/GB (Audi R8), 24h 01m 36.699s; **3** JJ Lehto/Marco Werner/Emanuele Pirro, FIN/D/I (Audi R8), 368 laps; **4** Soheil Ayari/Erik Comas/Benoit Tréluyer, F/F/F (Pescarolo C60-Judd), 361; **5** Allan McNish/Frank Biela/Pierre Kaffer, GB/D/D (Audi R8), 350; **6** Oliver Gavin/Olivier Beretta/Jan Magnussen, GB/MC/DK, (Chevrolet Corvette C5-R), 345 (1st GTS class); **7** Jan Lammers/Chris Dyson/Katsumoto Kaneishi, NL/USA/J (Dome S101-Judd), 341; **8** Ron Fellows/Johnny

O'Connell/Massimiliano 'Max' Papis, CDN/USA/I (Chevrolet Corvette C5-R), 334; 9 Darren Turner/Rickard Rydell/Colin McRae, GB/S/GB (Ferrari 550 Maranello), 329; 10 Sascha Maassen/Jörg Bergmeister/Patrick Long, D/D/USA (Porsche 911 GT3-RSR), 327 (1st GT class); 11 Peter Kox/Tomas Enge/Alain Menu, NL/CZ/CH (Ferrari 550 Maranello), 325; 12 Jaruki Kurosawa/Kazuyuki Nishizawa/Manabu Orido, J/J/J (Porsche 911 GT3-RSR), 322; 13 Stéphane Ortelli/Ralf Kelleners/Romain Dumas, MC/D/F (Porsche 911 GT3-RSR), 321; 14 Christophe Bouchut/Patrice Goueslard/Olivier Dupard, F/F/F (Ferrari 550 Maranello), 317; 15 Anthony Burgess/Philip Colin/Andrew Bagnall, CDN/USA/NZ (Porsche 911 GT3-RS), 317; 16 Luc Alphand/Christian Lavielle/Philippe Almeras, F/F/F (Porsche 911 GT3-RS), 316; 17 Werner Lupberger/Robbie Stirling/Kevin McGarrity, ZA/GB/GB (Nasamax DM139-Judd), 316; 18 Iain Donaldson/G Fisken/Lars Nielsen, GB/GB/DK (Porsche 911 GT3-RSR), 314; 19 Tom Coronel/Justin Wilson/Ralph Firman, NL/GB/GB (Dome S101-Judd), 313; 20 Rob Wilson/Frank Mountain/Hans Hugenholtz, NZ/GB/NL (Ferrari 360 Modena), 311; 21 Didier Andre/Benjamin Leuenberger/Christian Vann, F/CH/GB (Lola B2K/10-Judd), 300; 22 Bob Berridge/Michael Caine/Chris Stockton, GB/GB/GB (TVR Tuscan T400R), 300; 23 Nigel Greensall/Lawrence Tomlinson/Gareth Evans, GB/GB/GB (TVR Tuscan T400R), 291; 24 Tim Sugden/Ian Khan/Nigel Smith, GB/GB/GB (Porsche 911 T3-RS), 283; 25 John Nielsen/Casper Elgaard/Jens Moller, DK/DK/DK (Lister Storm LMP-Chevrolet), 279; 26 Clint Field/William Binnie/Rick Sutherland, USA/USA/USA (Lola B2K/40-Judd), 278 (1st LM2 class); 27 Sébastien Bourdais/Emmanuel Collard/Nicolas Minassian, F/F/F (Pescarolo C60-Judd), 282 (DNF); 28 Olivier Porta/Yojiro Terada/Patrice Roussel, F/J/F (WR-Peugeot LMP2001), 270; 29 Thomas Erdos/Mike Newton/Nathan Kinch, BR/USA/GB (Lola B01/60-Judd), 256 (DNF); 30 Joao Barbosa/Martin Short/Rob Barff, P/GB/GB (Dallara LMP-Judd), 230 (DNF); 31 Marc Lieb/Leo Hindery/Mike Rockenfeller, D/USA/D (Porsche 911 GT3-RSR), 223 (DNF); 32 Neil Cunningham/Adam Sharpe/Steve Hyde, AUS/GB/GB (Morgan Aero8 LMGT), 222; 33 Hiroki Katoh/Ryo Michigami/Ryo Fukuda, J/J/J (Dome S101-Judd), 206 (DNF); 34 Jean-Denis Deletraz/Mike Hezemans/Ange Barde, CH/NL/F (Ferrari 575 M Maranello), 200 (DNF); 35 Andy Wallace/David Brabham/Hayanari Shimoda, GB/AUS/J (Zytek 04S), 167 (DNF); 36 John Bosch/Danny Sullivan/Thomas Biagi, NL/USA/I (Ferrari 575 M Maranello), 163 (DNF); 37 Alex Caffi/Gabrio Rosa/Peter van Merksteijn, I/I/NL (Porsche 911 GT3RS), 148 (DNF); 38 Tristan Gommendy/Jean-Bernard Bouvet/Bastien Briere, F/F/F (WR-Peugeot LMP2004), 137 (DNF); 39 Jaime Melo Jr/Stéphane Daoudi/Jean-René de Fournoux, BR/F/F (Ferrari 360 Modena), 133 (DNF); 40 Jean-Marc Gounon/Alexander Frei/Sam Hancock, F/CH/GB (Courage-AER C65), 127 (DNF); 41 Gunnar Jeanette/Gavin Pickering/Renaud Derlot, USA/GB/F (Courage-IES C65), 124 (DNF); 42 Bruno Besson/Jean-Luc Maury-Laribière/Sylvain Boulay, F/F/F (Reynard 2KQ-Lehman), 122 (DNF); 43 Paul Belmondo/Claude-Yves Gosselin/Marco Saviozzi, F/F/I (Courage-AER C65), 80 (DNF); 44 Alexei Vasiliev/Nikolaj Fomenko/Robert Nearn, RUS/RUS/GB (Porsche 911 GT3-RSR), 65 (DNF); 45 Patrick Bourdais/Jean-Luc Blanchemain/Roland Berville, F/F/F (Panoz-Elan GTP), 54 (DNF); 46 Phil Andrews/Calum Lockie/Anthony Kumpen, GB/GB/B (Lola B2K/10-Caterpillar), 35 (DNF); 47 Jon Field/Duncan Dayton/Larry Connor, USA/USA/USA (Lola B01/60-Judd), 29 (DNF); 48 David Warnock/James Matthews/Paul Daniels, GB/GB/GB (Porsche 911 GT3-RS), 27 (DNF).
Fastest lap: Davies/Herbert/Smith, 3m 34.264s, 142.507 mph/229.343 km/h.

Indy Racing League (IRL) IndyCar Series

TOYOTA INDY 300, Homestead-Miami Speedway, Florida, USA, 29 February. Round 1. 200 laps of the 1.485-mile/2.390-km circuit, 297.000 miles/477.975 km.
1 Sam Hornish Jr., USA (Dallara-Toyota), 1h 57m 56.3961s, 151.094 mph/243.162 km/h; 2 Helio Castroneves, BR (Dallara-Toyota), 1h 57m 56.4659s; 3 Dan Wheldon, GB (Dallara-Honda), 1h 57m 58.0411s; 4 Toranosuke Takagi, J (Dallara-Toyota), 1h 57m 58.1383s; 5 Tomas Scheckter, ZA (Dallara-Chevrolet), 1h 57m 58.4210s; 6 Darren Manning, GB (Panoz G Force-Toyota), 1h 58m 01.0643s; 7 Buddy Rice, USA (Panoz G Force-Honda), 1h 58m 01.9628s; 8 Tony Kanaan, BR (Dallara-Honda), 1h 58m 02.1469s; 9 Scott Sharp, USA (Dallara-Toyota), 1h 58m 03.1846s; 10 Robbie Buhl, USA (Dallara-Chevrolet), 1h 58m 04.0687s.
Fastest lap: Hornish Jr., 24.6822s, 216.593 mph/348.573 km/h.

COPPER WORLD INDY 200, Phoenix International Raceway, Arizona, USA, 21 March. Round 2. 200 laps of the 1.000-mile/1.609-km circuit, 200.000 miles/321.869 km.
1 Tony Kanaan, BR (Dallara-Honda), 1h 33m 45.8490s, 127.981 mph/205.965 km/h; 2 Scott Dixon, NZ (Panoz G Force-Honda), 1h 33m 46.3834s; 3 Dan Wheldon, GB (Dallara-Honda), 1h 33m 52.8449s; 4 Alex Barron, USA (Panoz G Force-Toyota), 1h 33m 53.1710s; 5 Helio Castroneves, BR (Dallara-Toyota), 1h 33m 53.4272s; 6 Helio Castroneves, BR (Dallara-Toyota), 1h 33m 54.7655s; 7 Bryan Herta, USA (Dallara-Honda), 1h 33m 55.9079s; 8 Toranosuke Takagi, J (Dallara-Toyota), 198; 9 Buddy Rice, USA (Panoz G Force-Honda), 198; 10 Greg Ray, USA (Panoz G Force-Honda), 198.
Fastest lap: Manning, 22.3003s, 161.433 mph/259.801 km/h.

INDY JAPAN 300, Twin Ring Motegi, Motegi, Japan, 17 April. Round 3. 200 laps of the 1.520-mile/2.446-km circuit, 304.000 miles/489.221 km.
1 Dan Wheldon, GB (Dallara-Honda), 1h 49m 48.2611s, 166.114 mph/267.334 km/h; 2 Tony Kanaan, BR (Dallara-Honda), 1h 49m 49.7065s; 3 Helio Castroneves, BR (Dallara-Toyota), 1h 49m 53.3104s; 4 Darren Manning, GB (Panoz G Force-Toyota), 1h 49m 58.0141s; 5 Scott Dixon, NZ (Panoz G Force-Honda), 1h 49m 59.5378s; 7 Dario Franchitti, GB (Dallara-Honda), 199 laps; 8 Kosuke Matsuura, J (Panoz G Force-Honda), 199; 9 Scott Sharp, USA (Dallara-Toyota), 199; 10 Toranosuke Takagi, J (Dallara-Toyota), 199.
Fastest lap: Wheldon, 27.2016s, 201.165 mph/323.743 km/h.

88th INDIANAPOLIS 500, Indianapolis Motor Speedway, Speedway, Indiana, USA, 30 May. Round 4. 180 laps of the 2.500-mile/4.023-km circuit, 450.000 miles/724.205 km.
Scheduled for 200 laps, but stopped early due to rain.
1 Buddy Rice, USA (Panoz G Force-Honda), 3h 14m 55.2395s, 138.518 mph/222.923 km/h (under caution); 2 Tony Kanaan, BR (Dallara-Honda), 3h 14m 55.3954s; 3 Dan Wheldon, GB (Dallara-Honda), 3h 14m 57.5272s; 4 Bryan Herta, USA (Dallara-Honda), 3h 14m 57.6892s; 5 Bruno Junqueira, BR (Panoz G Force-Toyota), 3h 14m 58.9181s; 6 Vitor Meira, BR (Panoz G Force-Honda), 3h 14m 59.8530s; 7 Adrian Fernandez, MEX (Panoz G Force-Honda), 3h 15m 00.2396s; 8 Scott Dixon, NZ

(Panoz G Force-Toyota), 3h 15m 02.5903s; 9 Helio Castroneves, BR (Dallara-Toyota), 3h 15m 04.0474s; 10 Roger Yasukawa, USA (Panoz G Force-Honda), 3h 15m 04.5234s; 11 Kosuke Matsuura, J (Panoz G Force-Honda), 3h 15m 06.3554s; 12 Alex Barron, USA (Dallara-Chevrolet), 3h 15m 11.5117s; 13 Scott Sharp, USA (Dallara-Toyota), 3h 15m 12.9176s; 14 Dario Franchitti, GB (Dallara-Honda), 3h 15m 13.8878s; 15 Felipe Giaffone, BR (Dallara-Chevrolet), 179 laps; 16 Jeff Simmons, USA (Dallara-Toyota), 179; 17 Al Unser Jr., USA (Dallara-Chevrolet), 179; 18 Tomas Scheckter, ZA (Dallara-Chevrolet), 179; 19 Toranosuke Takagi, J (Dallara-Toyota), 179; 20 Richie Hearn, USA (Panoz G Force-Toyota), 178; 21 Sarah Fisher, USA (Dallara-Chevrolet), 177; 22 Robby McGehee, USA (Dallara-Chevrolet), 177; 23 Buddy Lazier, USA (Dallara-Toyota), 164 (DNF); 24 Marty Roth, USA (Dallara-Toyota), 128 (DNF); 25 Darren Manning, GB (Panoz G Force-Toyota), 104 (DNF); 26 Sam Hornish Jr., USA (Dallara-Toyota), 104 (DNF); 27 Greg Ray, USA (Panoz G Force-Honda), 98 (DNF); 28 PJ Jones, USA (Dallara-Chevrolet), 88 (DNF); 29 Robby Gordon/Jaques Lazier, USA/USA (Dallara-Chevrolet), 88 (DNF); 30 Mark Taylor, GB (Dallara-Honda), 62 (DNF); 31 Ed Carpenter, USA (Dallara-Chevrolet), 62 (DNF); 32 Larry Foyt, USA (Panoz G Force-Toyota), 54 (DNF); 33 A.J. Foyt IV, USA (Dallara-Toyota), 26 (DNF).
Fastest lap: Meira, 41.2086s, 218.401 mph/351.482 km/h.

BOMBARDIER 500, Texas Motor Speedway, Fort Worth, Texas, USA, 12 June. Round 5. 200 laps of the 1.455-mile/2.342-km circuit, 291.000 miles/468.319 km.
1 Tony Kanaan, BR (Dallara-Honda), 1h 53m 24.1239s, 153.965 mph/247.783 km/h; 2 Dario Franchitti, GB (Dallara-Honda), 1h 53m 24.3817s; 3 Alex Barron, USA (Dallara-Chevrolet), 1h 53m 25.3782s; 4 Sam Hornish Jr., USA (Dallara-Toyota), 1h 53m 25.4367s; 5 Adrian Fernandez, MEX (Panoz G Force-Honda), 1h 53m 25.5127s; 6 Vitor Meira, BR (Panoz G Force-Honda), 1h 53m 25.6567s; 7 Greg Ray, USA (Panoz G Force-Honda), 1h 53m 25.9190s; 8 Darren Manning, GB (Panoz G Force-Toyota), 1h 53m 27.7093s; 9 Felipe Giaffone, BR (Dallara-Chevrolet), 1h 53m 29.4264s; 10 Toranosuke Takagi, J (Dallara-Toyota), 1h 53m 29.5610s.
Fastest lap: Meira, 24.7679s, 211.483 mph/340.350 km/h.

SUNTRUST INDY CHALLENGE, Richmond International Raceway, Virginia, USA, 26 June. Round 6. 250 laps of the 0.750-mile/1.207-km circuit, 187.500 miles/301.752 km.
1 Dan Wheldon, GB (Dallara-Honda), 1h 38m 10.607s, 114.589 mph/184.413 km/h; 2 Vitor Meira, BR (Panoz G Force-Honda), 1h 38m 11.2357s; 3 Helio Castroneves, BR (Dallara-Toyota), 1h 38m 10.8115s*; 4 Bryan Herta, USA (Dallara-Honda), 1h 38m 12.8911s; 5 Tony Kanaan, BR (Dallara-Honda), 1h 38m 12.5701s*; 6 Buddy Rice, USA (Panoz G Force-Honda), 1h 38m 12.9233s; 7 Adrian Fernandez, MEX (Panoz G Force-Honda), 1h 38m 13.0959s; 8 Scott Dixon, NZ (Panoz G Force-Honda), 1h 49m 14.0318s; 9 Scott Sharp, USA (Dallara-Toyota), 248 laps; 10 Felipe Giaffone, BR (Dallara-Chevrolet), 248.
* penalised 1 position due to illegal overtaking.
Fastest lap: Sam Hornish Jr., USA (Dallara-Toyota), 15.9638s, 169.133 mph/272.193 km/h.

ARGENT MORTGAGE INDY 300, Kansas Speedway, Kansas City, Kansas, USA, 4 July. Round 7. 200 laps of the 1.520-mile/2.446-km circuit, 304.000 miles/489.241 km.
1 Buddy Rice, USA (Panoz G Force-Honda), 1h 42m 56.6727s, 177.183 mph/285.148 km/h; 2 Vitor Meira, BR (Panoz G Force-Honda), 1h 42m 56.6778s; 3 Tony Kanaan, BR (Dallara-Honda), 1h 42m 56.8742s; 4 Dario Franchitti, GB (Dallara-Honda), 1h 42m 57.4033s; 5 Bryan Herta, USA (Dallara-Honda), 1h 42m 58.0738s; 6 Adrian Fernandez, MEX (Panoz G Force-Honda), 1h 42m 58.2675s; 7 Helio Castroneves, BR (Dallara-Toyota), 1h 42m 59.1989s; 8 Sam Hornish Jr., USA (Dallara-Toyota), 199 laps; 9 Dan Wheldon, GB (Dallara-Honda), 199; 10 Alex Barron, USA (Dallara-Chevrolet), 199.
Fastest lap: Tomas Scheckter, ZA (Dallara-Chevrolet), 25.9677s, 210.723 mph/339.126 km/h.

FIRESTONE INDY 200, Nashville Superspeedway, Lebanon, Tennessee, USA, 17 July. Round 8. 200 laps of the 1.300-mile/2.092-km circuit, 260.000 miles/418.429 km.
1 Tony Kanaan, BR (Dallara-Honda), 1h 55m 34.6367s, 134.975 mph/217.221 km/h; 2 Sam Hornish Jr., USA (Dallara-Toyota), 1h 55m 35.0122s; 3 Helio Castroneves, BR (Dallara-Toyota), 1h 55m 35.1209s; 4 Darren Manning, GB (Panoz G Force-Honda), 1h 55m 35.8946s; 5 Townsend Bell, USA (Dallara-Toyota), 1h 55m 36.0738s; 6 Buddy Rice, USA (Panoz G Force-Honda), 1h 55m 36.0738s; 7 Mark Taylor, GB (Panoz G Force-Honda), 1h 55m 39.0957s; 8 Scott Dixon, NZ (Panoz G Force-Honda), 1h 55m 39.2829s; 9 Kosuke Matsuura, J (Panoz G Force-Honda), 1h 55m 41.3535s; 10 Adrian Fernandez, MEX (Panoz G Force-Honda), 1h 55m 42.2550s.
Fastest lap: Meira, 23.6263s, 198.084 mph/318.786 km/h.

MENARD A.J. FOYT INDY 225, The Milwaukee Mile, Wisconsin State Fair Park, West Allis, Wisconsin, USA, 25 July. Round 9. 225 laps of the 1.015-mile/1.633-km circuit, 228.375 miles/367.534 km.
1 Dario Franchitti, GB (Dallara-Honda), 1h 46m 49.4110s, 128.272 mph/206.434 km/h; 2 Buddy Rice, USA (Panoz G Force-Honda), 1h 46m 50.0700s; 3 Sam Hornish Jr., USA (Dallara-Toyota), 1h 46m 54.6577s; 4 Tony Kanaan, BR (Dallara-Honda), 1h 47m 00.5954s; 5 Vitor Meira, BR (Panoz G Force-Honda), 1h 47m 00.6940s; 6 Townsend Bell, USA (Dallara-Chevrolet), 1h 47m 03.5034s; 7 Alex Barron, USA (Dallara-Chevrolet), 1h 47m 03.7332s; 8 Adrian Fernandez, MEX (Panoz G Force-Honda), 224 laps; 9 Bryan Herta, USA (Dallara-Honda), 224; 10 Kosuke Matsuura, J (Panoz G Force-Honda), 224.
Fastest lap: Franchitti, 22.8049s, 160.229 mph/257.863 km/h.

MICHIGAN INDY 400, Michigan International Speedway, Brooklyn, Michigan, USA, 1 August. Round 10. 200 laps of the 2.000-mile/3.219-km circuit, 400.000 miles/643.738 km.
1 Buddy Rice, USA (Panoz G Force-Honda), 2h 11m 46.7517s, 182.123 mph/293.098 km/h; 2 Tony Kanaan, BR (Dallara-Honda), 2h 11m 46.8313s; 3 Dan Wheldon, GB (Dallara-Toyota), 2h 11m 50.3877s; 4 Vitor Meira, BR (Panoz G Force-Honda), 2h 11m 50.4331s; 5 Vitor Meira, BR (Panoz G Force-Honda), 2h 11m 50.4492s; 6 Bryan Herta, USA (Dallara-Honda), 2h 11m 50.8241s; 7 Scott Dixon, NZ (Panoz G Force-Honda), 2h 11m 50.8847s; 8 Townsend Bell, USA (Dallara-Chevrolet), 2h 11m 51.9529s; 9 Scott Sharp, USA (Dallara-Toyota), 2h 11m 54.1576s; 10 Helio Castroneves, BR (Dallara-Toyota), 2h 11m 54.4571s.
Fastest lap: Darren Manning, GB (Panoz G Force-Toyota), 33.2444s, 216.578 mph/348.548 km/h.

BELTERRA CASINO INDY 300, Kentucky Speedway. 15 August. Round 11. 200 laps of the 1.480-mile/2.382-km circuit, 296.000 miles/476.366 km.
1 Adrian Fernandez, MEX (Panoz G Force-Honda), 1h 38m 20.7207s, 180.588 mph/290.628 km/h; 2 Buddy Rice, USA

(Panoz G Force-Honda), 1h 38m 20.7788s; 3 Dan Wheldon, GB (Dallara-Honda), 1h 38m 20.8926s; 4 Kosuke Matsuura, J (Panoz G Force-Honda), 1h 38m 21.0572s; 5 Tony Kanaan, BR (Dallara-Honda), 1h 38m 21.6973s; 6 Dario Franchitti, GB (Dallara-Honda), 1h 38m 21.7368s; 7 Vitor Meira, BR (Panoz G Force-Honda), 1h 38m 22.0026s; 8 Ed Carpenter, USA (Dallara-Chevrolet), 1h 38m 22.0771s; 9 Bryan Herta, USA (Dallara-Honda), 1h 38m 22.4906s; 10 Darren Manning, GB (Panoz G Force-Toyota), 1h 38m 22.7177s.
Fastest lap: Meira, 24.6198s, 216.411 mph/348.280 km/h.

HONDA INDY 225, Pikes Peak International Raceway, Fountain, Colorado, USA, 22 August. Round 12. 225 laps of the 1.000-mile/1.609-km circuit, 225.000 miles/362.102 km.
1 Dario Franchitti (Dallara-Honda), 1h 34m 56.9156s, 142.182 mph/228.820 km/h; 2 Adrian Fernandez, MEX (Panoz G Force-Honda), 1h 34m 59.1585s; 3 Dan Wheldon, GB (Dallara-Honda), 1h 34m 59.5743s; 4 Darren Manning, GB (Dallara-Honda), 1h 34m 59.8433s; 5 Tony Kanaan, BR (Dallara-Honda), 1h 35m 04.4308s; 6 Helio Castroneves, BR (Dallara-Toyota), 1h 35m 07.6697s; 7 Vitor Meira, BR (Panoz G Force-Honda), 1h 35m 08.4156s; 8 Jaques Lazier, USA (Dallara-Chevrolet), 1h 35m 14.0080s; 9 Bryan Herta, USA (Dallara-Honda), 224 laps; 10 Alex Barron, USA (Dallara-Chevrolet), 224.
Fastest lap: Wheldon, 21.2880s, 169.109 mph/272.155 km/h.

FIRESTONE INDY 225, Nazareth Speedway. 29 August. Round 13. 225 laps of the 0.935-mile/1.505-km circuit, 210.375 miles/338.566 km.
1 Dan Wheldon, GB (Dallara-Honda), 1h 46m 11.0277s, 118.874 mph/191.309 km/h; 2 Tony Kanaan, BR (Dallara-Honda), 1h 46m 14.5830s; 3 Dario Franchitti, GB (Dallara-Honda), 1h 46m 15.0544s; 4 Buddy Rice, USA (Panoz G Force-Honda), 1h 46m 15.4729s; 5 Helio Castroneves, BR (Dallara-Toyota), 1h 46m 16.2896s; 6 Darren Manning, GB (Panoz G Force-Toyota), 1h 46m 16.4501s; 7 Adrian Fernandez, MEX (Panoz G Force-Honda), 1h 46m 17.9260s; 8 Bryan Herta, USA (Dallara-Honda), 1h 46m 19.3694s; 9 Scott Dixon, NZ (Panoz G Force-Honda), 1h 46m 19.7878s; 10 Vitor Meira, BR (Panoz G Force-Honda), 1h 46m 20.1453s.
Fastest lap: Sam Hornish Jr., USA (Dallara-Toyota), 21.2354s, 158.509 mph/255.095 km/h.

DELPHI INDY 300, Chicagoland Speedway, Chicago, Illinois, USA, 12 September. Round 14. 200 of the 1.520-mile/2.446-km circuit, 304.000 miles/489.241 km.
1 Adrian Fernandez, MEX (Panoz G Force-Honda), 2h 09m 31.3301s, 140.825 mph/226.636 km/h; 2 Bryan Herta, USA (Dallara-Honda), 2h 09m 31.4017s; 3 Tony Kanaan, BR (Dallara-Honda), 2h 09m 31.4540s; 4 Dan Wheldon, GB (Dallara-Honda), 2h 09m 31.5765s; 5 Vitor Meira, BR (Panoz G Force-Honda), 2h 09m 31.8714s; 6 Sam Hornish Jr., USA (Dallara-Chevrolet), 2h 09m 31.8703s; 7 Scott Dixon, NZ (Panoz G Force-Honda), 2h 09m 31.9410s; 8 Felipe Giaffone, BR (Dallara-Chevrolet), 2h 09m 32.4438s; 9 Scott Sharp, USA (Dallara-Toyota), 2h 09m 32.5179s; 10 Helio Castroneves, BR (Dallara-Toyota), 2h 09m 32.5896s.
Fastest lap: Meira, 25.1064s, 217.952 mph/350.760 km/h.

TOYOTA INDY 400, California Speedway, Fontana, California, USA, 3 October. Round 15. 200 of the 2.000-mile/3.219-km circuit, 400.000 miles/643.738 km.
1 Adrian Fernandez, MEX (Panoz G Force-Honda), 2h 14m 12.5029s, 178.826 mph/287.793 km/h; 2 Tony Kanaan, BR (Dallara-Honda), 2h 14m 12.5212s; 3 Dan Wheldon, GB (Dallara-Honda), 2h 14m 12.7114s; 4 Sam Hornish Jr., USA (Dallara-Toyota), 2h 14m 12.8106s; 5 Buddy Rice, USA (Panoz G Force-Honda), 2h 14m 12.9972s; 6 Dario Franchitti, GB (Dallara-Honda), 2h 14m 13.1753s; 7 Helio Castroneves, BR (Dallara-Toyota), 2h 14m 13.2579s; 8 Scott Dixon, NZ (Panoz G Force-Toyota), 199 laps; 9 Townsend Bell, USA (Dallara-Chevrolet), 199; 10 Mark Taylor, GB (Panoz G Force-Honda), 199.
Fastest lap: Vitor Meira, BR (Panoz G Force-Honda), 33.1860s, 216.959 mph/349.162 km/h.

CHEVY 500, Texas Motor Speedway, Fort Worth, Texas, USA, 17 October. Round 16. 200 laps of the 1.455-mile/2.342-km circuit, 291.000 miles/468.319 km.
1 Helio Castroneves, BR (Dallara-Toyota), 1h 49m 32.2547s, 159.397 mph/256.525 km/h; 2 Tony Kanaan, BR (Dallara-Honda), 1h 49m 32.6279s; 3 Dan Wheldon, GB (Dallara-Honda), 1h 49m 32.6297s; 4 Vitor Meira, BR (Panoz G Force-Honda), 1h 49m 32.7319s; 5 Adrian Fernandez, MEX (Panoz G Force-Honda), 1h 49m 33.7423s; 6 Scott Dixon, NZ (Panoz G Force-Honda), 1h 49m 34.2094s; 7 Mark Taylor, GB (Panoz G Force-Honda), 1h 49m 34.5919s; 8 Scott Sharp, USA (Dallara-Toyota), 1h 49m 34.6325s; 9 Townsend Bell, USA (Dallara-Chevrolet), 1h 49m 34.6840s; 10 A.J. Foyt IV, USA (Dallara-Toyota), 1h 49m 35.7269s.
Fastest lap: Bryan Herta, USA (Dallara-Honda), 24.3715s, 214.923 mph/345.885 km/h.

Final championship points

1 Tony Kanaan, BR, 618; 2 Dan Wheldon, GB, 533; 3 Buddy Rice, USA, 485; 4 Helio Castroneves, BR, 446; 5 Adrian Fernandez, MEX, 445; 6 Dario Franchitti, GB, 409; 7 Sam Hornish Jr., USA, 387; 8 Vitor Meira, BR, 376; 9 Bryan Herta, USA, 362; 10 Scott Dixon, NZ, 355; 11 Darren Manning, GB, 323; 12 Alex Barron, USA, 310; 13 Scott Sharp, USA, 282; 14 Kosuke Matsuura, J, 280; 15 Toranosuke Takagi, J, 263; 16 Ed Carpenter, USA, 245; 17 Mark Taylor, GB, 232; 18 A.J. Foyt IV, USA, 232; 19 Tomas Scheckter, ZA, 230; 20 Felipe Giaffone, BR, 214; 21 Townsend Bell, USA, 193; 22 Jaques Lazier, USA, 104; 23 Greg Ray, USA, 99; 24= Robbie Buhl, USA, 44; 24= Al Unser Jr., USA, 44; 26 Roger Yasukawa, USA, 39; 27 Tomas Enge, CZ, 31; 28 Bruno Junqueira, BR, 30; 29 Jeff Simmons, USA, 26; 30= Richie Hearn, USA, 12; 30= Sarah Fisher, USA, 12; 30= Robby McGehee, USA, 12; 30= Buddy Lazier, USA, 12; 30= Marty Roth, USA, 12; 35= PJ Jones, USA, 10; 35= Robby Gordon, USA, 10; 35= Larry Foyt, USA, 10.

Bombardier Rookie of the Year
1 Kosuke Matsuura; 2 Ed Carpenter; 3 Mark Taylor.

Engine manufacturers
1 Honda, 154; 2 Toyota, 114; 3 Chevrolet, 84.

Chassis manufacturers
1 Dallara, 142; 2 Panoz G Force, 130.

The Champ Car World Series powered by Ford

TOYOTA GRAND PRIX OF LONG BEACH, Long Beach Street Circuit, California, USA, 18 April. Round 1. 81 laps of the 1.968-mile/

3.167-km circuit, 159.408 miles/256.542 km.
1 Paul Tracy, CDN (Lola B2/00-Ford Cosworth XFE), 1h 44m 12.348s, 91.785 mph/147.713 km/h; 2 Bruno Junqueira, BR (Lola B2/00-Ford Cosworth XFE), 1h 44m 18.029s; 3 Sébastien Bourdais, F (Lola B2/00-Ford Cosworth XFE), 1h 44m 18.723s; 4 Patrick Carpentier, CDN (Lola B2/00-Ford Cosworth XFE), 1h 44m 29.149s; 5 Mario Dominguez, MEX (Lola B2/00-Ford Cosworth XFE), 1h 44m 29.875s; 6 Justin Wilson, GB (Lola B2/00-Ford Cosworth XFE), 1h 44m 48.993s; 7 Ryan Hunter-Reay, USA (Lola B2/00-Ford Cosworth XFE), 1h 44m 51.274s; 8 Alex Tagliani, CDN (Lola B2/00-Ford Cosworth XFE), 1h 45m 12.926s; 9 Mario Haberfeld, BR (Reynard 02I-Ford Cosworth XFE), 80 laps; 10 Rodolfo Lavin, MEX (Lola B2/00-Ford Cosworth XFE), 80.
Fastest lap: Bourdais, 1m 09.729s, 101.605 mph/163.517 km/h.

TECATE/TELMEX MONTERREY GRAND PRIX, Parque Fundidora, Monterrey, Nuevo Leon, Mexico, 23 May. Round 2. 72 laps of the 2.104-mile/3.386-km circuit, 151.488 miles/243.796 km.
1 Sébastien Bourdais, F (Lola B2/00-Ford Cosworth XFE), 1h 45m 01.498s, 86.544 mph/139.279 km/h; 2 Bruno Junqueira, BR (Lola B2/00-Ford Cosworth XFE), 1h 45m 05.350s; 3 Mario Dominguez, MEX (Lola B2/00-Ford Cosworth XFE), 1h 45m 06.707s; 4 Patrick Carpentier, CDN (Lola B2/00-Ford Cosworth XFE), 1h 45m 07.617s; 5 Alex Tagliani, CDN (Lola B2/00-Ford Cosworth XFE), 1h 45m 11.398s; 6 Justin Wilson, GB (Lola B2/00-Ford Cosworth XFE), 1h 45m 12.866s; 7 Paul Tracy, CDN (Lola B2/00-Ford Cosworth XFE), 1h 45m 18.545s; 8 Ryan Hunter-Reay, USA (Lola B2/00-Ford Cosworth XFE), 1h 45m 23.749s; 9 Roberto Gonzalez, MEX (Lola B2/00-Ford Cosworth XFE), 1h 45m 28.262s; 10 Nelson Philippe, F (Lola B2/00-Ford Cosworth XFE), 1h 45m 29.423s.
Fastest lap: Bourdais, 1m 15.021s, 100.964 mph/162.485 km/h.

THE TIME WARNER CABLE ROADRUNNER 250, The Milwaukee Mile, Wisconsin State Fair Park, West Allis, Wisconsin, USA, 5 June. Round 3. 250 laps of the 1.032-mile/1.661-km circuit, 258.000 miles/415.211 km.
1 Ryan Hunter-Reay, USA (Lola B2/00-Ford Cosworth XFE), 1h 59m 12.397s, 129.859 mph/208.987 km/h; 2 Patrick Carpentier, CDN (Lola B2/00-Ford Cosworth XFE), 1h 59m 18.262s; 3 Michel Jourdain Jr., MEX (Lola B2/00-Ford Cosworth XFE), 1h 59m 23.746s; 4 Jimmy Vasser, USA (Lola B2/00-Ford Cosworth XFE), 249 laps; 5 A.J. Allmendinger, USA (Lola B2/00-Ford Cosworth XFE), 249; 6 Bruno Junqueira, BR (Lola B2/00-Ford Cosworth XFE), 248; 7 Oriol Servia, E (Lola B2/00-Ford Cosworth XFE), 247; 8 Mario Dominguez, MEX (Lola B2/00-Ford Cosworth XFE), 246; 9 Rodolfo Lavin, MEX (Lola B2/00-Ford Cosworth XFE), 245 (DNF); 10 Mario Haberfeld, BR (Reynard 02I-Ford Cosworth XFE), 245.
Fastest lap: Hunter-Reay, 21.765s, 170.696 mph/274.709 km/h.

CHAMP CAR GRAND PRIX OF PORTLAND, Portland International Raceway, Oregon, USA, 20 June. Round 4. 94 laps of the 1.969-mile/3.169-km circuit, 185.086 miles/297.867 km.
1 Sébastien Bourdais, F (Lola B2/00-Ford Cosworth XFE), 1h 45m 50.461s, 104.923 mph/168.857 km/h; 2 Bruno Junqueira, BR (Lola B2/00-Ford Cosworth XFE), 1h 45m 51.708s; 3 Paul Tracy, CDN (Lola B2/00-Ford Cosworth XFE), 1h 46m 30.525s; 4 Patrick Carpentier, CDN (Lola B2/00-Ford Cosworth XFE), 1h 46m 42.817s; 5 Justin Wilson, GB (Lola B2/00-Ford Cosworth XFE), 1h 46m 48.890s; 6 A.J. Allmendinger, USA (Lola B2/00-Ford Cosworth XFE), 1h 46m 49.798s; 7 Alex Tagliani, CDN (Lola B2/00-Ford Cosworth XFE), 93 laps; 8 Jimmy Vasser, USA (Lola B2/00-Ford Cosworth XFE), 93; 9 Mario Haberfeld, BR (Reynard 02I-Ford Cosworth XFE), 93; 10 Roberto Gonzalez, MEX (Lola B2/00-Ford Cosworth XFE), 93.
Fastest lap: Junqueira, 1m 00.573s, 117.022 mph/188.329 km/h.

CHAMP CAR GRAND PRIX OF CLEVELAND, Burke Lakefront Airport Circuit, Cleveland, Ohio, USA, 3 July. Round 5. 97 laps of the 2.106-mile/3.389-km circuit, 204.282 miles/328.760 km.
1 Sébastien Bourdais, F (Lola B2/00-Ford Cosworth XFE), 1h 48m 16.056s, 113.209 mph/182.193 km/h; 2 Bruno Junqueira, BR (Lola B2/00-Ford Cosworth XFE), 1h 48m 31.186s; 3 Alex Tagliani, CDN (Lola B2/00-Ford Cosworth XFE), 1h 48m 43.640s; 4 Oriol Servia, E (Lola B2/00-Ford Cosworth XFE), 1h 48m 54.252s; 5 Jimmy Vasser, USA (Lola B2/00-Ford Cosworth XFE), 1h 48m 57.957s; 6 A.J. Allmendinger, USA (Lola B2/00-Ford Cosworth XFE), 1h 48m 58.414s; 7 Roberto Gonzalez, MEX (Lola B2/00-Ford Cosworth XFE), 1h 49m 14.719s; 8 Mario Dominguez, MEX (Lola B2/00-Ford Cosworth XFE), 96; 9 Rodolfo Lavin, MEX (Lola B2/00-Ford Cosworth XFE), 96; 10 Nelson Philippe, F (Lola B2/00-Ford Cosworth XFE), 95.
Fastest lap: Junqueira, 58.960s, 128.589 mph/206.944 km/h.

MOLSON INDY TORONTO, Canada National Exhibition Place Circuit, Toronto, Ontario, Canada, 11 July. Round 6. 84 laps of the 1.755-mile/2.824-km circuit, 147.420 miles/237.249 km.
1 Sébastien Bourdais, F (Lola B2/00-Ford Cosworth XFE), 1h 45m 36.930s, 83.749 mph/134.781 km/h; 2 Jimmy Vasser, USA (Lola B2/00-Ford Cosworth XFE), 1h 45m 38.326s; 3 Patrick Carpentier, CDN (Lola B2/00-Ford Cosworth XFE), 1h 45m 43.661s; 4 Mario Haberfeld, BR (Reynard 02I-Ford Cosworth XFE), 1h 45m 44.822s; 5 Paul Tracy, CDN (Lola B2/00-Ford Cosworth XFE), 1h 45m 46.595s; 6 Gaston Mazzacane, RA (Lola B2/00-Ford Cosworth XFE), 1h 45m 50.932s; 7 Alex Tagliani, CDN (Lola B2/00-Ford Cosworth XFE), 1h 46m 05.374s; 8 Ryan Hunter-Reay, USA (Lola B2/00-Ford Cosworth XFE), 1h 46m 20.105s; 9 Oriol Servia, E (Lola B2/00-Ford Cosworth XFE), 83 laps; 10 Alex Sperafico, BR (Reynard 02I-Ford Cosworth XFE), 83.
Fastest lap: Bourdais, 1m 00.304s, 104.769 mph/168.610 km/h.

MOLSON INDY VANCOUVER, Vancouver Street Circuit, Concord Pacific Place, Vancouver, British Columbia, Canada, 25 July. Round 7. 85 laps of the 1.781-mile/2.866-km circuit, 151.385 miles/243.631 km.
1 Paul Tracy, CDN (Lola B2/00-Ford Cosworth XFE), 1h 34m 42.849s, 95.900 mph/154.336 km/h; 2 Michel Jourdain Jr., MEX (Lola B2/00-Ford Cosworth XFE), 1h 34m 48.406s; 3 A.J. Allmendinger, USA (Lola B2/00-Ford Cosworth XFE), 1h 34m 48.988s; 4 Bruno Junqueira, BR (Lola B2/00-Ford Cosworth XFE), 1h 34m 49.393s; 5 Sébastien Bourdais, F (Lola B2/00-Ford Cosworth XFE), 1h 34m 57.080s; 6 Mario Dominguez, MEX (Lola B2/00-Ford Cosworth XFE), 1h 34m 58.683s; 7 Alex Tagliani, CDN (Lola B2/00-Ford Cosworth XFE), 1h 35m 15.017s; 8 Ryan Hunter-Reay, USA (Lola B2/00-Ford Cosworth XFE), 1h 35m 15.468s; 9 Mario Haberfeld, BR (Reynard 02I-Ford Cosworth XFE), 1h 35m 26.520s; 10 Jimmy Vasser, USA (Lola B2/00-Ford Cosworth XFE), 84 laps.
Fastest lap: Tracy, 1m 01.755s, 103.823 mph/167.087 km/h.

GRAND PRIX OF ROAD AMERICA PRESENTED BY CHICAGO TRIBUNE, Road America Circuit, Elkhart Lake, Wisconsin, USA, 8 August. Round 8. 48 laps of the 4.048-mile/6.515-km circuit, 194.304 miles/312.702 km.